Freedom and Authority in Our Time

TWELFTH SYMPOSIUM
OF THE
CONFERENCE ON SCIENCE,
PHILOSOPHY AND RELIGION

THE PAPERS included in this volume were prepared for the twelfth meeting of the Conference on Science, Philosophy and Religion in Their Relation to the Democratic Way of Life, which was held at The Men's Faculty Club of Columbia University on September 4, 5, 6, and 7, 1951. Each paper represents only the opinion of the individual author.

FREEDOM and AUTHORITY IN OUR TIME

TWELFTH SYMPOSIUM
OF THE CONFERENCE ON SCIENCE,
PHILOSOPHY AND RELIGION

Edited by

LYMAN BRYSON
PROFESSOR OF EDUCATION
TEACHERS COLLEGE, COLUMBIA UNIVERSITY

LOUIS FINKELSTEIN
CHANCELLOR, THE JEWISH THEOLOGICAL SEMINARY OF AMERICA

R. M. MACIVER
LIEBER PROFESSOR EMERITUS OF POLITICAL PHILOSOPHY AND SOCIOLOGY
COLUMBIA UNIVERSITY

RICHARD MCKEON
DISTINGUISHED SERVICE PROFESSOR OF PHILOSOPHY AND GREEK
THE UNIVERSITY OF CHICAGO

PUBLISHED BY THE
CONFERENCE ON SCIENCE, PHILOSOPHY AND RELIGION
IN THEIR RELATION TO THE DEMOCRATIC WAY OF LIFE, INC.
NEW YORK

1953

DISTRIBUTED BY
HARPER & BROTHERS
NEW YORK AND LONDON

All rights reserved including the
right of reproduction in whole or
in part in any form.

COPYRIGHT, 1953
BY THE CONFERENCE ON SCIENCE, PHILOSOPHY AND RELIGION
IN THEIR RELATION TO THE DEMOCRATIC WAY OF LIFE, INC.
3080 BROADWAY, NEW YORK CITY
Printed in the United States of America

Preface

These papers were prepared for and discussed at the Twelfth Conference on Science, Philosophy and Religion, held in New York City in September, 1951.

The oral proceedings of the sessions were recorded, and although it has not been possible thus far to arrange for their publication, the stenotype report is available at the Conference offices to qualified students.

The major change in Conference technique begun in the Sixth Symposium, *Approaches to Group Understanding,* has been followed in the subsequent volumes. The invitation for the Twelfth Conference included the following:

> The editors would use each paper as a basis for a chapter, not necessarily following the original form in every detail, but rather editing in the sense of clarifying the relationship between the various chapters that will make up the volume. Each author would, of course, be free to use his paper in its original form elsewhere, indicating the purpose for which it was prepared.

The papers in this volume were edited in accordance with this plan, and the comments edited and placed at the end of each chapter. In consequence, the printed comments do not necessarily give each writer's complete discussion of the paper in question, or his total statement on the subject under consideration.

As indicated in the program, papers had been expected from Dr. Charles S. Johnson, Professor Harold D. Lasswell, Professor Karl N. Llewellyn, Dr. Gerald B. Phelan, and Mr. Francis H. Russell. However, these men were prevented from completing their manuscripts for publication.

Father Robert C. Hartnett, S.J., in December, 1951, spoke at The Institute for Religious and Social Studies on "Freedom and Authority," in a series arranged by Professor F. Ernest Johnson, who kindly brought the paper to the attention of the editors. They much appreciate the opportunity to include it in the present volume.

Dr. David Iino, a former pupil of Professor Edgar S. Brightman, has translated a number of Conference papers into Japanese, and many thousands of copies have been sold in Japan. Dr. Iino wrote a paper on the subject of the Twelfth Conference, which is appended to this book.

The Conference volumes are listed on page viii.

The group that met at Amherst in 1944 and at Lake Mohonk in 1946, 1948, and 1949, again assembled there in October, 1950, in March and November, 1951, and April, 1952, for discussion of a number of suggestions that had been submitted to the Council of the Conference of which Dr. Harlow Shapley has served as president. The Council will meet again for further discussion in the autumn of 1952. Other proposals and criticisms of the activities of the Conference generally will be welcome.

The editors express their deep gratitude to all who participated in the Conference program, to those who attended the sessions, to the authors of comments, and above all to the original writers, whose work formed the basis of the Conference meetings and the substance of this volume. In particular they record their indebtedness to the officers of Columbia University, and to the officers and staff of The Men's Faculty Club where the working sessions were held. They again wish to thank Miss Jessica Feingold for her indispensable help in every phase of the Conference program. They wish to thank Mr. John W. Chase and Professor Roger L. Shinn for their editorial work on the papers and comments of this volume.

The participants in the meetings of 1951; and the authors of papers and comments are listed on pages 733-736.

At the close of the Twelfth Conference, a meeting of the members was held, and the following Board of Directors was elected:

William F. Albright	Charles W. Hendel
Lyman Bryson	F. Ernest Johnson
Harry J. Carman	John LaFarge, S.J.
Stewart G. Cole	Harold D. Lasswell
W. G. Constable	Alain L. Locke
Norman Cousins	Robert H. Lowie
Louis Finkelstein	R. M. MacIver
Philipp Frank	Richard McKeon
Simon Greenberg	John Courtney Murray, S.J.
C. P. Haskins	Anton C. Pegis

Preface

Gerald B. Phelan
Isidor I. Rabi
Roy W. Sellars
Harlow Shapley

Donald C. Stone
Gerald G. Walsh, S.J.
M. L. Wilson
Louis Wirth

At the Eleventh Conference, the committee headed by Dr. Carman reported on suggestions for reorganization of the Conference, looking toward its establishment on a permanent basis. Members agreed that a first step should be organization of a group of Conference Fellows, in addition to the members of the Board of Directors. The group of Fellows now includes:

Edgar S. Brightman
Van Wyck Brooks
Karl W. Deutsch
Irwin Edman
Hoxie N. Fairchild
Lawrence K. Frank
Hudson Hoagland
Charles S. Johnson
Clyde Kluckhohn

Jacques Maritain
Margaret Mead
Henry A. Murray
John U. Nef
F. S. C. Northrop
J. Robert Oppenheimer
Harry A. Overstreet
George N. Shuster
Ordway Tead

At the Twelfth Conference Dr. Ordway Tead was requested to serve as Chairman for the 1952 Conference. Professor Wendell M. Stanley agreed to serve as Vice-Chairman.

PUBLICATIONS OF THE CONFERENCE ON SCIENCE, PHILOSOPHY AND RELIGION

Science, Philosophy and Religion, A Symposium, 1941. (The papers prepared for the meetings held in New York City on September 9, 10, and 11, 1940.) Out of print.

Science, Philosophy and Religion, Second Symposium, 1942. (The papers prepared for the meetings held in New York City on September 8, 9, 10, and 11, 1941.)

Science, Philosophy and Religion, Third Symposium, 1943. (The papers prepared for the meetings held in New York City on August 27, 28, 29, 30, and 31, 1942.) Out of print.

Approaches to World Peace, Fourth Symposium, 1944. (The papers prepared for the meetings held in New York City on September 9, 10, 11, 12, and 13, 1943). Out of print.

Approaches to National Unity, Fifth Symposium, 1945. (The papers prepared for the meetings held in New York City on September 7, 8, 9, 10, and 11, 1944.) Out of print.

Approaches to Group Understanding, Sixth Symposium, 1947. (The papers prepared for the meetings held in New York City on August 23, 24, 25, 26, and 27, 1945.)

Conflicts of Power in Modern Culture, Seventh Symposium, 1947. (The papers prepared for the meetings held in Chicago on September 9, 10, and 11, 1946.)

Learning and World Peace, Eighth Symposium, 1948. (The papers prepared for the meetings held in Philadelphia on September 7, 8, 9, and 10, 1947.)

Goals for American Education, Ninth Symposium, 1950. (The papers prepared for the meetings held in New York City on September 7, 8, 9, and 10, 1948.)

Perspectives on a Troubled Decade: Science, Philosophy and Religion, 1939–1949, Tenth Symposium, 1950. (The papers prepared for the meetings held in New York City on September 6, 7, 8, and 9, 1949.)

Foundations of World Organization: A Political and Cultural Appraisal, Eleventh Symposium, 1952. (The papers prepared for the meetings held in New York City on September 5, 6, 7, and 8, 1950.)

Table of Contents

PAPERS

FREEDOM AND AUTHORITY IN PRACTICAL LIFE

I   Freedom and the Authoritarian Personality, *Harry A. Overstreet*   1
    COMMENTS BY:
    Rudolf Allers
    ✓*Hoxie N. Fairchild*
    Royal M. Frye

II   Spirit and Function of Organization, *James Marshall*   13
    COMMENTS BY:
    Edgar S. Brightman
    Daniel L. Kurshan

III   Notes on a Theory of Advice, *Lyman Bryson*   27
    COMMENT BY:
    Quincy Wright

IV   Authority and Freedom in Industry, *Leo Nejelski*   45

V   Workers' Control: Freedom and Authority in the Plant, *Adolf F. Sturmthal*   53

VI   Freedom and Authority in Labor Unions, *Mark Starr*   63

VII   Labor's Emerging Role in the Political Economy, *Kermit Eby*   79
    COMMENTS BY:
    Edgar S. Brightman
    Nels F. S. Ferré

VIII   The Exercise of Freedom, *Louis Harris* and *Julian L. Woodward*   87

IX   Social Security: Freedom from Want Without Want of Freedom, *George F. Rohrlich*   95

FREEDOM AND GOVERNMENTAL AUTHORITY, NATIONAL AND INTERNATIONAL

X Freedom and Authority in International Relations, *Hans Kohn* 103
    COMMENT BY:
    Robert H. Lowie

XI Individual Freedom Under the Law, *Luis Recasens-Siches* 109
    COMMENTS BY:
    Edgar S. Brightman
    Barna Horvath

XII Freedom and Authority, Retrospect and Prospect, *R. Gordon Hoxie* 121

XIII World Law and World Reform, *Susanne K. Langer* 137
    COMMENTS BY:
    Rudolf Allers
    Adda Bruemmer Bozeman

XIV Some Thoughts on the Soviet Concept of Authority and Freedom, *Ernest J. Simmons* 147

XV Liberty and Authority, *George S. Langrod* 159

XVI Freedom and Authority in International Organization, *Quincy Wright* 169
    COMMENT BY:
    Kenneth W. Thompson

XVII Methodological Equality and Functional Idealism, *T. V. Smith* 183
    COMMENT BY:
    ✓ *Hoxie N. Fairchild*

XVIII Ethics and Politics, *Roy Wood Sellars* 191

COMMENT BY:
Barna Horvath

FREEDOM AND LEGAL AUTHORITY

XIX Authority and Responsibility, *Edmond N. Cahn* 201
    COMMENTS BY:
    Rudolf Allers
    Barna Horvath

XX The Relation of Law to Freedom and Authority, *Julius Cohen* 217
    COMMENTS BY:
    Thomas A. Cowan
    Barna Horvath

XXI Freedom and Legal Authority: The Kinds of Authority of Law, *Edwin W. Patterson* 225
    COMMENT BY:
    Barna Horvath

XXII Legal Imperative and Moral Authority, *Glenn Negley* 237
    COMMENTS BY:
    Nels F. S. Ferré
    Barna Horvath

XXIII Freedom and Citizenship, *Helen Silving* 253

FREEDOM AND AUTHORITY AS CULTURAL AND SOCIAL PHENOMENA

XXIV Communication in Self-Governing Organizations: Notes on Autonomy, Freedom, and Authority in the Growth of Social Groups, *Karl W. Deutsch* 271

XXV The Problem of Freedom and Authority in Cultural Perspective, *David Bidney* 289
    COMMENTS BY:
    Robert H. Lowie
    Roy Wood Sellars

XXVI	Freedom and Authority in the Structure of Cultures, *James K. Feibleman*	309
XXVII	The Necessity of Authority to Freedom, *Gray Lankford Dorsey*	317
	COMMENT BY: *Edgar S. Brightman*	
XXVIII	Freedom and Authority as Integral to Culture and Structure, *Dorothy D. Lee*	335
	COMMENTS BY: *Nels F. S. Ferré* *Robert H. Lowie*	
XXIX	Freedom and Authority in the Social Structure: A Problem in the Interrelation of Institutions, *Rupert B. Vance*	345
XXX	Work and Freedom, *Eli Ginzberg*	353
	COMMENT BY: *Edgar S. Brightman*	
XXXI	The Role of Authority in the Interpretation of Science, *Philipp Frank*	361
XXXII	Freedom and Authority in the Realm of the Poetic Imagination, *Kenneth Burke*	365
XXXIII	Problems of Freedom and Authority in the Arts, *William G. Constable*	377
XXXIV	Psychiatry in Relation to Authority and Freedom, *Lawrence S. Kubie*	385
	COMMENT BY: *Rudolf Allers*	
XXXV	Persecution as the Pathology of Freedom and Authority, *Mark Graubard*	393
XXXVI	The Supposed Conflict Between Moral Freedom and	

Scientific Determinism, *William H. Kilpatrick* 409
    COMMENT BY:
        George E. Axtelle

POSTULATES OF THEORIES OF FREEDOM AND AUTHORITY

XXXVII   Freedom, Authority, and Orthodoxy, *Charles Frankel* 419
    COMMENTS BY:
        Rudolf Allers
        Edgar S. Brightman
        Simon Greenberg
        Barna Horvath
        Mortimer R. Kadish
        Chaim Perelman
        Quincy Wright

XXXVIII   The Concept of Political Freedom, *Franz L. Neumann* 441
    COMMENTS BY:
        Barna Horvath
        Roy Wood Sellars

XXXIX   The Universal Declaration of Human Rights: An International Effort at a Synthesis of Freedom and Authority, *John H. E. Fried* 451

XL   Authority as the Validation of Power, *Mordecai M. Kaplan* 461

XLI   Autonomy and Theonomy, *Edgar S. Brightman* 473
    COMMENTS BY:
        Swami Akhilananda
        Rudolf Allers
        ✓ Hoxie N. Fairchild
        Barna Horvath

XLII   Freedom and Authority, *Ben Zion Bokser* 485
    COMMENTS BY:
        Swami Akhilananda

Table of Contents

Nels F. S. Ferré

XLIII Authority and Freedom, *Nels F. S. Ferré* 491
  COMMENTS BY:
  Swami Akhilananda
  Edgar S. Brightman
  Barna Horvath

XLIV Freedom and Authority as Functions of Civilization, *Charles W. Hendel* 507

DEFINITION OF FREEDOM AND AUTHORITY

XLV The Nature of Personal Freedom, *F. Ernest Johnson* 543
  COMMENTS BY:
  Swami Akhilananda
  Rudolf Allers
  Edgar S. Brightman
  Stewart G. Cole
  Karl W. Deutsch
  Nels F. S. Ferré
  Roy Wood Sellars

XLVI The Dialectics of Freedom, *Rudolf Allers* 555
  COMMENTS BY:
  Swami Akhilananda
  Edgar S. Brightman
  Barna Horvath
  Ignatius Smith, O.P.

XLVII An Outline for a Comprehensive Inquiry into the Problem of Authority and Freedom, *Simon Greenberg* 577

XLVIII Metaphysical Background of the Problem of Freedom, *Sterling P. Lamprecht* 597
  COMMENT BY:
  Edgar S. Brightman

Table of Contents

XLIX   The Problem of Authority and Freedom and the Two Fundamental Alternatives of Thought, *Louis J. A. Mercier*   607
    COMMENT BY:
      Edgar S. Brightman

L   The Location and Dislocation of Freedom, *Mortimer R. Kadish*   623
    COMMENTS BY:
      Edgar S. Brightman
      Nels F. S. Ferré
      Barna Horvath
      Wayne A. R. Leys

LI   A Case Study in Freedom through Authority, *John LaFarge, S.J.*   641
    COMMENT BY:
      Swami Akhilananda

LII   The Freedom of Civilization, *Paul Schrecker*   647
    COMMENT BY:
      Barna Horvath

LIII   Authority: Intellectual and Political, *Gustave Weigel, S.J.*   659
    COMMENTS BY:
      Nels F. S. Ferré
      Barna Horvath
      Mortimer R. Kadish

LIV   Freedom and Authority in Education, *Robert Ulich*   671
    COMMENTS BY:
      Swami Akhilananda
      Rudolf Allers
      Edgar S. Brightman
      Barna Horvath

Table of Contents

LV Liberty and Authority: Constitutional Aspects of the Problem, *Robert C. Hartnett, S.J.*   687

LVI Altruism and Masochism, *William Pepperell Montague*   695
    COMMENTS BY:
    Rudolf Allers
    Stewart G. Cole

LVII Government in Islam, *Gustave E. von Grunebaum*   701
    COMMENT BY:
    John LaFarge, S.J.

Appendix Freedom and Authority in the Realization of Values, *David N. Iino*   717

Contributors to "Freedom and Authority in Our Time"   733

PROGRAM

Twelfth Conference on Science, Philosophy and Religion, September 4, 5, 6, and 7, 1951   737

Index   749

CHAPTER I

Freedom and the Authoritarian Personality

By HARRY A. OVERSTREET

*Professor Emeritus of Philosophy,
The College of the City of New York*

I

It was the Second World War that drove us out of our paradise of democratic innocence. Then, in a country we had supposed to be advanced in its culture, all hell broke loose—with racial persecutions, gas chambers, concentration camps, Gestapo, terror by day and by night, and an incredible propaganda of lies. We discovered to our amazement that in this country of advanced culture, there were many people who did not believe in a world organized in freedom and for freedom; who believed that it was right and good to force other people into submission—particularly the racially "inferior," and even, by mass executions, to put them out of existence. With horror, we saw an authoritarian state swell up from small beginnings into a Frankenstein monster that alternately issued commands and preachments, and that promised (to all except the racially damned) the beginning of a "thousand years" of happy regimentation.

In our own paradise of democratic innocence we had believed not only that all men were created equal, but that the dearest wish of men everywhere was for liberty in the pursuit of happiness. Now, suddenly and shockingly, we were brought to realize that multitudes of people believe that men were created vastly unequal and that life was best lived—and lived most freely—in the unfreedom of a strict obedience to authority.

First, this movement against equality and freedom seemed a passing aberration among a few gangsters. We laughed it away as perverse nonsense. But as the fanatical passion for a "new order" grew in strength, we began to realize that the power of this Fascist frenzy came from a deep, unsuspected need among millions of insecure people to be safe and significant in a system of obedience and command.

We saw among the German people the emerging lineaments of what we are learning to call "the authoritarian personality." And among the Russian people; although obscured by what seemed to be a revolutionary movement in behalf of economic and social freedom, the same authoritarian lineaments emerged, until today the domination-submission pattern is so clear that no one can mistake it.

Our effort to comprehend this curious phenomenon has made us psychologically less naive about ourselves. We have come to see that the authoritarian demand for an imposed conformity is present and threatens to impair or to destroy the democracy we had supposed was impregnable.

How can any people prefer unfreedom to freedom? Erich Fromm, in his masterly book, *Escape from Freedom,* showed that where the individual feels isolated and anxious, he tends to adopt "the kind of personality offered to him by cultural patterns; and he therefore becomes exactly as all the others are and as they expect him to be."[1] He *conforms;* and he gains his sense of security by this very unfreedom of conforming. Such freedom through unfreedom may seem to be a contradiction; but a person who "gives up his individual self and becomes an automaton, identical with millions of other automatons around him, need not feel alone and anxious any more." He has joined the crowd. Thereafter he is not only willing to take orders from those who lead the crowd; he glories in taking orders. For to be ordered to do things means that he, the insignificant one, has been noticed. He has been accepted. He can march abreast, his heels clicking in unison with the heels of his fellows.

Are we in our own country in danger of moving in this direction? We are accustomed to keep before us the image of ourselves as "a free people." But is this a realistic self-image; or is it mostly the after-image, shaped by schoolbook history, where we read of ourselves as brave pioneers in a new land, who decided to overthrow monarchy and govern ourselves? That schoolbook history was concerned with a people who lived in small face to face communities, where freedom was the freedom of neighbors to discuss and settle their affairs. These are not the people of the America of today. Bewildering complexity and a vast impersonality, heightened by large-scale competitions and antagonisms, have taken the place of the give and take of the small community. May it be that under these greatly different conditions of life a new kind of character structure is being formed; perhaps even an "un-American" one?

[1] Erich Fromm, *Escape from Freedom,* Farrar & Rinehart, Inc., New York, 1951, p. 185.

Thomas Jefferson wrote down his immortal lines riding in a leisurely stagecoach over the Virginia roads. The lines that will settle our human fates are being written under very different conditions: by men who fly in haste to far quarters of the globe in anxious efforts to quench angers and gain a short truce for keeping alive; by men who meet, as antagonists, to settle disputes that involve millions of workers, employers, and public; by men in Congress and in state legislatures, who, in a world grown suddenly huge, try, with their local outlooks, to legislate about matters that circle the globe.

In this world of greater dimensions and of incredibly more confusing conflicts, is the American still the self-reliant, rugged pioneer who "will be damned" if anyone denies him the right to make up his own mind and say his own say?

II

"The dominant fact about America at the mid-century point," writes Laurence Sears,[2] "is our search for security in a world that seems to hold little but threats. We are a frightened people." In a time of fright, individuals reveal most clearly their basic character structure. What does our present fright reveal of American character?

The story is not a reassuring one. The retort to the contemporary threat of Russia has been made in ways that hardly comport with a robust belief in individual freedom and in its protection by the due processes of law. The past two years among us have been characterized by a kind of creeping terror. It has come to pass in free America that men may have their characters assassinated and their means of livelihood taken from them without the basic right to defend themselves in a court of law. In the highest governing body in our land, a Congressional investigating committee that should above all have been solicitous to keep inviolate the rights of the individual, has been notorious in broadcasting accusations even before investigation, and long before a specific finding of guilt has been made. As a consequence, time and again, the accused has been forced to undergo the humiliation and unfairness of "trial by newspaper"; while the accuser has protected himself by hiding behind his shield of "immunity."

This reckless disregard of the individual's rights has also occurred

[2]Laurence Sears, "Security and Liberty," *American Scholar*, XX, Spring, 1951, p. 137.

in our civil life. A television actress has been dismissed from her job on an unsubstantiated and even uninvestigated charge—a charge brought against her by an unofficial and unauthorized body of accusers. The scholar, Owen Lattimore, accused of Communist connections but never proved guilty, has, time and again, been opposed by a number of citizens in his American right to say his public say.

All over the country anxiety has entered the teaching ranks, because of the ease with which mere accusation can be turned into dismissal. Capping it all, is the spectacle of loyalty oaths required of vast numbers of men and women who have never in the slightest degree laid themselves open to a suspicion of disloyalty. The result is that teachers are keeping their mouths closed, putting "freedom of inquiry" safely out of sight. They well know that charges can be recklessly made and that the nebulous ambiguity of accusations is so great that they would have little chance, even if they could afford the costs, to make their honest loyalty convincing.

As Laurence Sears points out, two of our most basic rights are being invaded: the right of dissent and the right to a fair trial. These were the first of the rights taken away in the Fascist countries. These are rights basic to freedom. When they are denied, dictatorial authority takes over. The free mind goes underground. All that remains above ground is the conformity of minds that like conformity and demand it of others.

III

The full danger is not seen, unless we realize that a great many persons are not only willing to submit to conformity (because there is an enemy in sight), but actually *prefer* conformity. These are the authoritarian minds in our own midst. They range from executive and legislative levels to the humblest ranks. They are found among columnists and newspaper editors, in chambers of commerce, and on boards of education. That there are multitudes of them is indicated by a number of straws in the wind [Summer, 1951]: by the fact, for example, that in the past election more invitations to speak were reported to have been extended to Senator McCarthy, the-accuser-behind-the-shield-of-immunity, than to any other political figure; by the fact that legislators, newspapers, and a large citizenry have approved conformity requiring laws and various oath signing acts; by the fact that one official—the Federal Attorney General—is permitted to issue a list of the organizations to which we are forbidden, on pain of punishment, to belong or to have belonged. Is this the beginning of a swing to authoritarian thinking in America?

Many of us continue to be hopeful about our democratic freedoms, believing that authoritarianism is so sinister that Americans will not willingly take it to themselves. We shall not really understand the full danger until we comprehend why authoritarianism—Fascism and Communism alike—has been so surprisingly successful in gaining popular support. We mostly labor under the illusion that Fascism and Communism were imposed upon unwilling people; and that all other peoples of the world would prefer our system, if only they could have it. It is our peculiarly dangerous nation-centered point of view. Caught in our trap of self-congratulation, we are unable to understand why authoritarianism has enrolled millions of willing people in its support.

The usual reasons given for the rise of Fascism and Communism are poverty and frustration. When we give these quite valid reasons we feel particularly safe about America. We have a way of forgetting the deep South, where dictators of one sort or another (we euphemistically call them "demagogues")—from Cotton Ed Smith to Huey Long—have ridden into virtually unrestricted power on waves of popular support. Here poverty and frustration have been real causes. But it has not required poverty and frustration to produce a large popular following for Senator McCarthy in states that could hardly be described as poverty stricken and frustrated.

We shall not appreciate the real threat of authoritarianism—particularly the Fascist threat—until we realize that the profoundest reason for the popular support for these new dictatorships has been a certain spiritual emptiness. Poverty and frustration, have, indeed, been real enough causes; but it still remains true that "man does not live by bread alone."

As we have studied man "in depth," we have come, in recent years, to realize that no individual is genuinely and lastingly happy, unless he has something beyond himself and greater than himself to care about, work for, and if need be, die for. This is perhaps why Theodore Roosevelt could make the trigger happy remark that war makes for the manly and adventurous qualities. In a world empty of great things to do, war can be a way of lifting people out of themselves, giving them a sense of the size of life, and granting them an involvement in greatness.

Our Western culture has made self-interest and the fight for ego-centered success the dominant ways of life. Out of this fight of self-interest with self-interest came the amazing willingness of millions of people to raise their arms in common salute and follow the commands of their leaders. Why? Men were distrustful of the old clashing selfishnesses. They rose to the call of what seemed to them to be a nobler devotion to something greater than themselves.

It is too easy to say that these people were deluded—that the call in Fascism was to a new and filthier selfishness of military arrogance and bestial cruelty; and in Communism to a fanatic intolerance and an unspeakable brutality that enslaved even while they promised to free. The reason for their delusion should be plain: human beings have to find a cause to live for, greater than themselves.

IV

Here is where the problem of our entire present world really begins: the kind of cause greater than themselves that human beings will respond to depends upon their *inner readiness to respond*.

Some individuals have been so conditioned by their life circumstances that they respond most readily to a call to hostility. These persons may be said to possess a "hostility pattern of personality." Others respond most readily to a call to give help. They may be said to possess a "goodwill pattern of personality."

Contrary to our usual conceptions, the call to hostility—to hate and to kill—can easily take on the guise of high nobility. To hate the enemies of one's country has long been enshrined in poetry and song. It is not surprising then, after the crash of Western cultures, to find millions of people engaged in a passionate enterprise of hating—hating the Jews, who supposedly were the enemies of the Fatherland; hating the capitalists, who supposedly were the enemies of mankind; hating democracy, which supposedly harbored capitalists and warmongers. Nor is it surprising that in their hating these people achieved a sense of noble fulfilment.

In Europe and in other parts of the world the potential for hating was enormous. It was as if depths on depths of bestial impulses had been suddenly released. Buchenwald and the labor camps of Russia are forms of men's passionate hating *in behalf of a cause*.

This, I think, is the significant thing to get hold of: hating in behalf of a cause, in all times and places, has made the individual feel lifted out of trivialities to a plane of involvement in great loyalties. It has filled his spiritual emptiness with a cause.

V

How the world will go, then—and how America will go—depends in chief measure upon what, among us, will become the predominant pattern of *readiness to respond*. Will it be the hostility pattern—the readiness to suspect, fear, hate, and oppose; or will it be the goodwill pattern —the readiness to trust and cooperate, to build a society where all are free and equal in their right to life?

We in America are suffering from much the same spiritual emptiness that has afflicted other peoples in the world. With the sudden rise of an unprecedented danger, our responses have taken the two characteristic directions we have described. Many Americans, with a trigger quickness, have responded by hating the enemy. They have called for measures of defense, not only, understandably, against the potential invader, but against fellow Americans whom they regard as in league with the potential invader. Other Americans have responded to the danger in a quite different way: they have met the danger creatively by seeking ways in which to avert in the future precisely this kind of danger. In each case *the readiness to respond* in the one way rather than the other has been the measure of the personality pattern.

There is much today to make us anxious about the way we shall go. A vast amount of hostility has been released among us. The hating of enemies has taken on the guise of high patriotism. He who does not hate enough is suspect.

How do these two readinesses—to hostility and to goodwill—measure up among ourselves?

VI

We now know a great deal more than we used to know about what creates in people "hostility" responses and "goodwill" responses. We now go back to the new born infant and take note of how he is received into the world. If he is "rejected," and/or "dominated" one of two things will happen: either he will submit to superior power (and suppress his fears and resistances within his subconscious) or he will rebel. In either case he will be on the way to building a hostility pattern that will reveal itself variously in his later life. If, on the contrary, the infant comes into an atmosphere of acceptance and affection, he will have every chance to build a pattern of reciprocal affection, which in later life will reveal itself variously as a pattern of goodwill.

Add to these contrasted influences in the family, the later influences in the school, the job world, and the community, and the same thing is found to be true. People who, in their adult years are quick with hostility responses; who look for the worst in others; who, if there is the slightest chance to accuse, will accuse; who chiefly hate and invite others to hate —these are people who have somehow, somewhere along the line received psychological wounds. In family, or school, or job life, or community, in one or all of them—they have either been made to feel of little worth, or they have been subjected to authority that has arbitrarily commanded their obedience; or they have suffered from both.

The fate of any culture lies in the relative amount of rejection or acceptance, domination or friendly cooperation that is found in the major institutions and relationships of that culture. We now can begin to understand why there was the vast potential of hatred among the Germans. Germany has been predominantly a land where the authoritarian pattern has prevailed. Typically, the father dominated in the home, the teacher in the school, the officer in the army, the army in the community, and in the nation at large. The prevailing right to dominate bred suppressed hostilities, that, when released into action became a national orgy of hating and persecuting. That the Jews were selected as the object of the hate was largely incidental. A hierarchic culture where the right to dominate was the widely respected and practiced right, would inevitably, in a time of crisis, go the way of hostility.

VII

What are the prospects among ourselves? The course our own democracy will take is to be found in the major life-relationships. It is of deep moment whether the prevailing pattern in the home is one of parent domination or of parent-child cooperation; whether the pattern in the school is one of authoritarian compulsion or of a friendly cooperation in learning; whether the pattern in the economic world is one of the will of

Freedom and the Authoritarian Personality

the stronger to dominate the weaker, or the will of both to work together for common advantage; whether the pattern of racial life is one of drastic subordination by a self-designated "superior" race, or one of respect for the equal dignity of individuals of all races; whether the pattern of political life is one of narrow-minded fight between partisans for patronage and power, or a joint effort, even in a party system, to work for the common good; whether the pattern of the religious life is one of jealous contention between systems of religious absolutism, or one of reverent effort, in unity of spirit, to make the Highest come alive among us.

In the above, we have a yardstick by which to measure the dangers and the hopes ahead of us. *If, in the major relationships of our life, hostility-engendering conditions prevail, the freedoms of democracy are profoundly threatened. If, on the contrary, in those major relationships, goodwill-engendering conditions prevail, the freedoms of democracy become assured.*

It becomes clear, then, that the basic support of democracy is a spiritual one. Democracy is strong in the degree that men are strong in their respect and liking for one another, and in their willingness to work cordially together as equals. It is weak in the degree that men learn to be suspicious of one another; to outsmart and defeat; to hate and overcome one another.

This, I think, points the way to the major task ahead of us if we do not want our hostilities to get out of hand. In many ways the authoritarian mind is taking over. I talked recently to a red baiter in an effort to find out from him why he was rousing the people of his community against those whom he called "Communists" in their midst. "Are these people you call Communists really Communists?" I asked him. He brushed the question aside, almost in anger. "Whether they actually are Communists or not," he said, "is immaterial. They have criticized our capitalistic system."

There is perhaps little that can be done with so unintelligently hostile a mind; but there is much that needs to be done to prevent such minds developing among our citizenry. We need, in short, to make not only informed citizens, but citizens with a certain bent of character. Thus we must think of citizen-making as taking place in all the relationships of our life.

Whether we shall go the totalitarian way of a compelled conformity, or the democratic way of freedom to differ, will depend upon how widely we can create, from childhood on, one particular form of readiness. Hitherto the churches have been the main proponents of a goodwill pattern of personality. We must now see that this way of life that religion at its best has sought to promote, must be promoted likewise by secular society. It is not enough, in short, that in a democracy men shall be free to vote. They must be so conditioned by all their life relationships that they vote with goodwill. This is something that cannot be acquired in a few days preceding each election. It is something that must proceed out of the entire enterprise of living together.

Comment by Rudolf Allers:

It is one thing to preach hatred against the Communists, to suspect every one not in agreement with certain preconceived ideas, to institute investigations, or to require "loyalty-oaths," and it is another thing to believe that the spreading of certain doctrines entails a threat for values considered—with what right is an ulterior question—as fundamental and constitutive of human dignity. One may dislike the procedure by which the first aim is pursued and still approve of the aim as such.

If there is a freedom of speech, there is also one of listening. If an audience, or any other group, as such or by means of its chosen representatives, refuses to listen to certain ideas or certain speakers, they are within their rights. A denominational college will not invite a professed atheist as a guest speaker, and if he tries to impose himself, the institution will do everything in its power to hinder his being heard. The college is in its right. Both, the general public and the college, were wrong, however, if they were to base their refusal on mere hearsay, on denunciation, or other such unsavory reasons. In other words, one cannot establish any general rule applicable in all cases without previous examination of the case. This may hold also of the famous list of "subversive organizations." It cannot be gainsaid that there exists a real danger; the cases of espionage have given testimony of this danger. A nation of which the majority definitely prefers a certain form of life, is entitled to take measures to ward off those who endeavor to introduce ideas obviously contradicting the commonly held convictions. The question of measures to be taken that such a danger be prevented or kept within limits, must be distinguished from the other question of the particular nature of the measures to be adopted.

It is not certain that removal of "domination" will, automatically, as it were, produce desirable results. There are many other factors at work; it is a dangerous simplification to see in the psychology which happens to be the fashion today, an all-powerful tool.

Simplification is one of the greatest dangers, *i.e.*, the "right to dissent"—but has anyone the right to dissent on certain basic principles? The authoritarian, too, dissents; he believes, for instance, in a fundamental inequality of men. Have we to allow him to propagate his ideas? And to act accordingly, if he may?

Comment by Hoxie N. Fairchild:

What I like best in Professor Overstreet's paper is his warning that our efforts to defend freedom bid fair to damage the very liberties of which we are the dedicated champions. Of course a good many intellectuals have recently said the same thing in much the same way, but it is well that this position should be set forth so clearly and vigorously in the proceedings of our Conference.

The connection between his remarks on this point and his advocacy of conditioning the American mind in the direction of goodwill is not altogether clear to me. One possible result of McCarthyism to which Professor Overstreet does not refer, is that good liberals may react against its stupidity and baseness to the extent of underestimating the peril in which our country does actually stand. We are threatened by an enemy against whom we have the right and the obligation to defend ourselves, and authentic agents of this enemy are actively at work among us. Doubtless we should resist Communism without hating individual Communists as human beings; but when human beings within, as well as without, our borders become enemies of humanity, we must expose and combat them, even while we try to perform the almost impossible feat of loving them at the same time. Let us think of atomic spies as charitably as we can. The immediate practical necessity, however, is to catch and jail them. This may be done without condoning the attempt to deprive patriotically liberal professors of their academic freedom. The masters of Soviet Russia, being quite unhampered by the faintest vestigial remains of religious commitment, would be delighted to have us substitute a goodwill campaign for the more mundane defense preparations which we have undertaken. By all means let us try to keep decent and rational, without shutting our eyes to the hideous fact that it is impossible in a Godless world to conquer a bestial enemy without acquiring some tincture of bestiality. The terrible price may not be too high, if we remember that there is a real and precious difference between dirty gray and pitch black.

But if Professor Overstreet means that the sense of human brotherhood is the long-range remedy for the ills of America and Russia and the whole world, the ultimate aim which we should cherish even while we perform the unloving acts necessitated by the present crisis, then I most warmly agree with him. I agree also that the world is suffering from "spiritual emptiness," and that "the basic support of democracy is a spiritual one."

Unfortunately we diverge again in our interpretation of the term, "spiritual." I do not share Professor Overstreet's faith in the power of human nature to create spiritual values by transforming human nature. For him, human beings are the mechanical products of their "life conditioning." Let us, then, establish a "goodwill pattern of personality," by placing our children amidst "goodwill engendering conditions" and seeing that such conditions continue to surround them as they move onward into maturity. "We begin to see that it is as simple as that," says Professor Overstreet. But is it really so simple? Where are the good men who will make the good environment which will make good children? The program is circular: in order to have a world of goodwill, we must have men of goodwill, and if children are to become men of goodwill they must grow up in a world of goodwill.

Of course the issue between Professor Overstreet and me is the issue between naturalistic humanism and supernaturalistic religion. This is the main cleavage which runs through our Conference, and there seems to be no way of closing it by means of argument. The most one can do—and it is a great deal—is to credit the man on the other side of the gap with complete sincerity, goodwill, and devotion to the cause of human freedom, and to recognize wholeheartedly the possibility that he may be right.

Comment by Royal M. Frye:

This is an arresting paper. It represents an excellent piece of analysis, and brings home to us a very serious situation. My only criticism of it is that it stops too soon. Like an absorbing play, even though it be a tragedy, we are startled when we find it is over.

CHAPTER II

Spirit and Function of Organization

By JAMES MARSHALL
Member, Board of Education of the City of New York
Nature of the Authority of Leadership

INSECTS ARE PROVIDED by nature with specialists ready trained, born to expertness as fighters, providers, guardians of the larvae and courtiers of the queen. Our experts learn through experience and schooling, and in the more technical fields are blessed with the certification afforded by university degrees. Then, time and again, trained experts and technicians who do not consciously conceive of themselves as engaged in public administration, who have had little or no training in the field of administration, are expected to perform the tasks of administrators.[1] Nevertheless, as Woodrow Wilson said, men must learn administration. It is not skill with which they are born.[2]

If administration is to be autocratic, then little is required other than that the high levels of hierarchy shall have the power or prestige—that is, in the sense of reputation for power—to obtain obedience.

If administration is to be leadership and not command, then it were well that the high echelons of hierarchy were Escoffiers or Rembrandts, sensitive to the flavor and shades of coloring in the group relationships. Such leadership requires not just an understanding of the organizational interrelationships of the hierarchy. It requires some knowledge of the psychological dynamics of group behavior, of belief systems, of status values, and of the learning process itself. The administrator who is a leader must also be a teacher. For such leadership he requires not only formal education in administration but also apprenticeship and on the job training.

---

[1] William A. Jump, "The Professors and the Practitioners," *Public Administration Review*, Chicago, 1947, pp. 208–210.

[2] Woodrow Wilson, *Congressional Government,* Houghton, Mifflin, & Company, Boston and New York, 1885, p. 254.

Leadership is not necessarily to be measured in terms of force and economic power. Tacitus, referring to the kings of the Germanic tribes, wrote: "These kings have not unlimited or arbitrary power, and the generals do more by example than by authority. If they are energetic, if they are conspicuous, if they fight in the front, they lead because they are admired. But to reprimand, to imprison, even to flog, is permitted to the priests alone."[3] The study of social organization of shops has also indicated that the natural leaders of the workers are not necessarily those vested with authority by management.

Perhaps we should describe more accurately what this administrative leadership is. The approach, at least on its higher levels, is well illustrated by Tolstoy's description of Kutuzov, the gray, fat, aged commander of the Russians in the great battle against Napoleon at Borodino:

> He gave no orders, but only assented to or dissented from what others suggested. . . . He listened to the reports that were brought him and gave directions when his subordinates demanded that of him; but when listening to the reports it seemed as if he were not interested in the import of the words spoken, but rather in something else—in the expression of face and tone of voice of those who were reporting. By long years of military experience he knew, and with the wisdom of age understood, that it was impossible for one man to direct hundreds of thousands of others struggling with death, and he knew that the result of a battle is decided not by the orders of one commander in chief, . . . but by that intangible force called the spirit of the army, and he watched this force and guided it as far as that was in his power.[4]

What Tolstoy called the "spirit of the army" is to civil administrators that equally intangible force, the morale of the organization. The principal function of the administrator, particularly as one approaches the highest levels of hierarchy, is to watch and guide this force, to be sensitive to the group dynamics of the department, the school system, the office, the plant.

How does an executive do this? In the first place, he must be sufficiently apart to have an over-all view. In the second place, he must be sufficiently *a* part of the organization to understand its group dynamics

---

[3] *The Complete Works of Tacitus,* The Modern Library, Random House, New York, 1942, p. 712.
[4] Leo Tolstoy, *War and Peace,* Simon & Schuster, New York, 1942, Chapter 35, Book 10, p. 898.

and the individual strengths and weaknesses of those upon whom he must primarily rely.

To the degree that the administrator must make important decisions to determine policy and engage in planning, he must be sufficiently apart from the hurly-burly of the line. To do this he must depend upon experts in the fields of administration as well as upon technicians. There must be a division of responsibilities. When General Marshall was worried that General Eisenhower was in danger of losing his "refreshing approach to problems" by overwork and overattention to details, he sent him an aide, with the instructions: "It is your job in the war to make him take care of his health and keep that alert brain from overworking, particularly on things his staff can do for him."[5]

This need for distributing responsibility—or authority—is recognized in the principle that decisions should be made at the lowest competent level. In dynamic terms, this means that as far down the hierarchy as possible people should be given the opportunity to feel that their responsibility in the enterprise is something vital.

This rule is probably breached more often than observed. A striking example is that of President Andrew Jackson, who "undertook single-handedly to supervise all of federal administration. An amazing mass of problems ranging from the disciplining of minor clerks to the location of a privy, were personally handled by the President."[6] Similarly, the chairman of the board of a great American corporation with scores of scattered branches, many of which do many millions of dollars worth of business in a year, insists on personally approving every expenditure of more than $500.

This does not make for responsible administration. It is a sign of anxiety and distrust on the part of the administrator. It fails to free him for his more important functions. "If there be one principle clearer than another, it is this: that in any business, whether of government or of mere merchandising, somebody *must be trusted,* in order that when things go wrong it may be quite plain who should be punished," Woodrow Wilson wrote. *"Power and strict accountability for its use* are the essential constituents of good government."[7]

---

[5] Harry C. Butcher, *My Three Years with Eisenhower,* Simon & Schuster, New York, 1946, pp. 247–248.
[6] Albert Somit, "Andrew Jackson as Administrator," *Public Administration Review,* Chicago, 1948, pp. 188–191.
[7] Wilson, *op. cit.,* pp. 283 f.

Just prior to the Yalta Conference, President Roosevelt and Prime Minister Churchill met on a warship in Malta Harbor. In a discussion between General Marshall and Sir Alan Brooke, the Chiefs of Staff of their respective governments, a question arose concerning the military government of Germany. Sir Alan asked General Marshall's approval of his proposal.

"I must first consult Washington," General Marshall replied.

"What do you mean you must consult Washington?" Sir Alan asked. "The President is here. The Secretary of State is here. You are here. Why consult Washington?"

"You see," General Marshall explained, "there's a fellow in Washington—and I don't know if he's a captain, a major, or a colonel—who has probably been studying this matter for several years. I want to know what he thinks. That's what I mean by consulting Washington."

In such a case the chief executive does not act as his own line and staff but shares with others the responsibility and the rewards of participation in decision-making. He respects their dignity and status and relieves them of much of the anxiety and antagonism so frequently incident to their subordinate conditions.

Authority or Responsibility

In the common parlance of administration, much is said of the "delegation of authority," "lines of authority," or "lines of command." If there is to be true accountability, there must be accurate definition of functions and the areas in which they are to be performed.

But the emphasis on *authority, command,* and *lines* is more pertinent to autocratic administration than it is to administration which seeks to achieve its ends through leadership. Far better would be the terms, "delegation of responsibility," and "areas of responsibility." "Authority belongs to the job and stays with the job. . . . delegation of authority should be an obsolete expression, yet we hear it every day."[8]

Administration, as religion and political science, has spoken of the duties and responsibilities of men. Nevertheless, by thinking and acting in terms of command they have fortified dependence on authority. By that very fact the sense of responsibility has been weakened. This attitude

---

[8]Mary P. Follett, "The Illusion of Final Authority," *Bulletin Taylor Society,* New York, 1926, XI, p. 244.

of command, the autocratic attitude, is understandable in a system which maintains the principle: "from the hour of their birth, some are marked out for subjection, others for rule."[9]

If, however, it is believed that all men are created equal or that the ends of society are liberty, equality, and fraternity, then an administrative attitude based upon command must create conflict and therefore tension in those who command, as well as in those who are commanded.

The power which administration needs to accomplish its ends is not power *over* but power *to do*. Power to do in terms of group behavior is achieved when the group assumes responsibility for accomplishing the purpose. When we speak, therefore, of an area of *responsibility,* we imply that the people having the responsibility in those areas *assume* an obligation. When we delegate responsibility, we are, in fact, giving the persons to whom it is delegated the authority to make decisions at their level of hierarchy.

It is ignorance of social dynamics to expect people at a lower level to assume responsibility for decisions, if they are commanded. One need only remind oneself of the extent of buck passing in autocratic organizations such as the military, to recognize the truth of this statement. For in such situations, lines of authority tend to become lines of evasion of authority, and responsibility tends to mean blame or censure—"I'm not responsible for that mistake, he is." As in the game of Hearts, the object is to leave some other player with the Queen of Spades, and avoid the penalty of being caught with the card.

Both in the production (or performance) and in the servicing spheres, there are four general areas of administrative responsibility. These are: (a) responsibility for determining the nature and scope of the job to be done; (b) responsibility for operation, for performance, for doing the job; (c) responsibility for checking the operation; and (d) responsibility for appraising the result and method of performance. Depending upon the extent of the operation, each area of responsibility may be subdivided. Where the operation is small as on a family farm, in a rural school, a neighborhood store, or a local office of government, it may be that one person is responsible for all of these areas. As the cook in the kitchen must plan the various courses of the meal, with an eye to the nutritional values of the whole, and time the various dishes of each course so that

---

[9] *The Basic Works of Aristotle, Politics,* edited by Richard McKeon, Random House, New York, 1941, p. 1132.

all are served warm at the appropriate time and neither overdone nor undercooked, so the administrator must interrelate the various areas of responsibility.

Policy-Making

The determination of the nature and scope of the job is primarily what we call policy-making. Parliaments, legislatures, boards of directors, of trustees, or of education, are the principal policy-makers in democratic situations, although they may be influenced by cliques among their membership and pressure groups from the outside. In autocratic situations the policies are determined by powerful individuals or groups, even though these may be influenced by a realistic appraisal of the temper of the people affected. The difference between a parliament or congress, on the one hand, and a politburo, on the other, lies in the relationship of the public and interested segments of the public to policy-making and appraisal, that is, participation in the discussions and planning before the policy is set; and then their power to require an accounting.

There is no clearcut line of demarcation between what constitutes the area of responsibility of the policy-making group and the administrator in determining the nature and scope of the job to be done. In parliamentary systems, such as the British and the French, the chief administrative officers of the government are part of a legislative body. They propose, vote on, and administer the laws which determine the areas with which the state intends to occupy itself. Autocrats and politburos combine the same functions. Even in the United States under the constitutional division of powers, the Congress engages in administration through budgetary controls and basic legislation concerning the organization of government. The question is not so much one of the legal right and the fiscal power of policy-making bodies to participate in administration, as it is the degree of restraint which they exercise in these areas with a view to fixing responsibility on administrative officers.

Although the lines between the responsibility to determine policy and to administer it may fluctuate and overlap, the functions are different. The status of the administrator is endangered and his accountability minimized, if the policy-making body assumes executive responsibility, that is, assumes the responsibility for getting things done. And if the executive takes over the major functions of policy-making, he becomes an autocrat.

However, after the last period has been placed to the final sentence of a statute, a resolution, decree, or order, there remains a considerable area of interpretation which is the province of the administrator. The executive authority must "fill up the details" of the law, as Chief Justice Marshall said; he must apply it and in doing so interpret it. "Legislators must not be too jealous to hand technical matters over to experts. No one can deny that there are experts in every legislature. . . . But there is a reservoir of accumulated knowledge and experience outside of the legislature which it is a pity not to use."[10]

And this reservoir of knowledge and experience is not alone in the minds of those whom we commonly think of as administrators. Experience has shown that the man at the work bench, in the warehouse and in the classroom, as well as he who comes to the government for its services and the shop for its merchandise, has valuable knowledge and experience which can be tapped. Much legislation, many rules and orders must be experimental. Those to whom they apply, as well as those who apply them, test their value and measure their efficiency.

The fact is that almost every decision made and every act in performance of the functions of an organization are in their major or little ways related to policy. The manners in which letters are written, telephone calls answered, inquiring callers received and replied to, are not simple acts of administration or routine of an office. They are expressions and interpretations of policy. If it cannot be said that the subordinate is deputized as a policy-maker, nevertheless he is certainly a policy-maker and breaker, and his interpretations and reactions to policy determine its effectiveness.

Consequently, it is important that policy-makers, whether their function be of a legislative character or administrative, recognize the part of the group in determining policy. This requires understanding of systems of belief, reactions to attitudes and methods, recognition of personality traits, status needs, and the expectations of the various roles performed by each level of the hierarchy. It is for these reasons, too, that he who watches morale most effectively must watch the effect of policy

[10] Cecil Thomas Carr, *Concerning English Administrative Law*, Columbia University Press, New York, 1941.

decisions in terms of group response. And it is because of the relationship between response and responsibility that some measure of participation in planning gives people a vested interest in the success of the outcome.[11] It is not uncommon today for governments to establish advisory committees to assist in administration. Some advisory committees today receive legislative sanction, such as the National Commissions established pursuant to the constitution of the United Nations Educational, Scientific and Cultural Organization, and the advisory committees on vocational education in several of the United States. These bodies have recognized authoritative voices in planning and appraising the work of governmental bodies. As the mass of government becomes more concentrated and the elected representatives are separated from the people affected by the mere force of numbers, advisory commissions made up of representatives of functional groups would seem to be imperative, if mass and distance are not to destroy democracy through inevitable apathy.[12] It would seem also that industry, whether in the form of private or state enterprise, needs to find a formula or formulas to bring greater participation of workers into planning and appraisal.[13]

Checking

Checking, of course, is necessary, because for various reasons men do not always fulfil their responsibilities or even accept them. This may happen because of personalities, because of the limitations of their intelligence or skills, because of misunderstanding, for many reasons. Administration itself can bring about indifference and carelessness. Perhaps equally important is the conditioning which workers have had in the course of their schooling which has made for apathy and negligence.

[11]F. J. Roethlisberger, *Management and Morale*, Harvard University Press, Cambridge, 1946, p. 24; Marion Redke and Dayna Klisurich, "Experiments in Changing Food Habits," *Journal of American Dietetic Association*, May, 1947, XXIII, 5, p. 403; and see Kurt Lewin, "Forces Behind Food Habits and Methods of Change," in "The Problems of Changing Food Habits," *National Research Council Bulletin*, Washington, 1943, 108, pp. 35-65.

[12]Alexis De Tocqueville, *Democracy in America*, Alfred A. Knopf, New York, 1945, II, p. 368; and see the author, "Citizen Diplomacy," *American Political Science Review*, February, 1949, XLIII,, 1, p. 83.

[13]Russell W. Davenport, "Enterprise for Everyman," *Fortune*, 1950, LXI, pp. 55, 58, 157; Joseph N. Scanlon, "Profit-Sharing Under Collective Bargaining: Three Case Studies," *Industrial Labor Relations Review*, 1948, II.

There is a constant danger that checking may increase carelessness and indifference, because it may develop dependence on checking—"let the inspector (or the auditor or proofreader) find the mistake." Checking often defeats its purpose, and substitutes for good workmanship.

There is a tendency on the part of inspectors and accountants to regard themselves as being on a higher level of hierarchy than in fact they are. This tendency results in status conflicts and stresses which may be more unsettling and cause more dissatisfaction, anxiety, and aggression than any order issued or policy set by high levels of the hierarchy. Where, therefore, a high degree of technical knowledge and experience is not essential, it may be well worth the trouble and expense to train people so that they may be shifted between production and checking. Of course this is more possible where hierarchies of salaries detailed for every function have not frozen the organization into bureaucracy.

Appraisal

After the planning and after the product has been checked and disposed of, or the services have been rendered, questions arise as to the efficiency of the performance and the quality of the product produced and the service rendered. It is essential that appraisal be made, if planning is to proceed. Industry, at least big industry, has some understanding of this need for appraisal and research. Considerable sums of money are set aside for research and laboratories. Comparatively little is done in appraisal and research by government.

The Taylor system of efficiency has affected American industry. It has spawned efficiency engineers who study with measuring tapes and stop watches industrial processes to bring about greater economy of motion. Many of these economies have run against worker resistance, because they have upset status relationships, unsettled belief systems, or have made unwanted, skills which were developed through generations. More recently, Taylor system devotees have extended the study of motion in industry to emotion in industry.

It is after all on facts—or what passes for them—that policy is decided. With appraisal we therefore return to policy-making. The facts may be obtained by such rough and ready methods as reviewing profit and loss statements; they may be derived from the degree of avoidance of "trouble" or by mere hunch. But they may be truly obtained through careful research, through scientific experiment, and statistical study. Research is also frequently done through the use of questionnaires. All of these methods may seem burdensome to the people whose work and behavior is the subject of the research. It may create resistances in them, born of anxieties which will impede and restrict the efficiency of the appraisal.

In any event, if men and women are to share in planning, they should share in the work of appraisal, or at least be given an understanding of the purposes of the appraisal. Here again we find a need for participation and planning; that is, if appraisal is to be most effective, it is preferable that the workers be involved in planning for the appraisal. It would be good practice to consult businessmen, their selected representatives, and others, concerning the questionnaires which they are asked to answer by agencies trying to gather facts or opinions upon which to base appraisals of the effectiveness of government.

Functions of Experts

Government and industry, as we all recognize, are complicated undertakings today. They are no longer simple units, but aggregations of many enterprises, sometimes delicately articulated, often with no functional relationship between their parts. Lighthouses and tax collection have been handled by the Treasury Department; mines and insular possessions have been the province of the Department of Interior. Education is far more today than the three R's in a one room schoolhouse, or even a ninety room schoolhouse.

In the larger organizations the chief administrative officers may have difficulty in keeping track of the many operations for which they are responsible. They must rely on specialists, experts, and technicians, men and women trained in the intricacies of the sciences, technology, craft skills, and in administration itself.

Some experts are part of the executive machinery without being administrators. They do the research work, make needed analyses and appraisals, provide the materials on which policies depend.

Experts in administration, however, have as one of their principal functions that of communications center. It is they whose area of responsibility includes transmitting and interpreting in the form of concrete work assignments the policies of the organization. It is they, too, who must report back the manner in which and the degree to which policy has been consummated and the cost thereof; and the extent to which the policies have been accepted and resisted by those who ultimately perform the services or make the product. These are the operating experts, the highly trained personnel, professional and skilled, who are the core of the enterprise.

We are so conditioned to the expert that we find it natural and acceptable that he should be called upon to function when technical knowledge is required. Sometimes, as in the case of the doctor and the teacher, we accept him with a blind faith not far removed from that rendered to his prototypes, the primitive medicine man and priest. For the culture of the race is founded on the expert who through magic could ward off the spirits of evil, and the wonder he inspired lingers about the atomic scientist and to a somewhat lesser degree about all experts today.

This is not always the case as it concerns the expert in administration, because his magic tends to impinge more often and acutely on the status of everyone. His authority is in a field in which power conflicts are more apparent and the power weapons of his subordinates more readily accessible; for he can at least be answered and met with words and apathy. More than any other expert, the managerial needs to know the mysteries of human behavior and to be able to officiate over them on a give and take basis.

The authority of the expert depends not only on his skill and the respect which his skill and knowledge induce, but also on his power and his executive status in relation to laws and rules. In our early years we learn that the policeman can enforce the rules of the state, the clergyman the rules of faith, and the umpire the rules of the game. The latter is especially interesting, because more clearly than in most situations, the rules which the umpire enforces are rules established and respected on a voluntary basis and enforced by mutual opinion. While it is true that "Popular opinion is ready to respect laws made by any well known authority," the range of free choice is more limited when the result of error may lead to durance vile, the imposition of monetary damages, or eternal damnation, than in the case of those voluntary enterprises in which we engage for recreation without compulsion or the threat of it.[14]

If, as we have said, the most effective administration in the long run, except in emergency situations, takes the form of leadership rather than

[14] Carr, *op. cit.,* p. 38.

command; and if this involves participation in the group as a member of it, not apart from it or above it; then perhaps the hierarchy of administration is more than a pyramid of individuals. It is rather a pyramid of groups, the administrator at each level being, among other things, an expert at leadership of those on the level or levels below him. Better administration encompasses the on-the-job growth of subordinates and a development of their feeling of belongingness, of acceptance, through the satisfactions that come through active rather than passive participation.

Communication is the heart of the matter, communication that brings understanding and a favorable response, communication which produces action with a minimum of hostility. This must of necessity be two way communication, if the belief systems, the status and the initiative of those involved are to be, perhaps modified, surely respected and employed.[15]

Neither in infancy, adolescence, nor maturity, is life possible except in a social setting,[16] and organized institutions are instances of social settings. Man requires society for his development and for the satisfaction of his moral and psychological, as well as of his physical tensions. Consequently, freedom can only be something comparative, its character determined by the interplay of personality and society, of individual and organization. We cannot conceive of freedom as a mere absence of restraint. If this were possible, it would not last long, because a new form of restraint would quickly fill the vacuum.

In organization, freedom means that an opportunity is granted to each member to contribute to the organization, to participate in planning and appraisal of some aspect of the organizational enterprise, no matter how humble. The greater the extent of participation, the greater will be the freedom. Without participation there is dependence. That is, and throughout history has been, the status imposed on most men in most organizations, and dependence is certainly not freedom. This can be

---

[15] Barnard, *op. cit.*, pp. 232–233.

[16] Rene Spitz, "Hospitalism: An Inquiry into the Genesis of Psychiatric Conditions in Early Childhood," *The Psychoanalytic Study of the Child*, International Universities Press, New York, 1945, I, pp. 53–74; "Hospitalism, A Follow-up Report," *ibid.*, 1946, II, pp. 113–117; "Anaclitic Depression: An Inquiry into the Genesis of Psychiatric Conditions in Early Childhood," *ibid.*, pp. 313–342; "The Smiling Response: A Contribution to the Ontogenesis of Social Relations," *Genetic Psychology Monographs*, 1946, 34, pp. 57–125.

put in another way. The positive side of freedom is that it is a condition affording opportunities to realize the most of one's potentialities. This is the vital thing concerning the relationship of freedom to organization.

Comment by Edgar S. Brightman:
On this admirably concrete paper, only one comment is needed, and that is a favorable one. A gem of wisdom is found in the sentence, "Taylor system devotees have extended the study of motion in industry to emotion in industry." This may be called the discovery of the person!

Comment by Daniel L. Kurshan:
This paper on the "Spirit and Function of Organization" is excellent; I am entirely in accord. I would have liked to have seen more about that aspect of authority which satisfies the dependency needs of the emotionally immature.

CHAPTER III

Notes on a Theory of Advice

By LYMAN BRYSON
Professor of Education, Teachers College, Columbia University

THIS TENTATIVE and fragmentary analysis of advice is offered to indicate what might be worked out as the basis of a guide for the scholars, scientists, and experts who move into the world of affairs on invitation. By reason of training and intellectual habit, they are capable of seeing clearly the abstract or schematic picture of what goes on and should be helped to do so. They should be able, if called on, to describe the behavior of policy-makers, and their assistants, to the policy-makers themselves, since administrators are not often given to the self-indulgence of abstract thought. One sure mark of the man of action is to use intuitions in place of abstractions, and this is true even in a society like ours, where skills are so generally explicit, and "know-how" is so much discussed. The man of thought is very different; he will make a small cosmos out of the smallest experience.

The expert who accepts an invitation from a policy-maker is entering a situation in which he can expect to observe the working of four or more distinguishable functions in the six or more stages of the decision-making process. We can take the functions first, understanding, of course, that one person may act at different times in different functions and that functions may occasionally be merged.

First is the making of the policy decision which we shall call the function of administration. It is final for the unit of action being examined. It includes the right, as will be explained later, to appeal to a free constituency, which is another way of saying that even the administrator who makes the final decision in any unit of action has the right and the responsibility of being judged by somebody. Swift remarked, "a flea hath smaller fleas that on him prey," and what was expressed as lyric annoyance is a true description of sober fact. Every decision, in any kind of organization, must please somebody who has a right to be displeased, no matter how final it may be for all subordinates. For the immediate purpose, however, we think of the policy-making decision as a terminal point in a process. The expert is called in to help eventually in giving that decision as much prescience and caution as is possible. The expert is not responsible, however, for making it; if he does, he is fulfilling the function of administration, not of advice.

The second function can be called execution. It is performed, if the unit is small, by the administrator himself; in larger organizations, there are executive assistants. It must be clearly understood that execution is here considered part of the policy-making process; it is not a merely mechanical performance in which the intentions of the policy-maker are automatically realized. Execution always involves a series of subsidiary decisions which arise in carrying out the powers that have been delegated to the executive by the policy-maker. Opposition, treachery, political manipulations, or useful inventiveness, may make or mar the policy as it is realized. The adage, "If you want something well done, do it yourself," is an admonition to an administrator not to trust his executives. The other adage, "A man who is his own lawyer has a fool for a client," may incidentally express the other side of the case. Or, we might find it in the Chinese maxim of political administration which states that the good administrator does nothing; he does nothing, in order to give his executives the opportunity to do their best. This ambivalence in popular folklore shows that the decision as to how much he shall personally intervene in the execution of his own policies, is one of an administrator's most sticky problems.

The third function is advice. Here the expert enters the situation; his work is almost wholly the giving of advice. How the location and content of his advice are to be determined will be discussed in connection with the stages of the decision-making sequence. At this point, while we are considering the functions, we can note that the function of advising is performed by all the members of an organization in some contexts, and this advice giving is almost never politically innocent. It is only the outsider, the expert who is paid primarily for his advice and listened to for his special professional knowledge, who can expect his opinions to have entirely objective standing.

If the invited expert is an academic person, whose experience of controversy has been scientific or scholarly, he is very likely to misunderstand much of what goes on around him, because he thinks of proffered opinions as opinions only. He weighs them in the same scales of objective valuation he expects his own opinions to be weighed in; he tries to examine them courteously but "impersonally." By living up to the ascetic ideals of his own intellectual discipline he heightens the value of his own work, of course, but keeps himself alien to the other elements in the decision-making process. We believe that he will be more useful in performing his special function if he knows the differences between his own behavior and that of his temporary colleagues, and this analysis is a suggestion of the kind of work that ought to be done to help him.

There is also a fourth function which we can call interpretation. It is not often the job of a designated person; either an executive assistant or an expert can perform it and is likely to do so without thinking that he is widening his own special task. The function is not clearly conceived, and is assumed by different persons thoughtlessly. This partly accounts for the fact that it is in this area of what we call interpretation that experts and executives most frequently fall afoul of each other without knowing why. The unspecified function is the cause of the trouble, as can be better understood when we examine the stages in the decision-making and decision-realizing process.

The decision-action process is a series of decisions whose nature and scope must be studied, if we are ever to conceptualize fully, and arrange logically, the cooperation between the elements of knowledge and power that make the world go round. What is said in these notes is at least sufficiently abstract to apply to any kind of business, whether government, industry, or the management of organizations. Power hunger shows itself openly in government and business; it may be disguised in a church hierarchy or a philanthropic society. Whether or not ambition is less potent in the competition of service, where money and material success are less obvious stakes, is a question we need not try to answer. But we need not put a cheap Machiavellian color on the matter; we can take each group of persons at their own valuation and make no moral judgments. The factors are about as we describe them in any single situation, and any one factor may be more or less present, according to pressures in the situation and the characters of the persons.

The first stage in decision-action is to describe the problem. In practice, most problems are partially formulated by the executive assistants in the regular administration of the enterprise. They note failures in the working out of previously initiated policies, report unexpected obstacles, complain of lack of tools, which may be in machines, money, or personnel; or, much more rarely, they may think of possible new objectives. The active administrator, for reasons to be suggested later, is not very likely to have much time for the discovery or the invention of problems. His primary function in all aspects of his job is to choose among suggestions received from his staff and from outside; the problems come to him in that form. Much of this flow of problems in the formulations of the executives is taken care of by routine decisions. When it is too difficult for that kind of "staff meeting" treatment, the expert may be called in.

A vague realization that the problem as now described is too difficult for staff routine decision is not enough, however, to determine the choice, the role, or the problem of the expert. In fact, there is often a period when some of the executive assistants may resist the suggestion of bringing in a consultant, because they have more or less routine suggestions of their own that they want to have favorably considered. The suggestion that only an expert can solve a problem is itself a suggestion, an "idea," and is immediately subject to all the kinds of scrutiny and resistance that meet every other idea. If the administrator accepts the idea in general, he is then open to new suggestions and may add a few of his own, leading to such a precise description of the problem as will make it possible to decide what kind of expert to call in.

Among executive assistants there is always competition. The energy of this conflict is one of the things with which an administrator works; it is also one of the factors that complicate the life and work of the outside specialist.

If the first decision by the administrator is that a consultant of specified knowledge shall be invited into the organization for the purpose of giving advice on a problem, that decision indicates that the problem is at least partly described in the administrator's mind. If he has not seen the problem clearly, he is merely indulging, for political or personal reasons, some member of his staff who offers a suggestion. The degree to which the problem actually is described before the advisory relation is established is of the greatest importance to the expert. There may be a later phase of the situation in which the expert can perform his own function only by stating that the problem has been wrongly described and that some other formulation, or indeed some other problem as yet undisclosed, must be tackled ahead of, or instead of, the one he has been assigned to.

Before this problem can arise for any expert, however, and before one is chosen, there is a choice to be made among the suggestions from executives as to the nature of the expert knowledge needed and as to the best available exponent of that kind of knowledge. The executive assistants will act as experts on experts and on expert knowledge. From among their suggestions, or on his own, the administrator chooses a person.

After being invited, and after accepting the assignment or agreeing to negotiate, the expert adviser is given a description of the problem. This first contact between him and his employers may be the locus of profound conflict or misunderstanding. If he accepts without question the problem, and the description of the problem which is given him by the administrator or by the designated subordinate, he is bound in his function as adviser to serve all the purposes of the administrator that are implied in it, or to make a clear rejection.

The question is raised at once, what right has an adviser to reformulate or to change the problem? The answer is still obscure, but it is evident from experience that each member of the relation between expert and executive, or expert and administrator, is likely to take it for granted that he has the privilege of naming and describing the problem. The expert, if not well trained by relevant experience in such affairs, coming probably from an academic situation in which it is the chief part of his work to rank problems in their respective importance and to formulate them for study, will try to go beyond the immediate presentation offered him to what he thinks is an understanding of ulterior policy considerations, so that he can (if still willing to associate himself with those purposes) help to achieve them. The administrator and executives have much more complicated and less innocent ideas about those ulterior policy matters and may not believe that it is necessary to disclose them.

They may, of course, listen watchfully to the expert's queries and suggestions regarding the nature of the "real" problem, and accept what can be used, provided it involves for them no embarrassment in their relations with each other.

Even at this early point in the process, the inexperienced adviser should begin to learn a few lessons about the competitive factors in decision-making. He may overlook them or fail to see them. In fact, men of academic background can often be seen trying to act as administrators in institutional leadership to which their expert knowledge fits them, without knowing or being willing to believe that what goes on around them is in any way different from scholarly or scientific discussion. Their expert knowledge fits them to understand the problems of the institution which may be school, library, business research department, or government bureau. They may have had an extensive knowledge of men in intellectual rather than power competitions. They may have a good second hand knowledge of practical affairs from reading and acquaintance. They may even have detected rudimentary power impulses in some of their academic colleagues, especially as manifested in malicious gossip. But they feel ashamed by the suspicion that men of affairs are not always wholly objective in what they say, as if, indeed, the morals of the seminar and the laboratory were the only morals extant.

The fact is, observable and inescapable, whatever moral judgment one may insist in passing on it, that the decision-making process is a field of personal ambition and sharp competition in all practical situations, whether business, government, or institutional. It might be argued that this is necessary and useful, that a scientific objectivity in the expression of opinions, the interpretation of facts, and the communication of ideas, among practical men would lead to worse, not better, results. We are not prepared to argue in that fashion any more than we are prepared to be shocked. The analyst has no moral obligation beyond stating the ascertainable facts in such a way as will be useful to other men of knowledge who mix in action and hope to serve a good purpose.

The administrator and his executives, generally through one person as a delegated intermediary, interpret to the expert a complex of administrative judgments as to the nature of the problem. The expert, after agreement as to the nature, or locus and formulation, of the problem, does his work by suggesting alternative courses of action and predicting the consequences to be expected from them. He is giving new dimensions of freedom to the thinking of the administrative group, because he is describing for them, and enabling them to entertain in their imagination, a range of choices they would not otherwise have considered.

It is evident that prediction of the consequences of a set of alternatives is a very difficult task which should always be performed with caution. The records would seem to indicate that the gifted man of action prefers to initiate a maneuver, and invent most of his planning as he goes. This has a number of psychological implications into which we cannot go at this point, related to the fact that men of action generally maintain their own morale by frequent rearrangement of goals, so that neither defeat nor victory can be too demoralizing. But when the expert, by definition not a man of action and therefore assumed to be more concrete in his expectations, is asked to describe alternative choices, he is expected also to tell the advantages and disadvantages of each choice. This is the same as asking him to predict, in spite of unpredictable circumstances, what will happen in any course of action. He is lucky if he can present plans in such a way as to indicate that future events will make new choices necessary, and that the road ahead is full of forks, each of which must be negotiated in the light of experience which cannot even be imagined until after arrival at that particular fork. He is not lucky if the administrator demands of him an absolute map of the future; some administrators think they are entitled to that kind of prophecy.

However, the expert is still caught in the process of decision-making, after he has described alternative courses of action, because he will probably discover that his ideas are subject to interpretation by the executive assistants before they are finally accepted or discarded. He may find that the executive who gives him the greatest degree of general approval and support interprets his suggestions in such a way as to produce results the expert did not intend. The expert can protest and argue; he may find himself silenced by the claim that his expertness goes only to the general idea, and that translating it into action requires another kind of knowledge which he does not possess, that is, knowledge special to the time and occasion and occupation in character.

After a decision is made by the administrator and a policy is explicitly chosen, then further interpretation in terms of action ensues, and the next decision will be as to which of the proposed practical lines of action will best achieve the policy's goal. The expert may be consulted on the alternatives here, but most of the suggestions will be offered by the various executive assistants; the administrator or one of his staff with delegated powers will choose. Subordinate decisions in a long series of budget-making, personnel selection and concurrent commands, will follow from this point forward.

We go back now to the essential character of decision-making in practical affairs and the understanding of it that will be most useful to the visiting consultant. A more or less conscious desire to dominate and get ahead in the administrative hierarchy pervades the behavior of all members of the staff. As we indicated before, this apparently cynical observation is subject to correction or reduction in any particular case. It can be observed, however, in the world of affairs, that the devoted and impersonal staff members who think only of the organization, never of themselves, seldom rise very high. And this may be better for the organization.

There are whole ranges of human endeavor in which competition in this sense does not enter; where the desire to excel is only a race for personal usefulness or service. It is also true, as I have insisted in many other places, that the goods that can be acquired by struggles for material power in business or politics are not of the highest order. We could even go so far as to say that the deepest satisfactions for men who constantly struggle for power and advancement in practical affairs seldom develop out of material success. All these statements are true and important; but the expert consultant who goes into the decision-making process, expecting to rely upon these reassuring facts, is immorally stupid. He is not exercising the ordinary prudence expected of any man of goodwill who has a practical purpose. If he discovers what ought to surprise him, namely, that the hierarchically ranged members of the staff achieve an objectivity in opinion which he is himself striving for, he has lost nothing but anxiety. If any of them turn out to be more basely human and he is surprised, he may have found out the truth too late. A kindly skepticism regarding the motives of all men in practical affairs is the usual attitude of experienced men of action; it becomes the expert quite as well if he can attain it.

The competitive modifications of opinion which we are accusing the members of the staff of making are, of course, partly unconscious, sometimes entirely so. The first to be looked at are the power ambitions of the executives. The difficulties of the administrator, the final arbiter, can be spoken of later. The executives who are, by our definition, all the members of the staff who have access to the administrator for purposes of policy discussion, will generally become quick advocates of some one of the various alternatives that are open in making the decisions listed above. They will have honest convictions about these alternatives and will in most cases be expressing those honest convictions. The administrator who cannot count on getting such honest opinions, either because he demands timid caution and "yessing," or because he has put men on his staff who are so completely political that they merely intrigue, deserves what he gets and is almost certain to fail in the long run. The administrator who is just and honest in his own opinions can expect a fair return in honesty. The executives, however, will almost certainly have something in their minds beyond the intrinsic worth of the opinions they back. They will also have more or less conscious mindsets that have organized in complicated fashion their desires to raise their own prestige and to make it likely that they will be allowed to help in further decisions and in decisions on other matters.

In scientific and scholarly disputes, or in consultative debates, it is more likely to be one opinion against another; one opinion wins if the question gets settled. In practical matters, the question almost always gets settled, but it is a man and not an opinion that wins. Every member of the staff wants to be that man, or to be associated with him. The description sounds more dramatic, of course, than the event generally seems to those who take part in it, but smiling friendliness and general acquiescence should not deceive the outsider.

The ambitions of the members of the staff, moreover, are not confined to motives of power. In many situations, the decision to call in an expert has followed deliberations in which members of the staff offered their own quasi-expert opinions and suggested courses of action. These suggestions were turned down, either by administrative fiat or by consensus; in any case, the executives are always inclined to resist the appeal to an outsider. His expertness is itself something of a criticism of their competence. Of course, situations may develop in which the adviser and his advice become a stake in the power game itself. At this point, the ambitious executive will affirm or deny the expert's competence without completely responsible regard for his real value. Academic veterans will probably have become indurated against the melancholy fact that some of their own colleagues on the campus will occasionally deride some other scholar's claim to eminence because of motives not strictly scholastic; that is, they may deny a man's scholarly attainments, in order to express their dislike or envy or fear of the man. The partisanships of executives are also colored by this kind of irrelevant feeling, but it is not so likely to sway them as are more clearly competitive motives. The expert then, may have allies and opponents, to both of which he has become a stake in the power game, but it would not be wise for him to count on simple friendships. His mere existence is a mild slur on the competence of the men he is dealing with and to whom he is giving the supposed benefit of his superior knowledge. Even the administrator, the decision-maker, may not be above claiming expert knowledge which helps to bolster his ascendancy over his executives and lessens his obligations to the outside adviser. What the administrator says is not likely to be listened to with complete objectivity by anybody.

There is a story that tells of the conversations which used to be held on the palace hill in Rome to entertain the Emperor Hadrian. He loved disputes about grammar and usage and word origins; professors were invited to dine with him and argue for his pleasure. Sometimes, he ventured an opinion of his own and on one occasion one of his experts rejected the emperor's theory summarily. The argument waxed hot and the emperor shouted. The deipnosophist shouted less and less as the exchanges went on, until at last the administrator, Hadrian, pronounced a final truth and his challenger was silent. "Aha," cried Hadrian, "my arguments have left you nothing to say." "Sire," replied the visiting expert, "who am I to disagree with the master of thirty legions?"

In the court at Rome, it would have been suicidal for the expert to have power ambitions of his own to match the knowledge ambitions of the emperor. In less deadly arguments, without his being well aware of it, his own pride in making decisions instead of merely outlining alternatives, may lead him into actions which are appropriate only if he is prepared to enter fully into the power contest. If he does so, his sense of objectivity and his reputation for disinterested knowledge are both likely to be damaged.

The problems of the administrator, the one who makes the final policy decisions, are one aspect of what has already been said. One of his most difficult procedural decisions, made generally by accident or intuition, is to choose the moment at which he will become a working member of the group that is examining the possible alternative lines of action. As long as he keeps out of it, he is only a useful future umpire. As soon as he joins the discussions, all ambitions are heightened because the dispenser of promotion and prestige is on hand to be impressed. If he makes choices at that time among alternatives he is inescapably choosing among advocates, as well as among plans.

On the other hand, if the administrator holds aloof too long, he is at the mercy of his executive assistants, because he must accept, as his range of choices, whatever they bring to him in the report of deliberations.

This is one of the most acute of the phases of the general administrative problem: How much should a manager be immersed in the actual diurnal round of his business in order to manage it? There is not likely to be any handy rule that will settle all cases. The principle needs far more thorough working out than it has received.

The special problems of the administrator can only be mentioned; they require much more elaborate treatment in other contexts. But it is useful, when we are plotting the difficulties of the outside expert in the swiftly changing patterns of an organizational process, to recall that the administrator has a primary task in keeping his own power as against rivals both inside and outside his own organization. It is a romantic notion of power, which ought to be blown out of an academician's imagination in his first experience as a committee chairman, that a man who struggles to get power can, having gained it, loll back and think about the good of his enterprise. He has, in fact, moved himself not to a seat of thoughtful leisure but to the center of a popular target. And to some extent, the greater the emoluments and the prestige of his position, the less he can think about anything but keeping it. All proposals for the single term occupancy of the White House are based on this fact, usually described in a more gingerly fashion. Exercising power is drastically interfered with by the need to hold it, unless you have agreed to get out on a fixed day. In politics, this is always a preoccupation of all but the innocent statesmen. In business, it is closely entangled with other motives and problems, because a business administrator's power may be diminished as much by the loss of his company's competitive position as by his own loss of position in the company. The two problems are often faced in the same decision. In any case, these things absorb time and attention that might otherwise go into thinking about function, as well as purpose.

In dealing with his executive assistants and the whole staff attached to him through them, the administrator has to give the example and the general direction of morale, as well as to make final choices among suggested alternatives. Sometimes he shakes morale by the seeming caprice of his choice, or by disagreeing with too many of his subordinates. As he listens to arguments, after he enters the deliberations, he is kept busy in settling the power disputes among his assistants in order to get the best ideas, to promote the fittest men, and to keep the appearance as well as the fact of justice. He must be alert to disentangle the knowledge values from the power bids of his advisers, whether they are executives or consulted experts.

He has also to think up ideas of his own. For this task, he has little time. His fitness to be the administrator, the man who makes the last decision and determines policy, is not determined by his fecundity in ideas. His ability to see the intrinsic, as well as the situational value of an idea suggested to him, is obviously far more important; other qualities which lie outside the scope of a theory of advice may count still more. It is evident enough that men of action, in business and politics, are often gifted with high intellectual powers, even beyond the needs of their work. They are not likely to exercise them for fun, as is the privilege of philosophers, artists, and teachers. But success in practical affairs is not commanded by sheer intellectual ability; other qualities of mind and character are also needed. Inventiveness does not seem to be one of them, and there is more inventiveness for sale in the market than there is of first rate administrative capacity.

The adviser, coming in *ad hoc,* has also some special problems of his own, for which he needs to be prepared. One is his responsibility to protect himself against being used to justify decisions already made. Just as some manager will, with naive dishonesty, call in workmen to "discuss" decisions already finally taken, so some administrators will ask advice when what they want is help. If the expert accepts the role of rationalizer, he may destroy his own integrity; he can often detect the hidden invitation to serve as mere helper in the formulation of the question he is asked to advise on. The first battle between adviser and staff, as we have already indicated, may be at that point, where the problem is described. Dr. John Gardner, of the Carnegie Corporation, has pointed out in a privately circulated memorandum that the expert is often challenged at the very outset of his work by the question of who has the right to say what the problem is. As a responsible practical manager, the administrator will usually assume that he has a right to tell a hired man what he is hired to do. On the other hand, as master of a field of knowledge, the consultant may well assume that he alone, and no other person of less knowledge, can understand the implications and history of a problem. Most men who have been consulted by business executives have discovered that much of what they think is pertinent is considered "theoretical" by business men, and that an attempt to extend the span of time of either hindsight or foresight is resented. No rule will suffice to guide the consultant here; he is the keeper of his own conscience.

There are limits on the criticism of one expert by another and the consultant has to decide what is appropriate for him to do in the competitive aspect of the world of knowledge. A more difficult question is what he will do in service to the public relations of the company he is temporarily working for. He may be asked by his own employer to issue a statement which, while technically truthful, is clearly planned to be a sales appeal. He may be asked by a newspaper or broadcasting station to comment on the general area in which he is working, as when physicians who are advising pharmaceutical manufacturers are asked to tell the public all about cures for the common cold. The problem is to keep honest. For the salesman or the advertiser to push his own product is honest; that is his economic function. But to what extent can the expert permit the use of his name and his personal prestige for the same purpose? He expects his findings, accurately reported, to be used. What about his professional standing?

The old rule, that doctors and lawyers do not advertise, does not help very much, because that has to do with whether or not they should advertise themselves. To what degree can a physician who has helped, as expert, to make a drug useful, allow his name to be used to increase public use of it? The answer is not suggested; the purpose here is only to mark the crossroads, with full stop signs.

Another aspect of the policy-making process which involves theoretical problems of freedom and authority, as well as practical problems of the relation between knowledge and power, is the definition of constituencies. Every person in a policy-making situation has his constituency, which may be free or captive. He has a group of people to whom he can appeal, in his own terms, for support and they can or cannot defy his administrative superiors. The analysis of this structural aspect of decision-making, when adequately done, will greatly help to solve the difficulties arising from the fact that our governments must deal more and more with technical questions, wherein legislators, voters, administrative officers, and elected executive officers have different kinds of competence, different degrees of freedom, and different private purposes. The same sort of complex relations on a smaller scale can be seen in industrial and other kinds of private organizations.

These concepts can be explained in terms of an ordinary hierarchy of authority in a political situation and the operation of constituencies will be understood as the mechanism by which democratic institutions restrain power. It is the criterion of freedom for any person in an administrative complex to discover whether or not he has a group to which he can appeal for help, which is not itself subject to the same superior pressures that he is subject to. For example, the head of a bureau in the state government of New York has a lesser degree of freedom than a member of the state legislature. The legislator can appeal to the voters of his district, who owe nothing but a reasonable hearing to the administrative officers of the state, whereas the bureau head, if he quarrels with his superiors, has no such independent group to appeal to. An appeal to an unorganized "public opinion" is of slight avail for the bureau head, for he has no special relation to any part or organ of the general body politic.

At the same time, the bureau head does have another kind of constituency, which we can call "captive." It is made up of his fellow administrative officials, both above and below him in the hierarchy. They are not a free constituency, because, although they may with more or less effect and safety take his side in a dispute against his superiors, they are subject to the same kinds of pressure that affect him. If they are his subordinates in a direct line, they are somewhat bound to him; if in an indirect way, they are bound by their own superior's action whatever it may be. If they are his coordinate or superior officials, they will be influenced by all the lines of authority and the inner struggle for power, and will more or less consciously have to calculate the effects of their own overt opinions on their own ambitions.

The term, "free," as applied to the voters in a legislator's district, does not mean that these persons are free of self-interest, prejudice, psychological pressures, and all the rest of the circumstances that bedevil the political thinking of all populations. They are a free constituency only in the sense that they have an established relation to the legislator which enables them, if they are persuaded, to exert pressures in his behalf, and they are not in any way affected by the administrative hierarchy in which he works. The bureau chief can organize support for himself inside the administrative system of the state, but his colleagues are not free to act as are the voters. To put it crudely, the governor, as administrator, can give orders to a bureau chief but not to a legislator.

One chief difference between a representative democracy and a totalitarian government, in purely technical terms, without regard to purposes or ideology, is here. In Russia, for example, in the present operational development of administration, since the Communist Party took charge of the country about five years ago, no official of any kind, appointed or elected, can be said to have a "free" constituency. The only free constituency is the people as a whole to whom in some measure the supreme government is responsible. No one has any legal machinery by which he can appeal to the country, or to any part of the country, as against his superiors or colleagues. It is the essence of a totalitarianism that all constituencies are captive. Anyone to whom any official might appeal for support in a dispute is himself a member of the administrative hierarchy and thus handicapped in his opinions, still more in his action. In a completely totalitarian country, a legislator cannot appeal to the voters as against administrative officials or against his legislative colleagues, because he is named to his post by the party, and only the party, through its regular graded channels, can express opinions. In a country with a more open system, like the United States, the tradition of allowing appeals to a free constituency is so deeprooted, and so close to our moral convictions regarding fair play, that an astute politician like President Truman will allow General MacArthur to dispute in public the administration's policies, although MacArthur has no legal constituency, and is actually under strict orders which could include an order not to discuss political or military matters in public. The fact that a rebellious and disgruntled military hero would not have been given open triumphs in Russia, but would have disappeared, is simple evidence of the causal fact that Russian political machinery offers no method by which MacArthur could have appealed to public opinion except by armed revolution. Caesar brought his legions with him when he crossed the Rubicon; MacArthur got his biggest triumph in a city controlled by the administration, with Democratic Party officials leading the cheers. The tradition is powerful and the machinery offers no obstacle; one could scarcely work without the other.

In more regular situations, the member of the Cabinet who disagrees with the President has no free constituency to which he can appeal; he has to rely upon arguments with his chief and whatever support he can get from his captive constituency which is made up of the President's other advisers and the subordinate ranks of the government staff. The member of Congress has the ideal type of free constituency in the voters of his district, who will, without any obligation or deference toward other members of the government, give him their judgment on what he does, in so far as they know about it and can understand it.

This is a concept of broader use, moreover, than can be seen in these commonplace political examples. Take, for example, the administrative hierarchy of a broadcasting network which is a profit system of the most modern kind. A vice president in charge of programs who has been reasonably successful in his past judgments will be listened to thoughtfully by the administrator above him. But if there is disagreement, the vice president has only a captive constituency, of the same sort as the one that can give limited help to a cabinet officer in the federal government. In the case of a performer on the air, however, even though he may be bound by contracts and have no administrative rights, there is always a free constituency to appeal to; it comprises his fans. He can appeal to this audience as against his editor and the same kind of relations give freedom to a novelist or a magazine writer. The principle can be extended. The meaning in larger terms is that any system which does not give to some members of the administrative or ruling group the chance to appeal to another free group for support must necessarily be authoritarian and monolithic.

The principle applies with special force to the function of the expert, the adviser, whom we were discussing previously. His free constituency is the company of scholars and scientists of which he claims to be a member. The administrator of a private organization is not bound to take the adviser's opinion, but the adviser can walk out of the assignment. In a free country, the adviser who is working for the government, can appeal to his scholarly colleagues and they can reply not only as specialists, but also as part of the general public, which in a free country is the locus of free constituencies. In a totalitarian country, there are no fully private organizations and the expert has no way of escaping the pressures of power. If he submits to these pressures, as he almost certainly will, the scientific and technological progress of the state is retarded. The administrator, whether in business or in government, is sure to profit in the long run by the amount of honest information he can get out of his advisers.

In this paper only two aspects of the function of advice have been touched on; the relation of the adviser to the inner hierarchy of power, and the relation of any member of a decision-making process to his possible support. It will be noted that nothing has been said about communication, although the difficulties of communication enhance every kind of difficulty mentioned. Such omissions of factors are justified only if the isolation of other factors makes for clarity. This is an area of human behavior which has been cluttered with generalizations, but is seldom subjected to analysis; there is not even a taxonomic basis for discussion.

The function of advice is one of the oldest in human affairs and certain abstract generalizations about it that could have been made in palaeolithic times are still true. Most of those generalizations, however, have not been made and, as far as can be discovered, no standard treatise in this field has ever been written. There are mountain piles of books on salesmanship, which is not disinterested advice, and a molehill of books on leadership, but nothing on the techniques and difficulties of trying to put knowledge at the service of power. The right relation of knowledge and power is, however, one of the key problems of our age. We need to give the closest scrutiny to the processes whereby decisions are made, and the effect on those decisions of rational information, if we are to master the difficulties of freedom in a time when power is so developed and knowledge is so dispersed. The function of advice is one of the crucial points in that relation and on that account may well be studied first.

Comment by Quincy Wright:

I have nothing but commendation for Professor Bryson's pioneering discussion of "advice." What he says applies not only to the outside expert brought in to advise an administrator, but also to the memoranda writers and the research workers usually to be found within modern large administrations. The memoranda writers and the decision-makers may come close together; in fact, the general staff, which organizes the former, may in certain circumstances equal or exceed in power the commander-in-chief who is the decision-maker. There are, however, memoranda writers whose function is distinct from that of administrators or executives. They foresee problems, analyze alternatives, and pile up documents under more or less explicit instructions from the administrator, thinking of future decisions, of which some are immediately at hand and others are dimly foreseen. The major problem of administration in a large organization is to get the prepared memoranda and those who have made them in contact with the decision-maker, at the time when a vaguely foreseen situation arises and a decision has to be made. It all too frequently happens that the connection is not made and the decision-maker is denied the benefit of memoranda and experts, utilization of which would have made the decision wiser. In such circumstances the memorandum writer may be called in belatedly to produce new memoranda in order to justify the decision already made.

What Professor Bryson is really discussing is the relation of action and thought, of manipulation and contemplation, of will and intellect, of power and knowledge, and the establishment of the proper relationship between the two in administration, whether in the field of government, of business, of religion, or of education.

Graham Wallas discussed the organization of thought and the organization of will in the *Great Society* a generation ago, but he did not make it clear how these organizations may be brought together. Writers on public administration, like L. D. White, have dealt with the relations of staff and auxiliary agencies to the administrator. The modern discipline of "group dynamics" is attempting a psychological approach to the problem. It seems to me that Professor Bryson gets to the essence of the matter by distinguishing "advice" (the anticipation of action in thought) and "execution" (the utilization of thought by action) from "decision" or the point, separating the two, at which thought merges into action. His insight into the relation of expert, executive, and administrator will ring true to anyone who has had experience in any of these positions. The issue is one of great interest in the general field of freedom and authority, for it is, in no small measure, in the decision-making process that free and unfree societies are to be distinguished.

CHAPTER IV

Authority and Freedom in Industry

By LEO NEJELSKI
President, Nejelski and Company, Inc., Management Counsels

THERE IS A sharp contrast between the freedoms experienced by the individual within his community and within the factory or office where he works. As a member of the community, he can vote for persons to represent him. He can criticize freely, or make suggestions, even initiate action to remove his representatives from office. So long as he does not damage other members of the community, he has freedom of choice and action.

Once he is on his job, however, his choices and actions become sharply circumscribed. His major goals are decided for him. His role within the organization is defined and he becomes subject to criticism, once he steps beyond his duties and responsibilities. If he belongs to a union, he is certain that his complaints will receive attention; otherwise he may, or may not, be heard. His advancement is largely beyond his control. In general, an observer who studied him only in these surroundings, would say that we are living in an autocratic or even despotic society.

This is one of the major inconsistencies that characterize life in these United States. The factors that enter into the historical development of this contrast are many, but it might prove useful to point out some of the main ones:

1. *Our concepts of ownership*
2. *The impersonality of profits*
3. *Intense competition*
4. *The fractionation of specialization*
5. *Lack of strong group identification*
6. *The primitive state of management skills.*

1. In industry, ownership is vested in the persons who supply the capital. These owners need never be identified by anybody but management. When the idea of the corporation was developed to make it possible for groups of investors to limit their liabilities without limiting the size of an enterprise, ownership became increasingly anonymous. It was easy to develop a habit of grouping men impersonally along with machines and materials.

As the size of industrial organizations has increased, specific owners have become increasingly difficult to identify, particularly in corporations whose securities are listed on public exchanges. Only by freezing the list of stockholders on specified days can these owners be identified from the records. Likewise the owners look upon their securities largely as means of producing revenue and gain, not as evidences of ownership.

From this, one can understand why such ideas of ownership often result in depersonalizing all phases of the work situation. Personal interest becomes minimal, and "objectivity" becomes the rationalization.

2. Another important factor is the impersonality of profits. Legally, the production of profits and providing fair returns to owners have been given as the reasons for corporate existence. The legal concept of profits takes only one form—money profits, a symbol of material value completely devoid of personality. Yet, the prospect of additional profit can be the sole reason for expansion of plants adding large numbers of personnel. On the other hand, threatening losses can lead to job insecurities, to shutting down of plants, and to paralysis of communities.

Seldom have industrialists questioned whether there are other values for which they are carrying responsibilities. Profits that are as cold as the dollar, and which ignore other phases of gain or return, cannot escape this aura of impersonality. If all the other facts or factors of the industrial situation are valued impersonally, then we can understand why impersonality also carried over into the considerations of the men and women involved in the same enterprise.

3. Intense competition also spreads a blanket of impersonality over the industrial scene. No industrial organization can withstand the onslaught of competitors, unless it is prepared to improve products or lower costs by better methods of manufacturing. This competition enables the consumer to exercise freedom of choice. But at the plant level, competition makes necessary the obsolescence of materials, machinery, and often human skills.

I am not arguing the individual and social gains of competitiveness. It is important that we recognize the effects of competition on the people who work in and manage industries. The development of television, for example, had crippling effects on the motion picture industry; the development of color television, in turn, brought the production of black and white television sets to an abrupt halt—all within a very few years. Not only have the results of this competition produced job dislocations, but they have also reinforced the tradition of industrial impersonality.

4. Large-scale industries have been made possible by specialization. Although specialization enables an individual to improve and increase his particular skills, it also tends to separate him from other persons, increasing his feeling of aloneness.

Perhaps the most profound effect of specialization is the increased need for supervisors and managers to integrate skills, multiplying the situations where people must be directed. Except where provisions are made in union contracts, chances of the workers' voices being heard in large organizations have been relatively small.

Competition and specialization also tend to make obsolete human skills. A specialist's security is endangered, if he is not able to recognize the skills that are coming into demand.

Broadly speaking, specialization has played an important role in our technological advances and in our increasing standard of living. In taking these positive aspects for granted and focusing on the problems, I aim to point up the areas calling most insistently for correction.

5. Along with impersonality in industrial organizations, the individual has not been able to identify strongly with his group. A job is regarded primarily as a means of making a living. There is a general tendency to overlook the fact that the job occupies at least one-third of the individual's life. Frustrations and gratifications that are a part of his work carry over into home and community.

During the war the threat of the enemy outside tended to develop a considerable amount of group identification. However, in times of peace, the methods of generating group spirit are still quite superficial. Group goals are of secondary importance to completing the job in hand and improving individual performance.

Recently group participation has received emphasis through profit-sharing programs. Group identification can be maximized primarily in situations where there is a high degree of job continuity and where everybody has an opportunity to share power, knowledge, prestige, growth, and the other values which individuals in all societies consider important. The autocratic methods of many managements do not permit the cultivation of these values.

6. Perhaps the most important factor with which we are dealing is the primitive state of management skills. When our economy was expanding rapidly, industrial organizations could prosper and grow in spite of unskilled management. Daring and drive were the most important managerial attributes. The momentum of a dynamic economy sweeps inefficiency and inadequacy before it; when the pace slows down, these shortcomings become glaringly evident. The very drive that carried many men to the top isolated them from the people they managed. Only recently has the evidence become clear that despotism in industry is as wasteful of profits and human values as is despotism in any other area.

As our sciences and technologies have advanced, the management of industrial organizations has become increasingly complicated. Similarly, world events and world trends have intruded themselves into management decisions. The American businessman, in the space of a few years, has been forced to recognize and consider military, political, and ideological factors that his predecessors could ignore.

It is a truism that our capacities to utilize the physical sciences have outdistanced our understanding of the people involved, as well as our capacities to integrate these people toward common goals that are meaningful for all. An increasing number of men in management, however, are becoming curious about how the sciences of man can assist in producing human profits, as well as money profits. In this there is some hope that the ideas of an industrial society and a free society can be harmonized.

Thus far, I have dwelt on the problems that make it difficult for the individual to find freedom in the industrial setting. There are many positive factors. I will attempt to elaborate some of these now.

In every industrial organization, some individual or group, must take the ultimate responsibility for important decisions. Capital is required to build a plant and install machinery. Markets must be defined. The amounts to be spent on selling, distribution, and advertising must be determined.

Once the basic decisions are made, somebody must structure and program the methods to be used in achieving these goals. The increasing complexity of business not only requires greater skill on the part of the management, but it also makes it necessary that those who make the important decisions be adequately informed on the major factors and influences with which they are dealing.

This does not mean that management should arrive at decisions, goals, and programs without assistance. The salesman in the field often has better evaluations of a sales program than the people at the home office; the worker at a machine very often can tell accurately why a production program gets out of gear.

Freedom in industry is not synonymous with maximizing permissiveness. Competition forces a flexibility in decision-making that must be the concern of at least one individual within an enterprise. In terms of survival, a high degree of permissiveness may be destructive rather than liberating. The ideal is a minimum of important decision-making and programming at the top, and a maximum of participation on the part of everybody in the organization. This participation should be as direct as possible, so that confusing problems of communications can be avoided. Likewise, direct participation can give each participant a better evaluation of his worth and importance than indirect participation. Participation must grow out of the assumption that each person has something worthwhile to contribute to the success of the total enterprise.

Some people in management look askance at this degree of participation, on the theory that it takes away from them some of the basic prerogatives. They overlook the fact that the increase in motivation and effectiveness throughout the organization more than makes up for the imagined loss of prestige at the top.

Genuine participation is particularly distasteful to people who are emotionally unstable or insecure. Groups that are accustomed to a working structure, even though autocratic, cannot abandon that framework without misgivings or anxiety. Participating in developing a new framework is an untested experience for them, with all of the uncertainty of the untried.

One of the great challenges to managements is to remain sensitive to a balance between direction and structure, on one hand, and participation, on the other. Leadership in the group need not come continuously from the top. Successful secondary leadership can come from any or all members of the group at various times. Research indicates that under varied circumstances, the focus of leadership can go from the designated leaders to several informal leaders within the group. In this way, too, human resources that might be submerged or lost can find fulfilment.

Genuine participation eliminates the rigid distinctions between managers and workers or between leaders and followers and permits a real regard for the human values usually associated with freedom. Without participation they cannot prevail.

Another important factor in management is the capacity to define goals clearly and to make them known and understood by all persons in an enterprise. This means greater clarity about long-range, as well as short-range objectives, than many managers take the time to attain even for themselves. As industrial organizations have grown, the needs for clarification and communication have become more dramatic and insistent. However, recent experiences are showing with emphasis, that people, although willing to be clarified on management's stand, want the opportunity to make up their own minds whether they agree with management. Only recently has management grown aware of this.

More precise methods of communication and more accurate ways of predicting results are needed. For example, very little is known about the human factors in communication. An encouraging sign is the new emphasis on communication from the "grass roots" up to top management. Polling techniques are being amplified by methods of intensive study and observation. More nearly precise methods of bringing to the surface the emotional contents of attitudes and ideas, should hasten the development of communication techniques at all levels of industrial hierarchies.

Still another area where management is directing its attention is to the human needs beyond the pay envelope. Money inducements are not all-powerful in getting capable men to change jobs or to take on greater responsibilities. In spite of higher wages, labor strife is still a major facet of our national scene.

In a study of labor-management cooperation conducted by the Twentieth Century Fund, these four objectives were defined as the goals of Labor:

1. Security
2. A chance to advance
3. More human treatment
4. More dignity on the job.

Appreciation of the dignity and worth of the individual and the development of management techniques that consider human needs, can go a long way toward bringing the values of freedom into industrial organizations. These cannot be superimposed from without. They must originate with those managements who are convinced that the disparities between our goals of freedom, and the absence of it in many industrial organizations, need not exist.

I can summarize by repeating a comment made recently by Harold D. Lasswell:

> Management techniques cannot result in the human values consistent with the goals of a free society unless they are rooted in *participation, clarification and appreciation.*

CHAPTER V

Workers' Control:
Freedom and Authority in the Plant

By ADOLF F. STURMTHAL
Professor of Economics, Bard College

I

BY ITS VERY NATURE, the labor movement is an attack upon property rights, regardless of whether this is intended or not. The collective agreement is an instrument designed to restrict in certain respects the rights which management exerts in behalf of the owners. By pressing for collective agreements, the labor movement sets limits to the exercise of legally recognized property rights—such as the freedom to make individual labor contracts, to hire and fire freely, to make unilateral changes in working conditions, etc. These restrictions are imposed upon the property owners or their agents—management—in the name of economic justice which requires, according to labor's views, that the disqualification which economic power can impose upon the propertyless individual workers be eliminated.

Up to the very recent past, however, and in large parts of the world, the ownership of property provided social and political privileges as well, while the propertyless worker was subject to social and political disqualifications. These disqualifications related to most, if not all aspects of life. It is perhaps sufficient to point out that in most countries of the world aristocratic principles of education reserved—and frequently continue to reserve—higher, and in many countries, even primary, education to children of the upper classes. Suffrage restrictions, based on property ownership, have been the rule even in Western and Central Europe, until some thirty-odd years ago. In the United States, on the other hand, educational opportunities and suffrage were opened up to all or most citizens of at least the white race about a century ago.

While labor in the United States has, since the rise of the AFL, concentrated on the struggle against the economic disqualification of the workers, labor abroad has directed its main effort against the social and political discrimination under which the workers suffered.

Freedom, for the American worker, has meant restricting the arbitrary exercise of management powers in certain fields—namely, those dealing with wages, hours, and working conditions. The authority which the American worker opposes is the unrestricted property right with regard to these matters. But to the worker abroad property itself appeared as the enemy of his freedom and as the embodiment of an authority that oppressed the working class.

From these differences of social and political history have followed important consequences, as far as the policies and ideologies of labor are concerned. American labor, at least since the AFL came into being, has aimed at a division of authority between management and the union, with the first determining the technical, financial, and commercial operations of the plant, and the union gradually obtaining control of the workers' job—wages, hours, working conditions, etc. European labor organizations, on the other hand, have attacked the very principle of authority based upon property rights. The abolition of private property, of the "means of production and distribution" and their transfer to the community, was to eliminate authority based upon property ownership.

II

From this starting point—which may be located in time as the last two decades of the nineteenth century—attitudes and practices on both sides of the Atlantic have followed a long and sometimes intricate evolution.

European labor's campaign for the transfer of property rights to the community has remained the main theme of labor action. But at some stages it has been accompanied by a realization of the fact that such a transfer would of itself not solve the problem of autocracy in the plant. It might merely replace one set of managers by another. Perhaps the clearest expression of this realization was the syndicalist movement (though it never had a clearly defined program). It is true that among the final objectives of Marxian Socialism was that of abolishing the differences between manual and intellectual labor, and thus to enable everyone to perform any function in society of which he was capable. But this was a final, distant objective, and it was not certain whether by itself it would change the fundamental character of authority in the plant. For the syndicalists, the overthrow of management absolutism was an immediate objective. Management was to be freely elected by the workers—including the technical staff—of the plant and remain responsible to its electorate. Enterprises covering large areas—such as the railroads—were to be administered by the trade union confederation, as were to be international transactions. Because the trade union leaders are elected by the members, the system of elected management would have been extended, though by remote control, into these fields as well.

These ideas, formulated in many different ways and with many variations in detail, originated mainly with French syndicalism. But they exerted a powerful influence abroad. In the process, however, they underwent considerable modifications. When they reappeared in Great Britain under the slogan of "Workers' Control," the monopolistic dangers involved in the original syndicalistic program had been realized. The emphasis now was on a share for the workers in management, with public authority representing consumers' interests to balance monopolistic trends in plant management. The British Guild Socialists who became the main advocates of these ideas, met with considerable success among British trade unions, particularly the miners and the railwaymen. From Britain, "Workers' Control" spread to the Continent. After the first syndicalist phase of the Russian revolution, "Workers' Control" became the official program of the Bolsheviks—modified by the peculiar circumstances of a terroristic revolution—and then formed the basis for the socialization program of the Austrian Socialists. This, in turn, exerted a good deal of influence upon the socialization program of the German Social Democrats after World War I, and upon the program for "industrialized nationalization" which the French trade unions developed in 1920. As a basic pattern these programs proposed that industry—or at least key industries, such as transportation, production, and transmission of energy, banking, etc.—be nationalized and that nationalized industries be placed under a tripartite administration in which the unions, the government, and the consumers, be represented in equal strength. Although the term, "workers' control," was still often used to describe this arrangement, little was, in fact, left of the original driving-force: the workers' delegates formed only one-third of the administration, and union delegates were hardly a full substitute for representatives of the workers in the plant.

III

Apart from the Soviet Union, these ideas remained mainly programs. British labor's nationalization efforts after World War I failed even in the most promising industry, coal mining; French union programs remained on paper owing to the political trends of France after World War I. Nor did German and Austrian socialization make considerable headway. Instead, in the latter two countries a much more modest step toward "workers' control" was made in the form of the works councils.

Under the German legislation, the works councils elected by all the employees of a plant were to fulfil a double function. They were, first, to act as shop stewards on personnel matters, primarily on dismissals; second, council representatives had the right to participate without vote in the meetings of boards of directors of joint stock companies and have access to the books. In their second function the councils were to be information agents for regional and national bodies on which the unions were to participate and which, under Article 165 of the Constitution, were to be the instruments of actual workers' participation in management. In this system "workers' control" had been once again transformed; it had become a "share in management," and it was now far removed from the workshop into regional or national bodies. It was precisely this part of the program which failed most completely. The shop steward functions were fulfilled by the councils with varying degrees of effectiveness; the regional and national economic councils failed to materialize in any effective fashion. But the idea survived in a modified form. In 1928, the German unions formulated a program for "economic democracy" which provided for union participation in the management of industries as a whole, roughly on the level of cartels.

While in Germany and France "workers' control" was gradually transformed into a program for high-level union-management cooperation, Guild Socialism was subject in Britain to a powerful onslaught by the Fabians. The attack was carried forward in the name of efficiency.

The Guild Socialists had poured a good deal of water into the original syndicalist idea, in order to prevent monopolistic developments. What emerged out of this process was workers' participation in management. To this modified concept the Fabians objected that in the struggle of the different interest groups within management, efficiency of plant operation and of business management was bound to suffer. Control should be in the hands of experts who alone could secure optimum results, if Socialism was to be economically superior to capitalism.

This was the starting point of a prolonged literary discussion, in whose midst Herbert Morrison, as Minister of Transport, submitted to Parliament a bill proposing that the London Transportation System be run by a board of experts—without workers or union representation. Morrison was sharply criticized by the unions—particularly by Ernest Bevin, leader of the Transport Workers—but in the long run he was victorious. When the British nationalization program was worked out in the late '30's, only token respect was being paid by unions and Labour Party to the old idea of "Workers' Control." On the boards of nationalized enterprises there were to be unionists as experts on labor relations and social welfare; but they were to be ex-unionists. Though proposed by unions, these members were to be appointed by the Minister, they were to be responsible to him alone, and they were to resign from their union offices upon appointment. This is the system which, from 1945 on, has been applied by the Labour Government when it nationalized coal, transport, electricity, gas, and, finally, steel. The only remnant of "workers' control" was a proviso for joint labor-management consultation on matters outside of the scope of collective bargaining, to be applied on all levels of the administrative hierarchy, from the pit or plant up to the boards of nationalized industries.

France, on the other hand, has remained loyal to the idea of labor representation in the management of nationalized industries. With some variation in detail, the tripartite character of the boards—union, government, consumers—has been retained throughout most of the nationalized enterprises. In only one case—the automobile factory "Renault" which has been nationalized as a punitive measure against the former management's collaborating with the enemy—are the labor representatives chosen from among the workers in the plant, perhaps because Renault is a single plant, not an entire industry. Usually it is the unions which provide for labor's representation on the board.

However, in fact, even this last remnant of "workers' control" is more apparent than real. The boards are part time, unpaid, and meet usually only once a month, for a few hours. This alone would be sufficient to insure that actual administration is not in their hands. Moreover, financial and economic circumstances, as well as the peculiar development of industrial relations and repeated political purges of board membership, have combined to place the nationalized enterprises under the *de facto* control of the government, or, more precisely, of some permanent high officials in the civil service. Workers' influence upon the management of most of the nationalized enterprises is hardly greater than under private management. Indeed, in some ways authority in the plant has become more anonymous and diffuse than ever before.

IV

As recently as at the Milan Conference of the International Confederation of Free Trade Unions (I.C.F.T.U.) in July, 1951, American trade union leaders protested against a resolution which seemed to them to make "codetermination" a common objective of all trade unions in the world. Not only did William Green, President of the AFL, some time ago, when asked about a statement of a German trade unionist that codetermination was widely practiced in America, reply by saying it was "unknown in America": United States labor leaders have asserted that they would not care to have "codetermination." They preferred, they said, to leave the responsibility for the enterprise to management, and to limit union influence to matters directly affecting wages, hours, and working conditions.

Sincere as these statements undoubtedly are, they are hardly a correct reflection of the actual state of affairs in the United States. True, since the '80's, as long as American unions were weak and still engaged in a struggle for survival, their concern was adequately described by the term, "pure and simple trade unionism." But since the New Deal, American labor has progressed considerably beyond the self-ordained limitations of Gompers's philosophy. It is sufficient to refer to the—unsuccessful—efforts of the automobile workers to influence General Motors price policy at the end of the war, or, better still, to the situation in the ladies' garment industry, in which we have almost reached the stage when the employers are asking for "codetermination."

This follows, as must be obvious, as a logical consequence from the very nature of American unionism, whatever union leaders may think about their own objectives. Nothing that happens in a business establishment or in a plant is completely unrelated to wages, hours, and working conditions. In attempting to influence the latter, the unions are inevitably led to deal—either by implication or openly—with all matters affecting the business. The greater the power of the union, the greater also its ability to influence the economic and financial policies of the establishment. Quite conceivably, such influence may in most cases not be sought by American unions as an end in itself, but rather be an unintended byproduct of the struggle for "job control," to use Perlman's classic expression. Nor do American unions choose legislation as the device by which they like to attain their objectives. But this does not alter the fact that American unions have, with a greater or lesser measure of success, restricted what is commonly called "management prerogatives." Nor can it be denied that by manifold work rules American unions have greatly affected the technical operations of plants. Directly or indirectly American unions aim at the "right to have a say" in most phases of American industry.

At the same time, American unions insist upon equality or near equality with business management in most public consultative institutions. During World War II this status became officially acknowledged in most phases of war production and, of course, wage policy. When, during the Korean war, the unions felt that equality or near equality was denied them, their refusal to cooperate speedily resulted in their victory.

V

The evolution of "workers' control" in Europe is significant in many ways. The effort to overcome "autocracy" in the plant has, on the whole, been defeated. It has fallen victim to the desire to avoid monopolistic trends and to establish efficiency. In the clash between economic democracy in the plant and the efficiency of autocratic rule, the latter has been victorious.

It is true that wages, hours, and working conditions continue to be jointly determined by unions and management. This applies not only to all British nationalized enterprises and legally to many of the French; even in those nationalized enterprises in France in which wages, hours, and working conditions are determined by law or decree, a process closely resembling collective bargaining is taking place. Nor does German codetermination eliminate collective bargaining in the industries affected by the new status of labor.

All this, however, is not "workers' control." The latter was to give labor a say in production, in commercial and financial matters. On this issue European labor's policy has been subject to a peculiar shift.

In the first place, the center of gravity has tended to move away from the plant to larger institutions. Major economic and social policies are more and more determined by consultation between the authorities, management, and the unions. This had become the practice in Great Britain during World War II, and, of course, under the Labour governments that followed in its wake. The French *"Conseil Économique"* under the chairmanship of the union leader, Léon Jouhaux, performs in a modest way a similar function. Such consultation is a major objective of German codetermination.

Secondly, experience so far tends to show that "workers' control" on the plant level functions most effectively within the area of working conditions and welfare, least effectively on economic and financial matters, where it has been undertaken at all. In both France and Britain consultation has been provided for between labor and management on economic and financial matters, while in France the workers have been given by way of "Joint Factory Committees" the right of decision on welfare problems. Experience tends to show so far that it is only on the latter level that "workers' control" functions effectively. Consultation on issues relating to the operation of the plant, to its economic and financial policies, on the other hand, has produced very few results.

Thirdly, to a considerable extent "workers' control" has become union control, as far as it exists at all. This is due, partly, to the desire of the unions not to foster developments which might oppose other workers' organs to the unions, partly to the lack of trained personnel in the plants which could argue on a level of equality with management representatives on economic and financial matters, lastly, and perhaps in connection with the preceding last point—to a lack of interest in the rank and file in issues not obviously related to wages, hours, and working conditions.

VI

In these aspects, nationalization does not seem to have made any profound difference. In some cases, union leadership has shown a good deal of eagerness to cooperate with the boards of nationalized enterprises, in order to make nationalization a success. But this has been by no means universal, nor are there clear indications yet that this feeling has penetrated far down into the ranks. In the absence of patent alterations in the administrative setup on the plant level, the workers have often failed to manifest any great changes in attitude. This, indeed, has been a source of great disappointment to Socialists.

Consultation is thus the main remnant or perhaps nucleus of workers' control in the plant. The consultive arrangements in England, the "Joint Factory Committees," in France and perhaps codetermination in German coal and steel, are the main institutional arrangements which, at least potentially, permit the workers to have a "say in management," outside of wages, hours, and working conditions. No one will claim that, as things stand at present, these institutions realize the old objective of the labor movement, aiming at supplementing political democracy by democracy in the plant. In some ways, all these devices seem to correspond in the plant to what the French prerevolutionary *États-Généraux* were supposed to achieve, namely, to *represent* "the people" *vis-à-vis* the powers that be. Whether at some stage the *"États-Généraux"* of the plant will follow historic precedent and claim exclusive powers—apologies are offered for all the shortcomings of the comparison—is a wide open question.

Another development that can conceivably be regarded as an outgrowth of the concept of "workers' control" is represented by such institutions as the so-called "Ladder Plan" in the British coal mines. This is an educational program designed to enable gifted young coal miners to advance gradually into higher positions in the industry. If implemented according to the intentions of the Coal Board, it would in due course break down—in one industry—the barriers which the "educational monopoly" of the higher classes put in the way of the social advancement of working class youth. This may very well prove to be in the long run one of the most significant achievements of nationalization. A careful reading of the writings of early French syndicalist leaders indicates that this approach would have been close to their heart.

Whether the frontal attack upon property rights in which European labor is engaged, is more likely to attain the objective than the slow pragmatic progress of American labor beyond the traditional limits of business unionism, is an open question. However, the peculiar social and political history of Europe may well have made it inevitable for the solution of the property problem to be the prerequisite for the clear realization of the issues of freedom and autocracy in the plant. The struggle for the nationalization of industry may then be but the first phase of an evolution which aims at democracy in industry; the main issues seem to emerge only after the stumbling block of property is eliminated.

CHAPTER VI

Freedom and Authority in Labor Unions

By MARK STARR
*Educational Director,
International Ladies' Garment Workers' Union*

THE EFFECTIVE CONTROLS exercised by Big Business were once the object of close attention and attack. Recurring agitations to protect small business and court orders to force particular corporations to dispose of part of their operations or subsidiary firms, do not alter the trend toward monopoly.

So long as the monopoly does not push the advantage of its power so far that a large enough number of consumers feel outraged, and so long as the community feels that efficiency is gained, Big Business enjoys its lucrative power. It is estimated that about two-thirds of American business does not compete in prices any more. The industrial leaders who hymn "free enterprise" endeavor to stifle it, hindered occasionally by the Supreme Court, as in its decision of May, 1951, which freed the retailer from selling brand goods at the "fair trade" price fixed by the producer.

New Forms of Competition

The new form of competition has to do with promotion. Instead of "the law of supply and demand" operating as the textbooks maintain, both supply and demand are manipulated with skill to secure optimum profit without sacrifice of goodwill. The price of cigarettes, for example, shifts by concerted action of the few big companies, but millions of dollars are spent to promote the use of cigarettes and to secure the popularity of one brand over another.

What the total expenditure on advertising does to the freedom of the customer to set his own standards of veracity and taste, and even what it does to our language and culture, are matters for investigation and warranted concern.

Opinion Shift to Blame Big Labor

However the discreet use of monopoly powers by Big Business and its effective public relations work have shifted the charge of monopoly in the past fifteen years to Big Labor. Just as the citizens earlier called for busting the trusts, so public opinion (agitated particularly by large-scale stoppages in the basic coal mining industry) supported the Taft-Hartley Act of 1947.

In high schools, forums, and in the public press, the fear of a labor monopoly is repeatedly expressed. In our schools students still suffer from much misinformation, despite improvements of recent years. There is all too little preparation for industrial citizenship in our colleges and adult education agencies. The hysteria of the headlines plays up strikes and exceptional strike violence. And organized labor is only beginning to develop public relations to meet the fear and ignorance which misrepresent its methods and aims. The record about the tiny fraction of the total man hours lost by strikes because of the increasing mutual understanding and respect between labor and management, deserves much greater attention.

It is not only the laymen who repeat the allegation that labor unions have established a monopoly. Professor Charles E. Lindblom in his *Unionism and Capitalism* endeavored to prove that monopolistic trade unions inevitably will destroy the competitive capitalist system.[1] But what has happened in 1950 and 1951 in the high relative advance in profits compared to wages, refutes the idea of union omnipotency.

Labor No Monolithic Bloc

The idea of a tightly knit labor combine directed by a few labor czars is a complete travesty of the true position. Out of about 42,000,000 wage and salary receivers (excluding the owner-operators, the professional self-employed, and the farmers in the 62,000,000 total working force of the United States) some thirty-five per cent are organized into unions. The 15,000,000 to 16,000,000 trade unionists do not form a monolithic bloc. The *Directory of Labor Unions*[2] lists 209 unions in the Ameri-

---

[1] Charles E. Linblom, *Unionism and Capitalism,* Yale University Press, New Haven, 1949.

[2] *Directory of Labor Unions,* United States Department of Labor, Washington, 1950.

can Federation of Labor, the Congress of Industrial Organizations, the Railroad Brotherhoods, and the independents. Internal differences based on craft, professional, regional, and personal rivalries are found within and between unions. Compared to the centralized authority and prestige of the trade union centers in other countries, both AFL and CIO are relatively weak, although undoubtedly increasing in their strength. The creation of the United Labor Policy Committee and the recognition of labor's claims to greater representation in making and operating controls, is, of course, evidence of the power of united labor. But it is only in emergency situations that labor acts as a single force.

But what the public has in mind are the services which are necessary to the operation of our modern cities, transport, light, and heat—the cessation of which would create a dangerous emergency. It may well be argued that if the thirty-five per cent of workers organized are located in strategic spots in industry, they can exercise tyrannical power and enforce their will upon the community.

The problem cannot be solved by a prohibition of strikes, because the worker with a gun in his back or a bayonet in his ribs can be more dangerous inside a modern power plant than he would be on the picket line outside. The awareness of the general public to the claims of the worker before they climax in a strike deadlock, the sense of community responsibility of labor and management, the institution of speedy grievance procedures and the establishment of wage standards related to changes in the cost of living, are the longtime answers. Prevention is better than emergency solutions of a temporary nature.

Problems of Security and Freedom

All that has been said does not make unnecessary careful examination of individual freedom, group authority, security, and welfare in the operation of trade unions. The unions are a powerful group in our modern community. To what extent is the individual subjected to group compulsions in the trade unions? How are leaders elected? What rights, as well as responsibilities, exist for the individual members? Do trade union practices conform to democratic ideals?

For example, what about the alleged tyranny of the *closed shop* and the *union shop*? (The closed shop means that the employer must hire through the union, and it is illegal under the Taft-Hartley Act. The union shop means that the employer hires and tries out a worker, who if given permanent status must join the union under the agreement with the employer.) On the face of things, to compel a worker to join a union, even if most workers have so voted, seems an interference with his liberty. Freedom, however, is never absolute. Group life involves rules and regulations based upon the welfare of the individual. Taxes must be paid, despite our disagreement with certain governmental policies. Our remedy consists of our power to elect. The parallel to the compulsory payment of union dues for the benefits received in a union shop is clear, but the non-union person can find employment elsewhere, and is not clapped into jail as is the person who refuses to pay taxes.

When after a signed declaration from the employee the employer deducts union dues from the worker's wage, that is known as the *check-off* system. Relatively few unions rely upon this method of dues collection; however, in some areas with workers widely scattered it is convenient. In practice it tends to strengthen the power of the union office, but is not a contravention of democratic principles.

The role played by the trade unions in extending the franchise and securing free public school education in the general advance of democratic rights, is not sufficiently well known. As a minority movement the trade unions for many years were declared illegal and fettered by court injunctions. Only gradually was recognition and the right to strike and picket obtained. Beginning with 1932 and continuing through the New Deal period, laws were passed placing union activity on a more legally secure basis.

A. The Norris-LaGuardia Act (1932) took from the Federal courts the right to stop strikes and other lawful union activities by injunction. It also abolished "yellow dog" contracts. (This was a document signed by the employee, declaring that he was *not* a trade union member and would inform the employer if he ever became one.)

B. The National Industrial Recovery Act (N.R.A., 1933) placed the government on record as favoring union organization.

C. The National Labor Relations Act (1935) guaranteed the rights of workers to organize and bargain collectively. It outlawed company unions and protected genuine unions and their members against unfair labor practices by the employer.

With the Taft-Hartley Act in 1947, a new phase of labor legislation developed, placing labor under government regulation and restricting the activity of labor unions.

A. The law makes it more difficult to organize. The employer—through the right of "free speech" can use his influence against the union, short of making direct threats or promising benefits. By merely alleging an unfair labor practice, an employer may postpone a representation election, and he may call for an election before a union is ready. Also, an active union member may be fired if the employer can show "cause" for the dismissal.

B. The law makes it more difficult to negotiate. Closed shop and preferential hiring are illegal. A union shop or maintenance of membership can be agreed upon by the employer and union if a majority of the workers vote for it. But the union may not ask the employer to fire a worker who has been expelled from the union unless he has been expelled for non-payment of dues. This permits a labor spy or a dissident and disobedient union member to continue membership. Also, individual signatures of workers are required before the check-off can be arranged.

C. Unions can now be guilty of unfair labor practices. A union may not threaten or coerce workers to join the union, charge excessive or discriminatory initiation fees; ask an employer to pay for work not performed, or call a jurisdictional strike or secondary boycott.

D. A union may now be sued if it or its "agent" violates the union contract.

E. To be eligible for services under the new law, a union must file an annual affidavit signed by each officer that he is not a member of the Communist Party. The union must also file a financial report.

F. Union contributions and expenditures in connection with Federal campaigns are prohibited.

Operation of this measure has not yet contended with mass unemployment and resultant union weakness. Nevertheless in unorganized areas of the South some of the textile corporations, utilizing the Taft-Hartley Act, have resorted to the old strikebreaking methods.

Misuse of Power

The question remains whether some unions misuse their power. One issue is discrimination: a few small unions have excluded Negroes. The

CIO and AFL leaders have actively campaigned to educate union members in fair play and decency. Another issue is the right of the member and local to criticize union leadership. Union members' participation in the control of their organizations is complicated. Naturally, democratic procedures depend upon the eternal vigilance and education of the members, and no outside check can be a substitute for this.

May I quote at length Dr. Philip Taft, Brown University, as an objective observer upon the complexity of democracy within the unions, in some comments he made to the American Economic Association in 1946.[3]

> As the union's power to gain its ends depends upon its ability to weld its members into a unified whole, so far as economic action is concerned, it must be equipped with means to reduce to impotence any divisive influences that appear. Moreover, extensive powers must be delegated to officers if many necessary functions are to be carried on with respect to economic action as distinct from struggle for office within the union. Officers must be given wide powers when dealing with employers, as a mass meeting is scarcely the proper atmosphere for negotiating a contract involving many detailed issues. . . . Serious limitation of the discretion of bargaining representatives would impose severe difficulties upon collective bargaining conferences, and would lead to a refusal by employers to make advance commitments. Union officers are as a rule experienced in negotiations, and they are in a better position than their members to appraise realistically the firm's ability to pay, its position in the industry, general economic conditions, and they are more likely to be more conversant than their members with industry and area practices. . . .
>
> The need for placing authority in the hands of union officers also arises from another source. A union is made up of districts and locals, each division subordinate to the other, and all to the general organization. . . . Wide delegation of power between conventions must therefore be necessary—power to enforce the rules, to protect the organization, to appoint agents, and to spend the funds of the union. . . .
>
> Some local groups may oppose the rule of the union that certain procedures be exhausted before a strike is called; the general organization

---

[3] Philip Taft, "Democracy in Trade Unions," *American Economic Review, Papers and Proceedings of the 58th Annual Meeting of the American Economic Association*, 1946. [The citation which Mr. Starr, for the sake of impartiality, quoted extensively, has been considerably condensed for the sake of brevity. The omissions are not intended to change the meaning or emphasis. Editors.]

may insist that its subordinate branches incorporate certain provisions in its contracts with employers; or the central office may require that grievance procedure written into contracts be utilized rather than that the issues be settled by economic pressure. If the union is to function effectively and if it is to fulfill its obligations to its industry and to its membership, considerable power must be delegated to the officers.

Delegation of power always creates the possibility of abuses, and the unions are microcosms which reflect the dilemma of the modern world—how to combine efficiency in administration with democratic processes. Delegation of power by the members of unions has become increasingly necessary as the unions have grown in size and importance, and as their negotiations have involved increasing and more complex problems. . . . This has led to greater dependence upon the officer and it has, in fact, intensified a long-run trend that has been evident for many decades. . . .

The demand by firms and even industries that the national organization underwrite contracts made by subordinates, the spread of collective bargaining and the growth of regional and national negotiations have all led to the strengthening of power of the central officers. Moreover, as the union grows in size the link between the membership and the officers becomes more tenuous. Once seized or accepted, power is not easily given up. . . . It is not easy to discover the reasons why some unions are more democratic than others, except that the membership and leaders exercise an influence in this direction. The need to place large responsibilities in the hands of the central organization makes it possible for a strong man to arrogate to himself much power. The United Mine Workers of America furnish a striking example of this process. . . .

The development of a bureaucracy seems almost inevitable irrespective of philosophy or political outlook of the leadership. . . . An outstanding characteristic of bureaucracy is its stability and long control. Robert Michels has observed: "Long tenure in office involves dangers for democracy."[4]

While this statement is true, the labor union cannot afford to eliminate officials, its skilled negotiators, those who understand the industry and its problems and who by training and temperament are the most qualified to lead the organization. . . . In most unions some difference exists between the stability of national and local officers. While the turnover of local union officers is not large, it is by no means unusual for local officers to be defeated for re-election. . . . On a national basis opposition to the re-election of officers appears infrequently, for the advantage is greatly

---

[4] Robert Michels, *Political Parties,* Hearst's International Library Company, New York, 1915, p. 97.

in favor of the incumbent as many union constitutions forbid the formation of an opposition strong enough to challenge those in office. . . . The power [of national officers] to proceed against members and subordinate locals is very great; and courts have in the past taken the position that in cases involving discipline, members of a union must first exhaust the remedies offered by the union before the courts assume jurisdiction;[5] as a rule, the courts will not intervene even when an honest error has been made. This view is summarized in Snay vs. Lovely[6] in which the court reached the conclusion:

> *Courts do not sit in review of decisions thus made by such officers even though it may appear that there has been an honest error of judgment, an innocent mistake in drawing inferences or making observation or a failure to secure all information available by a more acute and searching analysis.*

A close reading of this paragraph indicates that a union tribunal must follow certain forms and, as one attorney engaged in labor practice has observed: Unions have to go through a certain ritual, and the courts are hesitant to intervene if the external appearances of a fair trial are met.

It seems that the judicial attitude towards labor unions is founded on a fiction that is economically untenable. The courts have taken the view that "clubs, trade unions, professional associations, secret societies" are private organizations, and the test of a private organization is whether an institution is organized for a purpose other than making money. "*Corporations, partnerships, joint adventures, joint stock companies, and business trusts are frequently the objects of judicial control, but their activities naturally cause public concern.*"[7] To maintain that the activities of labor unions do not cause public concern is a piece of legerdemain beyond the comprehension of the non-legal mind. . . .

The top executive of a national union exercises tremendous power—and the term *"tremendous"* is used advisedly. . . . Here again it is necessary to stress that in the interest of sound management, the top officers should be given wide administrative authority, and cases can be cited—Local 604 of the stage hands—to show that the failure of the international to intervene constituted a dereliction of duty and failed to protect the membership. Once we grant the desirability of giving much power, we find ourselves facing the problem of how to protect the locals and their members against harassment. No assurance exists that the dele-

---

[5] Zachariah Chafee, Jr., "The Internal Affairs of Association Not for Profit," *Harvard Law Review*, Cambridge, May, 1930, p. 993.
[6] 276 Massachusetts 160 (1931).
[7] Chafee, *loc. cit.*, p. 993.

gated power will be used only to advance the interests of the union, rather than to solidify the power of the officers. It is unnecessary to assume that an opposition within a union is always motivated by high idealism. . . . Nevertheless, unless the union allows an opposition to present a policy and program hostile to the administration, the possibilities of democracy will be snuffed out. . . .

Several of the reasons for taking action against locals are based upon a desire to protect the interests of the entire union. Locals are subordinate to the national union, and they should conform to the rules and policies elaborated by the larger group. In union administration as in government, conflicts between localism or home rule and centralized authority are not rare. Yet it is obvious that some of the reasons for intervening listed below are not adequate grounds for undermining the autonomy of the smaller group and may lead to arbitrary exercise of power for selfish purposes. . . .

The following are some reasons for which locals can be suspended: Violation of International Constitution or orders of General Executive Board; failure to make required reports; failure to hold regular meetings; lack of effort to build membership; becoming demoralized so as to jeopardize the International; failure to be represented at the District Council; permitting attendance of members at meetings other than those held by the union at which union business is discussed; improper conduct; refusal to install a successor after an officer has been removed by Executive Board; refusal to bring members to trial when so ordered by the International; failing to enforce the penalty imposed by a proper tribunal within the union; resorting to courts before exhausting union remedies; issuing circulars or petitions that may injure the union. It was on such vague charges that the unions which originally organized the C.I.O. were suspended by the Executive Council of the A.F. of L. It is obvious that the power given to the officers is too broad and indefinite, and it can be used to stifle proper criticism of policies or conduct of the general officers.

Even broader is the power over individual union members. An examination of a large number of union constitutions showed a wide variety of offenses for which members can be reprimanded, fined, suspended or expelled from the union. Offenses could be divided into violations of prohibition of specific acts, and violations of prohibitions of general, vague and ill-defined rules. Union constitutions prohibit work below the union scale. This is definite and certain, and is designed to *"promote the welfare of the union and achieve the objects for which the union was formed."* . . . Yet union constitutions also punish such vague offenses as the commission of a disreputable act, slandering the organization or its officers, discussing union business except at authorized meetings of the union, signing circulars or petitions which may injure the union, undermining the union, commission of a dishonorable act injurious to the union, refusing to obey a lawful order of an officer, advocating secession or joining a dual union, and circulating literature attacking members without approval of the president or executive board. . . .[8]

Recently a New York court ordered the Brotherhood of Railway and Steamship Clerks to reinstate a member who had been expelled for circulating material which reflected on the honesty of one of the candidates in a local election. The court held that the manner in which the expulsion had taken place was *"repugnant to the principles of justice and fair play."*[9] It is true that loose charges and slanderous attacks may weaken the union, but these are risks inevitable in a democracy. There is no way to insulate society, a movement, or an organization against unfair criticism except by preventing all adverse discussion. . . .

Exposure of dishonesty can be punished under some union constitutions. In New York (Shapiro vs. Gehlman 244 N.Y. App. Div. 238, 1935) a member of Local No. 1 of the International Alliance of Theatrical Stage Employees and Moving Picture Machine Operators was suspended from the union after he had charged the business agent with malfeasance in office and conduct unbecoming a member. The business agent was exonerated, and the accuser was expelled for *"making or circulating false or slanderous statements against an officer or member."* This union held a closed shop contract, and the expelled was denied employment. He appealed to the court which found that the charges against the business agent were substantiated, ordered the member reinstated and awarded him damages. . . .

The provision that the rights of a union member are protected will be met if the union has established procedure and given the accused a copy of the charges, an opportunity to confront his accusers, and a chance to answer. If the union laws under which the accused have been expelled are contrary to public policy, the courts will set aside the verdict. . . .

The courts rightfully seek to lessen their intervention in the internal affairs of labor unions. However, with the increasing power of the unions, and the growth of some forms of union security, well-managed unions are of great importance to the worker. As has been stated at the outset, the officers need to be given authority to administer affairs and pro-

---

[8] Philip Taft, "Judicial Procedure in Labor Union," *Quarterly Journal of Economics,* Cambridge, May, 1945, pp. 276–285.

[9] *New York Herald Tribune,* November 8, 1945.

tect the union against disruption. At the same time, the member must be protected against oppression. The dilemma is one common to our society. . . .

Legislative interference with the internal policies may, however, lead to results that will seriously impair the ability of trade unions to perform their essential functions. . . . A bargaining and fighting organization must have permanent leadership that looks to the future of the organization. That opens the possibility of bossism and oligarchy. But in grappling with this danger of oligarchy, we mustn't overlook the opposite danger—this atomization which makes leadership a plaything for casuals. . . .

While the level of honesty, integrity and public responsibility is as high among labor leaders as other social or economic groups, the exercise of unrestricted power encourages abuse, arrogance and irresponsibility. Actions of labor leaders should be subject to review, and where decisions involve a serious loss or burden to individuals, it is imperative that an impartial body should exist for appeal. No union officer should be immune from appeal against his acts, and to my mind the labor movement should itself create an impartial tribunal—a sort of Federal Trade Commission—which would furnish quick and inexpensive review. Most unions regard such suggestions with extreme distaste, but only some such program, it seems to me, can ward off permanent and more stringent regulation of labor unions.

This quotation from Professor Taft has been given in length because it is a non-partisan and detailed analysis of principles and concrete cases. Union leaders demur emphatically against any general charge of undemocratic procedures: "Although there may be union executive groups who constitute a rubber stamp for the president, they are the exception. As a matter of fact, American trade unions are far ahead of any other element in American life in the operation of democracy," maintained Robert J. Watt, international AFL representative.[10]

What looks like dictatorship in a union may not be so. You may want to sandpaper Petrillo but his members like him tough and he is expressing the fears of his members against themselves making the canned music to play their own funeral march. Would professors like to take their places in the breadline while their students listen to the canned lectures of a few centralized experts? As citizens, we should reply to

[10]In a dissenting footnote comment to the final chapter "Report and Recommendations," in *Trends in Collective Bargaining,* Twentieth Century Fund, New York, 1946.

that fear by adequate provision for dismissal wages, plans for retraining and adequate employment compensation.

Professor Taft's thoughtful and scholarly comment shows the difficulty of reconciling democratic controls with the efficient administration of unions.

Even the fiercest critic of the third term for the late President Roosevelt does not advocate that the president of his bank should be automatically retired. The tenure of most corporation heads is more assured than that of union presidents. And there are by far more union delegates in the conventions which re-elect union presidents than shareholders present to re-elect, say, the president of General Motors. (Incidentally union leaders do not get salaries comparable to business executives, although the variety and responsibility of their work is as great if not greater.)

Professor Taft shows why collective bargaining demands executive powers and union discipline. The point can be well made that local autonomy varies according to the scale of the industry. A local of a railroad brotherhood could not make a local agreement but a printers or building trades local can and does. But with nationwide government orders and legislation (accelerated in wartime), the power of the union central office grows.

The functions of a union and union officers are changing and do not fit into accepted notions. Professor William F. Whyte, one of the best of our modern observers of workshop practices, wrote:

> Unions have played a much less obvious but also a vitally important role in the administration of the social system of the factory. Traditionally, we tend to view the union as a protest organization. According to this picture, management has the complicated job of deciding what actions should be taken in a wide variety of situations and the union officers simply raise protests when their constituents seem to be hurt by what management does.
>
> Research shows that this picture is not simply an over-simplification. Actually, it is totally misleading. In work now being done on the human relations problems of unions, we have been impressed by the remarkable complexity of the problems faced by local officers, not even to mention the higher officials. . . .
>
> In cases we are now studying, we find that the local officers spend far more time in discussion among themselves and with rank-and-file mem-

bers, trying to decide what action they should urge management to take, than they do in actually arguing the grievance with management. . . . Coming to this agreement involves a very complicated balancing of advantages and disadvantages to individuals and groups, plus an estimate of the reactions of such individuals or groups to a whole range of possible actions.

To handle such a job effectively requires a high degree of intelligence, social skill, and understanding of human relations and economic problems. No longer is leadership in our industrial institutions confined to the management hierarchy. Unions have made an exceedingly important contribution through multiplying the numbers of people in the work places who are given opportunity to develop social initiative and exercise leadership.[11]

An Impartial Tribunal

An increasing number of union leaders would accept Professor Taft's proposal of an impartial tribunal set up by the unions. The CIO and AFL might well initiate such a tribunal of academic and industrial experts who would be glad to assist labor in the preservation of democratic procedures in the unions.

But supplementary to this would be preventive action by the unions. Workers' education, producing a mentally alert rank and file with a grasp of labor history and philosophy, would be of tremendous assistance. Obviously education supports the *status quo* in any institution. Yet that should not rule out the duty of constructive criticism and the discussion of dissenting opinion in union classes. Indeed wise union leaders would encourage this.

What one can be sure about is that in the union journal and in union meetings channels for discussion and criticism ought to be forever kept open. Younger members, instead of being driven into permanent opposition (*and being built up and flattered by the Communists and outside agencies to be used as their tools, which has happened in the case of some right wing unions*) should be given posts of responsibility so that

[11] From a background paper, Conference on "Living in Industrial Civilization," May 17–18, 1951, Corning, New York. Published as "The World of Work," in *Creating an Industrialized Society*, edited by Eugene Staley, Harper & Brothers, New York, 1952. See also Joel Seidman, Jack London, and Bernard Karsh, "Leadership in a Local Union," reprinted from *The American Journal of Sociology*, November, 1950, by the Industrial Relations Center, The University of Chicago.

they can sober the fanaticism of youth with the realism of administrative experience. Union leaders and business agents should see that the economic power which they hold through the union shop is never used to penalize individuals who disagree with them.[12] Presumably, bureaucracy exists when means become more important than the end sought, and when rules and procedures are continued because persons have vested interests in their continuance. Unions should set up a court of appeal to which any member might go in case of suspected blacklisting by his union, just as he would go to the union if the employer tried to blacklist him. In some instances the unions should set up such a court of appeal composed of officers in other unions and of trusted friends of labor from educational and legal circles. While it would be best for the unions to set up a voluntary court of appeals, I have no basic objection to the National Labor Relations Board or the United States Department of Labor setting up an agency which would have power to hear appeals and to act. It seems to me that if the NLRB confers recognition upon a union, the union, in turn, is responsible for the wise and just use of power thereby conferred.

Fundamentally, the development of general civic intelligence and a keen desire to apply democracy to industry and to trade union practices, would be the real and lasting safeguards.

The Future

All that has been noted about the dangers of bureaucracy in the trade unions gains importance when, as in Britain, the unions have attained political power and where some of the basic industries have been nationalized. The alleged dangers of "the servile state" in which government monopoly ruled men's lives, were countered by the idea of worker control of industry in which the unions would become the agencies for operating industries. But G. D. H. Cole, the leading and most articulate of the Guild Socialists, has abandoned his former views and concurs with the policy of administration of nationalized industries by governing boards, the members of which are appointed by and responsible to Parliament. Nevertheless, he favors an increasing role for the joint con-

---

[12] A staff member of the International Ladies' Garment Workers' Union, Will Herberg, some years ago in *Antioch Review*, Fall, 1943, made an excellent critical and thought-provoking analysis of this danger.

sultation committees through which the unions will get the knowledge and experience necessary for the responsibilities of management.

The problems of new incentives, of "management by consent," of the relation of the consumer and the community to organized producers, are of vital concern to individual freedom and authority in a changed setting. The shift from suspecting all government actions as encroachments upon individual liberty is being made. Government can initiate and create collectively conditions of real freedom and security by social planning without the sacrifice of individual rights. The trade unions have, as one group among others in our community, provided some examples of this pattern of the future.[13]

[13]Those interested in further analysis of the problems of union administration, election, and salaries of union officers, etc., might well see "Understanding Union Administration," by Philip Taft, *Harvard Business Review*, Winter, 1946. "Democracy in Trade Unions," American Civil Liberties Union, 1944, 86pp., still is suggestive, although some of its details are outmoded. "Bureaucracy and Democracy in Labor Unions" by Will Herberg was reprinted in 1947 as a pamphlet for the Great Island Conference, New York. "Disciplinary Procedures of Unions" by Clyde Summers, reprint from *Industrial and Labor Relations Review*, October, 1950, examines the constitutions of 154 unions. One of the most recent and comprehensive descriptions of the ideals and methods of the trade unions is *The House of Labor*, edited by J. B. S. Hardman and Maurice F. Neufeld, Prentice Hall, New York, 1951. For a general summary of the history of Labor, see *Labor in America*, a high school textbook by Harold U. Faulkner and Mark Starr, Harper & Brothers, New York, 1949.

CHAPTER VII

Labor's Emerging Role in the Political Economy

By KERMIT EBY

*Associate Professor of Social Sciences,
The University of Chicago*

I

AMONG THE MANY irreversible changes characterizing the past two decades, perhaps one of the most profound has been the change in the American labor movement from a purely economic to an economic-political pressure group. Since the development is relatively new in this country and is still in process, it is looked upon with some confusion by the interested observer. As this political child begins to attain maturity it becomes increasingly important to understand where it came from and where it is going.

The confusion is easy to understand when one looks at the contemporary political and economic program of American labor. If you were to ask Mr. William Green or Mr. Philip Murray their conviction in regard to the American economic system, both men would state categorically that they believe in the American free enterprise system. Yet, when negotiations become bitter, they, like many other American labor leaders, would stimulate the loyalties of their men by pointing out that the malefactors of great wealth are standing in the way of an era of economic justice. For example, during one strike, Mr. Murray brought the Steelworkers to their feet when, championing the cause of non-contributory pensions, he cried, "I would like to ask Mr. Moreel of Jones & Laughlin if Socialism begins at $50,000!"

Similarly, if you were to ask Mr. Jack Kroll or Mr. Joseph Keenan, the respective heads of CIO's Political Action Committee and AFL's Labor's League for Political Education, what the official policy of their organizations is in regard to political action, they would reply that they seek to elect labor's friends and defeat its enemies.

If you should pursue the questioning and then ask, "Does this mean that you support Democrats only?", they would emphatically reply, "Of course not, we support men for public office irrespective of their party labels."

Idealistic critics of the labor movement have often taken such examples as an indication of labor's lack of an underlying political or economic philosophy which guides its decisions. To them, the choice of men and policy should be determined by a process of deduction from a preconceived ideal, whereas the labor leader will encourage *any* legislation which means economic or social benefits to workers, with much greater regard for its immediate gains than its ultimate implications. The cynics go even further and aver that all we have in American labor politics today is a kind of "advanced Gompersism."

Now if by these criticisms it is meant that the American labor movement lacks a dogmatic political or economic faith which takes precedence over the day-by-day tasks its leaders are called upon to perform, the critics are undoubtedly correct. I do not agree with their diagnosis, however, because I believe the American labor movement and those who lead it *do* have a philosophy, which I would call *pragmatic dynamism,* and define as the day-by-day meeting of the economic and social problems which affect the worker in a manner which will benefit him—and incidentally the society of which he is a part. Above all, it is a philosophy which takes the framework of the existing society as a point of departure. Thus, it is the philosophy of a working movement as well as a worker's movement. Its nature implies that labor's behavior in politics can be understood only as it is viewed within the context of the political process in which it functions.

Contemporary America is a society of numerous voluntary organizations and interest groups, and democratic process can be partially defined as a fusion of interests which occurs in the very attempt of these separate elements to gain greater dominance than they already have. Labor is one, but only one of these elements. If we recognize the voluntarism and pragmatism in the larger American political structure, we can begin to understand the apparent ideological vacillation of labor's leaders. Thus, when Mr. Murray or Mr. Green go to the bargaining table, their efforts are at all times conditioned by the fact that they must negotiate within the system that they seek to reform. Similarly, Mr. Kroll and Mr. Keenan must get a job done within a party framework which they do not control.

The thinking of the American labor leader is always governed by the questions: "Where are we now, and where can we feasibly get from here?" Future problems are to be worried about on arrival and not before. The person outside the movement often becomes blind to the operational meaning of the constant friction between competing forces, and in his zeal sees only his social dream. The labor leader, by the very nature of his daily operations, is continually made aware of the pressures which play upon his organization at any time. Out of this awareness come the conclusions that a theory without an organization to back up its implementation has little meaning, and that workers are more motivated by money in their pockets than by the most well ordered Utopian blueprint.

II

Thus, the first realization necessary to an understanding of labor's role in American politics is that it was born out of Gompersism and pragmatism, rather than Marxism or Fabianism. The second is that its conscious interest in politics evolved simultaneously with the Depression, the Roosevelt era, and the New Deal. It is clearly impossible to understand labor's and particularly CIO's interest in politics, if one does not remember that the CIO came into being in a period when it had the blessings of government. All of the men who were instrumental in the formation of the CIO-PAC never lost sight of Article 7A of the old NRA, which was the basis for the Wagner Act—nor have they forgotten what Roosevelt meant to the success of the formation of CIO, or to the passage of social legislation which came into being simultaneously with its birth.

Hillman and Murray and Green and Meany and men of their stature were top level operators. They had access to the White House during the Roosevelt administration, usually through the President and always through his wife. To them, FDR was something only slightly lower than the angels and slightly higher than man. He was the personification of the Great White Father, an artist in the field which was to them the master craft, and in which they themselves took great pride—the manipulation of men. It was therefore natural that their politics should be oriented toward keeping a friendly White Father in office, for he was a man with whom they, the lesser white fathers, could do business.

The Truman victory of 1948 meant a resurgence of the Democratic Party. It meant also the end of any immediate formation of a labor party, even of the most innocent variety; labor could still express itself through the majority party (which held in its ranks many white collar and farmer liberals who would not feel at home in a labor party) at its top level of organization. But withal, the American system of government not only has Presidential elections—it has off year elections in which the fate of the Congress is determined, and in which the interests of the electorate are much more likely to be local than national. In the most recent election [chapter written in February, 1951] there was no dramatization of the economic aspirations of the New Deal around a Presidential candidate. We did not have, as we did in 1948, a President tying into his election an economic program which was of direct benefit to workers. Instead, we had a series of more or less separate elections, involving everything from Taft-Hartley to the "World's Richest Cop."

It is precisely in this kind of situation that the effectiveness of a top level relationship breaks down. When election issues become independent and sectionalized, the votes are dependent not upon the influence of the big brass, but upon the sergeants, corporals, and not a few of the privates in labor's ranks. If the labor movement is ever to become really effective in influencing the political structure, it must recognize this inadequacy and develop an organization capable of carrying through in the precincts and wards and congressional districts. Herein rises the fundamental point, however, in any discussion of the labor movement and the political party, and it is the big question which Sidney Hillman and the big bosses of labor refused to face.

III

There are several forms which the relationship between labor and the Democratic Party can take. First of all, it can do as it has in Michigan: move in on the party organization and administer it directly or through friendly persons. Secondly, it can do as it has in New York, where it has developed a *modus operandi* by which it bargains with the Democrats on program, candidates, and operation of elections. Thirdly, it can do as it has in Illinois, continue to be the tail wagged by the Democratic kite, in which it takes whatever candidates the machine gives it and helps out in their election, without any very definite assurances of *quid pro quo*. Finally, it can do as it did in Ohio so disastrously in the past campaign: attempt to break with the machine's selection of candidates and force its own slate.

There are many other choices, as well as infinite varieties of the above mentioned, and each carries with it inherent advantages and disadvantages. The choice which I prefer is the gradual absorption of the Democratic Party machinery and the control of its organization, for I have long believed that the most significant decisions of politics are those which have to do with the selection of candidates and the formation of program, and I know that the major decisions in regard to candidates are too often determined by party loyalties, party supports, and party hackwork qualifications which are not of primary significance in qualifying for public office. The drawback to such avowed control of the party organization is the knowledge by the public that labor, in so many places a minority, has control of the political party. Consequently, as occurred in Ohio, labor becomes isolated and opportunity for alliances with other groups is dissipated. Thus, there may be some argument for organization such as labor demonstrated so successfully in Missouri in the past campaign. There it kept in the background and mobilized its forces quietly, as much as possible through other organizations and persons. I become a little less flexible than I like on this argument, for I have thought for a long time that responsibility must go with power and that the people have a right to know who calls the turns. Yet I know that if I push this argument further I will be coming out for a labor party and I certainly do not want to, because I also know that except in a few industrial cities labor cannot win an election alone, and certainly not as long as its members indicate the degree of independence which they did in the past election. If organized labor wishes to be successful in the future, however, it is not enough that it gain a voice in the selection of candidates. It must begin a process of recommending men for public office, in the sense of developing them for public life. Translated into terms of action, this means that organized labor must encourage its ablest people to seek positions on the boards of civic organizations, in nonprofit bodies, on school boards, and on the boards of trustees of educational institutions. Once these men gain a reputation for public service on the local level, they will have served their apprenticeship for higher positions and they will have what is so fundamental for organized labor —a knowledge of the movement they represent. Candidates do not spring full blown from the body politic. They must be nurtured, groomed, and, if you please, built.

Another problem to which such grass roots organization gives rise is the very practical one of financing the candidates who understand the problems and needs of the local communities. Such men lack independent fortunes, and thus it is my hunch that if we ever have a political party representing the worker it will have to be supported by small contributions. Labor will not have candidates of integrity, unless it is willing to support them much more adequately than it did in the past election. It is simply not fair to ask a man to be your servant and make it necessary for him to mortgage his home.

Finally, once it has selected the candidates and financed them, labor faces yet another problem and that is the development of a program attractive to the people it would influence. When I begin to speculate about the past election, I always end up wondering if one of the significant determinants of the voting attitudes of the worker was simply that the issues of the election had no primary impression on him. Although his costs have risen, he still has money in his pocket. Consequently he is responsive to other than economic factors in his whole environment. Labor, to be successful in politics, cannot be politically negative. In other words, it cannot be against Taft-Hartley, and at the same time shout that the trade union movement is stronger than ever. It cannot be part of the administration at the top levels, and criticize the hand that feeds it. Suffice it to say that in the area of program workers are not given a clear, succinct, and positive leadership identified with their interests.

It is exactly at this point that the advocates of a third or labor party advance their strongest case and argue that labor's program, that is, one serving its own interests, can find expression only when labor has a vehicle of its own. The advantages of such an organization, or of the gradual absorption of the Democratic Party and control of its machinery, lie chiefly in the fact that it can thus serve as an educational vehicle capable of arousing moral enthusiasm. There are many men in the labor movement who support this view, particularly in the secondary and tertiary levels of the auto and textile workers, but it will no doubt be a long time before their view prevails, because the top officers of their unions are much more interested in the day-by-day victories in collective bargaining than in the development of an educational vehicle strong on theory but weak on performance.

It is likely that the men who make the decisions for organized labor will continue to operate according to the principle of pragmatic dynamism, improvising as they go along, and operating differently in different areas. But perhaps the antithesis between the two points of view is not so decisive as it appears, for these men are not unconscious of the desirability of their own organization. To them the significant variable is not preference, but practicality. For the top men of labor the point of destination is never permanently defined, nor the area of debate ever permanently circumscribed. Above all, they accept history and the limitations which history places on their own movement. The relative strength or weakness of the position from which they bargain either in the political or economic arena varies with the conditions of the particular time, but it is precisely for this reason that it has developed an adjustable machinery and evolved a pragmatic philosophy. If conditions permit, that machinery can be adjusted to meet with the desires of those who envision a labor party.

Comment by Edgar S. Brightman:
This paper is an able and sound presentation of the role of labor. With its general attitude I am fully in accord, save for one point. Its social approach seems to me to underrate the ultimate criterion of all social processes in a democracy—namely, their effect on the individual person. "Pragmatic dynamism," yes—but dynamism for what? For what "will benefit the worker and incidentally the society of which he is a part." So far, so good. I know it is asking a great deal, but I think we have a right to ask that every responsible person, be he worker or manager, man or woman, test his dynamism primarily by the question: How is my conduct going to affect all the individuals in the society to which I belong? The question ought not to be, primarily, how it will affect me, and, secondarily, how will it affect the society. I am aware that this ethical demand is a very high one. But I am reminded of Spinoza; "all things excellent are as difficult as they are rare." But Spinoza was seeking the true basis for permanent happiness, not immediate pragmatic returns.

Comment by Nels F. S. Ferré:
Professor Eby has rendered a real service by his analysis. Pragmatic dynamism is concretely illustrated and the resulting relation between government and labor clarified.

Religion both takes the part of and criticizes capital and labor alike. Whenever relative right or justice demands its taking concrete stands on issues, religion thereby does not become partial, except as a human failing, but takes the part of the creative good in the name of the inclusive community. It may weigh whole systems in the balance and find them wanting, even though both capital and labor endorse their main operations and incentives.

I wish I knew how capital and labor, and religious leaders with them, could at the same time become humble and willing to learn in the presence of the unattained common good, and also fully committed to work ceaselessly for the partial good obtainable within one's group and from the give and take of the process of pragmatic dynamism.

CHAPTER VIII

The Exercise of Freedom

By LOUIS HARRIS AND JULIAN L. WOODWARD
Research Executives in the Elmo Roper Organization

ONE OF THE things we are proudest of about our American society is the system which guarantees certain personal rights to our people. Every school child is well versed in the more formal contents of the Bill of Rights in our Constitution, most students of constitutional law are aware of additional guarantees that are established by legal precedent, and those who study our customs and habits can point to still other guarantees—more informal and for the most part unwritten—which actually exist in our society.

We make a great deal of these rights. It is our claim that they distinguish our democratic system from the state of tyranny most of the world's people throughout history have lived under. We hear a good deal about our rights every July 4th, and studies of American character structure show that an abstract belief in them runs deep indeed in our national thinking. Observers from foreign countries, such as Gunnar Myrdal, have pointed out that our ingrained belief in human rights constitutes an offset or balancing factor in a society that has otherwise been described as "overmaterialistic."

Surveys of public opinion have consistently indicated that upwards of eighty per cent of the American people hold a firm belief in the traditional guarantees of the rights of individuals. Unfortunately, for a large section of the American public, these rights remain little more than abstract concepts to which scarcely more than "lip service" is paid. They are there; we believe in them; if they were seriously challenged we would fight to maintain them. But meanwhile they are taken for granted. Europeans who have lived under occupation regimes are surprised at our casual acceptance of rights they have learned to cherish above everything.

It is only the more articulate members of our society (probably no more than ten to fifteen per cent) who keep alert to the changing situation with respect to rights. This group does indeed have a frame of reference for evaluation—a sort of running inventory of publicized violation or near violations of rights. The inventory is not formally arrived at. It is rather a climate of opinion based on certain incidents or events which have come to the attention of those who reflect on the significance of news in relation to freedom.

What is happening in our courts of law at the moment is given heavy weighting. Because of the important role of the courts in protecting and insuring the maintenance of rights, we have also adopted in our thinking the curious symbolism of legal procedures. Legal cases dealing with individual rights are, by and large, considered more important than the specific individuals who are involved in the case. It is assumed that by trying one case which might be representative of tens or hundreds or thousands more like it, we are indeed settling an issue involving many times the number of people directly on trial. We rally our most fervent support for liberty and freedom when we have a "cause célèbre" to focus our attention around, for we tacitly assume that the decision will almost automatically be a pattern-setter for our society.

Thus, when we take our periodic inventories of American freedom, we tend to list off on our balance sheet individual cases which have either strengthened or weakened the cause of democracy. When we undertake to defend our system of rights, we cite progress in correcting violations of freedom and in maintaining freedom. We tend to teach the history of civil liberties in this fashion, and the annual summaries of the civil liberties situation, published by such organizations as the American Civil Liberties Union, tend to be inventories of this sort.

Curiously enough, the severest critics of our system also have adopted this framework of thinking in making their charges. Just as we tend to defend our system by pointing to case after case where individual rights have been preserved and maintained, the Communists, for instance, tend to point to individual instances where human rights have allegedly been violated, as proof that freedom does not exist in our country.

That this legalistic appraisal of the rights situation at any given time has its uses, no one would deny. But that it is the most significant part of the picture, might be questioned. Suppose that a complete inventory of all the cases involving violations of civil rights in America were statistically summarized, and a quantitative *and* qualitative balance sheet of court rulings were drawn up. Would we have an accurate inventory of human rights as they exist within this country?

This would be only one side of the coin—the side which indicated whether or not people had a certain right legally. But whether or not people actually enjoyed that right, might be an entirely different story.

For instance, take the recent Supreme Court decisions affecting the admission of Negroes to graduate and professional schools. When the Sweatt case at the University of Oklahoma was decided in favor of admission of the Negro plaintiff, the decision was hailed as a monumental advance in race relations in this country. And, indeed, it unquestionably will be looked on historically as a most significant point in the progress of Negroes in the South.

Actually, one year after the decision was handed down, only slightly more than 1,000 Negroes in the South were enjoying hitherto barred privileges of attending formerly all-white graduate schools. It will be a long and painful struggle to reach the point where aspiring Negro students will, in fact, enjoy the right to a proper graduate and professional education. And if one wants to assay the situation in terms of how the right actually *functions,* it might be argued that it is not fully enjoyed until the proportion of Negroes in graduate and professional schools is equal to the population proportion between Negroes and whites in each particular state.

In other words, another dimension might be introduced into the measurement of freedom: how many people actually enjoy the rights which are guaranteed for them through our judicial and legislative processes?

By introducing this third dimension of measurement, we will tend to overcome the severe bias of generalization now existent in saying that because lynchings have risen or declined, as the case might be in any given year, the rights of Negroes are rising or falling proportionately. By the same token, our answer to the false charges that the cases of the Trenton Six or the Communist Eleven or the Hollywood Ten *prove* that freedom does not exist in this country, does not have to consist of a recital of judicial cases, all to show that freedom is, indeed, very much alive and functioning.

In fact, by introducing an actual measurement of *exercise* of freedom, we point up an obligation of any free society: the necessity not only of insuring certain rights for people, but the educational necessity of teaching people how effectively to *use* their rights.

Data on the exercise of freedom are hard to come by. It is one thing to say that the right of free speech exists—it is another to find out what proportion of our population ever indulges in free speech on any public issue at all. As an illustration of the kinds of fact gathering we think are both pertinent and feasible, we now present a few bits of material gathered from public opinion surveys and from other sources. It would require much more information of this sort before one could say that we were accurately describing the situation in American life.

1. The right to vote is a good starting point. Surveys have regularly indicated that more people in this country cherish the right to participate in free elections than to enjoy any other freedom. The idea that rulers shall govern only with the consent of the governed, runs deep in American thinking. People like to feel that they "can always throw the rascals out." But, in spite of these sentiments, not much more than fifty per cent of the eligible ever turn out to vote at the polls in the United States at any given election.

It is interesting to note that in Western Europe, after the blackout of freedom under Nazi occupation, the turnout has consistently been between seventy-five and ninety-five per cent of the eligibles. In the recent French national election, for instance, despite a reported apathetic electorate (one qualified observer said the interest pitch was much lower than it was in the United States in 1948), just over eighty per cent of the voters came to the polls. This is one-third higher than we have ever recorded in an election in this country.

2. Ranking a close second to the right to free elections in the estimation of the American people, is the right to free speech. Some of our bitterest and most historic battles have been over the free speech issue. Of late, many have expressed fears that some groups are increasingly unwilling to risk economic security in order to exercise freedom of speech. A *New York Times* survey indicated that there is definite reluctance on the part of both college students and faculty members to engage in outspoken debate, for fear of being called subversive.

One might hazard the guess that perhaps ten per cent of our people have become more reluctant to express themselves within the past few years, and this would exclude the one per cent who are either Communist or Communist fellow travelers, whose right to preach the overthrow of the government has now been abridged under the law. However, many more people do not exercise the right of free speech on matters of public affairs, simply because they literally never talk about them. A Roper survey indicates that some twenty per cent of the American people simply never discuss public issues. And forty-seven per cent more who say they discuss them only occasionally, probably can be assumed rarely to exercise their freedom of speech.

Or take another aspect of free speech, the right to petition or communicate with one's elected representative. A recent Roper study indicated that eight out of ten people had never written or otherwise gotten in touch with their Congressman, Senator, or other public officials, to express their citizen wishes relative to a public issue.

3. Another deeply held American right is freedom of association. We have been called a nation of joiners. So far as politically active groups are concerned this is obviously a misnomer. One national Roper study reported that sixty-nine per cent of our people do not belong to *any* organization that takes stands on or discusses public issues, and only seven per cent belong to more than one such grouping. In 1947 only about half the people claimed to have even heard of the National Association of Manufacturers or the Political Action Committee of the CIO. It may also be noted that only ten per cent of a national sample reported that they had done any work in the past four years to help in the election of any political candidate. And less than a third had attended any meeting in that time at which any political speeches were made. The right to join political action groups (except those of a Communist tinge!) is there, but it is not over much exercised.

4. A fourth right that is buttressed by tradition and court decisions is freedom of inquiry. True, the right has been recently abridged on some university campuses, and in school systems whose libraries are not allowed to display certain magazines. But while these limitations are clearly bad, they are not as bad as the failure to engage in free inquiry when the opportunity does offer. How many of us take seriously the responsibility to become informed about public affairs. Fifteen per cent of Americans will admit that they just never read a morning newspaper, and another seven per cent say they never read a newspaper of any kind. It can be assumed that the number of actual non-readers is

much larger than those who admit to the fact. Thirty-six per cent do not read regularly any magazine "that contains news or discussions about public issues." Sixty-one per cent said they had not "had a chance" to read a book "during recent months."

5. A fifth right is freedom of enterprise. People are free to set up and operate their own businesses, but how many want to do so? Survey results indicate that about a third of the young people plan *never* to go into business for themselves. In a *Fortune* magazine survey of the "class of '49" at the colleges, an average of only two per cent had any intention of starting their own business enterprise on graduation or later. It is certainly not necessary that everybody exercise the freedom of enterprise, in order to maintain the right as a characteristic of our society, but one may maintain that if the number of new entrepreneurs in a generation falls as low as two per cent, the freedom may atrophy from disuse.

6. One might list other rights, such as freedom to worship (twenty per cent do not go to church at all), freedom to bargain collectively (union members are less than a fourth of all gainfully employed), or freedom of the press (how much variation in press point of view is there?). One can certainly raise questions as to the use we make of our opportunities in these regards.

So much for a hasty survey of very incomplete evidence about our current use of freedoms in America. Really only one point has been made—our rights are not so much exercised in practice as to give reason for any complacency about them. For if we have them and do not use them, one may argue that some day we will not have them. The statement is over simple, and certainly is not equally applicable to all the rights discussed, but we believe it contains at least enough truth to justify much further study of freedoms in operation.

For if the picture is accurate, we must recognize that our case for Democracy as the best form of government has a weakness in it. We want to convince other peoples of the merits of our system, but what will the "undecideds" of the earth say—the people of Asia, Africa, the Middle East—who have not experienced individual rights as we have in the Western world, but who know that the Russian Constitution and the American Constitution both purportedly guarantee that these rights shall be exercised by the peoples of these countries. They will state—
"We may know that the Soviet Constitution and its declaration of human rights is a mockery, because there is neither the guarantee nor the

practice of these rights." But they might further ask, "How much better is the United States, where we have heard of certain guarantees of rights not being kept, and where we know the positive exercise of these rights is not very widespread?" What then will these people who are newly oriented to self-rule believe about freedom and the actual working of Democracy in the United States? It is perhaps a matter for Americans to ponder seriously.

CHAPTER IX

Social Security: Freedom from Want Without Want of Freedom

By GEORGE F. ROHRLICH [1]
*Division of Program Analysis,
Bureau of Old-Age and Survivors Insurance,
United States Social Security Administration*

"FREEDOM AND AUTHORITY" have often been pictured as the two poles between which human striving in society has oscillated in pendulumlike fashion. Query, human striving after what: freedom *per se,* authority *per se?* I doubt it. I am inclined to think men have sought freedom at times and authority at other times only as either appeared to them, in turn, as the would be guarantor of "the good life."

Undoubtedly, "the good life," has meant different things at different times or in different parts of the world. By and large though, what it adds up to is to have what one needs, to enjoy it in his own way, and to be safe in counting on either. Leaving aside the purely spiritual and some of the deeper psychological aspects it amounts to what in our own day and culture we have dubbed "social security," and have paraphrased at times as the lasting accomplishment of freedom from want without want of freedom.

Should my initial supposition be correct, the attainment everywhere of this perennial goal, "the good life"—whatever be its contents at a given place and time—might conceivably enable mankind to transcend the zigzag maze in which its past has evolved in a future of growth without upheavals, stability without stagnation.

Let us look into the conditions for the realization of this lofty prospect, at least to the extent to which social security may bring it about.

---

[1] The views here expressed are those of the writer but do not necessarily represent any official position of the agency in which he is employed or of any constituent part thereof.

I

In the social realm, terminology is apt to be fuzzy, especially when it comes to defining goals of action. "Freedom from want" is, strictly speaking, an impossibility. Man is not built that way. Our wants are unlimited. New wants are born even before all the old wants are met. Were it otherwise, our capacity to satisfy given wants to the hilt would condemn us to stagnation.

Similarly, "want of freedom" is a state which we can never quite escape even in the freest of societies, and which we cannot hope ever to overcome in its entirety.

And yet, these terms, "freedom from want," and "want of freedom," connote realities in human life which are acutely felt, and which, at least at certain points, are susceptible to verification.

The basic want is that for enough food to keep alive. Hence, "freedom from want," at the very least, must mean that none should starve. This accomplishment in itself may constitute "the good life" at the lowest fringe of civilized living. Only as earthly possessions multiply and become sufficiently widespread among a people to permit a variety of enjoyments according to different tastes, does the issue of "freedom" arise in the form of freedom of choice. This is why hunger and destitution are not freedom's champions.

Within the more prosperous nations in which both the economic and civic development of the population have progressed to higher levels, the basic postulate of "none should starve," is expanded to include a complementary one: "none should have to obtain his sustenance at the price of his freedom." Our capacity for, and hence our potential want of, freedom—somewhat paradoxically—turn out to be a function of our comparative (absolute and relative) "freedom from want." This is the juncture at which freedom enters man's view as the necessary condition for individual self-realization.

Progressing toward the upper end of this scale, there comes a stage of development in which not only is a rather comfortable standard of living tagged as the lower margin of "the good life," but claim is made to it as a matter of earned right, and objection is raised to making its attainment contingent upon proof of need. Not only the material good things of life and their enjoyment in one's own way (freedom), but the *assurance* of both (security) become essentials of "the good life." With that expectation, the demand for "social security" is widely raised. Typically it aims at any or all of the following: the effective assurance of a job paying enough to meet regular needs and of the wherewithal to cope with the adversities of life, such as unemployment, illness, invalidity, death, and to anticipate without fear other occurrences, such as childbirth, a growing family, old age.

The form, too, in which this assurance may be desired or given varies. The slogans of "full employment," "employment stabilization," "guaranteed annual wages," indicate some of the lines of approach. If risks entail some loss of one's regular income, the desire for security usually takes the form of an assured substitute income through social insurance. On the other hand, hazards involving expenditure of money over and above the usual needs may be met out of savings, provided regular income is ample enough, or by a variety of public programs.

Once a society has set its mark that high, it has come a long way, indeed, from the social goal of "no one starves." If these extremes in expectation fall in the range of "the good life"—in one world and at one time—then what is there to guide us in our national and international policies aimed at helping to secure "the good life" as far as we can?

Before attempting to answer this question it might be well to spell out further what we are after and by what means we can go about it.

II

"Social" security refers, of course, to security within society. In this respect, it is both an axiom and a postulate. An axiom, because security cannot be attained outside of society, and is, in fact, *possible* only within it. But to make it *actual,* society must establish and maintain it. It is in this sense that social security is a postulate, a task to be accomplished. Marginal situations and times of crisis show this better than patterns of "normalcy." One may recall the feeling of present danger engendered by social unrest or enemy attack, or think of the sudden insecurity of the formerly so secure man of success who has fallen from fame and fortune. As a typical reaction, all of us have witnessed the phenomenon of group flight from frustrating social insecurity into the security of a place in the ranks, national grandeur, or other glory.

From the national point of view, defense, police, education, public health, indeed a nation's whole heritage of material riches and positive values, make up its security. They are, of course, interrelated. Lastly, though, their foundation is the nation's endowment with, and procreation of, economic goods, combined with a reasonably adequate share in them by each of its citizens. The two aspects are correlative: there must prevail at all times some sort of equilibrium between the nation's wealth and the distribution of that wealth and/or its fruits.

If the economy is successful in achieving constant growth of the nation's wealth, but fails to distribute sufficiently widely at least some of the gains, political upheaval will, in most cases, catch up with the rulers of that society sooner or later. If we claim for distribution and consumption what is required to keep the nation's capital intact, we undermine the powers of the economy for continued regeneration and further increase in wealth. To steer the course between the twin dangers is not easy. For one thing, we lack certain advance knowledge and precise measurements of the sum total of economic gains and losses following from our actions. Besides, we keep upsetting our security in terms of given ecological equilibria as we expand our humanity; witness our relentless struggle to save and prolong life even in notoriously overpopulated countries. To argue that we should do otherwise, would be to argue against man's destiny as a spiritual being. Finally, there are times of crisis, such as wars and other social and natural disasters, during which nations may be forced to live considerably beyond their means, thus heavily encumbering their future security, in order to safeguard their very existence.

The vectors of social security, *i.e.,* the media making for more of it, may be of different kinds: quasi-automatic, legislative, and external. The first has its place chiefly in an economy in which the play of economic forces is permitted to work itself out without major regulatory interference. What I have in mind is essentially a free enterprise economy in which the economic gains achieved are *over the long run* passed on in substantial measure to the population at large. The hitch is the long run, which may be too long to suit the needs and temper of the less prosperous members of a given society.

The legislative approach is open both to free enterprise societies in which it may be used as an accelerator or corrective of the economic automatism, and to controlled economies, in which it is the primary vector. Disregarding broader regulatory schemes, it consists in the enactment of social programs supervised or administered by public authority, and sometimes subsidized from general government revenues.

By the "external" vectors, finally, I am referring to foreign aid granted by more to less prosperous nations.

Passing over the problems of evaluation and choice as to the level and form and between different vectors of social security, the policy aim can be stated thus: to achieve with given means the greatest possible *total* results. At this point, national and international policies merge. While they deal with situations located at opposite or nearly opposite ends of the range of our problem, there is this in common to both areas: freedom has become the basic issue. How can we be sure, it is asked, that to legislate greater social security at home, and indirectly (through passing foreign aid bills) abroad, will not undermine freedom, rather than help it?

I doubt if we can be sure, but I believe there are sound arguments that gainsay such fears and at the same time provide us with some criteria to guide our actions.

III

Those who argue against an extension of social security by means of social legislation, usually base their opposition on two separate contentions. One is prohibitive cost, the other a concern lest individual self-reliance and incentive give way to government paternalism.

The economic-financial argument, though generally talked about in public discussion and especially in political debate, is really one for economic analysis to determine rather than political judgment. We cannot, of course, expect an economy to distribute over a long period of time more than it produces. But short of that limit, the question is not whether we can afford increased social security at home or abroad, but whether we prefer to allocate our net economic gains to this or to other purposes.

By contrast, the second argument charging a basic conflict between security, on the one hand, and progress and freedom, on the other, could conceivably apply well within the limits of economic capacity. If added social legislation would have an adverse effect upon individual incentive and productivity, it might actually narrow our leeway to the extent to which the national product is reduced, below what it would otherwise have been.

The argument boils down to this, that we ought to have a great deal of reservation in enhancing security, even where to do so is well within our means, because it may spoil our character. Strange anomaly: humane considerations have long forced us to recognize our responsibilities toward those in need of help. We extend to them a helping hand and try to salvage them, largely at public expense. But to those who ask for an orderly process of providing to meet common emergencies, partly out of their own contributions, in good time and before they bring about devastating results, some would raise a warning finger and say: "No."

It is hard to see how for those who would otherwise rely on public charity to meet a part or all of their needs, the substitution of social insurance would increase government paternalism or deprive them of self-reliance or individual initiative.

But, naturally, our greater concern must be with those above the bottom layer, the bulk of the population, our large middle class. Obviously, their freedom to enjoy *in their own way* what they have, is interfered with, in such measure as portions thereof are taxed away to support public welfare, health—or government at large. This is, initially at least, a comparative diminution of freedom. In nature, this loss of choice over the use of some of our means is of exactly the same type as that we inflicted on ourselves long ago, when we instituted compulsory education, traffic regulations, building codes, and more of the like. All of these are examples of actions which have expanded "the good life" (by eventually broadening our scope of action), not through greater freedom but through more authority.

Have they diminished our incentives to be educated, our concern for our safety? Indeed not. There is no limit for the eager student and the precautious citizen in carrying their zeal far beyond legal requirements. Have they reduced our self-reliance? Not on balance; to the extent to which public authority has relieved us of the worry; it has merely freed our creative powers for the next stretch and for other tasks.

Yet, there is one component which looms larger in our present day problem, such as care in old age, unemployment, invalidity, etc., than it did in the examples cited above: fear. I believe it is the lever of fear as the driving force for our individual actions which is really at issue in all this talk of incentives: fear of unprotected old age, fear of unemployment, fear of disability. These are considered the personal incentives and test stones of our self-reliance. I agree that a well rounded social security program would do away with these fears. It should. To equate incentive and fear of failure—which is what I think is being done—is to do grave injustice to the nature of the former. I doubt if the assurance of a basic minimum would stop the ambitious from reaching out for the stars. If fear has ever done anything to produce action, it has twisted and debased it. Often it paralyzes and prevents action altogether.

Fortunately, we have moved away from the motivation of fear in the way we run our greatest enterprises: government and education. Why should we protect its remaining preserve against further inroads?

IV

Yet security does have its dangers. Though last to appear in the threesome forming the foundation of "the good life," it may not—and probably will not—be the first to be sacrificed when the choice should arise of having to give up security or freedom or the material good things of life.

When men in frustration or despair have to give up one good to maintain another, I am inclined to think that, once property and other earthly possessions have come to mean a great deal, the threat to be deprived thereof may move such men to yield freedom (to enjoy what one has in his own way) in exchange for the expectation of assured possession. But I question that the denial of security in the first place would necessarily forestall a surrender to protective authority. Looking at extremes, history presents us with no less striking examples for the capitulation out of want than it does with cases of surrender born of satiety. Both cases have just this in common, that their common motive is fear. Let us beware of clinging to fear as an incentive to rely on and perpetuate wherever we are in a position to do away with it. We have progressed as we have conquered our fears.

What about our concern for freedom? I doubt if we can export it, or, for that matter, maintain it where it has struck roots, except as we insure the material conditions which make it meaningful. As we make life ever richer and increase the opportunities for individual self-realization, we underpin freedom.

Unfortunately, even the most modest version of "the good life," in the form of the injunction that none should starve, may be difficult to achieve in some of the less developed countries of the world; and others farther advanced, whose population had learned to aspire to a much higher level of living, might find that after the ravages of a war they are temporarily unable to provide the accustomed standard. Those are the danger points where our aid may be required—if a concern for freedom is to be implanted or maintained.

To instil the vision of freedom where it had never been known, and where the need for food is not met first is, I am afraid, a Sisyphean labor of love. Where it has been known, the surest way to keep the vision alive when it is in jeopardy, again, is to strengthen its material basis. The different levels at which "the good life" may need to be bolstered to give freedom a chance, may vary widely, from the very bottom where it is first engendered up to where it approximates our own material level of "the good life." The need is in terms of satisfactions once known and customarily aspired to.

For the sake of freedom, not the maximization of social security from "no one starves" all the way up, but the threat of its curtailment or failure to keep pace with mankind's ever growing horizons is to be feared.

CHAPTER X

Freedom and Authority in International Relations

By HANS KOHN

Professor of History, The College of the City of New York

INTERNATIONAL SOCIETY, like any other society, has to avoid the two extremes, anarchism and totalitarianism. International society, in the definition of thinkers like Machiavelli and Hegel, is based upon the principle of anarchy, the coexistence of sovereign individual entities which do not recognize any higher or superior binding law. Thus in their relations among themselves everything seemed permissible. Latent war, the *bellum omnium contra omnes,* seemed to be the natural state of international society, and actual warfare was restrained only by fear or prudence. Against this danger—following the example set by Hobbes for the relations among individuals within a state—a powerful world government was seen as a remedy. Such a rational world order enforcing peace was the mirage before the eyes of Napoleon, and may be the mirage before the eyes of Stalin. In *Mein Kampf* Hitler spoke of such a similar future world peace enforced by the German nation as the master race. But such an international authority would be bought at the expense of all the diversity, of all the freedom of development, which so far has constituted human history. The fundamental question of international society today is the same as that for modern civil society, namely, how to find that minimum of authority which would guarantee a reasonable order, without unduly sacrificing free and diversified development.

The tendency of modern Western society has on the whole, during the past centuries, stressed the preference for liberty over authority. In seventeenth century England, in the Puritan and, above all, in the Glorious Revolution, the foundations of modern liberty were laid. In the new mental climate of respect for individual rights and of tolerance for oppositional opinions, the realm of liberty was steadily expanded and the sphere of authority limited. It was the unique political genius of the English people who have on the whole struck for the past three centuries a happy balance between a maximum of liberty and a minimum of authority. In the eighteenth century liberty was widely believed possible, if at all, only in small and homogeneous communities. Yet the liberal system in England proved more conducive to a growth in strength, welfare, and inventiveness than the supposedly mightier nations across the Channel. The same principle of a very large area of liberty and a small area of authority, was applied by the British in ordering their empire, and in transforming it into a commonwealth of nations with a unique tolerance of diversity of thought and cultural trends, language, and religion. In spite of the severe limitations on central authority, the Commonwealth showed in the two trying tests of the World Wars an astonishing strength of cohesion.

The ideal of liberty as prevailing over authority within a balanced system (liberty under law) has spread from seventeenth century England and from the English settlements in North America in the nineteenth century to Europe and by the end of the century to Russia and Asia. In the twentieth century, however, counter currents became strong, emphasizing the importance of authority over liberty for the sake of peace, security, and the ultimate good of man. Communism and Fascism and other authoritarian trends promised, as Hobbes did, security in exchange for liberty. With the urgency of international peace in the wake of the great wars, the desirable goal seemed to many attainable only by a strong central authority which might force men into reforms. Social sciences chased after the will-o'-the-wisp of "the causes of war" and searched for panaceas in social reform, economic betterment, constitutional changes, fight against illiteracy, and, above all, national self-determination. Mankind was to be thoroughly reorganized and improved.

Though an authoritarian pattern imposed on a worldwide basis may insure peace, it might endanger the free development of diversified civilizations. For that reason any attempt to create a strong world authority might rather increase conflicts and tensions. The problem ahead is to allow the coexistence of various civilizations with reasonable security against the devastation of war and with little change imposed upon their ways of life. The maintenance of international security is the legitimate field of an international authority. All its other functions must be exercised on a basis of voluntary cooperation. The prevention of war, however, demands the application of authority and force, yet with a careful respect for the limits of this area. This is the task of the United Nations at present.

In the present state of the international community there is no agreement about concepts such as liberty or justice. They are viewed differently by the various civilizations, and sometimes even within one and the same civilization. Any attempt to seek liberty or justice internationally, to "liberate" peoples or groups, must lead to a heightening of tension and conflicts. Even the two world wars, when the contending parties attempted to remove "injustices," hardly solved any of the problems to general satisfaction. Whether the situation before 1914 or after 1918 corresponded better to the demands of liberty and justice, would have been very differently answered by the various parties involved in the old or in the new sovereignties. The newly liberated nations began to dispute among themselves about further liberation, and their disputes opened the way to new assertions of authority over liberty.

Nor would it be justified to try to impose one way of life on all communities. Modern Western civilization as it arose in eighteenth century England and Western Europe, has shown on the whole a spirit of tolerance which understands the value of different approaches to the one truth. Though there have been trends to regard modern Western civilization, with its emphasis on individuality and law, as desirable for all men, today most Western men will be grateful that there exist on earth non-Western civilizations with their own traditions, their own images of man, and their own attitudes toward nature and society. The values of Buddhism seem far remote from the activist and legalistic values of the West. Who, however, could claim that they are inferior, or that a Western scientist is superior to a Buddhist ascetic? Gandhi's activity, though unthinkable within the context of modern Western civilization, certainly does not suffer in an ethical comparison with the activities of any Western political leader. Dostoyevsky, who so savagely rejected modern Western civilization, enriched humanity by his deep probing into the recesses of the human or at least of the Russian mind. It is important for mankind that the full freedom of development in inward intensity, for the various civilizations, remain unhampered by any central authority.

Authority in international relations must be limited, at least for the foreseeable future, to the one task of preventing conflicts between the various civilizations and of thwarting aggression. The recent war in Korea has clearly shown that such a task is feasible. There is no doubt that both the North Koreans and the South Koreans, wished to "liberate" their "brethren" south or north of the dividing line and to establish a "just" regime without "oppression." The actual aggression was committed when the North Koreans with superior power and superior preparation invaded South Korea. It was then plain wisdom on the part of all nations interested in the preservation of peace, irrespective of ideologies, to come to the help of the attacked party. Thanks to Mr. Truman's clearsighted leadership, the United States and the United Nations acted in that way. But for a long moment they were not clear themselves about the implications of their action. They wished to go beyond their authority of preventing or thwarting aggression and to "liberate" North Korea. Soon, however, wiser counsel prevailed. It was recognized that the purpose of the action was the thwarting of aggression, not more. The success of driving the aggressor out of the invaded territory could be regarded as a great victory for the new principle of authority, within the right limits, in international society.

This success may mean a turning point in the fortunes of war and peace. Though the diversity of civilization makes a world government at present impossible, and the diversity of civilizations may be regarded by all except extreme rationalists as a good thing, what seems to be growing up is the efficient authority not of a world state but of a limited federal power. In his *Zum Ewigen Frieden,* Kant, who as the son of eighteenth century rationalism preferred the world state, nevertheless foresaw such a limited federation against aggression as the only possibility.[1]

The danger of war may remain ever present, as Kant says, in such a federal structure with very limited authority confined to the one purpose of preventing or repelling aggression. But even within one government showing an infinitely greater cohesion than a world government probably ever could, the danger of war exists. It existed in the Swiss Confederation and in the federal union of the United States. The best that can be hoped for is an authority enforcing the tolerably peaceful cohabitation of various groups. Western civilization with its tradition of

[1] Immanuel Kant, *Zum Ewigen Frieden,* II, *Abschnitt,* 2, *Definitivartikel, Absatz* 6.

tolerance, and within Western civilization the United States, has taken the lead toward such a development. Again Kant has foreseen it.[2]

For not a different or even hostile civilization, *Weltanschauung,* or system of government, should be regarded as the enemy, but aggression itself. Some people in the West regard Communism as *the* enemy. Communism is undoubtedly hostile to Western civilization, wishes to destroy and to supplant it by its own form of civilization. But Communism is not the only enemy of Western civilization. Ten years ago German National Socialism rejected and fought Western civilization in a manner as determined as Communism does, and with very similar arguments. Nor does General Franco or General Perón regard modern Western civilization with friendly eyes. They fear and despise it as much as the Communists do, but they have neither the strength nor the following to endanger it seriously.

If those nations whose system of values and of government is built upon the principle which grew out of the English revolutions of the seventeenth century, and which cling to this common heritage, will grow united and determined to lead the world in an attempt to organize against aggression, they do not need to fear the fanaticism of different and hostile civilizations. Authority in international society should prevent long periods of war and moral exhaustion. Without such an authority, the danger of submitting to aggression is great and tempting. An authority regarding aggression as the enemy to be combatted and held within bounds, would not only satisfy the desire for peace but also prevent submission.

Aggression has not always been committed by Communists, nor does it threaten today to be committed only by Communists. Wars between the Arab nations and Israel, between India and Pakistan, and in other parts of the world, are as possible as wars started by Communists. Aggression against Communist Yugoslavia demands action by the international authority, as much as aggression against a democratic state. When Fascist Italy attacked in October, 1940, the then Fascist Greece, this aggression should have been as much resisted as an attack on a democratic country. Some "liberals" have lately expressed the opinion that only governments of which they approve should be helped against aggression. This is a complete misconstruction of the task of authority in international society. It would make the exercise of this authority en-

[2] *Ibid., Absatz* 4.

tirely dependent upon ideological preferences, and so defeat its very purpose. When Italy attacked in 1935 the slaveholding empire of Ethiopia, action was as much indicated as in the case of German aggression in 1939 against a semi-Fascist Poland.

If authority in international relations be at the same time strictly limited to the one essential point and strengthened in its resolute action, irrespective of any ideological preferences or power interests, then a situation may slowly arise, in which some of the opposing civilizations will lose their fanaticism inherent in all primitive stages of civilization. In a feeling of growing security, the various injustices in the present situation may lose much of their emotional impact and may be more readily accessible to solutions of agreement and compromise, the only solutions which, as the example of the Glorious Revolution has shown, are enduring solutions. Communist and nationalist aggressiveness may be deprived of much of its incentives. With the limited authority at the center, the various civilizations and groups of nations would retain full liberty to develop their own concepts. With peace better assured, mutual understanding and intercourse might grow.

Comment by Robert H. Lowie:
  The general spirit of Professor Kohn's paper is admirable, and on practical grounds alone the reader feels inclined to agree that any supernational authority should be restricted so as not to cramp the individual development of the federated states. Further, to me the proposition seems highly commendable that victims of aggression merit protection, irrespective of the ideology they profess.

CHAPTER XI

Individual Freedom Under the Law

By LUIS RECASENS-SICHES
*Visiting Professor, Graduate Faculty,
The New School for Social Research*

THE SCOPE OF personal freedom and its relationship to authority should be ascertained in the light of the values underlying that idea.

Man Is Free Will

Each person is a being who has to make decisions about what he is going to be (what he is going to do) in the coming instant. Sometimes it seems as if we did not decide; but what occurs in these cases is that we are maintaining a resolution previously taken, and by not modifying it we confirm it.

Human life consists of a making of one's self. Life is not a being already made, nor yet an object with a predetermined trajectory. Life has not a readymade reality, such as a stone has, nor yet a predesignated route, like the orbit of a star or the vegetative cycle of a plant. Life is the making of itself; it is a task; its contents we have to create for ourselves moment after moment. Human life finds itself bound to settle the problem of its own being at each juncture. We have certainly not chosen the world we must live in; this is the dimension of fatality in human life. Yet we have a horizon alive with several possibilities, and this is the essential dimension of liberty. All human life consists in having to elect at each instant among the various roads which the environment offers. These roads are concrete and in limited number; but they are always manifold. Therefore, it could be said that man is free will.

Man neither *has* nor *does not have* free will, because free will is not something which one has or does not have, or has in greater or lesser degree, like muscular strength or memory. Free will is not a psychological power. Man *is* free will. When it is said that man is free will, it is meant that he finds himself always before a limited and concrete plurality of possibilities, and, consequently, stands in the necessity of deciding by himself, under his own responsibility, which to choose. Free will is simply the expression of a type of insertion of man in the world which surrounds him, not a fixed enclosing, like that of the screw in its nut, but an insertion with a certain margin of space, with a break in the circumference. This break, offers the person, in each of the moments of his life, a repertory of possibilities. To live, is to find oneself always at a crossroads, having to choose among directions. Therefore, man is free will. It is true that his life is forced to move in each one of his moments within the situation which constitutes its concrete circumstance. But he is not inexorably bound to follow a certain way. Even the life offering nothing more than a tragic path, will not face only one single possibility, but two: that of accepting a dark destiny and that of escaping from existence. I endorse, of course, all the condemnations which have been uttered against suicide. I refer to that hypothesis only to show that, even in the extreme case, there will be at least a choice of routes.

The concrete circumstance which offers such a multiplicity of paths at each one of the moments of life is composed of a combination of the very diverse elements: mental, biological, geographical, cultural, and social. The opportunities offered to a person will depend on his talent, on his health and strength, on his education, on his location, on his social station, on his economic means, on the collective atmosphere he breathes, and so forth. Consequently, there is in our life something predetermined. Yet each person is faced always with the possibility of different conducts, at each moment, whence he is free will.

The affirmation that man is free will differs just as radically from the classic indeterminist thesis as from the determinist one.

The traditional indeterminist supposes that man may do everything; and that all men may, in principle, do the same. That thesis does not start from human concrete reality, but from an abstract figure of man, conceived as something universal, situated in a vacuum inside which he can do anything, by virtue of a kind of creative potency. The thought I am developing shows that man finds himself in a concrete predetermined, limited circumstance, which is composed of multiple and diverse ingredients and of various singular combinations of them in each individual case. Man cannot do it all, but only may do some of the things which are possible at each moment. Nor can all men do the same things, because each one of them has a concrete circumstance to cope with.

Determinists, on the other side, maintain that man's conduct, in each case, is the single effect of a complex aggregate of factors that are usually transformed into motivations and among which the most vigorous triumphs at the end. Against that hypothesis—a gratuitous hypothesis, for it has never been fully demonstrated—I maintain that, even if man is situated within a definite shell, it has not been decided that he has to follow one of the paths which are offered in that shell. It is he who has to decide. For this reason man *is* free will. Will—in this meaning—is not a potency, is not a psychic resource; it is simply the expression of our ontological situation, as regards the world which circumscribes our personality.

This dimension of liberty grants man his quality as a person. Man is something real, he is a part of nature, he participates thereby in the natural laws of reality; but at the same time, he is different from all the other real beings, because he has a connection or contact with the realm of values, for which he has a special gift of mental perception. The ideal call stemming from values does not forcibly compel man to comply with them, but leaves him in freedom to decide for himself whether he will follow them or not. This weakness of the ideal principle is precisely what constitutes the grandeur of man, his qualitative greatness, his situation of power in the world. The ideal ought-to-be, proceeding from the world of the ideal, penetrates the person, flows through it, and issues in the form of real action; and, in traversing the person in this way, lends it a special dignity, which constitutes something radically new, in comparison with the other beings, namely, *personality*. Besides the characteristic of being *free,* the human person is also defined by another quality, namely, by the fact that his intentions, his purposes, his acts constitute the only ground for moral values. The strictly moral values do not aim or direct themselves to objective results, to works of real consistency—as occurs with other values, such as the esthetic, the utilitarian, etc.—but they aspire to dwell upon the acting person himself. Or putting it in traditional terms, man is a person, because he constitutes an end in himself, something that ought not to be employed as a mere means, that has a purpose in itself, and, precisely on that account, possesses *dignity*—something different from all other beings which have their purpose outside themselves. And this is so, because man is not only the agent for moral values, but also the seat where those moral values have to be accomplished.

The preceding statements constitute the philosophical assumption upon which the political problem of legal freedom has to be dealt with.

Freedom and Law

Both the meaning and scope of the rights of individual freedom depend on the valuation of the human person made by the law. This is a matter of ascertaining what the supreme ideal principle of the law (and, consequently, the supreme end of the state) ought to be. It is a matter of knowing whether the law has a meaning only to the extent of complying with the values which may be realized in the individual person. Or whether, on the contrary, the law (and the state) should be an end in itself, independent of the real individual men of flesh and blood who would thus function as mere instruments for the realization of that transpersonal end. It is a matter of knowing whether the law and the state are for man, or whether man is for the law and the state. These two antithetic and irreconcilable positions have been called respectively *personalism* and *transpersonalism*. This question inserts itself into another of greater volume and extent: that of valuation of culture and society, in relation to man. According to *personalism* (which might better be called *humanism*), culture and collectivity ought to converge upon man and take him as a substratum, for only by doing so have they a true meaning and are they justified: they ought to be converted into means to lift man up to his values. According to *transpersonalism* man would be a mere instrument to produce works of culture with an objective substratum of their own—science, art, technique, etc. —or for the aggrandizement or power of the state; man would be degraded to a pure mass paste, or dough, at the service of some allegedly objective functions, to be embodied in power, in state glory, in the race, in culture, etc.

One tries to ascertain what hierarchy there may be for human life among the different values, in relation to the substrata in which they are embodied. In human life are the supreme values those which can be embodied only in the spiritual person, so that all the others are subordinated to them? Or are those values superior in rank which are shaped in the objective outcome of human activity, so that the values in the individual ethical person are subordinated to them?

If it is understood that culture is based on man and is for him, then the values realized in the individual will be the highest ones; and all the other values will remain at the service of the individual. And in this way all the works of culture will have meaning only as means or instruments put at the service of man. But if it be understood that the substratum of the superior values is an objective transpersonal work, then man represents a mere means or tool for producing valuable works of culture, powerful states, etc.

According to *personalism* or *humanism,* the state (and, consequently, the law)—the same as science, technique, art, etc.—will have meaning and justification as an instrument for the fulfilment of the spirit of men (individuals) in order that in it they may embody the values for which they are destined. The state was made for the sake of man, and not *vice versa*.

It is not that personalism or humanism denies that in culture, in the law, and the collectivity are embodied very important values; but it maintains simply that those values are inferior to values realized in the person, namely, the moral values.

To the transpersonalist conception, humanism or personalism opposes the following arguments:

How can the individual be consecrated to ends which are not, at least to a certain extent, his? Only the individual is capable of proposing ends to himself and of acting to realize them, because he alone has consciousness. The collectivity ought to respect man's ends; and it ought to be structured in such a way that it be a means for those human ends. Without a true life of the individuals, in which are embodied the ethical values of personality—which are the highest ones—the collectivity lacks meaning and justification, and so the law and the state. The collectivity does not live, in the pure and authentic sense of this word; but those who live are individuals.

The opposition between personalism (or humanism) and transpersonalism is irreducible and unbridgeable. On a personalist conception many different political ideologies may be founded. While coinciding as to the goal, namely, to serve human ends, they diverge only as to the means for the attainment of that goal. Some political thinkers believe that the greater the volume of free activity the state concedes, the better will it serve human personality, and they consider that the spontaneous play of private initiative is the best source of social solidarity. Other political thinkers, who seek the same end believe that this is possible only by attributing to the state many faculties to organize in detail social cooperation and especially economics. And there are, of course, many intermediate doctrines between those two sketched attitudes. Among all those doctrines it is possible to establish communication or compromise, because, in spite of their great divergences, they have a common personalist or humanist inspiration.

But any conciliation or compromise between personalist and transpersonalist doctrines is altogether impossible.

The Foundations of Personalism

Although philosophical idealism has been superseded, something of it remains as a firm truth: that my consciousness constitutes the center, support, and proof of all the other realities. The consciousness is inescapably the instinctive center of our universe; because its vision is articulated in a perspective converging upon my mental pupil, which contemplates it. Human existence constitutes the primary and basic reality, as copresent and inescapable correlation between the self and the world, between subject and object. This is neither subjectivism nor idealism, precisely because it discovers human life as the copresence or coexistence of the "I" and the objects. To live, is to be occupied with a world in which I find myself necessarily; we—the world and I—meet each other, forcibly joined, in inexorable company. But the objects of the world, the same as I, occur in the reality of my life, which conditions all other realities, as far as they exist for me.

If all that is beyond me obtains expression only in my life, then the primacy in a conception of the universe belongs to the human existence. And from this it follows that the realization of values has meaning only in my life, which is individual life. So-called culture is an aggregate of things and works which man makes in his life; and, consequently, they have meaning only in his life and for his life.

Culture is constituted by human acts and works that aspire to realize ideas of value: it is integrated by actions and products which try to embody the truth, in the philosophic and scientific knowledge of the universe; to give sensible form to beauty, in art; to obtain the fulfilment of goodness in conduct, through morals; to obtain the reign of justice in society, through law; to utilize nature and overcome its resistances, thanks to technology; and so forth. Culture, then, has meaning only for man, who does not possess these values in full measure, and who, nevertheless, feels the need of striving to their conquest. Therefore, culture has no meaning for nature; nor has it either for God, Who is by essence absolute Wisdom and Truth, total Good, supreme Justice, complete Beauty, infinite Power. What need has God of science, if He knows everything in eternal actuality; and of morals, if He is pure Good; and of art, if He is perfect Beauty; and of technique, if He is Omnipotent? But, on the other hand, culture seems to us filled with meaning, in so far as we regard it as a human function and work. Because man does not know, but needs to know, science is constructed. Because man is a sinner, but it is necessary to redeem him from his meannesses, we have ethics. Because society must be organized according to justice, law is elaborated. Because man, who does not shelter within himself pure beauty, nevertheless desires to become related to it, art is created. Because man is helpless, but experiences the need of using and controlling the elements which surround him, technology is produced; etc. Therefore, man is necessarily the inborn center of culture and its point of final gravitation. And as the supreme values which can be referred to man are ethical, the idea of personal dignity must always rule above all his other tasks.

If each individual life is the basic reality; if, moreover, values, although objective, occur in our life; if the agent for realizing values is man, the only one capable of understanding them and dedicating himself to their call, it follows that the realization of values has meaning only for man. Things in which values dwell—among them society which is a mechanism or instrument—constitute goods, only to the extent to which they are conditions for his person being able to embody the supreme values, which are the ethical and spiritual ones.

It should always be borne in mind that the collectivity does not have a being for itself independent of the being of the individuals who compose it. On the other hand, the being of the individual consists of a free being. The collectivity ought to recognize his autonomy. The individual is not purely and simply a part of the whole. A member of society, he is at the same time superior to it because he is a person—which society can never be.

What has been said must not be misinterpreted in the sense that society is considered as something purely fortuitous. The individual is essentially social; even to the point that the isolated individual is not anything real, nor even possible, but a pure abstraction. The individual rests upon the values realized in history and transmitted to him by the collectivity; and almost everything he does rests upon those communal goods; and the most he can do sometimes is merely to raise himself a little above the historic level of those goods which the collectivity has handed over to him.

But although the social is something essential to man, the goods which are realized in the collectivity are only means for the realization of the supreme values, which belong only to the individual. Without society there is no man; but man—the individual man, the substantive reality—is axiologically superior to society. For society is something made by him and for him.

Legal Liberty

The law must be the condition which makes possible the fulfilment of man's moral destiny. Wherefore it has to guarantee the liberty of each individual; but it cannot be in any way the agent for the fulfilment of morality, which can be realized and has meaning, only in the degree in which it is carried out freely by each person.

On the other hand, the benefits which both the social and the legal order insure may constitute favorable conditions for man to ennoble himself by the realization of works of culture and his ethical values.

Personalism or humanism centers the legal order in the idea of human dignity, the first consequence of it being the affirmation of individual freedom. This freedom seems intangible in what belongs to the most intimate bosom of the individual personality (conscience, thought). It manifests itself also in personal autonomy. Thus, the law is what ought to guarantee to every individual his liberty, in order that he may be what he is, in order that each one may fulfil his own proper and untransferable destiny.

Though individual freedom must be guaranteed by the legal order, it cannot be taken as an all inspiring principle for the law. Here we are dealing not with the idea of freedom unlimited, but with the idea of the rights of freedom, that is to say, with legal liberty.

Freedom unlimited would be incompatible with peaceful social life, and inconsistent with any legal order. The most radical conceptions of liberty, Kant's, Humboldt's, or Mill's, for example, regarded liberty as limited, namely, limited by the recognition of other people's freedom.

Thus liberty does not appear as an all inspiring principle for the organization of the state, but as a claim upon the latter, demanding its respect toward the sphere of personal autonomy. Consequently, the law is asked to protect and guarantee personal autonomy by paying recognition to men's fundamental freedoms.

There still remains, however, one problem: What should be the scope of limited freedom? On the one hand, there are aspects or issues of freedom which must be considered as untouchable and sacred; for example, freedom of conscience and thought. The same might be said in regard to other freedoms very closely related to human dignity.

Other aspects of individual freedom may vary according to the diversity of historic conditions and changes. Our grandparents were not subjected to any traffic regulations, while we ourselves have lost the freedom to walk and ride at whim.

While the nineteenth century legal doctrine propounded that freedom be restricted only in so far as to insure the coexistence of other freedoms, both the doctrines and realities of today show, instead, a different attitude toward this problem. Only one thing is solely asked for, namely, the persistence of the essential freedoms, *i.e.,* those which are a necessary consequence of the individual's dignity. The greater complexity of the demands made upon the individual for the sake of the common welfare have restricted many of the freedoms enjoyed by our grandparents.

Yet no restriction should go as far as denying or making ineffectual the sphere of true personal autonomy. No demand for the sake of common welfare would be justified, if it encroached upon the fundamental rights and freedoms of man. There is nothing more universal than the individual himself, because what appertains to each appertains to all. Rather than thinking in terms of sacrificing each of us to all, we should think in terms of sacrificing all to each one. After all, collectivities consist of men of flesh and blood, men who are ends in themselves, men who each has to comply with his own destiny, men who think, feel, suffer, and have to make decisions, on their own responsibility to themselves.

Comment by Edgar S. Brightman:

Dr. Recasens-Siches has written a paper with which I heartily agree from start to finish, and which has much in common with the (however differently oriented) excellent paper by Professor Lamprecht. This Conference has always recognized respect for personality as a fundamental value. I could wish that the paper had defined personality more fully. I could also wish that the equation of *personalism* and *humanism* could have been avoided; for in the United States "humanism" often has a negative, atheistic, or naturalistic connotation absent from "personalism." But I am wholly in agreement with the arguments of the paper.

Comment by Barna Horvath:

I am in substantial agreement with most of the results reached by the eminent author in this paper: I share his moderate indeterminism, his individualistic personalism, and also his view that individual freedom is no all inspiring principle for the law.

The problem of personalism *vs.* transpersonalism is treated by the author in a lucid and persuasive way. I fully agree with the principle he defends, and differ from him only in emphasis and perhaps in argument.

But I find it difficult, I confess, to deduce this principle of personalism from the supposed *mutual dependence* of the world and the ego upon one another. It is somewhat hard to imagine how the "primacy of the human existence" might be deduced from such mutual dependence or coexistence. If "without society there is no man," the latter's "axiological superiority"—resulting from his unique freedom, not from his doubtful pre- or coexistence—may be at least distinguished from the (ontological?) (epistemological?) "primacy of the human existence."

Moreover, if the personalist principle is compatible with a policy favoring "the spontaneous play of private initiative," as well as with one striving "to attribute to the state many faculties to organize in detail social cooperation and especially economics," then personalism seems to be irreconcilable to that *excessive* transpersonalism alone which "deifies the state" and converts it from instrument to ultimate end of the individual person.

When the author mentions the traffic regulations, in order to show that liberty is no all inspiring principle for law, and that "demands made upon the individual for the sake of common welfare, have restricted many of the freedoms enjoyed by our grandparents," it may be asked whether this is because freedom is personal, whereas law is transpersonal, and, if so, whether personalism is not compatible with a certain amount of transpersonalism.

It seems to be equally important to draw a clear line of demarcation between the moral and the legal, the autonomous and the heteronomous, the personal and the transpersonal, and yet not to lose sight of their intimate interaction.

Although moral autonomy of the individual is the highest type of moral freedom, there is a broader sense of moral freedom, too (exemplified by hedonist and utilitarian ethics), which inspires, as the *Universal Declaration of Human Rights* seems to suggest, the whole operation of law. While it remains true that law may only establish conditions favorable to the highest type of moral freedom, but never directly fulfil its requirements, those broader fields of freedom which law may well directly cultivate, are the preliminary conditions for the emergence of the highest type. In this sense, there is a perpetual interaction between personal ends and transpersonal means.

Ends and means even change roles, sometimes with the tragic result deplored and opposed by the author, but sometimes with less unhappy and even unobjectionable results. The sacrifice of individual, personal freedom in the service of transpersonal ends is a historical fact: it is perhaps the highest act of freedom when the sacrifice is brought voluntarily for the sake of the freedom of others. How can we explain this unless by some allowance for a moderate transpersonalism? How can we deny that monuments of culture, including legal codes, may represent higher principles, levels, or standards than the achievements of the living? This does not contradict the author's view that present personal freedom should never be suppressed by the dead hand of any glorious past, culture, or collective effort, present, or future.

CHAPTER XII

Freedom and Authority, Retrospect and Prospect

By R. GORDON HOXIE

*Assistant Professor of History, University of Denver;
General Editor, Social Science Foundation*

For its fullest usefulness in these trying times any discussion of freedom and authority must be both retrospective and prospective, both reflective and pragmatic. Only by an historical view of man's age long quest for freedom and of his attempt to reconcile freedom and authority, can we come to a full understanding of both of these terms, and adequately assess our present and future means of facing the challenge to the free way of life. Only by both a sound philosophical reflection and a firm and courageous course of action, can we insure that the outcome of this present international trial shall be the fuller realization of freedom for all mankind.

I. *Retrospect*

A. *The United States*

Speaking with prophetic vision in the Constitutional Convention in Philadelphia in 1787, the great South Carolina statesman, Charles Pinckney, asserted that in the United States "there are fewer distinctions of fortune and less of rank than among the inhabitants of any other nation." He predicted that this was "likely to continue" so long as we possessed "immense tracts of uncultivated lands, where every temptation is offered to emigration. . . ."[1] Writing in a similar vein a century later when inequalities had become more pronounced, the British observer, Sir Henry Maine, noted,

[1] *The Records of the Federal Convention of 1787,* edited by Max Farrand, New Haven, 1937, IV, p. 31.

> There has hardly ever before been a community in which the weak have been pushed so pitilessly to the wall, in which those who have succeeded have so uniformly been the strong, and in which in so short a time there has arisen so great an inequality of private fortune and domestic luxury. And at the same time, there has never been a country in which, on the whole, the persons distanced in the race have suffered so little from their ill success. All this beneficent prosperity, is the fruit of recognizing the principle of population, and the one remedy for its excess is perpetual emigration ... it all reposes on the sacredness of contract and the stability of private property, the first the implement, and the last the reward, of success in the universal competition.[2]

Here then, were two significant speculative views, a century intervening, regarding freedom and opportunity in America. Both saw America as a land of *laissez-faire* opportunity. Sir Henry particularly acknowledged that here might be many abuses under such a system. Yet both agreed that opportunity would beckon for all, so long as there existed a frontier of Western land to which the populace might remove.

However, five years after Sir Henry had made his observation, the Superintendent of the Census in a routine bulletin wrote that the frontier had disappeared. This announcement marked the end of the great westward migration, of what Frederick Jackson Turner later termed the "safety-valve." Concurrently America underwent a tremendous industrialization, a growth of urban communities with a large industrial populace living on a bare subsistence basis. The resulting inequalities, coming at a time when the frontier no longer offered a new opportunity, caused many people to question the validity of a continued *laissez-faire* competitive system based only upon "the sacredness of contract and the stability of private property."

Demands arose in the first years of our century for the government to take action in the promotion of social justice. Such demands during the past half-century have been represented in the "New Nationalism" of Theodore Roosevelt, the "New Freedom" of Woodrow Wilson, and the "New Deal" of Franklin Delano Roosevelt. During these administrations a number of measures were taken to insure greater economic and social security and equality. For example, national income taxes

---

[2]Sir Henry Maine, *Popular Government*, Henry Holt & Company, New York, 1886, p. 51.

were instituted with an ascending levy on larger incomes. So also minimum wage laws, unemployment and health insurance, old age pensions, housing projects, and other similar activities were entered upon by the Federal government.

Such legislation was placed upon the statute books only after considerable controversy regarding the role of government and its relation to freedom. This has been a principal subject of debate during the first half of our century and at midcentury poses a vital issue. Yet this is not a problem of our times alone nor a problem limited to domestic issues.

B. *The Ancient World*

This reconciliation of government and liberty, of authority and freedom, has been a chief quest since the beginning of civilization. Life in the ancient autocratic state had no value to the despotic ruler. Yet even when a people was reduced to slavery, as was the case of the ancient Hebrews, there was an abiding expression of man's fundamental dignity. The Jewish people had a belief in a holy and just God Who wanted "judgment [to] run down as water, and righteousness as a mighty stream," and in a coming Messiah who would lead them out of captivity.

Aside from the Hebrews, in the ancient world the most complete attempts to establish democratic rule were in Greece and Rome. The very word, *demokratia,* comes from the Greek terms, *demos* (the people) plus *kratein* (to rule). Of course, democracy, or rule by the people, does not necessarily connote individual freedom. This historical discourse should, however, make it evident that democracy is that system under which freedom has been most fully achieved.

In Athens such reformers as Solon, Clisthenes, and Pericles, demonstrated that in a small city a government was possible which took its power from the individual rather than the despotic chief. However, even in Athens this concept of individual freedom was limited, for the freemen were greatly outnumbered by the slaves. Moreover, even at its height in the fourth century B.C., Greek democracy and political philosophy, as expounded by Aristotle and Plato, still subordinated the individual to the state. However, by endowing its citizenry with a wide degree of ultimate political control, Greece did make a contribution in man's eternal quest for freedom. The Greeks also left a philosophy of the dignity of the individual—Stoicism, which made self-realization the main objective of human endeavor.

The Roman state approached political democracy under the Republic, but even then when power was popularly exercised there was no concept of individual rights or civil liberty. The chief Roman contribution was in the establishment of law and order, rather than freedom and its reconciliation with authority.

Within the boundaries of the Roman Empire in Palestine, however, there arose a religious faith which sought freedom for all men. Christ Himself, like the Hebrew Prophets before Him, based His teachings on the worth, indeed, the sacredness of the human personality, and He believed that "Ye shall know the truth, and the truth shall make you free."

We must conclude that the ancient world, although it made a contribution in law and order, contributed little in the quest for freedom. aside from a brave new spiritual concept.

C. *The Medieval Period*

With the decline of the Roman state the medieval manor and the Christian Church became the principal institutions of government in Europe, and society became stratified into relatively fixed groups. Such freedom as existed for any of these groups could mean only immunity from some particular manorial or clerical obligation.

In contrast to the manor, however, the church emphasized that the citizen himself might have obligations higher than those imposed by the temporal ruler. By so doing, the church, sometimes consciously and sometimes unwittingly, was preparing the way for the development of the natural rights philosophy—a philosophy which insisted that there were certain inalienable rights from God and nature which the temporal ruler could not interfere with. Nonetheless, the reconciliation between conflicting loyalties was sought chiefly on the basis of the relative obligations and freedoms of particular groups. In its highest sense the reconciliation between freedom and authority was by divine law.

It must be concluded that the medieval period did little to advance the concept of individual freedom. It sought the reconciliation between freedom and authority chiefly on the basis of obedience to higher authority, and as such marked little change from the ancient period.

D. *The Late Middle Ages and the Modern Period—Changing Concepts of Freedom*

1. *Concept of Intellectual Freedom.* In the twelfth and thirteenth centuries we have the beginning of a new concept of freedom, an *intellectual freedom* brought about by scientific discovery and the diffusion of learning. Great institutions of higher learning were founded, such as those at Paris and Oxford in which were centered the revived study not only of philosophy, but also of the professions of medicine and law, and in which we have the dawn of modern experimental science through such teachers as Roger Bacon.

Moreover, side by side with the Latin tongue, the vernacular languages of German, English, French, Italian, Spanish, Portuguese, etc., gave a wealth of variety to reviving popular literature, particularly when written by such masters as Chaucer and Dante, and afforded new vistas of freedom to greater portions of the population. In the fourteenth century the humanist movement instituted the revival of the Greek and Latin literature with its spirit of the freedom of development of the individual personality. By 1450, movable type had been invented, greatly facilitating printing and affording further new vistas to countless thousands. New geographical discoveries afforded lighter horizons.

By the beginning of the sixteenth century, such writers as Erasmus and Sir Thomas More were challenging larger segments of the European population to greater intellectual freedom. As a result, through the spirit that the truth would make man free, man became less restrained by dogma, more prone to profit by new discoveries and to try new experiments, more critical of conditions about him, and more expressive of this thought and study.

This has been a continuous path from the sixteenth century to the present, but one marked both by high points of intellectual challenge and valleys of reaction. In particular, the eighteenth century stimulation of the Encyclopedists, and of Voltaire, Montesquieu, Rousseau, Beccaria, Adam Smith, and Franklin, may be noted. They engendered ideas of economic liberty, equality before the law, and denial of titled aristocracy, as well as general concepts of intellectual freedom, and the American and French Revolutions may be in large part traceable to their work—at least for their philosophical bases.

While there was a period of reaction following the French Revolution, freedom of thought renewed its course before the mid-nineteenth century. It was reflected in the discussion of such controversial issues as evolution and social progress, in a new emphasis on research and scientific instruction in colleges and universities. Finally, at the end of the nineteenth century, intellectual freedom brought the admission of women into the professions and public life.

Our present concept of intellectual freedom and the acceptance of education as a right of all free people regardless of race, color, and sex has been an achievement coming only after centuries of struggle. Indeed it has not yet achieved its fruition. Nonetheless, even its partial triumph represents a vital concept in a free state.

2. *Concept of Religious Freedom.* It is the Reformation which was most important in giving new emphasis to individual rights as a separate and distinct subject of freedom. The new Protestant sects gave birth to the idea of liberty of conscience, of freedom of worship, and toleration for at least their own particular sect. We cannot overestimate the importance of this new concept. Every earlier age had had as a distinguishing mark a great state religion, publicly professed, and financially supported by all the citizens. Whatever may be one's opinion of the Protestant Reformation of the sixteenth century, of the rise of deism and skepticism in the seventeenth and eighteenth, and of the existence of scientific rationalism in the nineteenth and twentieth, there is general agreement that each has contributed to a concept of religious freedom, to the idea that religion is essentially a private, not a public affair.

3. *Concept of National, Political and Civil, and Economic Freedom.* Nationalism and its accompaniment, national political democracy, are essentially modern concepts. The notion that people with a common language and culture should be organized as an independent state with uniform laws and customs, received little consideration before the fifteenth century; so likewise the concept that such a people of common ties should seek national political freedom was also a new concept.

The national state has proven the most powerful political organization thus far devised by man; it has steadily increased its functions, first at the expense of feudalism and the church, then under benevolent despotism, and finally under industrial democracy. At the same time, however, that government was enlarging its scope, the governed were working out new concepts and new guarantees of freedom. The Puritan Revolution, the French Revolution, the American Revolution, and the uprisings of oppressed populations throughout the nineteenth century, were all a part of seeking freedom within the national framework. Nor is this all, for the growth of the national state was accompanied by the rise of a capitalist economy, with its individual entrepreneurs demanding economic liberty. As a result, national, civil, political, and economic freedom became closely associated as national rights, so aptly expressed in the Lockean term, "Life, liberty, and property." Both national liberty and individual liberty have been supreme expressions of the desire for self-realization. The political history of most national states during the past four centuries may be expressed in terms of the series of compromises between the exaltation of the state and the exaltation of the individual. In some instances, however, these ends have found a common ground, when the state has sought to free itself from external forces. It was out of the joining of these desires for national and individual freedom that the American nation was born.

In general, the late eighteenth and the nineteenth centuries may be termed the classical period of freedom. Democratic reform became an accompaniment of the industrial revolution, and, indeed, received its greatest impetus from the economic grievances created by the industrial revolution. The democratic spirit expressed itself in (1) various attempts to relieve the distress of the lower classes; (2) in various reforms in the direction of religious toleration, universal education, and the reform of the criminal law; (3) in the anti-slavery movement; and (4) in the agitation for political democracy. It may be seen then that the concept of freedom became related to that of social justice, and the religious, humanitarian, intellectual, and democratic forces were joined in the formation of this new concept.

4. *Concept of Freedom as Social Justice.* Conditions were ripe for the spread of these new views of freedom. Concepts varying from the *laissez-faire* of Adam Smith, Bentham, and Mill, to the Communism of Karl Marx, were all presented as affording the fullest stage of freedom. Certainly, since about 1870, social justice has been a definite and continuous concept of the freedom idea.

The course of history during the past seventy-five years has brought a decreasing area of *laissez-faire* and an increasing area of government action. This has found expression in the Universal Declaration of Human Rights of the United Nations, wherein hope was held for "a world in which human beings shall enjoy" not only freedom of speech and belief but also "freedom from fear and want."[3]

The quest for social justice has brought varying degrees of state control. Even, however, under the most extreme forms of state control, such as in Russia, there is a rationalization that civil and political freedom have only been temporarily abolished in order to achieve this social justice. In this country, however, we still maintain a basic faith in the individual, a faith which differentiates us from the totalitarian state, a faith hearkening back to the ancient Hebrew-Greek-Christian concepts.

II. Prospect

Introduction

Many believed in the early nineteenth century that the reconciliation between freedom and authority had at last arrived. Writing during this period the German political scientist, Robert von Mohl of Tuebingen, believed he saw the answer to this long sought reconciliation in the American Constitution, political institutions, and free enterprise system. However, there were not such complacent views three-quarters of a century later, when the frontier had disappeared, when industrialization and urbanization had changed the social structure, and when the government began to enter at the opening of the twentieth century into a far more active participation in the economic and social life of the people. Two divergent schools became apparent as they viewed this scene. They were perhaps best represented by two professors of political science, one at Columbia and the other at Princeton. The former, John W. Burgess, viewed with alarm the seeming destruction of the balance between government and liberty. The latter, Woodrow Wilson, believed that governmental activity in social and economic spheres, was the harbinger of a new freedom.

Perhaps most influential of the Burgess disciples was Nicholas Murray Butler, who insisted that government was subordinate to freedom, that "free men have themselves erected government and have given it for

[3] O. Frederick Nolde, *Freedom's Charter, the Universal Declaration of Human Rights,* Headline Series, Foreign Policy Association, New York, 76, July–August, 1947.

domain and occupation a very small part of all that constitutes their activity, physical, intellectual, social, moral, economic, reserving the vast and unlimited remainder for themselves as the sphere of liberty."[4] Perhaps the great difficulty of this group was that they were seeking to answer the problems of the twentieth century with the liberalism, the combination of idealism and rugged individualism, of the nineteenth century. In the midst of the Great Depression which dogged the nation from 1929-1939, Herbert Hoover protested regarding the New Deal, "An emergency program for recovery is one thing, but to implant a new social philosophy in American life in conflict with the primary concepts of American Liberty is quite another."[5]

However, for an increasing group the sphere of government has come to be that of the furtherance of liberty, the concept of Wilson. Particularly during the mid-1930's there was the belief that through government regulation a new freedom and a new security might be attained. This new freedom had a positive concept of the enjoyment of a fuller life and a fuller experience in our culture, and it looked to John Dewey and Woodrow Wilson, and even to such Republicans as Lincoln and Theodore Roosevelt, and such nineteenth century liberals as Jefferson and Jackson, for its philosophical basis. The older freedom was referred to as constituting only freedom from restraint. On the other hand, public relief, social security enactments, and legislation to protect labor unions, were now introduced under the philosophy of a new freedom through government. Much of this legislation required a broader interpretation of the Constitution than had heretofore been given. What had once been merely a policing power, was extended to a paternalistic care on the part of the government for the safety and welfare of all, and public works and public education became important governmental functions. The entire galaxy of laws known as "social" legislation, the entire machinery of commissions and boards, became a part of the democratic enterprise.

No doubt the New Deal represented much the same crusading spirit with which Woodrow Wilson had asserted two decades before, "What I am interested in is having the government of the United States more concerned about human rights than about property rights. Prop-

[4] *The Rise of a University*, edited by William F. Russell and Edward C. Elliot, Columbia University Press, New York, 1937, II, p. 47.

[5] See Herbert Hoover, *The Challenge to Liberty*, Charles Scribner's Sons, New York, 1935, p. 5.

erty is an instrument of humanity; humanity isn't an instrument of property."[6] The New Deal also represented the Four Freedoms on which President Franklin Delano Roosevelt so inspiringly addressed Congress during the crisis of the Second World War—"freedom of speech and expression . . . freedom of every person to worship God in his own way . . . freedom from want . . . freedom from fear." "Freedom," he concluded, "means the supremacy of human rights everywhere." This, indeed, represented an inspiring idealism.

Yet in the past decade, as a degree of economic prosperity returned to this country, and as nation after nation which had embarked upon the road of the welfare state fell victim to totalitarianism, there was an understandable reaction against much of the planned economy, even in its milder forms in the United States. Walter Lippmann, as early as 1937, declared, "There is, in short, no way by which the objectives of a planned economy can be made to depend upon popular decision. They must be imposed by an oligarchy of some sort . . . Thus, by a kind of tragic irony, the search for security and a rational society, if it seeks salvation through political authority, ends in the most irrational form of government imaginable—in the dictatorship of casual oligarchs . . ."[7]

Now at midcentury a still more complex and crucial question has been injected into this relationship between government and freedom. In a world in which our very national existence is threatened, we must be strongly armed. Yet the garrison state poses a threat to individual freedom. We may well recall the words of James Madison written to Thomas Jefferson in 1798: "Perhaps it is a universal truth that the loss of liberty at home is to be charged to provisions against danger, real or pretended, from abroad."[8] In this present difficult period we must provide for dangers real rather than pretended, and with the minimum loss of individual freedom.

What is the true relationship of government and freedom? How are we to save the individual from being oppressed by the very machinery which has been established to promote his security? There justifiably arises in the minds of many the specter of a Leviathan. It is the in-

[6] Woodrow Wilson, *The New Freedom*, Doubleday, Doran & Company, Inc., New York and Garden City, 1913.

[7] Walter Lippmann, *An Inquiry into the Principles of the Good Society*, Little, Brown & Company, Boston, 1937.

[8] Quoted in Harold D. Lasswell, *National Security and Individual Freedom*, McGraw Hill, New York, 1950.

sistence of the conservatives that to prevent the state from reaching these dangerous proportions more emphasis must be placed upon the institutions of the church, the school, and the home, and that their influence rather than the government's must be more fully exerted.

Yet we must realize that ours is not an either-or decision between the best of nineteenth century liberalism and the best of twentieth century progressivism. Rather there must be a complementary union of the components of both. In the final analysis, there is far less difference between the Burgess-Butler-Hoover-Eisenhower school and the Roosevelt-Wilson-Roosevelt-Truman group than either has admitted. The conservatives have greater confidence in private agencies and greater concern for the preservation of individual initiative. The liberal group have a greater belief in public agencies and a greater concern for the preservation of individual initiative. Yet the observation of Burgess more than thirty years ago could have as well been the utterance of a Roosevelt or Wilson as of Hoover.

> The great problem of present constitutional development is the attainment of a proper balance between the individualistic element and the socialistic element in civil liberty, so that all that is beneficial in individualistic initiative and effort shall be preserved and encouraged, under such governmental direction and control, however, as to restrain it from transforming the political society into classes with a plutocracy at one end and a proletariat at the other.[9]

The end in view of both groups has been a fuller life, a fuller freedom for all Americans and for all other peoples of the world.

Freedom Begins at Home

With his great breadth, fine sensitivity, and patient understanding, John Dewey has told us:

> As we look at the world we see supposedly free institutions in many countries not so much overthrown as abandoned willingly, apparently with enthusiasm. We may infer that what has happened is proof they never existed in reality but only in name. Or we may console ourselves with a belief that unusual conditions, such as national frustration and humiliation, have led men to welcome any kind of government that

[9] John W. Burgess, *The Foundations of Political Science*, Columbia University Press, New York, 1933, p. 105.

promised to restore national self-respect. But conditions in our own country as well as the eclipse of democracy in other countries compel us to ask questions about the career and fall of free societies, even our own.[10]

We must face up to some harsh realities as we view this problem of freedom. In a world in which our freedom is threatened, literally millions of people apparently gladly gave up their freedom, trading it for promises of security. Here is a tremendous paradox—the strengthening and enriching of freedom had been man's chief quest since the beginnings of civilization. The First World War was seemingly fought to make democracy secure, and man emerged from it on the threshold of a new birth of freedom. Yet there is the disturbing and incontrovertible fact that when the political forms of this freedom and democracy were offered our fellow man, literally millions rejected it, fled from it under the promises of insidious totalitarian propaganda. We must ask ourselves why people have apparently gladly relinquished their freedom. Are basic elements lacking in the present culture of both Eastern and Western civilization?

Man today refers so much to government that he quite loses sight of the fact that there are broad areas in which the church, the home, and the school are daily operative, molding the fiber of which our democracy is made. If there can be no satisfying basic content in these elements of daily life, if there can be no security, hope, and enlightenment through them, is it not understandable that peoples fall victim to Communist promises?

The totalitarian states have only too well realized that the church, the school, and the home are the fundamental guardians of freedom. We need hardly be reminded of the totalitarian attacks upon these sacred institutions, how systematically the church and the school have been controlled, and at what early date the influence of the home has been broken both by intimidation and through youth organizations devoted to the worship of the state.

Yet as we view this picture there is also a positive side. The totalitarian states still have not satisfied the longings of the citizenry. There can be no doubt that today millions of people throughout the world yearn for a sense of neighborliness, for a strengthening of basic institutions. And herein lies our great opportunity—to make of our own institutions an ever more inspiring model for other peoples and to extend

[10] John Dewey, *Freedom and Culture*, G. P. Putnam's Sons, New York, 1939, p. 4.

the helping hand in strengthening theirs. As the late Dr. James Rowland Angell of Yale University declared, "There is no ethical development more important than the sharpening and enrichment of this conception of neighborly obligation."[11]

Now in a nation of such extent as ours and with such varying backgrounds and interests, the fostering of this spirit of neighborliness is, indeed, difficult, and it is even more difficult when we attempt to relate it to millions of peoples beyond our national borders. To give us a keen and vivid sense of the problems of all mankind will require a stimulation of our moral insight and sympathy, the rekindling of the pioneer spirit of living as a good neighbor and actively working to secure for all the necessaries for a full and happy life. Yet the spirit of our heritage should give us hope. The very foundation stone of our national existence, the Declaration of Independence, contains a concept which appeared in no previous milestone of freedom—the right not only to life and liberty, but also to the pursuit of happiness. This has been, this must be the essence of our way of life, a way of faith in the individual and of mutual helpfulness.

Our nation has recently given official cognizance to the importance of further extending this spirit of neighborliness through the Point Four Program. In our technological age two-thirds of the peoples of the world live on a bare subsistence basis. Here is a program predicated upon the American philosophy of helping others to help themselves, by giving them the skills and knowhow.

In the final analysis, there can be no cure for the world's ills and no permanent removal of the world's discontents until faith and the rule of the second commandment—love of one's neighbor—become the guide beacons in men's lives. If this is to be accomplished, there must be an appreciation, not only of a material environment, but of a spiritual and intellectual one as well. There must be an exchange of knowledge with all other regions. There must be knowledge not only in business and science, but also in the great areas of literature and art, of religion and morality, of history and political science. In all of this the school and the college can do much, but they cannot do all. There is a role for the family and the church as well.

If the family be weakened in respect to its economic or moral and spiritual basis, or if the church fails to offer its full spiritual service, the

[11] James Rowland Angell, *American Education*, Yale University Press, New Haven, 1937.

foundation of freedom is weakened. To safeguard these institutions and the minority, as well as majority groups which comprise them, full care and attention must be given to the protection of civil liberties. But there must be more than just insistence upon civil rights. There must also be a sense of material and spiritual security. The achievement of this must be the high purpose of all of us. In a world in which these objectives are achieved, we need have little fear that people will turn away from freedom when it is offered them.

Epilogue

It has been argued with some validity that the weakness and collapse of French democracy something more than a decade ago may in large part be traced to the failure of the private and public agencies, of the so-called spheres of liberty and freedom, to reach understanding if not unity. Fortunately there has never been such a wide gulf here in America, but it is abundantly clear that in this hour of trial when freedom-loving peoples throughout the world look to us for hope and direction, we must look to a more complementary relationship between freedom and authority.

It must be realized that the state is more than just the government, that it is also the church, the family, and the school, and that a balance between these groups and government must be maintained to secure the fullest freedom. Furthermore, the past decade of war and distrust should have taught us that freedom cannot be secure in one area of the world when it is violated in another, that there must be a full exchange of ideas as well as economic goods, that the end of government is not government but freedom, and that American conservatism and American progressivism must work together toward this end.

In the final analysis, freedom is constituted out of the way of life in which a people believe. If then, we seek to maintain a way of life affording free opportunity and social justice, we must keep ever before us our precious heritage of freedom, as well as the alleged demands of the times in which we live.

In a final lecture shortly before his death, Carl L. Becker left with us an abiding truth:

> When all is said, what is needed for the solution of the difficult national and international problems that confront us, and therefore for the pres-

ervation of our institutions and of the liberties they were created to serve, is more intelligence, more integrity, and a heightened sense of responsibility. . . . This is only to say that the preservation of our freedom depends less upon the precise nature of our constitutions and laws than it does upon the character of the people. In the last analysis everything depends upon the possession by the people of that *virtue* (virtue in the ancient Roman sense of the word), which Montesquieu declared to be the fundamental principle, the indispensable guarantee, of the republican form of government.[12]

To build and inculcate that character, that virtue, and that intelligence, is the heritage and duty and the trust of the home, the church, and the school. We must keep ever before us that it is here that freedom has its beginnings and its nurture, that we today stand before Almighty God as the guardians of this freedom to which man in God's own image aspires.

[12] Carl L. Becker, *Freedom and Responsibility in the American Way of Life*, Alfred A. Knopf, New York, 1946, pp. 121 f.

CHAPTER XIII

World Law and World Reform

By SUSANNE K. LANGER

WE SEE WITH growing dismay the increase of military organization in all countries in the world. The fear of war is not the only cause of our dismay; it is even more motivated by the effect of this militarism on individual lives in times of so-called "peace." Taxation increases so that most people find no margin of income left to improve their lives, or to carry out cherished ideas; restrictions and embargoes make personal projects difficult, and every move, if not flatly forbidden, requires a license, so that any original venture, no matter how harmless or even philanthropic, has to be examined first of all for possible conflicts with this or that trivial law or local ordinance.

Such governmental control is symptomatic of a shift in the general conception of law, from the idea of law as an instrument to protect individual rights, to the idea of law as an instrument whereby the government can immediately find, control, and utilize every person. In some countries, the latter conception is traditional; in other countries, however, personal freedom had once been achieved and honored, but is lost. In our own country the latter development is still taking place, but, other things being equal, its completion is only a matter of time: the power of law is becoming the power of the government to abrogate personal rights, to demand any percentage of personal income and allocate it according to political plans, to exact from all citizens vows of conformity in political thought, and interrupt men's personal careers just in the years of their launching, by forced military service.

In the apprehension of this disastrous trend we are considering the general relationship of freedom and authority, with the hope of discovering how the increasing opposition between them may be resolved.

The first step is, of course, to understand the situation that inspires the new attitude of private persons toward authority, and of governments toward human beings. I think this situation may be summed up by saying that all mankind is in a stage of transition from its age long economic organization by relatively self-sufficient units (tribes, principalities, countries, even empires) to a new economic organization of industries and commercial exchanges embracing the whole globe. The terrible tension that marks our age arises from a severe time lag between the economic order which has sprung up and spread out with the sudden growth of science, and the political order which still presupposes the old values of self-sufficiency and separateness. The political pattern today does not mirror the actual state of society; and since political institutions are the greatest and steadiest symbols of moral values, people's moral ideas and feelings today are largely unrealistic. Our interests are global, our consciences are tribal. Our activities reach round the world, our morality stops at a national boundary.

The old regionalism produced social solidarity, social rights codified into a system of laws, and especially the authority of civil government to implement the laws. In the security of such institutions the ideal and the reality of personal freedom developed; and under civil law, industry and commerce grew up.

In the new age of science, industry and commerce have grown to global proportions, wiped out the fixed local limits of economic needs and resources, outgrown every realm of civil government and therewith the controls of statute law. It has consequently become the prime function of government to uphold the claims of citizens to the legally unprotected goods of the world, forcing the issue, wherever necessary, by threats or acts of violence. There does not even need to be any mutual hate or warlike spirit to involve two countries in an international crisis; the rivalry is there, it is inherent in the economic exploitation of the globe, and there is no institution that provides "an instrument to which the wise and honest may repair." The only instrument of settlement is military power.

The cultivation of such power is, therefore, the necessary first concern of all societies that lay claim to anything tangible in the world. But military power rests on potential mass action. Governments, therefore, must regard their citizens as masses to be deployed; and they cannot regard them equally as individuals to be served. This is the cause of the shift from the conception of authority as protection of private rights to the conception of authority as the power to abrogate private rights, dictate arbitrary duties, forbid certain enterprises, and control speech and association. The demand put upon every sovereign state, to guarantee its nationals their power to act without legal right in the world at large, has made the sacredness of legal rights at home impossible to uphold.

As long as governments are absolutely free and increase in physical power, individuals must become less and less free to do anything but serve their governments. If, therefore, we want to save personal freedom in the new integrated economic world, we must have a different system of decisions and sanctions in that world; it is a staggering fact, but an ineluctable one that nothing short of world reform can stem the growth of modern militarism. A world geared for industry and commerce, whether private or public, requires a system of civil law as extensive as the interests to be protected; that is, an authority that can guarantee the integrity of each agent, and adjudicate the extravagant claims of all economic rivals.

Neither unnatural ambitions nor misunderstanding lie at the roots of our moral and political failure; the trouble lies in obsolete institutions. And I submit that the adoption and implementation of civil world law is the only world reform that is a reasonable political goal. Such reform demands a long-range policy to establish a political order suitable to the needs of our worldwide industrial civilization.

Almost as soon as you mention such a new order, someone is sure to say: "There's no use talking about it as long as certain states act the way they do." That is the obvious view for short-range policies. But a big project is not fitted to momentary conditions. The political picture changes every year, every month. There are times when no particular move can be made. At such times we must do just what we are doing here and now—study our purposes and pare them down to their essentials, and then hold on to those essentials as the measure of every specific move we advocate or make.

If the essentials of a policy are understood, you can keep its ultimate aims in sight; but if only the aims are stated, and stated vaguely, in words of emotional value—to make people free, give them security, bring peace, brotherhood, cooperation, and so forth—you have nothing to work with. It is notorious that in every major conflict both sides have claimed to be making the world free or safe for this or that.

In a long-range program of social reform there must be one goal on which all activities converge, and this goal must be such that its achievement, when it does take place, will be a definite social event, not a general condition like a "brave new world" or "a new sense of brotherhood." In other words, the aim of a reform must be institutional. Perhaps mankind cannot be reformed; but the institutions under which men live, can and often have been.

Every era of history has had its special, intolerable evil to combat. Such besetting ills of society are usually very old, and have always been accepted, until a change in economic conditions exaggerates them so they suddenly threaten the very existence of nations. In the Middle Ages, the desperate evil of the times was pestilence. There had always been illness, pain, even epidemics; but with the growth of the cities in Europe, the Black Death became a nightmare that threatened to depopulate the civilized world. The medical profession had to go into strenuous action, study the causes of epidemics, and educate an ignorant, superstitious, almost immobile public to accept a new knowledge that terrified the average person only a little less than the Black Death itself. But medical success in many directions finally begot one social success: sanitary laws and controls—that is, new social institutions. These made life viable again, despite the urban culture that had let pestilence get so far out of hand.

Another example of evil that grew suddenly from new economic conditions, and had to be met by social reform, is the heartbreaking episode of child labor in the early days of machine industry. Again there were pessimists who explained why the evil, which was rooted in the economic order itself, could never be stemmed unless humanity abandoned its machines and returned to hand labor, and optimists who thought they could move the hard hearts of employers. But certain coolheaded realists saw that the evil lay essentially with the law, which treated children as the absolute property of their parents, defining no personal rights of infants. These realists used moral appeal not to reform factory owners, but to enlist the voting public for their cause, which they carried straight to the legislative chambers. Industrialists are probably no better today than they were in 1800, and the factory system is here to stay, but the horror of child labor has disappeared with the reform of obsolete institutions. Today the civilized world is faced again with an old evil which has assumed a new, virulent form, so that it threatens to destroy us. That is the time-honored institution of international warfare.

Most people do not realize that war is an institution. They think of it as an outburst of passion, which could be avoided if men learned to control themselves and to understand each other. But wars are generally made by diplomats and not by public pressure. Wars are prepared, they are not spontaneous outbursts or diplomatic mistakes. Warfare is, in fact, the trump card in the game of international diplomacy. For this reason, the use of force is always planned for and prepared, even in times of peace. The threat of violence is the accepted means of backing claims in the concert of nations, as suit and judgment are in civil life.

International war, then, is an institution. In the accepted scheme of world politics it is taken as such, and invested with proper symbols of its dignity and importance. Nothing—no royal personage, no court of justice, no priesthood—enjoys more prerogatives than a military high command in time of war. A military hero is a popular idol, a pacifist is a despised person who may even be officially punished. War is the most celebrated and the most expensive institution in the world.

There have always been wars among sovereign powers. The world has taken their cost and their physical effects of death and ruin somehow in its stride. Civilization progressed in spite of wars. But today that world old pattern of absolute power and its assertion by violence is in a fair way to destroy civilization. Like the Black Death, the scourge of war has been stimulated by new social conditions to outgrow its normal size, and make all traditional ways of meeting and enduring it entirely inadequate.

The long-range policy I am proposing is not a moral campaign against conflict and violence as such, but an attack upon the institution of war among sovereign states—this accepted, prepared, and organized use of violence that threatens to destroy our world. We cannot change human nature, but we can change institutions.

Every institution, of course, serves a purpose, and cannot be simply abolished by fiat. We can do away with it only by instituting something else—some other device that serves the same purpose without the ruinous means. In this case, probably the only device that will serve us is the one long known in domestic affairs—a controlling authority, under whose auspices quarrels are normally settled by court action. Under civil order we may hate our rivals as much as we will and struggle to ruin them, but to speak of "cut-throat competition" is nonetheless a mere metaphor; the difference between a lawful and a lawless society is precisely that in the former, competition has to stop short of actual throat cutting, and in the latter it does not have to stop at anything.

The objection has often been made that war is a natural phenomenon and some men will always fight. I think there will, indeed, always be some violence—riots, even organized fighting, occasionally a full fledged civil war. But there is an all-important difference between international war and civil war. International war is an institution, prepared and implemented at enormous expense even in times of peace. Civil war, on the other hand, is a failure of institutions. The United States has had one of the worst civil wars in history, and still feels its economic and emotional effects. Yet the line between the Northern and the Southern states is still unfortified. There are no huge appropriations made each year to prepare for further violence. Civilization does not crumble under an occasional breakdown of its legal or administrative devices. What it cannot survive is the system of sovereign diplomacy, in which war is the official instrument of major settlements.

What we must achieve, then, is another instrument of political intercourse among nations—a civil order in which dealings are regulated under some impartial authority. But how can one even begin such a task? And what sort of global order should we set up? Some people speak of a limited world government; what should be its duties, and what the limits of its power? Some dream of a Christian world state, others of a Supreme Soviet, and still others of a two chamber parliamentary government speaking Basic English. Some believe its functions should be limited to "keeping the peace" (however one does that), and others think it should guarantee every person in the world a job with a living wage and a pension.

Obviously we have to operate with some principle by which we can construct a definite plan for a global authority. Now, one way of clarifying and simplifying the pattern of the projected civil order is to consider its prime purpose, which is to give us a universally valid, universally binding, and adequate law of nations. This moves the world court into the center of the picture. And the principle I would propose is this: *everything necessary to establish an effective system of world courts, facilitate resort to them, and make their decisions binding, is essential to civil world order; everything else is at present unessential.* If we make the administration of justice our central aim, the elements of world order are implied; we shall have to establish just as much legislative, executive, and protective power as the effective functioning of the courts require. This simplifies the whole project so one can keep its main lines in sight at all times.

The constitution of such a new order should be composed by the world's greatest jurists and statesmen. It is no task for amateurs. But its actual acceptance must be prepared and finally achieved by all citizens of the world who are free to participate in political moves at all. The slow pressure of votes with a conscious steady tendency in one direction, reinforced by occasional acts of statesmanship, could bring a civil world state into being. The need is obvious and much preliminary work has already been done. We do not have to overthrow any existing government, sweep away old constitutions and so on, to achieve our aim. A series of reforms, all with the same purpose, are a surer way to a new political pattern than throwing away the past and starting something new from scratch. One is too apt to get no further than the throwing away. It is wiser to use everything that can be used.

The greatest international institution that has existed in modern times is the United Nations. Five steps could turn it into a United World Organization: 1) Extend membership to *all* nations. 2) Make the General Assembly a legislative body with power to adopt a constitution. 3) Give the World Court the power of summons, and make its decisions binding. 4) Set up a high executive to administer world interests. 5) Internationalize all armed forces, setting up a federal guard (not enlisted by national units) and allowing the several nations reasonable national police guards of their own, for domestic use.

These are all radical steps, and not simple; but they are the goals toward which our activities must be directed. They all have the advantage of requiring reforms rather than experiments. The first—universal membership—is simply an extension of what already exists. The second—the institution of a legislative body—is a radical step, but it has the present General Assembly as its natural starting point. The third, which is at the heart of the whole project, would elevate a World Court that already exists, and simply means treating the functions of that court with full seriousness. The fourth, the establishment of a greater executive branch, would take place naturally by the growth of offices already established. The fifth reform—abandonment of vast military powers—is the most generally misconceived. Strange as it may sound, it would probably be easier than anyone supposes; for if the idea of a civil world order is good at all, the end of the diplomatic and military system would be its natural result. It would become as irrational to build bombers and manufacture atomic weapons as it is today to install cannon or flame throwers to protect rich men's houses. In the Middle Ages such defenses were necessary; rich men's houses were castles. Today, when a civil authority stands behind the policeman, we need not keep even heiresses in a tower. I do not think any government ever forbade castles, but we do not build them any more.

It is hard to imagine today that military power could ever be obsolete, and simply romantic. But in a civil world this would happen very soon. There might be disarming ceremonies in the General Assembly or there might not, but after a period of vigilance to prevent secret manufacture of atomic weapons, their immense cost and the bizarre appearance of plans to use them in a civil society would end the danger.

Above all, there would be means other than diplomacy and war to achieve one's ends—other forms of conflict and competition, no doubt, attack and revenge—but without mass destruction and the death of countless people not really interested in the ends. There would be lobbying and jockeying for positions and the same old fighting spirit. Humanity will probably never improve. But under a civil order, it could live, as now the greater part of it cannot. Besides, it might even improve. It is a great mistake to think that institutions merely reflect our sentiments and attitudes, and are made by them. In a way, the contrary is true. Sentiments and attitudes are largely inspired, and certainly given form and permanence, by the institutions under which we live. Religious rights define and develop our religious feeling; patriotic ceremonies beget patriotic feeling: and a civil world order would implement the ideals of universal brotherhood which now conflict with the political institutions that really exist. In every religious or moral advance, the symbol must precede the fact; and a United World will command loyalty as soon as it is a reality to which people can cleave.

The civil authority itself would not require great force. Authority has the latent force of the public will behind it; in this way it differs from Power, in the military sense. In a civil society the police force is such a small part of the population, that it could not possibly control a populace that really resisted it; but it can deal with serious defiance because actually its strength lies in the general public approval and support. Even a largely dissatisfied public may still acknowledge an established constitutional authority rather than risk anarchy, or the operation of pure power. The military force that would support the global administration would become essentially a guard of honor, symbol of every country's vested autonomy, the first army to seek no victories, but to implement the law of nations and protect a universal peace.

Comment by Rudolf Allers:
One cannot fail to be impressed by Professor Langer's optimistic idealism. One will also agree that some sort of long-range planning or of an encompassing vision is required. Nevertheless, one may be doubtful whether there is a chance of such ideas ever being realized.

Certainly, nobody looking at history can pretend that a definite social organization or institution has to be permanent and that its change is impossible. But there seem to be definite factors, inherent in human nature, which cannot be eliminated.

World court, world government, and so on, are fine sounding words. But can a court, can any authority, become effective without possessing effective power? The idea is not altogether new. It existed once before, in a different shape, of course, but with a similar intention. This was the idea of the Holy Roman Empire, of the "secular sword," ideally conceived as a power subservient to justice and peace. But the Empire never had the power it would have needed, even if its ideal had not been vitiated by many all too human elements.

Suppose all mankind were lifted up by a sudden inspiration, suppose disarmament were to become universal, suppose that a world court be established, and so forth. It is not improbable that tensions will persist nonetheless, simply because people are different and so are peoples. Maybe they will have neither cannons nor bombs; but men fought, long before such weapons were at hand. Means to fight are easily found.

Professor Langer sees a terrible danger in the trend toward conformity, and, especially, in the idea of forced military service. It is, however, conceivable that the implied dangers may be, if not totally avoided, at least, mitigated.

Comment by Adda Bruemmer Bozeman:
I share Professor Langer's fear of the undue extension of governmental authority, through military policy and otherwise. I disagree with most of the reasoning which she applies to this problem and with the analysis of alternatives which she offers.

1. "Law" cannot be understood exclusively as a device to protect individual rights. Governmental control is not exclusively directed against the enjoyment of individual rights. The initial oversimplification with which Professor Langer prefaces her whole argument, weakens, I am inclined to think, all of her conclusions.

Individuals have never existed by themselves alone. Their individual interests have always had to be adjusted to each other for the purpose of having a secured and ordered community.

2. Professor Langer rationalizes her trust in "reform through authority," on different pages of her paper, with the remark that human nature cannot be changed, but that we can change institutions. This strikes me as an unduly pessimistic view of human nature which is not borne out by either history or the science of man. It also strikes me as a total misconception of the relationship between institutions and men. What, after all, are institutions, if they are not expressions of human nature?

3. That international warfare in the twentieth century is a scourge, no one will deny. But twentieth century techniques being what they are, how can Professor Langer

take such a mild view regarding "occasional fullfledged civil wars"? Just what—in the interdependent twentieth century world which is the premise of Professor Langer's remarks—is the difference between civil and other wars? Why should one be more nearly accidental while the other doubtlessly is prepared? Why should one expect mankind to settle down nicely after having gotten over the one kind of war, while the other kind necessarily leads to ruin?

4. Having taken a very dim view of human nature and placed all hopes in new institutions established by authority from above, Professor Langer trusts that total world reform is possible through great vision. This vision would aim at "creating a universally valid, universally binding adequate law of nations."

All moral appeals for a change in basic orientation must, to be effective, have responses that are based on awareness of the need for a new orientation. Awareness, in order to matter, must be followed by action. Appeals for a worldwide reorientation must obviously have worldwide responses. These responses must be essentially voluntary. If the worth of the individual is the ultimate purpose of all community life (and Dr. Langer agrees with this on p. 129), an effective and purposive world community of twentieth century men must develop out of agreement. It cannot be established by force or by authority. Agreement must cover the purposes around which men are to rally in government or cooperation. This means that these purposes must be sufficiently meaningful to the great majority of men. We are obviously still far removed from any such basic agreement (see the difficulties that accompanied the drafting of the Covenant of Human Rights, the Convention for the Freedom of the Press, etc.). The criteria that determine the adjustment between man's freedom and his obligations to his fellow men, will for a long time to come be determined by more parochial community organizations on the basis of parochially accepted values. It will not be possible to standardize these criteria in such a way that genuine moral and political unity on a world basis can be achieved in the near future. In the meantime we need to ask a more limited question: how can societies that are different get along with each other? how can people who live under different systems of law, and have developed different hierarchies or scales of value, adjust these systems and preserve peace? In short, I feel strongly that world government and world law are illusions, because they rest on irrational expectations of what twentieth century men are, in this sphere, capable of. Arguing out of the realities of widespread moral agreement within their own national communities, the advocates of world government or world law *now* ignore the fact that there is no such solid agreement in the international community. The history of comparative government teaches plainly that joint experiences, common habits, and shared concerns must precede the establishment of all *basic* legal norms and institutions, if the latter are to be accepted without duress. It is only on the basis of such preliminary agreement on the substance of association, that law and governmental institutions have an educative influence on some aspects of political behavior by breaking old customs or introducing new habits.

CHAPTER XIV

Some Thoughts on the Soviet Concept of Authority and Freedom

By ERNEST J. SIMMONS

Professor of Russian Literature, Russian Institute and Department of Slavic Languages, Columbia University

I

THE CHASM THAT separates Soviet and Anglo-Saxon thinking on freedom and authority was sharply suggested toward the end of R. E. Sherwood's *Roosevelt and Hopkins*. Stalin indicated to Roosevelt at Teheran that the way to overcome the moral objections of the American people to the Soviet absorption of the Baltic states was to subject Americans to the right kind of propaganda campaign. And Vyshinsky put the matter more brutally when he said to one of the delegates that the American people should learn to obey their leaders. Herein is reflected not merely the bland assumption of the new totalitarianism, which in one form or another is as old as civilization, but also the central problem of the twentieth century: do the collective achievements and goals of an authoritarian power justify encroachment on the freedom of the individual? For the relationship between the individual and the state is one of the primary differentiating factors in the Soviet conception of freedom and authority and that of the West, but one nevertheless which has had a very powerful impact over the past thirty years on Western political and even legal thinking. A conviction that has dominated Western ideals and practice since 1500—the belief that the individual mind or conscience is the ultimate repository of truth, and that every individual, therefore, has the right to make his own judgments—is nowadays being questioned under the influence of the totalitarian belief that an organized group, church, party, or state, possessing some special insight into truth, has a right or duty to impose this truth upon the members of society by whatever means are most effective.

Several important Western historians of Russia have sought a basis for this totalitarian conception of freedom and authority in the beliefs and practices in the Russia of the tsars. Though this scholarly approach can be carried too far, it has some validity. Resemblances between the old village commune and the Soviet collective farm have frequently been pointed out. But there are also continuing traditions between the old and the new in dictatorial government methods, in the suppression of personal liberties, in the oppressive activities of secret police, and in such undemocratic institutions as censorship and vigorously state-controlled education. In all these respects the differences are those of degree and not of kind, for hundreds of years of secure autocratic rule had brought a greater measure of individual freedom, especially for the privileged classes, in the old Russia than presently exists for the masses of people in the Soviet Union. Yet Dostoyevsky could write in 1881: "Civil liberties may be established in Russia on an integral scale, more complete than anywhere in the world, whether in Europe or even in North America, and precisely on the same adamant foundation. It will be based not upon a written sheet of paper, but upon the children's affection of the people for the Czar, as their father, since children may be permitted many a thing which is inconceivable in the case of contractual nations; they may be entrusted with much that has nowhere been encountered, since children will not betray their father, and, being children, they will lovingly accept from him any correction of their errors."[1] Replace the word, "Czar," by "Stalin" in this quotation, and it would almost stand as an official description, in spirit at least, of civil liberties in the Soviet Union. In one sense, the difference between the dictatorship of the tsars and that of Stalin is that in the latter case the state has educated the masses through propaganda to some degree of acceptance of the dictatorship.

However, quite apart from civil liberties and governmental institutions, there existed in tsarist times certain indigenous intellectual and religious beliefs and practices which have helped to prepare the way for Soviet concepts of democracy, anti-individualism, the principle of unanimity, and a sense of community and world mission. The Slavophils, in particular, were the main conduits of such thinking. For ex-

---

[1] F. M. Dostoyevsky, *The Diary of a Writer,* translated by Boris Brasol, Charles Scribner's Sons, New York, 1949, II, pp. 1033 f.

ample, the well known Slavophil, Alexander Khomyakov, advanced as a typical progressive notion of Russian democracy in the nineteenth century the complete tolerance of the Russian common man for all peoples, whatever their race, color, or creed, and he added: "We shall be, as we have always been, the democrats among European nations. We are the representatives of humanity in its purest form . . . Russian culture puts greater trust in the voice of conscience than in the wisdom of civil institutions."[2] Such ideas about democracy in which the rights of the individual are overlooked, appear also in Soviet theorizing on the subject.

The will-less submission of the individual to the community seems to have been born out of the conviction of the Russian Orthodox faith, the religion of the great masses of the people for centuries, that truth resides in the brethren as a whole congregation. That is, the spirit does not express itself even in the agreement of the majority, but only in the agreement of all, and that the most the individual can do is to interpret the spirit in humility and to submit. This conception is reflected in the unanimity practice of Soviet democracy, in the self-effacement of the individual in the participation of the whole under the direction of the Communist Party. Another aspect of it is the Dostoyevskian idea that one suffers for the sins of all and all for the sins of one.

In short, the sense of the community in Russia has always been more significant than individual rights. In both the old and new Russia it has been traditional to exalt the place of the community in social and political life alike, and to stress the collective character of rights and obligations. And neither the old nor new Russia, unlike the West in its democratic thinking, has ever accepted the position of the individual as the supreme arbiter of life, or the individual conscience as the ultimate moral censor. Nor have the Soviet rulers, any more than the tsars, been able, as governments in the West have, to work out an acceptable compromise between freedom and authority, for freedom there has always tended to degenerate into anarchy and authority into despotism, with the result that rulers evince a general disrespect for law and citizens a tendency to evade it.

[2] A. S. Khomyakov, *Polnoe Sobranie sochinenii,* Universitetskaia tip, Moscow, 1900–1904, V, p. 106.

II

Though all these aspects are peculiar to both the old and new Russia, it should be understood that Soviet theorists, in developing the relation of freedom to authority, have transcended traditional Russian thinking on the subject by applying to it the doctrine of Marx. Properly regarded, Marxism is an outgrowth of nineteenth century Western liberalism, and as a program for action in the minds of early Russian Marxists it comprehended liberal views on such matters as authority and the freedom of the individual. The 1903 Party declaration of Russian Marxists included a Bill of Rights providing for unrestricted freedom of conscience, of speech, press, association, and the right to strike.[3]

And such rights were regarded as ends in themselves, and not merely as means to the end of Socialism. Even in the first few stormy years after the revolution, these traditional democratic freedoms, in the face of encroaching Party power, were hotly debated in public. The Communist theorists who argued for repressive measures then did not have recourse to Marxism; nor did it occur to them, as E. H. Carr suggests, to seek support in Rousseau's identification of society and the state, which posited an all-powerful "general will" from which it was treason for the individual to dissent.[4] On the contrary, they appealed to pre-revolutionary liberal Russian legalists, such as S. A. Kotlyarevski and V. N. Kistyakovski, who preached that no government, whatever its political form or social structure, could submit to its own destruction, simply in order to manifest its devotion to legal foundations. They argued, like democratic constitutional lawyers in a national emergency, that the powers of government cannot be limited by the subjective rights of its citizens, for the demands of the higher good of all must be the sole criteria for governmental action, and if this meant a deprivation of civil liberties, then the government had right on its side.

All Marxian doctrinal matters aside for the moment, two factors influenced the development of the Soviet state over its first fifteen years of existence in a manner inimical to the preservation of democratic liberties. The first was the civil war, the intervention, and the prolonged

---

[3] See VKP(b) v *Rezolyutsiyakh eyo sezdov i konferentsii 1898–1926*, Moscow, 3rd edition, 1937, pp. 16 ff.

[4] See Edward Hallett Carr, *The Soviet Impact on the Western World*, The Macmillan Company, New York, 1947, pp. 1–19.

hostility to the new regime of powerful foreign countries; the second was the internal struggle for power in the Communist Party. The first factor was logically, if opportunistically, used by the Party to justify the suppression of liberties, in order to preserve the new state against its various foes, and such actions were always taken in the name of the dictatorship of the proletariat. When these fears were ultimately removed and the government had reason to feel confident of its own power, sanction for further authoritarian rule was sought in the assertion that the Soviet Union was surrounded by predatory Capitalist states which at any time might attack to overthrow a budding Socialism. The Marxian anomaly of this situation has been frequently commented on: the coercive power of a so-called Socialist state, instead of beginning to wither away as it approaches Communism, is deliberately increased. Justification is found in Stalin's own peculiar interpretation of the conviction of Engels on this point—state controls will begin to wither away only when Socialism has spread throughout the major Capitalist countries of the world. Whatever real fears the Soviet government may still have of Capitalist countries, compromise with them was always a peaceful possibility. Accordingly, one is left with the conviction that both domestically and internationally permanent insecurity, like permanent revolution, is a necessary factor in the Soviet design for perpetuating its own arbitrary authority.

III

A kind of corollary to this situation has been the emergence of the monolithic power of the Communist Party out of the struggle that took place after Lenin's death in 1924. Stalin, of course, more than any single person, is the architect of this policy. And today, in a manner rarely evident before 1946, when the Party seemed more content to exercise its authority behind the scenes, it now openly and blatantly publicizes itself daily throughout the Soviet Union as the sole source of all action, thought, and all blessings. Nothing could be more symbolic of the present complete domination of the Party than its determination to rewrite the whole history of the Soviet Union as essentially the history of the Party. For example, a statement in the recent outline of his newly projected textbook of the history of the U.S.S.R., which will be compulsory reading for millions of Soviet students, reads as follows: "It is under Party guidance that the peoples of the Soviet land have achieved all their triumphs—political, economic, military, and cultural. The least separation of the so-called civic history of the Soviet State from the history of the Bolshevik Party is therefore impermissible in principle and profoundly harmful. The entire process of our country's development must be continuously and organically linked in the book with the Party of Lenin and Stalin so that the decisive role of Bolshevist leadership and its strength and invincibility may be shown vividly and convincingly through concrete historical facts."[5]

It is within the precise and narrow limits of absolute Party control that one must seek for any understanding nowadays of theory and practice in matters of authority and freedom in the Soviet Union. In short, there is a higher power, transcending government fiat or legal decrees, from which all human rights derive their ultimate sanction. Communism has often been called a faith, but it is little realized how completely the Communist Party has become a ruling theocracy in the Soviet Union. In his *Historical Materialism,* one of the early texts of Soviet Marxism, Nikolai Bukharin recognized this possibility when he wrote that "teleology leads straight into theology."[6] In fact, from the "idealism" of Marxism-Leninism, which is a natural concomitant of its supreme emphasis upon reason, there is but one step to faith in the supernatural, that is, to religion. This Communist religion goes much beyond the medieval Church, for it combines an infallible faith with a vast temporal power to enforce its dictates to which the Church could never aspire. In this Communist Church Marx is God, Lenin the son, and Stalin the living pope. The Politburo is the College of Cardinals, and the six million Party members a dedicated priesthood, bound to the faith with hoops of steel. The works of Marx and Engels are the Bible, and those of Lenin and Stalin the sacred patristic writings. Heresy is the worst offense, and the priesthood feels itself obligated, not only to guide the temporal and spiritual lives of the total population, but also to pry into their private morals. The heavenly goal toward which all the faithful strive, of course, is the Communist heaven on earth.

The Soviet constitutional limitations of authority and guarantees of freedom are comprehensible only when viewed in the light of this all-

---

[5] *Voprosy istorii,* July, 1950, 7, p. 61.
[6] Nicholas Bukharin, *Historical Materialism, A System of Sociology,* International Publishers, New York, 1925, p. 25.

demanding Communist faith. In fact, there is no separation whatsoever of the Communist Church and state in the Soviet Union; the Party is the ultimate source of all laws. For the dynamics of a state monolithically controlled by a single Party require by the logic of absolute power that all human endeavors contribute, according to their abilities, to the success of the Party's program, that is, to the further growth of its power. To expect anything other is to be politically naive. Freedom of choice in such a situation is at best freedom of choice between degrees of acquiescence, never freedom of choice between acquiescence and opposition. This extra authority that derives from Communist faith has imparted almost a mystical quality to the authority of the Soviet government. "Soviet rule," said a well known Soviet writer, V. Katayev, in a recent article, "is not only a form of government. It is also a moral category. Gogol speaks about a 'spiritual city.' We must speak about a 'spiritual government,' about the 'country of our spirit,' where the personalities of the Soviet man and of the Soviet citizen are not opposed to one another. They are fused together not only in time and space, but—and this is the principal thing—in a great and eternal feeling of world justice."[7]

It is necessary to state these facts, since in reality there exists an implicit contradiction between the Party and the government in the theory and practice (mostly in the practice) of freedom and authority in the Soviet Union. Authority and freedom, for example, are defined by law, but the Party is above the law, and will often take it into its own hands to violate guaranteed freedoms. Thus, in the 1938 edition of the Soviet Political Dictionary, democracy is defined as ". . . a peoples' government, political order, under which the power belongs to the people. Authentic democracy is possible only in a Soviet Socialist State. Soviet socialist democracy is actual peoples' government. All of the governmental power in the U.S.S.R. belongs to the workers of the cities and the country represented by the Soviet Union of Workers' Deputies. Stalin's Constitution is the only real democratic constitution in the world. In the U.S.S.R. humanity has for the first time in the world realized the equality of all workers regardless of sex, nationality, and race. The rights of citizens and political freedom under Soviet socialist democracy are provided by the economic strength of the land of socialism, the powerful apparatus of the Socialist State; and by the moral-

[7] *Literaturnaya gazeta*, November 7, 1947.

political unity of the Soviet people under the leadership of the working class headed by the Communist Party. The working masses of the cities and the country actively participate in the administration of the Soviet Government. The people and the government of the U.S.S.R. are one."

The aspect that strikes one as unusual in this definition is the emphasis placed on the identity of the government and the people, headed by the Communist Party, and on the conviction that the rights of citizens derive from the state and are supported by the economic strength of the land of Socialism. Nothing is said specifically of the rights of the individual to life and liberty, or of the right of the individual to dissent, even from majority decisions, if he cares to. In fact, the individual is lost sight of and the state is exalted.

In its fundamental essence, then, Soviet democracy is diametrically opposed to our conception which derives essentially from the thinking of eighteenth and nineteenth century English philosophers. Our notion of democracy is based on the rights of the individual against both church and state. The right to dissent—or in other words the protection of minorities—is the very heart of English and American democracy. And the rule of law means with us, in its democratic aspects, the enforcement of the rights of the individual against the state. Freedom for us means a minimum interference with individual liberty of action either by the moral coercion of public opinion, or by legal penalties imposed by the state.

The 1936 Soviet Constitution, it is true, also guarantees the rights of the individual, but always subject to the ultimate control of the Communist Party or, in actuality, the Party *summit*—the Politburo. To be sure, through a vast network of organizations, the Party constantly gathers information on popular reactions, probing the will of the masses; and it associates considerable sections of the people with it in the process of implementation and execution of government policies. However, ultimate political authority in the Soviet Union is a Party privilege only, exercised by the top Party organs without the possibility of any effective check by the people. In a sense, though not entirely so, the whole vast superstructure of government is a "democratic" façade, intricately contrived, to perpetuate the power of the Communist Party or, more precisely, that of its leaders. The most that can be said for "democracy" in this process is that, through the governmental structure, the people are actively associated with the propagation and execution of policy and are instilled with a growing sense of participation in the process of rule.

The rights of the individual, guaranteed by the 1936 Constitution, appear to be well enough protected through the normal operations of justice in the courts in matters of ordinary crime and litigation, but in those offenses considered to be crimes against the people, the Soviet Union is still a police state. Secret police, unwarranted search, arbitrary arrest, deprivation of movement, labor decrees, labor camps, etc.—all are violations of individual freedom inconsistent with the guarantees of the Constitution.

IV

From what has been said above, it should be clear that any appraisal of the operation and effect of authority and freedom today in the Soviet Union may require a political and ideological algebra not entirely suited to the solution of such problems in the West and America. It is easy to dismiss the matter by saying that Lenin and his followers set out to achieve for humanity the goals of freedom and equality by means of an organization that ended by denying these same principles. The means may have murdered the ends, but suppose these ends are passionately believed not only by the Communist Party, but by millions of non-Party citizens in the Soviet Union—and there is some evidence to this effect? Where faith begins, reason ends. It was faith and not reason that permitted the first Soviet Commissar of Education, Lunacharsky, to declare: "Our Central Committee can never make a mistake."[8]

Thus Marxism is the only truth, and the Central Committee, the Politburo, Stalin, are the "bearers of the word." In such circumstances the very controls that emanate from this authority may be accepted on faith by the masses; they may in fact become convictions.

Only some such explanation, it would appear, can account for Soviet accomplishments in the creative arts and sciences, and, if this view has any validity, in other human endeavors as well. For it is hardly conceivable that monolithic government authority, severely limiting individual freedom and supported by an all-powerful police system, could

[8] A. Krivosheva, *Esteticheskiye vzglyady A. V. Lunacharskovo*, Moscow, 1939, p. 125.

drive a whole nation to prodigies of human labor. And it is also difficult to accept the explanation that the Russian masses are conditioned to strict authority and are not particularly interested in individual liberties, so long as the material necessities of life are provided. Further, it is possible to argue that the numerous incentive appeals of the government would offer a still more plausible explanation for the various mass accomplishments which have taken place in the Soviet Union.

On the other hand, it is difficult to understand how the creative spirit of man as manifested in the arts and sciences can function successfully while completely regimented, unless it draws its inspiration from faith in the system that controls it. Though it is customary in America to dismiss Soviet creative accomplishments as trivial, much of high worth has been achieved in the arts and sciences. Nor is this to deny that in the creative arts in the Soviet Union there are many timeservers who prostitute their talents to the latest Party "line." But there is still a very respectable residue of achievement on the part of great artists and scientists whose sincerity of belief in Communism it is hard to doubt.

That is, the proposition must be squarely faced, with all its implications, that Soviet creative artists and thinkers may have come quite seriously and honestly to accept as convictions what at first may have been regarded by them as hostile controls of the Communist government under which they live. Are we too far removed from the kind of religious faith that turns the ends achieved by instruments of control into fighting convictions? Though art cannot serve propaganda, propaganda can serve art by giving it a renewed meaning and purpose, and a new virility. After all, the cathedrals of Notre Dame and Chartres are in a real sense glorious artistic monuments to Christian propaganda. The religious controls over Christian art in the Middle Ages did not prevent the flourishing of the creative spirit. A Shostakovich in the Soviet Union today might be just as sincere in recanting artistic heresy and in accepting Party dictates in music as a Fra Lippo Lippi who, with Christ in his heart but a spirit too weak for the temptations of the flesh, finally humbled himself before the controls of the Church and went back to his paintbrushes with renewed faith in God.

And one might point out another analogy that has bearing on the problem. In the Middle Ages society was sure of the Church; it provided a definite pattern of life that took men hopefully from the cradle to the grave. Men did not wish to escape the controls of the Church;

on the contrary, these controls had become convictions, for they had come to be accepted on faith.

To a considerable extent the same may be true in the Soviet Union with regard to the Party. Life is officially represented as sure, and the future is always presented in a hopeful light as all struggle toward the great "Age of Communism." Under such conditions, for the creative spirit art and life become one. There is no more desire to escape from a Socialist art than there was to escape from a Christian art in the Middle Ages. Your good Soviet Communist would wonderingly ask: "What is there to escape to?"

Clearly, the relation between freedom and authority in such a system is that between faith and the source of faith. But the source is the Soviet Communist Party, and as it can compel both secular and spiritual obedience, there can be no freedom of choice to believe or not to believe. Opposition is always "minority opposition," which is condemned because the exercise of authority is always represented as for the good of the collective—for all. And collective privileges ("freedoms"), from the state always require collective responsibilities to the state. There can be no limit to such absolute authority, except through the desire of the leaders to preserve their personal power.

Conclusion

To point out the influences throughout the world of the Soviet conception of freedom and authority would be a special task, outside the scope of this paper. On the one hand, some of the most advanced and salutary economic and social legislation over the past twenty years in the West and America would have been unthinkable without the tremendous challenge of Soviet Communism. On the other hand, democratically minded peoples must view with alarm the growing tendency among the free countries to fight the worst authoritarian abuses of Soviet Communism by employing variants of its own methods. In more ways than one the Soviets seem to be turning the old axiom that "Power corrupts and absolute power corrupts absolutely," into a new modern axiom that "Power expands and absolute power expands absolutely."

CHAPTER XV

Liberty and Authority[1]

By GEORGE S. LANGROD

Research Director, French National Center for Scientific Research

I

IN SPITE OF its juridicization and of its institutionalization, more and more evident everywhere, freedom should be considered before anything else as a *state of mind,* or under its psychological aspect. It seems that this aspect is always triumphant, if one wishes to look at reality as it is. Man is free, if he feels free, if external pressure does not succeed in troubling the moral and spiritual order of his soul. Thus, a prisoner can feel freer than a man who is free, but "dehumanized," because of his inability to benefit by the faculties theoretically his in a given social framework.

However paradoxical that may sometimes seem, nevertheless, real facts prove that, freedom being everywhere and always a conquest of the individual conscience, a product of the autoregulation of man—it is he who remains at bottom the only master of his own freedom. It is he who "rises above things to rule them by law";[2] it is in his conscience that freedom finds its best refuge and its surest guarantee.

The best proof of this statement is found in the fact that liberty consists of something different for every social being one observes. For the "man on the street," to be free means less the right to vote, to enjoy constitutional rights and a democratic regime, than not to be reduced to poverty, to fear, to insecurity; to be able to rest, to talk, and to live without too great a social pressure.

For a pure intellectual, it is primarily a matter of "freedoms" (in the

[1] Translated from the French. Editors.
[2] Emil Durkheim, *De la Division du Travail Social,* Alcan, Paris, 2nd edition, 1902, p. 381.

plural)—well defined and guaranteed, established on political and social grounds.

The notion of freedom modifies its content according to the geographic parallel, extending from West to East and from North to South. It is essentially a relative notion, variable and unstable, changing in space and time, dependent on a series of the most varied factors. But what remains stable and universal to an understanding of the essence of freedom is precisely its psychological basis, its subjective character. One must have—let us emphasize it once more—the feeling of freedom, in spite of the difficulties and untoward external accidents, in order that the social mechanism may be able to act in its favor. Unless it contributes at least indirectly by its existence to an environment favorable to freedom's birth, it turns unavoidably in empty space.

Whoever has been a prisoner, for instance, can show a series of phenomena to uphold this thesis. When the author of these lines found himself for five years in a closed prisoner of war camp in Germany (1940-1945), he had enough leisure to study closely the psychological aspect of the problems of freedom. Indeed, the external conditions having been, during that period, diametrically opposed to freedom of any kind (for five years the interned men were not once able to leave the barbed wire enclosure), an inner work of great intensity was in fact able to liberate some of all exterior constraint, transforming them, as time went on, into beings more "free" subjectively than the free citizens of the Hitlerian dictatorship. In spite of the total isolation from the outside world, of the permanent compulsory association with 180 men in one room of a barracks, of particularly hard daily material conditions —an intellectual life was organized in pursuit of the realization of the thesis: *in litteris—libertas*. Everything, literally everything, depended on the moral level of the prisoners who—in order to get a rest from the crowd of cointernees—managed to get themselves locked up for several days in the disciplinary prison of the camp, so as to find in the *restricted prison* a relief from the life of the larger prison. This serves to prove the fundamental relativity of the problems under discussion; it demonstrates the inner arsenal every human being can use in the struggle to acquire the feeling of freedom. Without this feeling, all the institutional realizations on the social plane serve no purpose, because everything depends on the feeling of a man about the real value of his subjective conquest, his personal psychological contributions, founded upon his moral strength, which he can employ and which he knows how to oppose to the external difficulties on the plane of his freedom.

II

But—speaking objectively—freedom, while being indisputably a state of mind, equally constitutes a problem on the basis of human ecology.

On the one hand, man has great difficulty in realizing the victory considered above, when he lacks a favorable atmosphere, an adequate psychological climate. Generally, in spite of the fact that by an effort of his will man can—either isolated or in a group—raise himself above his surroundings, in order to create *in himself* the subjective environment of freedom, he needs a state of relations with men and human groups that would facilitate his individual freedom. That which is often called "social freedom" to a large extent is essentially a question of the particular environment. There seems to be a kind of "organizational freedom," that may result in the transforming of a primitive state either into degeneration, or into anarchy. Opposed to this is the alternative of collective conscience founded on moral autonomy and a specific rule of order.

Moreover, independent of the problems of a psychological order, one must realize that the human environment, like the general external conditions of the life of man, prevent him inevitably from benefiting fully from his theoretical freedom. There is then—from this point of view—an inevitable difference between freedom in its pure state, as it presents itself *in abstracto,* not taking into account human ecology, and in its possible practical exercise. For reasons of order—physical, economic, moral, juridical, deontological, and others—man finds himself constrained to an autolimitation of the effective use of his freedom. If this does not destroy it in itself, freedom, nevertheless, finds itself considerably diminished in fact. In current language, one confuses almost always these two problems: freedom *in se,* as a theoretical faculty of acting or of abstaining; and its *exercise,* as a practical possible benefit. It seems indispensable to make a clear distinction between the two, the ecological aspect of the entire question helping the orientation, and the delimitation of the problems in question.

On the other hand, it is necessary in a society to "put order into disorder."[3] One must regulate the deportment of man so that he should not decompose and destroy the social WHOLE. In spite of the commonplace character of this statement, one must repeat it, in order to oppose energetically the considerations of freedom and authority as fatally antagonistic values. There is nothing more dangerous to the idea of liberty, and nothing more harmful on the social plane, than the idea of authority. One must realize that freedom is not at all an *absolute* value of an almost religious nature. Its institutionalization (following the organization of authorities of all kinds, of the state, or purely social or moral) precisely *limits* it (in relation to a given state or to an ideal being pursued) and *augments* it (in the psychological order) by reinforcing and guaranteeing it. There are here an interdependence and a basic interpenetration of phenomena.

There is no question of a fundamental inevitable *conflict* between freedom and authority. If one believes it, if the average man thinking about freedom, searching for it, or fighting for it, sees in every kind of authority a factor opposing it, because limiting it, it is nothing but a misunderstanding issuing from a false conception of freedom as a value in itself, preexisting or resulting fatally from transposing a *method* (convenient to present things in a fundamental problem). It seems sometimes, indeed, more efficacious, from the methodological point of view, to present this totality of social questions under this contradictory form by underlining the antagonism effectively conceivable between their extreme incarnations, between the limits imaginable *in abstracto* of the phenomena of life, both individual and collective. In order to simplify the explanation and facilitate the comprehension, one prefers, consequently, to conceive these phenomena in the frame of a contradiction, of an antagonism as the basis of the reasoning. Then one searches for a compromise between these extreme notions: order is anarchy in all phases of life; man is inclined to construct diametrically opposed solutions. (Does he not, for instance, tend to the knowledge of truth for which he searches forever, and with no respite, although, at the same time he does nothing but avoid it and hate it? He also erects prisons for himself and for his fellow men, attempting at the same time to escape, in order to be free.)

It is thus evident (and at heart everybody realizes it) that there can be no liberty without authority and no authority without liberty. If one

[3] Cf. Bonald, *Essai analytique*.

of these notions becomes thoroughly and effectively antagonistic in regard to the other, if it degenerates into an enemy of the other—we face a pathological situation, a *moral cancer* producing the decomposition and the degeneration of observed social cells. Every separation of these two notions (that in the last analysis constitute a grimly inseparable WHOLE), presents a symptom of a serious illness of the social body, which, although it is not uncommon (like cancer), does not cease, nevertheless, to be fatal, contagious, endemic.

For instance, it would be easy to demonstrate this thesis by discussing the history of various historical groups, established either by mere opportunism or as a result of considerations of a particular philosophical order. It would show the deepseated antagonism between freedom and authority. The author believes himself well placed to present one instance: the Communist regime (Marxist-Leninist) under which he had to live in his country (Poland) from 1945-1948. Though drawing on personal experience, he abstains from all political prejudice and proposes to render a faithful account of all observed facts.

Wishing to enlarge upon the content of the classical notions of liberty, the Communist regime—in the name of freedom—demands that man though perhaps given the impression of greater political independence, at the same time becomes so weak economically that anxiety, terror, insecurity, the feeling of his frailty in relation to omnipotent capitalists, not only kill all sense of freedom, but all possibility of its efficacious exercise is destroyed.

In order to realize, in a more or less distant future, a "total" freedom in a classless society, Communism—acting in the name of the people-dictator—suppresses methodically all environment of freedom of man, which it sacrifices to a future collective good. Consequently, Communist authority is transforming itself into a veritable mechanism of oppression of the individual, and even into the mortal enemy of all individual freedom—this under the pretext (perhaps valid) that a greater freedom for *everybody* will come of it one day. The press finds itself regimented, public opinion suppressed, all independence of thought and speech excluded *a priori,* all rights of political opposition banished, the right to strike, the freedom of work, of independence of scientific research, of worship—condemned once and for all. Freedom exists in a relation proportioned inversely to the means of modern propaganda; Communism, in utilizing all the methods of propaganda, creates an environment of permanent social pressure that—thanks to the power of its technical means, to the brutality of its methods, and to its genuine efficiency—surpasses any comparable example that has ever existed in the history of mankind.

The specific structure of the government and of the administration belongs to the one omnipotent party, with its pitiless control of the whole of man's life. Everything in this regime becomes totalitarian: the collective economy, the religion of rate of production, the worship of the leaders of the people (the heads of the government), they always present signs of "public" authority. Submission to this totalitarianism must be total, aggressive, enthusiastic, and without visible mental reservation. This submission embraces the "civic" behavior of man (taxes, elections, political and social opinions, trade unions, scientific teaching and research, etc.), as well as the details of his domestic life, his strictly private behavior, his children's education, his desires, even his thoughts. This degree of ceaseless social pressure—coinciding with the carefully created "great fear"—kills forcibly any climate of freedom. The disjunction between "freedom"—such of it as remains in the doctrine and is guaranteed by the constitutional texts of the Soviet Union and of the "peoples' democracies"—and the "authority" (as it is in reality), becomes, in its turn, "total." Authority exists as the unique distributor of unequalitarian freedom.

The cult of technocracy, the contempt for human personality, the iron centralization of all collective life, the vilification of any individual initiative (excepting that which is regimented, checked, and blindly obedient to the government)—these constitute the essence of the governmental tactics of the regime. Every spontaneous action of man (considered by Henri Bergson as the first condition of freedom) disappears. Man finds himself morally enslaved; degraded to become part of a replaceable spring of a planned and centralized mechanism. His insecurity is linked with the impossibility of any outside knowledge, of all legal defense against the arbitrariness of power, of all criticism (except autocriticism).

Consequently, an abyss gapes between the democratic façade of the whole and the anthill society, dehumanized, technocratic, founded on the fundamental inequality of the "subjects." There is privilege for the few, persecution for all others. This state of things has, in reality (contrary to doctrinaire statements and surface appearances), nothing to do with the position of a man in any given social class: the industrial worker suffers as much—if not more—than the farmer, the artisan, the merchant, the intellectual. On the ideological plane, the sincere Socialist suffers more than the former bourgeois. Equality seems introduced for the living generation only in suffering, in fear, and in extreme poverty.[4]

[4] It is necessary to repeat, in order to avoid all misunderstanding: this somber picture is an attempt to be strictly objective and constitutes only one "laboratory" model of the disappearance of freedom in conflict with authority. The author admits willingly the possible sincerity of the Communist leaders, and does not wish to express himself as far as the truth or lack of truth in the Bolshevist doctrine as far as the program of economic and social reform of the capitalist society is concerned. He admits also the evident success of a series of Communistic innovations, on the social, cultural, economic, and administrative plane, and does not underestimate a democratization of ways and manners and of certain institutions. But nothing seems to him more striking than this modern instance that one must analyze most deeply, by confronting it constantly with other regimes, actual and anterior, on the plane of freedom. The practice of the Communist regime gives us the best opportunity to measure the distance between abstraction and life, between the façade and the content, between the "totality of man" in a regime of effective liberty and the antihumanitarian totalitarianism of power in a dictatorial regime. As mentioned above, freedom could maintain itself in it, as a purely subjective state of mind by taking refuge in the individual conscience and by opposition to the outside environment; but it seems evident that precisely in this regime (as well as in like regimes), even the conscience of man is not free any more, the dictatorial authority penetrating into it continually and by every means of pressure—psychological or physical—prison itself constituting no more a refuge against this pressure.

Every unilateral way of approaching the problem of freedom threatens fatally to empty it of its real content, in spite of the appearances capable of leading into error.

We have seen instances cited and lived, proving that it is as unfair to exclude *a priori* the existence of all subjective freedom in conditions that oppose it objectively, as to be satisfied with a façade purely external and decorative, covering an entirely opposed content. It would be also as unjustified to confuse freedom in itself with its effective exercise, as, for instance, to identify them with the arbitrariness or the caprice of the individual with the possibility of his doing anything he wishes. Finally, it seems as unfair to conceive freedom universally according to the *French* tradition—as stamped with a particular taste for revolt, for struggle against power, of rebellion—as to approach it according to the *Anglo-Saxon* tradition only, identifying it with the subjective right of the individual to defense against every possible arbitrariness of the public powers. It is necessary to examine here, briefly—in the light of the above-mentioned instances—the danger presented inevitably by unilateral concepts of freedom, for instance, on the exclusively juridical plane, as well as on the exclusively psychological or exclusively economic one.

It is clear that if one approaches the complex problem of liberty only under its juridical aspect, one runs more serious dangers than those suspected by the generations of the nineteenth century. One runs, in effect, the risk of justifying by conformity of acts to the legal form (the rule of law in force)—all that hides under a formally correct regulation of the opposition to freedom.

This result is the more frequent, the more modern peoples keep their love of legality —*the taste for form* alone. Thus, in the name of law and of their freedom in strict conformity with a preestablished regulation, the Hitlerians in power were able with impunity to kill by gas millions of innocent beings, in exterminating entire populations. The conscience of the absolute value of the correctly established juridical rule, had degenerated to the point where it was enough to establish, in the Third German Reich, the rule that, for instance, a Jew had no right to live (even in a ghetto isolated in the fashion of the Middle Ages), in order that a whole civilized nation could tolerate passively "in its majority and support actively in its minority," crimes of "genocide" against humanity, that its rulers put into practice with efficacy on the scale of a whole continent. Thus, the juridical regulation of freedom becomes—if one is satisfied to omit the psychological and moral aspects of the problem—the best way regularly to oppress peoples and individuals.

Besides, the law when in the service of force becomes elastic, *standardized*, gets reduced more and more to "general clauses," directives of the legislator sanctioning the executives to act freely. Consequently, the notion of legality tends to be confused with the expediency of power, the juridical form remaining hanging in empty space and in the service of the strong against the weak. There is nothing more dangerous than this degeneration of law into a legitimate illegality, into a legal oppression, because covered with an appearance of legality (thanks to the art of juggling with the juridical form).

And if, for instance, one wishes—as do the Communists in justifying their regime of terror—to free man from a freedom *without content,* by widening thus sensibly the content of the classical notion of freedom, one comes to results that are equally nefarious for freedom itself. Freedom—political, cultural, social—finds itself sacrificed to the progressive search for a future economic freedom *ut supra*. This search demands a meticulous regulation of the conditions of compulsory labor (even hard labor)—whence the factual enslavement of the mass of the workers; a collectivization of the whole of life—whence Kolkhozian, syndical state bureaucracy and the total submission of man to force (the ruling powers); the improvement of production—whence a veritable worship imposed on the workers for planned work as a goal in itself; the order controlled and unified like the one introduced into any prison; a dictatorial power—strong, centralized, authoritarian, brutal, without checks and effective popular control—whence the rejection of all social harmony, of all arbitration between contrary forces, of all equality, of the objective equity and impartiality of the judge; of all trace of a Lincolnian democracy (and not merely of the democratic appearance and phraseology). Consequently, dictatorship consists on this plane in a *dosage* of freedom, distributed at will by the dictator of the moment, who divides it into fractions, considering it either as a reward or as one of the numerous technical means for reaching his goals. When it opposes his plans in any way, he modifies this distribution as he pleases. Thus it becomes understandable that the search for the conceivable *comfort,* well-being of generations to come, finds itself—consequently—conditioned by the exclusion of all effective freedom from the living generation on which one imposes the absolute faith in expected results, which it will not verify or which it will verify only in part.

One could have illusions about the fact that in every regime of antiliberal dictatorship (whatever it may be) at least the *men in power* incarnating absolute power, could be considered as free in relation to all others. But, even on that plane, it is not so. First of all, because their participation in power, founded on physical force alone, remains fatally shortlived and subordinate, on the condition that a stronger one does (or not) take the upper hand and at the same time corner all freedom. Then, because this freedom which is theirs, finds itself forcibly conditioned in advance at its base, by a net of varied bonds resulting from their being dependent on forces without which every dictatorship crumbles. Finally, because these regimes organize methodically, in modern times, as is proved by the Communist instance, periodic purges, in order to prevent all sclerosis of the dictatorship. Dictators then kill each other, the encompassing permanent insecurity going beyond the limits of those governed, and sparing nobody, dictators included.

These few observations should be sufficient to convince the reader that—as it has been said—in order to try to get at the problem of freedom, one must, at all costs, avoid all partial and unilateral concepts. Freedom presents itself to us as a resultant of the moral autonomy of man and favorable exterior conditions, like a synthesis searched for, two coexisting orders of values, different but complementary (FREEDOM:AUTHORITY). These values can be defined only by a *reciprocal filling,* all pure values being empty, and require for definition resort to other values. When one wants to get close to reality, one must—however difficult it may be—take simultaneously into consideration diverse values, in order to penetrate thus into the whole of observed social relationships, and to approach it from different points of view. Thus only can one try to avoid a lack of equilibrium, falsifying all analysis, a deformation of the dilemma presented by its imaginary breakdown.

(When, for instance Communism criticizes severely the unilateral and hypocritically partial Occidental concept of liberty, according to the constitutional Western rules and the practice of so-called bourgeois countries, it chooses—to combat this fiction—the *opposite extreme:* its liberty becomes as hypocritical, if not more so, because *toto orbe* far from real freedom. The establishing of a constitutional façade, *whatever it may be* or wherever it may be, changes nothing. It seems almost funny (if it is really unconscious) that the Communists understand this *in others,* and never at home, although it is self-evident. But truth is the same everywhere; in order to reach it, one must have the widest possible analytical basis, the most complete semantic clarity, the rejection of all methodological dogmatism and of all preconceived ideas, an environment adequate not only *to be free* but also to be able to study freedom.)

The dualism LIBERTY:AUTHORITY is a key problem of the whole social life, as well as one of the bases of political science. Its age is that of all philosophic speculation. It is at bottom an eternal problem, ever treated anew in all philosophical and political writings, every author in this domain, from the greatest to the smallest, bringing it up at some point in his life. The whole social life oscillates, indeed, between these two notions and depends before everything upon the way in which people manage to resolve the possible conflict between them. It would be presumptuous to suggest that by a monographic study we could enrich our knowledge of the problem in question, by adding to it new fundamental observations: everything seems already to have been said on this subject on the plane of theoretical knowledge of the problem. What one can do, is to try regrouping ideas that have often been expressed, thus facilitating a better understanding, thanks to a more convenient systematization. One can also utilize certain results of direct observation of particular social phenomena, by searching in them—thanks to the inductive method—for certain light as to possible solutions of the entire problem. One can, finally, make a serious effort from the point of view of semantics, the notions discussed being badly understood and lending themselves to confusion. Thanks to a series of such contributions, it would be possible to attempt to look for a synthesis that would supply a better concept of the social life of the future. That is the maximum profit that one can expect from such an endeavor to emerge from the actual chaos of ideas and apparently inextricable complications, created by misunderstandings in the application of current notions and by the abyss separating doctrine from life. One will thus, perhaps, get nearer—on the plane of reasoning—to more adequate solutions to the doctrine of freedom, as to its free exercise, as to its more equitable order in a better society.

CHAPTER XVI

Freedom and Authority in International Organization

By QUINCY WRIGHT

Professor of International Law, The University of Chicago
Freedom of the Individual

FREEDOM REFERS to the capacity of individuals and groups to make choices. The freedom of individuals may be limited subjectively, 1. by a sense of necessity or apprehension of impending catastrophe leaving no time for deliberation, 2. by ignorance of the alternatives open or of the probable consequences of their application, 3. by inertia inducing a customary or habitual response which may not be adapted to the situation, or, 4. by unquestioning obedience to prohibitions and directives supported by the opinion of the group. Individual freedom may be limited objectively, 1. by the obstruction or violence of other individuals, 2. by lack of resources or means to pursue a preferred course, 3. by a culture or religion unfavorable to personal initiative and the will to make decisions, or 4. by the compulsion of law or discipline of the state or other group of which the individual is a member.

The four subjective limitations are parallel to the four objective limitations. President Roosevelt's Four Freedoms suggest guides for moderating these limitations. Those arising from necessity and violence may be moderated by suitable laws, policies, and measures of police, assuring "freedom from fear." Those arising from ignorance and poverty may be moderated by improvements in technology, economy, education, and social security, assuring "freedom from want." Those arising from inertia and cultural unprogressiveness may be moderated by "freedom of speech and communication," assuring broader sources of education and information, and more varied social contacts. Those arising from superstition, oppression, and arbitrary law may be moderated by institutions, assuring fair procedures in the administration of justice and "freedom of religion and conscience."

Discussion within the United Nations has tended to distinguish the first two types of freedom protected by "social and economic rights" from the last two protected by "civil liberties." Both are included in the Universal Declaration of Human Rights approved by the General Assembly in 1948. While the latter have been emphasized in traditional "Bills of Rights," including that of the United States Constitution, the former have been given much attention in Twentieth Century Bills of Rights and are emphasized by Socialist and Communist thought. In all countries, however, and at all times some freedom of citizens from fear and want has been considered a primary interest of government. Democracies have usually considered a minimum standard of living and a minimum level of education a condition of their successful functioning. Other forms of government have not been indifferent to the living conditions and ideologies of their subjects, if for no other reason, as insurance against revolt and military weakness.

The rule of custom may be moderated by development of an active public opinion. Such a public opinion has been considered essential to democracy. In totalitarian governments the rule of custom has often been broken by propaganda, indoctrination, and legislative innovations in the interest of government policies.

The guidance of choices by the value system established by culture, religion, and tradition, has often been considered a manifestation, rather than a limitation, of freedom. A free society, however, fears arbitrary impositions of the dead hand of the past and self-interested impositions of authority. Consequently, free societies separate church and state and tolerate a diversity of values. The law of a free state therefore assures wide freedom to pioneer in religious and moral ideas. The common law of such states often accepts as the criterion of justice, the maximum freedom of individuals consistent with equal freedom of others.

Freedom of the Group

When the term, "freedom," is applied to groups, the same definition and the same subjective and objective limitations apply. But individual and group freedom may be in conflict. The group's subjective freedom increases in proportion as it is organized to make decisions and to assure the obedience of its members. Its subjective freedom is, therefore, a function of its internal authority, and tends to increase as the freedom of its members diminishes. Its objective freedom depends on its relation to parallel groups and to supergroups. The competition of parallel groups for freedom tends to establish an equilibrium of power among them or to subordinate all to, or to dissolve all in a supergroup with a "higher" culture, law, and organization. Power rivalry tends to create "garrison states" minimizing individual freedom. The union of groups or the assimilation of groups in supergroups may have this effect but need not if the process is gradual and voluntary.

Freedom and Authority

The terms, "authority" and "power," can be applied, not only to the relation of a group to its members, but also to the relation of an individual occupying a superior position in the hierarchy organizing a group to those below him. "Authority" and "power," therefore, resemble freedom in that both refer to the capacity of individuals and groups to make choices, but authority and power add the idea of inducing or compelling others to accept choices. Authority and power may be distinguished. Authority wins compliance by superior wisdom or prestige, while power compels adherence by coercion. In legal and political writings, however, this distinction is often neglected.

A court's authority is defined by its "jurisdiction." Within its jurisdiction, a court of last resort escapes the first two limitations of freedom. It has ample opportunity to deliberate and is informed of all the alternatives which may be chosen. The court is, however, obliged to apply the law, supposedly embodying accepted principles of justice, as its rule decision. Thus, in exercising its jurisdiction, the court's intellectual and moral freedom is confined to discovering and interpreting the law.

The law defines a sphere of freedom, but it is not expected that choices within it will be capricious. Decisions should conform to rules of the culture. It is expected that choices will be influenced by the individual's conception of his interests, of the most suitable means to obtain them, of social propriety, morals, and religion, established by the culture of the group, as manifested by tradition, by custom, by institutional precepts, and by public opinion. The law sets limits to the freedom of the will, the culture to freedom of the intellect. In free societies the law gives a wide sphere within which individuals and groups can make choices; and the culture permits great variations in the objectives toward which and the standards by which that freedom may be exercised.

The group imposes itself upon the individual mainly to prevent encroachments upon the equal freedom of others and to preserve order, settle disputes, and provide essential services and facilities of cooperation. In totalitarian and primitive societies the presumption is opposite. Instead of general freedom being presumed and limitations defined, restriction is presumed and freedom exists only in so far as explicitly permitted. Permission is often given in the form of privileges to particular individuals, groups, classes, or castes.

Authority of Universal Organization

What should be the authority of universal organization in the contemporary world? Should the world community organize itself so as to maximize the freedom of individuals? Should it seek to maximize the freedom of nations? Should it seek to maximize its own freedom by increasing its power and authority?

Traditional international law has assumed that each nation is free to make law, to deal as it wishes with its subjects, and to pursue a foreign policy, even employing force. These freedoms are limited only by the equal freedom of other states. The result has been an emphasis upon territorial sovereignty, limitations of political contact to governments, formalization of diplomatic intercourse, limited rights of the state to protect nationals abroad, freedom of the seas, and sharp demarcation between states of peace and states of war. The latter confers upon belligerents extraordinary rights and upon neutrals extraordinary duties. The freedom of the individual is reduced to what his own state accords him. The world community exists only as a theoretical assumption of international lawyers or a generalized expression for the equilibrium of power which tends to arise under these conditions of international anarchy. While war remains a possibility, permitted by law, the state cannot rely upon law for security, but must be always ready to defend itself by its own arms and alliances. Such efforts have at times produced a stable balance of power giving moderate security to all.

In a world shrinking under the impact of invention, with war becoming more destructive and more probable, and with the power of great and small states becoming more disparate, defense preparations induce states to become "garrison states" in time of peace and to engage in total mobilization in time of war. This tends to reduce the field of individual liberty and to increase tensions. At the same time, aspirations for peace, democracy, individual liberty, and higher standards of living, spread throughout the world's population as information increases.

With these opposite movements of necessity and desire, traditional international law, supported by a balance of power, suffered two disadvantages. First, it could not protect the freedom of states. Second, it subjected the individual to the loss of much freedom in all states and of all freedom in some states, thus frustrating his aspirations for security and prosperity. It is, therefore, not surprising that the United Nations was established to realize four new purposes. These purposes are not entirely novel, but through the United Nations they have been more clearly stated and more widely accepted by governments in the twentieth century than ever before. These purposes, stated in Article 1 of the Charter were:

(1) To maintain international peace and security,
(2) To develop principles of equal rights and self-determination of peoples,
(3) To achieve international cooperation in promoting and encouraging respect for human rights and for fundamental freedoms for all, without distinction as to race, sex, language or religion, and
(4) To be a center for harmonizing action of nations in the attainment of these ends.

These purposes were to be implemented by the acceptance of certain principles of law by the members of the United Nations. The members are obliged to respect the sovereign equality of other members; to settle international disputes by peaceful means; to refrain from threat or use of force in international relations; to assist the United Nations and to refrain from giving assistance to any state against which the United Nations is taking preventive or enforcement action (Art. 2); to accept and carry out decisions of the Security Council (Art. 25); and to take joint and separate action in cooperation with the organization, to promote universal respect for, and observance of, human rights and fundamental freedoms for all without distinction as to race, sex, language, or religion. Other obligations concerning social and economic cooperation are also specified (Art. 56).

Legal Authority and Effective Power

It is clear, however, that the effective power of the United Nations has not matched its legal power and its authority has gained only imperfect acceptance. Some believe that if the freedom and capacity of the world community were augmented by the establishment of effective world government, that government would function to preserve peace and justice, properly distributing freedom among individuals and nations.

Others fear the possible tyranny of such a government, and perceive no means of establishing it except by a universal war from which a world government of the Soviet type would be as likely to emerge as one of the American type. Consequently, they urge abandonment of the aspirations of the Charter, and reaffirmation of state sovereignty guided by enlightened self-interest. Such a system, they hope, would balance power among states of widely differing ideology.

Still others urge a long-run policy of developing a universal culture which attributes high value to the aspirations of the Charter, and an active world public opinion which insists upon realizing these aspirations. Appreciating, however, the time necessary to develop such a universal culture and world public opinion, this group would support short-run policies to prevent war and to stabilize power relationships. To that end they would utilize national diplomatic, military, economic, and propaganda policies; the organs of the United Nations; and such world opinion as exists. At the same time they urge moderation of action, so as to avoid frustrating progress toward the long-run objectives.

The obstacles in the path of either effective world government or a stable balance of power are obvious. The difficulties in the way of the third alternative, which has in the main commanded support of American opinion and has been the policy of the Department of State, are perhaps less clear.

Long- and Short-Run Policies

These difficulties lie in the considerable measure of contradiction between the long-run and short-run policies advocated. Whatever may be the world's aspirations, the actual situation is that of a divided world, in which opinion in the democracies will not tolerate a world government on the Soviet model, and opinion in the Soviet Union, or at least in the Politburo which controls it, will not tolerate a world government on the democratic model.

Both positions are backed by physical forces capable of mutual destruction, and whatever may be the professions, or even beliefs, on each side concerning the possibilities of peaceful coexistence, each suspects that the other would like to wipe it out. Each is, therefore, convinced of an urgent necessity to augment its power position. The resulting arms race induces anxious calculation as to which side time favors. The United States watches the more rapidly growing population of the Soviet Union; the increasing integration of European and Asiatic satellites into the Soviet system; the manifestations of revolutionary opinion and violence in Korea, Southeast Asia, Iran, and elsewhere; the development of atomic weapons, airplanes, snorkel submarines, and other instruments of war in the Soviet Union. At the same time, the Politburo observes the success of ECA in stemming the tide of Communism in Western Europe; the defection of Jugoslavia; the organization of a military alliance among the Atlantic powers; the association with them of Western Germany, Jugoslavia, Greece, and Turkey; the success of the United Nations and the United States in dealing with violence and threats of violence in Iran, the Balkans, Indonesia, Palestine, Berlin, and Korea; the gradual mobilization of the superior resources and industrial plant of the non-Soviet world for military production; the establishment of air bases on the periphery of the Soviet bloc; and the qualitative and quantitative superiority of the West in science, technology, and military material. While the actual thoughts of this group are obscured by the vociferousness of their propaganda, it is difficult to believe that they do not actually fear that time may be against them. Such a reaction is particularly suggested by the Marxist theory which declares that conflict between Capitalism and Socialism is inevitable.

In his testimony before the Senate Armed Services Committee and the Foreign Relations Committee on June 1, 1951, Secretary Acheson dealt with the proposition that it is expedient "to take extreme risks now because time may not be on our side." He thought this wrong and said, "the basic premise of our foreign policy is that time is on our side if we make good use of it."[1]

He did not, however, point out that if Stalin and the Politburo agree with him, it would be rational for them to strike sooner rather than later. Fortunately, the uncertainty of the situation permits Russia to believe that time favors it, even while the United States believes the opposite. This uncertainty mitigates the immediate danger of World War III, but it favors the long continuance of power rivalry, continual acceleration of the arms race, continual reduction of the zone of uncommitted states, accentuation of the bipolarity of the world, differentiation of opinion in each half, and increasing anxieties and tensions. American short-run policies seem consequently to be faced by the alternatives of present surrender, hot war, or cold war. None of these seems likely to advance the peace and security, individual and national freedom, and general cooperation for economic and social progress called for by the United Nations Charter.

Dangers of Power Politics

Even if a lull in the arms race permitted the development of independent centers of power in Western Europe, India, China, or elsewhere, creating conditions more favorable to a stable balance of power, such as existed in the nineteenth century, still maintenance of such an equilibrium would in the present state of military technology require intensive defense organization, and intensive coordination of opinion, production, and culture within each regional group. Universal vulnerability to sudden attack arising from new military inventions, and the extraordinary anxieties arising from the grave consequences of such attack, mean that the military balance of power, even if there were more than two major centers of power, requires a degree of military and economic preparation, of regimentation of the population, and of subordination of lesser powers to greater, which militates against a universal order of the kind contemplated by the United Nations Charter.

Perhaps the major hope for avoiding World War III lies in the uncertainty of all calculation concerning which side time favors, in the

[1] *Department of State Bulletin*, Washington, June 11, 1951, XXIV, p. 926.

destructiveness of war which makes each hesitate to initiate hostilities even if time seems adverse, and in the belief by each side that the other faces ruin from within and will eventually yield without war. But it seems clear that the necessities of short-run policies are not favorable to the achievement of long-run objectives of the Charter.

Dangers of Internationalism

The contradiction between the short-run necessities and the long-run aspirations of the Free World, is no less clear, if attention is given primary to the latter. The long-run policies to achieve the objectives of the Charter require an abundant and universal communication of authentic information, especially that concerning United Nations activities and decisions, and effective education in all nations favorable to the United Nations and its purposes and principles. Such a long-run policy also requires continuous utilization by the member nations of the organs of the United Nations and the Specialized Agencies and reliance upon the procedures of the United Nations for security.

Regulation and limitation of national armaments, development of effective forces available to the United Nations, good faith in meeting obligations, and acceptance of procedures to assure rapid decisions by United Nations organs, is essential, if such reliance is to be justifiable. Countries which seek in good faith to forward these objectives may, however, become progressively less secure so long as some great powers do not cooperate. Reliance upon law for security may be suicidal, when the law is not supported by efficient procedures or adequate power. China in 1931, Ethiopia in 1935, Czechoslovakia and Poland in 1939, Norway and the Low Countries in 1940, and Korea in 1950, were overwhelmed by aggression. In the long run, the forces behind law and order liberated them. But perhaps they would have suffered less, if they had relied less upon law and more upon their own arms and alliances.

So also subordination of national commercial, financial, and cultural policies to procedures of international cooperation through the United Nations and the Specialized Agencies may militate against effective national, bilateral, or regional action in pursuit of policies which at the moment appear to be in the national interest. While, in principle, all nations can increase both their security and their prosperity by universal cooperation, in practice, such gains may fail to be achieved, because the foundations for universal action are inadequate and action on a lesser scale is neglected.

Observance in good faith of the spirit of the United Nations, in the fields of opinion and education, requires that governments give their public free access to transnational and United Nations communication and education. Such communication and education may, however, permit the spread of interested propagandas from hostile nations, modify the spirit essential for effective defense programs, and create a state of public opinion inclined to rely upon goodwill or the United Nations for security. Furthermore, the development of such tendencies among some sections of the population is very likely to develop countermovements of intensive nationalism among other sections, creating a division of opinion in itself unfavorable to effective defense.

Totalitarian countries will not suffer either of these cosmopolitanizing or denationalizating tendencies of public opinion, but will take advantage of these conditions, if they manifest themselves elsewhere.

The Soviet Union and its satellites have not joined the Specialized Agencies, have maintained a strict censorship against information from outside, and have controlled policy and opinion rigorously, without regard to either the spirit or the letter of the United Nations Charter. In view of the apparent inconsistency of Communist ideology and Soviet foreign policy with the long-run aims of the Charter, and in view of the vulnerability to information from outside of Soviet culture and opinion, it is not to be expected that the Soviet Government will reduce censorship. It is rather to be expected that it will utilize any opportunities offered by the United Nations to disseminate propaganda, such as the "Stockholm Peace Appeal," designed to forward revolution, pave the way for aggression, and frustrate achievement of the long-run aims of the United Nations.

A Balanced Policy

A general understanding of this situation may reduce its dangers. Continued contact of the representatives of the Soviet Government with those of other countries in United Nations organs may provide a useful avenue for diplomatic discussion, and, if conditions within the Soviet Union should change, may perhaps facilitate a gradual modification of Soviet policies. Yet the contradiction between policies based upon the long-run aims of the United Nations, and the short-run policies of all countries intent upon security, is likely to continue. Whatever may be its inadequacies for long-run security, immediate necessities require all states to strengthen themselves to play the game of power politics.

After analyzing the problem of world stability as it appeared in 1942, the present writer wrote:

> It appears that the policies appropriate to a balance of power order are in most cases very different from those appropriate to an effective international legal order. This suggests that *gradual* transition from a balance of power system to a juridical and cooperative international system is not likely and that states may find themselves in serious difficulties if they pursue policies adapted to the latter type of order before enough of them do so actually to establish that type of order.
>
> Such transitions have, however, taken place in the past during short periods of time. The twentieth century can witness the advent of a new system of world politics, better adapted to its technology and its democracy, if statesmen of the principal powers *simultaneously* adopt policies appropriate to such a system. These changes can take place only with able leadership and only at a moment when world opinion is convinced of the disastrous consequences of the past system. That opinion cannot be expected to endure without suitable supranational institutions.[2]

It is possible that the opportunity presented at the San Francisco Conference of 1945 three years after this was written, was not made the most of. At the present time such simultaneous adoption of policies appropriate to an effective world legal order is not feasible. Statesmen will have to do what they can to prevent the necessities of immediate policy from wasting opportunities which may arise for further progress toward the goals of the United Nations. It would appear that the leadership of the United States seized the opportunity offered by the Korean invasion to make such progress by effective action both to maintain the Charter and to develop it through the Uniting for Peace Resolution.

Peace is a consequence of a proper balance between individual freedom, national freedom, and the organization of world authority. Too much individual freedom may result in anarchy, weakening the nations, and preventing effective world organization. Too much national freedom disrupts world authority and may result in oppression of the individual in many nations. Too much world authority may result in a

[2] Quincy Wright, *A Study of War*, University of Chicago Press, Chicago, 1942, p. 1497.

universal tyranny dangerous to both individual and national freedom. The maintenance of an equilibrium among these factors is a matter of great difficulty. National governments must be tolerant, alert, and ingenious. Peoples must look beyond national horizons to the world as a whole. International organizations must be patient and intelligent. Overcentralization should be avoided by maintaining some competition, not only between nations, businesses, and ideologies, but between international organizations in different fields. Non-political supranational institutions of commerce, religion, and education should be free to criticize national and international policies independently.

With complicated checks and balances, peoples, associations, nations, and international institutions may become continuously aware of the dynamic complexities of the world. With a leadership wise, cautious, and determined, utilizing the many organizations, private and public, national and international, devoted to the purposes and principles of the United Nations, disaster may be avoided in the short run, and opportunities may be utilized in the long run.

The future has many possibilities. The public opinion of democratic countries must be well informed, if the leaders of national and international governments are to provide necessary defense without giving unnecessary provocation to potential disturbers of the peace, are to utilize opportunities to negotiate and conciliate without consenting to dangerous appeasements, are to facilitate general cooperation without ignoring the machinations of those who seek to subvert from within, and are to guide policy by the spirit of the Charter, utilizing its organs and seeking to strengthen its procedures, without so weakening national policies and national morale as to encourage aggression and jeopardize freedom.

Comment by Kenneth W. Thompson:

The great merit of this paper is that it courageously faces up to the probable conflict between long-range goals and short-run policies in international affairs. Most men of great faith ignore this conflict or deny that it exists. In doing so they raise false hopes and illusions which sooner or later lead disillusioned believers down into valleys of deep despair. In most democratic societies the nation's pulse can be charted in sharp peaks and troughs of optimism and fear. Tragically enough, this is a crude but accurate description of what has happened to public opinion in this country since the end of the war.

It early becomes apparent that for Professor Wright the paramount contemporary issue is the problem of world political unity. There are three philosophies of international relations which grapple with this basic issue. They are the utopian, eclectic, and realistic philosophies. Two of them attempt to adjust their principles to the facts of international politics; the other says, if theory conflicts with the facts, so much the worse for the facts. The utopian school maintains that the domestic scene is characterized by peace and harmony. Here the most powerful and conspicuous institution is government. In contrast, the international scene is marred by unremitting rivalry and strife. Its sphere is marked, not by powerful government, but by the conspicuous absence of effective authority. To bring the international orbit into line with national order, all that is needed to remedy this social lag is an effective constitutional world government.

Because his paper is drawn from the two major philosophies which furnish the truest guides for international affairs, the critical evaluations which can be offered here are limited. Because the eclectic philosophy is the prevailing view for Professor Wright, it is responsible for his tendency to overlook vital political considerations. Critics who find fault with the first and third of the dominant philosophies, sometimes assume that the extent and scope of the eclectic position safeguard it against intellectual error. I find three respects in which this is not true.

First, the obstacles to freedom, inherent in threats from other individuals are moderated not in the first instance by law and public policy, as Professor Wright alleges, but by the vitality and influence of the individual himself. Freedom is not the simple attainment of one's place within an easy harmony of nature and society. Freedom in one sense is an eternal dilemma. The individual seeks freedom and security through attaining at least that power and influence essential for survival and security. But my power, by which I safeguard my freedom, becomes, in turn, a threat to your security and freedom. Each man interpreting his own predicament sees in the striving of others a challenge to his own well-being. The best one can expect is a rough and uncertain justice in which the sphere most vital and intimate to you is demarcated from the one that is crucial and basic for me. In the family, nation, and among nation-states, the line drawn separating your interests and mine represents the imperfect attempt of men to achieve what Aristotle called distributive justice. It is tempered and leavened by goals of political morality. But its methods are the balancing of strength, the determining of vital interests and the postponing of overt conflict. Freedom is not earned, once and for all, through permissive laws or policies of state. It is achieved, placed in jeopardy, and regained many times for each generation.

A second quarrel with Professor Wright is sociological in nature. The nation-state is the repository for good or ill of all man's deepest loyalties. If a deliberate choice is conceivable, it is the state which will make it. More important, sociologists maintain that there is no international community today. There is only a frail, undifferentiated international society. A society, in contrast to a community, is a fellowship of porcupines huddled together for the moment in paralyzing fear and trembling. Its only bonds are contingent ones; its common interests are provisional. True community requires mutual confidence and trust. The overwhelming weight of sociological inquiry rejects the notion that the economy of world politics approximates a true community. It is at its strongest a rudimentary society. If the world order is a community, certain techniques are practical. If it is a society, others are required. On this count, the problem is a profound one of political means and ends, and not an exercise in semantics. In an international society there is no alternative to foreign policy based on the balance of power. In a world community, foreign policies could be founded on abstract principles of justice.

Finally, as there are defects in the utopian and realistic philosophies which are frequently enumerated, there is a fundamental shortcoming in eclecticism which threatens to thwart its otherwise positive undertakings. This error is its tendency to undervalue the diplomatic and political enterprise and overvalue the practical relevance—in modifying persistent rivalries—of progress toward universal culture. The tendency since World War II has been to divert attention from the practical art of diplomacy to projects and plans for textbook revision, exercises in political definitions, and the translation of national classics. Commendable in their own right, these projects on paper or in practice do little to ease the tension between East and West, the problem which transcends all others. The first step toward world community is probably not the building of universal culture and world public opinion, but a toughminded political settlement. Its attainment awaits a return to diplomacy with its ameliorating function and purposes. There is faint evidence that this objective has been given first priority in the Department of State, any more than it has in the philosophy of eclecticism.

Professor Wright's reply:

I have also read with great interest the comments of my colleague Dr. Kenneth W. Thompson. His distinctions are suggestive, but they are rather of a philosophical and qualitative character than of the relativistic character of science which I think is more useful for analysis. The distinction which he makes between realism and Utopianism is of little value unless the relative amounts of Utopianism and realism in any exposition can be measured. Furthermore, such terms are hardly sufficiently precise to permit of such quantification.

World politics, like all human affairs, is influenced by group opinion, as well as by effective mechanisms. The realist looks at the mechanism and tends to ignore the opinions on which they lean. But the human significance of governments and armies lies in the goals which they serve, as much as in their size and efficiency. The former may shift rapidly. Today the army may support the Tsar, tomorrow, kill him. Today it may support the policy of the United Nations, tomorrow, oppose it.

On the other hand, the Utopian looks at the changeability of opinion without sufficient awareness of its ineffectiveness, unless it operates through an organization with resources of power. As Pascal said, "Justice without force is anarchy; force without justice is tyranny. The problem is to unite justice and force."

It may, therefore, be desirable to escape such tendentious terms as realism and Utopianism, and seek to define in situations the elements of opposition and cooperation, of inertia and aspiration, in terms of both opinion and organization. All of these elements may be expected to coexist in greater or lesser degree in any situation.

CHAPTER XVII

Methodological Equality and Functional Idealism

By T. V. SMITH

Professor of Citizenship and Philosophy, Maxwell School, Syracuse University

NO MAN COGNIZANT of the morphology of ideals can escape their strange ambivalence. Take Liberty, for instance. Take Authority, for example. Liberty matured to the left, becomes laxity and license; to the right, dominance and monopoly. Authority developed in one direction begets submission, in the other rebellion. There is perhaps no ideal uncontaminated by such ambivalence, nor is there any whose meaning can be fixed so fast as to resist at the center the attrition of its own extremes. Even Courage, high virtue that it is, becomes foolhardiness when pushed to the one side; and cowardice, when jostled to the other.

The Platonic definition of courage, and of every virtue, as knowledge, was calculated to hold the meaning fast against the flux. And the Aristotelean doctrine of the mean was, too, a strategy to fix virtues firmly in the center, where they seem indigenously to belong. It is out of such efforts to hold ideals against the flood that it has become historically modish to exhibit ideals in trilogies. Logical distinctions run to twos, but axiological ones tend to run in threes. There are, for instance, Truth, Goodness, and Beauty; there are God, Freedom, and Immortality; there are the Father, the Son, and the Holy Ghost. In the democratic purview of our present discussion there are Liberty, Equality, Fraternity—and the greatest of these is Equality.

We shall get large light, I think, upon the triune trooping of ideals by inspecting this pivotal, this latter ideal of equality, in its own context. Much as the Holy Spirit mediates between the Father and the Son in Christian theology—if I may become Pope to myself and authorize my own exegesis—even thus Equality stands between Liberty and Fraternity, in the democratic litany. It stands indeed in its own context much as Mother does between Home and Heaven, in the trilogy of our Christian firesides.

I

Equality it is, we now pointedly affirm, that saves Liberty from license. License is primarily the appropriation of something for oneself at the expense of somebody else. We hardly brand ourselves as licentious, not unless we take the standpoint of another; others it is who say that we have misused our liberty, when we trespass theirs. As a virtue, then, it is not liberty that men continually and justly demand; it is *equal* liberty. Without this qualification liberty is always in danger of sliding into excess. Acceptance of the limitation thus prescribed by equality is the surest safeguard against license. So deeply is this so that the liberty ideal, rather than awaiting correction, advances to accept equality in its very formulation. Such accommodation is the only way ideality has to prevent war among its members. Liberty thus matures as equalized access to the benefits, and, in the event, to the burdens, of common life.

Also true it is, on the other hand, that the Equality ideal saves Fraternity from fanaticism. The lovingkindness of liquidation of little brothers by Big Brother is a familiar outcome of insistence upon unmediated brotherhood as the ultimate ideal. It is not Fraternity in its naked gregariousness which civilized men want; it is not, that is to say, the fraternity of slaves, or of men cowering in a concentration camp; the brotherhood we want is fraternity of the free, of those *equally* free. Without the protection of such qualification against mutual encroachment, brotherhood would spell constant intervention by earnest "do-gooders." Without equal access to means of self-development, fraternity would be a poor thing indeed, odiousness anointed with unction. Free men who are equalized as to benefits and not unequalized as to burdens, they alone are brothers in any sense that is honorific. Freedom makes brotherhood tolerable, and Equality makes it possible for civilized men.

II

This is enough to suggest with what strategy ideals must be handled to prevent their occasioning the most unideal outcome. But the illustrations which we have used face us now with a predicament, the central predicament indeed of all personal development and the predicament also, in the destiny of our national life. Our classic temple of justice at Washington has over it, engraven in stone, "Equal Justice under Law." That is more emphatic as to our thesis than will appear at first glance. Justice enshrines the root word, "ius," which itself connotes "equality," and law is addressed to equal treatment of all who come under it. So the maxim comes close to saying, "equal equality under equality." The implicit pleonasm, not uncommon wherever men try to articulate first things, but emphasizes the predicament which arises from the fact, the simplest of all facts, that men are *not* equal. Actual inequality would be less troublesome, if men could be made equal, as Rousseau thought it the business of legislation to do. Next, however, to the certainty that men are not equal is the further fact that nobody can make and keep them equal. That impossibility might, in turn, be palliated, if we could yet say in all conviction that men *ought* to be equal. Even the obligation itself, however, is more than doubtful. Ought is debilitated when applied to what is not and to what can never be. Ought implies a "can." But apart from this true enough dialectic of Immanuel Kant, it is not expedient to affirm that men ought to be equal in even the elemental sense that things would be better on the whole if men were equal, or if they could be made equal.

Eschewing, therefore, such dialectics, let us merely fall back upon, and set out from, the simple observation that the more concrete and commonsensical we make the test, the more certain it becomes that no two men are equal, ever have been equal, or ever will be equal. Not in strength certainly, nor in speed, nor in virtue, nor in efficiency, nor in character, nor even in imagination. In no specifiable regard whatever are men equal. "There is only one time," says Lillian Smith in *Killers of the Dream,* "when men are equal and that is when they are dead." How, without reflecting on deity, can we even say that men are equal "before God," when they are as a matter of fact not equal? What, then, *does* the Equality ideal mean? Wherein does it get its democratic significance—if not centrality?

III

Equality is not a substantive claim; it is a methodological device. And that to what end? To the end indeed of its very opposite. Equality is a device to ascertain the *in*equalities of men. Men are unequal, but not importantly unequal, because of color, or lineage, or language, or religion. Differential treatment based upon these otiose differences is unfruitful and unjust. But men must be treated equally, especially early in life; that is, they must be given a chance to show the meaningful differences that are in them. This chance should be an equal chance, as in education; it should indeed be as far as possible the *same* chance, in order to disclose the real differences. If men are not given an equal chance to develop their differences, many of the differences will never appear. They will in fact disappear, only to function mischievously, *i.e.,* to poison all social relations. If men are given the chance, then mankind can abide the inequalities thus disclosed. Indeed two magnificent benefits flow from the disclosure of genuine inequalities among men.

The one benefit is negative, the other is positive in form. The negative one is to transform the aggressiveness of men which flows naturally enough from the universal observation that men seem to themselves to get too little of the assets and too much of the debits of associated life. This discrepancy clearly appears to each unjust. And the only proper response to injustice is resentment to begin with and is aggression to end with. It is hard to build a social order upon such psychological foundation, and it is impossible to maintain a social order so founded.

Such is the very foundation upon which Communism builds. The class struggle exists to foment and to exploit precisely this adverse feeling. Men take out on the "System" the malevolence which they feel but which they cannot in detail discharge. The resulting "struggle" is the writing large of what men cannot indite in the small. On the other hand, a man who has to acknowledge—and there is a grain of candor in every man—that he had his chance to develop what was in him and either would not develop it or did not have the wherewithal for development, that man is readied to accept his lot and to make the best rather than the worst out of his situation. Who has not known men to say that they, too, had their chance, but did not exploit it, and so to admit that if they have any complaint coming, the complaint is against themselves? Only equality of opportunity grounds such feeling of acceptance, but it does do precisely that. As Leonardo da Vinci copied into his notebook:

> Let him who cannot do the thing he would
> Will to do what he can. To will is foolish
> Where there's no power to do. That man is wise
> Who, if he cannot, does not wish he could.

There is this inchoate prudence in all men, the prudence of final acceptance. Reliance upon it as motive is our chief resource short of force. Such self-assessment is the beginning of personal responsibility, and personal responsibility is the beginning of wholesome acceptance. It is of enormous advantage to social order, a very propaedeutic to self-respect, that men should feel in themselves the will to accept constructively what befalls them, rather than to project it upon other men as envy or upon the "System" itself as rebellion. This is the first, the negative, benefit of functional equality, the equality of opportunity.

The other benefit, the positive, is even greater. It is the exploitation by themselves of whatever talents men have. There never exists too much talent in any for the good of all. The final, the creative, the self-sustaining joy is to let one's energies out to the full, to test one's powers to the limit, whatever that limit may be. The fact that it is different in different men is not relevant, save as envy makes it crucial. And if that envy be allayed, as indicated, then each makes the best of his talents, whatever those talents be. The only way to find out what those talents are is to have the chance to discover them, the encouragement to disclose them, and the prompting to fulfil them. Society would grow narrow and cooperation stale, if all men had the same capacities. It is the very fact of unequal capacities that makes variety possible, and the further fact of full and joyous realization that makes the human venture robust.

The self-sufficient joy of fulfilment prevents those who are superior in ability from gloating over the lot of those lesser endowed. This same fulfilment helps save those of inferior ability from apology and resentment toward those who are more fully equipped. And the key to both alike is, as now appears, the methodological device of equal treatment for the sake of unequal performance.

IV

What is needed to complete the story is the further observation that hardly anybody is superior in all regards, or inferior throughout. A democratic society proceeds upon the assumption, verifiable enough in observation, that one who is inferior in physical strength may be superior in courage, or one who is inferior in imagination may be superior in perseverance. This makes it possible for each to get what he craves, an earned deference for his own superiority; and it makes it possible for society to get what all require, the unearned increment of variety.

Leadership, therefore, and the deference which is its due, is not a matter of all or none. Each man may lead in that wherein he surpasses, and each must follow with reference to what he lacks. And as a resultant at any given time each man and citizen stands on his own anthill of superiority, with a perspective which begins with modest self-assessment and ends with an unenvious, a joyous, view of the functional whole. The joy of self-realization mingles thus with the greater joy of participation in a society whose final cooperation takes the form of dynamic competition. It is the fulfilment of Goethe's dream, from the mount of felicity:

> . . . could I but stand
> With a free people, and upon free land!
> Then might I to such moment of delight
> Say, "Linger with me, thou that art
> so bright!"

V

The myth of equality, like the mythology in which every great ideal functions, is an extension of factuality, not its outright denial. We begin where we are. It is the business of imagination to supplement the given. Every ideal is a precipitate of imagination. As where we are is always unsatisfactory to an animal whose reach, like that of man, exceeds his grasp, imagination is beset with the tendency to substitute the Best for the better, and thus to despoil both. Supplementation, not substitution, is the genius of imaginative projection. Whoever understands this, as the law of ideality, is prepared to treat every ideal as a methodological device, a device to enhance rather than to depreciate that which is "given" in the economy of nature. This is our hint to the wise as to the ideals of "Liberty" and "Authority"—and as to their mediation. Not to find mediation is to make insistence upon a chosen ideal the denial of ideals that are coeval and co-honorable. As Equality has been made to mediate and thus to allay the strife between Liberty and Fraternity, fulfilling both through its methodological fecundity, so every ideal can at once reduce the strife of the system of which it is a part and fulfil the potency of what itself projects. Every idealist knows "the simplicity which lies this side of the complex," though not every idealist can resist the temptation to monistic fanaticism which this simplicity constitutes. It is the mission of the growing idealist to know at length "the simplicity which lies the other side of the complex." To know this simplicity is the goal of the spirit, but it is arrived at by a strategy which only the magnanimous soul ever discovers. Whoever can discover it, and can abide the discovery, transforms his fate into a freedom which is self-sustaining, self-corrective, and self-fulfilling. Not to discover it is to make of liberty our own precious license; is to make of authority our own preferred presumption; and is to make of any and every ideal authorization for indulgence in the most unideal conduct.

Comment by Hoxie N. Fairchild:

I wonder whether the most important thing to be said about the triads "Truth, Goodness, and Beauty," "God, Freedom, and Immortality," "Father, Son, and Holy Ghost," "Liberty, Equality, and Fraternity," is that they are axiological *distinctions*. In all of these groupings the synthetic element would seem to be quite as important as the analytic. The terms in each triad are by no means identical, but they are inextricably interdependent and overlap so greatly that they seem to be human attempts to triangulate one real, but not humanly expressible value by taking three shots at it.

In the democratic triad, at all events, the three terms are so closely intertwined that it is hard to agree that "the greatest of these is Equality." Equality, as Professor Smith himself shows in Section II, is no less subject to misunderstanding and corruption than liberty and fraternity. And when it is misunderstood and corrupted, it is quite as dangerous as either of the others. Even without invoking the authority of Saint Paul, one might more cogently argue that the greatest of these—the one which comes closest to saying what cannot be said—is fraternity. For without love, liberty "is always in danger of sliding into excess"; and without love, to provide equality of opportunity is merely to give every animal the right to develop his rapacity to the fullest possible extent. This is said with full recognition of the fact that fraternity may become sentimental or bigoted, unless safeguarded by rational interpretations of liberty and equality.

In Section II, the not unfamiliar point that democratic equality can mean no more, and no less, than giving all men an equal chance to become whatever they are capable of becoming, is tellingly set forth. I would demur, however, that the notion of men being equal before God is not meaningless for those who believe that every human soul is equally precious in God's sight. Indeed I doubt the fruitfulness of any conception of equality for which this belief is not fundamental.

The discussion of equality as "a methodological device" in Sections III and IV is interesting. In such thinking as this paper represents, the hard head and the soft heart are often curiously mated. Perhaps, for example, Professor Smith is overoptimistic in supposing that men who fail in a society of equal opportunity will have the honesty and courage to blame no one but themselves. Doubtless, however, the chances of such a result will be greater in a democratic society. To my mind a more serious difficulty arises from Professor Smith's passion for progressively increasing individual variety through a "dynamic competition" from which will somehow emerge a social harmony. Apparently the ghost of Herbert Spencer has not yet been laid.

CHAPTER XVIII

Ethics and Politics

By ROY WOOD SELLARS
Professor Emeritus of Philosophy, University of Michigan

How can authority be put into harmony with freedom? That is a recurrent question which has had different historical contexts. The most usual answer has been in terms of constitutionalism. The Greek city-states had their written and unwritten constitutions of which the best known is that of Athens. This was, itself, the result of a social evolution. A supplementary device was appeal to Natural Law or Reason. A combination of constitutionalism and of Natural Law, was characteristic of the Middle Ages. The freedoms stressed were those of the group or order. Then came economic and social change and the rise of nation-states; and with these appeared centralized authority, strong men, and an increase of statute-law. Authoritarianism and control became the order of the day. Back we come to a new constitutionalism and that stress on freedom which is called liberalism. Governments were to be held responsible to the citizens and Bills of Rights were formulated. In this period our own country was born.

To many, this is the end of the story. But it is not as simple as all that. Freedom from arbitrary government is a high good which is rightly extolled. But it must be recalled that government is tied in with other institutional arrangements and that it is more of a means than an end in itself. Should a responsible government limit itself to the maintenance of law and order? Or should it entertain notions of furthering the general welfare? Should it become a welfare state? There is much need for definition and analysis here.

Early liberalism went with individualism, the emphasis upon *freedom from* authority in religion, politics, and economics, and upon something of a faith in automatic progress. As society became increasingly complicated, it was found that independent liberty and property rights tended to get in the way of needed conditions for positive, or concrete freedom. People required health, education, some measure of security, and such other things as art and beauty and leisure.

In economics, this "new liberalism" moved between interventionism and a gradualistic, evolutionary type of socialism. In this setting the problem of the relation between authority and freedom had long been discussed in terms of centralization and decentralization, federal control, and local autonomy. How was bureaucracy to be mitigated? What was the role of the expert? How was a living consensus to be obtained? Even before the First World War there was a large literature on these subjects. The whole theme was that responsible authority had to be rational authority and freedom had to harmonize with a normative climate of justice, opportunity, and a large measure of equality. Institutions required constant supervision and even reform.

It is clear that the presuppositions of neo-liberalism and of experimental gradualistic socialism were moral, rationalistic, and largely secular. Democracy meant government by discussion and not merely rule by a majority. A minority might in its turn become a majority. Emotion and prejudice were to be held in check by reason and experience. Despite the recognition of historical relativity, human dignity was a finality; and so, in their fashion, were such principles as equality, freedom, and justice, though they needed integration and practical interpretation. The more morality was clarified, the more certain principles stood out. Consideration for others was of its essence. The moral genius was one who had imaginative sensitiveness with respect to his fellow man. The good side of Christianity has, in my opinion, been this; and not its supernaturalism. For America, Jeffersonism had this moral element.

The new liberalism was but a ferment in education, politics, and economics. Institutions were resistant, supported, as they were, by inertia, customs, privileges, intellectual presuppositions. Liberalism had become an ideology which seemed to many a little aloof from current issues, a trifle shopworn, so to speak. And then came an era of competing ideologies. Counter-revolutions confronted revolutions. Reason had to defend itself against irrationalism and mysticism. Party dogma was faced with charismatic leadership. Secularism was challenged by theological revivals. Philosophy, as always, became an integral part of the cultural debate. War was succeeded by power politics in which propaganda and ideology were essential weapons.

I suppose the technical philosopher must now ask himself, as never

Ethics and Politics

before, the difference between social philosophy and ideologies. The Marxist theme has been that ideologies reflect economic situations. The Mannheim conception, developed on this, is that particular ideologies are regarded skeptically as the ideas and representations advanced by opponents, as more or less conscious disguises of the real nature of the situation. Thus, the Communist regards the use of the terms, "free world" and "freedom," by the Western powers, as, to say the least, too unqualified. Are there not institutional controls of all sorts? And do these powers desire basic reform in backward countries? And the Western powers counter by emphasis upon party dictatorship and the control of the press back of the Iron Curtain.

In my opinion, any social philosophy which deserves the name must be thoroughly grounded on careful analysis, reaching from epistemology and ontology to ethics and religion. It must give grounds for its adhesion to such principles as reason and experience. It must be able to point to the inadequacies of irrationalism and intuitionism. It must be a part of a systematic growth, always open to criticism. For instance, it will not adopt a view of human nature of an *a priori* sort, either too optimistic or too pessimistic to fit the facts. Suppose we go into this last point in a little more detail, as ideological controversy makes so much of it.

Neither Hobbes nor Spinoza in the seventeenth century had a perfectionist view of human nature. They laid stress upon personal *conatus* or drive. Hobbes is particularly explicit in his rejection of the traditions that man is a completely socialized animal. And John Locke, though less pessimistic than Hobbes, was an individualist who accepted the fact that disputes would break out in civil society, and that government and enforced law were necessary.

Much of the history of English ethics concerns itself with a qualification of the selfishness theory of Hobbes. And it cannot be said that it ever went to the extreme of unmitigated altruism. The idea was that of a rational balance between egoism and altruism.

It was really economic liberalism that was most optimistic in a grim sort of way. Being against all controls, it argued that competition would bring the best results. A certain proportion of the entrepreneurs would fall by the wayside but enterprise would be served. As for the laborers, their tendency to multiply would keep wages low.

Much is usually made of a brief moment in French thought when the Enlightenment allowed itself to dream of human progress. Reason was to be the guide in human affairs. But it is usually forgotten that Rousseau, the champion of democracy and the General Will, was an admirer of feeling, rather than of reason. And he is concerned to outsmart the selfish will of each and of particular groups in some mysterious, mathematical fashion.

There was considerable optimism in the nineteenth century, especially after the Napoleonic wars, because of technological advance and improvements in health and standards of living. The members of the middle class got a fairly high opinion of their own qualities and virtues, but tended to keep a critical view of the vices of the poor. It is true that doctrines of original sin had less vogue, but that was because of increased secularism.

As has frequently been pointed out, Marxism opposed itself to utopianism, and took a sociological approach in which classes and economic institutions dominated. While Marx himself had moral fervor, he felt that a moralistic approach separated from a realistic analysis of the social scene, could easily mislead. Individuals were largely what their position in society made them. Their ideology *tended* to be that of their class. It is a sociological theory of human nature.

What have been the attitudes and procedures of philosophy with respect to such ideologies? Essentially, an attempt to keep balance and get at the facts. Human nature has deep roots and it develops differently under varying conditions. It is being probed by biologists and psychologists. Social psychology is helping to add perspective. Social philosophy —to distinguish it from ideology—is characterized by comprehensiveness, method, and readiness to consider the results of all the special sciences. The consequence is that it is less apt to go off at a tangent under the influence of crises.

Suppose, then, we look briefly at some contemporary ideologies in the light of social philosophy. The following list will be sufficient: Fascism, Communism, neo-liberalism, and Christian supernaturalism, Thomistic and Calvinistic.

Fascism is defeated but smoldering. In essence, it is a complex of authoritarianism, irrationalism, militarism, nationalism, and the leadership principle, with racialism usually added. The more novel element is that of the theory of leadership. The leader is assumed to have valid *intuitions,* not reached by reason, and testable by discussion and evidence.

It is generally held that some encouragement to this *mystique* was given by Bergson and Nietzsche and even by James's *Will to Believe*. These thinkers fought what they regarded as too superficial types of rationalism. But all of them, I believe, would have been horrified by Fascism.

Because we are interested in the harmony of authority and freedom, it should be noted that Fascism stressed authority. The result is totalitarianism in a monolithic way with the values of the leader dominant. Attempts to curtail free speech and to outlaw minority opinion, or frighten it into silence, cannot, I think, be rightly called Fascistic. They are primarily anti-democratic and have motivations, such as fear for national security, dislike of what groups regard as heretical opinions, readiness to repress attacks upon accepted privileges. Under these circumstances the great need is for *criteria*. Legislatures and courts have a great responsibility at these times.

In any discussion of Communism one must make a distinction between Marxism and the Communist party. Marxism had three dimensions: the political, the economic, and the general philosophical. The political side was dominated by the tradition of the French Revolution; the economic by a critique of English classical economics; the general philosophical by a modification of German, left wing Hegelianism. Because of this breadth and complexity Marxism is an intellectual challenge.

As is well known, social democracy toned down both the revolutionary emphasis and the economic theory of Marx. I suppose the most usual criticism of Marxism is that it did not take into consideration the possibility of interventionism. It set up classes as entities and conceived of them in terms of exploitation and struggle. Perhaps the topic most relevant to our subject is the postulated inevitability of the movement from capitalism to some form of socialism. The result of such an outlook is the demand for orthodoxy; and orthodoxy encourages control and the repression of questioning. The imperatives and coercions here tend to spread to the political field. Much the same phenomenon manifested itself in the past when religious orthodoxy had prestige and a fairly intimate alliance with political authority. A lesser degree of the same sort of thing has accompanied orthodoxy in science and philosophy. The only cure is to give prestige to investigation and rational discussion. Only in this approach lies freedom. If the emphasis were upon truth, even those with strong convictions would continue to support rational examination. Unfortunately, other values of a more personal or a more institutional sort operate.

It is undeniable that political and social tensions cause an appeal to power. Extremes are apt to polarize out of such a situation; and then reason has short shrift. There have been hopes attached to what has been called a *third force,* but the third force has usually turned out to be myopic and traditionalistic. Perhaps a stalemate of extremes might encourage the exploration of positive programs, and activate methods favorable to group understanding. There has been progress in the psychological study of group dynamics. Freedom, undoubtedly, is a moral right, but it needs intelligent implementation.

Neo-liberalism, the last of the three secularistic ideologies mentioned, has always adhered to the machinery of democracy, but has been criticized as too relativistic and too much inclined to dwell upon procedures and legalism. I am, myself, inclined to favor a little more moral absolutism, in terms of the recognition of human dignity, justice, and equality. Such absolutes may well have the functions of guides in the maze of problems confronting mankind. Such is the outlook of what I would call a *humanistic absolutism.* It is absolutistic in the sense that it recognizes the moral equality of human beings as such. This means that the ethical outlook cannot cease to treat them as ends. And experience has shown that conditions of freedom give support to this recognition of human dignity. But this does not mean that I am lapsing into the perfectionalism that the neo-Calvinists condemn.

The anti-secular, or religious, ideologies are relevant to the questions I have raised on two counts. First, they press hard, in their zeal, upon those whose humanism is naturalistic, for they reject the setting of nature and history as too truncated. And, second, social philosophy must justify the credentials of its own asserverations.

In the Calvinistic type we find fused a rather rhetorical stress upon man's intractable badness and a denial that man can do much for himself. A certain amount of this doctrine may be a healthy tonic, but, surely, it can be overdone to the point of discouragement. It is justified to condemn facile optimism in human affairs, but a pessimism used to enforce supernaturalism must be able to defend its premises rationally.

Here, of course, we have the fundamental philosophical question. I can merely indicate my rejoinder. It would take the lines of developing a new, evolutionary naturalism, stressing levels and emergence. Morals, I take to be a social emergent, clarifying itself as it goes from communal mores to rational principles in the service of a growing universalism. Here it is increasingly self-conscious and builds on the recognition of human dignity and the consequences of actions, both in the way of the distribution of happiness and unhappiness and in the way of the consideration of persons.

The polemic of anti-naturalism would be raised to a higher philosophical level, if it did not dwell so persistently on the old, mechanical naturalism alone. There are newer, more adequate forms of naturalism; Kierkegaard was quite right in criticizing Hegelian impersonalism; and existentialism is justified in stressing the human problem of decision. But the ultimate freedom of choice, confronted by tragic alternatives, should be guided by as rational evaluations as possible. It may well be that liberalism was too smug and the tragic sense of life damped down. Ethics and politics need quickening, but, surely, there is no need to escape from reason and experience.

A word on the more sedate Thomism which is seeking to absorb the more flamboyant, Christian existentialism in the doctrine of creative *esse*. The naturalistic humanist moves back to categories other than those of passive matter and active form and, in the modern conception of energy, finds a base for self-existence, or *aseity,* which his own self-consciousness affirms at its peculiar level of being. It has been a question whether emphasis upon God does not tend to drain human life of its intrinsic vitality and self-confidence. And, on the context of freedom, it must be noted that ecclesiastical institutions have claimed authority justified by their credentials. Both secularism and ecclesiasticism have been jealous of the other's claim. Philosophy is a judicial part of this cultural debate. It must claim freedom from authority of an imposed sort, if it is to perform its responsible job.

To keep authority legitimate and in harmony with freedom is, I conclude, a persistent problem which only vigilance can keep under control. On the whole, the tradition of liberalism has been most effective in this work. What we would seem to need today is a positive and reactivated liberalism pushing on from release of authoritative controls to constructive endeavor, to *freedom for* a worthwhile life. It is the duty of philosophy to lead in this cultural debate, for it concerns itself with political and ethical fundamentals. This can be done by naturalizing Natural Law as a term for normative principles intrinsic to the very nature of the moral life as this is clarified and universalized. In this sense, authority, to be rightful, must be responsible to normative principles, and further their practical interpretation and application.

Comment by Barna Horvath:

As against contemporary ideologies, the author adopts *humanistic absolutism,* differing from neo-liberalism in adding to it "a little more moral absolutism, in terms of the recognition of human dignity, justice and equality." His particular point of view is best characterized by what he calls the moral, but what may be said to be also the intellectual, task: "to have an eye on principles, as well as upon diverse situations."

He mentions the "fundamental philosophical question"—one does not see clearly whether he means freedom or supernaturalism—in connection with Calvinism. His "rejoinder" is "evolutionary naturalism, stressing levels and emergence." He takes morals to be "a social emergent, clarifying itself as it goes from communal mores to rational principles in the service of a growing universalism."

In the author's opinion, "existentialism is justified in stressing the human problem of decision," but he objects that "there is no need to escape from reason and experience." Thomism is answered by the assurance that "the naturalistic humanist . . . in the modern conception of energy, finds a base for self-existence, or *aseity,* which his own self-consciousness affirms at its peculiar level of being."

As philosophy "must claim freedom from authority of an imposed sort," consequently, "religion with its emphasis on God," and "both secularism and ecclesiasticism . . . jealous of the other's claim" to authority, are to be judged by the tribunal of philosophy as to whether they do not "tend to drain human life of its intrinsic vitality and self-confidence."

I agree with the humanism of the author, in the sense that governmental authority has to be justified from the point of view of humble people.

But I heartily disagree with him in judging Marxism which he seems to absolve from any responsibility for the politics of the Communist Party inside and outside the Soviet Union. Professor Sellars calls Marxism "an intellectual challenge," whereas, in my opinion, it did not stand the test of scientific criticism. His only objection is to the orthodoxy of "scientific socialism" which he likens to religious orthodoxy. I feel that Marxism is intellectually responsible for *deceiving the masses,* and many intellectuals, by masquerading as science, furthermore for the *decline of individual freedom* and the *rise of authoritarianism,* and lastly for party dictatorship, terror, and mass criminality, as methods of government.

Professor Sellars's reply:

Professor Horvath's analysis of my paper is, in the main, correct and is appreciative of the perspective I had in mind. My outlook is humanistic but I wished to oppose the moral relativism which has no criteria to apply. I am quite ready to criticize the politics of East and West, but find it so hard to find out the facts about conditions and intentions. That holds for the East with hardly any qualification, but of the West with considerable qualification. What are the motives and assumptions underlying specific policies in the United States? I cannot be naive enough to be satisfied with general statements about freedom. After all, we are nationalistic, and our democracy is linked with a highly developed technological capitalism.

As for Marxism, I am critical of its dialectical formula, stemming from Hegelianism, and of unqualified historical materialism. I am what is called a critical realist and a believer in emergent levels. No, I would not absolve either Marxism or the Communist Party from doctrinaireness and dogmatism. I prefer reasonableness, however, to toughness, which will usually be in evidence anyway. And I always agreed with those who held that Pitt did not handle the French Revolution intelligently, and so produced Napoleon.

CHAPTER XIX

Authority and Responsibility

By EDMOND N. CAHN

Professor of Law, New York University

THE SPECTACLE presented by human life being what it is and always has been, there are not many occasions when sounds of really hearty laughter have been heard in heaven. One such instance is reported in the Babylonian Talmud.[1] We are told that at a session of the rabbinical sages, Rabbi Eliezer got into a heated argument over a fine point in the interpretation of the law. After exhausting all his resources of precedent, distinction, analogy, and citation of textual authority without convincing any of them, he became desperate and cried out, "If the law agrees with me, let this tree prove it!" Thereupon the tree leaped a hundred cubits from its place. But the other judges calmly retorted, "No proof can be adduced from a tree." Then he said, "If the law agrees with me, let this stream of water prove it!" At this the stream of water flowed backwards. The others rejoined, however, "No proof can be adduced from a stream of water." Again he called out, "If the law agrees with me, let the walls of the house prove it!" Whereupon the walls began to fall, but Rabbi Joshua rebuked them, saying, "When scholars are engaged in a legal dispute, what right have you to interfere?" And so they did not fall, out of respect for Rabbi Joshua, nor did they resume the upright, out of respect for Rabbi Eliezer, but remained standing and inclined. Finally Rabbi Eliezer said, "If the law agrees with me, let it be proved from heaven!" At that moment a Heavenly Voice cried out, "Why do you dispute with Rabbi Eliezer, seeing that in all matters the law agrees with him?" For a space the assembly sat transfixed, but almost immediately Rabbi Joshua rose from his seat and exclaimed, "The

---

[1] *Baba Mezia* 59b, in *The Babylonian Talmud, Seder Nezikin II*, edited by I. Epstein, The Soncino Press, London, 1935, pp. 352 f. I have paraphrased the passage and pruned from it the reference to Exodus 23.2, which has many controversial interpretations, some of them summarized in *The Soncino Chumash*, edited by A. Cohen, The Soncino Press, Hindhead, Surrey, 1947, p. 487.

law is not in heaven! It was given on Mount Sinai. We pay no attention to a Heavenly Voice."

Soon thereafter one of the rabbis happened to meet the prophet Elijah (who, having been alive when he was transported into the celestial regions, remained able to converse with mortals). The prophet was asked, "What did the Holy One, blessed be He, do at that point?" Elijah replied, "He laughed with joy, saying 'My sons have defeated Me, My sons have defeated Me.'"

This is a happy episode, an episode hard to match for its affirmation of the right of anyone confronted with the duty of reaching a judgment to assume responsibility for his own decision. Miracles cannot deprive him of that right or relieve him of that responsibility, and so he must construe the law as best he can without deferring even to the intervention of a Heavenly Voice. But when such a person has justly disregarded the Heavenly Voice, or *vox dei,* is he necessarily bound to heed and obey the community mores, or *vox populi?* That is the problem to be opened up here.

One of the statutory requirements which must be complied with by an alien before he can become a citizen of the United States, is that he "has been . . . a person of good moral character."[2] The statute, however, does not define what constitutes "good moral character." How is a judge to formulate a standard by which to guide his decision?

Responsibility and Clarity

There is a time to judge, a time to suspend judgment, and a time to refuse to judge. A judge who decides before he has heard both sides and has deliberated conscientiously is guilty of a denial of justice. A judge who decides matters beyond the orbit of his official competence is likewise guilty. And guilty too is a judge who, because the matter seems hard or obscure, refuses to render such judgment as his own capacities make possible. Each of these is an offense against the solemn responsibility that, at least under our system of government, should accompany every grant of coercive power.

The flight from personal responsibility for the decision of moral issues is as old as human society. Customarily, the escape consisted in shifting the burden to some deity or to his priests, or perhaps to the dictates of a

[2] 8 U.S.C. §707 (a) (1946).

political creed or of a party elite. Fanaticism is another time-honored device for evasion of responsibility: the fanatic's obsession provides a single and simple touchstone by which he can test any issue that arises.

American liberals on and off the bench, moreover, have felt special incentives to avoid the burden of deciding moral questions for themselves. They are prompted by an historical incentive—the example of judicial dogmatism during the first part of this century, culminating in the Supreme Court crisis of 1937, and by an idealistic incentive—the principle that governmental prohibitions should be spelled out clearly and explicitly before anyone infringing them can be judged or punished. If the meaning is uncertain, the legislation will be considered "void for vagueness."

Now "void for vagueness" was and is an unimpeachable libertarian concept—in its traditional usage. The judge refuses to judge in such a case because the accused received no intelligible notice from the statute that his act had been forbidden, nor an intelligible specification of the nature of the charges he must prepare to meet on a trial. "Void for vagueness" then affords an impervious shield to the rights of the people.

But of late, "vagueness" has been developing a new and different meaning, a meaning that can be used to discharge, to shift, or evade, or even to repudiate the judge's responsibility. The traditional or primary requirement of certainty was invoked in the interest of the individual accused; this evolving secondary requirement is invoked in the interest of the tribunal. If the statute is considered to be vague, how can the judge define the pertinent issues of fact for the jury's guidance? If he cannot, what is the value of its verdict? And if it is the judge who must determine the facts—because the case on trial is not, strictly speaking, a prosecution for crime—what rule can he formulate for the major premise of his decision? Justice is supposed to influence the content of the legal rule and its use in particular cases, but a rule there must be.[3]

This secondary application of "void for vagueness" covers a lurking danger. A judge who dislikes a statute because it burdens him with difficult or uncongenial duties can escape responsibility where justice requires more than the usual cerebration or sympathetic investigation or moral courage on his part. He may even reason that if decisions in individual cases arising under a statute seem to vary too much from time

---

[3] A commendable statement of this position was made a century ago by Judge Oran M. Roberts in Duncan v. Magette, 25 Tex. 245 (1860), at pp. 252 ff.

to time and court to court, the diversity of outcome is of itself enough to demonstrate the statute's fatal vagueness.

The telling point here is that this kind of analysis, beneficial as it is in some applications and harmful as it is in others, appears more and more frequently in respect of those statutes which have a direct reference to morality. It crops up in connection with such statutory terms as "good moral character," "injurious to public morals," "obscene," or "crime involving moral turpitude."

There remain two other avenues of evasion. One is for the judge who —congenitally or advisedly—thinks too little; the other is for the judge who—to his own dismay—thinks too much, that is, to put it better, "considers too curiously." The unthinking judge can escape his responsibility in these matters by deluding himself that he discharges it, never questioning his own familiar biases or his absolute command of the eternal verities. Whatever he is wont to dislike is, by his test, *per se* immoral, and the pleasures he does not lust for are *per se* acts of sin and turpitude.

The thoughtful judge, on the contrary, may come to trust his own moral judgment far too little. He is too sophisticated to ignore the existence of the problem of moral standards, too well read to forget their relativism, and perhaps too modest to insist on conformity by others to what he deems to be virtuous. His democratic loyalties may seem to compel him as judge to accept and enforce the standards of the popular majority. And so he sets about to call "moral" what the community would approve, and "immoral" what it would condemn if it were somehow placed in the seat of judgment. And then—

And then his oracle stands uncommunicative and mute. Or if the popular voice can be heard at all, it utters commands in a riotous confusion of tongues, each denouncing the others, and all contradictory and irreconcilable, babbling at him without message, guidance, or sense. What, in such a plight, is this thoughtful judge to do?

Crime and Character

For a variety of reasons, I shall take Judge Learned Hand as the specimen of the good and thoughtful judge confronted with this dilemma. Judge Hand went on the United States District Court in 1909. In that same year there appeared John Chipman Gray's *The Nature and Sources of the Law,* one of the finest products of American juristic thought. Professor Gray wrote:

> We all agree that many cases should be decided by the courts on notions of right and wrong, and of course everyone will agree that a judge is likely to share the notions of right and wrong prevalent in the community in which he lives; but suppose in a case where there is nothing to guide him but notions of right and wrong, that his notions of right and wrong differ from those of the community,—which ought he to follow— his own notions, or the notions of the community? . . . I believe that he should follow his own notions.[4]

Gray, as I understand him, placed the responsibility for decisions of right and wrong on the shoulders of the judge, and insisted that the judge formulate his decision only after consulting external sources in order to refine his internal evaluation.

At that stage of his career Judge Hand apparently would have been disposed to agree with Professor Gray. At any rate, for the twenty years following his appointment to the bench Judge Hand's opinions[5] in cases involving deportation, exclusion, or naturalization of aliens, were direct, forthright expressions of his intelligence and sympathy for humanity. In 1929, a turn toward a different direction was taken.

It was in a case involving an Italian named Iorio[6] who, after residing in this country and returning to Sicily to visit his mother, obtained an American visa without revealing to the American Vice-Consul that he had incurred several minor fines and jail sentences in the United States for the possession and sale of liquor. The Government, noting that after his return to this country Iorio had resumed his illicit trade, proposed to deport him, and the case came before Judge Hand's court on Iorio's appeal.

Yet the judges who heard Iorio's appeal could not convince themselves that he had been guilty of "moral turpitude," such as would require his deportation under the statute. The right decision was reached—by means of wrong reasons. Judge Hand wrote:

---

[4] John Chipman Gray, *The Nature and Sources of the Law,* The Macmillan Company, New York, 2nd edition, 1938, pp. 287 f.

[5] The early opinions are listed and classified in "A Table of Opinions of Judge Learned Hand, 1909–1946," *Harvard Law Review,* LX, 3, 1947 (an issue dedicated to Judge Hand).

[6] United States *ex rel.* Iorio v. Day, 34 F. 2d 920 (2d Cir. 1929).

> We do not regard every violation of a prohibition law as a crime involving moral turpitude. While we must not, indeed, substitute our personal notions as the standard, it is impossible to decide at all without some estimate, necessarily based on conjecture, as to what people generally feel. We cannot say that among the commonly accepted mores the sale or possession of liquor as yet occupies so grave a place; nor can we close our eyes to the fact that large numbers of persons, otherwise reputable, do not think it so, rightly or wrongly.[7]

Thus the scapegoat of the "common conscience" or community opinion carried off the burden that the judges quite understandably considered too heavy for their own shoulders. But the trouble with a scapegoat is that the convenience of the arrangement tempts us to foist every burden on it, including those that we could quite easily handle without outside help. And this is what Judge Hand found himself doing in the next such case[8] that came along.

In February, 1938, a man named Berlandi pleaded guilty to concealing liquor with intent to defraud the Government of whiskey taxes, and in May, 1938, he pleaded guilty to conspiring with others to commit exactly the same offense. Federal laws provide that an alien who has more than once been sentenced to more than a year of imprisonment because of conviction of "a crime involving moral turpitude"[9] shall be deported. Berlandi was ordered deported and his appeal came before Judge Hand's court.

This time the other two circuit judges, Augustus N. Hand and Robert P. Patterson, disagreed with Judge Learned Hand. The court's opinion, written by Judge Augustus N. Hand, distinguished the moral situation from that in the *Iorio* case. Prohibition had been repealed, and Berlandi was simply trying to profit by evading taxes, that is, by cheating the Government and thus increasing the fiscal burden on all other taxpayers. So the majority of the court, affirming the order of deportation, considered the case to be one of fraud and entertained no doubt that fraud is a badge of moral turpitude.

Judge Learned Hand, however, found himself caught in the net he had woven when he wrote the *Iorio* opinion. Candor required him to say that he wished:

---

[7] *Ibid.*, at pp. 920, 921.
[8] United States *ex rel*. Berlandi v. Reimer, 113 F. 2d 429 (2d Cir. 1940).
[9] 8 U.S.C. § 155 (a) (1946).

it was commonly thought more morally shameful than it is to evade taxes; but it is certainly true that people who in private affairs are altogether right-minded see nothing more than a peccadillo in smuggling, or in escaping excises on liquor. . . . We must try to appraise the moral repugnance of the ordinary man to the conduct in question; not what an ideal citizen would feel.[10]

No one can doubt that if Judge Hand had seen fit to follow Professor Gray's admonition and had applied his own notions of right and wrong, he would have agreed with his colleagues. But by subordinating his own moral principles to those of the marketplace, Judge Hand seriously distorted the function of the court as pedagogue and moral mentor in a democratic society. Instead of exercising such influence as he could to raise the morals of the marketplace to a level approaching his own, he expressed an attitude of resignation in the face of fraud.

From the pen of almost any other judge, these views would be less dangerous. But as the *New York Times* said (May 18, 1951) in its editorial tribute to Judge Hand on his retirement, "His decisions and opinions have had the respect—and sometimes the very humble respect—of justices . . . on the Supreme Bench." This editorial appeared less than two weeks after a decision of the Supreme Court dealing with the issue of "moral turpitude,"[11] a decision in which three dissenting Justices—Jackson, Black, and Frankfurter—took Judge Hand's views in the *Berlandi* case as their point of departure. Indeed there can be no doubt that his opinions are read with respect.

The Supreme Court decision just mentioned involved another alien vendor of whiskey, Sam DeGeorge, who had defrauded the Government of more than $10,000 in alcohol taxes. The majority of the Supreme Court ruled that conspiring to defraud the United States is a "crime involving moral turpitude."

However, the three dissenters reached the position, which Judge Hand had only prepared for them without articulating it for his own account, that the statutory phrase, "moral turpitude," is unconstitutional, because it is "void for vagueness."

But what has all this to do with the ascertainment of "good moral character" for the purpose of granting naturalization to aliens? There would appear to be a real difference in kind between one provision im-

---
[10]United States *ex rel.* Berlandi v. Reimer, *op. cit.,* at p. 431.
[11]Jordan v. DeGeorge, 71 S. Ct. 703, 341 U.S. 223 (1951).

posing the penalty of deportation and another provision specifying the conditions for granting of the privilege of citizenship. The nature of the judge's duty, moreover, is very different in the two situations. Under the deportation statute the judge has only specific convictions to consider; he is not concerned with other features of the alien's biography. But when considering an application for naturalization, the judge must evaluate not two dramatic instances of overt conduct but the whole human personality.

Notwithstanding these rather weighty disparities, Judge Hand has made it clear in his naturalization decisions that his criterion of "good moral character" follows the standard which he announced in the deportation cases concerning "moral turpitude." In judging "good moral character," he consults the "moral feelings now prevalent generally in this country" or "the common conscience prevalent at the time."[12]

But again and again Judge Hand has reported with dismay that he cannot identify the community's moral feelings: "Our duty in such cases, as we understand it, is to divine what the 'common conscience' prevalent at the time demands; and it is impossible in practice to ascertain what in a given instance it does demand."[13]

Of course it is impossible to find out what the common conscience demands "in a given instance." It is impossible not only because there is no way of nailing down the community's general standards of moral evaluation, but even more significantly, because the community cannot conceivably know the myriad circumstances of a unique individual biography.

By means of its legislation the community says to the judge, "Ascertain whether this man has had good moral character for the past five years." Judge Hand's approach returns that task to the community, a sort of *renvoi* which leaves the societal purpose unfulfilled.

Hard Cases and Bad Law

As the old maxim has it, "Hard cases make bad law." This seems true of Judge Hand's *Iorio* opinion. But it may likewise be said that "Bad law makes hard cases," and, assuredly, in the light of the standard he chose to adopt, Judge Hand has had to decide some very difficult issues

---

[12] See United States v. Francioso, 164 F. 2d 163 (2d Cir. 1947).
[13] Johnson v. United States, 186 F. 2d 588, 590 (2d Cir. 1951).

of "good moral character." Destiny has presented him with a variety of borderline situations in the vaguest area of all—sexual morality.

In 1935 Judge Hand joined in an opinion written by Judge Swan holding that, without evidence of extenuating circumstances, a single act of adultery by a married man was sufficient to demonstrate that he was not of good moral character under "generally accepted moral standards of the community."[14] In 1947, however, Judge Hand had to consider the case of a man named Francioso who, after coming to this country and settling in Connecticut, had married his niece there, though he knew when he married her that Connecticut law would treat the marriage as incestuous.[15]

This is the case in which Judge Hand declared that "good moral character" should be determined by the same kind of resort to community feelings as "crime involving moral turpitude." It is doubtful, however, that anyone reading his opinion would conclude that he had made a serious effort to ascertain the community feeling, except perhaps from his reference to the circumstance that a priest of the Roman Catholic Church had solemnized the marriage with the consent of his bishop. Otherwise the opinion reads like a reflective exposition of Learned Hand's own reasons for not passing judgment of condemnation on the applicant Francioso.

When the next case involving sexual mores came before him, Judge Hand resumed the search that had so often ended in futility, the search for a judgment in minds other than his own. Here the applicant, one Adolf Schmidt, a teacher in the College of the City of New York, thirty-nine years of age and unmarried, openly stated to the Government examiner that he had occasionally engaged in sexual intercourse with various unmarried women. Who can blame Judge Hand for referring wryly to Schmidt's "unnecessary frankness"?

This time again Judge Hand adhered to his community-feeling criterion. He felt compelled, however, to concede that there was no practicable way "to conduct an inquiry as to what is the common conscience on the point." And so Mr. Schmidt was held to be a person of good moral character "so far as we can divine anything so tenebrous and impalpable as the common conscience."[16] The outcome was obviously correct, but

[14] Estrin v. United States, 80 F. 2d 105 (2d Cir. 1935).
[15] United States v. Francioso, *loc. cit.*
[16] Schmidt v. United States, 177 F. 2d 450 (2d Cir. 1949) at pp. 451, 452.

rarely does one observe a judge insisting with such tenacity on a rule of decision while he himself effectually demonstrates its worthlessness.

Finally, at the beginning of 1951, Judge Hand held that a Simeon Machnowitz Johnson had not succeeded in showing that he was a person of good moral character.[17] Johnson had failed to support his legal wife and for a space of years had been living with a married paramour. Again the judge expressed despair as to the possibility of ascertaining the "views of the common conscience" and he added:

> Nor is it possible to make use of general principles, for almost every moral situation is unique. Theoretically, perhaps we might take as the test whether those who would approve the specific conduct would outnumber those who would disapprove; but it would be fantastically absurd to try to apply it. So it seems to us that we are confined to the best guess we can make of how such a poll would result.[18]

These cases have dealt with problems of sexual morality. A 1947 decision by Judge Hand arose in an entirely different moral area.[19] In September, 1944, one Louis Repouille applied for citizenship. In October, 1939, he had deliberately put his thirteen year old son to death by means of chloroform. The child was an idiot and a physical monstrosity, blind, mute, and deformed, incapable of feeding itself or of controlling the movements of its bladder and bowels. Repouille had four normal children whose nurture was seriously prejudiced by the effort and money involved in caring for the unfortunate one. He was convicted of manslaughter in the second degree, with a recommendation of utmost clemency, and the trial judge suspended execution of the prison sentence.

Here again Judge Hand rehearsed the familiar reasons why a determination of the community standard was impracticable. Then he moved swiftly to the conclusion "that only a minority of virtuous persons would deem the practice [of euthanasia] morally justifiable, while it remains in private hands, even when the provocation is as overwhelming as it is in this instance." How that minority was ascertained to be a minority, in fact, how the "virtuous persons" were identified in order to be consulted, the reader of the opinion will not discover. He will

---

[17] Johnson v. United States, *op. cit.*
[18] *Ibid.*, at pp. 588, 590.
[19] Repouille v. United States, 165 F. 2d 152 (2d Cir. 1947). Dissenting in this case, Judge Jerome Frank invited Judge Hand to test his standard by applying it with some semblance of statistical consistency; Judge Hand warily avoided the challenge.

discover, however, that Judge Hand at least took the course of caution, for by the time Repouille's case reached the circuit court more than five years had elapsed since the date of the mercy killing. Thus, the judge was able to add: ". . . the pitiable event, now long passed, will not prevent Repouille from taking his place among us as a citizen."[20]

Two Responsible Courses

The reader needs no elaboration now as to what I consider the two irresponsible courses in the ascertainment of "good moral character." They are: (1) any evaluation of moral character made without critical examination of all the biographical circumstances and of the judge's own familiar presuppositions and biases; and (2) any evaluation of moral character for which the judge assigns responsibility to the feelings, standards, or conscience of the community. What are the responsible ways to deal with this problem? I see two; they are quite different in result.

One way is to hold the statute unconstitutional in so far as it requires proof of "good moral character." An argument can be made in support of this result, comprising the following propositions: (a) The statute in this respect is "void for vagueness" because it establishes no standard which can be practicably administered; (b) ascertainment of "good moral character" is not a proper judicial function, since it involves judgment without benefit of rules; (c) since the Constitution requires "an uniform Rule of Naturalization,"[21] the statute is unconstitutional because uniformity is impossible to attain in its application; (d) the statute is unconstitutional because its requirement that the general desert of an individual be adjudicated is incompatible with our democratic tradition that all procedures be directed to the ascertainment of an individual's particular desert in connection with specific sets of relations or specific combinations of conduct. The crux of these arguments is that Congress has called upon the federal judge to act as a sort of father confessor or psychoanalyst or theoretical ethicist, not as the wielder of the judicial power.

Yet, the foregoing arguments show at most that the statute is undesirable, not that it is unconstitutional. The statute does in fact call on a

[20]*Ibid.* at pp. 153, 154.
[21]*United States Constitution,* Article I, § 8.

judge to do something for which virtually no one, on or off the bench, is ideally equipped; nevertheless, misgivings as to one's competence do not ordinarily furnish a constitutional gravamen for avoiding one's duties.[22] Unless and until the language of the statute is amended to achieve more precision, the judge who deems its present form to be constitutional should be ready to shoulder the responsibility it imposes on him.

In executing that responsibility there is little reason to fear that a judge, relying on his own deliberate reflections and the call of his own conscience, will apply erratic, capricious, or idiosyncratic moral standards. Our judges are products of our society, and as Professor Gray noted, they will generally think along with the beliefs of some substantial segment of the citizenry. A man who uses a moral standard that no one shares in a population of 150 million probably does not belong at large, much less on the bench. Irrationality we need hardly fear; we have more cause to fear the making of decisions by a judge who deems himself the mouthpiece of an unidentifiable, amorphous, and irresponsible mass.

A judge evaluates "moral character" in one way or another every time he listens to a witness testifying before him. That is the way he decides whom to believe and what testimony to disregard. What is new and special in connection with naturalization is the heightened duty to judge after most painstaking investigation of all the circumstances, after sympathetic understanding of unique individual motives, and after careful criticism of the judge's own customary biases.

Generally speaking, it is the best and finest of judges who afflict themselves with the whips of doubt while their inferior colleagues remain in a state of complacency. What the community needs most is the moral leadership[23] of such a man as Learned Hand and the full benefit of his mature and chastened wisdom. The community is perhaps not at fault

[22] At least so Justice Jackson thought when he wrote the court's opinion in West Virginia State Board of Education v. Barnette, 319 U.S. 624 (1943) (the second Jehovah's Witness "flag-salute" case).

[23] In an analogous situation arising under provisions of the French Civil Code, certain theorists of the sociological school have urged the courts of France to follow a course which would in effect parallel Judge Hand's; but their proposals have gone unheeded. As Ripert puts it, "Les tribunaux résistant à ces pitoyables suggestions. Ils savent qu'ils sont les censeurs des passions humaines et non leur serviteurs. Ils ne croient pas que la mode fasse la justice." George Ripert, *La Règle Morale dans les Obligations Civiles,* Librairie générale de droit & jurisprudence, Paris, 4th edition, 1949, pp. 40–73.

when it calls upon him and those like him to test and determine the good moral character of aliens who wish to join its ranks.

The path of personal responsibility, thorny though it be, remains the only path anyone has ever found to wise and righteous judgment. In the end, the sages could discover nothing more specific to say than:

> In every good work trust thy own soul; for this is the keeping of the commandments. . . . Let reason go before every enterprise, and counsel before every action. . . . And let the counsel of thine own heart stand: for there is no man more faithful unto thee than it. For a man's mind is sometime wont to tell him more than seven watchmen, that sit above in an high tower. . . . (Ecclesiasticus 32.23; 37.10, 13-14.)

Little enough it seems, yet this little is quite sufficient to make us lift our heads and throw back our slumping shoulders. Need we be told again what we have always known? There is no nobler sight than a good man in session with himself and prepared to answer for the outcome.

Comment by Rudolf Allers:

The essay by Professor Cahn raises incidentally an issue which has little to do with authority, but quite something with both freedom and responsibility, that, namely, inherent in the attitude of the community in regard to certain individuals. It is not a legal question, or only remotely so.

Suppose a man is guilty of an action which is characterized—by any criterion whatsoever—as one of "moral turpitude." Suppose, the time when this action took place is many years past. It may be that the action has no longer any legal consequences in the sense that it would be prosecuted, if of such a kind as to render prosecution legal. Is then this person to be viewed as not having been and not being a person of "good moral character"?

This seems to me a question not so much of legal procedure—though it has this aspect, too—but primarily one of morality. And also one of empirical anthropology. In the kingdom of heaven there is more joy over a converted sinner than over ninety-nine just men. This is the law of the *civitas caelestis*. What is the law of the *civitas terrena*?

Comment by Barna Horvath:

Professor Cahn expounds a thesis highly interesting and stimulating even to those who are unable to accept his conclusions without reserve. He holds that the judge has to shoulder the responsibility the statute imposes on him, by interpreting phrases of the statute, such as "moral turpitude" or "good moral character," according to his own individual opinion, instead of trying to explore the common conscience of the people.

Perhaps it serves some useful purpose to ask how the subject matter of this paper is related to the general theme of this Conference. When Professor Cahn urges the judge to shoulder responsibility, he seems to fight for the *freedom* of the judge, his emancipation from the authority of public opinion. Responsibility, in this context, takes the place of freedom. From the point of view of the individual litigant, as well as from that of the legislature, however, the individual conscience of the judge, interpreting those phrases of the statute, is established as *authority,* replacing that of the common conscience. The problem might be formulated, perhaps, as that of whether the statute authorizes the judge to interpret those phases according to his own individual conscience or according to the common conscience.

But Professor Cahn uses another language when he speaks of the evasion of responsibility. By declaring the statute "void for vagueness," by never questioning his own familiar biases or his absolute command of the eternal verities, the judge is said to *escape* responsibility, no less than by accepting the moral standards of the popular majority.

The paradoxical conclusion seems to be that the judge *frees* himself from responsibility by succumbing to authority. This language seems to suggest that the judge is free (from responsibility) when he is bound (by authority), whereas he is bound (by responsibility) whenever he is free (from authority).

There is no doubt, however, that Professor Cahn means by responsibility the freedom of the judge from the authority of public opinion; but he looks at it from the angle of shouldering a burden. By using such language, he points out wisely that the exercise of freedom is tied up with the burden of responsibility, while in the legal field freedom is protected by, and in so far turns into authority.

To proceed to the particular issue treated in this paper, I find the following apparent contradictions in the argument. The dissenting opinions of Justices Jackson, Black, and Frankfurter who held that the statutory phrase, "moral turpitude," is unconstitutional, are mentioned with apparent disapproval. Yet the author himself calls it later a responsible way to hold the statute unconstitutional, as it is "void for vagueness"—a course characterized formerly as a "lurking danger" of escaping responsibility.

A more serious contradiction appears between the characterization of the "unthinking judge" and the author's optimism that a judge "relying on his own deliberate reflections and the call of his own conscience" will not "apply erratic, capricious, or idiosyncratic moral standards."

Have we, indeed, "more cause to dread the making of decisions by one who deems himself the mouthpiece of an unidentifiable, amorphous, and irresponsible mass," or by one to whom "whatever he is wont to dislike is, by his test, *per se* immoral, and the pleasures he does not lust for are *per se* acts of sin and turpitude"?

This legal-political, rather than philosophical, question is the real issue of this paper. Whether the optimism of the author is warranted in this or that country, I do not know. Generally speaking, I would doubt it, as greatness, in my experience, is something exceptional, whether among judges or men in general.

Moreover, the example of totalitarian justice warns us that vague phrases in statutes and their free judicial interpretation may serve as the instrument of *dictatorial,* instead of liberal, programs. I am sure Professor Cahn himself would ask us to bind the judge, rather than to rely on his individual conscience, were he aware of a reactionary wave of the average judicial conscience.

The dilemma of the judge who *would like* to listen to *vox populi,* but is *unable* to clear it up with any degree of exactitude, is a sure sign of high judicial culture. In my view, such a judge does *not* escape responsibility; on the contrary, he shoulders its double weight. The solution of the dilemma seems to be simple. The law does not want the judge to take public opinion polls; it wants him only to try to harmonize his own with the common conscience as far as he is *aware of it.*

But if this be true, then what is the problem? If (a) even the judge's individual opinion will reflect public opinion, while (b) he is unable to state the latter precisely, what is the difference between the author's and the criticized judge's position? When a judge follows public opinion more liberal than his own individual conscience, why is this bad from the liberal standpoint? If the facts are the same with either formulation, why is it preferable for the judge to purport he is voicing exclusively his own, instead of public, opinion? Is he more responsible in carrying the burden alone?

I am the last to deny that judicial decision is, in the last analysis, a morally relevant act. In so far the judge is responsible for it, whether he invokes the statute and public opinion, or not. But I would hesitate to stress, in a democracy, the basically *aristocratic* principle that judges should refuse to listen to the *vox populi,* even when this latter be more liberal or more lenient than is their own conscience.

The hard core of both the judge's and the author's complaint is, however, that there is *nothing* to blend with the judge's individual opinion. The weight of the author's objection is that the judge both *admits* the impossibility of finding out the state of public opinion and *claims* his judgment to be dependent on it. He is tormented by the insincerity of his purported dependence on public opinion, where there is no public opinion. The judicial mind is tormented by its suspense in the gap between being the creature or the creator of public opinion.

We may relieve the judicial mind somewhat by stating that, at least theoretically, there is no dilemma at all. All he is asked to do is to take into consideration trends of public opinion, to the extent he can find them out. To the extent that he finds nothing in public opinion to agree or disagree with, his own measured opinion is *vox populi*. It is a novel product of the deepest currents of national conscience, working through his own frame of mind by way of education and tradition.

CHAPTER XX

The Relation of Law to Freedom and Authority

By JULIUS COHEN

Professor of Law, College of Law, The University of Nebraska

IF LAW IS a form of authority; if authority implies coercion, and coercion restraint; if the essence of freedom is the absence of restraint—it is obvious that, implicit in any discussion of law, is the problem of freedom. To the extent that law restrains man from interfering with the activities of others, *he* is not free. But to the extent that the restraint permits the activities of *others,* then *they* are free. Thus, where law exists, freedom is created at the same time it is denied. By denying one the freedom to kill, law gives everyone else that much more freedom to live; by denying one the freedom to steal, law gives everyone else that much more freedom to enjoy his possessions. By denying one the freedom to spend all of his earnings (taxation), the law gives others that much more freedom to travel (roads), to obtain an education (schools). Indeed, the freedom to do what law permits one to do would be non-existent if it did not, at the same time, effectively prevent everyone else from interfering with that freedom. Freedom, thus conceived, is a relational concept; the references above to "him," "others," to "one," "everyone else," suggests that, when it is protected by law, it consists of rights *against other* human beings. When so viewed, "freedom"—like "property" and other abstract concepts of law—loses a certain aura of the mystical, and permits of translation into concrete positive terms.

If law is merely an *instrument* of authority, that is, a *means,* it is obvious that its concern is only with the effectiveness of its authority, and not whether the authority is employed for good or bad ends. The goodness or badness of ends is a problem of ethics or morals; law as an instrumental means is amoral. If the freedom to kill, to steal, or to spend all of one's earnings is granted; if the freedom to resist being killed, or having one's property stolen, or the freedom to travel over roads or receive an education is denied, the law which enforces these patterns of human relationship is still law, no matter how much it offends one's sense of justice. Whether there is law, then, depends on whether there is an enforceable system of freedoms and restraints. Whether there is *just* law depends on (1) the distributive scheme of the restraints and freedoms, *i.e.,* on who gets what restraints and corresponding freedoms, and on the nature of their human consequences; and (2) a measurement of these consequences against a given scale of values. To determine the first involves empirical research—a venture into the realm of the "is"; the second involves a search for a normative steering gear—a venture into the realm of the "ought."

Despite the influence of the utilitarianism of Bentham and Mill, of the pragmatism of Duguit and Dewey, of *Der Zweck im Recht* of von Jhering, of the sociological jurisprudence of Pound; despite the impact of their "functionalist" and "realist" satellites in this country—all of whom share the common view that the consequences of law should be measured—there has been more talk than performance in this direction.

The inability of the social and psychological sciences to attain even a small degree of the stature of the physical sciences, is primarily due to the comparative complexities of the subject matter with which they deal. The factors are so complex that doubt still remains in respectable circles whether the establishment of invariant relations between them is, indeed, ever possible. But until such relations are established, how can the human consequences resulting from the distributive scheme of our restraints and freedoms be reliably measured? How ever to know that the given consequences actually flow from the distributive scheme? In the absence of such knowledge there remains only guess work, or shrewd hunch, or the unverified hypotheses of the "experts"—obviously slim fare for those few amongst the policy-makers (the legislators, the administrators, the judges, etc.) who seek firmer grounds upon which to base their actions. These policy-makers are ill equipped to undertake experimental studies of their own—even those of the "short-run" variety —concerning the consequences of their decisions; legislators and administrators, though better equipped than courts (by way of access to resources, personnel) have not been in too experimental a mood. It would seem, then, that the first hurdle—the ascertainment and measurement of the consequences of our distributive scheme of freedoms and restraints

—remains in a stage that is both formative, and needless to say, formidable.

But assuming, *arguendo,* that significant inroads can be made by the social and psychological sciences in the determination and measurement of these consequences, equally formidable is the second hurdle—that of ascertaining whether these consequences are consistent with the value goals which most people seek to attain.

There are those who are of the view that the determination of the consequences of our freedom-restraint relationships will, by and of itself, somehow yield information concerning the "fairness," "goodness," or "justness" of this distributive scheme. By no amount of legerdemain, however, can one ever obtain a valid "ought" conclusion solely from "is" premises. The advocates of this position are either ignorant of the obvious logical fallacy which it involves, or are the victims of a crypto-idealism which identifies "fairness," "goodness," or "justness" with whatever happens to be the *status quo*—a view which would justify the cruelest, most tyrannical oppressions as "just," merely by pointing to the fact that they exist. Obviously, although knowledge of the *status quo* and its consequences is necessary for its evaluation, it is, in itself, not sufficient. There must in addition be some method for determining whether the freedom-restraint relationships which exist are in or out of tune with our basic moral values. This involves a thorough search for and discovery of these values, an exposure and articulation of those that are implicit in our expressed and tacit choices, and finally their systematization and harmonization into a rational system—in short, the application of scientific method to the field of ethics. Clearly, no amount of such systematization and harmonization of our basic values will yield any *absolute* moral rules with which to test or measure the adequacy of our existing freedom-restraint relationships. Ultimate ends are matters not determined by reason; they are matters of choice. But if the light of reason is permitted to shine on our choices, it will aid us in clarifying what they involve. Man is not always aware of what his values really are until he is given a clearer picture of their implications and consequences. Often the restraints which, at first blush, seem to jibe with our basic values, turn out, upon reflection, actually to be in conflict with them. Just as it is the purpose of the natural sciences to make us aware that often what we *think* we see is not what we actually do see, so it would be the purpose of a scientific ethics to make us aware that the freedom-restraint relationships that we often think are proper or just, may not actually be consistent with our moral values.

There are those who would suggest that the variability of moral judgments makes it impossible to systematize or harmonize them. But variability in itself does not preclude the establishment of system or harmony. To the contrary, it is the very existence of variables that prompts the search for the invariant relations that will account for and explain them. If the variation of human eyesight is not incompatible with the existence of standards or principles for the correction of vision, why then should the variation of human judgments suggest the absence of standards or principles for the correction of values? Just as judgments concerning the correction of vision must take account of differences in vision, so judgments of right and wrong must allow for differences in circumstances of time, place, etc. As in the natural sciences, the search is for the discovery of more and more general principles under which the variables may be harmonized and subsumed.

But how proceed? One might start with certain crude hypotheses concerning the nature of these moral values, develop their implications and then ascertain whether these latter jibe with our actual experiences. If they do not, it is a signal for the need to revamp the hypothesis so as to account for inconsistencies. As in physics, the course is from general principle (hypothesis) to fact (particular instances of what people actually desire); and from fact back to principle again. Thus, we might begin with the hypothesis that freedom from economic insecurity is held as a basic value by most people. Facts of experience might reveal, however, that the hypothesis is valid only under certain circumstances—for example, when it would not be at a cost that would require the sacrifice of other strong moral principles, such as those against stealing or cheating. This would require an extension or revamping of the original hypothesis to permit the factual exceptions to be encompassed. Just as the object of the physical sciences is the constant search for more accurate and more inclusive principles that best express the realities of physical nature, so in ethics there must be a constant search for more accurate and inclusive moral principles that best express man's emotional and volitional nature. The better the generalizations in the physical realm, the less they will conflict with any possible physical observations; the better the generalizations in the realm of values, the less they will be in conflict with any possible moral observations.

The Relation of Law to Freedom and Authority

For those lawmen who are concerned not only with the impact of our existing freedom-restraint relationships, but with the ascertainment of their ethical implications—the road ahead, is, indeed, not an easy one. For this latter task, however, the lawman's talents could well be tapped. There is his training in critical, logical analysis; his penchant for synthesis. He is at home with normative propositions, because a great deal of his work-a-day life consists in endeavoring to persuade policy-makers that existing policy *ought* or *ought not* be changed. It is the first task—that of ascertaining the consequences of our freedom-restraint relationships—that for him poses the real problem. For this, the age of specialization makes it virtually necessary that the lawman lean almost exclusively on the shoulders of the "experts"—the theoretical economists, sociologists, anthropologists, and psychologists, to tell him *what* to measure; and on the shoulders of the statisticians to tell him *whether* and how. That the shoulders of those who deal scientifically with human factors are still despairingly soft, cannot be gainsaid. It obviously does not follow from this that reliant muscles can never be developed. But it does follow that, until they are, the real meaning of "freedom" is, at best, still determinable; it awaits much more experimentation and knowledge than we now have to make it determinate. And until more is done to discover, clarify, and systematize the basic values by which law itself is to be judged, law must primarily remain what Hobbes long ago suggested —an instrument of force for settling what otherwise would be open to dispute.

Comment by Thomas A. Cowan:

The task of commenting on this closely reasoned and compact paper on *The Relation of Law to Freedom and Authority* is indeed formidable. The paper presupposes a whole philosophy of science, and raises problems of methodology so comprehensive in character that one is well advised to exercise considerable restraint in commenting on it. Accordingly, I propose to address myself exclusively to the discussion on the relation of the "is" and the "ought" in law. As indicated by Professor Cohen, this is in effect a problem of the relation of law to a possible science of ethics.

The separation of actually existing tenets of the law from the moral principles or objectives it strives to attain, is a problem inherited from classical times. Modern perspective, however, views the separation as resulting from incomplete insight. The organic view that "is" and "ought" can be separated in law, only as a result of an abstraction, and that such abstraction is no longer fruitful, is coming more and more to represent the "modern" insight. It is argued, for example, that every legal fact represents an actually existent legal choice; that in law, at least, all judgments are value judgments, and every legal synthesis in the form of precept, rule, principle, or system, is a congeries of value judgments; and that the science of law (imperfect as it is) is a more or less coherent series of judgments as to what ought to have been done in the law's past, what ought now to be done, or what the law ought to do in the future. Hence, social scientists attempting to study volitional choices of human beings must be warned that they ignore the vast experience of the law in dealings with human volition at their peril.

As consequence of these reflections on Professor Cohen's paper, there emerges a suggestion that the way to make a start on the experimental science of ethics is to tackle legal problems. The value aspect of the matter will inescapably receive paramount attention. To test this statement in the concrete, consider a possible experiment in the law of crimes and of criminal administration. The problem of petit larceny suggests itself. The enforcement of the law of petit larceny (a moral necessity) runs immediately into the problems of expense and effectiveness of enforcement (economic necessities). Experiments could be devised to determine the most efficient method of enforcing the law of small thefts. Important byproducts of such an undertaking would be objective data on the relative value of enforcement as against ignoring violations of the law, of changes in criminal statutes, and other value judgments important for law reform. The immediate effect of the studies might be to save casualty insurance companies huge sums of money, and to leave the enforcement agents of the law free for other more important tasks.

Comment by Barna Horvath:

This lucidly written and thoughtful paper raises two kinds of problems. One of them concerns the clarification of the legal sense of freedom and authority, as well as their relation, and is directly pertinent to the topic of this Conference. The other group of problems concerns the necessity and difficulty of empirical and normative research into the conditions which contribute to make a *given* legal order just or conducive to "real" freedom.

Accepting the basic statement that "the essence of freedom is the absence of restraint," is the author's view correct that freedom, in the legal field, "consists of rights *against other* human beings"? If this is admitted, freedom can hardly be distinguished from authority. Whoever has a right against another human being, whether claim or capability, is authorized to exercise it. More akin to freedom are privilege and immunity, as legal exemptions from duty and liability. This use of the legal term is nearest to the Roman *status libertatis* or to the basic principle of *una et eadem libertas* of the nobility, in the *Tripartitum* of *Werboeczy* (1514). But whatever is *due* from others, or to others, and whatever *can* be done against others, or against ourselves by others, is always subject to *chances,* adverse or propitious, and is, therefore, not the citadel of legal freedom. This latter is that inner core or kernel of autonomy which consists in our free choice as to enjoyment of the *objects* of rights, legally protected and safeguarded by rights, but in itself legally irrelevant. It includes our freedom to renounce our rights, but its clearest example is to do as we like (within limits) in our home, to whistle or listen to music, to wear blue or green neckties or no necktie at all, etc. Legally free, in this narrowest sense, is the behavior which has no legal consequences at all (but is the remote goal of all legal safeguards).

It is a matter of dispute whether this legal freedom is the creature of law or the residue of the original freedom invaded by law. There is no doubt that law serves (may serve) as its bulwark, but it does not follow that man is *authorized* by law to be free. He is authorized, and other agents, topmost among them courts, are authorized, to exercise rights, claims, and capabilities, or jurisdiction against offenders, in order to safeguard and protect freedom. Legal *authority* is best understood in terms of (Kelsenian) normative logic, as the higher norm from which the validity of a lower norm is derived; or as the validity of *res judicata (autorité de la chose jugée).*

The dividing line between legal freedom and authority is *private autonomy.* Some of the classical human rights and freedoms belong to genuine legal freedom, others are

The Relation of Law to Freedom and Authority

instrumental to it. Freedom of thought, conscience, opinion, are rightly considered as the cradle of all human freedoms and rights (Jellinek). Next to them stand privacy, home, correspondence, movement, and residence, freedom from arbitrary arrest, detention, or exile, due process. All of them are clearly definable safeguards of private autonomy (or rather its very essence) which does *not* invade that of other people. On the other hand, there are other rights which *necessarily* invade the sphere of interest of other people, and are, therefore, *no* genuine freedoms, although sometimes instrumental, but eventually also detrimental, to genuine freedom. Such rights are the freedom of expression, speech, assembly, and association, participation in government, social security, property, work, standard of living, education, etc.

If we accept this dividing line of private autonomy, we get a clear picture of the difference between legal freedoms and rights. Rights, as such, are never mere freedoms, because they encroach upon the freedom (autonomy) of other people, and include inasmuch an element of coercion. "Absence of restraint" does *not* include restraint put on other people. But rights are, on the other hand, indispensable instruments of genuine freedom, inasmuch as they merely reject encroachments by others on our own freedom. In this idealistic sense, they are almost inseparable from freedom, because to repel the encroachment on our freedom is no encroachment on the violator's freedom. But the danger of this idealistic formulation is only too well known. Whenever both parties, or only one of them, are mistaken about their or his rights, whenever issue is joined, both parties soon learn that they have something to lose by litigation.

Rights are correlative to duties, and, as the author shows by some examples, the character of law as good or bad, just or unjust, depends precisely on the question, whether it grants "much more freedom" by imposing certain duties and denying, thereby, certain freedoms. We may add, the *authority* of law depends on this question. For authority differs from coercion, precisely in that it is freely, voluntarily respected, and this can only be the result of general satisfaction.

CHAPTER XXI

Freedom and Legal Authority: The Kinds of Authority of Law

By EDWIN W. PATTERSON
Cardozo Professor of Jurisprudence, Columbia University

"FREEDOM" AND "AUTHORITY" are important words because they designate important sets of ideas in the modern world. As they refer to sets of ideas rather than a single class of objects, people have taken different meanings from them and have drawn different sets of conclusions. Unfortunately, in one sense, the most important and basic terms of political science (as perhaps also of any science) are the ones most difficult to define, because they have been given many different meanings. Semantics and semeiotics have made the sophisticates aware of the differences in meaning of the words we use, of the different functions of language, and of the possibility that apparent disagreements between men *may* upon analysis turn out to be merely verbal. Yet the possibility often has turned out to be worthless. It would be a mistake to believe that the road to agreement ends just over yon semantic hilltop. The present essay is written with no such expectation. It will begin with an exploration of some of the meanings of freedom in Western civilization—that is, of freedom in relation to legal authority. It will then offer several different meanings of the authority of law.

Three conclusions about the relations of freedom to legal authority will be submitted at the outset. The first is that the maintenance of a suitable kind of legal order in society is, and as far as we can now see ahead will be, an indispensable means to the maintenance of any kind of individual freedom that is practical and valuable. Another is that freedom, some freedoms of the individual from governmental restraint, should be one of the ultimate ends or objectives of the exercise (or non-exercise) of legal authority. A third is that the practical and good content of freedom (in relation to legal authority) is dependent in the main upon the certainty, expediency, and justice of the making and administration of law.

I

One of the traditional views of freedom is that man finds his best kind of freedom in a politically organized society, and, therefore, freedom is merged in political authority. Rousseau's cry that man is born free yet everywhere he is in chains, aroused eighteenth century thinkers, from politicians to romantic poets, to a passionate devotion to freedom. Rousseau, however, became reconciled to the view that man can attain his true freedom only by living in a community of men and in accordance with the general will; that is, eventually under some political authority. Hegel, who is said to have rejoiced over Napoleon's victory at Jena because of his sympathies with the French Revolutionists, made freedom one of his ends of social evolution, yet ended by finding that man attains his highest fulfilment, and, therefore, his best freedom in the state. From this point on the reasoning became somewhat artificial: the individual wills the legal regime and all that follows from it; the condemned criminal has willed his own execution or imprisonment. The narcotics peddler who is sent to jail for five years would scarcely recognize his going as an exercise of his freedom. The theory that the individual who lives under a legal regime thereby consents to all of its provisions and to all of the consequences which follow from them by implication, is a political fiction that has few adherents today. It is no longer felt necessary to justify every legal invasion of an individual's freedom by showing that he had already willed it or consented to it, and, therefore, his freedom was really not being invaded at all. The "implied consent" theory of the relation between freedom and authority is like the merger of the lady and the tiger.

Immanuel Kant postulated freedom as the ultimate end of law and the state. The only justification for the exercise of legal restraint upon one man's freedom is to protect thereby the freedom of another or others. Legal authority should only hinder the hindrance to freedom. Now this sounds like a rather sensible conception of the relation of freedom to legal authority, until one discovers that Kant meant the moral freedom of the man of goodwill to exercise his faculty of reason by formulating his maxims of conduct in conformity with the categorical imperative.

Freedom and Legal Authority: Kinds of Authority of Law

This is a pretty attenuated kind of freedom, the kind that a saint might exercise in the depths of a dungeon. Here freedom and authority are reconciled by making freedom an abstraction, a postulated inner state of mind. It is hardly adequate for an age which conceives of the state as having an important task to perform in promoting individual welfare. For practically Kant's conception was taken to mean that the state should maintain internal peace and order, and provide a means of enforcing private obligations—and that was about all.

A similar conception of the limited function of the state appeared in nineteenth century philosophies which treated freedom as an intermediate rather than an ultimate end. Jeremy Bentham's view that the state should promote the greatest good of the greatest number, might have led to a collectivist state; yet because he regarded individual liberty as the best means of bringing about subsistence and an abundance of economic goods for the individual, he found the chief object of the civil code to be the protection of the security of expectations—in short, of property and contracts. Bentham borrowed his economic theory from Adam Smith. As the conception of "free enterprise," it is still very much alive.

Freedom of speech and the press is, in nineteenth century liberalism, another intermediate end of legal authority. The ultimate end is good government, the choice of good officials; freedom of speech is a means of informing the electorate as to the merits of candidates and issues; it protects novel utterances from suppression by conservatives. Thus Pound lists freedom of speech as a means of promoting political progress, just as freedom to utter and to publish generally, is a means to literary, scientific, and cultural progress generally. Does it follow, then, that as a means to an end, this kind of freedom may be modified, curtailed, even discarded, whenever it appears that it is not producing good results? This is at present a very lively question among liberals, both those on and those off the Supreme Court. Clearly the Supreme Court has during the past fifteen years been far more sensitive to restrictions on freedom of speech than to invasions of freedom of economic enterprise. Mr. Justice Douglas emphasized in the "sound-truck" case that freedom of utterance is almost a judicial absolute. For a time it seemed that freedom of speech via sound-truck was likely to send some people to the madhouse; yet a way has been found, apparently, of protecting the unwilling listeners in their freedom not to listen. Now it is probably true that the complete abolition of freedom of speech would be an irreversible decision, that is, one that the party in power would not allow to be set aside at the next election. Once gone, it is gone forever—or until the next revolution. Still it is only a means to an end, and must be limited by that consideration, as well as by the need for protecting other values.

A fourth kind of political philosophy concentrates upon promoting the welfare of the individual, or at least of some group or class of individuals, and ignores freedom as a major end. Plato sought to depict in his *Republic* a society in which each individual would find his place and stick to his knitting. In Aristotle's political society, also, one finds that the state is to play a considerable part in promoting individual welfare—through education and recreation—but there is no emphasis on individual freedom. As man finds his highest and best fulfilment only in political society, political authority is inevitable, necessary, and sometimes good. Some may argue (as one admirer of Aristotle already has) that he took account of individual liberty when he laid down the two kinds of justice, commutative and distributive, that are to guide the relations of men to each other in society. Still Aristotle would, it seems, have regarded individual freedom as a rather empty concept. Freedom for what? Both Plato and Aristotle wanted the intelligent and the virtuous people to prevail in society; they would have but little patience with a restless and untidy democracy. So one can find philosophies of law in which freedom is given a minor part.

Should every political philosophy include in its ultimate objectives or ends of political authority (the state) the maintenance, compatibly with other ends, of an area of individual freedom from legal authority?

Now someone may argue that this is an academic question, because no political organization could possibly provide a nurse maid for everyone with respect to all of his or her activities, and so the most comprehensive and drastic socialist welfare state would have to leave individuals free to make many choices of their actions or inactions. A man might have no choice as to his job or his pay or his place and time of work; yet he might be free to choose beef or pork at the state owned food store, free to attend the state opera or movie or go to the zoo or to stay at home and choose what he would read from among the offerings of state censored books and periodicals. These choices of practical freedom might become trivial, just as the Kantian moral freedom may become abstract and empty. The question posed above is not academic, if one asks, should the maintenance of some substantial area of practical freedom for the individual be deemed by the makers of laws to be *one* of the objectives of the state?

The answer here is an affirmative one. The reasons are primarily twofold: 1. The political organization of society and its means of control, law, are too unwieldy to make many kinds of choices for the individual. 2. The individual's satisfaction in his freedom, even to make mistakes, is one of the ends that the state should promote. Individual freedom includes the right, power, and privilege to be a little bit foolish at times. The kind of freedom here discussed is a "freedom from" governmental control, rather than a "freedom for" some further good of the individual or society. The idea put forward is similar to Bentham's presumption against the enactment of new laws, on the ground that every law causes some pain, and must, therefore, be outweighed by a greater increment of happiness. With the increasing activity of the government to satisfy the physical needs and the creature comforts of the population, the preservation of the individual's separateness and wholeness may somehow be overlooked. These other needs are not merely the spiritual ones, which are respected in our nation by freedom of religion, nor even the intellectual needs, which are protected by freedom of publication and by academic freedom. Wherever a governmental intervention, direct or indirect, is the subject of discussion and choice, the choice should be made in such a way as to leave to the individuals affected as much area of selection as possible.

II

The authority of law is sometimes seen by lay observers as a single thing, a combination of force and caprice. The chief purpose of this essay is to show that this view of legal authority is inadequate and incorrect. The initial step is to examine the meaning of authority in general. First of all, we should note that authority is not the same as force, and that force is not the same as evil. These two identifications—authority is force and force is evil—have beclouded some philosophical speculations about the relation of the state to its individual citizens, and about the establishment of a world legal order. As to the latter, our Korean adventure is a grim reminder that international wrongs sometimes cannot be righted or prevented, without the use of force. As to the former, the Russian philosophical anarchists were wont to argue that the use of force in the world is the source of all injustice in society. Professor John Dewey, after attending many wearisome discussions of this theme, refuted it by pointing out that force can be used to attain good ends as well as bad ends, can be used to operate rationally, or can be allowed to run amok. Law, then, is a reasoned organization of force:

"Law is a statement of the conditions of the organization of energies which, when unorganized, conflict and result in violence—that is, destruction or waste."[1] The force used by the policeman in subduing and capturing the robber who was about to hold you up (assuming he obeyed the limitation of the common law and used no more force than was reasonably necessary under the circumstances!) would be a good kind of force. Here even a Kantian would recognize the use of force as a necessary hindrance to a hindrance of your freedom.

But the authority of law is not identical with the state-force which law commands. Austin's over-narrow conception of law as a command of sovereign to subject, a command that carried a threat of force, was supplemented by his conception of the sovereign as the political body whom the subjects habitually obey. The habit of obedience of the bulk of the population supports and maintains the regime of law. Another explanation is Hegel's, who said that the power of the state rests ultimately upon the deepseated feeling of order of the people. While the effectiveness of any particular law may rest upon the threat of using force if necessary, the authority of the legal order is not dependent—at least, not necessarily—upon the fear of coercion, but rather upon the attitude of the greater part of the community toward the regime as a whole.

Despite this, authority, whether legal or otherwise, is in some sense arbitrary. It is arbitrary, when taken in opposition to reason or individual taste. Thus, if a state has made the death penalty mandatory under certain circumstances, the reasons for and against capital punishment cannot change the law, though they may still be relevant in its administration. In a great many affairs of life one has to rely upon authority for guidance. Shall we go to see a certain play or movie? Perhaps the reviews of pro-

---

[1] John Dewey, "Force, Violence and Law," *Intelligence in the Modern World: John Dewey's Philosophy*, edited by Ratner, Modern Library, Random House, New York, 1939, pp. 486, 489. See also, Mr. Justice Holmes, Sir Frederick Pollock, *Holmes-Pollock Letters, the correspondence of Mr. Justice Holmes and Sir Frederick Pollock, 1874-1937*, edited by John Graham Palfrey, Harvard University Press, Cambridge, 1941, II, p. 36.

fessional critics or the recommendations of friends will often be decisive. On questions of morals, as on questions of etiquette, people consult "authorities." So the law has authoritative influence, apart from its being enforceable.

From the foregoing discussion, one can draw some conclusions as to the kinds of authority of law. In making this classification, the present writer is not relying upon any particular authority, but is assembling ideas taken from various "authorities." There seem to be four such kinds, the first two of which are common to all law, while the last two apply to particular items of law. The four are: 1. Authorization or legal validity. 2. Political authority. 3. Personal authority or authorship. 4. Traditional authority.

1. *Authorization, or Legal Validity.* This is the conception of authority of the lawyer and the judge, and ordinarily the only one that they are concerned with. The problem is presented whenever a claimant in litigation produces facts and a legal norm or norms which sustain a conclusion supporting his claim. If the validity of the legal norm is challenged, then it must be traced to some authoritative source. The source may be either a legislative act or a judicial (or administrative) decision. The action of the legislature or the court must be authorized by some higher authority —a statute of the supreme legislative organ (*e.g.*, the Parliament and King in England) or a provision of a written constitution, in the United States. Beyond some such legal authority, the professional lawyer, *qua* lawyer, does not go. (Never? Well, hardly ever!) Now this practice of tracing legal authorization is one which Austin tried to explain (with his theory that a law is a command of the sovereign), and which Hans Kelsen has greatly clarified.

Kelsen brought out the distinction, mentioned above, between *power* norms and *decisional* norms, between norms that empower an official (or a body of officials) to create legal norms, and norms that prescribe how and what they shall legislate and adjudicate, and also prescribe what subjects (non-officials) shall do or not do. As the constitution does not prescribe what rules the legislature shall enact, nor what rules the courts shall use in arriving at their decisions, both legislatures and courts are authorized to create law. The view that courts "make law" is scarcely disputable today, and yet it would not ordinarily be safe tactics for an advocate to urge a court to make new law, because judges are unwilling to avow that they are making law when they are doing it. The power to make new law is, of course, a two-edged sword, for while it may enlarge one man's freedom it may constrict another's. That it has not proved disorderly, has been due in part to political traditions and the restraints of a professional legal system.

2. *Political Authority.* Political authority is the authority of the state and the government as a working organization; it consists of the attitudes of officials and of citizens toward the legal order as a whole and toward any particular item of the legal system: are they set (respectively) to enforce it or to obey it? A lawyer equipped with Kelsen's theory of legal validity might enter a law library to investigate the validity of a particular administrative regulation, and emerge triumphantly the next day with the conclusion that it is valid, only to find that a revolution had overturned the constitution which he presupposed to be valid and on which his conclusion depended. Thus political authority is not merely a lawyer's presupposition, but a complex factual situation. The theoretical freedom that a complete revolution gives to those holding political power to create new laws, is rarely exercised to its fullest extent. The revolutionists usually continue the great bulk of civil, penal, and procedural law in effect, unchanged.

The conception of political authority is also applicable to a particular law, such as the National Prohibition Act of 1919–1933. Many private citizens of excellent repute (otherwise) refused to aid the enforcement of this law, by refusing either not to buy alcoholic liquor from bootleggers or to testify as witnesses, or to vote as jurymen to convict those who were clearly guilty of violations. Yet the Act continued to have legal validity until deprived of that quality by a superseding law. The view that a law becomes obsolete and invalid from disuse, has gained little or no support in Anglo-American jurisdictions, chiefly because of the uncertainty introduced by the test of obsolescence. In the United States, we have a peculiar specimen, a so-called law with political authority but without legal validity. This may happen when the Supreme Court declares a statute to be unconstitutional after it has received the enthusiastic support of most officials and citizens. Such was the case with the National Recovery Act of 1933, which came to an end with the "sick chicken" case.

3. *Personal Authority or Authorship.* The wisdom or expertness of the person or persons who created a law or a body of laws, or who ap-

proved and promulgated it, is another kind of authority of law, perhaps the oldest kind. Among primitive tribes the chief or headman is obeyed because of his personal authority.[2] Many ancient and medieval laws were revered because of this kind of authority: the laws of Solon, the laws of Ethelbert, etc. Although the Emperor Justinian had but little to do with the compilation of Roman law that bears his name, and Napoleon had probably even less to do with the set of codes that bears his, in each case the personal authority of the famous ruler enhanced the prestige of the laws. The opinions of Lord Mansfield on commercial law and of John Marshall on constitutional law are still given exceptional respect. In the United States, each state court of last resort has the final say as to many matters of private law (within broad limits set by Federal and state constitutions) and the common practice in state courts of citing judicial precedents of other states, may be ascribed in part to the respect given to those other courts as interpreters and adapters of the English common law. Thus, a legal doctrine of State A, though it has no legal validity in State B, may have an influence on State B's law. In the United States today, the personal authority of laws is felt chiefly among the professionals, the lawyers and judges. Perhaps it is unfortunate that the American public knows of only a few of its ablest judges: Marshall and Holmes and who else? The naming of statutes after their proponents, as in the case of the Wagner Act and the Taft-Hartley Act, does not signify respect for these men, unless the law becomes hallowed by tradition.

4. *Traditional Authority.* The fact that a law or a body of law has prevailed in the community over a long period of time, gives it a kind of authority that may be called "traditional authority." The authority of the English common law in the United States during the nineteenth century was partly of this kind. That which was settled long ago, before the present controversy arose, is free from the bias and caprice of the present judge or judges; and it represents the wisdom of our forefathers who lived under it. Take a dispute as to land law between two owners of adjoining lands: would they not rather have it settled (the facts being undisputed) by the guidance of some long standing rule of the common law than by the judge's untutored sense of justice? The question is not just rhetorical: some litigants would prefer one, some the other. Still

[2] See Robert H. Lowie, *The Origin of the State,* Harcourt, Brace & Company, New York, 1927, p. 5.

the preestablished traditional law is a kind of protection against the bias or arbitrariness of an individual judge, and is thus a protection of individual freedom.

From the foregoing account, one can see that the relation between freedom and legal authority is more complex than that of mere logical opposition. It is true that "no legal prohibition against doing Act X" means ordinarily (*i.e.,* excluding indirect legal hindrances) "legal freedom to do Act X." Yet practical freedom to do Act X, often requires something more: one's legal protection from interference by others in one's doing Act X, or one's legal protection in acquiring the means of doing Act X. Thus, legal authority may foster freedom by making some freedoms for the individual human life an ultimate objective, and by making freedom a means, as in the case of enforcing anti-monopoly laws, in order to give consumers the benefits of competition. Freedom of speech and of the press are fundamental means not only to the exercise of cooperative intelligence, but also to the maintenance of a free ballot box, that is, individual freedom to vote the opposition into power. The strict judicial interpretation of penal laws which often shocks the layman, is a kind of legal protection of individual freedom; a man cannot be punished for an act that was not a penal offense when he committed it.

If, then, we conclude that men can best attain their practical freedom in a state governed by law and administered by those who are loyal to the maintenance of such freedoms, the scope and content of man's practical freedoms depend in large part on determining the proper ends of the legal order, and on adapting it wisely to the best attainment of those ends.

Comment by Barna Horvath:
One great merit of this paper is to point to interpretations of freedom by political philosophy that are clearly unsatisfactory. We may heartily laugh with the author at the "merger of the lady and the tiger," performed by the "implied consent" theory, or at the "attenuated kind of freedom" that "a saint might exercise in the depth of a dungeon." We may ponder over the grain of truth in doctrines that "treat freedom as an intermediate rather than an ultimate end," or "ignore freedom as a major end."

The author well distinguishes the *authority* of law from its enforcement. The former is dependent, in his opinion, "on the attitude of the greater part of the community toward the regime as a whole." The distinction of four kinds of authority of law is also highly interesting. Legal validity or authorization seems to be the technical-logical *norm* element, while political authority seems to be the somewhat narrowly conceived sociological *fact* element in the authority of law. The third and fourth kinds of authority seem to be additions to this sociological element: personal authority or authorship and traditional authority obviously strengthen the "complex factual situation" on which the

Freedom and Legal Authority: Kinds of Authority of Law

authority of law is said to be dependent. Professor Patterson mentions highly interesting cases of the divergence between political authority and legal validity.

It is of particular value to explore the relation of freedom and legal authority within limits of adopting the narrower, more palpable, almost technical definitions of these terms. Our topic in this section of the Conference is *Freedom and Legal Authority;* the wording of this title suggests that we should take at least authority in a technical legal sense. The *first* kind of authority, distinguished in this paper, is most technical, for the professional lawyer (we are told) does not go beyond it. But the author shows convincingly that the *second,* less technical, *sociological fact* element cannot be neglected either. He proves this by the example of a lawyer who would rely entirely on the first *technical norm* element of legal validity, only to be ridiculed by an overnight revolution. I should like to add, in all fairness, that this ridicule can hardly be addressed to Kelsenians (or to them alone), as they have to investigate, not only the technical validity (or authority) of a norm as derived from another norm placed higher in the legal hierarchy, but also the correspondence with facts of the norm-system as a whole.

It is the charm of any discussion or speculation about freedom and authority that their meaning oscillates between a palpable naturalistic and postulated idealistic one. It is particularly in the meaning of authority that the external, heteronomous, and—as the author correctly remarks—arbitrary element is ineradicable. Facts themselves are no authority any more than a club is an argument. But authority is conveyed to us always by external facts and even a club may be laden with heavy argument. Nevertheless, Professor Patterson emphasizes himself that "the authority of the law is not identical with the state-force which law commands." Is it, then, dependent on the "attitude" of the majority or on the "wisdom" with which it is adapted to proper ends? The *third* and *fourth* kinds of legal authority, distinguished in this paper, would allow such an idealistic interpretation, because the personal authority of great codifiers and judges, as well as that of tradition, are attributed mostly to individual wisdom or to the accumulated reason of ages (both of which may prove, of course, deceptive, and this testifies again to the element of arbitrariness in all authority).

CHAPTER XXII

Legal Imperative and Moral Authority

By GLENN NEGLEY

Chairman, Department of Philosophy, Duke University

I

THE LEGAL IMPERATIVE is that factual configuration which supports and endorses the command of law as execution in action. Lest this appear a simple tautology, it must be remembered that an imperative is not constituted by the manner of statement thereof. A law is not constructed merely by submitting a wish or a desire to legalistic formulation. Not every statement which commands, "Thou shalt," or "Thou shalt not," is such as to demand and elicit obedience. A command which does not *in fact* command is not *in fact* a command. Nor can we allow that a law, which claims imperativeness as an essential element of its definition, be admitted the status of law in fact unless it evidences an imperative in fact—unless, in short, it commands *action*.

This reasonable demand, that a law which is not in fact a law be called something other than law, does not simplify the task of defining law. But the confusion is considerably less than that which results when the distinction is neglected, for it allows us at the outset to disencumber our analysis of a vast amount of pseudo-legal formulation which has hopefully, and sometimes dramatically and aggressively, laid claim to the legal imperative. The imperative of law is not simply the imperative of grammatical form. Linguistic structures are indeed important; the absence of clarity and precision in the statement of law will nullify whatever force and effectiveness it might otherwise have had. However, had it not a force and effectiveness distinguishable from, and antecedent to, its semantic construction, it would hardly derive them from linguistic symbols.

We cannot, therefore, accept the kind of evasion which tries to avoid the problem of the imperative by asserting that the law is what the judges say it is, that it is what the courts declare, or that it is what is done officially. There is, for example, the point of view typically expressed by John Dickinson: "Whatever forces can be said to influence the growth of the law, they exert that influence only by influencing the judges."[1] To this, Cardozo would add that there will be as many estimates of those forces as there are judges on the bench. Leon Green states a similar view in different language: "In so far as the sources of law are apparent, they are found in the judgments of the individuals who are entrusted with the power to pass these judgments."[2] We can certainly agree with Green that authority is not to be found in the language of the law, and we might also agree that the judge is the most responsible individual in society because it is his judgment which proclaims law. But proclamation does not constitute law. When two judges or ten judges of equal responsibility proclaim incompatible judgments, then what is the law? It would but continue the circle of evasion at a more naive level to answer that the judgment of the court of highest appeal will constitute the law. All courts can err in their proclamation of law, because all men can err in judgment. Err about what—other than the nature and source of that authority which they assume will contribute the necessary element of imperation to their proclamation? Without that imperative, their proclamation is not law, regardless of the merits of the judicial process of judgment and the linguistic formulation of that judgment—or the individual responsibility of the particular judicial agent. Holmes should perhaps have said that the *imperative* of law is not in logic; it is in experience, for the imperative is indeed the life of law. The logic of the judicial judgment presents that judgment to experience for verification; if verified, it can be called law. The authority which the judicial decision evidences will derive from the factual references of the premises upon which it is based; imperation will not flow from the logical or judicial process of judgment itself.

Dickinson emphasizes the distinction between "rules" and "discretion," a classification long employed by Pound, who assigns three meanings to law: (1) the legal order; (2) the body of authoritative guides;

---

[1] John Dickinson, "The Law Behind Law," *Columbia Law Review*, New York, XXIX, p. 113.

[2] Leon Green, "The Duty Problem in Negligence Cases," *Columbia Law Review*, New York, XXVIII, p. 1014.

and (3) the judicial process.[3] This distinction asserts that, while the judicial discretion which makes law is not authoritative, yet somehow the law which results from the operation of the judicial process is authoritative. This is a miracle and can be accepted only on faith.

Perhaps we are rather to be asked to believe that the law accumulates authority because the judgment which proclaims it is grounded in equity, morals, or reason. We do indeed hope that judicial process is to be grounded in rational value discrimination, but that judgments of morals invoke their own power of imperation we can hardly verify. It must be insisted that such descriptions leave law subject to authorities which do support their claims on factual grounds, even though the fact be but brute force.

If any specific meaning is to be conveyed by the term, "law," it must therefore be distinguished from those forms of statement which are properly designated entreaty, plea, argument, exhortation, wish, desire, hope. A law does not wish hopefully; it does not entreat; it does not argue; a law commands in form and in fact. That statement which commands in form but not in fact cannot therefore be properly designated a law.

That the law cannot derive its essential imperative quality from either divine or moral sources has been clear in the practice of American and English jurisprudence for a hundred years or more, if not always clear in the minds of the practitioners. The gradual waning of faith in revelation and morals, and even in reason, either singly or in combination, has left legal theory and practice with the embarrassing task of commanding in form, while admitting ignorance or denial of the fact which alone could give ground to the command. One result has been that legal speculation more and more turned inward upon itself, expending its effort on the examination and manipulation of its own formal symbols and procedures. Concern for the nature of law in fact, and for the substantial ground from which law must derive its imperative, or enforceability, has become so slight that one could in general anticipate only a reaction of annoyance if such questions were introduced into the introverted studies of schools of legal training. That the law should manifest a reason for

[3] Roscoe Pound, *Social Control Through Law*, Yale University Press, New Haven, 1942. Different classifications will be found in other works of Pound; the problem formulated is the same.

being what it is, that it should evidence observable and verifiable grounds for the command it attempts to exercise—these are notions almost alien to those concerned with law.

The erosion of old Absolutes without the discovery or construction of firmer foundations is likely to leave a very shaky and unsubstantial superstructure. It is not remarkable that men now so generally accept without argument the assumption that law is no more than a formal pattern for the arrangement of undisguised power configurations. Thus formalized, the law soon comes to lack any discrimination as to the factual grounds which are contributing the essential imperative to the law. Those who counsel at law evidence little or no concern about whether the demands made upon law derive from observable fact, artificial pressure, or the sheer force of individual will to power. Perhaps this may be understandable on grounds of practical expediency; but it is manifestly legal suicide. The introduction of such quaint concepts as justice and equity into a discussion of legal conflict is more likely to bring a glint of cynicism than a gleam of interest to the jaundiced eye of today's legal practitioner.

The possible consequences of such artificiality in legal procedure are not immediately evident when the procedure is confined to a social structure in which rules of order have already achieved a high degree of autonomy through homogeneity of institutional organization. But when the procedure is extended to encompass facts not so institutionally ordered, as in international adjudication, the frailty of artificiality becomes glaringly apparent—and dangerous.

In the presence of this artificiality, power has assumed the status of significant symbol. Law is then but a formalization of manipulations and configurations of power interests, and monopolies of power will contribute to the law whatever power of imperation it manifests. This current form of the problem of the authority of law is even more discouraging than the older statements which tried to describe that authority in terms of divine revelation or reason or moral principles, for now we are apparently trying to make ourselves believe that there is really no problem of the source and ground of that authority.

The problem, however, remains; the sequence of events will not allow us for long to ignore the fact that law, as constituted of those principles of action which men obey in social intercourse, is determined finally by the evidence of an imperative whose source is matched in obscurity only by its effectiveness when called into action. It does not seem naive to ask, "Why are laws obeyed?" This is, in effect, to ask what makes a law a law. More pertinent to legal speculation would be the question: "On what grounds can it be anticipated that this law will be obeyed?" for it is clear that if some reasonable assurance of obedience cannot be assumed, the law will in effect not be a law at all, and the judicial process will be an embarrassment of futility.

The nature of fact is neither determined nor altered by a selection or change of symbolic designation. Taste in symbols has evidenced all the whimsy of fashion. For Blackstone, the imperative of English law followed from the fortuitous circumstance that legal construction was a discovery and writing out of the laws of nature which conformed to the will of God. "This law of nature, being coeval with mankind, and dictated by God Himself, is of course superior in obligation to any other. It is binding over all the globe, in all countries, and at all times: no human laws are of any validity, if contrary to this; and such of them as are valid derive all their force, and all their authority, mediately or immediately, from this original."[4] If it should be thought that Blackstone's reliance upon a beneficent deity represents a simplicity of conception confined to his age, it might be well to consider the implications of the report of a conference of the Federal Council of Churches held in 1947, in which the important legal concept of property was given this basic premise: "Property represents a trusteeship under God."[5]

Yet, for all the disparagement to which such statements are now customarily subjected, they are hardly less descriptive than the concept which has of recent times borne the weight of symbolizing the legal imperative: sovereignty. While Bentham and Austin did great service emphasizing the essential nature of law as command, neither was apparently much interested in exploring the factual basis of that command. Legal theory contented itself with the hearty affirmation that law derived its imperative from the will of the sovereign. After all, everybody knew what sovereignty was; it was the will of the State or the will of the people, or something like that. Probably the most succinct statement of this point of view is that of Jellinek: "The rights and duties of indi-

[4] Sir William Blackstone, *Commentaries on the Laws of England*, I, 41.

[5] As a typical example of the Scholastic view, see Francis Peter LeBuffe aud James Vincent de Paul Hayes, *The American Philosophy of Law*, Crusader Press, New York, 4th edition, 1947. This work modestly claims to be *the* American philosophy of law, all others being castigated as "alien."

viduals receive their potency and authority from grounds set forth in objective law. The State finds the grounds for its own rights and duties in itself."[6]

Throughout the period of the development of national states, this casual assumption of national sovereignty as the source of the legal imperative allowed systems of law to attain intricate internal development by the simple expedient of establishing legal systems as equally nationalistic. Thus, the entire problem of the ground or source of law was designated as political and could be ignored by those concerned with legalistic interpretation.

It is becoming increasingly evident what the acceptance of this vague and ill-conceived idea of sovereignty as a sufficient ground of the imperative of law has meant to legal theory. It was a happy holiday from worry as long as the legalist could with nationalist fervor assert that his "sovereign"—whatever it was—was rational and beneficent and therefore a good and adequate source of the necessary authority of law. "The happiness of the people, therefore, is the only true end of government. No ruler does avow, no ruler dares avow, any other."[7] There is not, however, enough fervor in the most optimistic of jurists to obscure the fact that sovereigns do indeed command for purposes other than the happiness of the people. Sovereigns in the form of political leaders may be vicious, irrational, and ruthless. Sovereignty, in the form of the will of a people—whatever that may mean—may be stupid, irrational, ruthless, or horribly mistaken. What then of the law which derives its authority from this sovereign source? Of what force are its interpretations, its complexities, its rationalizations?

Precisely this kind of predicament has been described most astutely by Ernst Fraenkel. His description of the status of law under National Socialism is so clear a warning that it shakes the superstructure of every nationalistic system of law. "The entire legal system has become an instrument of the political authorities. . . . Whether the decision in an individual case is made in accordance with the law or with 'expediency' is entirely in the hands of those in whom the sovereign power is vested.

---

[6] George Jellinek, *Gesetz und Verordnung*, Mohr, Freiburg, 1887, p. 196. Compare Bentham's cavalier assertion that the fact of the establishment of government he assumes as "notorious, and the necessity of it as alike obvious and incontestable."

[7] Sir William Markby, *The Elements of Law*, Clarendon Press, Oxford, 6th edition, 1905, p. 30.

Their sovereignty consists in the very fact that they determined the permanent emergency."[8]

The arguments which grounded the imperative in sovereignty, while ill-conceived as descriptive explanations, at least had the merit of appealing to reason. It is difficult to hold a brief for some of the theories which try to objectify moral prejudice in terms of Natural Law; but, in many instances, the reference to Natural Law represented a sincere effort to establish principles of legal order on rational value determinations.

The effort is utopian and visionary, it must be agreed. But the regard for values which dictated the proclamation that "when a long train of abuses and usurpations, pursuing invariably the same Object, evinces a design to reduce them under absolute Despotism, it is their right, it is their duty, to throw off such Government, and to provide new Guards for their future security," is surely preferable to a determination of social procedures by sheer, undisciplined force. Here is at least a recognition of the fundamental necessity of legal procedures and judicial process. The good motives of its founders, however, are not sufficient safeguard for law against the depredations of monopolies of power; nor is it enough to show that those principles of law are derived from reasonable or acceptable value discriminations. The imperative of law cannot be established on moral grounds, and the realization of this fact but increases our sympathy for those who think they are so doing when they are ultimately faced with the arbitrariness and expediency of unlegislated force.

If the circumstances appear bleak in respect to the status of national systems of law, they are even more distressing in that area which bitter facts have forced upon our attention—international law. Austin recognized the results to law of his acceptance of a nationalistic concept of sovereignty and refused to give international law the status of positive law. He interpreted international law as merely a series of agreements enforced and maintained only at the sufferance and will of the participating sovereigns. International law evidences no imperative, its propositions are not commands; it is, therefore, not law in any factual sense.[9]

---

[8] Ernst Fraenkel, *The Dual State,* Oxford University Press, New York, 1941, p. 57.
[9] See Thomas Erskine Holland, *The Elements of Jurisprudence,* Clarendon Press, Oxford, 5th edition, 1890, pp. 114 f.:

> But there is a third kind of law which it is for many reasons convenient to coordinate with the former two kinds, although it can indeed be described as law only by courtesy, since

The most deplorable result of the acceptance of territorial sovereignty as an adequate explanation of the source of law has been that our reasoning in respect to the principles of international law has progressed very little, if any, since those principles were formulated in 1625 by Grotius. There obviously has never been a "sovereignty" which could be assumed as the source of the imperative of international law. Thus, those who still insist that there is, or should be, such a thing as International Law, are forced to adduce some other source for its authority. The only rationalization available has been that of falling back upon the very dubious and certainly outworn concept of "natural law," the very premise assumed by Grotius. Maine long ago described clearly how the acceptance of the Grotian theory is dependent upon a conception of territorial sovereignty. "The theory of International Law assumes that commonwealths are, relatively to each other, in a state of nature; but the component atoms of a natural society must, by the fundamental assumption, be insulated and independent of each other."[10]

In international affairs, the failure is even more obvious and complete and much more critical. In the recent trial of war criminals at Nuremberg, we witnessed an unprecedented effort on the part of the prosecution to demonstrate that there were good and sufficient grounds for indictment and conviction, and that the executions were thus the administration of a legal imperative, not the summary act of a military victor.[11]

---

the rights with which it is concerned cannot properly be described as legal. It is that body of rules, usually described as International Law, which regulates the rights which prevail between State and State (*civitas* and *civitas*).

See also Herman Finer, *America's Destiny*, The Macmillan Company, New York, 1947, pp. 76 ff. and J. L. Brierly, *The Outlook for International Law*, The Clarendon Press, Oxford, 1945, p. 21.

[10] Sir Henry Maine, *Ancient Law*, John Murray, London, 9th edition, 1883, p. 172.

When we say that the British Commonwealth of Nations or even Great Britain alone has moral obligations toward the United States or France, we are making use of a fiction. By virtue of this fiction international law deals with nations as though they were individual persons, but nothing in the sphere of moral obligations corresponds to this legal concept. . . . In any case, the reference to a moral rule of conduct requires an individual conscience from which it emanates, and there is no individual conscience from which what we call the international morality of Great Britain or of any other nation could emanate.

Note Hans Morgenthau, *Politics Among Nations*, Alfred A. Knopf, New York, 1948, p. 188:

This makes clear the only possible ground upon which could be established the claim that legal imperativeness is resident in national sovereignty; when thus stated, the fictitious nature of the ground is immediately evident.

[11] Thus, Robert H. Jackson, chief of counsel for the United States of America at the Nuremberg trials, there argued:

Unless we are prepared to abandon every principle of growth for International Law, we

Legal Imperative and Moral Authority 245

The utter emptiness of the concept of sovereignty as the source of a legal imperative was adequately demonstrated in the fact that it served neither as a defense for the accused nor as a ground for the prosecution. However, it is not clear from the numerous arguments of the war criminal trials that there was available for application any more substantial substitute for sovereignty of the victor than moral conscience of the victor. This is mere semantic manipulation, and not very adroit manipulation at that.

II

That the concept of sovereignty has seemed to suffice for nationalistic systems of law, has been due to the fact that the question of legal authority was muffled by the clamor of noisily developing sovereignties. Numerous attempts to give the concept of sovereignty rational description have not, on the whole, been characterized by marked success; but they have at least made an extremely important contribution to the investigation of the imperative of law in the various efforts to explore and define the fact of "will." Sovereignty, as the source of authority in the state, must be defined as will; therefore, the authority of the state which transmits itself through law is an expression of the will of the state. This traditional statement, of course, is not illuminating unless the terms, "will" and "state," have some definiteness of meaning. The democratic representative declares himself to be the representative of the will of the people, the only rightful source of sovereignty. The dictator asserts that, as leader, he is the embodiment or spokesman of the state; his will is the source of sovereign authority. An oligarchy may lay claim to authority, and hence to the will of the state, through the possession of the instruments of power.

By far the most persistent and influential of the claimants to the

---

cannot deny that our own day has the right to institute customs and to conclude agreements that will themselves become sources of a newer and strengthened International Law. You judge, therefore, under an organic act which represents the wisdom, the sense of justice, and the will of nineteen governments, representing an overwhelming majority of all civilized people.

The desperation of this effort to find an imperative is evident in the assertion of the fiction described by Maine and Morgenthau in the face of overt and persistent manifestations of fact which contradicted the fiction. The contortion of terminology merely elaborates the fiction, as when a nonexistent agreement is referred to as an "organic act" or custom is referred to as being "instituted."

authority necessary to provide a legal imperative have been natural law and natural rights. The reference to natural law as a ground for the authority of civil law represents a direct appeal to morals. Whether natural law has been described in terms of a rule of justice, the rule of reason, *lex aeterna,* utility, or the inalienable birthright of individuals, each concept represents an effort to establish an objective ground or source for the authority of law, and the objectivity of the ground supposedly derived from its moral or "reasonable" connotation.

Natural law is the phoenix of legal speculation; however often it is criticized to extinction, it rises again, an old spirit in a new and vigorous body. Untouched by the scathing fires of ridicule, "the law of nature" appears anew as a "higher law prevailing in every legal state," the hope of international law and order.[12] Over thirty years ago, Morris R. Cohen asserted that "to defend a doctrine of natural rights today requires either insensibility of the world's progress or else considerable courage in the face of it." In the face of a crucial threat to the system of legal order, it is doubly damaging that law should be supported on grounds which we have every reason to believe will be rejected by reason when practice demands verification. The conflict between appeals to natural rights and prevailing concepts of sovereignty marks the final absurdity characteristic of almost every recent instance of international dispute.

A rational man cannot believe what his reason has indicated to be unreliable. In procedure, the application of the classic norm of natural law will inevitably result in determination according to the pragmatic criterion of "under the circumstances," rather than in consideration of the more speculative ideal of "reasonable man." The appeal to natural law has become clearly and unmistakably an appeal to a moral basis for the imperative of law, and this development has at least served the purpose of clarifying the confusion between law and morals which has plagued legal speculation and ethical theory throughout the course of Western history. It was an absence of distinction inherited from the Greeks and vastly confused by Christian tradition; the assumed correlation of reason, morals, and law became so fixed in our thinking, our terminology, and our analysis that it persists to this day. The distinction

---

[12] See, for example, "Statement of Essential Human Rights," *The Annals of the American Academy of Political and Social Science,* January, 1946, XXIV, and of course the innumerable sources which use natural law doctrine as a support of particular religious creeds or hierarchies.

between law and morals is, in a very real sense, the determining factor in the description of the legal imperative; if this distinction cannot be maintained, then the law will have to be defined as very different from what we now assume it to be.

In the face of a strong current of criticism of the command theory of law, it may be somewhat hazardous to argue that law by definition must exhibit a real imperative. A real imperative must be defined as a command which, upon demand, could exert the coercion necessary to fulfil the command in action. Only thus can the command be accepted as a real rather than a formal command,[13] and only thus can a law be accepted as a real law rather than simply as a statute, a decision, or a miscarriage. This definition of law indicates immediately the distinction which it is necessary to maintain between moral principles and legal commands. No moral action can result from circumstances in which the agent is subject to coercion. Morality is attributed to an act in which an individual evaluates and elects an alternative of behavior because he judges that alternative to be "reasonable," "best," "right," or "good." Rational systems of morality do not command; they exhort. The moralist must not command his listeners to action, for if he were to attempt to enforce his command by coercion, he would cease immediately to be a moralist in the effort to be a legislator.

The law, however, must command; it cannot be mere exhortation. What constitutes the ground of the imperative of law is the subject of discussion here; but it is hardly to be denied that the law *can* and *does* legitimately command for a number of reasons which could in no wise be acceptable as the basis of moral action; among these might be mentioned expediency and the rule of the majority. It is clear that the law does command for such non-moral reasons; it is not clear why the law has the authority to issue such commands.

It would indeed simplify matters if the legal and the moral were coterminous; this would be the kingdom of heaven. In fact, such a condition properly describes the kingdom of heaven; it is only in divine law that such a happy conjunction of reason, morals, and law can be postulated.

---

[13] It is this necessary factual distinction which indicates that clarification of the so-called "logic of imperatives," to which a great amount of attention is now being devoted in certain quarters, is not likely to contribute much to the definition of the legal imperative, although it may well have certain applications to procedural problems.

Political and legal thought of our recent past has concentrated attention on the perfection of the private, individual will. We have attempted to convert men to an obedience of law by preachment and moral suasion; the greatest moralist of all, Kant, made it perfectly clear that moral action was dependent upon the prior establishment of legal order. The legal imperative cannot be grounded in morals. The law thus prosecutes and executes for an act of bad will; in this respect, it is not legal prosecution, but moral persecution. As we have seen, this doctrine holds also for the theoretical fiction by which we explain the relations of nations at the level of international law. The inadequacy of this view becomes apparent in those cases in which the law cannot isolate the particular will responsible for the act, as in almost all cases in international law.

Anglo-American legal theory has thus admitted surreptitiously through the back door what was so ostentatiously thrown out the front. Our legal system has developed gradually a permissive irresponsibility of corporate bodies because action, responsibility, will, and duty have been consistently defined in terms of subjective motivation. The reason for this mistaken definition which vitiates the very purpose of law follows directly from the effort to ground the imperative of law in morals. If the imperative of law derives from moral conviction, then we must surely look for the source of that imperative in the consciences of individuals. This is a considerably less realistic and reasonable explanation of the imperative than that suggested by the doctrine of sovereign authority. The description of law as grounded in national sovereignty at least had the merit of recognizing that value structures and legal systems were alike appropriate to particular institutional configurations. The fact that these institutional configurations were then fictionalized as "individuals" or "persons" in the construction of international law was a most unfortunate failure of analysis. This has resulted in a confusion of moral responsibility and legal liability.

The question of individual liability for corporate action was the most debatable issue in the so-called war criminal trials. That the problem was clarified in these prosecutions is doubtful. References to international law and the Family of Nations echo rather hollowly. The arguments in these trials present a confusing admixture of legal terminology and citation, enforced by moral righteousness, and proclaimed with the authority of a military victor. Morally, the defendants were "guilty," but since we stopped burning witches, we proclaim not to stomach moral persecution. It has been argued, and not without reason, that these trials represented convictions by a military tribunal; an odor of moral retribution made the executions palatable to English and American sensibilities which would have cringed at sheer summary execution. Legal theory is reduced to sheer absurdity, when it is argued that "although a soldier, in killing an enemy soldier, is for obvious reasons usually exempt from responsibility for murder, this rule of exemption nevertheless requires that the killing, even if done in warfare, be lawful."[14] *Silent leges inter arma.*

We have now apparently accomplished the dethroning of the absolute of national sovereignty, albeit without ever having adequately described its nature. Into the breach we have thrown the unarmed hordes of individual conscience and moral camouflage; the resultant confusion is dramatically portrayed by quotations from two contemporary legal theorists. Glueck, in the work cited above, seethes with moral indignation, for which most of us feel sympathy. "It would be a heartening demonstration," he declares, "of a long overdue international firmness of purpose to maintain the people's peace through living law, if once and for all there were cast into the teeth of war-worshippers and warmongers the cynical words of Field Marshal General Count von Moltke: 'Perpetual peace is a dream, and it is not even a beautiful dream.'" Yet, how then shall we evaluate the ringing words of that most morally conscious of American jurists, Holmes?

> But in the midst of doubt, in the collapse of creeds, there is one thing I do not doubt, that no man who lives in the same world with most of us can doubt, and that is that the faith is true and adorable which leads a soldier to throw away his life in obedience to a blindly accepted duty, in a cause which he little understands, in a plan of campaign of which he has no notion, under tactics of which he does not see the use. . . . War, when you are at it, is horrible and dull. It is only when time has passed that you see its message was divine. I hope it may be long before we are called again to sit at that master's feet. But some teacher of the kind we all need. . . . We need it everywhere and at all times.[15]

What better evidence could be adduced to document the observation that the assumed correlation between moral conviction and legal im-

---

[14] Sheldon Glueck, *The Nuremberg Trial and Aggressive Warfare*, Alfred A. Knopf, New York, 1946, p. 105.

[15] *Speeches*, Little, Brown & Company, Boston, 1934, pp. 58–63 (delivered, 1895).

perative is a myth? Similar moral convictions may adjust satisfactorily to contrary legal systems; similar legal systems may tolerate contrary moral convictions. Identity of value structure, in other words, does not imply identity of legal imperative, nor does difference of value structure necessarily imply conflict of legal imperatives. Moral authority will not, therefore, provide a legal imperative. It is this factual premise upon which future speculation on the nature and source of civil law can fruitfully proceed; it is the only premise which offers any promise of order through law at the level of international relations.

Comment by Nels F. S. Ferré:

I have read and reread Dr. Negley's paper. Frankly, I am now more interested in why he says what he does than in what he says. His paper, to me, is a tragic illustration of the ill which besets our age: the inchoate, rationalized rebellion against the moral and the spiritual. The divorce between power, sovereignty, and national will, and the ends of power, reign, or community, is tragic and deleterious. Dr. Negley himself rejects the founding of law in the former concepts. Similarly, he rejects the individual conscience. Recourse to natural law seems to cause ambivalence in his thinking. Mere reason is likewise no stable guide. What then? Will he actually leave us with a negative insistence that law and morality must be kept apart?

I am convinced that law centers in the will of God for the good of all. Democratic majority cannot make right, for instance, any law for the persecution of prophets or minorities. The eternal law is our duty as historic groups, small or large, or even as individuals, to act with maximum creative concern for all, allowing them freedom, privacy, and chance for maturation, as well as the opportunities and means for the fullest possible social participation, up to their intellectual and moral maturity.

Natural law consists of the kairic or epochal configurations or patterns of social process which serve the needs of any age. There once was no state, for example; the state then had a function in history as the sovereign wielder of sanctions; the day of the sovereign state is almost over. Natural law is not fixed, but is the epochal application of the eternal law. Not to serve the state, on its positive side, in its sovereign day, is to transgress natural law. To prevent international laws, with the final power of sanctions, in the name of the sovereign state, when its day is done, is likewise to transgress natural law.

Positive law is the concrete enactment of legislation and its enforcement, and is to be judged right or wrong in relation to its embodying and carrying out natural law. Naturally, in order at all to clarify our position, the whole organismic setting of man, nature, and history would have to be elucidated, but although the future calls for a careful distinction between moral freedom and positive law, as Dr. Negley points out, it calls all the more for a rooting of the commandments of men in the law of God, the legal in the moral.

Comment by Barna Horvath:

The most interesting point in Professor Negley's thought is perhaps that although he is looking for the legal imperative as a "factual configuration," he seems to be less concerned with the "factual grounds" than the "substantial ground" or "reason" for the command that the law attempts to exercise.

In other words, Professor Negley seems to be an adherent of the command theory, but no adherent of the power theory of law. His definition of law is that of a "real imperative" defined as a "command which, upon demand, could exert the coercion necessary to fulfil the command in action." His crucial problem, "Why are laws obeyed" is easily answered, so far as it is a question of *fact*. Laws are obeyed by the bulk of the people habitually, as a piece of that habitual conformism to various social norms which is the result of education. This general habitual obedience makes coercion in exceptional cases possible. But descriptive explanation of the fact of obedience, will hardly satisfy the author who is looking for the *reason* rather than the *causes* of the whole phenomenon.

The paradox of looking for reasons, instead of causes, in explanation of facts, throws some light on the general problem of this Conference. Authority is meant sometimes as the counterpart of freedom, although it is not the opposite of freedom in the sense in which necessity, coercion, or causality are its opposites. For, whereas these are defined by the very absence of freedom, authority, seems to be something freely accepted and obeyed. Very likely, this is the driving force in the argument which is not satisfied by the explanation of legal authority, in terms of causes or proximate reasons, but only in terms of ultimate reason. However, authority is *not* the same thing as freedom: it is a midstage between freedom and coercion. Legal authority, accordingly, derives in part from "inexorable" fact, and in part from freely accepted reason.

A command theory which rejects the power theory of law, seems to move on similar lines. It wants to justify coercion and finds this so difficult that it is not satisfied by explanation in terms of fact, power, or even morality. But *is* there any other way of explanation?

The impasse of speculation on the source of legal authority is brought out by the author's statement that "law does command for such nonmoral reasons" as expediency or the rule of the majority, but "it is not clear why the law has the authority to issue such commands."

I think the difficulties which seem to the author to be insurmountable are inherent in a somewhat narrow definition both of law and of morality.

The connecting link between moral and legal principles is the general principle of justice, which, in its turn, authorizes a set of principles known as the general principles of law recognized by civilized nations. We have to conclude that the authority of law may be derived, both as fact and principle, from its indispensable function as an instrument in realizing all kinds of practical purposes, from the lowest to the highest.

CHAPTER XXIII

Freedom and Citizenship

By HELEN SILVING [1]

Member, The New York Bar; Attorney, Office of Alien Property, United States Department of Justice

FREEDOM, IN THE sense of a right to participation in government, is normally assumed to be a right of citizenship. In the sense of a right against the government, it is in many respects predicated upon citizenship. From time immemorial, enlightened governments granted to the resident alien certain basic rights. However, these rights were never equal to those of the citizen. The Old Testament accorded protection to the so-called *"guer,"* the resident stranger, along with the widow and the orphan (Exodus 22.21). But the *"guer"* was not generally included in the community of the children of Israel. The Roman law in a special body of law, the *jus gentium,* regulated the interrelations of strangers, the *peregrini,* both among themselves and with the Romans.[2] This law was superior to the notorious *leges Barbarorum* which Rome enacted for foreign tribes abroad, the Barbarians; however, it was deemed inferior to the *jus civile,* the enjoyment of which was considered a personal privilege of Roman citizens.[3] At common law, *Calvin's Case,* (1608, 7 Co. Rep. 1), the basic case which also laid the foundation of American nationality law, arose from the rule that an alien could not maintain an action in England for the possession of land. The French Revolution, which is generally held to have originated the idea of the "rights of man," proclaimed this idea in a "Declaration of Rights of Man and of the Citizen." At present, there is no country in which the rights of aliens are exactly coextensive with those of citizens.

Citizenship everywhere determines the extent of men's rights. There-

---

[1] The views expressed in this article are purely those of the author, and as such do not reflect the views of any governmental agency.
[2] Gaius, I, 2.
[3] *Justae nutiae,* property *ex jure Quiritium,* oral obligation in the form of *sponsio, etc.,* were such privileges of Roman citizens.

fore, the problem of citizenship may be regarded as preliminary to that of right or freedom. It is in a very broad sense "jurisdictional."

Conversely, when speaking of the relation of freedom to authority, one frequently uses the phrase, "freedom of the citizen," almost unconsciously implying freedom to be an attribute of the citizen. Here "citizenship" is used in relation to *"civitas,"* "state," or "government." Clearly, the laws of citizenship, and their corollaries, the laws for aliens, are more than any other laws in any country pertinent to the form of government, the nature of the relationship of freedom to authority.

The Meaning of Citizenship and Its Crises: Statelessness

The term, "citizenship," like any other legal term, is a generalization inferred from the connection in any given legal system of certain hypothetical facts as legal conditions, with certain legal consequences as rights or duties attaching to such conditions. Such conditions may be birth within a certain territory, descent from certain parents, marriage, naturalization, etc., from which follow by way of consequences military duty, the right of suffrage, the right to acquire and hold land, etc. The sum total of such conditions and consequences defines a country's concept of "citizenship."

As may be readily seen, the concept of citizenship is never the same in any two legal systems, for in no two systems are all legal conditions and all legal consequences the same. Nor has the concept of citizenship been the same throughout history within any given legal system. Even division into distinct groups of general concepts in the field of comparative nationality law is more precarious and should be more cautiously used than in any other field of comparative law. Thus one finds that the usual akinness of American and English law is absent where the basic philosophy of nationality is concerned. Indeed, American nationality law in a significant respect, *i.e.,* with regard to expatriation, is closer to French than to English nationality law. Today only few countries adhere to a pure *jus sanguinis* or a pure *jus soli,* and the combination in which these principles occur in the several countries varies widely. The laws concerning the nationality of married women have been revised everywhere to a larger or smaller extent. Soviet Russia formerly granted political rights to aliens. Germany under the Nazis deprived entire groups of her nationals of all political rights. It would seem that now, more than ever before, a general statement that a person is a national of a certain state, may convey such entirely different meanings as to be practically meaningless. Yet, on an international level, a country or a court is generally satisfied with another country's designation of a person as its "national" irrespective of the substantive meaning of the designation.[4] Thus, we have witnessed the peculiar cases of German Jews during the Nazi era being considered abroad as German citizens, although their "citizenship" had not the remotest resemblance to "citizenship," as we understand it.[5]

This situation puzzled jurisprudes a great deal, and they proceeded to remedy it by their usual device of classification and nomenclature. They said that there are in fact two concepts of citizenship, "citizenship" proper, which is variable and differs widely in the various countries of the world, and "nationality," which is a constant concept used in international relations in matters of protection, extraterritorial jurisdiction, etc.[6] Of course, citizenship and nationality normally coincide. However, in the United States there are "nationals" who are not citizens,[7] and in Germany under the 1935 legislation there were German "nationals" who were not Reich citizens.[8] "Nationality" in international law is mostly tantamount to protection, but the ideas which governments hold concerning such protection vary widely. The United States has a very substantive

[4] The principle that each state determines for itself who its citizens are is set forth in Article 2 of the Convention on Certain Questions relating to the Conflict of Nationality Laws, signed at The Hague on April 12, 1930; see also United States v. Wong Kim Ark, 169 U.S. 649, 668 (1897).

[5] Thus, German Jews were regarded as German nationals for the purpose of determining the nationality of a company which they owned, although they were residents of England and one of them had served in the British army. Lowenthal and others v. Attorney-General (1946) 1 All E.R. 295. The issue in the case, of course, was not whether German nationality had any meaning, but rather whether British courts should give effect to expatriation by Germany during wartime.

[6] See statement of the difference in Charles Cheney Hyde, *International Law Chiefly As Interpreted and Applied By the United States,* Little Brown & Company, Boston, second revised edition, 1947, II, § 342, pp. 1064–1067.

[7] Section 604, Nationality Act of 1940, 8 U.S.C. § 604.

Throughout this chapter, which was written in 1951, reference to United States citizenship is based on the Nationality Act of 1940 and not the present Nationality Act of 1952.

[8] Reich Citizenship Act of September 15, 1935 (RGBl.—Official Journal of Laws of the Reich—I 1146).

concept of protection, in that by Federal statute the President is bound to use means not amounting to acts of war to protect a citizen.[9] On the other hand, the idea which the Nazis had concerning the protection of their nationals of Jewish descent is best evidenced by the law which expatriated such nationals when they left Germany.[10]

The ideologists and revolutionists of all ages have always been anxious to do away with citizenship, together with the state from which it derives, and with wars as contests both of enemy states and of enemy citizens. Thus, they invented internationalism, a strangely appealing idea, which, however, in two classical cases in which it was tested by history, created the very opposite reaction to the one originally intended. Its ultimate product was excessive nationalism and xenophobia. Both the French and the Russian revolutions started by a ringing humanitarian appeal in the name of the solidarity of people dedicated to the same ideology throughout the world, irrespective of citizenship. Both ended by a violent nationalism and hatred toward strangers. "No, gentlemen," exclaimed Vergniaud in 1792, "it is not for ourselves alone, it is not for that small part of the globe which is called France, that we have made the conquest of liberty." The framers of the French Revolution proceeded to declare their akinness to the "philosophers" of all nations. On August 26, 1792, the Assembly voted to grant citizenship rights to men who "by their writings and their courage have served the cause of liberty and prepared the liberation of peoples," and specifically conferred the title of French citizen upon Dr. Joseph Priestley, Thomas Paine, Jeremy Bentham, William Wilberforce, Thomas Clarkson, Jacob Mackintosh, David Williams, N. Gorani, Anacharsis Cloots, Corneille Paw, Joachim-Henry Hamilton, M. Madison, H. Klopstock, and Thaddeus Kosciuszko.[11] There is evidence that aliens served as representatives in the Assembly. We know that particularly from the act which later excluded them from representing the French people. In 1793, Barère declared: "To call aliens to the national legislature is to exclude Frenchmen from it."

---

[9]15 Stat. 224, 8 U.S.C. § 903b. The extent to which the United States will go in protecting a citizen is evidenced by the Vogeler case.

[10]Eleventh Regulation under the Reich Citizenship Act of November 25, 1941 (RGBl. I 722).

[11]Session of the revolutionary Assembly of August 24, 1792, *Arch. Parl.*, t. XLVIII, cited in Marguerite Vanel, *Histoire de la Nationalité Française d'Origine*, Ancienne Imprimerie de la Cour d'Appel, Paris, 1945, p. 109; Lamourette, same session, p. 114; pp. 115–116.

About a year after Vergniaud's appeal, aliens in France were required to register and were then ordered to be arrested.[12] Many years later, the Zimmerwald Manifesto declared in 1915: "In this intolerable situation we have met together, we representatives of Socialist parties, of trade unions, or of minorities of them, we Germans, French, Italians, Russians, Poles, Letts, Rumanians, Bulgarians, Swedes, Norwegians, Dutch, and Swiss, we who are standing on the basis, not of national solidarity, with the exploiting class, but of the international solidarity of the workers and the class struggle . . ." Article 20 of the Constitution of the Russian Socialist Federated Soviet Republic of July 10, 1918,[13] proclaimed: "Proceeding from the solidarity of the toiling people of all nations, the Russian Socialist Federated Soviet Republic grants to aliens who are present within the territory of the Russian Republic for the purpose of performing labor and who belong to the working class or to the peasant class which does not exploit other people's labor, all political rights enjoyed by Russian citizens and authorizes the local Soviets to grant to such aliens Russian citizenship without cumbersome formalities." This provision was adopted by all subsequent laws of the Union of Soviet Socialist Republics (1924, 1930, 1931) [14] until the present Nationality Act of August 19, 1938.[15] The latter no longer contains a provision for the enjoyment of political rights by aliens. The present attitude is most clearly reflected by the provision enacted in 1947,[16] prohibiting intermarriages between Soviet citizens and aliens. Thus another utopia of internationalism ended in nationalism and hatred.

History can be perverted. But, unless all records are destroyed, laws

[12]Law of 26 *Nivose An* II (December 26, 1793). This act speaks of citizens born in foreign countries. *Ibid.,* p. 121; August 1, September 6 and 7, 1793. Cited *ibid.,* p. 122.

[13]RSFSR Laws 1918, text 582. Translated from the German translation in Walter Meder, *"Das Staatsangehoerigkeitsrecht der UdSSR und der Baltischen Staaten,* 1950, p. 17, in *Geltende Staatsangehoerigkeitsgesetze, herausgegeben von der Forschungsstelle fuer Voelkerrecht und auslaendisches oeffentliches Recht der Universitaet Hamburg,* Wolfgang Metzner Verlag, Frankfurt-am-Main.

[14]Nationality Act of October 29, 1924 (USSR Laws 1924, text 202); Nationality Act of June 13, 1930 (USSR Laws 1930, text 367); Nationality Act of April 22, 1931 (USSR Laws 1931, text 196), cited *ibid.,* pp. 22 ff., 26 ff., 29 f.

[15]Vedomosti 1938, Nr. 11. Cited in Vladimir Gsovski, *Soviet Civil Law, Private Rights and Their Background Under the Soviet Regime,* University of Michigan Law School, Ann Arbor, 1949, II, pp. 293, 294.

[16]Edict of the Presidium of the Supreme Soviet of February 15, 1947 (Vedomosti 1947, Nr. 10). Its provisions were incorporated into the RSFSR Code by Edict of April 2, 1947 (*ibid.,* Nr. 13). See Gsovski, *op. cit.,* 1948, vol. I, pp. 116, 117.

remain for posterity to read. The reading of the legislative attempts at internationalism and world citizenship in conjunction with the laws which replace them, teaches a lesson in realism. Nations and nationality laws are here to stay. All we can do in the name of humanity is to make these laws humane, and perhaps grant international aid to those who do not partake of the benefits of any citizenship—the people without a country, stateless persons. For they are internationalists by fate, not by conviction. Everywhere they have all the disadvantages of alienship and none of the advantages of foreign citizenship.

Stateless persons find themselves in the peculiar position of being both the original wards and the ultimate victims of internationalism of the Soviet type. Until 1938, the Soviets had a most laudable provision which excluded statelessness within the Soviet Union: everybody within the Union who had no foreign citizenship was declared to be a Soviet citizen.[17] In 1938, this provision was abolished.[18] On the other hand, like the French, the Soviet Revolution created innumerable cases of statelessness by elaborate provisions for punitive expatriation.[19] Such provisions are also contained in the Polish Nationality Act of 1951, the Rumanian Nationality Regulation of 1948, etc.[20]

Of course, the enormous increase of statelessness is not exclusively attributable to actions of Soviet Russia and her satellites. Nazi Germany contributed considerably to the number of stateless persons by provisions for expatriation on political[21] and racial grounds.[22] Nor are democratic countries entirely free from blame. Provisions tending to increase the phenomenon of statelessness have been enacted in Switzerland, France, England, and the United States.

If there is any field of law where internationalism is appropriate, it

[17] Article 3 of the Act of 1924, above; the same article of the Acts of 1930 and 1931, above.

[18] Article 8 of the Act of 1938 (above) provides that persons who under this law are not citizens of the USSR and possess no proof of a foreign citizenship are considered as stateless.

[19] Provisions for expatriation of emigrants were contained in laws prior to the 1938 Act. For present law on the point see below.

[20] For Polish law see below. For Rumanian law see Regulation Nr. 125 concerning Rumanian Citizenship, Art. 17, Official Journal of Laws Nr. 154 of July, 1948, cited in Guenther Beitzke, *"Das Staatsangehoerigkeitsrecht von Albanien, Bulgarien und Rumaenien,"* 1951, in *Geltende Staatsangehoerigkeitsgesetze,* cited above.

[21] Law concerning Expatriation and Revocation of Naturalizations of July 14, 1933 (RGBI. I 480).

[22] Above, note 10.

is the field of statelessness. Stateless persons have no nationality; they are the proper citizens of the world. Let then the United Nations declare them to be their direct nationals. Of course, the United Nations cannot offer to such persons perhaps the most important element of citizenship: a territory from which they could not be expelled. However, a declaration of the United Nations conferring citizenship upon stateless persons would serve notice upon the world that these persons are not outcasts at the mercy of every state. Such declaration would give substance to the provision of Article 15 of the Universal Declaration of Human Rights, that "Everyone has the right to a nationality."

Apart from the implications of statelessness, citizenship in recent decades has grown to tremendous importance, an importance not dreamed of in the years preceding the First World War, when people could travel all over Western Europe without a passport, and when people in the United States "forgot" to secure naturalization.

How can the significance at present attributed to the mere quality of being described as a "citizen" be explained? In the minds of men there attaches to the term, "citizenship," a certain magic idea of right or privilege, on the one hand, and loyalty, on the other. Though "nationality" is much older than the French Revolution, yet the latter initiated that peculiar connection of nationality as a system of rights with nationalism as attachment to both the legal entity of a state and to the sociological entity of a "nation," which is typical of the modern ideology of citizenship. The French revolutionary came to associate his civic ideals of liberty, equality, and fraternity with "patriotism." France also initiated the identification of the sovereignty of the people with the sovereignty of the state.[23] The feudal system and England contributed the concept of "allegiance." The notion that citizenship implies rights and feudal allegiance persists in men's ideology, even though in many countries the basis of this notion has been largely destroyed. Not everywhere today does citizenship impart rights in a substantive sense. Also, the concept of allegiance has been fundamentally revised.

Totalitarian countries found that it is possible to camouflage a total lack of rights by a formal grant of the citizenship title. Indeed, as one party states, they can, without commitment, confer not only citizenship but actual voting rights. The party determines the policy and selects the

[23]Paul Lerebours-Pigennière, *Précis de Droit International Privé*, Librairie Dalloz, Paris 1946, pp. 25, 26, 61.

candidates. The vote, which cannot influence the course of government, is devoid of its traditional meaning and function. Under such conditions, Hitler's Germany could well afford being plebiscitarian, and Soviet Russia does not hesitate to grant voting rights to all citizens, even without distinction of social origin.[24] "Citizenship" in such systems maintains the illusion that the state *is* "the people," that the individual is a socially important factor.

Consensual Citizenship

Citizenship, a jurisdictional element in determining the extent of man's freedom, may, in turn, itself be determined by either free will or authoritative fiat. It may be based on consent of the individual, or on an authoritative grant of grace by the sovereign state. The nineteenth century terminology referred to "contract," as opposed to unilateral grant. Present-day theory prefers to use the antithesis of individual right as against "public interest," and at times conveys a similar thought when speaking of citizenship as a matter of civil status, as opposed to citizenship as "an institution of public law."

An analysis of the recent development of nationality legislation will no doubt lead to the conclusion that the predominating trend is toward stress on the "public law" character of citizenship. However, some nationality laws continue to adhere to the principle of free will and individual right. Here I shall emphasize the elements of free will and individual right still prevailing in certain nationality laws; in the succeeding section I shall describe the public interest ingredients of such laws.

France and the United States more than any other countries reserve a large part in the determination of citizenship to the free will of the individual. Both adhere to the right of voluntary expatriation. Nationality is automatically lost by acquisition of a foreign one. No release is necessary.

In the Soviet Union this right is implicitly denied. The laws preceding the Nationality Act of 1938 provided—and this may be assumed to apply also under the present Act[25]—that persons naturalized in the Soviet

[24]Sections 134, 135 of the Constitution. See Gsovski, *op. cit.*, I, pp. 58, 59.
[25]The present Nationality Act of 1938 (Vedomosti, Nr. 11) consists of only eight articles. Many provisions of previous acts may be assumed to be still in force.

Union have neither the rights nor the obligations flowing from their former citizenship.[26] There is no corresponding provision for the loss of Soviet citizenship upon acquisition of a foreign citizenship. On the other hand, release from Soviet citizenship is made more difficult than ever before. It can now be granted only by the Presidium of the Supreme Soviet of the USSR, and is an act within absolute governmental discretion. The Polish Nationality Act of 1951 specifically declares that "a Polish citizen can acquire foreign nationality solely after securing permission of the Polish authority,"[27] the proper authority being the State Council.

An intermediate position is taken by Switzerland[28] and England.[29] Nationality is not automatically lost by acquisition of a foreign one. But if the conditions of release are fulfilled, the citizen has a legal right to be released. The conditions are that the *de cujus* no longer reside in the country of release, that he possess (or in the case of Switzerland, that he have the assurance of acquiring) a foreign citizenship, and that he have legal capacity.

The American and French principle is now accepted in the provision of Article 15 (2) of the Universal Declaration of Human Rights, that "No one shall be . . . denied the right to change his nationality."

The contractual nature of citizenship may be read from provisions concerning "apparent citizenship." In the French Nationality Code[29a] there are provisions for the protection of rights acquired on the faith of citizenship where such citizenship does not in fact exist. The famous English case of William Joyce may be rationalized on the ground of apparent citizenship. Joyce was convicted of treason as a person owing allegiance to the King, although he never was a British subject in fact,

---

[26] Article 11 of the Nationality Act of 1924; Article 4 of the Nationality Acts of 1930 and 1931.

[27] *Ustawa z dnia 8 stycznia 1951 r. o obywatelstwie polskim (Dziennik Ustaw, No. 4, Poz. 25)*—Act of January 8, 1951, concerning Polish Citizenship (*Official Journal of Laws,* No. 4, Item 25); Article 11.

[28] Article 7 of the Federal Law of June 25, 1903, concerning the Acquisition and Renunciation of Swiss Citizenship, as amended by Federal Law of June 26, 1920, *Amtliche Sammlung der Bundesgesetze und Verordnungen der Schweizerischen Eidgenossenschaft, Neue Folge* (ASNF), Bd. 19 S. 690, 36 S. 639.

[29] Section 19 of the British Nationality Act, 1948 (11 & 12 Geo. 6. Ch. 56).

[29a] Articles 26, 39, 42 of the Code which is part of the Ordinance of October 19, 1945, *Journal Officiel,* October 20, 1945.

but merely held himself out as such and invoked British protection by using a British passport obtained by fraud.[30]

Judicial protection is an important element of the individual's "right" of citizenship. In spite of the emphasis placed on the public law character of nationality in the French Nationality Code, actions concerning nationality continue to be adjudged by civil courts.[30a]

Under Section 188 of the Supreme Court of Judicature (Consolidation) Act, 1925,[31] the courts in England have jurisdiction to determine the question of whether a person is a subject of His Majesty and any questions preliminary thereto.

In the United States, not only are questions of nationality adjudged by courts, but even jurisdiction to naturalize is a judicial and not a political power, and a court may not prescribe qualifications for citizenship in addition to those provided for by Congress.[32]

But in France, as well as in England, naturalization is a matter of purely executive jurisdiction. The Minister of Justice in France must state the grounds if he rejects an application for naturalization or renaturalization as not meeting statutory requirements, but he may, in his discretion, reject an application which does meet the requirements, without stating any reason therefor.[33] In England, the Secretary of State is not required to assign any reason for granting or refusing a certificate of naturalization, and his decision is not appealable.[34]

In Germany, administrative tribunals have jurisdiction to adjudicate nationality matters, these being regarded as belonging to the sphere of public law.[35]

In summarizing, it may be said that nationality today is not entirely a matter of "public law," in the sense of being wholly authoritative and discretionary with the government. In several countries the part of the individual in nationality matters is in many respects of equal significance

---

[30] Joyce v. Director of Public Prosecutions, 1946, 1 All E. R. 186. However, the decision was mainly based on the ground of temporary allegiance incurred by domicile within a foreign country.

[30a] Article 124, Nationality Code.

[31] 15 & 16 Geo. 5. Ch. 49, as amended by omission of the term, "natural-born," preceding the word, "subject," in the British Nationality Act, 1948.

[32] State v. District Court of Sixteenth Judicial District for Garfield County, 61 Mont. 427, 202 Pac. 387 (1921).

[33] Articles 115, 116, Nationality Code, 1945.

[34] Section 26, British Nationality Act, 1948.

[35] See Makarov, *Allgemeine Lehren Des Staatsangehoerigkeitsrechts*, 1947, pp. 357 ff.

to that of the state, and the individual's right of citizenship or to citizenship is vindicated in a manner similar to that in which private rights are asserted. To this extent, it is proper to say that government based on consent is a reality rather than a mere fiction.

Citizenship as an Institution of Public Law: Dual Status and No Status

In contrast, there is another area of the law of citizenship—the area of public law—in which the interest of the individual concerned is frequently disregarded, particularly his interest in being neither stateless nor a person of dual nationality.[36] Dual nationality may interfere with the freedom of the individual as much as does statelessness.

The determination of the citizenship of women and children is now frequently dictated by public policy considerations rather than by the interest or desire of the individuals concerned. The French Code of Nationality has introduced a novel system of repudiations which may prevent the occurrence of an otherwise automatic attribution of nationality.[37] These repudiations may be exercised only at strictly defined periods. Because people are frequently unaware of the importance of such repudiation rights, the status desired in the public interest will in most cases prevail. Such status often conflicts with that obtaining under other legal systems.

Public policy considerations are even more noticeable in the discrepancy between the rules governing acquisition and those governing loss of citizenship, a discrepancy which frequently leads to statelessness. Citizenship is granted on the basis of a mere presumption that certain conditions are fulfilled, and is later withdrawn upon proof that these conditions did not in fact obtain.

It is also important to note the rise of specifically political expatriation grounds. In Switzerland, by Resolution of the Federal Council of November 11, 1941,[38] the Federal Justice and Police Department is authorized to annul a naturalization or renaturalization within ten years of its occurrence, if the applicant is proved to have a "patently un-Swiss men-

---

[36] The special treatment of nationality law as part of the "public law" may also result in a dual status within an identical legal system. Discussion of this phenomenon will be omitted here as very technical.

[37] Articles 19, 24, 38.

[38] Article 20, ASNF. Bd. 57. S. 1257.

tality." In England, since the Act of 1914, a naturalized subject can be denaturalized if "he has shown himself by act or speech disloyal or disaffected towards His Majesty."[39] In France, the government may oppose an otherwise automatic acquisition of citizenship by a person born and domiciled in France on the ground of a "lack of assimilation" (*défaut d'assimilation*).[40] In the Soviet Union under the present Nationality Act,[41] nationals, whether natural-born or naturalized, may be deprived of nationality (a) by court decree in instances prescribed by law, or (b) by special discretionary order of the Presidium of the Supreme Council of the USSR. The present Polish Nationality Act contains a provision[42] for the involuntary expatriation of citizens residing abroad who have violated their duty of loyalty to the Polish state, or who have acted to the detriment of vital interests of the People's Poland. This provision is strangely reminiscent of the Nazi legislation expatriating persons who had "injured the interests of Germany through conduct violating their duty of loyalty to the German Reich and the German folk."[43]

In the United States, though the methods of losing nationality have been broadened, denaturalization remains subject to an important limitation. Naturalization, once granted, cannot be revoked for acts or attitudes occurring thereafter. It has been held that "the power of naturalization vested in Congress by the Constitution, is a power to confer citizenship, not a power to take it away."[44]

Significant to an evaluation of the governmental philosophies underlying involuntary expatriation are the procedures employed. In the Soviet Union expatriation is generally pronounced by court decree. But the fact that, in addition to such judicial expatriation, a discretionary non-judicial method of expatriation is also available, reflects on the over-all system. In Poland expatriation is an executive function. In England and in France naturalized persons can be expatriated by executive

---

[39]Section 7, British Nationality and Status of Aliens Act, 1914; Section 20(3)(a), British Nationality Act, 1948.

[40]Articles 45, 46, Nationality Code, 1945. This is not, strictly speaking, a denaturalization.

[41]Article 7, Nationality Act, 1938.

[42]Article 12, Nationality Act, 1951.

[43]Law concerning Expatriation and Revocation of Naturalizations, above, Section 2.

[44]United States v. Wong Kim Ark, above, at p. 703. But see Section 25(d) of the Internal Security Act of 1950 (8 U.S.C., Section 705(d)).

action.[45] However, in England, the person to be denaturalized has a right to an inquiry by a committee appointed by the Secretary of State. The chairman of this committee is required to be "a person possessing judicial experience."[46] In France, the person to be denaturalized is given an opportunity to present evidence and briefs.[47] In the United States, denaturalization is necessarily a judicial function; since naturalization is effected by a judgment, it cannot be revoked by legislative or administrative fiat.

Political Philosophies Implied in the Methods of Acquiring Citizenship

Philosophies of government are more importantly reflected in the methods of losing citizenship than in the methods of acquiring it. The influence of these philosophies upon the choice of the principal method of acquiring citizenship, the method of acquisition at birth, *jure sanguinis* or *jure soli,* is negligible.

The choice of principle is, in the first place, dictated by practical considerations. Immigration countries will normally prefer the *jus soli,* emigration countries the *jus sanguinis.* Tradition also plays a large part in the selection.

In relying on tradition, the usual phenomenon of picturing a tradition as uniform and ancient is also noticeable in this context. However, as is frequently the case with legal concepts, the sharp line of demarcation drawn between the *jus soli* and the *jus sanguinis* is more the creation of jurisprudence than of law, so far as particular periods of history are concerned. The two principles are generally found side by side. True, the Pentateuch, beginning with God's promise to Abraham to make him "a great nation" (Genesis 12.2), consistently accepted the *jus sanguinis.* So did the Roman law, as traditionally interpreted. However, it might be appropriate to inquire into the legal basis of Paul's describing himself as a Roman in invoking Caesar's jurisdiction (The Acts, 22.3). The

---

[45] In France, under the Nationality Act of 1927 (Article 10, al. 1), denaturalization was a judicial function, and the defendant was granted the procedural benefits accorded to accused persons in criminal cases by the Law of December 8, 1897. This was changed by the *décret-loi* of November 12, 1938, and the Law of July 16, 1940 (Ordinance of May 24, 1944).

[46] Section 20(6) and (7), British Nationality Act, 1948.

[47] Article 121, Nationality Code, 1945.

feudal system in its original form did not sanctify the *jus soli*. Citizenship under it was rather a matter of personal jurisdiction of the king. Neither the *jus soli* nor the *jus sanguinis* has been exclusively accepted in modern times.

Whatever arguments based on political philosophy may be advanced in this context, would seem to me to favor the *jus soli*. This principle makes the fate of individuals independent of that of their parents, and may for this reason be said to be more democratic. It has less tendency to become racist and nationalistic than the principle of *jus sanguinis*.

Political philosophies are more fully disclosed in provisions concerning naturalization, for these provisions bear on the status of aliens. It would seem that the Soviet Union, in declaring that naturalization is granted irrespective of nationality or race,[48] is more liberal than the United States which still declares individuals belonging to certain races as ineligible to citizenship.[49] However, it is too easily forgotten that naturalization in the Soviet Union is entirely discretionary with the government, so that, in order to comply with the above provision, the government need only omit any reference to nationality or race in denying a petition for naturalization. By contrast, our courts in granting citizenship have no such discretionary power. Thus any legislative development toward a more liberal policy is no mere verbalism, but a meaningful reality. In this connection it may be also worth mentioning that a great American judge, Mr. Justice Murphy, expressed doubt concerning the constitutionality of racial exclusion.[50]

Of all the methods of acquiring citizenship, the one most discussed at present in the light of political philosophy is the acquisition of citizenship by marriage. The contention is made that under a system of equality of men and women marriage or its dissolution should not affect the nationality of either spouse. However, there is a certain inconsistency between a system of perfect equality in nationality matters and the rule whereby the husband determines the domicile of the wife.

Under a system of perfect equality of husband and wife in nationality matters, the problem of the nationality of children from nationally mixed

[48] Article 3, Nationality Act, 1938.
[49] 8 U.S.C. § 703.
[50] Justice Murphy concurring in Oyama v. California, 332 U.S. 663, 664 (1947), stated:
> The proposition that the "plenary" power of Congress over naturalization is uninhibited, even by the constitutional prohibition of racism, is one that is open to grave doubts in my mind. Racism has no justifiable place whatever in our way of life, even when it appears under the guise of "plenary" power.

marriages presents a major difficulty. Various solutions have been tried. Salient among them are: determination of the child's nationality by free parental agreement; at times, in the absence of agreement, by judicial decision; predominance of the nationality of the country which enacts the law at issue; and an entirely novel factor, the child's own choice expressed during minority, *e.g.*, a Polish child may without parental consent express a choice of nationality at the age of thirteen.[51]

Allegiance

The concept of "citizenship" is generally assumed to imply "allegiance." Traditionally, allegiance was believed to be both a condition and a consequence of the citizenship status.

In France the feudal basis of allegiance to the king was replaced by a voluntary act of joining the social contract, in the revolutionary era concretely evidenced by the "oath of citizenship" (*serment civique*), the establishment of domicile in France, or enrollment on the civil register. Thus allegiance became dedication to principles, not to a person or to a symbol. The revolutionary idea in France was considerably modified by the emergence of nationalistic ideas. In the United States, however, it was adopted in a relatively pure form.

In the United States, citizenship is an eminently political concept, invoking political and constitutional rights and duties, rather than tribal or nationalistic associations. The nature of our type of citizenship, in contrast to the old British one, is indicated by a comparison of the United States oath of allegiance with the British oath. The former is an undertaking to "support and defend the Constitution and laws of the United States of America,"[52] the latter a promise to "be faithful and bear true allegiance to His Majesty King George the Sixth His Heirs and Successors according to law."[53] The bond which unites United States citizens and attaches them to "the United States" is not, and cannot be, a bond of blood, or race, or of the ancientness of a common history, but rather a "philosophical consanguinity" of principles. It carries the potentiality

[51] Article 8, Nationality Act, 1951.
[52] 8 U.S.C. § 735. As amended September 23, 1950, c. 1024, Title I, § 29, 64 Stat. 987, it now reads: "I hereby declare, on oath . . . that I will support and defend the Constitution and laws of the United States of America against all enemies, foreign and domestic; that I will bear faith and allegiance to the same. . . ."
[53] First Schedule, British Nationality Act, 1948.

of an ideological internationalism, while preserving intact the separate existence and sovereignty of nations. Of all the countries of the world the United States is the one which grants most civil rights to resident aliens.[54]

The recent revision of the British nationality legislation has also done away with the ancient feudal element of allegiance. The old common law concept of British subject has indeed given way entirely to a purely statutory concept, which derives meaning from the various nationality laws of the countries of the Commonwealth.[55] It is to be expected that in the new concept of "citizen of the United Kingdom and Colonies" (the latter being one of the Commonwealth countries) an opening is made for a connotation similar to that covered by the term, "United States citizen." The traditional freedoms of the British subject justify such expectation. Yet, one feature of the present English concept of allegiance seems not to be compatible with this idea. In the United States, allegiance being profoundly ideological, is indivisible.[56] The same is true of the French concept of allegiance.[57] In England, on the other hand, the recent Nationality Act reverts to the old common law idea of the divisibility of allegiance. It admits dual allegiance even in cases where the second allegiance is a voluntary one.[58] This carries the danger of making the concept of citizenship rather mechanistic.

[54] An authority on constitutional law, Professor Robert L. Hale of Columbia University, succeeded in spelling out some slight differences in the treatment of citizens and aliens. See Hale, "Some Basic Constitutional Rights of Economic Significance," *Columbia Law Review*, 1951, LI, 271, pp. 258 ff.

[55] A "British subject" or a "Commonwealth citizen" under the present Act is "every person who under this Act is a citizen of the United Kingdom and Colonies or who under any enactment" of any other Commonwealth country "is a citizen of that country." Section 1(1), (2).

[56] "It is fundamental that one can owe allegiance to a single country only." United States v. Karnuth, 19 Fed. Supp. 581, 583 (D.C.W.D., New York, 1937).

[57] The indivisibility of allegiance in France is best evidenced by the provision expatriating persons who conduct themselves as citizens of another country of which they are also citizens. Article 96, Nationality Code.

[58] J. Mervyn Jones, "British Nationality Act, 1948," in *The British Year Book of International Law*, 1948, 174, points out that "many persons of unimpeachable British associations became naturalized in foreign countries for purely business reasons, and it was no longer felt justifiable to cause them to lose their nationality automatically in such circumstances." It seems to be forgotten that naturalization in a foreign country usually involves an oath of allegiance to that country.

Concluding Remarks

It may be appropriate to recall in this context the puzzling juxtaposition and opposition of two books of the Old Testament, Esther and Ecclesiastes. The former, a "naughty" book (Luther), presents a capricious and ignorant tyrant sentencing to destruction an entire nation of strangers within his kingdom, whose very identity was unknown to him. The put of relatively large-scale physical changes in response to an input of nature and the human mind, discovered evil in the fact of "man"—"man" in general—with "power over another to his hurt" (Ecclesiastes, 8.9).

CHAPTER XXIV

Communication in Self-Governing Organizations: Notes on Autonomy, Freedom, and Authority in the Growth of Social Groups

By KARL W. DEUTSCH

Associate Professor of History, Massachusetts Institute of Technology

THE DISCUSSION IN this paper will be centered on the social sciences.[1] Yet its background can be found in four areas of experience:

First, in the social sciences, as data on the structure and behavior of various political and social organizations[2]; second, in history, as data on the behavior of various peoples and civilizations, and as ideas found in the history of philosophy and of religion[3]; third, in the theory of communications and control, as data on problems of self-steering processes and devices[4]; and fourth, in psychology and neurophysiology, as data

---

[1] Some of the literature, and a discussion of a number of terms have been given in earlier papers: Cf. Karl W. Deutsch, "Higher Education and the Unity of Knowledge," *Goals for American Education,* Lyman Bryson, Louis Finkelstein, R. M. MacIver, Editors, Conference on Science, Philosophy and Religion in Their Relation to the Democratic Way of Life, Inc., New York, 1950, pp. 55–139, and the further development of some of the points raised there in "Mechanism, Organism and Society," *Philosophy of Science,* July, 1951, XVIII, 3, pp. 230–252.

[2] Cf. R. M. MacIver, *The Web of Government,* The Macmillan Company, New York, 1937; F. Neumann, *Behemoth,* Oxford University Press, New York, 1942, 1947; J. Towster, *Political Power in the U.S.S.R.,* Oxford University Press, New York, 1948; K. Mannheim, *Freedom, Power and Democratic Planning,* Oxford University Press, New York, 1950; David Riesman, *The Lonely Crowd: A Study of the Changing American Character,* Yale University Press, New Haven, 1950.

[3] A. J. Toynbee, *A Study of History,* I–VI, Oxford University Press, London, 1935–1939; Hans Kohn, *The Idea of Nationalism,* The Macmillan Company, New York, 1943; E. H. Carr, *Nationalism and After,* The Macmillan Company, New York, 1945; A. Cobban, *National Self-Determination,* Oxford University Press, London, 1945; H. Innis, *Empire and Communication,* Clarendon Press, Oxford, 1950; etc.

[4] N. Wiener, *The Human Use of Human Beings,* Houghton Mifflin & Company, Boston,

on the behavior of the human or animal body, and of human beings.[5]

Different investigators, drawing upon these various resources, have produced a growing body of thought, which appears to have applications to social science. The present paper will be confined largely to this latter field, and within it to the problems of self-steering or autonomy and their possible significance for some of our ideas of democracy, authority, and freedom.

I. *The Structure of Autonomy*

We may assume tentatively that self-determination or autonomy is a special case of the problem of steering, and that problems of steering show significant similarities, whether they are found in the case of a man walking, or a ship navigating at sea, or a social group formulating and executing policy.

One fundamental problem of steering, common to all cases, is an output of relatively large-scale physical changes in response to an input of information. This requires not only a set of physical facilities for steering, but also a set of intake channels functioning like sense organs in an organism; and it requires further a set of internal communications channels linking the intake of information to the output of steering behavior. The maintenance of such a system of intake facilities and inner communication channels represents a second type of problem.

A third characteristic common to all steering systems is the presence of *values*, that is, of priorities in the reception and transmission of messages in the intake facilities and inner communication channels of the organization. Such values need not be formulated in words; they are implicit in the character and arrangement of the system. No steering system could be even imagined, which would receive and treat impartially all information in the universe. If it is to function, the organization must somehow discriminate, at least to some extent, between the near and the far away, between message and noise, and between the relevant and the trivial. If it does so abstract and discriminate, according to any

---

1950; *Cybernetics*, The Technology Press, Cambridge, 1948; "Bibliography on Cybernetics," Electrical Engineering Department, Massachusetts Institute of Technology, 1951 (multigraphed).

[5] D. O. Hebb, *The Organization of Behavior*, John Wiley, New York, 1950; J. Ruesch and G. Bateson, *Communication*, McGraw-Hill, New York, 1951; etc.

relatively stable pattern, then this pattern represents, in a sense, the operating values of the organization.

1. Autonomy and Inner Communication

What, we may ask, is such "an" organization? What holds it together and what separates it from its surroundings? In the case of a single ship or a single organism, such as a single human or animal body, the answer seems quite simple: there are physical bonds holding the unit together, and physical gaps separating it from everything else. Selfhood in a single organism would then consist in being held together by such bonds and being surrounded by such gaps.

If this would have been a doubtful test already in the case of the famous Siamese twins, Chang and Eng, who were two distinct persons although their bodies were linked, it becomes far more doubtful in the case of any social group or organization. What holds members of such groups together is their "social cohesion," or accurately, their *complementarity* of communication, their ability to transmit relevant messages more nearly accurately to each other than to anyone else.[6] Such complementarity may be implicit in the physical pattern of the organization, as in the layout of telephone lines, or of streets in a city. Or it may be given by the specific social structure of the organization, such as the chain of command in an army, or the routing of documents in a research organization. Finally, it may be embodied in the communications habits or character structure of each individual, as in the cases of language communities and peoples.

As some degree of external separateness and inner communication is implicit in the functioning of any self-steering system, they are, in that sense, part of its operating values. We may look upon such values from the outside as observers, or from the inside as participants. In the latter case, such operating values may appear to us as our own feelings. In our bodies, we may experience them as feelings of health, good coordination, and freedom from external physical restraints. In our organizations we may experience them as *esprit de corps*. In our social groups, tribes, and

---

[6] Cf. Karl W. Deutsch, "Nationalism, Communication, and Community," *Perspectives on a Troubled Decade: Science, Philosophy and Religion, 1939–1949*, Lyman Bryson, Louis Finkelstein, R. M. MacIver, Editors, Conference on Science, Philosophy and Religion in Their Relation to the Democratic Way of Life, Inc., New York, 1950, pp. 339–365; and *Nationalism and Social Communication*, The Technology Press, Cambridge, public. sched., 1952.

nations we may experience them as a sense of "we-feeling" or "belonging," or in more extreme but frequent cases, as "ethnocentrism" or "in-group" feeling.

The common characteristic is the differential treatment of information: its markedly more efficient transmission within the group or organization, than its reception from without. Would an increase in this differential bring with it an increased cohesion of the group? We cannot answer, "Yes," without qualifications. The differential could be increased by improving the transmission of information within the group, or by reducing the acceptance of information from without. It is the former, rather than the latter method, which promises significant gains in autonomy. A thicker skin is not a substitute for health. Nationalists have often considered dislike of foreigners an inexpensive substitute for genuine mutual knowledge and sympathy among their own people, but usually it has been complementarity and cooperation among their own people which proved indispensable to self-determination. Thus, according to a recent investigation, the landowners of Virginia came to think of themselves as Americans after 1763, not because they had cut themselves off from Britain during the preceding years, but rather because they had come to form a so much more closely knit community in their own country.[7]

Selfhood at this extremely simple level, would be located mainly in the set of channels of inner communication; if these should cease to function the group would no longer hold together.

2. *Autonomy and Feedback of Data from Observation*

Inner communication and relative external separateness are necessary conditions for autonomy, but they are not sufficient. If an organization is to be self-steering, its communication channels must include a feedback loop. A feedback loop is an arrangement of channels such that the input of information to the organization includes data about the organization's own performance in the outside world, and in particular, of its own position relative to a goal situation in that outside world. This information about the extent to which the organization has as yet fallen short of its goal (or to which it has overreached it) is then fed back into the steering of the further output of the organization.

[7] Carl Bridgenbaugh, *Seat of Empire,* Colonial Williamsburg, Inc., Williamsburg, Va., 1950, pp. 7–9.

Seeking such a goal may be merely implicit in the configuration of communications channels, or the goal may be explicitly known as a value to the members. In either case, selfhood at this level would be located in the set of channels making up the feedback loop.

3. Goal Changing and Memory

The simplest type of self-steering involves the seeking of a single goal. An organization might have far more autonomy, however, if it could change its goals. Goal-changing feedback requires some sort of second order feedback loop, which, *e.g.,* accepts information about the reaching or approaching of the first goal and uses this information *to change the configuration of the channels themselves,* so as to put a new goal in the place of the first. Values at this level appear in the organization as priorities among the various first order goals; and selfhood, or the highest type autonomous control within the organization, would now be located in the channels making up the goal-changing circuit.

Goal-changing feedback with much richer results depends on facilities for memory and recall. If information from the outside can be stored and recalled later so as to be fed back eventually into the determination of subsequent output, a wider range of control becomes possible. Such storage may be in the heads of individuals, or in written records, files, and libraries. Memory, the past, tradition, thus become operating values. Selfhood at this new level depends on memory, and is lost with the loss of the latter.

The importance of memory is the greater, and the effects of its loss the more severe, because a functioning memory implies the probability of eventual *individuation.* Two organizations might set out with exactly the same structure, and yet the different experiences from the outside world would eventually produce different stocks of memories in each, and eventually different kinds of behavior even in the presence of identical stimuli. Then such organizations might function in some respects similarly to individuals with peculiarities of personality; and as their memory-guided behavior might influence their intake of subsequent memories, such organizations might be capable of considerable internal evolution.

4. Initiative and Consciousness

Memory—however short—is the foundation of novelty and of initiative. The essential steps toward initiative in an organization are taken as four.

First, that some information should be stored analytically, that is to say, in parts which can be recalled independently.

Second, that on recall the parts should be recombined in new patterns.

Third, that the new pattern should be matched by a new secondary symbol which would match the most characteristic features of the new pattern, but without preserving any longer the traces of its combinatorial origin; this step is decisive in producing *novelty*. We might say that novelty is produced by sequences of analysis, combination, and abstraction.

Finally, the fourth step, that the new pattern should be fed back into the determination of the subsequent behavior of the organization; this feedback of novelty into behavior, we may call *initiative*.

If the new behavior should lead to the production of a new pattern in the material or social surroundings of the organization, we might even speak of *creativity* or creative behavior.

All these performances, carried out by individual members or by the teams and facilities of the organization, would still be at their most primitive levels. Yet they would represent from their very beginnings a new level of autonomy, now resident in the channels carrying these new functions.

The consideration of secondary symbols (step three, above) may now lead us to the problem of consciousness, and its possible meaning in the performance of organizations. Consciousness in an organization may be viewed as the attachment of secondary symbols to some of the primary messages or symbols (*i.e.,* messages or symbols originating in the outside world). They are fed back into the memory facilities, or directly into the determination of the behavior of the organization. In either case they may change the statistical weight of the primary messages and change significantly the over-all performance of the system. The result may be greater accuracy in the treatment of information from within the organization or from the outside world, or it may be the opposite. Consciousness may be "false consciousness," grossly misrepresenting the character or performance of the organization to itself and to its members.

If secondary symbols of consciousness become attached to operating values which hitherto merely had been implicit in the configuration of the system, these values become conscious for us. They may now be confronted with other values, criticized and tested, and either reinforced or modified. The set of operating values as whole may then become more consistent and effective.

Consciousness, clearly, seems a higher function of control, even though it may sometimes take up critically scarce facilities or impose critical delays, so that the "unconscious" or "intuitive" performance will appear swifter or more accurate. Consciousness itself may be considered a value, and the highest type of selfhood of an organization would reside in the particular set of communications facilities in which the secondary symbols of consciousness are produced, carried, and processed.

5. *Will and the Problem of Commitment*

If memories and values can be tested by consciousness, they can also be deliberately frozen. Here the problems of consciousness touch upon those of will.

We may speak of *will* wherever a decision has been taken so as to assure preponderance to predecision data over postdecision ones. By a *decision,* is meant here a significant physical change in the connections or performance characteristics of channels of communication. Preponderance for predecision data means assigning greater weight to earlier incoming information and recalled memories, and to those of their implications which may be subsequently worked out without upsetting the main trend of the original data. Earlier data contradicting this main trend are forgotten or repressed, and so are, even more easily, contradictory new data coming in after the "decision has hardened." The deadlines of newspapers, the freezing of designs for industrial mass production, the carrying out of battle plans, are examples of the problems involved.

The advantage of "will," or of a temporary freezing of a given pattern is in the ability of the organization to commit its resources. Frozen patterns of behavior sometimes can be applied immediately. The more time is at a premium and resources are scarce, the more important it may be to commit them promptly rather than let everything be dissipated in a long weighing of alternatives.

Yet the gain is temporary, and the price of perpetual "emergency behavior" is high. Frozen designs do not make for the best designs; the wailing sirens and the racing fire truck do not make for smooth traffic flow. "Will power," "total commitment," "iron firmness," while they may stand for important policies at times, are poetic metaphors for an ominous capacity: the capacity *not* to learn beyond quite narrow limits. An organization following such policies for long becomes not more self-steering or autonomous but less: it may become the prisoner of its own past.

6. *Learning Capacity and the Range of Outside Contacts*

In the short run, the ability of a social group or organization to endure depends perhaps on its cohesion and on its ability to maintain itself under immediate conditions. In the long run, however, its ability to survive may rather depend on its capacity for adapting itself to a wide range of changes in its environment and for adapting the environment to its own needs. Organization and environment might then continue to transform each other, with the initiative probably more often with the organization than with the environment.

The capacity required for such an outcome, may be called the capacity for learning. Learning has occurred when a previously consistent type of response to a particular kind of "stimulus" is replaced by another response without any significant change in the stimulus. Learning, in this sense, always involves the rearrangement of some physical facilities. The facilities so rearranged may be distributions of matter or of energy. They may be states of nerve cells, or connections between them, in the body of a man or animal. They may be physical facilities or configurations of communications channels in the case of a city, an army, a nation, or any other social organization.

The learning performance can then be measured in two ways. First, it can be measured in terms of the difference between the prelearning output of the organization as against the new output, under comparable input conditions. How much better does the football team play after training than before? How does the export-import balance of a recently industrialized country compare with its former balance?

This method of measuring learning performance has the disadvantage that we cannot tell for sure whether the newly "learned" performance will continue into the future. We may then resort to the second method of measuring learning performance more indirectly, in terms of internal structural changes. This second method alone could not be trusted; however, the two methods together, where both can be applied, should give more dependable results than either in isolation. As their inner structure often can be inspected, social groups and organizations might form a class of cases to which this combination of the two methods might well be applicable.

If we can measure learning performance, we should be able to predict probable learning performance for certain cases. Here we may take as our goal an estimate of the probable ensemble of the adaptations of an organization over a whole range of different future "challenges." The *learning capacity* of a social group or organization is in some ways *related to, or proportional to, the uncommitted* (e.g., *readily reassignable*) *resources of the organization*.

The learning capacity we are discussing here is that of the organization as a whole, as distinct from that of its individual members. The learning capacity of all the individual automobile drivers in a traffic jam could be reckoned in terms of the changes in the equipment of their cars, or the improvement in their personal driving habits, and their aggregate effect on traffic flow. The learning capacity of a city or a traffic organization as a whole, on the other hand, could be estimated in terms of the rearrangement of the streets, lanes, intersections, underpasses, road signs, and traffic lights, all of which determine a large part of the over-all patterns of traffic flow.

There is a qualitative element in learning capacity, as it depends not only on the amount of uncommitted resources, but also on their configurations. Yet, the range of configurations of internal elements increases with the greater amount of uncommitted resources and of facilities for their quick and varied recommitment.

Estimates of the learning capacity of an organization for some time in the future can again be derived from our two methods. First, it can be estimated by extrapolating the results of outside tests of over-all performance: the learning capacity of rats is tested in a maze; that of armies, in battle. Secondly, capacity can be estimated from an analysis of inner structure. The greater learning capacity of rats compared to frogs can be predicted from the greater size and complexity of the rat's nervous system; or the greater learning capacity or adaptability of one army rather than another, can be predicted, if, other things being equal, it has greater facilities of communication and transport and a greater "operational reserve" of uncommitted manpower and equipment. As over-all performance tests are expensive in armies, the prediction of probable learning capacity from structural analysis and the suggestions for probable improvements by the same method, may have considerable practical importance.

Of the many kinds of possible inner structural rearrangement one is perhaps of particular significance—the capacity of an organization so to rearrange its channels and resources that it gains *access to new kinds of input* or, in human terms, to new dimensions of experience. To learn to open up new contacts with its environment—indeed to discover new series of environments—this is perhaps crucial in the long-run development of an organization. Simple physical growth has often been described in terms of metabolism. Now we may perhaps add some notion of a second, though related, type of growth: an increase in the range and volume of an organization's intake of information, and its internal feedback so as to produce a further widening of the flow of new experiences, a further increase in the effective intake facilities of the organization.

A third type of learning capacity might remind us of certain patterns of growth suggested by A. J. Toynbee. They would involve such inner rearrangements of facilities as would increase an organization's capacity for recommitting its resources in the future. They might increase the number and effectiveness of higher order feedbacks, including the facilities for self-steering, for consciousness, for novelty, and for initiative. This ensemble of learning capacities might then well resemble Professor Toynbee's "increase in self-determination," with its transference of activities from the external to the internal environment, and its further stages of inner transformation.[8]

These higher types of learning capacity may well be critically important for those social organizations which are intended to continue to function despite large changes in the environment and over long periods of time. Our community, our country, our nation, our church, philosophy

---

[8] A. J. Toynbee, *op. cit.*, pp. 112–217. "Growth means that the growing personality or civilization tends to become its own environment and its own challenger and its own field of action." *Ibid.*, p. 217.—This extreme formulation perhaps should not be accepted without qualifications. As it stands, it might suggest an organization ever more cut off from the universe around it, as if caught up in some illusion of self-sufficiency. Growth, it is suggested in the present paper, is also an increase in openness and responsiveness to the infinite realities around us.

or denomination, and our common family of all mankind, all these we know to have endured for decades, centuries, or millennia. We may wish that they shall retain their separate distinctness. Yet such is perhaps a paradox of persistence and of growth, that those organizations may well have the best chances for ultimate survival, which have learned to keep themselves open to ever new contacts with a universe which we may still believe to be inexhaustible.

II. *Freedom and Authority as Aspects of Organization*

It is for these organizations intended to endure that the problem of freedom and authority has been most seriously posed. The various answers to this problem may perhaps be worth evaluating, in terms of this overriding aim of enduring growth and self-determination.

1. *Freedom as a Range of Choices*

The underlying problem of long-range growth becomes visible as soon as we begin to search for the greatest freedom of each individual. Freedom we may well define as a range of choices, provided that the choices are real. By real choices are meant choices based on the presence of actual opportunities for action, offered to individuals capable of using them and aware of their existence.

Certain ranges of choices, and thus kinds of freedom, may have to be traded for each other. The wider range of automobile travel, as compared to walking, implies at the same time the narrower range of the automobile's dependence on hard surfaced roads. Similarly the wider range of choosing among one's employment opportunities under governmental policies of full employment, may well involve a narrower range of certain business or investment transactions left to private individuals. Yet if all men are considered as ends in themselves, or as children of God, and hence as potentially equally valuable, it should be possible to estimate any major over-all gain or loss involved in such exchanges.

So far nothing seems to stand in the way of the pursuit of ever broader vistas of individual freedom—except the inescapable fact of death. The only answer which we have found has been to extend our "I" beyond ourselves, to identify ourselves with something that is greater than we are and that will live longer.

We thus regain freedom by extending our identification into space, and particularly into time. But then our previous calculations of the greatest freedom within our lifetime can no longer be trusted. We must now take account of future generations. For their sake we must conserve some resources and perhaps renounce some present opportunities for enjoyment and consumption.

On this claim of the long future, Edmund Burke based some of the strongest of his arguments for conservatism and authority. As the predictions of no single generation can be trusted—for every single generation is but one of "weak and giddy men"—the long future must call on the long past. Authority then seems to be the voice in which this past and this future speak together.

2. Authority as a Strategy of Deference

In a context of communications, we may think of *authority* as a property of those messages to whom preferred treatment is given for reasons other than for the sake of their own content. We defer to authority for various reasons. Authority may reside in a single individual whose messages are arbitrary. Or it may reside in a leader who has become the object upon whom his followers have projected their own hopes and expectations until he seems to them endowed with a gift of charismatic leadership. Authority may be diffused among the members of a "veto group," whose messages must be listened to and deferred to. Or authority may be still more widely diffused among the members of a peer group of one's equals, among whom "it does not pay to get out of line."[9]

In all these cases a strategy of deference has been established, in regard to certain classes of messages. However, this strategy of deference may be internalized, so as to become part of the personality structure of certain individuals. Authority to them now speaks with an inner voice. It may appear to them as the voice of tradition, or as a code of thought and conduct, or as a spirit of a community or group, which imposes upon them a strategy in the selection of those values and preferences which they may henceforth espouse.

So far as the treatment of messages is concerned, it would seem on this showing that, among the members of a social group or organization, authority is simply an operating preference writ large. It represents a

[9] Riesman, *op. cit., passim*.

particular aspect of the inevitable necessity of having some channel configuration, some stable pattern in the distribution of messages and channels. Without it, it would seem, the communication system would be flooded by what communications engineers call "noise," and what some political scientists have recently called "anomy."[10] Authority, according to this reasoning, is simply indispensable. The only problem is to make it strong and stable, to give it some small share of consistency, and to anchor it in the slowly learned habits and personality structures of the population. Where this has been accomplished, authority has been made legitimate.

Yet there remains a doubt. Why must deference be established as a strategy? Why must it be attached to external sources? Or why, when it has become internalized, is it so often felt to be in conflict with other aspects of the human personality? "Freedom," said Rousseau, "is obedience to the law which we prescribe to ourselves." Authority is the law which we definitely do not prescribe to ourselves. There is something of the voice of the strange, of the other, in the voice of authority, no matter how familiar the message may have been. It is the not-we, the not-ourselves that is speaking here, and even where it has become internalized we can still recognize the harshness in the tone. True, we may try to flee to authority when we are discouraged or desiring to "escape from freedom." But we flee to it as to any port in a storm, and not as to home.

Why do the spokesmen of authority sound so often like men on the defensive—and never more angrily defensive than when they try to copy the posture of attack? Is it not because this specific claim to authority must only be made when it is already on the verge of being questioned?

This specific assertion of authority in an organization suggests that the distribution of preference and deference is no longer automatically implicit in the pattern of its channels, and that it is no longer automatically accepted by all members. Certain operating priorities in a communications system are ceasing to function. The more often from then on the voice of authority is heard, the more it will sound like glass that has been cracked.

In the language of Professor Toynbee, we may expect to find explicit assertion of authority at the point where a creative minority is changing into a dominant minority, trying to awe or frighten those whom it can no longer charm. Where social communication and self-government are

[10] Cf. *e.g., ibid.*, pp. 13, 288–289.

growing, there freedom and authority may appear as two equally necessary sides of the same process. Where these conditions do not obtain, where, in the words of W. B. Yeats, "the center cannot hold," there the ever louder assertions of authority cannot restore the harmony that has been lost. Here the cry for authority may well change into the cry for naked power.

3. *Autonomy and Power*

Power to most of us means the answer to the questions: "Who is the stronger? Which side in a conflict must give in?" This concept of power seems constructed as an analogy to the physicist's notion of hardness. Which material will scratch which other, and not be scratched in turn? From the results of tests a hardness scale has been constructed on which all minerals are ranked with the diamond, the hardest of them all.

This scale finds its curious counterpart in the peck order in the chicken yard. It may seem a long way from the chicken yard to negotiations between some conflicting interest groups in domestic politics, or to international conferences involving war and peace and touching on points of national honor. Yet, if we listen, we can hear as in an undertone the old refrain: "Who is the stronger? Who must give in?"

Power in an organization is the ability to force another organization to give in. When two organizations meet head on, each of them tries to substitute directly or indirectly the output of its own steering channels for the output of those of its rival. If a conflict ensues each organization is trying from the outside to operate on the inner steering channels of its enemy. Each may try in effect to destroy the other organization's *integrity,* that is, the intact state of its facilities for self-steering, as well as to destroy its *dignity,* that is, its ability to learn at a non-disruptive rate of speed. As the bitterness increases, the opponent's autonomy must be broken; in short, he must be "taught a lesson." The phrase is revealing. There is a dangerous connection between cruelty and a certain kind of teaching. Both are attempts to do violence to the inner processes.

Would this kind of power preserve at least our own autonomy by destroying the autonomy of those groups and individuals standing in our way?

On balance, the answer must be, "No." If the conflict should be hard, we might have to allocate to its conduct all the disposable resources and all the learning capacity which our organization can muster. But our current output which we are now trying to make prevail, actually was determined by the past of our own system. To make the outcome of this past prevail, may very likely mean to freeze it. In reallocating every ounce of strength that can be recommitted we may well cut down on our facilities for intake and for inner recall and recombination, that is, we might cut down our sources of new information and of inner novelty. We should be cutting down our receptors and the creative parts of memory, in order to give the effectors all power. What we would be actually doing in this case would be destroying the autonomy and learning capacity of our own organization.

The consequences might become visible even in the power struggle. Our risks might become blind, even though we called them "calculated." There might be increasing breakdowns of the flow of outside information to our side, as well as increasing failures in the evaluation of such intelligence as still comes in. At the same time we might find it increasingly difficult to devise new policies in situations calling for new combinations of ideas. Intelligence and policy-making depend less on the number of people sitting behind desks, and more on the quality and the autonomy of the persons and organizations charged with the processing and treatment of such information.

Perhaps such thoughts are not completely academic. In many countries in the world today there seems an inclination to step up the output and let the intake go, to speak rather than to listen, and to shoot rather than to think.

III. *Self-Determination and the Strategy of Growth*

A more realistic concept of power could perhaps be developed from the notions of strength and growth. Power, in this broader view, might be based on the ability to integrate,[11] both in the worlds of thought and of action. It would involve the ability to mobilize resources, tangible and intangible, from within our organization, as well as from among its

---

[11] Cf. "The Concept of Integrative Behavior," in Karl Mannheim, *Freedom, Power and Democratic Planning*, Oxford University Press, New York, 1950, pp. 199–206, with references.

neighbors, and to contribute to their resources in turn. It would stress the ability to make allies into partners, and ultimately to make partners into something not very unlike fellow citizens.

1. *The Dimensions of Growth*

The problems of freedom, authority, and power might be looked at as special aspects of the strategy of growth. In organizations intended to endure for longer periods of time such growth would involve at least four dimensions.

It would involve economic growth, that is, the increase in such facilities of production as manpower, capital equipment, land, skills, and knowledge.

It would involve growth in autonomy—Professor Toynbee's "increase in self-determination." This would include an increase in the facilities, tangible and intangible, for cohesion within our group, and a corresponding increase in the facilities for the intake of new information and for communication and steering.

All this, in turn, would necessarily involve a growth in learning capacity, a growth in the range of goals, in the range of inner initiative and creativity.

Finally, all these would imply a growth in the organization's range of integration, that is, an increase in its ability to incorporate patterns, ideas, individuals, and whole sub-organizations different from itself, without loss of its own identity and yet with a gain toward its own richness and vitality.

2. *Touchstone of Growth: The Individual*

As John Stuart Mill knew so well, the development of a state or an organization is inseparable in the long run from the development of the type of individuals it produces or permits to grow. All we can say here about this topic is that an organization which is characterized by inner richness and autonomy, by self-awareness and world awareness, and by growing ranges of creativity and integration, should furnish a hospitable home for the development of the type of individuals who would carry on those tasks and who might surpass them in the inner life of their own persons.

There is perhaps one more question we may still take up. How can an organization increase its range of integration and yet retain its own identity? Our search for an answer may lead us here to one of the most interesting aspects of the theory of communications: to the problem of spirit.

3. Strategy and Spirit

We have often reason to suspect that the word, "spirit," when it is used in a serious sense, has something to do with values, but that it means much more. Perhaps we may try to make this notion more explicit from the viewpoint of communications. While no mind and no organization can operate without values, *spirit* denotes second order value. It is the set of preferences about sets of preferences. The *spirit* of a man, or a people, or an epoch, is the configuration of rules, according to which their value systems are patterned and operated. Spirit is related to values as strategy to tactics, or as policy to operations. A change in "spirit" means, therefore, a strategic change in the patterns of behavior. And, under suitable conditions, it can be communicated.

As it is second order value, the notion of spirit and indeed the strategic value pattern of spirit can be communicated beyond the confines of the original value system from which it was abstracted. It may thus suggest a framework for the integration of several different value systems which partly contradict each other. At the same time, spirit does not need to touch the first order value systems at every single point; and it may, on the other hand, include second order abstractions from other ranges of value and experience which may be quite unfamiliar to most of the individuals in every one of the constituent first order groups or cultures which it has helped to integrate. Spirit, in other words, is capable of being received and of aiding effectively in bringing about major changes; but it need not be capable of being exhausted.

What has been suggested here in analytical language may perhaps be more familiar in another guise from the data of history. The great styles of art and of music and the great religions of the world have demonstrated many times that a pattern of spirit can transcend the limits of individuals, organizations, groups, and cultures. Each of these great strategies of value transcended the region that gave them birth and transformed themselves in the process. We have around us the inescapable evidence. We have perhaps for the first time a chance at making a very weak and tentative beginning at understanding at least a few of the aspects of the process; and we have before us the tremendous storehouse of the world's living traditions of ethics, philosophy, and of religion. We know that time and again a spirit of integration has characterized some period in the past. Perhaps there is good reason to believe that it can happen again.

CHAPTER XXV

The Problem of Freedom and Authority in Cultural Perspective

By DAVID BIDNEY

Associate Professor of Anthropology and Philosophy, Indiana University

1. *The Relativity of Cultural Freedom*

ACCORDING TO Franz Boas, "Freedom is a concept that has meaning only in a subjective sense. A person who is in complete harmony with his culture feels free. . . Obedience to a ruler, law, or custom is not exacted but rendered freely. For this reason, the concept of freedom can develop only in those cases where there are conflicts between the individual and the culture in which he lives. The more uniform the culture, that is, the more intensely all the individuals of a community are subject to the same customs, the stronger will be the feeling of lack of restraint. . . . With all this, the *concept* of freedom is not found in primitive society. The individual, on account of the lack of knowledge of diverse forms of thought and action, cannot form by himself the concept of something new, not intimately connected with the range of his experience, and, therefore, the possibility of a free choice does not exist."[1]

Thus we see that from the perspective of a cultural anthropologist, Boas maintains that the concept of freedom is entirely subjective and relative to a person's conformity or lack of conformity to a given culture. A person feels free, in so far as he finds himself in complete harmony with his culture; he feels "unfree," in so far as he finds himself in conflict with it and does not wish to submit to its demands. No one is "absolutely" free, because every culture imposes certain limitations upon one's conduct. We are subjectively free, in so far as we accept these limita-

[1] Franz Boas, "Liberty Among Primitive People" in *Freedom: Its Meaning*, edited by Ruth Nanda Anshen, Harcourt Brace & Company, New York, 1940, pp. 51, 55.

tions; we do not feel free, if we do not wish to submit to these limitations. It is significant to note, furthermore, that, according to Boas, primitive man has not the *concept* of freedom, owing to his lack of comparative knowledge of other cultural alternatives, but this does not preclude him from having the psychological experience of freedom.

This sound psychocultural principle, it would appear, underlies all recent and contemporary attempts at thought-control initiated by totalitarian governments. To limit a subject's knowledge of other cultural alternatives, deliberately to distort the truth concerning other peoples and to depict one's own cultural institutions as the only satisfactory and "free" institutions, is to preclude the possibility of alternative choices and to preserve the feeling of freedom in conforming to the dictates of the state.

On this basis, if the concept of freedom is entirely subjective and relative, then all peoples may be said to be free, provided they *feel* free, no matter what the conditions under which they live. A slave who accepts his lot without complaint is as free as his master—or freer if the latter feels the limitations of his own position. And yet, this view appears to run counter to common sense and common experience. We do seem to feel that there is also some objective basis for evaluating freedom, in addition to the purely subjective feeling resulting from conformity to a given culture. A slave is not free, even though he accepts his lot cheerfully. And the fact that a given society conforms to its culture, need not prevent a student of culture from comparing the limitations of that culture in relation to others, and evaluating the degrees of cultural freedom to be found in them. As Boas himself suggests, or implies, the consciousness of the concept of freedom involves a comparative knowledge of other cultural alternatives. To the extent, therefore, that one is conscious of the ideal of freedom, one may envisage cultural alternatives which enlarge the scope of freedom. The feeling of restraint under a given culture need not be conceived merely as a subjective reaction of discontent, for it may be derived from a knowledge of cultural possibilities which give fuller expression to the individual's desire for freedom. Does it not make sense to speak of the development of human freedom? And if it does, we must assume that there is some objective, rational standard for evaluating degrees of human freedom and man's progress in the quest for freedom.

2. Types of Freedom

Obviously the concept of Freedom is a complex one rather than a simple one. I propose to distinguish three basic types of freedom, namely, psychobiological, cultural, and moral freedom.

Psychobiological freedom is action in accordance with one's innate abilities, powers, and inclinations. One feels free in so far as there is no external restraint or compulsion which hinders him from doing whatever he has an inclination to do. Genetically, psychobiological power is subject to development in time. The infant is not free to walk and talk at birth; only with the maturation following upon growth does he acquire the abilities and powers which he then feels free to exercise. The human organism has different freedoms relative to the ages of life and to the powers and inclinations associated with each age. This is the "natural liberty" of which the seventeenth and eighteenth century philosophers spoke, and which they attributed to man living in the "state of nature."

Secondly, cultural freedom comprises all those liberties of action which are permitted to man living under a given system of culture. Cultural freedom presupposes psychobiological freedom or power, but involves, in addition, the patterning of human conduct in socially recognized ways. Every culture, as anthropologists have noted, is a system of freedoms and restraints, prescribing patterns of freedom and proscribing actions which are thought to be socially harmful. Universally, theft, murder, and incest are forbidden, with reference to members of the in-group or one's own society. The kinds of cultural freedom which are permitted vary, of course, from culture to culture. The members of a given culture are usually conditioned to accept the limitations of their culture, and hence feel little or no restraint or compulsion in conforming to its imperatives. It is only the exceptional individual who is prepared to fight against the folkways and mores of his society; for the majority freedom lies in obedience to custom and cultural folkways. In all cultures there is some tension between the desires and inclinations of the individual and the respectable, socially approved norms of conduct. Where this tension is not restrained and suppressed, it gives rise to crime—to action which violates socially approved norms. Crime thus involves a conflict between the demands of psychological liberty and cultural freedom.

Thirdly, there is moral freedom which may be defined as action in accord with the rational good of the individual or his society. An individual is said to be morally free, in so far as he acts in conformity with the requirements of his "true good" and his "true self." Thus moralists have pointed out that a man who does not curb his passions is a "slave" to them, because such a person may see the better and follow the worse. The life of the passions, as Spinoza has demonstrated, is but human bondage. From a social and political point of view, man in society is free, in so far as he acts with reference to the good of his fellow citizens. The free man, as Kant has insisted, acts out of respect for the moral law and the Categorical Imperative, which enjoins him always to treat other human beings as ends and to respect their human rights. This moral law, philosophers, from the time of Plato and Aristotle, have regarded as the "law of nature" or the law of reason to which man is subject, regardless of the civic or cultural laws of the political state. Moral freedom, both theologians and moral philosophers agree, involves a knowledge of the truth concerning the nature of man and the proper virtues of man, and action in accordance with these rational ideals. Moral freedom and rational enlightenment are thus closely bound together.

Moral freedom and cultural freedom do not coincide. Moral freedom is based upon the notion of a rational norm or ideal which may be approximated, but is never completely realized. Cultural freedom, on the other hand, is something which varies historically with different cultures, and is subject to reform in accordance with changing ideologies and social circumstances. A person may feel culturally free and yet be considered as morally non-free with reference to the kind of life he leads.

What may be culturally permissible, for example, sexual fertility rights, may be morally reprehensible and intolerable.

The distinction here drawn between psychobiological, cultural, and moral freedom, corresponds to the distinction drawn by Rousseau in his *Social Contract* between natural liberty, civil liberty, and moral freedom.[2] In his *Discourse on the Origin of Inequality*,[3] Rousseau clearly made the point which exercised such great influence upon Kant, namely, that "it is not so much the understanding that constitutes the specific difference between man and the brute, as the human quality of free agency. Nature lays her commands on every animal, and the brute obeys

---

[2] Jean Jacques Rousseau, *The Social Contract and Discourses*, Everyman's Library, E. P. Dutton & Company, London, 1913, 1923, Book 1, Chapter 8.
[3] *Ibid.*, p. 184.

her voice. Man receives the same impulsion, but at the same time knows himself at liberty to acquiesce or resist: and it is particularly in his consciousness of this liberty that the spirituality of his soul is displayed." Man's moral freedom, he points out in his *Discourse on Political Economy*[4] is based upon man's rational ability to formulate laws in the interests of the public good. By subjecting himself to the requirements of moral law, which he himself has instituted, man is able to enjoy a maximum of freedom in social harmony with other members of society. *Rousseau, however, tends to identify moral and civil or political freedom.* The general will is the expression of public reason in public law. Hence every citizen is said to be morally, as well as politically free, in so far as he obeys the general will as expressed in civic law. From this assumption it is an easy but inevitable step to the conclusion that "whoever refuses to obey the general will shall be compelled to do so by the whole body. This means nothing less than that he will be *forced to be free*" (italics mine). By identifying moral and political freedom by means of the concept of the general will as embodied in the state, Rousseau tended to confuse the ideal, Platonic norm of the good and the actual decrees of the state, thereby justifying political compulsion of the individual in the interests of the higher morality and freedom of the state.

It is this confusion of the metacultural ideal with positive, cultural law which has since, through the influence of Hegel and Marx, also served as a justification or validation of the iron discipline and intolerance of the totalitarian state in which virtue is identified with conformity to the general will of the state.[5] Rousseau himself recognized the difficulty of determining just what the general will represents under particular circumstances. All we do know is that the general will is, for him, a kind of Platonic ideal; "the general will is always right and always tends to the public advantage; but it does not follow that the resolutions of the people have always the same rectitude."[6]

He points out that "There is often a great deal of difference between the will of all and the general will; the latter regards only the common interest, while the former has regard to private interests, and is merely a sum of particular wills."[7]

[4]*Ibid.*, p. 256.
[5]Rousseau, *Discourse on Political Economy*, p. 260.
[6]*The Social Contract*, Book 2, Chapter 3.
[7]*Ibid.*

In answer to the question as to how the general will may be known in cases in which it has not expressed itself, Rousseau replies: "for the rulers well know that the general will is always on the side which is most favorable to the public interest, that is to say, most equitable; so that it is needful only to act justly, to be certain of following the general will."[8] In practice, therefore, he leaves it to the ruler rather than to the people to decide what is the general will and the general interest. Had Rousseau recognized the disparity of the moral ideal and cultural facts, he would not have regarded the state as a moral person actually embodying the general will, and would have separated the demands of moral freedom from *de facto* cultural freedom permitted by the state. As it is, he grants the state or the sovereign power "an absolute power over all its members."[9]

This doctrine, as noted, logically prepares the way for the modern doctrine of totalitarian state power in the name of moral freedom.

3. *The Concept of Authority*

Closely allied to the concepts of cultural and moral freedom is the concept of authority. We have noted that cultural freedom is prescribed by a given system of culture. This means, in practice, that a given society collectively or through its leaders permits certain forms of activity and prohibits others. Similarly, as regards moral freedom, there is a principle of limitation involved, but in this case the individual himself, by means of his conscience, or the general consensus of public opinion, prescribes the norm of conduct. In either instance there is a principle of limitation at work which defines the sphere of individual and social freedom. This principle or factor which regulates the freedom of the individual or of members of a given society, may be designated as the factor of authority. *The concept of authority may thus be defined as an attribute which the mind attributes to a person (or principle) who is recognized as qualified to exercise a regulative or directive power over the behavior of others.* It should be noted that the concept of authority involves two distinct notions, namely, that of competence and that of directive power. An authority is one whom an individual or a society regards as competent or qualified to regulate conduct and issue directives.

[8] *A Discourse on Political Economy*, p. 259.
[9] *The Social Contract*, Book 2, Chapter 4.

The Problem of Freedom in Cultural Perspective

A principle, whether it be a law, custom, or ideal, is said to be endowed with authority, in so far as its validity is recognized and it serves as a means of regulating human conduct. The measure of competence or qualification is relative to cultural conditioning, so that the objects of authority will vary with diverse cultures. The shaman exercises authority in primitive cultures, but would not be recognized in our culture where the scientist enjoys high prestige. Thus authority is an attribute which varies with cultural perspective and social belief. It is only in so far as we postulate some regulative, ideal norm of absolute truth, as in science or religion, that we also postulate the notion of absolute, transcultural authority. As a regulative ideal, such transcultural authority makes for a gradual increment of cultural freedom for the individual as well as his society.

It follows from the preceding that there may be as many kinds of authority as there are spheres of competence which are socially recognized. A political authority is one who is recognized as qualified to rule or govern a given state. A religious authority is one whose jurisdiction is accepted in religious matters. Some authorities are ranked higher than others, and the hierarchical order will vary again with different cultural systems. In the Middle Ages the theologian outranked the philosopher and the practitioners of the arts. In our modern culture the scientist outranks the theologian. The problem of ultimate authority is a highly complex one which mankind has not yet resolved.

In general, so far as Western culture is concerned, two basic trends may be observed. Owing to the influence of the Hebrew-Christian tradition and the acceptance of the Old and New Testaments as books of divine revelation, there developed a tendency toward a theocentric culture, according to which all authority was conceived as derived from God, the author or originator of man and nature. The Bible, as the revealed will of God, was to serve as the authoritative source for the regulation of human affairs. In Christian societies, the Church was the interpreter of divine revelation, and its authority was, therefore, recognized as supreme. The doctrine of the divine right of kings was a product of theological thought, and was based on the assumption that the authority of the king derived from the authority of God, the author of all things.

As over against the doctrine which made God and divine revelation the measure of, and source of authority over, all things, we have the humanistic tradition originating among the Sophists of ancient Greece, according to which man is the measure of all things—and all authority in human affairs is derived from man himself. In the sphere of political theory this humanistic tendency received its classic expression in the period following the Renaissance during the seventeenth and eighteenth centuries. In the philosophies of Hobbes, Spinoza, Locke, Rousseau, Hume, and Kant, the democratic, humanistic principle was put forward that political authority is derived from the consent of the governed and is justified by its utility in promoting the interests of society. The concept of "the state of nature," whether it was taken as referring to a supposed historical state based on contemporary ethnographical evidence or whether it was merely a fictive, logical postulate, served to draw attention dramatically to the problem of the origin of political and cultural authority and was employed to demonstrate the purely human, historical origin of political authority and its function in the service of society. This doctrine was to have revolutionary import in Western culture, and led to the development of modern democratic states in which political authority is ultimately derived from the consent of the people and is justified by its utility in promoting the welfare of their citizens. One of the characteristics of the modern age is the general tendency to justify or validate political authority, whether it be democratic or autocratic and dictatorial, by appeal to the consent of the governed.

It appears from the above analysis that authority, by its very nature, requires justification or validation, because, as said above, authority depends on recognition of competence or qualification. With reference to primitive cultures, as Malinowski has pointed out, myths serve to provide the necessary validation for the authority of tribal rulers and the sanctity of custom, by referring the origin of cultural institutions and traditions to some remote, prehistoric past and preternatural events. Authority in civilized societies or among literate peoples is justified either by religious belief or by some rationalistic philosophy which is just as "mythological" to those who do not accept the validity of these beliefs or rationalizations. Those who do not accept the authority of a given state are inclined to contrast "authority" and "freedom," as if they involved two opposing principles; those, on the other hand, who do accept the authority of a given state or culture see no such conflict, and find their freedom in conforming to the established authority. It would appear from our discussion that those who tend to oppose authority to freedom set up a false antithesis, as authority depends for its function upon the free recognition of its competence on the part of those who submit to its direction. There may be a conflict between some forms of authority and the demands of moral freedom, but such conflict is brought about because the individuals concerned recognize some different transcultural principle of authority.

Furthermore, authority involves not only competence but also power to regulate or direct. Authority without regulative power is a contradiction in terms. This power may, however, be either intrinsic or extrinsic. Power is said to be intrinsic, in so far as the object of authority exercises such power directly and by its very nature, *e.g.,* the authority of a doctor depends upon his actual ability or power to heal and cure, the authority of a teacher depends on his ability to teach and on his actual possession of a knowledge which is valued by his community. Power is said to be extrinsic, if it be adventitious or superadded to some person who of himself alone does not possess it, *e.g.,* he who commands an army has extrinsic power which he may utilize in promoting his authority. Such extrinsic power is a means to an end, in the sense that it enforces personal authority and executes its will. Political authority is complex in that it combines intrinsic and extrinsic power; the ruler must be qualified to rule and have intrinsic power in this sense, and his authority is upheld and supplemented by extrinsic power of police and soldiers. The intrinsic power of a principle or ideal is that of a final cause or unmoved mover— its power is that of affecting some intelligence which acknowledges its authority. Ultimately, political authority is a species of moral authority designed and recognized to promote the social good, and its authority depends on its moral function rather than upon the physical force by which it may be supplemented to enforce obedience. Political authority, as Rousseau and Kant maintained, depends on respect for or recognition of, the law and the general interest on which it should be based (but, contrary to Rousseau, is not necessarily based); it does not depend primarily on the physical force which may be utilized to enforce it. Extrinsic power neither confers authority nor serves to validate it. As frequently put, might is not right. *Authority is a right of governing in virtue of certain qualifications; the mere fact of exercising the extrinsic powers of government does not automatically confer the right to do so. Power without authority is tyranny.*

4. Totalitarian Culture and the Concept of the Totalitarian State

In the foregoing analysis the point was made that there may be as many kinds of authority as there are spheres of competence which may be socially recognized. On this assumption, political authority is but one kind of authority. Just what the scope of political authority is and what are its limits, is a debatable question. According to the democratic philosophy of the eighteenth and nineteenth centuries, the function and authority of government extended only to the protection of individual rights; the function of government was to protect life, liberty, and property, and all those various cultural activities of the individual which may be comprised under "the pursuit of happiness." Government was to provide the necessary conditions of security for the exercise of individual freedom, and hence that government was best which governed least and exercised a minimum of control over the life and thought of its citizens. This meant, in practice, that the authority of the government was strictly limited, so far as the cultural life of a nation was concerned. In particular, government had no authority or jurisdiction over religious matters, and church and state were sharply separated. Similarly, education was not in the province of government, and educators could feel free to teach, subject only to the self-discipline of their own organizations which set the necessary standards and qualifications. On this basis, it may be said, there was a plurality of authorities each claiming a measure of autonomy or freedom in the pursuit of their own interests. This is still the creed and practice of democratic states, even though modern democracy now recognizes the obligation of government to take a more active part in promoting social justice and the economic welfare of its citizens.

As shown elsewhere,[10] what is new in modern political theory and practice is the emergence of an ideology of power. Instead of power in the service of ideals, we now have the doctrine of ideals in the service of power. Underlying the new ideology of power is the metaanthropological assumption developed by Friedrich Nietzsche and Karl Marx that moral values always serve the special interests or will to power of some dominant group or of some subservient group in quest of power.

---

[10] David Bidney, "Ideology and Power in the Strategy of World Peace," *Learning and World Peace,* Lyman Bryson, Louis Finkelstein, R. M. MacIver, Editors, Conference on Science, Philosophy and Religion in Their Relation to the Democratic Way of Life, Inc., New York, 1948, pp. 200–219.

The Problem of Freedom in Cultural Perspective 299

The concept of a common good in which all members of a given state may participate, is dismissed as a delusion of metaphysical idealists. The state is thought to be essentially an instrument for the protection of the interests of the dominant economic class and is a product of society at a particular stage of development.[11] Only when the "dictatorship of the proletariat" has achieved its goal of a classless society through the liquidation or elimination of all opposition, may one look forward to a "withering away" of the state as an instrument of coercion.[12] The modern, materialistic ideology of power is based upon the premise that cultural ideals are rationalizations of the political will to power. Hence ideological conflict is an inherent part of the struggle for power in international affairs. According to the Marxists, all ideology is a function of economic conditions, and every culture system is integrated about given historically determined economic institutions. Thus, contrary to the "delusion" of the liberals and democrats that a given culture system may comprise a plurality of partially autonomous cultural interests, the Marxist sociologists maintain that every culture system constitutes an integrated cultural whole dominated by economic institutions. Every ideology is but a reflection and rationalization of the dominant economic institutions prevalent at the time and of the class whose interest they promote.

This belief in complete cultural integration and in cultural determinism tends to bring about its own verification. The belief of contemporary Communists, following in the general tradition of Marx and Engels (though Marx himself was never quite an orthodox Marxist) that every culture is an integrated whole and that its ideology is a function of its economic institutions, has led in practice to systematic efforts *to make* their culture conform to their theory of economic determinism. In other words, the theoretical belief in *total cultural integration* as an historical, cultural fact, had led in practice to the elimination of individual cultural deviation and to the effective prevention of the expression of heterodox views. Thus the modern Communist states have embarked upon a program of cultural "integration" which embraces every aspect of the life of the individual. The modern totalitarian state is but a logical expression in practice of the theory of the total integration of

---

[11] Friedrich Engels, *The Origin of the Family, Private Property and the State*, International Publishers, New York, 1942, p. 155.

[12] V. I. Lenin, *State and Revolution*, Little Lenin Library, Universal Distributors, XIV, New York, 1932.

culture. In conformity with their theory of the state as an instrument of coercion, they utilize all the powers of the state to bring about complete cultural uniformity and compliance. *As cultural ideology is conceived as an instrument of political power, it becomes the function of the state to exercise complete or total political control over all aspects of cultural life, with a view to making it theoretically consistent and an instrument in the conflict of ideologies.* Thus is set up a vicious cyclical process in which a totalitarian theory of culture leads to totalitarian governments, and totalitarian government, in turn, leads to rigid cultural dictatorship. Underlying the whole process is the assumption of a monistic concept of authority based upon economic power. It is rather ironical to reflect that Plato in his *Republic* had looked forward to the day when philosophers would be kings, in order that political power might be united with wisdom. In its modern version, philosophers have become kings and have set themselves up as authorities over the total cultural life of their states. It would appear that it makes a great deal of difference as to *which kind* of philosophy prevails and *who* the philosophers happen to be.

It is of interest to note in this connection that the concept of totalitarian culture and totalitarian government may be arrived at either from a materialistic or idealistic position. We have seen that Rousseau, by conceiving the state as a moral person embodying the general will, arrived at the conclusion that the state has absolute authority over its members and may coerce them in the name of moral freedom. Thus, in so far as the state is conceived to embody actually the moral ideal of society, one is led to justify a political dictatorship of culture in the name of some ideal of the good. Similarly, in the *Republic* Plato took it upon himself to exile the poets and artists from his state, because they tended to deal with myths, rather than with philosophical and scientific truths. Plato, as a philosopher-king, thus set up a kind of intellectual dictatorship in the interests of justice and the idea of the good. Rousseau, who was much influenced by a study of Plato, conceived of the general will as comparable to the Platonic idea of justice and the ideal social good, but without the specific content of the latter. Instead of universal ideas which have to be discovered and intellectually intuited, Rousseau posited an abstract general will which has to be willed into existence by the state. But Rousseau's general will and Plato's ideal of justice are equally absolute, infallible ideals which determine the goals of moral freedom, and justify the total cultural dictatorship of the state and its absolute authority over the life of its members. In the historical materialism of Marx, on the other hand, the state is conceived as amoral, as an instrument of power in the hands of the governing class. Nevertheless, as the ultimate goal is a moral, classless society, the dictatorship of the proletariat is also justified in the interests of this moral ideal. Once more we have a philosophical-political dictatorship, only this time we have a different elite class, the proletariat, which constitutes the membership of the Communist Party. Thus we have a meeting of extremes, for both absolute idealism and absolute materialism justify totalitarian culture and totalitarian government.

5. *Absolute Freedom versus Absolute Authority*

Historically, the modern world has been confronted by two extreme doctrines concerning the nature of man and the relation of freedom and authority. On the one hand, the liberal, democratic philosophers in their reaction against political tyranny and religious intolerance, sought to establish the inalienable rights of the individual as over against historically instituted, political authority. The common note of their philosophical anthropology was the doctrine of the natural equality of man as over against the Aristotelian theory of natural inequality. The individual was said to be endowed with certain inalienable rights which it was the function of the state to protect. These natural rights were attributed to man by reference to the laws of nature or reason, and hence did not originate with the state. Among these natural rights, according to John Locke and the Founding Fathers of the American Constitution, were life, liberty, and the protection of property. In the nineteenth century, under the influence of the theory of evolution and the emergence of a science of evolutionary sociology, the doctrine of absolute individualism was supported by appeal to the laws of cultural evolution. Thus Herbert Spencer and William Graham Sumner found themselves in accord with Adam Smith for entirely different reasons, in insisting upon the doctrine of *laissez-faire* and non-interference with economic enterprise, as contrary to the laws of nature and natural laws of cultural development. The basic pattern of the thought of the so-called liberal, democratic philosophers was their inclination to maintain the doctrine of the absolute rights of the individual in his economic and other cultural pursuits, as over against the authority of the state.

For the great majority of the people this doctrine of absolute rights to freedom introduced a new form of economic tyranny in place of the former political tyranny. With the development of the industrial revolution in the eighteenth and nineteenth centuries and the increase of population, the irresponsible freedom of the individual proved to be the right of the exploitation of the many by the few, because freedom of enterprise depended on control of economic resources. In the sphere of economics, as contrasted with the purely intellectual pursuits, the freedom of the individual in democratic society proved to be delusion, so far as the great majority were concerned, as the right to freedom of enterprise was not joined to any effective power to do so. Individual freedom no longer seemed to be in harmony with the general interests of society as a whole, although the liberal sociologists prophesied that in the long run it would prove to be to the advantage and progress of society.

The appeal of the Marxist doctrine of historical materialism lies in the fact that it emphasized social responsibility and justice, as over against the rugged individualism of the democrats. Contrary to the doctrine of the absolute rights of the individual and the fixity of human nature, Marx and Engels put forth the theory of historical materialism, according to which there is no fixed human nature or essence, because the nature of man is said to be conditioned by social and economic institutions. Hence there can be no inalienable human rights with which so-called human nature may be endowed. Human nature was essentially a social product historically conditioned and molded by society, and all the so-called rights of man were therefore derived from the state. Because capital was the root of all evil, state ownership of economic resources was the panacea which would transform competitive, selfish man into altruistic, social man. The spurious freedom of democratic society would be replaced by the real or effective freedom of Communist society, for the state would provide economic security and freedom from exploitation.

During the first half of the twentieth century the socialistic doctrines of man and society, and especially those of the Marxists, have exercised great influence upon the democratic societies of Europe and the Americas. All democratic societies have now come to realize that the doctrine of the absolute rights of the individual, particularly in the economic sphere, are not compatible with the best interests of the society as a whole. There has been a growing realization that individual liberty carries with it social responsibility and that the interests of society take precedence over those of the individual. There has been a decided change in the conception of the functions of the state, and a recognition of the responsibility of the state to promote the welfare of its citizens, not merely by providing a minimum of security for individual enterprise, but also by positive leadership in ameliorating social conditions and correcting social abuses. The democratic state is becoming increasingly a moral person concerned with the actual welfare of all classes of citizens rather than with the special interests of one class. In this way, the democratic states have sought, and are continuing to seek, to reform themselves by adopting some of the economic principles of socialistic theory, while avoiding the excesses of totalitarian dictatorship. The Communist states, on the other hand, have so far shown no similar spirit of compromise, but have, on the contrary, continued to exaggerate their ethnocentric differences, the more democracies approached some form of economic socialism. It would appear as if the totalitarian ideology of power and the notion of a *perpetual crisis* and[13] permanent revolution prevent any long-term peaceful solution, notwithstanding the repeated assertions of their proponents that both systems are compatible. Unless contemporary Communist states are prepared to discard their form of Social Darwinism in favor of a doctrine of international cooperation based on the recognition of cultural diversity, the prospects for world peace in our time are not very bright.

6. Conclusion

The basic thesis of this paper is that freedom and authority are complementary, polaristic conditions or principles, essential for the proper functioning of any sociocultural system. Within the context of any culture, freedom and authority are complementary principles which mutually limit one another. Generically and positively, at its lowest common denominator, the concept of freedom refers to the exercise of power; negatively, freedom refers to any unrestrained or unimpeded activity. One may, however, distinguish three levels or modes of free-

[13]Bidney, *op. cit.*

dom, namely, psychobiological, cultural, and moral freedom. The concept of authority involves two essential elements: 1) sociocultural recognition of competence or qualification to govern or regulate conduct; and 2) the effective power to regulate that conduct. Every exercise of authority requires sociocultural validation and recognition and is therefore relative to sociocultural conditions. Authority may, however, be conceived in monistic or pluralistic terms. According to the pluralistic theory, there are as many kinds of authority as there are spheres of socially recognized competence. This thesis implies the notion of the *relative autonomy* of spheres of authority. Historically, the Western democracies have separated the expression of political, from religious and educational authority. According to the monistic theory, on the other hand, the state is the final authority in all spheres of cultural life. This presupposes the notion that the state is the embodiment of absolute truth. What is new in modern totalitarian culture is the fact that we have here a secular absolutism and ideological intolerance instead of the religious intolerance of an earlier age. "Philosopher-kings" have replaced the theological-kings of the past. We now have ideological dictatorship in the interest of political dictatorship.

The basic presuppositions underlying modern democratic culture, with reference to the problem of authority and freedom are, first, that political authority is derived from the consent of the governed, and second, that political authority is independent of other aspects of cultural authority. By contrast, totalitarian authority derives from the principle that there is one supreme authority, namely, the state, which is qualified to integrate all aspects of cultural life.

It is important to bear in mind that no matter what the political organization may be, it is still possible to have a mode of totalitarian culture. That is to say, even a democracy may have a form of cultural totalitarianism if its members are sufficiently intolerant of cultural divergencies and cultural minorities. The blessed term, "integration," often serves to make acceptable a form of total cultural authority which its so-called liberal adherents reject in others in the name of dictatorship. That is why Democracy must not be held up as if it were an absolute good not subject on occasion to the evils and diseases which afflict other political systems.

The great modern discovery, it seems to me, is the principle of social freedom as a prerequisite of, and integral element in, social justice. This implies the utilization of political authority to promote social freedom. Authority need no longer be looked upon merely as a principle of limitation which restrains the exercise of individual freedom. *What is emerging is a new, positive conception of authority as the principle of the plenitude of freedom.* On this basis, authority becomes the instrument of freedom rather than of restraint.

The fundamental theoretical and practical problem is to determine the limits of freedom and authority in relation to varying social and cultural conditions. There are no inalienable freedoms which are not subject to limitation in the interests of the social good under critical conditions. From the perspective of ethnology in particular, it is significant to note the diverse ways in which culture may serve as a medium of regulating human conduct and self-expression. Cultures differ widely in the scope of freedom allowed to the individual and in the theoretical and practical sanctions they provide for the exercise of authority. We of the West must be especially careful to avoid the ethnocentric fallacy involved in setting up the individualistic standards of our democratic societies as a universal norm for all peoples. Freedom, in its various modes, is something which may not be imposed upon others; it must be experimentally acquired by the people concerned as a product of their cultural experience.

The crises of our times, it would appear, reveal a tendency to swing between a theory of the absolute rights of the individual as over against the absolute rights of the state, between the contrary poles of cultural totalitarianism and the "dreadful freedom" of individualistic existentialism. There is a tendency to set up petrified cultural absolutes based upon the arbitrary will of given men, on the one hand, or to deny the authority of cultural traditions and long-established social imperatives in order to affirm the will and freedom of the individual. The thesis of this paper has been that progressive freedom requires a dynamic, pluralistic conception of the relation of freedom and authority which recognizes the absolute authority of the moral and scientific ideal together with the relativity and temporal character of all our cultural and social expressions in approximating toward this ideal. Natural science offers a model of a progressive, self-reforming discipline which combines rational authority with freedom of initiative and creativity. Similarly, a normative and scientific theory of culture and society would follow this model in recognizing the polarity of freedom and authority and would make provision for the establishment of new norms of freedom and authority, in accordance with the empirical, practical, ever-changing cultural requirements and aspirations of man in society.

Comment by Robert H. Lowie:

There are two minor points on which I should like to register dissent. It seems to me unwarranted to say that "In our modern culture the scientist outranks the theologian"; the statement has validity only for certain circles, whether in the United States or elsewhere. More important, I find it necessary to qualify the formulation of my revered teacher, the late Professor Boas, which Dr. Bidney quotes with approval. Inasmuch as even primitive societies have contacts with one another, there can be no question of a thoroughgoing "lack of knowledge of diverse forms of thought and action." To be sure, the tribes in contact are sometimes, as in the North American plains, so many samples of one pattern, with only minor variations. But this emphatically does not hold true in all instances. For instance, in Arizona the Hopi and Navaho have had intercourse with each other for a long time, but their ethos is quite distinct. Professor Mandelbaum has discovered parallel diversity on the Nilgiri Plateau in India; probably the differences are still more profound between the dominant herdsman and the subject peasantry of several East African societies, *e.g.*, in Ruanda and Ankole. In the interests of precision a rephrasing of the statement thus seems indicated.

Professor Bidney's reply:

I am grateful to Professor Lowie for his constructive comments. I agree with him that Boas's statement concerning the "lack of knowledge of diverse forms of thought and action" on the part of the individual in primitive society is in need of "rephrasing." With his profound and original interest in the processes of acculturation and historic diffusion, Boas could not possibly have been unaware of instances of culture contact such as those to which Professor Lowie refers. Yet, if we accept as fact Boas's statement that "the concept of freedom is not found in primitive society," some explanation is required to account for this lack. Boas suggests that the individual in primitive society has a *very limited* knowledge of cultural alternatives, and feels a *minimum* of restraint or conflict in conforming to his culture patterns. Owing to the limitations of his knowledge and experience of other cultures, it is suggested, primitive man has failed to formulate the concept of freedom, even though he does have the subjective experience of freedom in conforming to his culture. I have interpreted Boas's statement to mean not an *absolute*, but a *comparative lack* of knowledge of cultural alternatives.

I should like to add here the thought that even if primitive man did have the concept of freedom, this would not affect Boas's main thesis at all, namely, that the individual in harmony with his culture feels free. Boas unnecessarily complicated his thesis by introducing the linguistic and epistemological problem as to whether primitive man has the *concept* of freedom.

As regards the statement that "In our modern culture the scientist outranks the theologian," I was there referring to the dominant trend or climate of opinion in contemporary Western society. So far as academic life and the general, ideal orientation of Western culture is concerned, this does seem to be the case.

Comment by Roy Wood Sellars:

I find myself in almost complete agreement with the analyses of this paper. I like the author's distinction between the three types of freedom. The contrast between the adjustments of cultural freedom and the critical challenge of moral freedom is important. Dr. Bidney's handling of Rousseau is suggestive. Rousseau's General Will hovered between the institutional and the moral. I should like Dr. Bidney to indicate his own moral criteria. Would he revamp the idea of Natural Law or revise utilitarianism? One other point. He suggests an ultimate authority as additional to a pluralistic play of diverse authorities. How could this be institutionalized? Or would it find expression in enlightened public opinion?

I am somewhat skeptical of the correlation of Nietzsche and Marx. I think that Dr. Bidney and Popper are both right in distinguishing between Marx's theories and their application in present-day Communism. On the other hand, American democracy is tied in with capitalism, and we must bear in mind the difference between democratic ideals and their actual working. In power politics we shall have our loyalties in practice, but we must try to be objective as thinkers and grasp the lights and the shadows. I regard Dr. Bidney's appraisals as very fair.

Professor Bidney's reply:

With reference to the question raised by Professor Sellars as to whether I would "revamp the idea of Natural Law or revise utilitarianism," my reply would be: *neither*.

The authority of the moral ideal can never be institutionalized, because to do so would automatically reduce the ideal to the factual, the *ought* to the *is*. The moral ideal is something which connotes a limit or goal of cultural endeavor, something which is gradually discovered and invented in time and approximated in our social institutions, but is never achieved. That is why a progressive society must always allow scope for individual freedom of thought and some cultural deviation. The authority of the moral ideal does not find expression in public opinion, which again is a cultural fact and as such differs from the ideal.

As regards Nietzsche and Marx and their correlation, what they have in common is the thesis of voluntarism and the relativity of ideology to the quest for power. This does not, of course, imply a complete identity of perspective. Nietzsche, as is well known, had much in common with the classical idealistic tradition, and Marx evaluated power in materialistic terms.

CHAPTER XXVI

Freedom and Authority in the Structure of Cultures

By JAMES K. FEIBLEMAN
Graduate Professor and Head, Department of Philosophy, Tulane University

I

RECENT STUDIES HAVE begun to encounter evidence of the complexity and importance of culture in social life. The smallest human isolates are individuals, the largest are cultures. All social abstractions have to do with these as limits or with intermediate organizations counted from them. The proper item for analysis is the culture, not the social group.

Philosophy, in the old sense of a subjective study involving supernatural or transcendental knowledge, was inimical to the physical sciences; but this is not true of philosophy in the new sense, and it is not true for the social sciences. A finite conception of ontology is not inimical to empirical social science. These propositions involve the proposal to set forth a certain theory concerning the relations of ontology to human cultures. The result will be a method of analyzing cultures as to their relative strengths which will reach down to the individual—inherently a false isolate—and relate him to the culture of which he is so integral.

II

Ontology is the widest system in any finite set of systems. It would perforce have to be an abstract body of knowledge and make the claim to truth, tentatively or absolutely. Its own terms of description are the categories of traditional metaphysics, Bentham's "supremely abstract entities," or, in modern logical and mathematical systems, the undefined terms in the unproved postulates of the system. Rival ontologies exist theoretically and practically, and assert their respective positions in both abstract and concrete forms. They exist theoretically in the written and spoken words of the professional philosophers. Their concrete existence is somewhat more practical, for they exert force as actual elements of cultures. But before we can be more detailed about this, we shall have to explain what we mean by culture.

Culture is the common use and application of complex objective ideas by the members of a social group working with tools, folkways, and institutions. Such complex ideas are held unconsciously by the individual members, and are manifested socially both by the myth of the leading institution and by the ordering of the institution. Every culture contains some system of religion, philosophy, art, science, politics, education, economics, communication, transportation, and family. The question of the order of importance of these institutions is paramount in a culture. For the myth of the leading institution is its theory of the real, the religion of the culture in terms of which the arrangement of the other institutions is determined. The complex ideas are said to be objective, because they issue from the external world and are referred back to it. Another name for them is the implicit dominant ontology—ontological because they refer to ultimate states of being, and dominant, because they take precedence over all thoughts, feelings, and actions. Thus every culture has its own implicit dominant ontology, but the environing conditions for every culture differ. Thus a culture is the actual selection of some part of the whole of possible human behavior considered in its effect upon materials, such as tools and institutions, made according to the demands of an implicit dominant ontology, and modified by the total environment.

Ontologies are found empirically in two places: in the unconscious of the individual and in the social order of institutions.

We are all susceptible to the power of certain conceptions of which we are for the most part unaware. We consider everything else in the light of them. This is what we call common sense, or the implicit dominant ontology. It requires a tremendous effort for the individual to be able to make himself aware of his unconscious ontological beliefs.

We have integrated the individual with the social when we have said that ontologies exist in candid cultural form. An implicit dominant ontology is found in the myth of the leading institution of the culture.

Thus authority is dictated from above, while freedom is a product of the lower levels of the *modus operandi* institutions, so to speak: the political, for instance. The institutions lower in the scale are those which provide the freedom when they function well—the family, transportation, communication, economics, education, politics; while those which are higher provide the authority—religion, philosophy, art, science. The first division of cultures is institutional; it is not the class struggle but the institutional struggle that is the most significant.

The culture is dominated by the institution it places first in order. For example, the Church was the leading institution in the Europe of the Middle Ages, while economics and politics are the leading institutions of Soviet Russia. In the Middle Ages, the implicit dominant ontology included the superiority of certain absolute values over the human values, original sin and the partially evil nature of man due to the fall, and a variety of idealistic philosophies based upon a realm of essence held to be superior to actual existence. In Soviet Russia, the implicit dominant ontology includes the superior reality of the means of production, the class struggle, the superior values of the proletariat, and the nominalistic philosophy based upon a realm of existence superior to essence.

Beliefs and institutions are mechanisms as they function in a culture. For this functioning they need a certain amount of freedom, plus a definite degree of systematization. It is in terms of the feeling of common sense, of rational sanity rather than implicit belief, that the changes in a culture threaten to occur. When the lives of men of common sense are invaded by forces beyond common sense, that is, by the products of high abstraction, there is a threshold of violent reaction just in proportion to the extent of the invasion.

It may be difficult if not impossible to analyze the content of one's own myth without getting outside the circle of belief of which that myth forms the center. For everything in a culture is affected, from the merest details of economic life to the most grandiose conceptions of the professional philosopher. The term, "myth," as we use it, is intended to convey no opprobrium, it means a symbolic account containing a theory of reality (or the *eidos*). It is revealed in the folkways, as well as in the order of institutions, and it is pervasive through the quality which is termed the ethos.

We shall find a good example of how ideas sweep through an entire culture, changing everything before them, in the alterations now taking place in our own times. Although no doctrine has explicitly trumpeted the shift, we see one taking place throughout the culture. The shift is from substance, as the master analogy, to function. Not what a thing is, but what it does, has received the emphasis. The abandonment of some forms of nominalism in philosophy and the revival of realism, may be interpreted as an effect rather than a cause. In logic, the shift from substance to function is evident in the exchange of Aristotelian syllogism for Boolean algebra as a starting point. Newtonian substance in physics has been replaced by the relations of relativity theory. On the more practical side we have the conception of property as function (for use) for property as substance (inalienable ownership).

III

Philosophy can no longer be limited to the abstract speculations of the professional philosophers. What is new is the pursuit of research and development in technical philosophy (including logic, metaphysics, and ethics) at the empirical level. Therefore, we shall need to say a few words about the empirical problem and its approaches, and then try to show what this adds to the work of the speculative ontologist.

The organization of things and events *qua* organization, is also evidence of the force of ontology in existence. Those organizations whose postulates include false ontological propositions (and this must be true of every actual organization to some extent), are those which must suffer diminution, degradation, and perhaps extermination. An organization exists and acts according to the forces of its ontological postulates. Now a culture is one kind of organization, one whose implicit postulates are ontological; so that it is possible to assert that culture is applied ontology.

The empirical ontological problem, then, can be formulated as follows: given the institutions, tools, and folkways of actual cultures, to find the ontologies which underlie them. Cultures are all of a piece, and will give the same ring when struck in any vital spot. The task requires painstaking inquiry into, for instance, the graded meanings of the leading institution and its myth. It relies upon the use of the projective techniques furnished by empirical psychology, to interpret the implicit dominant ontology in the unconscious of the individual. For the ontology there reveals itself indirectly, never directly. The investigator has to back up, so to speak, from the encounter with the details of actual conditions in a given state, nation, tribe, or country, to reconstruct an ontology whose application could have given rise to such conditions. He will have to subtract the environmental factors, which are brute and irreducible, constituting the framework within which the choice and application of beliefs was made; and he will have to reconstruct an hypothesis on the basis of the solid remainder.

The history of philosophy is the chronological recital of a succession of theoretical ontologies whose practical role does not seem to have been well known. All we get are social interpretations of the effects of the times upon the philosophers. We do not get the dynamic interaction of the societies and philosophies. The philosopher must work with the materials and depend upon the findings of the empirical ontologist. In this sense, too, the cultural anthropologist and the sociologist are field workers in ontology; and philosophy, to the extent to which it is held down to actual human cultures, is nothing more nor less than a social science.

IV

The fundamental theory of ontology involves inquiries which can in a certain sense never be answered with any finality or absoluteness. Yet actual cultures are themselves the frozen answers to ontological problems. Unless such answers are made tentatively, they tend to block further inquiry. This is the sense in which philosophy can act as a liberating force, as Russell pointed out. It sets us free of fixed abstractions which we have been accepting as implicit beliefs. But the forces of tradition, which are the conditioned habits of cultures, are against change of any kind. In short, cultures inhibit further inquiry, by giving final answers to ultimate questions.

We see this at work in the process of education. It has often been observed that young children are natural metaphysicians. Within the narrow limits of their vocabulary, they do ask penetrating questions, such as how far does space extend or who made God. The process of education, however, transforms such basic inquiry, and smothers the hunger it represents, with the petty behavior patterns of our complex society: the rat race which consists in paying taxes, going to church, earning a living, running for street cars. The authorities who administer this system have the temerity to consider the ultimate problems adequately solved. The scientists and the artists are the only ones who are able to save or recapture what Professor Albert Einstein has somewhere described as "the holy curiosity of inquiry," an attitude paradoxically so foreign to the established religions.

A well ordered culture requires tolerance. The harmony of institutions in a culture varies with its right ordering, and the product is a certain degree of elasticity: the structure of the culture will withstand a large degree of stress without cracking. (The structure of culture in this sense is not to be confused with the political organization of a state or nation.) Witness the emergence of tolerance in the sixteenth century, illustrated in the flourishing of such figures as Bruno, Mauvissière, Greville, Gentilis, Florio, and Montaigne. The period of Western culture began with such manifestations. It is challenged now by the class struggle, by signs of intolerance, showing strains in the folds.

For all cultures have faults, potential cracks which lie athwart the structure, such as inherited and outmoded economic distinctions. Any undue pressures from without, exerted on the whole, will test the strains. Intolerances will develop. For a culture must expand or shrink. Expansion admits of difference, which is a measure of the richness of culture. But shrinking calls for similarity, when cultural adhesion demands conformity, and a unilateral culture develops which has strength in one direction only. Such stiffness is the old age of culture, a condition of hardening which may be reached prematurely.

V

Although cultures are themselves the results of inquiry, their custom is to stand in the way of further inquiry. If curiosity is almost as basic as food and sex, frustrated inquiry may be almost as disastrous to society as frustrated sexual desires are to the individual. The difficulties of actual societies may to some extent be characterized as akin to neuroses resulting from blocked inquiry. But the fact is that individuals and human cultures do not live on the unsolved problems of philosophy, but on incorporated and institutionalized solutions. Put otherwise, the texture of the everyday practical world in any complex culture like our own, consists in the working abstractions to which we have become so accustomed that we think of them, if we think of them at all, as the ultimate in what is concrete and down to earth.

It is the purpose of what Emerson labeled perpetual inquiry, to insure that such acceptance is never irrevocable. For an individual or an entire culture can progress only to the extent to which change is allowable. Cultures are supported by individuals who are able to peep for a little outside their own cultures, that is to say, at other cultures and at the extracultural aspects of nature: the physical elements, the lower organisms, the galaxies. Science in this connection is the business of opening up extracultural influences to human culture. Hope for progress depends upon the assumption that while we must work with what we have, nothing is absolutely settled.

Militant faith in bad solutions is conventional practice. An official metaphysics means a dark night of absolutism. It is not on record that either the scientific method of inquiry or the philosophical attitude of skepticism ever led to war. To be a realist, it is mistakenly thought, one must be a Platonist. To be religious, means to most people to embrace the dogma of some existing church.

But it may be that our failures and frustrations are due to an ambition for which hitherto we have not found the proper methodology. We ought to start by taking tiny steps toward ultimate goals, implementing final causes by more efficient methods. We ought to investigate the natural society. The cultural domain comprises the laws and the structure of the natural society. Some work toward the discovery of these has already begun, but it is in a tentative stage only. One has been suggested by Professor Lyman Bryson. The rate of change in any culture is a function of the complexity of the culture, so that the greater the complexity, the faster the change. Murdock and others in the cross-culture survey at Yale have discovered more than seventy institutions and folkways which appear, on historical evidence only, to be invariants for all cultures, primitive as well as advanced.

Every institution in a culture, and many folkways, represent specific answers to ontological questions. The first empirical assignment of the ontologist is to work back from the institutions and folkways of various cultures—from the specific answers, in other words—to the abstract formulations of the questions. Then the movement is to be reversed and he is to go forward again to the hypothesis of better answers. Such is the empirical side of scientific culture theory, considered in its synoptic aspect, and this aspect proves to be nothing less than applied ontology.

VI

Let us summarize in a few sentences the way we have come. The analysis of culture yields a structure, indicated by the hierarchy of institutions, and particularly by the leading myth of the culture, the implicit dominant ontology, carried by the leading institution, and accepted implicitly by individuals at the unconscious level.

Now the values which accord most closely with the leading myth are those which are allowed in the culture, and give the effective range of its actions. Thus political and ethical ranges are allowed by the lower levels, *i.e.*, the economical, and required by the higher, *e.g.*, the leading institution. Thus freedom emanates from below, while authority is imposed from above. As the unconscious of the individual is where the cultural values are accepted, it is here that the restrictions of authority are encountered as obstacles and the freedom of choice is felt as a liberating force. In a developing and growing culture, differences require a minimum of authority, while in a declining one, uniformity makes possible a maximum of authority, which is not felt in most quarters as any loss of freedom. Do not tell me what you are free from, Nietzsche said, but rather what you are free for. The measure of our demand for the freedom which makes diversity possible, is a measure of the state of our culture.

CHAPTER XXVII

The Necessity of Authority to Freedom

By GRAY LANKFORD DORSEY

Assistant Professor of Law, School of Law, Washington University

FREEDOM, OF COURSE, is plural, not singular. All the undesirable things we are free from, and all the desirable things we are free to do we tot up as the measure of freedom we enjoy. One thing man is never free from—dependence upon others. Through cooperative action men produce their joint and several needs and protect themselves and their resources.

This necessity for cooperative action is the particular source of the necessity of authority to freedom, for in order to cooperate men must know what behavior will be expected of them and what behavior they may expect from others in each concrete situation within the area of cooperative action. For these expectations to be known and fulfilled, there must be rules which are commonly followed. The system of rules, or norms, may be simple or extremely complex, depending upon the number and variety of goals a particular group seeks to achieve and the variegation of the division of labor they deem necessary to achieve them.

This may appear to be advocacy of the social compact theory of society. In a sense, it is. Indeed, how avoid it in the face of the fact that man, of all the animals, has been given the faculties of reason and true speech through which to accomplish the cooperation necessary to his existence? But I do not suppose every member of the group to have consciously subscribed to an articulated, detailed compact. Assent to the behavioral implications of a social compact is more probably imbibed through social intercourse. In fact, it is hardly proper to give the name, "assent," to socially acceptable action so induced, because non-assent is not normally presented as a possibility. Further I recognize coercion, conquest, oppression, demagoguery, etc., as often operative in securing action in accordance with a particular set of rules. Nevertheless, if there is to be any cooperative action, the action, whether voluntary or forced, must be in accordance with some non-contradictory plan. It is such a plan I speak of when I say that authority is necessary to freedom.

The Formulation of Authority

Man lives with his own body and mind within a social and a natural environment. But, in so far as he makes use of his unique characteristic as man, he never acts or reacts *directly* in response to either his internal or his external environment, but in response to his *interpretation* of them.

Man unmistakably has a hunger drive, yes. But it does not cause him to eat. It makes its demand upon him. He decides. He may refuse proffered food, even accepting death instead. Man's hunger does not cause him to eat that which will best satisfy it. He chooses. He may become undernourished on confisserie and patisserie if he wants. He accumulates information from his own experience and, through speech, the experience of others about what hunger is, and about what should be done to satisfy it. He creates a concept to include that which satisfies hunger, namely, food. He studies how much, how often, and what kinds of substances it is best or desirable to take aboard in response to the demands of hunger. He looks about him to see how best he can supply himself with the substances he admires for the purpose. If he wants a certain grain, must he plant it himself? in this kind of soil or that? on the hillside or in the valley? how plant it? how care for it? when reap it? how preserve it? how prepare it? He must learn of the soil, the sun, something of the hydrologic cycle.

But he has many more needs which, as we have noticed, he cannot satisfy by his unaided efforts. If someone else grows his grain for him, what must he do for that man? how repay? in what measure? And likewise with respect to all the others by whose labors or knowledge he benefits. What should be the relation between him and each of these various other persons?

And within the area where he labors, what should be the relation between him and others who work to produce the same article? Should each procure his own raw materials, buy all the necessary tools, manufacture the total article and peddle it to consumers? Or should he specialize upon producing in great quantity one piece of the total article? What should be the relation between him and each of the other persons engaged in the same assemblyline production? Should each man own the machine upon which he works and the whole group hire men to buy materials, schedule the production, and sell the product? Or should those who have accumulated large amounts of the medium of exchange, or who have induced others to put large amounts in their care, furnish the facilities, engage men to run them, and engage others to procure the materials, plan and supervise the production, and sell the products? Other combinations of relations, of course, are possible.

What relations should exist between a man and other men with respect to his own body and mind? Should any person be authorized to restrict his movements? Should others be authorized to limit the scope of his mind by preventing certain knowledge from reaching him and by preventing him from acting upon or expressing certain kinds of ideas?

Some gifted man (or group of men) on the basis of *all* his knowledge formulates one or a few basic propositions about the nature of man, his needs and impulses and his environment, and how he meets his needs in that environment. Probably the most clearcut example is the proposition upon which Marx and Engels erected the *Communist Manifesto*. I quote the preface by Engels:

> That in every historical epoch the prevailing mode of economic production and exchange, and the social organization necessarily following from it, form the basis upon which is built up, and from which alone can be explained, the political and intellectual history of that epoch; that consequently the whole history of mankind (since the dissolution of primitive tribal society, holding land in common ownership) has been a history of class struggles, contests between exploiting and exploited, ruling and oppressed classes; that the history of these class struggles forms a development in which a stage has now been reached where the exploited and oppressed class—the proletariat—cannot attain its emancipation from the sway of the exploiting and ruling class—the bourgeoisie—without, at the same time, and once for all, emancipating society at large from all exploitation, oppression, class distinction and class struggles.

Here, man is assumed to be a creature whose mind is capable only of interpreting the demands of his class environment or, at most, anticipating the course and the ultimate conclusion of the historical, dialectical class struggle. The enlightened man will understand his own needs and impulses as being the result of his class environment. (After the Second World War, the leading philosophical journal in Russia called on Soviet psychologists to study the "new man" which had emerged in Russia out of the experience of struggle as a united class to build socialism and protect it in war.)[1] He will understand his environment as being characterized by the continuing class struggle, and he will take account of that knowledge in his every act as he seeks to fulfil his needs and satisfy his impulses. The needs of his physiochemical body are especially emphasized—those which the products of the basic economic production relations will meet.

Upon the basis of such a proposition (that is, any proposition resulting from an exercise of the process, not the particular Marx-Engels product) men formulate a complete system of rules for all the myriad relations of society. This process, I believe, is casuistical and, therefore, may be to a large extent anonymous, or have the appearance of a social unfolding. The position that socially acceptable or required behavior in every concrete behavioral situation evolves out of a common recognition of the "needs of society," or the consciousness of the people's destiny, or of the demands of the collective will, is not at all incompatible with the position that a major society articulates in its every branch certain general propositions.[2] *These general propositions, or accepted implications of them, are the criteria for judging acceptable behavior.* This process may become so smooth and habitual as to be overlooked until a serious challenge is made of the general propositions on the basis of which a people has for years been making its decisions. Witness the new awareness of fundamental principles the challenge of Communism has brought about in the United States.

It is necessary that the formulation of a society's system of norms should be casuistical, because human imagination cannot anticipate every situation which will arise. It is desirable that the formulation should be casuistical, because a decision with respect to a particular behavioral situation is then made on the basis of more adequate knowledge than would otherwise be available. (This is the wisdom in one of the primary

[1] *New York Times,* July 28, 1949.
[2] Pitirim A. Sorokin writes: "All the important recent works on culture recognize the integration of a major culture into a single system based on a major premise and articulating it in all its main compartments. Spengler's 'Decline of the West' (New York, 1926–1928), A. J. Toynbee's 'A Study of History' (New York, 1934–1937), A. J. Kroeber's 'Configurations of Culture Growth' (Berkeley, 1945), and F. S. C. Northrop's 'The Meeting of East and West' (New York, 1946) afford examples of such works." *The Reconstruction of Humanity,* Beacon Press, Boston, 1948, p. 98, n. 2.

rules of Anglo-American law, namely, that the court will make no decision, except upon a *bona fide* case or controversy.) It is further desirable that the formulation should be casuistical, because the opportunity for change is more readily apparent.

A society's system of norms defines the individual's freedoms. A general norm may state that the individual should have freedom of speech. A specific norm will state that persons in official capacities should not be allowed to judge beforehand what a man may say or print. On the other hand, specific norms will state that no person shall be allowed to spread a false alarm of fire in a crowded theater, or to incite a mob to violence; or that an employer may not print or say certain things to his employes before a labor election, and that union members may not say or print certain things about a place of business with which they are in dispute.

The freedoms of the individual will depend upon the fact that other persons are required to do and to refrain from doing certain acts with respect to him. Needless to say, the corollary of his freedom is the duty to perform the acts required of him and to refrain from the acts proscribed to him, in order that others may realize their freedoms. His acts, with respect to the system of norms will fall into three general classes: things he must do, things he must not do, and things he may do.[3]

A man may have certain inalienable rights, but he can actualize them only after their behavioral implications have been formulated in a body of authority and that authority is followed by a group of persons in cooperative action. That man has certain inalienable rights is, in fact, not a self-evident truth, but a conclusion about the nature of man which a few men arrived at and many have agreed with. It is the kind of general proposition which can be the basis or part of the basis for a complete system of norms.

To recapitulate: Cooperative action of a number of men is necessary to the freedom of any one man; authority, in the sense of a hierarchical body of norms, is necessary to cooperative action, and therefore to freedom. But also necessary to cooperative action, evidently, is action in accordance with the authority.

[3] The conception of the origin of norms followed here is Dr. Northrop's, with the exception of the suggestion that the body of the system is casuistically filled in.

The Functioning of Authority

Persons endeavoring to take cooperative action will have certain institutions charged with securing action in accordance with the norms, when that action is not voluntarily forthcoming. The organized force of the community is then placed at the disposal of these institutions.

The never ending debate about the proper balancing of authority and freedom arises mainly out of the formation and functioning of these institutions. There are these principal tasks to be performed: selecting the goals which will be achieved by the group effort; planning the division of labor which will best achieve those goals; directing the group effort; accumulating and dispensing necessary information; determining what acts are absolutely essential to the success of the common effort and requiring those acts of the appropriate persons, all or some; determining what acts will frustrate the common effort and preventing all persons from doing those acts. In any one society some of these functions may be kept more or less decentralized, as in the United States production goals evolve out of a multitude of decisions by private producers.

It is a part of the system of norms (which I have called authority, and believe to be authority in its truest sense) to delineate the organization of the institutions which perform these key functions and the method by which individuals will be selected to fill up the institutions; to delimit the functions which each institution shall perform and the kind and scope of action it can take in doing so. The body of authority delineates the limitations and the degree of representativeness of the institutions which are the central nervous system of a society.

A society, however, with respect to the particular form it takes, is not a natural organism. Unfortunately a society's central nervous system is capable of planning, directing, and coercing only for the benefit of those individuals who control the central nervous system. This is a familiar quagmire. I shall not enter it, but pick up my path on the far side.

This brings us to the fact that to a greater or lesser degree authority conflicts with freedom, and this in two respects. One instance is general and results from the imperfection of man's knowledge. To the extent man errs, his freedoms will be at odds with the perfect freedom he would enjoy if he knew himself and his world perfectly.

The other instance is personal. To the extent that the individual's judgment varies from the general judgment, the freedom he demands and authority are in conflict. This personal variance will result from two general causes: shortsighted self-interest; and disagreement with some or all of the general propositions upon which the body of authority rests. The product of the first cause are the common criminals. We need not be concerned that these persons are denied some freedoms because the difference between their conception of freedom and that of their society arises not from principle but from avarice. With the other group we need to be deeply concerned.

Nation-states are presently the most inclusive social groups. It is the national group that is bound together by a common fund of natural resources, a common plan for the division of labor, a common system of institutions. In the present world it is the nation-state which maintains the basic system of productive-protective relations. Therefore a man gets the freedoms that go with the system of relations and the state upon which he is dependent for survival, possibly by choice, but more often *through accident* of birth, by conquest, or by revolution.[4]

Therefore, a great many persons find themselves living under "freedoms" they despise and consider false. In a very real sense the body of authority under which these principled dissidents live is not valid for them.

Here, to my mind, is the gravest conflict between freedom and authority. There can be no doubt that the principled dissidents have some obligation to the other persons in the system by whose cooperation they benefit. Complementarily, as long as the principled dissidents perform their obligations and refrain from frustrating the common cooperative effort, it would appear inescapable that they should have certain rights which the other persons in the system should respect.

But how much is due them? Should dissidents be given every freedom to speak, publish, move about, assemble, that others enjoy, even if the dissidents utilize these very freedoms to promote a change in the body of authority which defines them and the institutions which actualize them and protect them? If the change they seek is through parliamentary

[4]For more on my conception of the state see my chapter, "A Porch from Which to View World Organization," *Foundations of World Organization: A Political and Cultural Appraisal,* Lyman Bryson, Louis Finkelstein, Harold D. Lasswell, R. M. MacIver, Editors, Conference on Science, Philosophy and Religion in Their Relation to the Democratic Way of Life, Inc., New York, 1952, pp. 359-377.

means? through subversion and economic blackmail? through organized sabotage and violence? Or is there justification for segregating the principled dissidents physically, for exterminating those who show signs of leadership? Above all, is there justification for keeping them by force for the benefit of their labor when they wish to sever all connections and leave?

By what criteria shall we decide such questions? There's the rub! Principled dissidents quarrel not simply with the application of norms to them, they deny first premises. Even the benefits of freedom, social status, material wealth, seem bitter and false to them, because they cannot accept as true the basic propositions from which those benefits flow. Is it right to judge them by national justice because of the general consent of even a vast majority of *other* persons? Must they be accounted rightfully subject to a nation's justice, simply because they are found within a certain geographical territory? or because they were born to these parents rather than to those? Above all, should the question of whether they are subject to a nation's justice be decided in accordance with a criterion which is itself national?

National and Supranational Freedom

If freedom and justice are at the present time *entirely* national, then there is no freedom outside of national freedom for anyone to make a decision about whether a particular person is subject to a particular nation's justice. And it would be meaningless to say that a decision on the matter was just or unjust, except in terms of the legal and moral principles of the nation within which the decision is made. Freedom and justice result from a conception of truth. If there is only national truth, then there can be only national freedom and justice. If there is truth beyond, there can be freedom and justice beyond.

It is only natural that the set of fundamental propositions upon which a group of persons bases their cooperative effort should purport to exhaust the truth about the nature of man and his universe. If any such set actually did so, and men were able to recognize truth, we might expect a single worldwide cooperative social group. But some men seize upon one part of the truth, others upon another. Because of human bias, it is extremely difficult to convince any national group that they have not the whole of truth in their grasp, simply by pointing out a piece of truth some other people have got hold of. The tendency is (1) not to listen, (2) simply to deny it is truth, (3) to explain it in terms of their own conceptions.

However, one bit of truth is inescapably necessary. That bit of truth is the premise with which this paper began, namely, that man is the kind of creature who can meet even his most dire needs and elemental impulses only by cooperative action with other men on the basis of a common interpretation of needs, impulses, and of environment. (Communism, which denies such a capacity in man, in its own birth and growth is the most striking illustration of the exercise of this faculty.)

Here, then, is truth which goes beyond the nation. It follows that the most primary need of man is to select such an interpretation and to live accordingly. I hold it consequent that there is a generally valid norm, beyond the nations, which all men if they would be honest must admit, namely, that: every man should be free to make or choose the interpretation, the fundamental propositions, the body of authority, he will accept and to live according to them, consistent with the same right for all other men.

Of course very few men will undertake a completely new interpretation of man's nature and environment and of the consequences for human cooperative behavior. Most will passively accept the interpretation of others. Yet a man with strong social conscience, courage, and imagination may arrive at conclusions so radical as to comprise the basis for a whole new ordering of men in society, a new culture, different institutions of the state; or he may make a contribution to the knowledge upon which his society is based, reinforcing its fundamental propositions or, perhaps, altering them. A man of equal social conscience and courage but of less imagination is apt to see what strikes him as social injustice in his own society, and to espouse the body of authority of some other society which tags as unjust the acts or conditions which have incensed him. Only later, perhaps after he has betrayed the trust of associates or done them violence, will he become aware of the errors in his new allegiance.

These principled dissidents are persons who are part of one national society and yet by conviction owe allegiance to another. Should the issue of whether such persons are subject to national justice be decided by a criterion which is itself national? I answer in the negative. If we admit the general validity of the norm that every man should be free to live according to that truth and social justice which he shall select, then it is meaningful to say that the actions of any nation are unjust which deny that freedom to any individual.

If this is true, then we need a body of supranational authority, a set of supranational norms. The beginnings of such an authority have long existed in international law. It is the fashion at the moment to attribute the ineffectuality of international law to the fact that sufficient coercion has not been brought to bear, as it is in national law, to induce unwilling persons to act in accordance with the norms of the body of authority.

It does not follow, as too many proclaim, that the solution is simply to have the courage or the faith to form supranational political institutions and to commit to them overawing armed forces. This shallow solution overlooks the fact that institutions can function only if their human molecules act in accordance with a common authority or plan, and that armies or police possess no force unless their human muscles obey the commands of a common authority. Force serves justice, only as it is used to secure the social articulation of some authority which defines the measures of freedom, status, and estate appropriate to each man.

A Proposal for International Democracy

Our first problem with respect to supranational freedom is not to start killing those who appear to us to be threatening that freedom, nor is it to erect institutions to protect supranational freedom, nor to endow those institutions with power capable of world immolation. The first problem is to reach a decision upon what supranational authority is to guide our efforts.

Soviet Communism offers a logically neat answer to the problem: eliminate all nations and establish throughout the world among all people Communist authority, Communist freedoms, Communist social justice, Communist production relations. The United States and many other countries reject this way of securing worldwide cooperative action among men.

Communism has the initiative at present, because it has a definite program of belief, faith, and action. The program of Communism's opponents is far less definite and far less common. Every action of every Communist meshes perfectly with the actions of every other Communist. Communists offer specific freedoms. Of course the freedom that is advertised in the show window is the freedom from exploitation of a man's labor by others. Any man who has at some time worked long hours for a low wage with no prospect of anything better, can imagine what a lift the promise of this freedom—if accepted at its face value—could give to a man's heart. Also in the package, of course, is the complete domination of mind and body by the dictatorship of the proletariat, but its presence may not be known until the sale is made, and the individual is safely captive, and begins to pay for his purchase. Or, being forewarned, the individual may discount a rumored evil and weigh it against grievances he has known, and these greatly exaggerated by his own bias.

The Communist plan for world conquest is multiform, liquid, subtle. The Communists have the force of traditional organized military units, but these have been used more as threat than in action. They are avid and clever proselytizers, tireless infiltrators and organizers. They are skilled in the incitement and control of mass emotion, skilled in economic and parliamentary maneuver. They are reputed masters of sabotage and guerrilla warfare, and they plan far in advance, assigning specific targets, such as central power plants, to teams of Communists who must rehearse their mission.

Above all, Communists have the initiative, because they are sustained by the driving force of moral conviction. Communism purports to have shown them the truth about man. It claims to be the new truth and the new justice, and it tells men that they cannot be wrong so long as they follow its program. Here is the stuff of which courage and hope are born.

The nations that oppose the spread of Communism prepare in alarm but they prepare to strike in only one dimension, with traditional organized military units (and in this their cooperation is troubled), while all else is denunciation, frustration, rage, recriminations, resentment, discouragement, apathy.

Such folly! Let us defeat Communist truth with Democratic truth, defeat Communist freedoms with Democratic freedoms, defeat Communist justice with Democratic justice, defeat Communist evangelism with Democratic evangelism. Let us undermine the moral conviction of the Communists and strengthen our own, evaporate their force by inducing defection, confusion, apathy, and build our strength on the conviction that we serve truth and seek freedom and justice for all.

These things are attainable. But we can accomplish them only through cooperative effort. And in order to have cooperative effort we need a body of authority to guide our actions. Further, that body of authority must derive from truth we can all accept, whether Asian, European, African, or American. It must be universal truth.

I propose a Democratic Manifesto. But it must be a Manifesto of International Democracy. Its fundamental proposition must tear the bonds from the mind and spirit of man that the *Communist Manifesto* places upon them.

I suggest the following as the fundamental proposition of International Democracy:

> That man, of all the animals (in the words of Grotius), "has received for his protection no natural weapons or protective covering, but instead reason and speech; that alone the easiest of prey to wild beasts and the elements, man, through cooperative action in society has become the master of the earth"; that this cooperation is not automatic or accidental but must be accomplished by man through the exercise of those faculties unique with him: through reason arriving at an understanding of his own needs and impulses and of the total environment within which he functions, through speech sharing and modifying the various opinions, in order that where agreement is found cooperative behavior may satisfy the common needs and impulses; that on the basis of such an area of agreement and its implications for human behavior man forms a system of relations for producing his needs and protecting his person and social, political, and legal institutions in harmony with those relations; and that, consequently, the only universal justice, that justice which International Democracy seeks, is to give to every man the opportunity within the bounds imposed by the necessity of cooperative behavior, to choose or form his own interpretation of man's needs, impulses, and environment, and to associate freely with others as they may agree, pursuing their common goals in accordance with the implications of that interpretation, without infringing the equal right of other men to do likewise.

Consequences of International Democracy

Many of the implications of this proposition would need to be thought out in time and under various circumstances. Consultation should be held among all non-Communist peoples about the adequacy of this proposition and the content of a Manifesto of International Democracy. Some implications of the proposed proposition are immediately apparent. For instance, we can immediately answer a question posed earlier, namely, whether any nation has the right to keep principled dissidents for their labor when they wish to sever all connections and leave. As the fundamental proposition includes in its implications the universal norm that every man should be free to make or choose the body of authority he will accept, we must answer this question in the negative. On the basis of universal justice, not just our own national justice, we can say that it is unjust for Russia to restrain bodily those Russians who seek to escape their homeland.

On the other hand, the conclusion with respect to persons who are unwilling thus to migrate, would appear to be that they must accept the kind of freedom and justice which goes with the institutions and the system of productive-protective relations whose benefits they are unwilling to forego. This conclusion, however, needs considerable qualification.

In the first place, a man's choice of what freedom he will enjoy, what truth and social justice he will live by, is to a high degree today limited to those sets of freedom, truth, and social justice which the various states offer. The individual's freedom must always be exercised "within the bounds imposed by the necessity of cooperative behavior." There will always be some individuals who will feel restrictions which the common authority places upon them are unjust. Yet, to insure the freedoms of others which these restrictions make possible, obedience must be required. The most that can be done for those who feel themselves injured is to keep open to them opportunities to change the authority or to disassociate themselves from the group. As a practical matter, few men are able to exercise even the limited choice between various national freedoms. It is always difficult to migrate. Furthermore, other nations will not always take in those who want to come to them.

As there cannot be complete mobility of nationals, we must seriously qualify the conclusion that all persons who are unwilling to migrate must then be accounted justly subject to whatever measures of coercion the nation puts upon them. More detailed supranational norms are needed to specify when a person may be rightfully accounted subject to a particular national justice.

Of course the application to Russia of any norms based on the Democratic Manifesto would have to await the establishment of a body of authority of International Democracy. Doubtless, institutions endowed with the organized force of the world community would also need to be established to insure effective worldwide cooperative action. There are, however, certain norms of International Democracy, in accordance with which the nations opposing the Communist solution can profitably direct their own affairs immediately.

One is concerned with the reverse of the coin with respect to principled dissidents: whether they must rightfully be accorded all freedoms of movement, assembly, and speech that other members of a national society enjoy, until they are personally proved guilty of some punishable act, such as treason. Specifically, let us consider the case of the Communists in the United States. These persons have exercised their most fundamental, universal right—to choose the interpretation of man, his needs, and impulses, and his environment, and the resulting body of authority under which they want to live. We should recognize that right because of its basis in supranational truth.

But by their own act these persons have rendered any non-Communist national body of authority invalid for them. Therefore they have no further claim of right to any of the freedoms which that authority specifies. However, the United States under the norm of International Democracy stated above, certainly would not be justified in withholding civil rights from domestic Communists, unless it offered them full opportunity to leave our national society and join a Communist society.

One other major qualification results from the fundamental proposition of International Democracy. If man seeks his destiny through an interpretative process, then he must communicate with other men, in order that they may share experience and their interpretations of that experience.

We have then, another general norm, namely, that every man should be free to communicate his ideas to others and to receive theirs; and because of the emotional coating men give to ideas, I believe this norm should include the right of advocacy. It follows that the United States (or any nation with respect to principled dissidents in its midst) would not have the right, under the universal justice of International Democracy, to withhold freedoms from Communists or others if they sought only to convince others by open and honest communication and to change by open parliamentary means the productive-protective relations and the institutions of government.

To the extent that the plan of Communism departs from this open and honorable method of propagation, the nation which has offered them free egress has every right to withhold whatever freedoms from these principled dissidents it deems necessary in order to protect the effective functioning of its own system of relations and institutions. Of course every man should receive the fullest protection of all his civil rights, and be given every constitutional protection in the course of the process of determining whether he has indeed chosen Communism in preference to United States democracy. But we are simple fools to allow one who has alienated himself from us by choosing Communism to remain among us scoffing at our justice, our truth, our authority, seeking to destroy them, and yet invoking them when it suits his purpose. We are even greater fools to feel that we are somehow obligated to accord him the "constitutional rights" that he has rejected.

We must reach the same conclusion if we look only to our own legal norms. The doctrine of conspiracy, firmly established in our law, declares that every party to a conspiracy shall be held guilty of every act which any party has performed. There can be no question that, among the Communists, each is tied to the other in a conspiracy to overthrow all non-Communist governments, to destroy all freedoms except Communist freedoms.

Geography and Nationality

These two specific examples of the implications of the fundamental proposition for a Manifesto of International Democracy illustrate the need for complete reconsideration of the criteria of nationality. Geographical location should receive a much less central place in determining the nationality of an individual.

Serious consideration should be given to discarding entirely the notion that a nation is geographically fixed. Is the notion really any more than an outmoded feudal heritage? Eliminating geographical location and area from the determination of nationality and from the concept of nation would dissolve the greatest dilemma facing the peoples opposing Communism. This dilemma arises out of a conflict between the obligations imposed by international law and practice, and increasing awareness on the world scale that persecution and injustice to some must be counted an injury to all.

The highest obligation of a nation under international law is to respect the sovereignty of other nations, and probably the most serious breach of this obligation is to interfere in the relations between a people and their own government. On the other hand, when a ruthless minority has seized control and maintains its control by mass executions, forced labor, and torture, then the growing awareness that "justice and freedom are indivisible" demands that something be done.

United States policy has reconciled these two demands in this way: it offers to and does help any people to resist and defeat the overthrow of their government by internal subversion and violence or by external aggression; but once a government has fallen under Communist control it honors its obligation under international law and abandons to their fate all those persons within that country who oppose Communism. This enables the Communists, once they have taken over the government of Russia, Poland, Czechoslovakia, China, to consolidate their hold on that geographical area and the persons they choose to allow to continue to live in it, and gather their strength for the next bite.

Some who recognize the necessity of wresting the initiative from the Communists propose military action against those countries. This is wrong for a number of reasons. One is that under the universal justice of International Democracy we must respect the right of those who are convinced of the truth of Communism to live according to its tenets, except as those tenets abridge their own obligation to recognize the right of others to do the same. Another reason is that, even according to our own doctrine, at present all the persons we supposedly seek to aid are still nationals owing allegiance to the governments we seek to overthrow.

Suppose that all non-Communist peoples unite in the policy of International Democracy that a nation has no claim upon principled dissidents; that these persons must be allowed to disassociate themselves from the nation of which they have been a part? Principled dissidents would then be counted free to leave the authority they hate, and there would be some chance for them to have a place to make a new start. Suppose a man took a share of land with him when he rejected one national authority and placed himself, with his land, under another. Consider the possibilities for freedom and peace in a world in which the natural resources of nations did not lie in contiguous land, water, and air, but were scattered about the face of the earth, so that transactions with one's own next door neighbor might be international intercourse. War as we know it would be strategically, logistically, and psychologically impossible. The suggestion that an emigrant should continue to hold the same land is merely one of the extreme possibilities of International Democracy. The program, of course, would have to be worked out by all interested peoples on the basis of what is presently possible.

If principled dissidents are no longer to be considered nationals, we are then free to aid them to resist police violence, avoid execution and forced labor. Indeed we have an obligation to use every means to induce the Communist government under which they live to recognize their rights under International Democracy. We are justified in propagating to the fullest the program of International Democracy in these countries. We are justified, in view of the announced aggressive program of Communism, in encouraging, planning, and directing economic disruption, and, if advisable, even sabotage and guerrilla action, in order to induce the Communist governments to honor their obligations under International Democracy—which is as equitable for them as for others. All these measures are less than the launching of full scale war, and promise more in the effort to bring about greater measures of freedom, justice, and peace in the world. We should fight a war if we must to insure the supremacy of a program of International Democracy over the program of world Communism—but only if we must.

In the meantime the program of International Democracy must be constructed. The peoples of Asia, Europe, the Americas, Africa, Australia must consult and agree upon this or some other fundamental proposition about man and his universe. They must fashion a Manifesto of common faith and belief. The body of authority must be casuistically filled in. The institutions will practically form themselves and acceptance and support of the program of International Democracy will grow to irresistible proportions in a short time if the fundamental proposition strikes truth. Here lies hope and strength for freedom and justice!

Comment by Edgar S. Brightman:

The theme of this paper is an important truth—but it is only a half truth, and, taken alone, a dangerous half. For while authority *is* indeed necessary to freedom ("me this uncharted freedom tires") the dialectic of social reality requires the complementary principle of "the necessity of freedom to authority." Especially since "we need a body of supranational authority," we need free, democratic safeguards if we are to avoid the fate of Orwell's *1984*. These safeguards are hinted at in Dr. Dorsey's "Democratic Manifesto," but should, in my judgment, be made more affirmative and integral to the argument.

CHAPTER XXVIII

Freedom and Authority as Integral to Culture and Structure

By DOROTHY D. LEE

Professor of Anthropology, Vassar College

I

MY FUNCTION IN this Symposium is to show how concepts of freedom and authority vary from culture to culture. I have therefore chosen for presentation societies where the concepts do vary; where, if the concepts are present at all, they may be related not to each other directly, but only to the whole in which they are rooted. I shall speak of cultures where freedom—whether recognized conceptually or not—is the same for all aspects of the universe, including man; where authority may lie in natural law or cultural tenet; where authority, as taboo or regulation, may mean freedom, not interference; where chieftancy or other political leadership may not mean authority, except as maturity and ability to guide; where authority can never be delegated, but lies in the structured interdependency of roles, or in hereditary right, or in organic incorporation of culturally patterned experience.

It is not easy to recognize freedom in other cultures when this is not emancipation from, not freedom of choice and not freedom from limits. In our culture, it is difficult to recognize as freedom, the positive freedom to perform an established function, what we would term the filling of an *ascribed* role. Culture itself is considered by social scientists to be interfering with the natural desires and the expression of the individual. The "don't" is prohibiting, the taboo is an interdiction; the "do!" is a command, the regulation is restrictive; the "must" is an obligation. And when other cultures are presented, they usually bristle with regulations and taboos. There has, therefore, come to be the impression that people in primitive societies have little, if any freedom; that they have to conform to traditionally imposed behavior, and to fulfil the obligation imposed upon them by their ascribed role.

For example, Raymond Firth, writing of the Tikopia of the Solomon Protectorate, uses with great frequency terms implying external compulsion. On one page chosen at random I found ten such terms. But when we investigate intensively the wealth of incidental detail which he gives and when we delete the interpretative terms which come from our culture, we find performance of function rather than fulfilment of an obligation. For example, Firth calls an obligation the contributions of food to the chief when he is to give a feast in the name of the clan. Now, there is no coercion to contribute; and when a man does not do so, he suffers, not through punishment, but because he misses out in the enjoyment of participating in the general contribution. Firth tells of a man from another clan, who took advantage of his position as a neighbor to participate in this contribution. To Firth, the giving was an obligation, but obviously to this man it was a privilege. Again, when Firth describes the functions of men in respect to the clan of their wives, he speaks of the obligation to act as cooks at the great feasts of the wives' kinship unit; in his description, this function appears as onerous and unpleasant. When he describes the place of the sons of these men within their mothers' kinship group, he calls them guests of honor who receive gifts and services. But he does not say that it is an "obligation" to be a guest of honor, though this position is as structured as that of cook. Further, a man has the privilege of functioning in the role of his dead father; and Firth tells of a feast where the chief sister's son, the chief guest of honor, chose to perform the function of cook in place of his dead father.

In both examples there was freedom of choice involved. When people were free to refrain, they *chose* to give food and service. But I do not believe that the freedom of the Tikopia lies in this area of possible freedom of choice. The Tikopia are free, because they are *free to perform* a clear function which holds meaning and value for them; not because they are *free to choose to perform*. What we conceive as an imposed behavior, is apparently undertaken willingly because it is good and satisfying.

In our society we see culture as interfering with the freedom of the individual, and express this view in our speech. The terms we use, such as ascribed role, prescribed behavior, inhibition, prohibition, interdiction, obligation, when we speak of culturally patterned behavior, beg the question in that they presuppose that such interference is there. In the vernacular, we imply the presence of external limitation of freedom, in terms of external time limits, or limits coming from external plan. We say, "It is five o'clock, *I've got to run*," or, "*I've got to* do my hair because I am having guests to dinner." This is the way the growing child hears his mother phrase her behavior at home; and it is usually in terms of such external interference that he has his culture presented to him. It is this phrasing of culture which underlies the discussion about toilet training, which has been going on among child specialists; but whether the infant is toilet trained early or late, firmly or permissively, the training is still given as an interference, not as a privilege. In Burma, where the individual has personal autonomy unparalleled in our culture, the baby is nevertheless reportedly toilet trained by the time he is six months old. But there, as in China, the training is presented to the child as a way *to do;* the baby is gently guided into being socially acceptable, which he wants to be above all else. In this way of presenting culture to the infant the cultural tenets, the rules and taboos, are actually a map of procedure, guiding and freeing, and offering the training and discipline necessary to satisfying conduct.

In such cultures, the *must* and the *don't*, which for us interfere with personal freedom, are an aspect of guidance. We use them in this sense in our society, but we discount this use when we evaluate the terms. For example, we say in giving directions, Don't take the first turn to the left. This is guidance, giving the individual the freedom to proceed. In this way, the Navaho mother brings up her child with a continual "no," "don't," by way of showing him how he can proceed safely through life. Nature and its immanent divinity, for the Navaho, are potentially dangerous; and culture offers a guide for safe and harmonious relations between the individual and nature. The *must* and *don't* then release for action. It is not the authority of the mother which guides to action; it is her knowledge and wisdom.

Among the Wintu Indians of California, the *must* and *must not* are used only in connection with the necessity immanent in nature and culture, and they are used by people who have ability to guide but not the power to enforce. So a chief, having reached that point in the scalp ceremony where a young captive boy must be shot to death, says to his people, "The boy moves to compassion; but we must not (cannot) act otherwise." A father brings up his motherless daughter with this kind of *must*. "You are now a woman," he says; "you must gather wood; a woman is one who gathers wood." Here the *must* of guidance and custom is clearly distinguished linguistically from the personal command and request. The authority of action lies in the cultural regulation; and culture itself is guidance.

II

In many cultures, freedom and authority do not occur as concepts; there are often no words for these, or at any rate, no words are reported. But they do occur as realities recognizably equivalent to our own concepts. Thus I speak of them in the three societies I present below.

Freedom and Authority in Pre-British Burma

To the Burmese, freedom meant and still means, personal autonomy. Observers have been struck by what they call the fierce independence of the Burmese. This freedom arises largely from the pattern of responsibility for the course of one's own life, for progress in status during the present life and along the stages toward higher incarnation to the point where no incarnation would be necessary. A man was free to achieve deeds of merit, and thus strengthen his *kan*, his luck or personality or potency, through which he could withstand evil. Deeds accumulated from a past existence, were responsible for his *kan* at birth; and he could maintain and enhance this *kan* through maintaining a favorable balance of merits over demerits in the present life. So whatever life brought, the poverty or wealth of one's family of birth, low or high status, health, good crops—all was of one's own free doing; "as you desire, so you get," said the Burmese.

A corollary was an extreme sense of personal inviolability, and its counterpart—a respect for the autonomy of others. A British magistrate, Hall, says that a villager seeing a man about to cross a bridge which he knew to be broken, would not give warning, as he assumed that the traveller knew what he was about. No one would try to stop a man who was seen to be attempting suicide; no one would offer help to a man obviously in dire straits, for this would reflect on the man's ability

Freedom and Authority as Integral to Culture

to run his own life. In the village culture of pre-British Burma, there was almost no hired labor of any kind; and in the monasteries, where work had to be done by young novices for the monks, because they could not occupy themselves with mundane things, the monk did not say, "Do this," but, "Do what is lawful," reminding the boy to act according to the cultural tenet, not ordering him.

Authority lay in the way of life of the village. There was a way to act within the structured system of the family; a way to act as a member of the village, as a Buddhist, as a Burmese. If the Burmese found no clear guidance in the culture, he could go to the headman for arbitration or to consult him; he inherited the right to go to this particular headman, just as the headman inherited the right to guide this particular group of people who lived in a "circle" of adjoining villages. His "authority" lay in this reciprocal right; and it consisted in an interpretation of the village law, in giving counsel, in arbitration. He made no dictatorial pronouncement, and he did not coerce. He had no police force and he needed none.

We can see how contrary this was to the picture of authority and freedom among the British, when we consider what happened when the British assumed control of Burma. For greater efficiency, they rearranged the boundaries of the circle of villages, thus including people who had no right to the leadership of a particular headman. They found the hereditary element irrational, and changed the headmen into appointed officials; but, in the eyes of the Burmese, these officials had no authority of any kind, because authority was an inborn, not a delegated, right. As the British saw no clear evidence of law, or the enforcement of law, they imposed duties on the villagers from above; and soon they had to install a village police force.

The British believed in law as rule and authority; but to the Burmese, law was authority only in the sense that a dictionary is an authority in our culture. The British, fully intending to base legislation upon Burmese principles, were thwarted at every turn by what they considered the disorganization and irrationality of Burmese law. In the end, they installed British judges and introduced their idea of human freedom: a jury of Burmese who could pass judgment upon their peers. It did not work, because the Burmese would not be bound or coerced by fixed principles of procedure, externally imposed. For example, if a woman accused a man for rape, they, knowing her, might convict her instead for seduction.

The British misunderstood the basis of freedom and authority; they did not see that authority maintained, and guided to, freedom.

Freedom and Authority in Greek Culture

Greeks have a word for freedom, and they use it frequently. It is a term for political emancipation and freedom from coercion. Freedom is also an inner quality, so that, throughout the years of Italian and German occupation, the Greeks remained free, for there was no inner submission to the external coercion. They gave expression to this freedom, when they defied Hitler, knowing that they would certainly be defeated, and perhaps exterminated. Little boys gave expression to this freedom when they courted death, playing pranks on German officers and defacing posters.

Greek freedom is a dimension of the Greek *philotimo,* the self-esteem that is upheld and enhanced by fulfilment of role as a member of a family or a village, and as a Greek. The *philotimo* incorporates self-control, fortitude, hardihood, simplicity, and moderation; it means strong discipline. But discipline itself is a freeing, guiding, positive element; it is not interfering, but enabling. With such discipline, the Greek can be free to act according to his *philotimo,* without calculating the risks involved, the price to be paid. When a man speaks of going to war, without first finding out what provision will be made for his family, or for himself in case he is incapacitated; or when he speaks of working to earn a dowry for his sister, even when the betrothed does not demand it, so as to uphold the family *philotimo,* he uses terms expressive of free act.

Work within the structured role is life to the Greeks; diligence is an expression of freedom to perform one's function. But work under external compulsion is not good; speed induced by external time limits is insupportable, interfering with personal freedom. Greeks wear watches as ornaments; but only those unfortunates in industry and other urban occupations use them for the limitation of activity. The term for "to hurry" is literally "to coerce oneself." There is no dualism of "work" and "leisure"; leisure is a dimension of all work, the feeling of internal freedom while at work or at rest. Greeks who emigrated to this country took up shoe-blacking; men who despised cooking as an occupation for men became cooks in their own restaurants, rather than have to follow the dictates of outsiders.

Greek parents say that the first thing they teach a baby is obedience; but this is obedience as role, within the structured unit. The role itself is not an interference, is not felt as constricting; it is a part of being. A man does not *assume* the role of brother or son-in-law; he *is* one, and that is why he *acts* as one. Role guides, motivates, and frees. Authority is within the role of being a father; it belongs to the structure of the unit; it is internal. To all such authority the Greek tenders obedience in filling his role as a free individual. But the authority of the central government is external; Greeks do not recognize it as part of a structure of interrelated roles. To this, Greeks owe no obedience. Their guide is expediency, in deciding whether to obey or to circumvent. The honored village teacher has now been supplanted by an appointee from the central government; and his authority is not recognized. Authority obtains its validity only from place in the structure of an organic—not a created—whole. And in obeying this authority, the individual does not forfeit freedom, but rather acts freely in the performance of his established function.

Freedom and Authority in Tiv Culture

The term, "freedom," seems to have no relevance in connection with the Tiv of Southern Nigeria. Certainly we cannot speak of autonomy, as there is no *autos,* no individual self. When the British established their rule over the Tiv, they found people who were continuous with their social unit, present, past, and future, and with the environment; with what they called "the land." A man could not perform an act, even unknowingly and involuntarily, could not think a thought, make a wish, have a hope, or a resentment, without possibly opening the way to pollution of what they called "the land"—whether fields or people or animals.

It was not enough to follow the positive guidance of culture to live securely. Man could offend without intending to, or wanting to, without his knowledge, and without any memory of such offense. He could offend one of the many natural spirits or ancestral spirits, and thus release contaminating evil; or he could offend one of the potent men in his immediate social unit and bring upon himself the angry retaliation of these people. All this was unpredictable.

The main stress of the cultural tenets was in teaching avoidance of harm; a Tiv tells us that the first word a baby learned to say was "don't."

There was a "do" also, taught later in life, for increasing personal potency so that evil could be withstood. There was a series of progressive initiations into akombo rites, beginning approximately at adolescence, through which a man acquired the knowledge and the right needed for the performance of specific acts of prevention, purging, and expulsion; and there was a series of parallel procedures, through which a man gradually incorporated his social unit, thus increasing his potency so that it kept step with his progress in akombo initiation.

Yet the picture was not permeated with the insecurity, the inability to act, which we would expect to find if such conditions prevailed in our society. If we do speak of freedom in connection with the Tiv, we can say that the Tiv were free to act, because the function of the ordinary Tiv lay in the present act, in performance; it was not concerned with effectiveness, with results, with the future. In our society, we can act freely only when the way is clear; when what is ahead is predictable and rational and possibly within our control. To the ordinary Tiv, these things were not important. A man was free to act as a husband, clearing a plot for his wife's garden; and a woman was free to cultivate her beans, irrespective of the akombo dangers to the crop and lurking evil magic. The uncertainty of the harvest was irrelevant; it was not the concern of these people. The ordinary Tiv was not even certain of how he should act or how he did act; of what he thought or perceived; it was not his function to be certain.

It was the man in authority who was responsible for all these. It was his function to see to it that the normal course of events was not interfered with; it was he who was responsible for the effectiveness of the acts of the people of his unit; for good harvest, for normal rainfall, for the fertility of the wives, for normal health. The well-being of the family unit was incorporated in the potency of its elders and in the even greater potency of its headman. The well-being of the land was embodied in the potency of the chief; as he throve, so did the land thrive. If red monkeys destroyed the crops, the chief was responsible; he had allowed himself to grow weak. If adultery or a murder was committed within the family unit, it was the headman who was responsible, because he was the unit. In such cases, the elders met in council to shift the responsibility to the concrete culprit. They told the man what he had done, and whether he had knowledge or memory of such an act was irrelevant, for certainty came only through authority, and not through the evidence of one's own senses.

Authority did not come to a man through his being an elder, or headman, or chief. Elders and headmen were recognized as such because of their achieved potency, wisdom, knowledge, their organic incorporation of the social unit. Chiefs were elected in rotation from the council of headmen; so that sometimes they had less authority than the headmen in their council. Men in authority diagnosed, fixed guilt, pointed out a course of action, advised, arbitrated; but they did not punish, coerce, or enforce. People came to them for reference, clarification, counsel, approval, of a proposed course of action.

When the British rearranged districts, so that a chief was set in authority over people unrelated to him, they created an empty shell, as it was impossible for any one to be an authority to people with whom he was not organically continuous; just as it is impossible for a heart to pump blood to a strange body. When they chose young, thrusting men as chiefs, they again attempted the impossible; for a man had to grow in authority, along established procedures and experiences. Authority among the Tiv completed, assured, validated, individual performance; but when the individual sought the authority of the headman, he was not going to something external, because the headman was regarded as the unit itself, of which the individual was a part. If we must relate authority to freedom, we can say here that authority was necessary to freedom; but to discuss Tiv society in terms of freedom is, I believe, to introduce an irrelevant principle.

Bibliography

1. Raymond Firth, *We, the Tikopia,* American Book Company, New York, 1936.
2. D. D. Lee, "Wintu War Dance: A Textual Account," *Proceedings of the Sixth Pacific Science Congress,* held at Berkeley, Stanford and San Francisco, 1939, IV, p. 143 (Free translation).
3. D. D. Lee, "Conceptual Implications of an Indian Language," *Philosophy of Science,* Baltimore, 1938, V, 1, pp. 97–98.
4. Based on the writings of:
   J. S. Furnivall, *Colonial Theory and Practice,* Cambridge University Press, Cambridge, 1948. L. M. Hanks, "The Quest for Individual Autonomy in

the Burmese Personality," *Psychiatry,* Washington, XII, 3, pp. 285–300. H. Fielding Hall, *The Soul of a People,* Macmillan & Company, Ltd., London, 1906; *The Inward Light,* The Macmillan Company, New York, 1908. Sir George Scott (Shway Yoe), *The Burman, His Life and Notions,* Macmillan & Company, Ltd., London, 3rd edition, 1910.

5. World Federation of Mental Health, *Mental Health Implications of Technological Change,* section on Greece (in press, September, 1950).

6. Roy Clive Abraham, *The Tiv People,* published on behalf of the Government of Nigeria by the Crown Agents of the Colonies, London, 2nd edition, 1940. *Akiga's Story, The Tiv Tribe as Seen by One of Its Members,* translated and annotated by Rupert East, Oxford University Press, London, 1939.

Comment by Nels F. S. Ferré:

I have read with high interest and appreciation Professor Lee's paper. Her claim seems vividly illustrated that freedom inheres in authority, not as external compulsion nor as internal restraint, but the authority which releases the self to fulfil an organic role, within which it participates meaningfully and satisfyingly in social and natural processes. When the processes are understood in the light of an eternal Purpose—the Unity of the universe —and when freedom finds its final consummation in God's inclusive community, we discover a unity for thought and a meaningfulness for life which give depth of perspective to cultural pluralism. The study of the unity and diversity of meaning or of behavior among peoples and in different ages, has profound implications.

Comment by Robert H. Lowie:

Dr. Dorothy D. Lee's paper is extremely valuable, not only because of the intrinsic interest of the data presented, but because of certain implications. The thesis she defends may well be applied to a series of phenomena within Western culture. For example, is a Swiss woman less "free" because suffrage is denied her? There seems to be wide concurrence in the statement (even on the part of Swiss suffragists) that Swiss women themselves do not desire to vote, regarding the potential right as merely an added burden. I know of at least one instance of a husband's favoring female suffrage while his wife deprecates it. To take another example, Germans have repeatedly protested against the current alien judgment that they are less free than the French and the Anglo-Saxons. They argue that such a view one-sidedly stresses only one possible type of freedom, that belonging to the public sphere.[1] At times they advance the coercion exerted by Main Street in America or of a fixed etiquette in England—not felt as authoritarianism in these countries, yet very definitely resented as an infraction on individual liberty by Germans. Finally, there is the old question in how far Protestantism, with its acceptance of the Bible as the supreme court of appeals, is less authoritarian than Catholicism, with its reliance on the Church. I do not venture to argue these matters now, but should like to point out that the relativistic attitude of Dr. Lee's paper has indeed some vital meanings for modern society.

[1] See *e.g.,* Max Scheler, *Die Ursachen des Deutschenhasses,* Leipzig, 1917, pp. 127 ff.

CHAPTER XXIX

Freedom and Authority in the Social Structure: A Problem in the Interrelation of Institutions

By RUPERT B. VANCE

Kenan Professor of Sociology, Institute for Research in Social Science, University of North Carolina

SOCIAL THEORY of late has suffered from a failure to give sustained attention to the analysis of power and power relations in the social system. Power has a bad name; it is associated with tyranny, dictators, and totalitarianism. Power, it is thought, should be subject to analysis, only so that it can be analyzed out of existence. This is certainly not a realistic point of departure from which to attack the problem of authority and freedom in modern society.

Freedom and Authority

If the individual is to have a measurable degree of freedom in our society, he must have a measurable degree of power. An institution or a system must have social power to perform social functions, just as a machine must have a source of energy. Power in organized society is not necessarily synonymous with coercion or the ruthless use of force. Rather power in a functioning social system is institutionalized, that is, it is *legitimate* power.

Modern democratic societies differ from the authoritarian societies of the past, in that they have given authority to the exercise of individual freedoms. To guarantee these freedoms to the individual, the society had to specify where individual rights end. "Your fist ends where my nose begins," is a good folk saying, which specifies that fist shaking is persuasion, but a blow is not. For all of us to have rights, my rights must end where yours begin.

Sincere equalitarians have sometimes been troubled by the fact that power is not equally diffused among the members of a democratic society. Certainly the exercise of power is not equally diffused in any society nor should this be regarded as either desirable or possible. A distinction must be made between the source of power and the exercise of power. The source of power is in the community; and theoretically power could be equally diffused among the individual units of the common society. But power cannot be *engineered* in this fashion. Power is built into social structures; it is exercised through offices arranged in a hierarchy. This hierarchy of offices, with its gradations of power, does work for the organization's members, who may be presumed to benefit from that work. Any social organization which gets work done can well be called a power structure.

Power Structures in Society

Every society and every social organization—whether a corporation, social club, political party, or church—can, accordingly, be analyzed as a power structure. If power is regarded in the neutral terms which physics sets up for the analysis of energy, then we can regard power structures as mechanisms for so channeling the energies of men that the diverse work of society gets accomplished.

Moreover, groups have power in our society, because they have authority to operate within their selected and often limited spheres. By authority we mean *legitimate* power or, as Professor R. M. MacIver says, "the established *right* within any social order to determine policies, to pronounce judgments on selected issues, or more broadly to act as leader or guide to other men . . . Power itself has no legitimacy, no mandate, no office."[1]

By social power, we mean the capacity to control or influence the behavior of others—or better still, to participate in decisions which change the behavior of others. Authority exists in every group and in every sphere in which this use of social power is sanctioned. "There is," as Professor MacIver says, "authority in religion, in education, in business, in science, in the arts."[2]

[1] R. M. MacIver, *The Web of Government,* The Macmillan Company, New York, 1947, p. 83.
[2] *Ibid.*

How Institutions Govern

All institutions and all associations, according to this view, must participate in the function of governing in our society. Professor Charles E. Merriam has well described the function of voluntary associations in the governing of society:

> A congeries of associations operate to produce the net result in the community. Many have their own parallel plans for social action in their own sphere—in family, in church, in industry, in agriculture, and in the professions.[3]

The public government is not aloof from all these permutations and combinations. The government is the instrument of all these groups taken together for the realization of security, order, justice, and welfare, within the framework of the common good.

The difficulty lies, Professor Merriam feels, not in the self-government of the main social groups but in their desire to impose their government upon others. In a sense the bulk of government is nongovernmental; functions, rather than structures, are the staples of social direction. The real directives come from such social techniques as education and medicine, from industry, agriculture, and labor. To formalize all these associations into responsible political governing agencies, will accomplish nothing, Professor Merriam believes. With the proliferation and professionalization of all groups, the task would become complex and unworkable.

Participation in authority is, unavoidably, one of the most difficult of the problems of political association. The sharing and diffusion of authority, coordination, and cooperation require the concurrence of many opposing elements in democratic social structure. Lawyers may forget, says Professor Merriam, that there are adjudications behind and beyond the law; managers and administrators may forget that management is not a monopoly of administration but a commonplace of social organization.

[3] Charles E. Merriam, *Systematic Politics*, University of Chicago Press, Chicago, 1945, pp. 236–241.

Freedom and the Social Structure

From the sociological point of view, then, the problem of human freedom, that is, freedom of social action, is the problem of social structure, broadly conceived. Gerard DeGré has phrased this position very neatly:

> Man as a political animal lives his life in groups and the concrete freedoms which he enjoys derive their sustenance and vitality from the backing of his group *vis à vis* other groups . . . A sociological theory of freedom therefore must take as its starting point the *socius*, that is, the individual as a member of a group, class or a social type rather than the abstract individual as such, that forms the nucleus of the concept of freedom held by Romanticism.[4]

The power structures of modern society are such as to pose this whole problem of authority and freedom in terms of the interrelations of our major social institutions. The minimum degree of freedom exists under a maximum concentration of power in one institution. Totalitarianism can be regarded as a society in which individuals stand naked and unprotected against one institution—the monolithic state which has outlawed or absorbed other institutions and voluntary associations.

Freedom, it must be realized, would be equally lost, if men faced a total church or a total industrial system unprotected and unsupported by other institutions. Democracy must be regarded as that form of society in which individuals have the protection of many institutions against the encroachment of the one. That no institution attain monopoly power, we support a pluralist society of many voluntary associations which citizens freely join and as freely abandon.

Liberty and authority have been regarded as extremes on a social continuum, reading left to right from freedom to tyranny. This is not the adequate and sufficient statement. Social life can function only as a synthesis of these two principles. We look askance at the society in which the authority of any one institution exists unchecked. We must take the same point of view toward the doctrine of individual liberty. As Harold J. Laski wrote:

> So long as it was conceived as a body of absolute rights inherent in the individual and entitled to be exerted without regard to their social

[4] Gerard DeGré, "Freedom and Social Structure," *American Sociological Review*, October, 1946, pp. 530-531.

consequences, liberty was divorced from the ideas of both equality and justice. The individual became the antithesis of the state; and liberty itself became, as with Herbert Spencer, a principle of anarchy rather than a body of claims to be read in the context of the social process.[5]

We should be clear as to the danger to freedom of social action which would exist in a hyper-individualized or atomized society, lacking in authority. This minimum degree of group integration is also correlated with a low degree of freedom and comes closest in theoretical terms to resembling Hobbes's atomized state of nature, the "war of all against all."[6]

The optimum conditions for the development and maintenance of freedom of social action, as DeGré points out, is found in the Pluralist society. This is "characterized by the presence of large, well integrated groups representing significant divisions of interest and values."[7]

In the course of history the family and the church have lost in power and authority. The family, which once gave the patriarch power of life and death over its members, has been known in our society occasionally to request curfew laws of the municipal community that it may get its teen-agers off the streets by midnight.

The church was once an international and a universal institution—a monolithic structure, supreme over matters of dogma, faith, and, within limits, over behavior. Where there was no secular state to enforce toleration, freedom of religion and liberty of conscience were held under the restraint of authority. The irreconcilable conflict of absolutes has given way to the relativism of secular power—political authority to decree religious freedom. If we remain uneasy under this system, in view of the potential unity of our Judeo-Christian tradition, we still must recognize it as the *modus vivendi* of our compromise of freedom and authority in the institution of religion.

As the family and the church have lost in power and authority, the state and economic institutions have gained. War remains the greatest menace to the conception of the balance of freedom and authority, for it tends toward the integration of economic institutions and the state, and thus tends to place all activity under state regulation. The state must remain the one institution possessed of the ultimate sanctions of author-

[5] Harold J. Laski, "Liberty," in the *Encyclopedia of the Social Sciences*, IX, p. 443.
[6] See DeGré, *op. cit.*, p. 533.
[7] DeGré, *op. cit.*

ity, but it must be restrained by individuals free to act in voluntary associations. Here the chief safeguards are political parties, themselves operated as voluntary associations.

The Place of the Political Party in Democratic Power Structure

In a democratic social system, the political party must be regarded as the power structure whereby the citizen gains access to the supreme power structure of his society—the government. The broad determination of policy is a function of the conflict of political parties; the administration of policy, once it is determined, is a function of those many power structures we call bureaucracies. In terms of the wishes and claims of individual citizens, both parties and bureaucracies come to act with remarkable *inertia,* but of the two, political parties are more responsive to individual action. The average citizen takes much too lightly the function of the political party in preserving the balance between freedom and authority.

Professors Merriam and Gosnell have phrased this neatly:

> The party is in a sense a political church which does not require very regular attendance or have a very strict creed; but still it provides a home and it looks after the individual if he pays the minimum of party *devoirs* consisting in acquaintance with and occasional support of some one of its lords even though a minor one.[8]

As Graham Wallas wrote, the party must be a familiar institution: "Something is required, something that can be loved and trusted, and which can be recognized at successive elections as being the same that was loved and trusted before. A party is such a thing."[9]

A political party then is a form of organization, whereby large numbers of persons of diverse interests are enabled to support a common program. There are two reasons for supporting a party: (1) Its program and policies suit the special interest group to which we belong in the pluralism of social structure. Therefore, its program should suit many groups. (2) It becomes an end and good in itself, capable of transcending during the conflict the immediate claims of special interest.

---

[8] Charles E. Merriam and H. F. Gosnell, *American Party System,* The Macmillan Company, New York, 1923.

[9] Graham Wallas, *Human Nature in Politics,* Alfred A. Knopf, New York, p. 123.

Parties, according to Robert Michels,[10] manifest an inevitable tendency to develop as *oligarchic power structures*. Party leaders and bosses developed a vested interest in maintaining the party organizations as a power structure. Certainly the great danger both to party leaders and to the public is that realistic clashes of interests within the party will drive out those diverse groups which afford it strength. The Republican Party must not lose all labor support; the New Deal must retain some "tame business men." Such necessities dictate some of the strategies of party conflict. In fighting the other party there can be no compromise; in internal policy, sweet reasonableness must prevail between conflicting interests.

Professor Merriam has characterized the party as a type of social group concerned with social control, as exercised through government. (1) It rests upon social and economic interests and fundamental psychological tendencies. (2) It develops its own organization, attracts its own personnel, acquires its own professional standards and technique—in time its traditions, tendencies, and predispositions. Like other groups its momentum carries it on after its immediate purpose is achieved, for parties represent social capital in which much has been invested and much may be lost.

In the United States, we have kept the large party which seeks to serve many groups, rather than to develop splinter parties devoted to single interest groups. We have found it easier to change an old party as a going concern to a new program, rather than to let it die and found a new one.

Professor Merriam phrases the logic of party unity in this fashion:

> In the party those who have been acting together in the narrower circles of leaders, governors, inner clique and in the broader circle of those interested for social and economic reasons may go on acting together for other and newer purposes.[11]

The party is a paradox. It is in government, but not of it. We cannot evade the necessity of exercising the public authority over the power system which gives citizens access to power at the same time it gives them freedom of group action. The party is not mentioned in the Constitution, but nowhere in our democratic system can it be regarded as either a private club or as a monopoly of the state. It is an arm of legal

---

[10] Robert Michels, *Political Parties: A Sociological Study of Oligarchical Tendencies in Modern Democracy,* Hearst's International Library Company, New York, 1915.

[11] Merriam and Gosnell, *op. cit.,* p. 382.

government and, in the one party system, is almost equivalent to government itself.

Totalitarianism as a legal one party system, with that party a monopoly of the state, must remain a contradiction of the democratic resolution of freedom and authority. The parties are no longer voluntary organizations competing for the favor of citizens. Instead, the party is forever a minority—a closed group open only to those who show themselves through long apprenticeship to be fanatics. Citizens are no longer free to form parties as voluntary organizations either to initiate or oppose government policies.

A pluralistic society of many voluntary associations to which individuals may resort for support and protection, remains the best guarantee against the abuse of power and authority, which individuals and groups may otherwise exercise in the name of major institutions. The state makes use of its authority to sanction the rights of these groups, and sets limits to their powers. And, finally, individual citizens acting in concert, possess in the political party as a voluntary association, a power structure giving them access to the powers of government itself.

CHAPTER XXX

Work and Freedom

By ELI GINZBERG

*Associate Professor of Economics,
Columbia University*[1]

THE FIRST CLASSIC formulation of economic theory, presented by Adam Smith in the latter part of the eighteenth century, emphasized the significant relations that exist among individual freedom, individual well-being, and national wealth and security. Smith contended that as individuals obtain freedom to determine for themselves their own pattern of work and life, both individual and national welfare will be enhanced. He argued that a man, reaping the reward of his own labor, will do his best; and if every man does his best, the nation will prosper.

As England and, somewhat later, Western Europe and the United States, committed themselves to the doctrine of *laissez-faire,* its limitations began to be revealed. Smith had argued that it was man's natural right to determine the location and field of his employment. All efforts to interfere with this natural right, either by government or corporate bodies, dangerously jeopardize individual freedom. But while industrial capitalism was still a new institution, perspicacious students realized that political freedom could be appraised only within the context of a specific economic environment. The freedom guaranteed the individual to work at whatever he wanted and wherever he wanted (as long as someone was willing to pay him for his labor) had little substance at a time when unemployment was rife.

Depression was perhaps the major, but surely not the only, challenge to Smith's optimistic doctrine. There was a considerable accumulation of evidence that many people who worked very hard and very long were unable to provide for themselves even a minimum standard of living, certainly not a reasonable degree of well-being.

[1] I desire to acknowledge my indebtedness to Dr. John L. Herma, Research Associate, "Conservation of Human Resources" Project, Columbia University, for his assistance in the preparation of this essay.

The first half of the nineteenth century witnessed the serious limitations of a policy of *laissez-faire* arising from the twin evils of depressions and below-subsistence wages. But fortunately unemployment was a periodic rather than a perpetual menace, and general increases in productivity worked toward the reduction of industries dependent on paying starvation wages.

It is against this background that Marx, both of the *Communist Manifesto* (1848) and of *Das Kapital* (1867), must be appraised. Marx was convinced that although depressions were periodic, their frequency and intensity were increasing. Marx prophesied that an ever larger number of workers would be thrown on the scrap heap of unemployment; and, further, that for an increasing number of workers, wages would be forced down to an absolute minimum for subsistence, and even below. Marx concluded that the mass of mankind could not hope for an adequate standard of living until capitalism had been ushered out by a revolution which would enthrone socialism. Believing the essence of the problem to be "economic," Marx insisted that, in the last analysis, all significant differentials in political power were based upon control over the means of production. If individual ownership of the means of production could be brought to an end, then and only then, could freedom be a reality, not a sham. Marx established a very simple equation: social ownership of the means of production equals social and individual welfare.

The "External" and "Internal" Problems of Work

For the purposes of this analysis, it is well to note that Marx pointed up two problems of work and freedom under capitalism. The first, and the most important, was the exploitation of the workers that the free market made possible by enabling employers to obtain twelve hours of work while paying wages for six hours. Since the workers did not control the means of production, they would starve unless they were willing to permit employers to extract such a large amount of "surplus labor." According to Marx, the only real "freedom" accorded the workers was to trade starvation for exploitation.

Marx's other main concern with the problem of freedom and work revolved around factory life itself. In the *Communist Manifesto,* he describes working conditions in these terms:

> Masses of laborers, crowded into factories, are organized like soldiers. As privates of the industrial army they are placed under the command of a perfect hierarchy of officers and sergeants. Not only are they the slaves of the bourgeois class and of the bourgeois state, they are daily and hourly enslaved by the machine, by the overlooker and above all by the individual bourgeois manufacturer himself.

For eighty years until the Great Depression of 1929, there was little interest in England or in the United States in the doctrine of exploitation or, for that matter, in the entire Marxian theory. During this period history had denied the two fundamental assumptions, namely, that more and more workers would be thrown out of employment and that ever larger numbers would be ground down into abject poverty.

A considerable number of British contemporaries of Marx knew little and cared less about the interrelationship of economics and politics but they were nevertheless much concerned with the impact of industrialism upon the individual worker. Their revulsion against the dehumanizing of man by the omnipotent machine is now a central problem of industrial psychology. Most contemporary students of the problem of work and freedom are concerned with what we might call the "internal" problem —the adjustment of the worker within the factory—rather than with the major "external" problem of the role of work within the society at large.

This paper will attempt to support the contention that despite the many shortcomings in the formulations of Adam Smith and Karl Marx about work and freedom, their approaches contained one important aspect of truth. They recognized what most romantics of the nineteenth century and professors in the twentieth century overlooked—that a meaningful consideration of work and freedom must be set within the broad framework of the total pattern of life rather than limited to the factory and its hours and conditions of employment.

The importance of the "external" environment can be illustrated by an extremely simplified, summary consideration of the role of work under varying political constellations. The German Government (Bonn) broadly adheres to an economic policy of minimum interference with the market. The result has been large-scale unemployment. The Government apparently did not weigh the probable effect of *laissez-faire* policies on the maintenance of employment. But it was mass unemployment that gave Hitler his chance. It may well be that a good test of the "democratic" orientation of a modern government is its willingness to concern itself with unemployment. Certainly the leading democratic nations have done so.

An interesting insight into the relation between work and freedom in the American tradition can be found in a position of our trade unions. Even at the height of World War II, the trade unions fought the National Service Bill. Labor felt that until all alternative solutions had been exhausted it was dangerous to grant the Federal Government power to order individuals from one job and community to another. The depth of labor's feeling was indicated anew in early 1951, when even a suggestion that the Office of Defense Mobilization might favor the enactment of similar legislation was sufficient to have the labor representatives withdraw completely from active participation in the work of the defense agencies.

Great Britain, which was confronted during World War II with an even more stringent manpower situation than the United States, enacted legislation governing the "direction of labor." Minimum, rather than maximum, use was made of this broad grant of power to the Government. And it was Ernest Bevin, the most respected of the British trade union leaders, who was responsible for the actions taken under the terms of this Act. After the war the Government, committed to a general policy of economic planning and with small margins for adjustment, was for a considerable time loath to see the Act rescinded.

Totalitarianism gained its first success through Hitler's astuteness which led him to direct his early efforts to overcoming mass unemployment. Hitler preached the doctrine that women belong in the home, which helps to explain why Germany failed to mobilize women during World War II. Moreover controls exercised over the entire labor market were relatively weak. In part this reflected the unwarranted optimism of the Germans following their early successes in Russia (1941-1942). In part it probably reflected the extreme compulsion exercised over the many millions of "foreign laborers" in Germany, making other controls less essential.

As far as Soviet Communism is concerned, we must first take note of the permeation of the dominant political ideology throughout the whole of Soviet life. At this late date, nobody can doubt that Communism is a religion, not merely an economic and political philosophy. Lord Keynes once remarked that the difference between capitalism and Communism could be identified with reference to the punishments for economic failure. In England a bankrupt loses social status; the director of a Soviet trust who makes a mess of things is summarily liquidated. A contemporary comparison can be drawn. Although even a democratic society exercises a degree of informal and formal censorship over the work of nonconforming members, one need only admit this fact to recognize the significant differences between this and conditions in Soviet Russia. The unpopular author in the West may have to find another job; in Russia he may be exiled for five years!

In the case of corporate states in which there is a close alignment between the secular and the ecclesiastical power, such as the Iberian Peninsula, Ireland, and certain countries in South America, there is much less preoccupation with work and freedom than in democracies. The corporate state is concerned with doctrinal orthodoxy and social stability. Within these limits people can be free and work as much or as little as they desire or find necessary. The state is perfectly willing to sacrifice the gains of rapid economic progress, in order to avoid the unsettling consequences which frequently attend such progress.

The Ends of Work

The impact of the general political structure on work and freedom can be appraised in another way—in terms of the ends of work. Russian Communism has operated, from the very beginning, under the shadow of war—recovery from World War I, fear of World War II, active participation in World War II, and high mobilization since. Likewise, throughout the entire development of Nazi totalitarianism military aggression usurped a central role. It is difficult to distinguish between the inherent characteristics of a regime and its specific historical circumstances; but it would be an error to assume that war has only an incidental relation to either Soviet or Nazi totalitarianism. Politically and economically—and perhaps most important, ideologically—a war environment is conducive to the establishment and maintenance of a totalitarian regime. In times of national danger it is relatively easy to gain general consent as to the ends of economic activity. In addition, a defense or war economy provides the leadership with a conducive environment in which to gain and maintain support, or to ban public debate and to insist upon rigid discipline.

This sketch of conditions during recent decades in totalitarian countries indicates the significant differences between their way and the way in which democracies determine the goals of work. Starting with the basic premise that peace is the normal and desirable condition and that the best society permits the individual the greatest degree of self-determination, democratic countries are loath to grant their governments any large-scale control over the allocation of economic resources. It has been one of the weaknesses of democracy that it fails thus to protect itself until it is actually under attack. Moreover, whenever the external threat appears to be lessened, a democratic people is quick to restrict again, often too quickly, the power of its government.

But perhaps the most important distinction between a totalitarian and a democratic society is found in the respective roles of the populace in the determination of national policy. Under totalitarianism, the people are manipulated so as to insure that they do as the leaders desire; in democratic countries, they are active participants in the society and are even called upon to approve the broad outlines of national policy.

The Means of Work

These striking differences with respect to the way in which the ends of work are determined are paralleled by important differences in the means that are used. Operating in terms of a national economic plan, with goals which have been emotionally charged, it becomes a matter of overwhelming necessity for the totalitarian leaders to accomplish their plan. With the welfare of a totalitarian society defined in terms of the accomplishment of specific ends, it follows that only incidental consideration is given to the human cost of accomplishing these ends. A parallel can be found in military life. As General Bradley emphasized in his recent book, *A Soldier's Story*:[2]

> In time of war the only value that can be affixed to any unit is the tactical value of that unit in winning the war. Even the lives of those men assigned to it become nothing more than tools to be used in the accomplishment of that mission. War has neither the time nor heart to

[2] Omar Bradley, *A Soldier's Story*, Henry Holt & Company, New York, 1951.

concern itself with the individual and the dignity of man—men must die that objectives might be taken.

The use of the military analogy helps to illuminate another aspect of totalitarian life. It explains why the leadership is able to establish strict control over deviants. The nonconformists threaten the security of the state; in short, they are traitors. This attitude extends not only to those who refuse to hew to the ideological line, but also to those who fail to accomplish their specific responsibilities. A worker who fails to meet a production quota is considered in much the same light as a sentry who falls asleep at his post—both endanger the group.

The contention has been advanced that the extreme sensitivity of the Soviet leaders about those who deviate even slightly is only in part a reflection of their determination to keep an ironclad control over society. In part it reflects the convenience afforded the state in utilizing the "slave labor" of those condemned for deviation. It is difficult, apparently, for the state planners to develop effective incentives to secure the required labor supply for certain strategic production. Although this problem is shrouded in darkness, there is ground for suspecting that political orthodoxy and economic necessity reinforce each other.

In contrast, a democracy is automatically preempted from accomplishing its ends through the use of coercive measures over the individual. Only in times of great national danger is a limited grant of power given the government to determine who should work and under what conditions. This does not mean, of course, that a democracy operates without compulsions. In a totalitarian society, there is the use of direct coercive action; in a democracy, law and custom provide rewards and punishments. Most important, in a democracy the legal system cannot be manipulated to suit the convenience of those in power.

Conclusion

The foregoing analysis supports the basic contention that the significant aspects of work and freedom must be sought in the "external" environment of the social structure, rather than in the more limited and restricted "internal" environment of the factory. Whether the individual can determine for himself his field and place of work depends on the external environment. Likewise, it is the external environment which establishes the criteria of nonconformity and the punishments. Further, it determines the degree to which the individual can participate in decisions affecting national policy. Finally, these external forces determine the extent to which the individual is the master of his earnings and his free time.

Once the role of these external forces has been delineated, it should be apparent that the range of adjustments possible within the internal environment—the typical concern of industrial psychology—must assume a secondary importance.

Democratic countries, taking their freedom for granted, have concentrated on the improvement of the "internal" environment. The people in most totalitarian countries have never had any direct knowledge of the values inherent in a democratic regime. Hence, their frame of reference is restricted to assessing the extent to which their leaders are providing them with small increases in their standard of living. The productivity of modern technology makes it relatively easy for the totalitarian leaders to satisfy at least this part of their followers' aspirations.

The democracies learned that freedom without work was dangerous. They are now faced with the threat of work without freedom, for this would be the implication of a totalitarian victory. During recent decades the democracies have struggled with an increasing degree of success to reach a new balance between freedom and work. The peoples in totalitarian countries have still to learn the potentialities inherent in freedom.

Comment by Edgar S. Brightman:

I have nothing but praise for Professor Ginzberg's sound, penetrating, and realistic presentation of his thesis that "a meaningful consideration of work and freedom must be set within the broad framework of a society, and must never be delimited to the factory alone." There is one remark, however, that I want to add: the framework might profitably be made still broader, to include man's metaphysical environment—be it called Nature, Matter, Energy, Spirit, or God. To ignore this framework is not only to neglect many facts of experience and science, but also to slur over the deepest motives for work and freedom.

CHAPTER XXXI

The Role of Authority in the Interpretation of Science

By PHILIPP FRANK
Lecturer on Physics and Mathematics, Harvard University

IF WE LOOK at science as a human enterprise as we look at art, religion, or politics, we notice two facts which seem difficult to reconcile. On the one hand, science is a doctrine which is based on experience about sense observations. It can be applied to technology, and becomes in this way the basis of all advances in industry and warfare. If a doctrine of science is successful in these respects, we say that it is "valid"; in the opposite case we call it "false." In this way and only in this way can science distinguish between right and wrong. But, on the other hand, the history of old and new times has shown that authorities, organized or unorganized, have tried to direct the way in which the results of science have been formulated, taught in schools, or presented in print. As the results of science can be checked by their technical failure or success, it is difficult to understand how any authority can modify or influence these results.

We may call the results of science that can be checked by sense observation and technical application the "technical results" of science. It is obvious that no authority can alter these technical results. When the Church condemned the Copernican system, the computation of the position of planets on the sphere was not touched. When the Nazi government in Germany ostracized Einstein's Theory of Relativity, the results concerning the production of atomic energy, the technical results, were recognized and taught in all Nazi schools. When the Communist Party in the Soviet Union condemned the Theory of Relativity, because of its connection with the "idealistic" philosophy of Ernst Mach, the technical results were taught in the Soviet schools. It is clear, therefore, that any interference of authority in science has never dealt with the technical results but with other aspects of science. We have, therefore, to ask what are the aspects of science besides its technical results?

When Copernicus advanced his heliocentric system which removed the earth from the center of the universe, the technical results of his system were by no means different from the Ptolomaic system. When Einstein presented his theory of relativity, there was no technical result which could not be derived from the older hypothesis of a world ether. We know, however, very well that there have been spirited controversies between the advocates of these new theories and the supporters of the older conceptions.

What was the source of the fervor with which the struggle between the old and new theories was carried on? Certainly not any interest in technical progress—which was non-existent. We notice also in both examples the interference of organized power groups (government and church), as well as of public opinion. As technical results did not provide a purely scientific criterion, the fight could be carried on without a decision by the "authority" of science. This lack of a "verdict" by "experts" gave other types of authorities a possibility of intervention. But why should these powers intervene?

This can be made clear from one example which is even much older than Copernicus. In Plato's *Laws,* we read of the scientific problem whether the celestial bodies, sun and planets, are made of the same stuff as our earth, of the same fluids and rocks, or of other material. In Plato's time no scientific method existed which could check any of the answers by direct sense observations. The Athenian Stranger, who is Plato's spokesman in the *Dialogues,* advocates strongly the theory that the sun is made of a very subtle stuff, a rather immaterial substance, perhaps even a soul. His chief argument is the great advantage that this hypothesis affords to everybody who wants to prove the existence of the gods, while the opposite opinion, according to which all celestial bodies consist of terrestrial matter, would lead to a world view which we would call today "materialism." Plato was so convinced of the moral harmfulness of this "materialistic" hypothesis, that he recommended imprisonment for everybody who teaches this astrophysical doctrine. In this case we see clearly that a certain hypothesis about the chemical constitution of the sun was not rejected by Plato because of its technical results, but because it lent itself to a "materialistic" interpretation which, in turn, was believed to have a bad influence on human conduct. As between two "astrophysical" theses no decision could be made on the basis of observable facts, Plato did not see any objection to making the choice on the basis of the effect on moral behavior.

We see exactly the same scheme in the attitude of the Church toward the Copernican system. As no decision could be reached on the basis of astronomical observations, one was free to make the choice according to what was a better basis of teaching moral behavior. It seemed obvious that an interpretation is the better in this respect, the better it fits into the traditional interpretation of the Bible, and the more it is in agreement with the traditional Scholastic philosophy upon which all indoctrination in religion and morals was based. The decision about the acceptance of a scientific theory, in such cases, can only be made and will always be made by those powers which decide what kind of human conduct is desirable. This means that the ultimate decision rests with "authority" and not with scientists.

In such cases the interference of "authorities" is not only understandable but necessary. Probably the same kind of interference has taken place at all periods of history. One has in our present time heard much about the way the totalitarian governments have interfered in the formulation of scientific theories. We shall not speak here about the administrative and judicial form in which the interference has taken place. According to the degree of government pressure upon the citizens, this interference can occur in different forms. The advocate of an undesirable doctrine may in some case simply be excluded from dinner parties with the "right people," or he may be excluded from some job, or he may be imprisoned, or may be tortured, and eventually executed. All this may vary in different cases, but the logical structure of the interference will be about the same in all cases.

Summing up, we have to say that every condition of indecision in the general principles of science will bring about interference of authorities. They regard it as their duty to support the teaching and the advances of such doctrines as have a healthy influence on morals and religion. The search for technical results is to a high degree free, but the philosophical interpretations of scientific theories have been always under the strong influence or even pressure of "authorities."

CHAPTER XXXII

Freedom and Authority in the Realm of the Poetic Imagination

By KENNETH BURKE
Bennington College

THIS ARTICLE, frankly, is an attempt at special pleading. It would question the wisdom of the harsh Us-Against-Them attitude that threatens to become absolute sovereign of all mankind today. However just each side might be in its own eyes, or in the eyes of God, or History, or any other ultimate court of appeal, can there be hope in such a drastically antithetical way of approaching the expedients of human relationship?

While this article deals specifically with the field of the Poetic Imagination (as shaped by the resources of symbols in general), it also considers the moral worth of such Imagination; whereat arises our plea for the attempt to uphold a many-termed view of motives.

We here call such symbolic behavior "sheer exercising." We try to ground it in the notion that a free speculative tinkering with terms is the birthright of man, as the symbol-using species. Next we consider how one's immediate involvements restrict this range. But since this second stage is the one in which men are prodded to put aside their capacity for "sheer exercising," we next ask how the abandoned principle might be restored, though with a difference.

Eulogistically, we call our solution the "esthetic of the Shakespearean drama," having in mind the playwright's constant readiness to help one see and feel beyond the limits of any particular social role or situation.

Where Freedom and Authority Are One

Let us start with an ideal simplification. A child, let us say, has learned the words, "kill" and "eat." He experiments with them and plumbs their resources. He will imagine situations that are in essence "killing-and-eating" situations. Out of such "freedom," there might arise conceits of this sort:

> My mother has killed me,
> My father is eating me,
> My brothers and sisters sit under the table
> Picking up my bones,
> And they bury them under the cold marble stones.

Here, certain aspects of killing and eating are abstracted and made absolute. Much is omitted. One cannot even be sure of the attitudes implicit in these conceits. Do the lines indicate some "primal masochism" in their inventor? Or "sadism reversed"? (That is, did the inventor first think of killing and eating others, but did he leave such notions unformulated until he hit upon some conceits that in effect pronounced a retaliatory sentence against himself?) Or, more paradoxical yet, maybe the conceits were of a *prima donna* sort. That is, they may subtly "flatter" the victim, since they picture him as the center of attention. In this case, the conceits would be not cruelly self-pitying, nor pursued by a judgment against the self, but self-congratulatory. (The omitted aspects, *e.g.*, of pain, may not necessarily be "suppressed" or "repressed." They may simply not come within the range of the inventor's knowledge or imagination.)

Or we could think of a possible progression whereby the lines went from one motive to another. Or though the lines were invented one day in response to one motive, they could be repeated another day for a motive quite different.

But running through them all, there is what we might call the "technical" motive, which concerns "kill" and "eat" purely as terms. Put them in a verbal context that allows for subjects and objects, and for the "breakdown" of an act into imaginal parts (in this case, the picking and the burying of bones)—and the inventor has certain "material resources" which he can exploit.

His responsibility, in this respect, is to the materials only. Ideally, he need merely experiment with the terms, "kill" and "eat," isolating and projecting whatever aspects of them he is able to conceive as contributing to a design. Ideally, at this point, no personal motives are involved.

Here, freedom and authority are one. For the "authority" is automatically established by the resources of the terms—and the ranging within such limits is in itself "freedom."

This ideal simplification is also the ideal of "perfection." "Perfection" exists as a motive in so far as one seeks to exploit the resources of his material as such. Let a man have a gun; and if he shoots it, not because it gives him a sense of power, or because it might prepare him to defend himself, or because it has secret analogies with sexual prowess, etc., but simply because *there is a certain range of things that can be done with guns qua guns*—there you have "perfection" as a motive.

"Perfection," in this sense, implies "autonomy." Freely to explore the nature of a medium as such, is to love perfection and to be autonomous. Might the medium blow up the world? Then, to love that medium, in its perfection, is to abide by it, even to the extent of blowing up the world.

Or one might come upon an *idea* or an *image* that, when released in a given social context would be capable of great harm. But as regards our ideal of "perfection" (= "autonomy" = "the identity of freedom and authority"), one should freely explore the resources of such idea or image though the result be the blasting of us all.

The ideal limit of "perfection" is reached when you carry the variation even to the extent of its opposite. Vary the theme of heroism until you come upon cowardice; or vary the theme of cowardice until you come upon heroism; or vary the theme of weakness until you come upon power; or vary the theme of . . . , etc.

Vary the theme of autonomy until you have crossed beyond autonomy.[1]

---

[1] As for our choice of the somewhat bloodthirsty examples: In grounding our argument we take hypothetically forbidding cases, and ask how a good word might be said even for them. The resourcefulness of symbols, we say in effect, is not in itself either morally good or bad. It just is. And its existence is a major reality for human relations, because man is the distinctively symbol-using species. So we begin with an Edenic garden of autonomy in which no self-consistency can be questioned by terms alien to its particular universe of discourse. Symbolic self-consistency can be loved in and for itself. When considering poetry, one properly begins with this, rather than with any notions of art as substitutive, compensatory, secretly vindictive, and the like. Such motives operate, to be sure, but only as special cases of symbolism. And any poetic species must be located first of all in terms of symbolic resources as such.

Where Freedom and Authority Fall Asunder

What, then, of the "fall"?

Our talk of autonomous "perfection" (in which freedom and authority were one) concerned the realm of the expert. No one, praise God, is monster enough to be, to perfection, the expert. Hence, as seen from another point of view (the civic point of view, man as citizen, man as fellow man), the "fall" is in effect a salvation.

Thus enters the sociology of human affections. Or, if you will, we go from Poetics to Rhetoric, Ethics, Politics, and the like. Our ideal Lover of Perfection has his ax to grind. There is, initially, a responsibility to the material, in and for itself, regardless of where it leads. But there are also man's personal goadings, or personal limitations.

In one case, those Mother Goose lines we quoted at the start will be localized by a sadistic drive. In another, by a masochistic urge. Or by a prima donna itch. Etc. Though our inventor is exploring the resources of his terms, and though the resources may themselves be absolute, they are conceived within the limits of *his own* resources. Through him they are "screened."

To take the extreme: Is something in order? The poet may even imagine it wholly disordered. He may imagine it upside down, inside out, and backwards. In such imaginings, he can be scrupulously responding to the resources of the materials themselves, concerned with the ultimate stretching of a terminology.

A purely dramatic consideration also figures here: One most vivid way of symbolizing a "value" is by bringing to our imagination the acts of an agent who *violates* that value. For the poet can awaken our consciousness by touching our conscience (and the most extreme way of doing so would be by a work, *implicitly* ironic, in which he evangelically *called for* the vicious act as though it were the correspondingly virtuous act).

In the stage we began with, the poet did not himself need to know exactly where play-acting ceases and the corruption, or perversity, begins. Nor did he need to ask whether (as the poet, John Brooks Wheelwright, used to say) an idea might propagate like rabbits in Australia.

However:

As things actually work out, such far ranging among the resources of given materials (given terms) is not likely often to be done through sheer artistic exercise. Nor will it be read as such. To varying degrees, we read like the naive child who, seeing a trick crime in a movie, tries it out really, on his trusting playmate. And one writes similarly.

And here, freedom and authority fall asunder. Here, rightly or wrongly, the poet's art is outside the realm of "autonomy," inside the realm of police and politics (generally "morals").

Here is the realm in which the artist settles personal scores, or bootlicks, or even answers opponents such as never were. He is a hunted man (productively so—for take away the morbid goads and terrors, and his free exercisings would most likely become quite trivial).

He strikes, he squirms, he slinks down dark alleys, he lies in the very act of truth-telling, he rots ingeniously, he does not merely fear tyrants, he goes in search of them, himself guilt-laden, bearing personal guilt, as shaped by the general guilt of the social pyramid by which his particular society contrives to act together.

And he is homeless. For his art is his home. And in so far as mere self-consistency is not enough, his art has been driven out. Freedom and authority have fallen asunder. He must, subtly, either bootlick or rebel.

Again and again, he will be made uneasy, finding that, as judged by his tests, Official Pronouncements draw the lines at the wrong places. *His* freedom is at odds with *Somebody Else's* authority.

Where Freedom and Authority Are Re-united

If the first stage was "innocence," and if the second stage was a "fall" into the discord of Babel, then the third stage must be reclamation by "virtue." It must be a return, but with a difference.

The attitude, as reduced to a formula, would be:

To thank God for the enemy, who assists by cooperative competition. To seek for ways of widening the encompassment, until it includes the enemy. To find the modifications that will bring things back into order, by treating the jolt in such a way that it becomes a subtler contribution to rhythm. To so change the rules that the cause of the embarrassment is transformed into a necessary element of the solution.

If there were but one rule for writing, it should be this: Let the poet write each sentence as though he were seeking to pay a sincere compliment, to something or to someone, including the Reader. Let him approach everything in terms of its peculiar order of perfection.

Thus, always, above all, the poet must *exercise* in his art.

Has he made a hero? Let him, next time, burlesque that hero. Has he discovered a perfect fool? Let him, next time, discover the wisdom of that fool. Has he blessed? Next time let him restate the blessing as a curse.

Let him *multiply* his moments, if only as an exercise. Let him be, not two-faced, but many-voiced.

In brief, let him have spirit. Let him be the float, not the sinker.

Yet, he must mull over. He must lurk and linger. And it may be that, to do so, he must in a sense be like lead, and refuse to budge outside the narrow orbit of the few concerns which he feels competent to handle perfectly.

Even so, there is no harm done, if critics and readers supply the dialectical sophistication. And supply it, not just when reading so-called "imaginative" literature, but also when confronting the Thunderous Headlines. Even while allowing the poets and the newsmen to be as drastically one-sided as their calling may seem to demand (the sharper the conflict, the more "dramatic" the news), we need not take all such utterance as stark reality.

What of the Marxist calculus, for instance? Confronting those who would make of it everything, should we feel obliged by antithesis to make of it nothing? Unless we would cheat ourselves, let it be one voice in our dialogue. We should not silence it. Rather, we should ask ourselves: By how many other voices should it be modified?

Or, put it another way: Enjoy ideas, too, as music. Love them for their gesture. As *moods*. As poetic *moments*. Or at least, first "screen" them through such a way of seeing, as though they were sheer arbitrary images, before you begin believing in any of them literally. (Lest they take over, like rabbits in Australia.)

When the day's "reality" is handed to you, in the papers, or over the air, first ask yourself, *just as an exercise:* Suppose I wanted to present that same information in such a way that it had exactly the opposite effect, as a mood-maker, an "attitude-former." Whereupon, even without authoritative knowledge of the facts themselves, you can contribute somewhat toward a discounting of a medium which prods its experts each day to hunt up and put together the best and biggest batch of conflicts that money can buy.

Confronting the sincere, honest, patriotic citizens who, having scared themselves and us beyond necessity, would next burden themselves and us beyond necessity, let us rather, if only as a stunt, help break the malign continuity by a tentative act of sheer linguistic exercising. And not with too much counter-belief either, except the counter-belief based on the sound notion that the world's issues cannot be as drastically localized as any such selection of conflicts might lead us to believe.

In a recent number of *Der Monat,* Karl Jaspers writes convincingly on the *Redlichkeit* of Kierkegaard and Nietzsche. He means, or I hope he means, also a kind of *conscientious irresponsibility* in expression: a willingness to follow any idea to the end of the line, not because you thought it was the whole story, but because you liked the dialectic exercise as such. (True, both Kierkegaard and Nietzsche finally got caught in their own traps—and we must let that fact have a voice, too, alas!)

The great playwrights of Athens found it natural to end on a satyr-play that burlesqued their own solemn gesturing. Why not just a modest measure of such "exercising" always? And, at present, at least enough to break the morbid solemnity that hangs over the relations between East and West? Otherwise, all Freedom gone, each great Bureaucratic Structure of Authority confronts the other with the unbending dignity of a corpse.[2]

Where, Then?

Confronting the problem of freedom and authority, in its range from the private act of a poet to the great public opposition between worldwide structures of governmental authority, at least in speculation we cannot allow a whole system of international morality to take form in terms of a blunt Us-Against-Them alignment. Not thus does a speculative body antithetically "contain" the opposition (like trying to hold the flooding Mississippi within ever higher and higher levees—an "arms race" that must eventually be lost, even if we must wait until the river has been raised as much as a mile above the level that would otherwise be natural to it).

One may ask: What if the yielding is all on our side? If one side is saying yes-*versus*-no, can the other safely say yes-no-and-maybe?

First, it is questionable whether a policy of gradations would be an-

---

[2] A friend said: "Riding in a military plane, in the last rays of twilight, I saw clouds ahead that looked like the chiselled profiles of corpses stretched on mortuary slabs."

swered by a policy of flat antithesis. Second, even if it were, one cannot reduce it to flatly antithetical terms without in the end making oneself the victim of a false simplicity.

An administrator, let us say, finds that, by the nature of rhetoric, a policy of flat antithesis provides him with the strongest public backing. But as soon as he begins negotiations in an actual situation, the very attitude that he helped establish returns to plague him, as the public demands simple yes-no solutions for yes-no-maybe situations.

Thus, the "sheer exercising" may in the end be a far better way of protecting a great nation's prosperity than the mutual self-hypnosis of an Us-*versus*-Them alignment.

This is a time (because it is always such a time) for us to remind ourselves that All the Returns Aren't in Yet. There is still time to seek for ways of inquiring in terms of a dialogue with more voices than just two flatly pitted against each other. Each doctrine can still be modified or enriched by cautious respect for the contributions made by other doctrines. To doubt this is to doubt the very essence of culture, as a mutual search for truth.

The progress toward truth (comprehensive, summarizing truth), like a spring under the skyscrapers of Manhattan, must somehow still go on—truth, still welling forth, down there in the dark, the brooks still wholesomely flowing, unstoppable, in the dark, down there, somehow.

In Sum

Let the esthetic of Shakespearean drama be the norm. For the present purposes, its principle might be stated as:

(1) Ideas, like proverbs, cancel one another out, without losing their validity.

(2) Ideas are like personal Characters—and there is room for very many, in the gallery of portraits.

(3) Have yes and no, but keep them on the run; and between yes and no, insert all notable degrees.

There is nothing self-destructive about such an "esthetic." Indeed, mankind can become at home in it. Or if it cannot, then men's ideas, as too naively believed in, and backed by the ominous new machines, are but the first stage of our Destruction.

And as for the notion that ideas can cancel one another without losing their validity: There is nothing glib or paradoxical about it. For the implications of an idea depend not only upon itself, or upon the material conditions that "implement" it, but also upon the other ideas with which it happens to be combined (and upon the material conditions that effectively resist it).

Taking the simplest of these problems, we offer one example of its solution:

We recall an earnest liberal who head-shakingly regretted that, in the script of the movie, *Nature's Half Acre,* much stress was placed on the "law of nature" whereby all natural organisms lived by the devouring of other natural organisms. "Fascist" implications were seen in this point of view. But they are there, only if the idea of dog-eat-dog, as a law of nature, is not matched by a distinction between "nature" in general and *human* nature. In fact, the situation offers a sound basis upon which to build a doctrine of universal human cooperation, in accordance with a *distinction* between the resources available to non-verbal organisms and those available to the symbol-using species, *homo dialecticus.*

Meanwhile, however, each side seems to have done all it could, to discourage and silence those aspects of itself that could most sympathetically treat with the other side.

Whereupon, unless this tension is relaxed, how figure out feasible ways of not blowing up the world, the otherwise so poignantly delightful world?

Recapitulation

By way of review, consider an example of this sort: A poet, let us say, loves resonance of diction. But within his particular limitations, he can best attain such resonance by the use of invective. Thus, in exploring the resources of invective, he would enjoy "freedom"; and internal principles of self-consistency would supply the controls that amounted to "authority." Here, freedom and authority would be one.

In so far as his invective had practical consequences beyond its nature as "free exercising," the *poet's* freedom would confront a *public* authority. The conditions are now set for Freedom and Authority to become *rivals.*

If our hypothetical poet's artistic skill at invective placed him in political jeopardy, we would attempt to defend him thus:

First, we would demand that he himself practice a wider range of "free exercising." We believe that, if he but brought himself to school himself in the full resources of his craft, he would find many devices whereby the resonance of invective can be transformed into the resonance of praise. Or he can discover intermediate stylistic devices (of irony, comedy, fantasy, and the like) which will subtilize his invective, thereby disclosing other kinds of stylistic resonance. (Recall, in *Lear*, how we are gratified by Kent's wrathful outpourings against Oswald; yet recall how our attitude toward Oswald in turn is subtilized, when we see that this poor excuse for a man has his own kind of loyalty, albeit loyalty to a villainess.)

But even if the poet's craft requires him to be a specialist within narrow limits, something can still be saved, if criticism supplies the more complicated interpretative frame needed for the rounding-out of a fragmentary poetry.

And however compelling our ideas may be in the practical realm, we suggested that one might seek to let in the whole pantheon of even mutually antagonistic ideas, as an aspect of the "free exercising" so natural to the symbol-using faculty.

Next we suggested that, in the end, such "freedom" in the realm of theory would form the soundest basis upon which to build a structure of practical authority. For no single terminology can be equal to the full complexity of human motives. (Each terminology arises to handle certain local conditions of time or place. And to guard against specious simplicity here, we might remind ourselves that human motivation must be at least as complex as an income tax report.)

Finally, in following out such notions, we came upon that most menacing (because most dramatic) of all dangers besetting man as the symbol-using animal: the tremendous rhetorical device of antithesis. And, now that the conditions of international rivalry are being presented in terms of one overriding antithesis, we suggested that the purely esthetic discipline of "free exercising" might help release us all, and without malice, from so dangerous an oversimplification.

In sum, then, it is the tactics of this article to ground "freedom" not in "God," or "nature," or "politics," or "economics," or "the human spirit," but in the resources natural to symbols (antithesis being the great picturesque temptation natural to symbols). Without embarrassment to our position, the grounding in symbols could, in turn, be referred to a super-personal author of all human symbol-users—but such speculation is outside the scope of this essay.

Similarly, "authority" is grounded in the limiting principle of self-consistency, which infuses the symbolic order as a canon.

Certain political and economic orders may, in one period or another, under given objective conditions, be better fit for translating the nonexistent "absolute union of freedom and authority" into their nearest possible practical equivalent. But, as regards the resources and limitations of symbols, let us be on guard ever lest the specious clarity of antithesis deprive the intelligence of its basic admonition: All the Returns Aren't in Yet.

CHAPTER XXXIII

Problems of Freedom and Authority in the Arts

By WILLIAM G. CONSTABLE

Curator, Department of Paintings, Museum of Fine Arts, Boston

BROADLY SPEAKING, there are three elements present in every work of art: 1. The emotion and ideas that inspire it. 2. The subject, which may be defined as the object or concept that set the artist's mind and emotion to work. 3. The convention or set of means used to convey the idea or emotion. To give an illustration, the subject might be a view of Fifth Avenue; among the ideas and emotions it inspired could be, for example, a purely sensuous pleasure in certain colors and shapes, or a profound sense of the character of all human effort and the fundamental imbecility of mankind; and the convention used might range from a photographic naturalism to a completely abstract series of blobs and streaks of paint.

Needless to say, these three elements are not always in practice separable. The emotion experienced by the artist is a function of the subject; and a change in subject may alter the emotion. On the other hand, a wide range of subjects may produce the same kind of emotional reaction in the artist. Again, the convention used may arise directly out of the subject, or from the emotion; but the artist may deliberately adopt a convention without much reference to either subject or emotion. At the same time, these three elements are always present, and the effect on each one of them of freedom and authority is likely to be different.

Not until the early nineteenth century did the idea fully develop that the artist ought to be free in every aspect of his work. This idea was largely a child of the Romantic movement, and derived from the conception of the arts as primarily a means of self-expression, to the extent of arguing that a public is quite unnecessary for an artist, except as a means of making a living; and that the artist (or his agent) must bully or cajole people into buying what he chooses to produce.

Emergence of such ideas was favored by social and industrial changes in the nineteenth century. The large-scale manufacturer came to regard the artist as a superfluity at best, and as a fool at worst; the artist regarded the manufacturer as one who corrupted public taste and had sold his soul in the search for profits. Such a situation was very different from anything that had existed in earlier days. Then, the artist was regarded primarily as a particular kind of craftsman. He often was highly regarded and honored; but his business was to supply something that somebody wanted. Ordinarily, the artist produced a piece of work for a definite and known patron, much as a high class tailor does today. In the Middle Ages, much of his work was for the church, though he served also great noblemen and civic bodies. In any case, the subject was always carefully prescribed, sometimes in elaborate detail; and even when this was not done, the artist almost invariably followed closely some written source. Religious and civic works, especially, were meant to be read for instruction and edification, and the text had to be correct. Contracts sometimes specified the materials the artist was to use, and guild supervision was constant over the conditions in his workshop, and the quality of the work he turned out. With the rise of the lay patron and the decay of the guild system during the Renaissance, the degree of control relaxed somewhat, especially on the technical side. But it was still customary for the patron to prescribe in minute detail exactly what was to be painted, a program sometimes being drawn up by a dilettante or scholar without any reference to the artist. After the Council of Trent, control by the church over religious painting, which had declined in the fifteenth and sixteenth centuries, was intensified. The great teaching and missionary orders made great use of the arts, and saw to it that subject and treatment suited their purposes; and the whole problem of decency in the treatment of nude figures in religious work became of importance. Moreover, in the seventeenth and eighteenth centuries a new type of authority in the arts developed, that of the Academies, typified by the Academy of Painting in Paris, and the French Academy in Rome established by Colbert, which were under government control and imposed strict rules as regards themes and their treatment upon members and students.

These examples show that authority in the arts is no new thing. One point to be noticed is that in the past control was mainly exercised before or during the production of the work of art, and not by action after it had been produced. There were exceptions to this, famous cases being the haling of Paolo Veronese before the Inquisition for introducing trivial and unedifying details into religious subjects, and the criticism of the nude figures in Michelangelo's *Last Judgment*. Substantially, however, the control was that of the patron, public or private, before the work was finished. A second point is that in the long run professional control, such as that of academies, affected the artist very little. It generally reflects artists' opinion of the day before yesterday, the revolutionaries of today becoming the academics of tomorrow. Moreover, such control has never managed to cover more than a fraction of the artists active at one particular time; it has usually been exercised in purely professional, rather than religious and political matters; and so has seriously affected the artist only when it was directed by some authority concerned with those fields.

In general, control in the past has been exercised almost entirely on subject matter. Emotional interpretation and the convention used to express it, were largely left to the artist. Thus Duccio and Giotto, working within the narrow range of the iconographical schemes of their time, are yet very different. Even in the period following the Council of Trent, when the church became a mighty patron of the arts, strictly controlling them as a means toward edification and devotion, the range of personal expression among artists was remarkable; so that painters such as Annibale Carracci and Caravaggio could flourish at the same time. The same holds true even among the portrait painters. Working amidst the rigid ceremonial of the Spanish Court, Velazquez and Goya could produce portraits conforming to every regulation for official work, but make them devastating revelations of the individuals concerned. The examples quoted have all been taken from painting; but the same holds good for sculpture, music, and literature.

Turn now to the present time. The visual arts are playing an increasingly important part in daily life, in the form of advertisements, illustrations in books and newspapers, the comics, the movies, and television. The place of the artist as a designer for industry is expanding rapidly. The artists involved are mainly anonymous; but they work much as did artists before the nineteenth century, in terms of a definite commission or job, of which the specifications are often highly detailed and rigid. By their side are the practitioners of the so-called fine arts who (except the architects) mainly still hold to the nineteenth century concept of the artist producing what he chooses to produce, and hoping to find a buyer for it. The patrons of today, however, who control the artist before and during production, differ from the patrons of the past who did the same thing, for they are rarely consumers themselves, but middlemen who sell the product to the public. In order to do this, they have to see that that product does not offend on political, religious, and moral grounds, the majority of their customers. So within various industries, notably the film industry, censorship boards have been established. It is not that the entrepreneur-patrons are much interested in morals, politics, or religion, as such; but they want to avoid getting into trouble. Moreover, they must guard against not only loss of sales due to action from the public on its own initiative, but to the action of censorship by bodies outside the enterprise. These are of two types: (a) those established by religious, political, and other organizations; (b) those established by governmental bodies. Thus, though the ultimate control of the artist seems to rest with the public, in fact the public attitude is in part interpreted and perhaps controlled by boards of censorship, official or otherwise.

The position of the independent artist is comparatively simple. He is not exposed to the action of outside authority until he exhibits a work of art, when the self-constituted or public censors may descend upon him. At the same time the possibility of such action will in some cases undoubtedly influence him.

Apart from the situation in the arts, there have to be taken into account the social and political conditions of today. If the totalitarian theory be accepted, then complete control of the arts in subject, emotional content, and convention of expression, is inevitable. It is reasonably clear that the Soviet government is interested mainly in control of emotional content. What the artist feels and makes the spectator feel is important, as appears from charges of a work of art being "bourgeois in sentiment" or "capitalist in feeling." In 1936, works of art of all kinds were on exhibition in Leningrad and Moscow, and are so today, I am told. But by the spoken or written word they are being used as awful warnings or as laudable exemplars. So it was with the Nazis. Hitler's famous purge of "decadent art" is still a vivid memory. Such labels as "decadent," "bourgeois," "anti-social," were aimed at thoughts, ideas, emotions. These were apt to be critical of established standards, to make men think and ask

Problems of Freedom and Authority in the Arts

questions; and that above all the Nazis wished to prevent. So it was with the Fascists. Italians being what they are, purges of art galleries and direct interference with artists was difficult; but every effort was made to divert artistic energy into the creation of works of art which would strengthen the hold of Fascism on men's minds.

Totalitarian regimes shrewdly realize that the arts can be among the most important powers in shaping men's minds. They have not been misled by silly wisecracks, such as "art is bunk," made by some politicians in democratic countries. This is not to say, however, that the democracies should follow totalitarian regimes in setting out to exercise authority over the arts. The basis of democracy is the freedom of the individual, especially freedom to speculate, to form his own opinions, to express those opinions, to argue with and (if he can) persuade other people; and by orderly and established methods which he himself accepts, to put those opinions into action. In such a process, the arts can play a vital part. Experiment and speculation are the breath of life to them. The artist's tentacles are out in every direction, especially in the metaphysical subsoil of men's minds. What he sees and feels today, many men are going to see and feel tomorrow. For example, the disasters of the past forty years were all foreshadowed in the turmoil of the arts; and there is little in our material environment today that was not unconsciously imposed upon us by an artist. This, of course, is not the only or even the most important function of the arts. That lies in the inspiration, the delight, the disillusionments, and discomforts they can bring. But these functions cannot be performed, unless the artist has freedom to feel as he does feel, and to give that feeling outward and visible form.

If the potential contribution of the artist to democracy is realized and accepted, the question of the control of the artist in a society that aims at being democratic has importance. In the immediate past, in such societies control was exercised primarily in the interests of decency and public morals. The normal machinery for control was the courts of law which in their nature represented the whole community and no particular section of it; and they evolved a series of more or less objective tests. Sometimes inquiry would be made as to *why* a work of art had taken the form to which objection was taken; and if, in the opinion of the court, the form was an integral part of a legitimate intention (and the idea of legitimacy was widely construed), that form would be likely to be accepted. A classic case is the judgment of Judge John M. Woolsey on Joyce's *Ulysses*. Also, works of art that had become a recognized part of the world's cultural heritage were excepted from action. Mr. Bowdler could publish a Shakespeare for family use; but nobody has yet taken action to suppress the complete text.

Admittedly this system, which is still in operation, had its drawbacks. The activities of Watch and Ward societies can be very irritating; and a great deal of grossly lubricous work exhibited by official bodies, such as the French Salon, are flaunted in the face of the public. But by and large, the system has not worked badly. A playwright may be forbidden to use the word, "damn," but there are fifty other ways of expressing the same sentiment; and a wisp of drapery can cover a multitude of official sins. The experience of the past has been vindicated by that of the present; that interference with subject and means of expression do not seriously hamper the artist, if he is left free to feel, and to put that feeling into such terms as may be allowed him.

Unfortunately another form of control has reared its head: that of public authorities and of more or less organized nongovernmental bodies who seek to exercise authority, not only over the outward and visible signs, but the informing emotion. The ideas from which such action derives have been expressed in many quarters. Mr. Dondero has attacked in Congress every phase of contemporary painting which is not conservatively academic, on the ground that it is a vehicle for Communist propaganda, only differing from the Soviet authorities in that they find just the same kind of painting bourgeois or capitalist. The outcome of such an attitude is illustrated by the forbidding of a collection of contemporary American painting formed by the State Department to be sent abroad. Again, the Pope, in a speech to the International Congress of Catholic Artists, specifically making the quality of art dependent upon its moral content, condemned all surrealist and abstract art whose meaning is not perceived immediately by normal persons. To tie down the artist to the comprehension of the "normal" man (whoever he may be, outside the mind of a statistician) is merely to deny to the arts their ordinary function of leading the way to enlargement of human knowledge and perceptions; and if, as here, the meaning to be perceived by the "normal" man is also to be regulated by some particular moral code, the arts are put in a strait-jacket.

The same kind of thinking is behind recent attacks on various films.

The release of *Oliver Twist* was held up in the United States, owing to representations that the character of Fagin is a manifestation of anti-semitism; and the *Miracle* has been the object of attacks on the ground that it is "sacrilegious" from the Roman Catholic point of view. All that has been said makes it clear that the battleground is the meaning and emotional content of the film.

The important point is that these views are not merely expressions of individual personal opinions; they represent a claim to exercise authority over the emotional content of the arts, in accordance with the political, social, or religious views held by some group. There is no criticism here of the motives inspiring the groups mentioned. Moreover, that their views and beliefs should be made known as widely as possible, is of the greatest importance. The artist in a democracy, no more than the theologian, should claim exemption from challenge. What is open to objection is that the action invokes an exercise of authority, in order to prevent challenge, on the part of the artist of the beliefs of other people. In other words, it follows the line taken by totalitarian governments. As such, it not only cuts at the root of the artist's potential contribution to civilization, but ultimately at the basis of democracy itself.

CHAPTER XXXIV

Psychiatry in Relation to Authority and Freedom

By LAWRENCE S. KUBIE
*Clinical Professor of Psychiatry
School of Medicine, Yale University;
Faculty, New York Psychoanalytic Institute*

IN WHAT I have to say here I will be trying only to explain the contribution of the psychoanalytic theory of human nature to our understanding of human reactions to authority and freedom.

About these two abstractions, the psychoanalyst would note first that they are banners; and that we react to banners in patterns which are determined largely by our concrete experiences. Abstractions tend to be emotionally meaningless, unless they tap the reservoirs of our own memories, whether we can recognize and recall specific happenings, or have "forgotten" (*i.e.,* repressed) them. Especially toward authority and freedom do we respond with a complicated intrapsychic struggle, the workings of which can be observed in ourselves, our children, our friends, and the people who work with us. What ultimately comes out of such a struggle in any human being represents the history of a man's whole experience with authority, submission, and defiance. The balance between the acceptance or rejection of authority is a condensation of all of our conscious and unconscious loves and hates. Consequently, to understand this aspect of any personality requires that we understand all of his feelings about individuals and situations out of the past and present. In fact, the individuals and the situations who become the immediate targets of our present emotions always carry a heritage from the past. In the conflict over freedom and authority, as in everything, today is the screen on which all of our yesterdays project their images. Thus the man who wields authority today is an embodiment of all of the authority, real or imaginary, which has been exercised over us in the past by parents, teachers, nurses, etc. The authority of the top sergeant may carry the flavor of the authority of an older brother, uncle, father, grandfather, or even of an older sister or mother; sometimes either/or, and sometimes all of these. To such condensed symbols of authority it is impossible for us not to have complicated and conflictful feelings. We may reject it, saying, "I will allow no one to dictate to me." Yet in that same moment we may cling desperately and with terror to that same authority. Consequently, we sometimes provoke exhibitions of the very authority against which we react.

Thus, a five year old girl with blazing blue eyes and a tousled shock of golden hair said, "I will always do anything I want to do, and no one will ever make me do anything I don't want to do." Yet, while nursing these fantasies of omnipotence, that same youngster did not dare to leave her mother's side to go to school or to a party.

Consider a three year old boy walking with his father on a sunny Sunday morning. Suddenly he stops and looks up at his father and says, "Reach up." The father asks, "Why?" In all seriousness the little boy answers, "I want to see if you can touch the sun." Two years pass; and one morning the same small boy solemnly regards his father who is standing beside a very tall uncle. The little boy looks perplexed and unhappy, then draws his father down to whisper miserably in his ear, "Why is he so much bigger than you are?" More years pass, and the once little boy is now 6'4". As he views his image reflected in the shop windows, he feels a shock both of surprise and of dismay. "Not *that* big fellow. That can't be I." He is unable to accept his own maturity as represented by his stature. Still more years have to pass before he is able to cut the mooring lines which bound him to his own infancy; and to accept both his maturity and his size. For the first time now he can look down on his middle-sized father with tolerant affection.

Those four steps condense four phases in human development. First comes the infancy of man in which he wants his own grown-ups to be omniscient and omnipotent, *i.e.,* to be able to reach up and touch the sun. Even when he rebels he needs and welcomes this symbol of their authority; because from their power, as represented largely by size, he derives a feeling both of security and of reflected power. In most people we find traces of this early stage throughout life. Second, comes the discovery that there are some adults who are even bigger than the parent, that father is not all powerful and omnipotent, that he cannot touch the sun. This is the little boy who makes the bitter reproach, "Why is he bigger than you are?" Third, comes the struggle over accepting or rejecting one's growing power and maturity, as evidenced by the rejection of one's own reflected image as it becomes uncomfortably big. Finally, comes the acceptance of maturity and authority, the ultimate phase which only few people reach.

These four stages in man's growth affect profoundly his relationship to authority, filling him with confusion and conflict. This occurs whether authority is represented in physical size alone, or in a Hitler, or in a dogmatic party line or religious philosophy, or in a dictatorial pseudo-scientific attitude. The earlier universal roots of this conflict lie in the simple fact that the human child remains small for long years in a world of towering adults with whom he cannot cope on equal terms. It is as a reaction against our childish rebellion and dependence that we overvalue size itself, building Empire State Buildings, manufacturing taxicabs and automobiles which are impractically big, setting fantastic store by genital size, and always linking together those two strange words, "bigger and better." Consequently we tend to cling to infantile dependency, even as we try to free ourselves from it.

The complexity of our attitude toward authority, and the extraordinary contradictions which infuse it, are further illustrated by the person who in all trivial details of life is intransigent in his insistence on his independence, but who remains perpetually dependent in all important matters. The young adult may be full of wordy rebellion against a father on whom he remains economically dependent. Another example is the *Ewige-Student* of the old German universities, a phenomenon not unknown on our own campuses, particularly among graduate students. Here is the man who seems always to be rebelling intellectually; yet if we trace the history of his rebellion we find that it runs in interesting cycles. He begins each new field of study as the best student in the group. He soon knows every word his chief has written or uttered. Yet as he nears the point at which he should launch himself as an independent investigator or practitioner, he becomes restless. He soon begins to reject his teacher's teachings. He regurgitates everything which up to that point he has accepted submissively, until finally he rejects the whole subject, to make a fresh start in another field of study. By implication he says to the chief, to whom only a few months ago he was completely docile, "Your whole field of work is no good." Thus his belated defiance and his refusal to submit further to authority fuse in the same instant with his resumption of the role of the dependent child, as he starts to grow up all over again in a new nursery under a new father-figure. An able young physician has done this five times. In more subtle forms we see this same paradoxical and ambivalent attitude toward authority in all aspects of life: a single symbolic gesture expressing the ultimate in defiance, another the ultimate in submission, yet both occurring simultaneously.

Curiously enough, in politics we encounter the same paradox. Both at the extreme right and at the extreme left we find men who are willing to accept arbitrary abuses of political and economic power at home while attacking it at a distance. The powerful father who is near at hand is always regarded as a benign protector: the distant powerful figure is always an ogre. The reverse is also found: men reacting with exaggerated violence to even the slightest hint of a violation of civil liberties at home, while tolerating the most savage abuses of human liberty at a safe distance of several thousands of miles.

One finds this same paradox in overt homosexuality both among men and among women: *i.e.*, the ultimate in defiance and the ultimate in submissiveness expressing itself in the same sick bodily dance.

The issues of authority and freedom have implications for knowing, as well as for doing. Are there areas of thought in which we must be guided to our convictions by authority, rather than evidence? By implication, the answers to these questions involve the basic problem of faith as a phenomenon in human life. Is faith higher than evidence? or evidence higher than faith? or do we accept the usual shoddy evasion that they have separate mandates, separate and equal spheres of influence? Here again one finds that the reactions to authority can be full of inconsistencies which occur because the same individual may be submissive toward one person or type of ideas and rebellious toward another.

These few examples merely emphasize the fact that in questions of freedom and authority, as in so much of life, we are full of perplexing and confusing paradoxes.

It may, however, be useful to describe a few of the general principles which derive from this summary. In the first place, our reactions toward authority and toward freedom have simple, earthy, concrete roots in the experiences of our childhood, through the long years of dependency, and in the attitudes of mingled love and hate that we generate toward those adults who were the original representatives of authority and of restrictions on our freedom. Out of this arise the curious compromises between overt rebellion and masked submission, or overt submission and masked rebellion, which make up the intricate mosaic of our conscious and unconscious attitudes toward authority and freedom. How we behave in the end, the causes that we espouse, the principles that we adopt, the philosophical rationalizations which we give to those principles, all of these represent the algebraic summation of innumerable affirmative and negative attitudes, conscious and unconscious compulsions and phobias, which unfortunately are by no means always congruous.

This can be summarized in another principle: namely, that the ultimate restrictions on human freedom are imposed less by external authorities than by unconscious internal forces. In every one of us is generated a system of unconscious internal commands: obligatory, compelling, unreasoning processes. These are the forces which make automatons out of human beings, pulling the strings to which we dance, forcing us to behave in ways for which we may be able to find no adequate rationale.

Clinically these obligatory compelling inner forces may take various forms. Sometimes they are manifested in severe mental illness. For instance, if I am sick and have to crawl on my knees, I may attempt to explain this behavior by a conviction that some secret foreign agents are operating on my mind, influencing it by cosmic rays and compelling me to do this. Here we are dealing with a *psychotic* disturbance in human freedom. On the other hand, I might crawl on my knees not out of sickness, but because I am being initiated into some college fraternity. My group, the club, thus gives a social sanction to what would otherwise be a foolish act; and, in return for something which I want from them, I delegate to this group a limited authority to command me. The performance is determined almost wholly on a conscious level; and, if we grant the premise that it is desirable to get into the club, and desirable also for the club to make me pay for this privilege by furnishing amusement to its members, the act remains within the bounds of "reason." (Yet you will realize that concealed in this ritual of initiation are subtler forces which use the ceremony as a socially acceptable way of mocking the authority of the adult world. Here again, therefore, submission and rebellion are expressed in the same gesture.) Or I may crawl on my knees because a church has decreed that there is merit in so doing, and that in this way I may achieve salvation and forgiveness for sin, or even healing. As I accept that which the church says as being a revealed form of truth, within the limits of this assumption what I do remains an act of free submission on my part: acceptance, submission, and freedom again intertwined in the same act.

But there is another and deeper form of enslavement, an enslavement to a compulsive internal mechanism which we do not seek to explain away, which we know to be *sick*, but which we cannot resist. Thus, is normal to wash our hands when they need it, but not a thousand times a day, as some patients must do. Such patients say to us, "We know that this is foolish—a neurotic symptom. We want to stop it, but we cannot. Help us to stop." They are not psychotic. They have not taken leave of reason. Their understanding of reality is quite intact. Yet some unconscious force is so compelling that the sufferer must obey it, or experience an overwhelming inner discomfort. Such easily recognized compulsive symptoms are only a special case of an even subtler, more universal, manifestation of the compulsive distortion of human life. These are the compulsions which consist of an inflexible and insatiable exaggeration of normal forms of behavior.

Thus it is normal to eat, normal to sleep, normal to love, normal to be angry, normal to be ambitious, normal to desire approval, normal at times to take chances, normal to compete, normal to seek social companionship, normal to enjoy solitude, normal to be concerned about one's appearance, etc., etc.: yet there is no normal form of behavior which cannot become the channel of unconscious mechanisms which exaggerate it, overdrive it, and distort it, by making it rigid, insatiable, and stereotyped. This occurs whenever internal psychological forces which are inaccessible to simple, direct conscious introspection (*i.e.*, the forces that we call "unconscious"), exercise a predominant control over what we are doing, thinking, and feeling. When this happens our acts, our thoughts, our feelings, become slave-labor; enslaved, however, not to an external but to an internal tyranny. This is a form of universal slavery which is no respector of social or economic or political considerations. It is the price we pay for the fact that in no culture on earth has mankind learned how to bring children up in such a way that they do not bury alive the moral conflicts with which every child struggles unsuccessfully, conflicts which subsequently continue to plague them throughout the rest of their days in secret and distorted forms.

To the psychoanalyst this is the ultimate tyranny. To the psychoanalyst, the ultimate freedom is the fifth freedom: the freedom to know what goes on inside us. Until we solve this most basic problem of education, of morals, and of spiritual development, all other efforts to seek human freedom are relatively superficial makeshifts.

I doubt that the full implication of what I have in mind can be clear. I may seem to be making light of man's pursuit of political, economic, religious, and intellectual liberty. This is not what I intend. What I do intend, however, is to try to indicate that the pursuit of liberty is not a simple matter on any level, that men are often in two minds about it; and that, furthermore, they may attain the four external freedoms yet remain slaves to the tyranny of their own unconscious processes.

It will be obvious that it is impossible to study this freedom anywhere except in a free community, *i.e.,* one which is free intellectually, spiritually, religiously, politically, economically. Therefore, although the preservation of external freedom is not the ultimate answer to human freedom, it is its necessary prerequisite. *External freedom* sets the stage on which it will be possible for men to study the solution of the problems of *internal freedom*. The first is a challenge to political scientists; the second to the scientist of human thought and feeling. But this scientist cannot solve these problems in a laboratory that is burning down, nor in any atmosphere except where he is unfettered, free to pursue his goals over uncharted seas to unanticipated destinations. This then is the pursuit of the fifth freedom, the freedom from the tyranny of unconscious compulsions and unconscious fears.

Comment by Rudolf Allers:
Professor Kubie seems to have fallen prey, to some degree, at least, to the "genetic fallacy," that is, the idea that by the discovery of causal or genetic factors one arrives at a full understanding of a phenomenon. It is not definitely proved that adult behavior is determined only by the vicissitudes of early life.

Childhood is indeed important, but not all important. Nor can one be certain that all situations a person encounters in his later years are analogous to those of infancy; hence it may well be that his behavior will be determined by experiences after childhood.

CHAPTER XXXV

Persecution as the Pathology of Freedom and Authority

By MARK GRAUBARD

Graduate School, College of Science, Literature and the Arts, The University of Minnesota

PERSECUTION IS the expression of a pathological disturbance in the relationship of freedom to authority. Each society adjusts its freedoms at particular levels, and necessarily does the same with its authoritative power, with its conscience and even its subconscious values and judgments. Social changes in value or in institutional adjustment are brought about in ways that represent a broad spectrum. Its band ranges from slow, invisible, but cumulative shifts and realignments, to changes that erupt with violence. The bulk of change seems to consist of the slow, imperceptible, but constructive irregular adjustments and modifications which, as in biological evolution, soon loom on the historical horizon as vast divergences from the previously existing arrangements. Similarly the lines of demarcation between freedom and authority shift slowly and gradually in every society. Occasionally, that shift occurs explosively. Occasionally, too, the slow, continuous process of adjustment develops a sudden lesion. Under such conditions when the inflammation grows intense, there may occur a genuine conflict which often expresses itself in persecution.

Students of history of science are so uncompromisingly opposed to persecution for differences in belief that they are not inclined to consider objectively the particular circumstances of such tragic conflicts. Nevertheless, that is exactly what has to be done, if one is to inquire how and why people act as they do. Moreover, persecution for belief is usually carried out by the learned, or at least by the leading lights of a functioning society, by the spokesman of the accepted faith, or the vanguard of a movement newly installed in power. Hence it should be subjected to intensive study with particular care.

By persecution, we mean a state of emotional tension in which force is employed to suppress, punish, or eradicate opposition to those views or values which the culture, or its delegated power, considers basic. Moreover, the degree of persecution will usually vary with the intensity of the generated tensions, and that, in turn, will depend on a variety of factors, not least among them being the particular natures of the creed and the challenge; the manner in which it is made, hence the personality of the challenger; the circumstances, such as the times, the sense of security of the group in power, and the personalities of its leaders or spokesmen.

Persecutions in the history of science bring out relationships between freedom and authority in their starkest nakedness. The people involved on both sides are often seekers after truth. The conflict is not a matter of life and death, as conflicts over social or moral tenets seem to be. Economics seldom can be dragged in to befog such conflicts. After the big battle is over, it is often easy for all concerned to see how silly and futile the whole furor appears. The issues, in so far as they deal with a scientific situation, can then be reexamined in their stark objectivity. Hence the pathology of freedom and authority, and therefore by inference, the normal relationship between the two, may be better understood.

I. *Persecution and Personality*

Much persecution in science can best be classified under the heading of *Persecution and Personality.* In such instances the personality of the persecutee, as deviant and challenger, is of utmost significance. For convenience, the topic of *Persecution and Personality* can be subdivided into three subtopics:

1. Persecution by Impasse; 2. Persecution by Invitation; and 3. Innovation Without Tears.

(1) *Persecution by Impasse*

Persecution by Impasse involves situations in which a tragedy unfolds, as if in accordance with its definition by the ancient Greeks. The hero goes about doing that which he had been doing all along and which is the very goal of his life and interests. For many years his labors are praised, and he feels appreciated. Suddenly he finds that an idea he has expressed or a discovery he has made disturbs people and creates hostility. He wants no conflict and feels that he has done no wrong. Yet, there is the hostile crowd, the humanity that he loves and wishes to serve.

There are its leaders whom he adores, and here stands he bewildered and helpless, because he cannot change himself, his thoughts, his oft-lauded efforts and abilities, nor can he denounce their fruits. An impasse is created, and the furies of irrevocable and inexorable tragedy in the manner of Greek fate are let loose and cannot be halted.

SOCRATES

The seventy years of Socrates's life (469-399 B. C.) practically spanned the peak of Athens's greatness. At the time of Pericles, Athens enjoyed more freedom than any other known civilization; yet Phidias was arrested for sacrilege and died in prison; Anaxagoras, held then in great esteem as scientist and teacher of Pericles, was exiled for "sacrilege and Persian leanings"; Aspasia, Pericles's mistress, was tried on the charge of "sacrilege"; Protagoras was exiled, and his books were publicly burned; and Socrates was put to death for advocating new gods, and for corrupting the youth. Whence this persecution in the midst of much freedom?

There was freedom in Athens then, and the arts and sciences prospered. Aeschylus, Sophocles, and Euripides, were practically contemporaries. Hypocrates, Herodotus, and Thucydides flourished. The Pythagorean school followed its mystic numbers and diets, and Parmenides and Anaxagoras philosophized freely. The sophist Protagoras plied his sharp wits, and Aristophanes mocked whom he pleased.

Socrates's main concern was virtue, not knowledge. "When I was young, Cebes, I was tremendously eager for the kind of wisdom which they call investigation of nature."[1] But Socrates gave that up later. People should study a little science because it is useful. But "he deprecated curiosity to learn how the deity contrives celestial phenomena. Their secrets could not be discovered by man . . . attempts to search out what the gods had not chosen to reveal must be displeasing to them."[2]

[1] Plato, "Phaedo," *The Dialogues of Plato,* translated by B. Jowett, Random House, New York, 1937, I, pp. 480 f.
[2] Xenophon, "Memorabilia," *Works,* Macmillan & Company, Ltd., London, 1897, III, vii, p. 6.

He was not interested in advancing a pet philosophic system. His goal in life was to seek out the meaning of the good, of duty, truth, justice, the nature of the soul, and above all, spiritual consistency and responsibility. He is justly famous for his keen and merciless interrogation. No man was too great for his scalpel or too foolish or humble for his patient discourses. No act was beyond the sharp power of his mind; no hold was barred, no corner too dark, no conflict or inconsistency too personal to be exposed. His patients' or victims' torments did not exist for him. He would have been amazed if told of their discomfort, and would have argued most logically that they had no reason to be hurt.

His accusers were not villains. Anytus was a decent and moderate democrat, with no personal grudge, and only wished to see Socrates exiled. Meletus was a religious fanatic, but an Athenian nonetheless. The fact is that the jury could not help but sympathize with Socrates's victims, in the same way as the American public sympathized with Mr. Truman in 1948, when he was attacked for being a common, ordinary American by men who considered themselves superior. The more Socrates went on with his apology, the more the five hundred good and doubly selected men of the jury grew in hostility, because he was in reality finding *them* wanting.

Socrates had to be loyal to his master, Reason. How was he to know that twenty-three centuries after him, Freud, himself a believer in the rational method of science, would suggest that reason is often rationalization, and that human acts or beliefs are often the results of criss-crossing conflicts, repressions, and projections? Besides, Freud or no Freud, do we not know that man lives also by values and emotions not necessarily open to rational control or modification? What would not Socrates have done to poor Thomas Jefferson for his "We hold these truths to be self-evident"?

Socrates was bewildered. His goals were good and noble. His method was sound. But here were "these men . . . who instead of being angry with themselves are angry with me." The jury, too, had little freedom to choose. They admitted his greatness, they admired his genius, but they were human beings and not angels.

GALILEO

Galileo was also a man who had been held in high regard by his fellow citizens, both as man and as scientist. When he invented the telescope in 1609, he already enjoyed an international reputation. After the invention of the telescope, Galileo announced to the world in rapid succession the true topography of the moon, many hitherto invisible stars, the satellites of Jupiter, the "knobs" of Saturn, the crescents of Venus, sun spots, and solar rotation. Collectively these discoveries challenged the established astronomical conception of a static, circumscribed universe, carved out in perfection. Small wonder then that the human mind was staggered by the impact of Galileo's observations, and that the defenders of the established pattern of belief reacted violently. Who were the ones who felt the blow? Not only the common people but the teachers of science as well, whose defense of the accepted notions was far more sophisticated. Among them were Maestlin, Kepler's teacher (who was a great Copernican but who exclaimed, "I will never concede his four new planets to the Italian from Padua, though I die for it"); Welser of Augsburg and Clavio of Rome, two great mathematicians; the celebrated scholars, Julius Libri of Pisa and Cesare Cremonius of Padua; Francesco Sizzi, the astronomer of Florence; and the astronomer Christman. These great scholars, who were at home with the mathematical intricacies of Euclid and Ptolemy or the depths of Plato or Aristotle were in no different position than one's learned and pious grandfather who when confronted with keen arguments against his faith exclaims: "What am I to believe in? Have I lived a fraud all my life?" Such cries of anguish can be packed with dynamite.

Galileo did have many defenders among lay scholars, as well as theologians. His *Sidereal Messenger* was published in 1611. A commission of church dignitaries examined his claims and recommended complete acceptance of his views. Pope Paul V granted him an audience and expressed his admiration and friendship, and other high officials followed suit.

But the problem remained. In 1613, Galileo's devoted pupil, Father Castelli, had an argument with a Florentine professor of physics, who brought in the Bible to refute Galileo. Galileo wrote a letter in which he implied that the Bible deals with God's revelation and the soul's salvation. But God also gave man reason to study nature, His grand handiwork.

The Scriptures have few and only contradictory statements on astronomy. Besides "in discussing natural phenomena we ought not to begin with texts from a scripture but with experiment and demonstration."[3] The common people and the lower clergy were restive. They lacked the strength and sophistication to accommodate the new and not be shaken by it. Hence real trouble was brewing and Galileo's first trial took place in 1616. He was ordered to abandon the Copernican theory and abstain from "teaching, defending, and discussing it," under the threat of imprisonment. There was no recantation or punishment. Copernicus's work was suspended "until corrected," and the corrections were minor. Cardinal Bellarmine advised Galileo to be cautious and "to write freely but be careful to keep outside the Sacristy."

Galileo was a deeply religious man, firm in his loyalty to the Catholic faith. He stayed on in Rome, because he saw no reason why his beloved church could not be in league with science and accept Copernicanism. He saw no conflict between them, only harmony. *He* managed all right, why could not every good Christian? He was warned by friends. His patron the Duke ordered him home.

For sixteen years all was quiet and the conflict lay dormant. In 1630, Galileo completed his *Dialogues on the Two Principal Systems of the World,* the Ptolemaic and the Copernican, and obtained the papal imprimatur. Pope Urban VIII was his great friend and a true lover of science. As Cardinal Barberini he had defended Galileo in 1616, and as far back as 1612, upon receipt of Galileo's *On Floating Bodies,* he had written the author: "I shall read it with great pleasure, both to confirm myself in my opinion which agrees with yours, and to enjoy with the rest of the world the fruits of your rare intellect."[4] Galileo rejoiced when this man became Pope in 1623, and renewed his campaign to make the Church give its blessing to the Copernican hypothesis. He went to Rome to see the new Pope, who listened attentively to his plea for the revocation of the ban of 1616. We know from Campanella that six years later the same Pope said: "It was never our intention, and if it had depended upon us, that decree would never have been passed."[5] Yet, the Pope promised Galileo nothing, gave him a medal and much praise,

---

[3] J. D. Bethune, *Private Life of Galileo,* W. Hyde & Company, Boston, 1832, p. 75.
[4] J. J. Fahie, *Galileo,* J. Murray, London, 1903, p. 184.
[5] K. von Gebler, *Galileo and the Roman Curia,* Stanley Paul & Company, Ltd., London, 1879, p. 134.

and bestowed a pension on Galileo's son, born of an unsanctioned alliance.

But the storm could not be averted. Galileo had two loves and thought they could live in peace side by side. But it could not be. The Pope, who had flirted with science all along, no doubt spent many sleepless nights castigating himself for catering to his selfish love of mathematics and experimentation while his flock endured confusion and bewilderment as a result of the new speculations. To whom did he owe his stronger allegiance? To Galileo and science, or to the flock entrusted to him by Christ? He kept completely out of the second trial, and let it seek its natural course. Galileo was a true penitent. He did not betray science or miss becoming a hero, nor did he perjure himself as some historians claim. "I am a true and zealous Catholic," he said, and submitted. He knew he failed, but tried to remain loyal to both loves. During his imprisonment he wrote his greatest work and surely had cause to do the most praying. A few decades later his two loves made an excellent adjustment and neither suffered thereby.

(2) *Persecution by Invitation*

Under *Persecution by Invitation* we shall consider two cases in which the individuals presented strong temptations for punishment.

BRUNO

Giordano Bruno met his tragic death at the stake in 1600, after an imprisonment of eight years. The charges against him were apostasy from his order, association with heretics, and unorthodox attitudes to the dogma of the Trinity and Incarnation. These charges need not have been serious, and the judges offered him his freedom, if he abjured eight petty propositions advanced in his books. But Bruno refused and chose death.

Nowhere in the documents of the Inquisition is there any mention of Bruno's defense of Copernicanism or his scientific interests. Although he had praised Copernicus, Bruno wrote that he "sees neither into the eyes of Copernicus nor into those of Ptolemy but with his very own eyes in matters of judgment or conception."[6] He was primarily a philo-

---

[6]Giordano Bruno, "La Cena de la Ceneri" (Ash Wednesday Supper), *Gessammelte Werke*, edited by Ludwig Kuhlenbeck, Leipzig, 1904, Dialogue I.

sophical poet, a speculator with untrammelled scope and boldness in mystic cosmologic schemes. He shared all the contemporary beliefs in magic, incantations, occult forces, secret sympathy, and amulets. He saw in nature a Universal Mind and a Universal Soul. His leitmotif was—the universe is infinite. It has "no center and no circumference but the center is everywhere and every part is outside some other part."[7]

Born in 1548, Bruno entered a Dominican monastery at the age of fifteen and became a priest in 1572. He was nonconformist in many respects, and the Provincial drew up charges against him in 1576. He ran away to Rome where he says the Inquisition "sought a quarrel with him on 130 points." He escaped after throwing the suspected informer into the Tiber, it is said. And casting off his garb, he went to Genoa. The Genoese Republic sued him on some counts, and he was off to Venice. He was soon in Padua, and put back on his Dominican garb. He visited Milan, Lyons, and finally arrived in Geneva in 1579. Calvin ruled there, and Bruno tried to become a Calvinist but was soon involved in some quarrel, landed in prison, apologized and was let off. He went to Lyons and Toulouse, somehow began calling himself Doctor in Roman Theology, and launched a campaign against Aristotle on many points. He arrived in Paris in 1581, and lectured there on his specialty, mnemonics or the art of memory, and on alchemy. King Henry III befriended him, and Bruno dedicated a book on memory to him. The king had a vile reputation but Bruno praised him, because he bestowed a lectureship upon Bruno at the Collège de France. As usual, he was well received at first but soon "tumults were brewing."

Bruno went to England feeling that the "barbarians who dwelt at the ends of the earth must assuredly be only too glad to welcome so highly qualified a teacher as he."[8] Received at Oxford with open arms, he soon began heaping his customary abuse upon one and all who displeased him. It was in London that he wrote his best known works. He soon returned to Paris, was well received at the University, and in no time used such vile language on Aristotle that a fight ensued in which he showed up a coward as well. Having vilified and antagonized everybody in the West, he left for Germany and Bohemia. There the same stories

---

[7]Bruno, "Infinite," Dialogue III. See D. W. Singer, *Giordano Bruno: On the Infinite Universe and Worlds,* Henry Schumann, Inc., New York, 1950, pp. 302-327.

[8]William Boulting, *Giordano Bruno, His Life Thoughts and Martyrdom*, Stanley Paul & Company, Ltd., London, 1914, p. 81.

were repeated. He finally landed in Venice as tutor in magic, memory, alchemy, and the secret arts, to a scion of a noble family, Giovanni Mocenigo. The man was so shocked by Bruno's vulgarity, cynicism, and general looseness that he reported him to the Inquisition. Hostile though Venice had always been to Rome, he was extradited and imprisoned.

Bruno was a hater, quarrelsome, and a man without principles. While in Germany, he praised Luther in a eulogy beginning: "Thou hast seen the light, O Luther." In Geneva, he tried his best to treat Calvin similarly. In Italy, he sought to reenter the church. He could not even be kind to Copernicus for the span of an entire sentence. He quarreled with everyone who befriended him. He simply did not know how to say, "I disagree with you," let alone, "I beg to differ." Anyone who failed to drown him in gifts of money and in flattery, was a swine, a vulture, a thief, a fool. It seems difficult to avoid the conclusion that had he defended a consistent philosophy and had his personality been a bit gentler, he would in all likelihood have finished his years unmolested.

PARACELSUS

Not much different in type, though considerably milder in form, is the case of Paracelsus. But here we are dealing with a man who had great scientific insight[9] and was essentially possessed of a great love of humanity and of deeply religious sentiments. His was a loose and broad outlook, lacking in specific contribution, yet stimulating much thought at the time. He introduced many new chemical substances into medical practice and showed great insight into the art of healing. Yet when he attacked anyone there were no holds barred and no terms too vulgar to use. "O, you hypocrites who despise the truths taught you by a true physician, who is himself instructed by nature and is a son of God himself! . . . Woe for your necks on the day of judgment. I know that the monarchy will be mine. Mine, too, will be the honor and the glory. Not that I praise myself; nature praises me."[10] This goes on and on *ad infinitum* and *ad nauseam*.

He was a dyed-in-the-wool rebel and was ever busy hating. He hated Geber and Aristotle, Galen and Avicenna, Rhasis and Albertus Magnus,

[9]See A. M. Staddart, *Life of Paracelsus*. McKay, London, 1911.
[10]*The Hermetic and Alchemical Writings of Paracelsus,* edited by A. E. Waite, Elliot, London, 1894, I, p. 39.

the universities and the authorities, in fact, everybody outside his own ego. But what was all the hating about? He believed most intensely in alchemy and astrology, in magic and necromancy, in fact, in everything that constituted the folklore of the time. The fulminations were merely the outcroppings of a rambunctious, termagant ego, bursting at the seams with bitterness toward others.

Invited to lecture at Basel, he was popular at first, but students soon deserted him. Paracelsus blustered and threatened, sued the city for a prize he thought he should have been awarded, and left Basel with aggravated bitterness. Strangely enough, he treated the poor without charge, and late in life dedicated himself to missionary work. He wandered widely, and never really enjoyed peace or any recognition. But when a man cannot open his mouth without pouring out venom and abuse, just what is one to expect of his victims or bystanders?

(3) *Innovation Without Tears*

Let us now consider the obverse of the coin. In Nicholas Copernicus and William Harvey we have two key innovators, each of whom revolutionized a thought pattern which lay at the very center of a well knit outlook. Yet in each instance the personality and methods of the innovator were such as to render hostile responses impossible.

COPERNICUS

Copernicus studied civil and canon law, as well as medicine. He had a teacher at Bologna who advocated bold ideas in astronomy, and Copernicus collaborated with him. Although Copernicus was never a good or diligent observer, at the age of twenty-seven he was invited to lecture on astronomy in Rome. Fourteen years later he was invited by the Lateran Council to assist in the planned reform of the calendar, a rare honor. But he politely refused, on the grounds that the true motions of the sun and moon were not yet satisfactorily known.

Because his uncle was bishop of the Cathedral of Frauenburg in Prussia, Copernicus was elected a canon as a young man. He served well in that capacity and rose on the ladder of the chapter. He practiced medicine free of charge to the poor of the parish, and did some portrait painting as well. He always pursued his amateur work in astronomy, and for a decade or more before his death and the publication of his great *De Revolutionibus Orbium Coelestium* in 1543, he circulated fairly widely a brief account of his theory in manuscript form.

In 1525, Melanchthon's nephew Peucer had already declared that Copernicus's fame was solid and widespread, and in 1533, Pope Clement VII ordered his secretary Widmanstadt to report to him on the theory. In 1536, the great scholar, Cardinal Schonberg, wrote Copernicus for a transcription of his manuscript at the Cardinal's expense, and urged its publication. Protestants and Catholics praised the novelty and cleverness of his ideas, though Protestants and Catholics were also in the camp of the opposition.

In the preface Copernicus relates that he long withheld publication, because he feared the scorn that would greet "the novelty and absurdity of my opinion." But friends urged him to publish, a cardinal, a bishop, and others. And if some people "should dare to criticize" his work "because of some distorted passage of Scripture . . . I care not at all. I will even despise their judgment as foolish." In 1540, Copernicus asked Andreas Osiander, a Lutheran theologian and mathematician, whether "it would be possible for him to publish his theory of the Earth's motion without exciting hostile criticism."[11]

Osiander replied: "For my part I have always felt about hypotheses that they are not articles of faith, but bases of calculation, so that even if they be false, it matters not, so long as they exactly represent the phenomena of the motions" . . . It would be very difficult to find a more intelligent statement in the annals of science, assuming that by false he meant imaginary or unreal. Yet the author of the Introduction to the *De Revolutionibus* is frequently attacked nowadays as an appeaser or opportunist.[12]

The humility of Copernicus's character is seen in all his comments, acts, and letters. "It often happens that someone grasps a thing quite correctly but cannot make clear to others a concept which is clear to himself. I fear that sometimes this happens to me . . . I acknowledge freely that I can err."[13]

His skill in human relations was correspondingly excellent. He was

[11] Angus Armitage, *Copernicus, the Founder of Modern Astronomy*, G. Allen & Unwin, Ltd., London, 1938, p. 64.
[12] Edward Rosen, *Three Copernican Treatises*, Columbia University Press, New York, 1939.
[13] Herman Kesten, *Copernicus and His World*, Roy, New York, 1945.

involved in many activities, and made friends everywhere and retained them. He was not molested nor was his idea, anywhere, until Galileo brought to focus its contradictions with the accepted belief pattern of the times.

HARVEY

The situation with William Harvey is remarkably similar. Here was a humble, kindly, and modest man, full of adoration of Aristotle and Galen, but without blind submission to their authority. Writes Doctor Ent: "He never hostilely attacks any previous writer but ever courteously sets down and comments upon the opinions of each."[14] Harvey was physician to Charles I, and shared the tragic king's tribulations patiently and quietly. Though a member of the Court he never partook in intrigue. No wonder Hobbes said that Harvey "was the only man who conquered envy in his lifetime."[15]

Yet Harvey's ideas were thoroughly revolutionary. He had formulated his notion of the circulation of the blood by 1616, but did not publish his great and beautiful opus until 1628. In the interim he demonstrated and dissected, lectured, and won over friends and colleagues. His introduction to his masterpiece, *On the Circulation,* shows the greatness of his spirit, his humility, decency, and wisdom. His noble conduct to a reputed witch and his supervision of the examinations of witches before their trial demonstrate that freedom from bitterness and hatred can be a true guiding light to decency and justice. Harvey's theory, which contradicted the basic concepts of the workings of the body, discomfited every physician. It upset the entire medical concept of the body and its workings. The opposition published many books and treatises, because the world of science was keenly disturbed. Harvey's answers were models of sympathy, respect, and scientific honor. He soon won over many of his bitterest opponents.

The relationship of personality to persecution indicates that while some situations are extremely difficult to control or mollify, others are foolishly created or inflated by a victim who begs for trouble. Other situa-

---

[14] William Harvey, "On Generation," and "Introduction," *Works,* edited by Robert Willis, Sydenham Society, London, 1847.
[15] D'Arcy Power, *William Harvey,* T. Fisher Unwin, London, 1897.

tions, dangerous on the surface, can be suppressed or averted. As we know from anthropology and psychology, the human mind is highly plastic. Hence there is no must about any particular conflict or irreconcilability. The mind can make unlimited adjustments, a feature of man which is both useful and harmful, depending on the circumstances. Needless to say, the times, in which the clash occurs, are of prime importance. Adjustments that seem impossible at the moment are easily negotiated in time.

II. *Persecution by Creed*

Let us now consider a second large segment of persecution, in which the individual plays no role whatever. This type falls under the heading of *Persecution by Creed*. In this category we include the medieval wave of persecution known as the witch mania, and its contemporary twin images, race mania and class mania, hence Nazism and Communism.

Every society has a mass of frustration seeking an aggressive outlet. The bulk of social frustration, which means the bulk of individual frustration composing it, is neutralized by the great force toward equilibrium which seeks to appease or undo it, in order to establish peace at the bidding of the will to live. But here and there the equilibrating force working against frustration fails in its effort, and a search for an aggressive outlet ensues. Medieval witchcraft declared: "You see this evil about us, the plague, poverty, and misery. You know who is the cause of it all? The witch, the sorcerer, the devil's accomplices, and the dabblers in his hidden forces. Catch them, and burn them, and all will be well."

In most cases the suspects were people who aroused suspicion, for no real evidence could possibly exist. Hence they were people who had somehow acquired "common fame," that is, popular distrust. People who were too rich and mean, sloppy or frivolous women, men who were too cocky or obviously unique, and often people who were merely available by chance, or fitted the needs of the mosaic. Thus hundreds of thousands were caught in the trap and had their lives snuffed out. As individuals they stood no chance. The personality of the victim mattered little in the vast majority of cases.

Only four hundred years later another mass delusion swept over Europe, the Nazi terror. This one was a logical outgrowth of a theory of race. When Gobineau published his *Essai sur l'inégalité des races humaines* in 1855, he little knew that he was laying a tricky system of pipes for blood to flow, and for human bitterness to pour into. His successor, Chamberlain, came closer to it, but Hitler and Rosenberg completed and perfected the job. Here was a typical modern outlet for the hate and bitterness which the defeat of Prussian nationalism generated. Man cannot apparently kill or even hate without a suitable rationalization, no matter how hot and tense is the force of hate within. Modern biology could easily be made to provide that rationalization. Once a man or a culture begins to see race as the cause of differential progress, evil, goodness, or glory, it becomes a culture fortress not easily stormed or dented. Within such a trap man lives, reasons, struggles, and dies. Unlike witchcraft, no ready witnesses were needed here. The victim was a Jew or a Pole or Gypsy, was he not? Then die he must! The crowd yelled, and the victims died. Whether they were Harveys or Brunos, kind or humble, meek or learned, mattered not at all.

Today the class struggle theory operates the concentration camps and the factories. While Gobineau was merely a snob who concocted a vague speculation, Marx was a Bruno with a theory into which he poured endless hatred of his people and his friends, his contempt for the workers, peasants, and, above all, the middle classes. His concoction suited well the Russian intelligentsia who had many forces contributing to their frustration, such as Tsarist tyranny, lack of opportunity, the poverty of the masses, cruelty, and ignorance. Communism learned all it could from medieval witchcraft and from Nazism, but it is essentially a mirror image of both. All the world's poverty, misery, and wars, according to both, are caused by the witch of Wall Street, and the ruling cliques, tolerated by the easily deluded idiotic masses. But class hate seems far more vicious even than Nazism, because its defense of persecution is more fluid. Hence today the victim is Trotskyism, tomorrow Titoism, or social Fascism or cosmopolitanism or opportunism or left wingism or idealism, and what not. Such flexibility is a tyrant's paradise. Moreover, it has demonstrated more often than any hate movement that the personality of the victim is of absolutely no account. Today's hero is tonight's reptile, swine, renegade, anti-Stalinist, or American spy. In the face of such fluidity and in the face of Marxist or Leninist contempt for reality, those who wish for the final elimination of persecution are doomed to stand helpless for a long time.

III. Persecution by Ambivalence

There is another form of persecution which we may term *Persecution by Ambivalence*. The common man has always respected learning and skill. In ancient society the prophet, seer, teacher, or diviner was held in high esteem, and so was the magician, the man of knowhow. But, people felt that one must be wary of such men. They had powers the common man did not possess and they mastered deep secrets. Beware lest they go too far, and cause great harm.

Similarly, people today also respect science and learning. But they suspect it as well. The story of Frankenstein is as human as the Biblical story of the tree of knowledge. We go on admiring George Washington for a century or so, and then rejoice when a muckraking book about him appears. We laugh and scoff a bit, and then return to our old habits. It was all right for Molière to mock the medical profession, but he was sure to call a physician when he or his children took ill. Similarly, people go to hear sermons and would not dream of marrying or burying someone without a church representative. But they like a joke about a minister or about sex, even though they will defend with their lives the institution of the family or prevailing morals.

It would seem that people get tired of paying homage and respect and welcome some relief. A joke, an occasional persecution of a long hair, be he astrologer, alchemist, scientist, or prophet, brings solace to their ego and restores their self-respect. Such is the ambivalence of a human response.

IV. The Pathology of Freedom and Authority Today

How does all this discussion of pathology affect us today? In my opinion it concerns us in many ways. Consider the spread of loyalty oath legislation, loyalty investigations, and the fight against subversion. Unwillingness on the part of scholars to analyze objectively the forces that brought these phenomena to the fore can only aggravate an already tense emotional situation. Actually there has not yet appeared in America a single honest study of these phenomena. To my knowledge, not a single university professor has stopped to think why the people of California, who built their marvelous university and never before bothered the faculty with oaths, have suddenly changed their attitude. It is my guess that the legislature represents the people far better than Dr. Tolman or the AAUP. Instead of honest analysis, we have had nothing but defiance, condemnation, fulmination, loud crys of Nazism and tyranny.

The people have gone through a great deal of tension and panic, and have hoped for much after 1945, only to get treachery and aggression, watch more countries fall under the heel of tyranny, and see 75,000 of their own sons suddenly snatched away from their homes, some forever. They also saw shocking espionage in the State and Justice Departments and in the atomic energy projects. They also know by now that Communism has singled them out as the next candidates for conquest or oppression. They know well what Communism, Russian style, means. They have not had any help or guidance from the intellectuals as they did in their resistance to Hitlerism. They are bewildered and even terrified, and apparently think that oaths or some such measure—which to sophisticates seems silly and ineffective—will help. Delicate situations such as the present one, if not studied with sympathy and honesty, can lead to the social inflammation called persecution. To retain our freedom and unity, let us beg the analysts to desist from inflaming the embryonic bitterness, and thus let other approaches and analyses be tried.

CHAPTER XXXVI

The Supposed Conflict Between Moral Freedom and Scientific Determinism

By WILLIAM H. KILPATRICK
*Professor Emeritus of Education,
Teachers College, Columbia University*

IN DISCUSSING a topic as old as this, one cannot hope for striking novelty. However, certain new emphases in thinking seem to call for a fresh consideration of the effort to study morality in continuity with the rest of life and experience, while at the same time upholding the highest possible standards of personal integrity and moral responsibility.

Two assumptions seem prerequisite to any proper understanding of normal human behavior and moral responsibility: (a) the possibility of effective choice, and (b) reasonable freedom to exercise such choice. Two questions thus present themselves: (1) Does man, normally, have the capacity to engage in real and responsible choosing? (2) If yes, what bearing has scientific determinism[1] on such choosing? Does determinism deny freedom to choose?

First, as to the process we call choosing, what are the pertinent facts as we observe life in operation? How, for example, do a brick, a candle moth, and a normal man differ as regards choosing?

As for a brick, clearly it does nothing that we call either behaving or choosing. Left to itself, it stays put. By contrast, a candle moth flies about, apparently "at will." It is explicitly active; if we try to catch it, it seeks

---

[1] The word, "determinism," as here used refers to the ordinary scientific "law of causation," not the inclusive cosmic determinism or predeterminism which asserts, in the words of the *Rubaiyat*:

> Yea the first Morning of Creation wrote
> What the Last Dawn of Reckoning shall read.

If such predeterminism were true, life and responsible morality would have to be conceived in a very different way from that in which our customary goal-seeking sees it. In a *Philosophy of Education*, recently published, I have given five arguments against such a predeterminism.

to escape. Suppose, however, that the moth is in a dark room and that a candle is suddenly lighted. The moth seems unable to resist the attraction of the light. Even if it escapes the first burning, it will return again and again until its wings are consumed. The moth seems to have no choice but to destroy itself; it cannot learn and so cannot resist the attractive danger of the flame.

How is it with man? Clearly, he is essentially different from the brick; he will not stay put. Action, goal-seeking, choice of ends, planning of means for attaining his ends—these are the characteristics of man. While some men are in certain respects somewhat like the candle moth, most men can—at least within limits—learn from experience and change their acts, or exercise choice, accordingly.

Before going further with man, let us introduce a dog into our series. Wherein is the dog superior to the candle moth? In at least two respects: the dog has a greater variety of abilities; and the dog learns better. If something hurts a dog, he tries next time to recognize the danger and avoid it.

Wherein is man superior to the dog? We can name at least three respects: (1) Man has more numerous and, in significance, greater abilities; (2) man can learn better than the dog, certainly with better discrimination; (3) normal man has self-consciousness far beyond what the dog can show.

With self-consciousness man is aware of himself as a continuing entity among other like entities around him. He not only thinks about the goal he is pursuing, but of himself as pursuing it and of the quality of his pursuit. In this way man can judge himself and his effort as others about him would judge it. He can study his present experience to improve his acts. Out of these varied aspects of self-consciousness man has discovered, or invented, or created, tools, language, customs, institutions, critical study—in a word, his culture and his civilization.

How does the individual man come by such self-consciousness? It seems to be a product of his selfhood. Each man has to develop (acquire, learn) selfhood through his intercourse with others who have previously developed such selfhood. This process, briefly, consists in re-forming the initial private self—the guiding center of activity—into a compounded self-other selfhood now capable of far more adequate guiding. This transformation, begun in early childhood, consists in coming to understand one's self in terms of what one sees in others, and, simultaneously, to understand others in terms of what one has first seen in himself. Through such a self-other compounded selfhood the human individual can increasingly see himself as others further along see him. In this he has acquired the self-consciousness,[2] which greatly facilitates fuller and better guidance of one's life activities.

It may be well to add a word regarding the further moral development of the individual. Out of self-consciousness the child notes what others are doing and wishes himself to do the like. He likes nothing better than to show others what he can do. In this way he learns, increasingly, how to direct his acts with self-conscious intent. When he has fairly well begun on this new trait of *consciously self-directed activity,* his mother follows, bringing to his attention some things he may do, and some he may not do; and she begins to hold him *accountable* for doing as he has been told. In time he learns, more or less successfully, to accept this accountability. He begins to build the conception of *right and wrong,* and he grows in personal responsibility for doing what is counted "right."[3]

We are now ready to answer more precisely what is meant by choosing. The process is not simple. There is no proper choosing except as the person faces a situation of possible alternatives. The person then contrasts the expected outcome from these respective alternatives, and usually finds that he prefers a certain outcome to the others and then acts accordingly. So to see and act is to choose. We can write out in five steps a more deliberative choice:

1. The person recognizes that the confronting situation has alternative possibilities of treatment, each with its own probable outcome.

2. He lists all the alternatives that seem worthy of consideration, that these may be duly studied.

3. He develops for each alternative its probable outcome.

4. He weighs the several probable outcomes, to see which seems most desirable.

5. If the resulting differences of outcome are significant, he accepts for

---

[2] Anyone interested to study further on this point can find it discussed in J. Mark Baldwin, *Social and Ethical Interpretations,* The Macmillan Company, New York, 1906; George H. Mead, *Mind, Self, and Society,* University of Chicago Press, Chicago, 1934; and the writer's *Selfhood and Civilization,* The Macmillan Company, New York, 1941, Teachers College Bureau of Publication, 1947.

[3] What is thus to be obeyed as "right" is in early childhood decided by parents or others in authority; later this authoritative deciding is, typically, so accepted by the doer; and still later what to do may be decided by the doer's own critical thinking.

action—he chooses—that alternative which promises the most desirable outcome.

Some may feel that this analysis slights the factor of wishing. However, it is certainly wrong to think that choosing and wishing mean the same. Wish indicates present inclination, often without reference to feasibility. The practical danger is to follow one's unexamined wish with later regrets which proper deliberation—proper choosing—would have foreseen and refused. A person of proper integrity of character and responsibility will not allow any mere wish to determine either his choices or his acts. To the precise contrary, he will bring to each situation as it arises a prior commitment to the highest good to all concerned that can be got from the situation. When he finds by careful inquiry which of the possible alternatives promises the best, that finding decides his choice. And it is exactly this kind of choosing which is contemplated as the highest instance of the analysis above given.

But if "mere" wishing is denied, a deeper and wiser wishing is active throughout the whole process. The values that one has built into his character enter strategically into the total choosing process as above outlined. In step 1 of that analysis it is the previously built-in values which initially furnish the sensitivity to note this as a situation calling for attention and then supply the urge to action. In this sense, the built-in values constitute a true advance commitment, a wish commitment we may say. In step 4 the weighing of one alternative against another goes forward precisely on the promise therein involved to take care of the values felt to be at stake. And in such weighing any mere wish, apart from the values at stake, could be only a betrayal of these values. It is thus the most reliable logic possible which is desired in steps 3, 4, and 5 alike; anything else is actual betrayal. But in and through it all is the commitment of the person to the values felt to be at stake.

We may next ask about freedom. Specifically, in the light of the discussion so far given, what does *freedom of choice* mean? There are at least two senses in which the term may initially be used. First, whether the person under consideration is psychologically and morally capable of going through the steps given in a way to constitute full proper choice. Second, whether the circumstances allow the implementation of the choice as made. An infant, lacking the psychological equipment for full choice, or a drug addict, lacking the strength of character to resist a ruinous urge, fail of the first sense of *freedom*. As to the second sense of freedom, there are today in Czechoslovakia, for instance, many people of integrity and moral responsibility who in the first sense fully reject the Communist regime, but find themselves unable, under the existing circumstances, to act upon their rejection. They are free in the first sense, but not in the second.

We are now ready to take up the crucial issue of our topic. What, if any, bearing has the scientific conception of determinism on the question of freedom of choice? By determinism is here meant, as earlier stated, the ordinary "law of causation," the fundamental belief of scientists: (1) that each event is determined by otherwise existing "causes," and (2) that like "causes" always produce like effects. To be sure, "cause" and "causation" are now understood differently from what formerly prevailed. But outside of microphysics the "law" is generally accepted not only in physics, but also *mutatis mutandis* in such studies as psychology and anthropology. The pertinent facts seem to support the principle; and without such a principle effective study in the area seems practically impossible.

Let us next consider how determinism, the ordinary "law of causation," is not only not the denial of moral freedom, but is in fact the necessary basis alike of any dependable character and of any reliable and responsible morality.

What do we mean by dependable character? Do we not all believe that the stronger and finer a person's character, the more surely we can rely upon that person to behave as he has come to think he should? In this we are assuming that character in the degree that it is present, brings forth behavior after its kind; that is, we are assuming the law of causation at work.

And again, when we object to bad conduct in the young because we fear that bad conduct will result in building bad character, we are again assuming the law of causation. Our growing study of child behavior and child development exactly supports these conclusions. The more consistently we assume the law of causation both for the study of behavior, its causes, and its effects, and for the building of character, the more we feel convinced by actual experience and observation that the law of causation does apply to behavior and to character building. If in matters of character and behavior like causes did not produce like results, there would be no such thing as a reliable and responsible morality, and similarly no reliable way of educating the young.

But there is still more to be said. Go back to the analysis of the act of choosing. In step 1 and more explicitly in step 3, the process followed assumes a dependable law of causation, namely, that each of the alternative plans of action will, if applied under the given circumstances, bring about its own outcome in life. And finally in step 5, unless the person has a dependable character as above discussed, there is no assurance that he will implement the choice indicated in step 4.

Some, however, will claim that, if character and choice depend on the law of causation and like "causes" always produce like results, then man's choice and act in any given situation are exactly fixed by his character and the situation as he sees it; so that he has no freedom. To these objectors this consideration seems to make man's behavior as fixed as that of the candle moth.

The answer turns on a closer attention to the meaning and possibility of freedom. It is true, as these objectors claim, that in no sense can a man get out of himself, out of his own character, to act. In this sense a man's choices are determined precisely by his character as this interacts with the confronting situation.

But because of self-consciousness and what that can do for man, this determinism is no denial of the kind of freedom necessary and sufficient to support freedom of moral choice and moral responsibility. Determinism still holds, but self-consciousness gives the possibility of acquiring through the working of determinism a true and morally responsible freedom of choice. Note the phrase, "possibility of acquiring"; the bare possession of self-consciousness does not suffice to give this desirable *freedom of moral choice*. It does, however, give the possibility, under favorable conditions, of acquiring this freedom.

Because the whole thesis of the paper turns on what has just been said, it may be wise to repeat the argument in greater detail. Let us consider three contrasting instances of differing degrees of freedom.

A. A drug addict or a confirmed alcoholic is not free. The character he has built gives him bondage, not freedom. He cannot resist temptation. In this respect he repeats the experience of the candle moth; left to himself he will continue his addiction until he is completely ruined.

B. Consider a more typical man, who in most respects is both properly behaved and practically effective, but in certain respects has failed to reach generally recognized standards. He may, for instance, be too easily made angry; or he may be unduly partisan in his political or religious outlook;

or he may shape his daily life by certain superstitions; or he may, if he can get away with it, be dishonest in business dealings. Such a person may come in time to renounce his bad trait; but in so far as he refuses to review and reconsider his particular weakness, that is man not free but bound—whatever intelligent freedom he may show in other matters.

C. A man, however, may be possessed of an inclusively strong high character of personal integrity and moral responsibility. Such a one is concerned in each situation as it arises to find out and do what *ought* to be done, and accordingly to study this situation to learn what in it is the right thing to do. He is willing, as he studies, to change and improve upon what he has hitherto thought and done, even improve upon what has hitherto been conceived.

In these three instances we see three degrees of moral freedom. A and C represent the extremes of a scale; B represents a middle position, a position more or less like most of us. Those occupying the middle of the scale are capable, under favorable conditions, of learning better self-control. Many do in fact as they grow older go higher up the scale.

Perhaps some will still insist that the man C is no freer than either A or B. The only difference is that he is bound by his character to behavior that we *approve,* while A and B are bound by their characters to behavior we disapprove; each is equally bound. In answer, if C were in fact bound always to specific, known outcomes, nameable in advance, this and nothing else, we should have to accept the criticism as argued. But the significant factor is that C is by his character free to study and *then* to act according to what he finds from his study. In as complex a world as that in which we live there will be many times when no one knows in advance, neither C himself nor anyone else, what C's study will bring forth. Progress is possible, and C may well find something never before known or suspected. True, if the situation confronting C is simple, say whether he will steal or not, we can with fair certainty foretell that a man like C will not steal. Otherwise we could not have the dependability on which to build a viable society. But in a changing world, with precise outcomes forever uncertain, such a man as C will have full freedom of study into doubtful situations almost every day of his life.

A more searching question relates to the men not as high in the scale as C. How far will the typical man have freedom? And how can he increase this degree of freedom?

Answers to these questions will differ according to the character of the civilization under review. There have been groups, and still are in certain remote regions, where there has existed almost no freedom to think in any novel fashion. This was not so much because existing codes forbade novel ideas, as that custom had educated the youth to full acceptance of the tribal way of thinking and acting. There was no effective freedom to think variantly. Tribal man had achieved self-consciousness—gradually we may suppose—from the early days of *homo sapiens;* but creative thinking lagged greatly. For example, the Old Stone Age, we are told, went 30,000 years without improving upon its chipped flint implements. It was Athenian Greece, with its many and varied cultural contacts, that first compared one culture with another in a way to become culturally self-conscious in any significant degree. This achievement of critical thinking we can accept as the greatest single advance in intelligent action man has ever made.

In Western civilization there has been a growing proportion able and disposed to run their lives on such a basis of inductive critical thinking as means real moral freedom. They are disposed to follow the argument wherever it may lead. Thus is Kant's "self-determination of rational beings" increasingly realized. The Enlightenment apparently had this in mind in its opposition to habit. Rousseau said explicitly, "The only habit the child should be allowed to form is that of having no habits"; and Kant said, "the more habits a man has the less is he free and independent." We cannot now accept this opposition to all habits. What we wish is that our habits shall fit into a holistic pattern ruled by reason and sense of right.

We may sum up the discussion of the A B C scale by listing a series of factors for leading one up the scale, each factor to be preceded by the phrase, "other things being equal." The first one would thus read as follows: Other things being equal, *the better adjusted the personality,* the higher up the scale one can go. Several such factors are here named: 1. the better adjusted the personality; 2. the more of pertinent information one has; 3. the fewer one's prejudices; 4. the more logically one can think; 5. the less susceptible one is to popular hysteria; 6. the greater one's skill of deliberation; 7. the higher one's I.Q.; 8. the more creative one's thinking; 9. the better organized is one's character to obey reason; 10. the higher one's devotion to criticized right; 11. the more intelligent one is as to wherein and how things are right or wrong.

In conclusion, there is no final or necessary conflict between moral freedom and scientific determinism. Any moral self-conscious individual has possible moral freedom in the sense that he can learn from experience and so can, within limits, be held accountable for his acts. But many have built such prejudices and such binding habits, that these in too great degree control the individual rather than he them. However, if favorably treated in time—this is where appropriate education should enter—each innately normal human being can be helped to learn a high degree of effective moral freedom. And for the prosecution of this desirable goal the principle of determinism supplies, not a hindrance, but the necessary basis.

Comment by George E. Axtelle:

I am so much in accord with the general point of view of Professor Kilpatrick's paper that it is difficult to say more than, Amen. However, a few remarks regarding the basic concepts of natural law and of freedom may have some relevance to the discussion.

Professor Whitehead has noted four concepts of natural law; law as immanent, law as imposed, law as the observed order of succession, and law as conventional interpretation. Clearly the latter two have really nothing to say about the problem of freedom, for they make no assumptions about the nature of things. The conception of law as imposed, however, must find the problem of freedom a great enigma. Whitehead's development of the doctrine of immanent law[1] suggests a metaphysical scheme which not only explains the more recent developments of the sciences, but also provides insight into the basic character of association and sociality throughout nature, the creative process of growth and experience, and the central place of freedom and intelligence in that process.

According to this point of view, nature is profoundly social in character, and freedom itself is an expression of this sociality. Nature is social, in the sense that individualities are perforce in association, and in association in such a way as to modify the characters of those associated. We see nature itself as expressing numerous levels of individuality. Each level of individuality is the expression of a pattern of order or organization of individuals of the next lower level, and of membership in a pattern of order or association of the next higher.

Each individuality is a novel entity in that it occupies a perspective from which it organizes its relations, which is unique. As both the constituents and the environment of an individual undergo continuous change, individuality must be seen as a process of creative growth. Freedom then is at the heart of the nature of individuality and of change. It is a process of creative expression of character.

At the human level, this process is, as Professor Kilpatrick has described it, one of reflective choice, discrimination, judgment, and at the same time one of cooperative organization in the pursuit of common ends. At the human reflective level, intelligence, participation, and communication are central in freedom, because the subtleties and complexities of relations are lifted to a conscious and social level. Organization of relations, the development of order are not automatic. They are the fruit of imagination and reflection, not only at the personal level but at the level of cooperation and culture.

[1] *Cf.* Alfred North Whitehead, *Adventures In Ideas*, The Macmillan Company, New York, 1933, pp. 142–144.

Those individualities survive and prosper which can assimilate in coherent patterns the materials of their environment. At the human level this assimilation and continuous reorganization, both of environment and individual character, involves the heaviest demands upon the intellectual and imaginative resources of the culture. To be oneself, to be free, means the continuous growth of experience in meaning and control, both individually and as a society. To exercise control, individually or collectively, means to know the characters of things, how they behave, *i.e.,* their natural law. If things (including ourselves) possessed no consistent characters, and behaved in no consistent manner, *i.e.,* if there were no natural laws, we would be unable to establish effective relations with them. Our lives would be sheer hazard. Not to know their characters or how they behave, would mean the same thing.

I do not believe that these observations differ in any important way from Professor Kilpatrick's paper. Their relevance to the discussion lies, I believe, in the fact that they suggest a metaphysical scheme which is essential to explain not only the more recent developments of the sciences, but provides insight into the basic character of association and sociality, throughout nature, the creative process of growth and experience, and the central place of freedom and intelligence in that process.

CHAPTER XXXVII

Freedom, Authority, and Orthodoxy

By CHARLES FRANKEL
Associate Professor of Philosophy, Columbia University

A RECENT WRITER has remarked that philosophy is a little like lawn mowing or shaving: the same old growths keep reappearing and have to be cut back every day.[1] There are apparently moments, moreover, when it is all one can do to hold the gains already achieved, much less to extend the field under cultivation. Certainly the present moment in philosophy seems to have become primarily one for holding actions. With respect to a great variety of issues, philosophical fallacies which one might have thought had been laid to rest by past generations have arisen refreshed and in a fighting mood; and much of what once seemed to be an acceptable point of departure for further inquiry has now once again come into dispute.

Nowhere is this more the case than in connection with discussions of freedom and authority. The breakdown of the institutions and intellectual tradition which treated "freedom" and "authority" as antithetical, has led, on the popular level, to a renewed quest for orthodoxy. And, in a more formal fashion, it has led to the resurgence of the ancient argument that some initial agreement as to the universally mandatory ends of life is the indispensable prerequisite to a rationally ordered society.[2] Indeed, the increasing popularity of the belief that metaphysics and theology are essential to political philosophy, and an officially established position on first and final things indispensable to political order, has become one of the distinguishing features of our anxious times.

The popularity of this point of view is not, I am afraid, a passing phenomenon. A passion for orthodoxy has quite generally appeared when

[1] A. N. Prior, *Logic and the Basis of Ethics,* Oxford Press, Oxford, 1949.
[2] Representatives of this view are, I am sure, well known: In philosophy, Professor Jacques Maritain; the "New Critics" in literary criticism; Robert N. Hutchins and Mortimer J. Adler in educational circles; in political and social theory, John U. Nef, J. M. Hallowell, R. M. Weaver, and M. J. Hillenbrand.

men have felt overwhelmed by their problems. Pressure toward conformity is usually strong furthermore, in societies which feel themselves endangered, as ours most certainly is, by an external enemy. War may or may not be the health of the state; but it is certainly just what the doctor ordered for metaphysics.

As frequently happens when old doctrines are revived, this one has been given a new twist. For perhaps the first time in the history of ideas, a version of metaphysical absolutism is being urged, with every evidence of sincerity, in the name of democracy. An increasing number of men, frightened by what seems to be the unity and dedication of a rival state, have apparently come to the conclusion that a democracy can achieve the same virtues, but without the same consequences, merely by having a more spiritual outlook on things.

I propose in this paper to consider this point of view in a more or less systematic fashion, and to bring together some of the principal arguments which empirical philosophers have used against it. The widespread currency of the view that the problem of freedom and authority is initially metaphysical has, I think, sidetracked consideration of the problem as one for cooperative empirical inquiry and urgent institutional reform. Under the circumstances, some effort to determine the kind of problem which the question of freedom and authority is *not*, would seem to be in place. The major point I wish to make is that an empirical and relativistic philosophy provides the only way in which men with diverse backgrounds and differing interests can find a common ground for rational agreement.

I

In substance, the new partisans of philosophical absolutism make two charges against philosophies which deny the necessity of metaphysics or theology: (1) that such philosophies, having denied the validity of any principle of authority, are unable to make warranted moral discriminations of any kind (which means, among other things, that they cannot genuinely distinguish between "freedom" and "slavery");[3] (2) that

[3] There seem to be at least three senses in which this "denial of authority" is alleged to have taken place: (1) a denial that there is anything to appeal to in rational support of belief or moral decisions; (2) a denial of hierarchy—or, in general, a denial that there is any reason why some should command and others obey; (3) a denial that there is any organized institution, or any person, whose decisions must be regarded as infallible. It is

such philosophies are the major historical cause of the decline of freedom in the modern world.

I shall consider each of these charges in turn.

In one obvious sense of "authority," the charge that empirical philosophies have denied the validity of authority, is plainly false. In general, it is of course obvious that a rational choice can be made only by reference to limits which are, at least for that choice, unalterable. It is also plain that these limits must recommend themselves on moral and rational grounds. For if they seem to depend only on the fact that those who enforce them have the greater physical or propagandistic power at their command, men will not feel free, but enslaved. In the sense in which "the existence of authority," means the existence of such acceptable limits of behavior, it is therefore plain that freedom requires the existence of authority.

In this sense, however, it is also highly doubtful that empirically inclined advocates of freedom have ever denied the necessity or reality of authority. Indeed, only one major philosopher in the empirical tradition actually placed "freedom" and "authority" in unequivocal opposition; and this philosopher, Hobbes, was not an advocate of freedom, but of political absolutism. What empirical philosophers opposed in fact were institutions which claimed an irrevocable hold over individuals; and as such institutions were the almost exclusive instances of social authority in their day, it is perhaps natural that they should have viewed the struggle for "Freedom" as a struggle against "Authority." In fact, however, there was a very clear principle of authority contained within traditional empiricism.

At least until the nineteenth century, the authority required to support rational choice was provided by the conception of Natural Law. On the one hand, this conception expressed an aversion to higher metaphysical or theological speculation: these, it was felt, were attempts to convert simple and evident principles into mysteries, and thereby to justify the monopoly of power by privileged groups. On the other hand, Natural Law was associated with a kind of inquiry to which, at least in principle, publicly available evidence was relevant and sufficient: it might, for ex-

---

characteristic of philosophical absolutists, from Plato on, to argue that the denial of authority in any one of these senses logically implies the denial of authority in the other two senses; and that the recognition of the legitimacy of authority in each of these senses is a necessary condition—indeed, the defining condition—of political order.

ample, be based on sciences such as economics or psychology, or, again, on certain simple moral axioms, self-evident to any rational man. At least in one sense of "authority," therefore, the charge that empiricism has deliberately rejected all conception of authority, is historically inaccurate.

Strangely enough, the present-day critics of empiricism now rest their charges against it not on the ground that it depends exclusively on Natural Law, but on the ground that it has rejected Natural Law. This is, of course, largely the case. The political impulse which led to the doctrine of Natural Law has persisted in empirical Liberalism. But the development of an increasingly empiricist interpretation of science has undermined the alleged scientific or axiomatic foundations of Natural Law, with the result that it has been progressively replaced in empirical philosophies by utilitarian and pragmatic considerations.

Judging from the observations of certain of the contemporary critics of empiricism,[4] it is this appeal to pragmatic considerations which justifies the charge that empiricism has rejected the very conception of "authority," and has thereby made "freedom" a meaningless term. But it is revealing, I think, that when the belief in Natural Law was at its peak, it was similarly attacked for undermining "authority," and was held to be an insufficient basis for action unless supplemented by some Supernatural Law. This may at least suggest that the issue at stake is not the acceptance or rejection of authority, but a decision between differing ideals of authority.

In fact, the contemporary introduction of pragmatic and utilitarian considerations is not a denial that such things as "objectivity" or "rationality" are possible in moral judgments, but the considered proposal of an alternative definition of these terms. To argue that empiricism denies all conception of authority, simply because it rejects the absolutist definition of this term, is to beg the question. The question, rather, is whether, as empirical philosophers have maintained, there is an alternative ideal of authority, which can be defined without reference to metaphysics or theology, and which will be both essential and sufficient to guide responsible moral judgments, and to legitimate (or "illegitimate") the exercise of political powers.

---

[4]Cf. M. J. Hillenbrand, *Power and Morals,* Columbia University Press, New York, 1949, and J. M. Hallowell, *The Decline of Liberalism as an Ideology,* Kegan Paul, London, 1946.

It is to this question that we now proceed.

It is plain, I think, that empirical standards are *essential,* for not even the critics of empiricism can avoid appealing to empirical materials in supporting specific moral decisions. Indeed, I doubt that even the most extreme critics of empiricism today really deny this. What they do deny is that purely empirical criteria are *sufficient* to test the relative worth of particular moral decisions. The arguments in support of this assertion are, of course, innumerable, but I think it possible to state the main lines of certain more representative views.

We may grant (let us imagine a temperate advocate of absolutism saying) that every one, empiricist and anti-empiricist alike, must make judgments of the relation of means to ends. These are empirical judgments. But this does not touch the crucial issue, which has to do with the choice of ends. And on this empiricism gives us no help whatsoever. Indeed, it does a good deal of harm; for with respect to ends, all that the empiricist offers is a mania of indecision, or a frankly arbitrary choice. And, in practice, this means either a spineless opportunism or the appeal to power.

Certain points in this argument are true and give it its air of plausibility. Certainly the one thing on which all empiricists are agreed is that statements about the relation of means to ends are the only responsible type of moral discourse. And it is of course true that if one does not hold some ideal, one cannot come to any moral decision. The empiricist must therefore admit that, in coming to a specific moral conclusion, he introduces at some point a value about which no questions are asked. Just as in the sciences certain beliefs are regarded as operationally *a priori* to a specific inquiry—that is, not in question in *that* inquiry—so in moral judgments certain initiating imperatives function to control decision.

But this admission is not a confession of guilt. The fallacy in this argument against empiricism is that it assumes that to say that factual beliefs are logically *dubitable,* is the same as to say that a particular belief is actually *doubtful.* But these are not the same at all. The proof of the first, broadly, is the logical analysis of methods of empirical inquiry; the proof of the second is a specific bit of factual evidence. For this reason, we neither must in theory, nor do we in fact, doubt a specific belief because it is logically dubitable. For if all the evidence we have is in favor of a belief, and we have none against it, why should we doubt it? And if, on the other hand, some evidence should come in which does make it doubtful, are we to blame this on the empiricist theory of knowledge? I should myself imagine that we should blame it on the evidence—or, better, on our belief.

In effect, therefore, the empiricist reminder that our beliefs are logically dubitable, far from necessitating that we shake in indecision, simply warns us that we should try to keep our beliefs responsive to experience. An empiricist can be as assured about any given value as an absolutist; indeed, the significant difference between the two in this respect is that the absolutist is formally unwilling to risk the test of further experience. So far as I can see, this makes the empiricist the more "objective" of the two, in a quite usual sense of that word.

Indeed, from the point of view of empiricism, an irrational ideal is precisely one which is held in such a way that empirical evidence is believed to be irrelevant. Logically, it is always possible to consider a particular ideal as a means to some still further ideal. And if a specific ideal, hitherto unquestioned, becomes questionable, doubts about it can be rationally resolved only by introducing another unquestioned value or set of values, and considering the newly questioned value in its role as an instrument to these ends.

This does mean, of course, that empiricism can offer no justification of a system of values "as a whole." And this seems to be the source of a second objection to the empiricist account of the status of ideals. Thus, it is frequently argued that empiricism can be employed only to examine a particular exercise of power, but not to justify the principle of Authority itself.[5]

This is true. But the demand for a categorical justification of Authority seems to me like asking for a justification of breathing—I want to know, whose breathing do you want to justify? In general, all I can do is refer to those physiological laws which give breathing a fairly influential role in keeping body and soul together. Similarly, hierarchy may not be necessary for all forms of joint social activity, just as breathing is not necessary for stones; and, in certain cases, it may actually interfere with other highly desirable ends, just as breathing sometimes interferes with eating. But I do not know how to show that hierarchy is either necessary or unnecessary, save by considering a specific hierarchy as a means to a specific end.

---

[5]This seems to be a central issue, for example, in Professor Jacques Maritain's *Scholasticism and Politics,* G. Bles, The Century Press, London, 1945.

What I want to know as a citizen, for instance, is whether some particular order from higher up serves a desirable purpose; and this I can always determine, in principle, by empirical methods. Indeed, if I succeeded in justifying the principle of hierarchy in general, I would be a little embarrassed by my riches: for such a categorical justification would lead me to suspect that every time I disagreed with some specific exercise of authority I was in the wrong.

There seems to be still a third sort of argument against the empiricist elimination of metaphysical or theological considerations. Empiricism argues that questions of right or wrong conduct, or good or bad government, cannot be answered without at some point consulting human interests. At least two kinds of reason are usually adduced to show that this is objectionable. The first is that it is "anthropocentric," "subjectivistic," that it makes man the measure of all things.

Now of course it is true that, for empiricism, an element of choice or preference is uneliminable from moral judgments. But to admit that choice is an element in moral judgments is not to say that these judgments must be capricious. Choices are natural events, which take place in accordance with (at least theoretically) ascertainable laws and have identifiable consequences which do not depend on the hopes or desires of the choosers; and sober men will be guided in their choices by such considerations. Indeed, this is what the empiricist means by "rational" choice. An irrational choice is precisely the kind of *isolated* choice which is ungoverned by consideration of causes and consequences, or relationships to other values. In short, from the empiricist's point of view, it is the absolutist who proposes that we choose our values at will, and then that we sanctify our wilfulness by calling it divine.

This brings us to the second reason why the empiricist reference to human interests seems to be objectionable. What is the justification it is asked, for measuring the worth of human decisions in terms of their consequences for human interests? How do we know that "happiness" is good? Do we not need some "transcendent" justification of such a criterion?

Actually (despite confusing formulations by a great many empiricists), the empiricist use of such terms as "interest" or "happiness" really concerns statements, not within a moral system, but about the kind of evidence to which one would appeal in order to vindicate such a system. The empiricist is answering the following sort of question: When disagreements arise over values, to what sort of evidence would one appeal to settle the question rationally? And, in general, his answer is that one would, among other things, consult human interests.

The defense of such an answer rests on a number of grounds, *e.g.*, that, in cases where men are ordinarily said to settle their disagreements rationally—*i.e.*, by appealing to evidence—this is in fact what they do; that the effect of a given course of action on human interests is in principle a publicly observable affair; that appeal to "transcendent" entities or specially revealed norms in stultifying, as it raises issues for which there is no common evidence; and the like.

Such a method provides a conception of "ultimate" social authority which serves the same normative purpose for which absolutists provide their own alternative conception of authority: that is, no institutions will be acceptable as "legitimate" which are not subject to its test. An institution cannot be "justified" unless it is "justifiable"; and it cannot be "justifiable" if it forbids empirical inquiry as to whether it genuinely serves human ideals. In this sense, there is, by definition, no "authority" for despotism; and the ground for saying this is more than a mere counting of noses, or a totting up of "satisfactions."

II

Against the background of the above discussion, I should like now to deal with the charge that empiricism is the major historical cause of our present troubles.

Sometimes it is asserted that our present troubles are the logical consequences of empiricism, following "in the way that conclusions follow from premises."[6] This charge seems to say that men drew the logical consequences of empiricism and applied them in practice, so that individuals like Hitler and Stalin got to be the way they are from their interest in philosophy and their inordinate passion for logic. Of course, it might be argued that the implications of a philosophy will be realized in history whether or not men take any active part in the process. But this is hardly a view which will convince anyone of the reality of human freedom, about which those who make this charge claim to be especially concerned.

There is, however, a more subtle variant of this indictment, which

[6] R. M. Weaver, *Ideas Have Consequences*, University of Chicago Press, Chicago, 1947.

holds that our present troubles are the result of the psychological impact of empiricism. Empiricism, it is alleged, has bad consequences when it is believed; in short, it is "unworkable." This argument has been offered, interestingly enough, not by "pragmatists" but by no less a philosopher than Professor Maritain.

I cannot avoid a twinge of surprise that those who criticize "anthropocentric humanism" should take this tack. But actually there are at least two flaws in the argument. The first is that men do not think their beliefs are true unless they derive from "transcendent" truths. This rests on a confusion of two quite different things—a belief that one holds true ideas, and a belief in a particular interpretation of the meaning of "truth." I doubt very much that most men will stop believing in the truth of their ideas because one conventional interpretation of "truth" has been rejected. But even if this is the interpretation which they implicitly hold, and even if they were shaken by an attack on this interpretation, it is still not the case that they *cannot* act effectively on any other basis. The second flaw in the argument, in short, is the presupposition of a fixed human nature, unaffected by historical or social conditions.

In the end this argument reduces to the assertion that men have been historically predisposed in favor of the absolutist ideal of logical certitude. But is it not then a paradox that those who dream of total escape from the trammels of history should convert historical facts into eternal necessities? The empiricist assertion that transcendent truth is unattainable, has contributed to skepticism only because the conviction has persisted that there is no possible definition of truth but the absolutistic one. It is, therefore, extraordinary that absolutists should call empiricism "unworkable." Perhaps it is true that you cannot be happy unless you get to the other side of the rainbow: but if a man tells you that you would be better advised to try for Southern California, it seems strange to call him "impractical."

There is, finally, a broad assumption about the conditions of political behavior which holds that general unity on ultimate values is an essential condition of "social cohesion." It is plain, so the argument runs, that joint activity in a free society will, to as great an extent as possible, be voluntary. But large-scale voluntary cooperation presupposes the widespread acceptance of the same general ends-in-view. For, by empirical standards, a rational resolution of a disagreement over values can be attained only where some other value is found which is held in common. And if none is found there is nothing to resort to but force.

Something like this argument seems to be entertained, not only by the partisans of the new absolutism, but also by a considerable number of other social scientists and political philosophers. The following brief considerations may help to suggest how very doubtful this argument is.

1. Formal agreement on first principles is by no means sufficient to insure agreement on concrete programs. And because what is wanted is a set of decisions about which there can be no question, this can mean only the establishment of an allegedly infallible and legally unquestionable group of interpreters. The result is not voluntary agreement, but only social conformity.

2. Formal agreement on first principles is not even essential to practical agreement as to such "tried and true" moral and political principles as good faith, equity, the rejection of hearsay evidence, or the right of *habeas corpus*.

3. There can also be agreement on the desirability of proximate ends, such as the elimination of poverty or intolerance, the achievement of which is more than sufficient to engage large-scale, concerted action. Furthermore, where there are disagreements about the desirability of these ends, one of the major impediments to rational discussion is the refusal of one party to submit its ends to a common test, on the ground that these ends are absolute; and one of the major aids is the general acceptance of a common *method*.

4. Men who disagree about a given value need not hold the same ultimate end-in-view in order to resolve their dispute. All that is necessary is that each hold some other interest to which the value in dispute can be shown to be instrumental. Voluntary cooperation is thus possible, even though each of the cooperators may have a different purpose in mind.

5. Furthermore, it is important to distinguish between *difference* between values and *disagreement* over values. It is perfectly possible for two men, even living side by side, to entertain different values without there being any issue between them at all. One can prefer baseball, the other Bach, but there is no issue so long as each can pursue his interests, for what is involved here is the expression of a taste and not a program for joint activity.

6. Of course, one of the men may feel that he cannot be happy in his own tastes unless they are universal. This is a medical problem. Fre-

quently, however, this sort of situation is confused, especially by philosophers, who have a way of making a principle out of their tastes, with straightforward disagreement over values. It is important to see, however, that it is not in this case the one man's liking of baseball which prevents the other man's liking Bach. It is rather that one man's liking for persuading others prevents these others from going about their business.

7. Finally, there are, of course, cases where genuine disagreements over values cannot be mediated, because no common value has been found. This is, it seems to me, the germinal political situation. But even here it is a false disjunction that if men can find no common value they have no other recourse but force. Under certain specifiable conditions it is rational to compromise, or to submit the disagreement to some conventional form of solution, such as an election, or a decision by the courts. If the disputants hold other values as well, if they prize them equally highly and if they are independent of the value in dispute, it is clearly unreasonable for them to risk their all for the sake of the one value that is in dispute. It need hardly be said that such "compromise" should be sharply distinguished from what has come to be called "appeasement," in which a man gives up a value which is, in fact, basic to his other values.

There has frequently been an apologetic attitude toward compromise on the part of Liberals, as though it reflected a kind of moral weakness. Nevertheless, the notion that successful compromise is not a defection from principle, but the finest achievement of political life, has been the distinguishing characteristic of the liberal attitude toward politics. The objective of a liberal society is to construct an institutional framework for human decisions, such that collisions of interest are localized, and ultimate and unresolvable disagreements avoided. In short, "social cohesion" with a minimum of coercion would seem to be the function of a pluralistic society, offering a variety of values, rather than of a society initially committed to a unitary scheme of fixed and final ends.

The "problem of freedom and authority," therefore, is not a problem which can be settled by bemoaning the decline of respect for "Authority," or by insisting that men pay their respects to a particular metaphysics or theology. It is the problem of providing an institutional framework which provides at least minimal conditions for rational choice: men must be confronted by decisions between alternatives which are not ultimate but relative—in short, *choices;* they must have ways of getting at the relevant facts; they must have the power to implement their decisions. To enlarge these conditions, and even to maintain as much of them as we already have, requires the large-scale reform of our centralized political and economic institutions, which are increasingly failing to provide a form of contingent and empirically examinable control over our lives. Those who are interested in freedom, it seems to me, will look for a reform of our economy which will place men in situations such that they can attain some more relevant knowledge of the conditions of their work, and some more immediate control of its consequences. They will also be prepared to consider the possible advantages of governmental decentralization and devolution. And all of this, or a good part of it, will in all likelihood have to wait upon the reduction of international tensions, and the effective containment of the Soviet threat.

This is all elaborately complicated and difficult, and it is no doubt tempting to think we can avoid these problems by manipulating words. But we should not mistake a symptom of our illness for a diagnosis of it. Those who, on one side, now talk of choice as a kind of undetermined leap in the dark, only reflect the state of alienation in which countless ordinary men and women are now being asked (meaninglessly) to make choices. And those who, on the other side, urge the return to some orthodoxy, reflect not a desire for freedom but only the desperate wish not to feel constrained by situations which increasingly fail to offer a choice between anything but relative evils, and sometimes do not even offer a choice as to that. Freedom *from* choice is not freedom *of* choice. We are not yet so badly off that we have to fall in love with our disease.

Comment by Rudolf Allers:

The position of empiricism and relativism has found an able and eloquent advocate in Professor Frankel. His arguments are a challenge to all those who hold what he terms an absolutist and orthodox view.

It is, perhaps, unfair, to answer that the relativist is not less "orthodox" in what concerns his last principles, and not less absolutist in maintaining their validity. He might reply that he readily admits this, but that his principles differ from those of his opponents, first, by their greater generality or formal character, and, secondly, by their origin in observable facts. However I cannot see that this difference is decisive. Something absolute must underlie any conception whatsoever. Nor can I convince myself that the appeal to facts is as unequivocal as it is believed to be. It is difficult to ascertain what is a fact and what is a "finding" clad in the terms of a preconceived theory or belief.

There is another notion which requires clarification, that, namely of the "natural law." This term has had one signification prior to the seventeenth century and another after this time. The turning point is, more or less, the moral and political philosophy of Thomas Hobbes.

Originally, "natural law" meant an ability on the part of human nature to discover certain principles which were believed to be rooted in the eternal law of God. Within this view, there was alive precisely a preference for metaphysical and theological speculation, and not an aversion. Only when the concept of the natural law changed into that of a law of nature, that is, of human nature as it is encountered under the varying conditions of man's existence, a law of which one hoped that it would parallel finally the laws of which science was so proud, only then did the notion take on the signification of which Professor Frankel speaks. This interpretation of the natural law is to be found, *e.g.*, in d'Alembert's writings: we have discovered the "true system of the world," we are going to discover the true system of society.

The idea of natural law, as it appears with the "absolutists" is, however, more like that of the ages prior to the modern period.

The reference to the recent developments in mathematics and logic seems to me not conclusive. It would carry weight only if it could be shown that the principles in these fields of inquiry are the same as those in others. This is not, of course, the place to raise this question. It should be evident, nonetheless, that it has to be answered before the argument can be considered as valid.

It seems to me a somewhat unjust reproach that the "absolute" way of thinking rejects or despises factuality. It definitely does not. But it is keenly aware of the dependence of all interpretation on previously adopted principles, and wishes to submit these principles to a searching examination. It is obviously true that this examination ends with the statement of certain "first principles"; but so does all inquiry, and so does any view whether it be empiricist or other.

It seems to me that the "absolutist" may go a long way together with the empiricist. All that regards the study of interests, ideals, as they factually exist and are effective, constitutes problems which are as much of concern to the one as to the other. I would venture to contend that the ways do not separate because they turn into different directions, but because one goes on while the other comes to an end.

I may be permitted to comment incidentally on the relation of skepticism and empiricism. It is true that the former is opposed to the "absolutistic" conviction and that its nature is to deny the possibility of attaining any "transcendent" truth. This is not tantamount to saying that absolutism is the "condition" of skepticism. The empiricist cannot disregard the fact that a longing for transcendent truth has been alive in mankind forever, and that it is, so far as we can know by experience, going to stay with us forever. By what criteria is the empiricist enabled to declare that this "interest" is less relevant or less justified than another?

Professor Frankel's reply:

I am grateful for the attention which Professor Allers has given to my contribution, and impressed with his obvious desire to find areas of agreement between us. The length of his remarks is such, however, that I shall have to confine myself in general to what I think are his essential points.

Professor Allers seems to have one major reason for objecting to my position, which he repeats, in one way or another, a number of times: namely, that "something absolute must underlie any conception whatsoever." Professor Allers no doubt means to point out that in any inquiry something must be taken for granted—a position with which I would be foolish to disagree, and which I emphasized in my paper. But to be unquestioned in one context, is not the same thing as being unquestionable in every conceivable context. It is the latter, I take it, which is normally meant by an "absolute." And it is precisely the failure to make this distinction which leads to the confusion of "authority" with "orthodoxy." Hence I do not see what Professor Allers has done besides reiterate the very point in question.

Similar considerations, it seems to me, apply to Professor Allers's other objections. For example, though I devoted a good deal of time to arguing why I consider such questions superfluous, Professor Allers does not answer these arguments, but simply repeats that "human interests . . . are themselves in need of some 'measure,'" and asks, "Why *should* man seek the good?" Assuming that it is really the good that he is seeking, I am afraid I do find this an "absurd" question. What else should man seek? The "bad"? In short, empiricism does not deny anyone "the right" to ask questions as to "transcendent truth," etc. It merely assumes that when men ask questions they hope to find answers to them, and that there are, in consequence, certain rules to be followed in formulating questions.

Comment by Edgar S. Brightman:

The trouble with leaning over backward is that your head may meet your feet, and you may start going around in circles. This, I fear, is Professor Frankel's situation. He loses no time in creating a contradiction. First he repudiates any "initial agreement as to the universally mandatory ends of life." Then he declares that "an empirical and relativistic philosophy provides the only way in which men with diverse backgrounds and differing interests can find a common ground for rational agreement." The only way—*extra quam nulla salus!* Either this means that "common ground for rational agreement" and "empirical and relativistic philosophy" are "mandatory ends of life," or they are not. If they are not, there is no contradiction; but the words then lack meaning. If they are mandatory, here is a new orthodoxy. Professor Frankel fails to see that some agreement is necessary for an ordered society, and that he is proposing such agreement.

Now, may I ask Professor Frankel how in a society in which orthodoxies (including his own) exist, can we persuade society to repudiate all orthodoxy but his own? Until he answers this question, the rest of his very challenging paper seems socially and democratically irrelevant to his main points.

Professor Frankel's reply:

On rereading Professor Brightman's remarks, I am relieved to find that his criticism is not really so unrelenting as his tone suggests. He asserts that I "lose no time in creating a contradiction." But a few lines farther down he agrees that there may be no contradiction at all, provided that "common ground for rational agreement," etc., are not regarded as mandatory ends of life. The consequence, however, according to Professor Brightman, is that my "words then lack meaning." I fail to follow. All I have said is that *if* men want to find a common ground for rational agreement, they will have to employ in practice an empirical and relativistic philosophy.

I find myself a bit startled by Professor Brightman's final query. I find nowhere in my paper that I have suggested that anyone must repudiate any "orthodoxy"; I have only suggested that political and intellectual authority does not *require* such orthodoxies, and that the insistence upon applying them to such issues as the one to which this Conference is addressed is frequently disruptive of intellectual cooperation and social compromise. If this is "democratically irrelevant," then, I am afraid, so is the principle of the separation of Church and State.

It seems to me that Professor Brightman has unwittingly begged the very question at issue—namely, the traditional identification of "authority" with "orthodoxy." Apparently because I am critical of the *necessity* for *orthodoxies,* he assumes that I fail to recognize that "some agreement is necessary for an ordered society"; apparently because I propose a method for coming to specific agreements on fact, he feels that I am proposing an orthodoxy of my own. I can only repeat that, far from failing to recognize the importance of "agreement" to "an ordered society," I have tried to suggest how various and complex such "agreements" can be, and how much widespread agreement on empirical fact can contribute to that particular kind of "ordered society" which can be called "rational."

Professor Brightman's rejoinder:

Professor Frankel's reply is ironic and conciliatory, but, I regret to say, leaves me gravely in doubt as to the meaning and utility of his basic principle. That principle is that: *"If men want to find a common ground for rational agreement, they will have to employ in practice an empirical and relativistic philosophy."* My essential point is this: If the words, "empirical" and "relativistic," are not precisely defined, and each man may take them as is right in his own eyes, then I do not see that they afford much ground for agreement. If, however, they are defined as seems right in Professor Frankel's eyes, it is hard to see why they do not turn into a very specific working hypothesis which is a kind of orthodoxy. To many minds the empirical suggests the naturalistic, although I do not myself share this identification; and to many minds the relativistic suggests a basic skepticism. I want to urge that the freedom of democracy and of this Conference requires a broader tolerance for difference of method than is clearly stated in Professor Frankel's formula. I want to plead for a respect for difference of opinion which is based on the dignity of personality, rather than on a single restricted theory of method.

Comment by Simon Greenberg:

Dr. Frankel's paper is an excellent summary of the position of those who maintain 1) that the present state of the world is in no way due to the pragmatic, utilitarian, relativistic frame of mind that characterized Western thought; 2) that a return to any given orthodoxy is not desirable, for it cannot answer our problem; 3) that empiricism is still the only and the safest way for man to find his way out of the current moral, social, and political morass. He seems to imply, however, that all those who do see some relationship between the moral bankruptcy of Western civilization and the relativism which Western philosophy, the physical sciences, and particularly the social sciences introduced into all realms of human thought, rejoice at man's present plight, because it gives them the opportunity to put forward their own pet orthodoxy.

We can agree with much that he has to say about the inadequacies of the orthodoxies of the past for our present purposes. But I would have wanted him, however, to be more convincing in presenting his case in behalf of empiricism.

He denies the "ancient argument that some initial agreement as to the universally mandatory ends of life is the indispensable prerequisite to a rationally ordered society." However, he states that, "In general it is of course plain that a rational choice can be made only by reference to limits which are, at least for that choice, unalterable. It is also plain that these limits must recommend themselves on moral and rational grounds." I, for one, would have been grateful to Dr. Frankel if he had at this point introduced an example or two to illustrate his argument. . . .

We do not maintain that a principle necessarily becomes practically more effective, if it is metaphysically or theologically rooted. The fact is that the religious leaders of America failed as miserably as its political, philosophic, and social leaders, to prevent, as an example, the Civil War. But religion explains man's failure to follow the course best suited to his own mundane welfare, by man's inveterate inclination to sin, to choose death rather than life. Religion sees its most difficult task to be, not that of convincing man that this or the other path is to his own best interests, even in terms of his physical welfare upon this earth, but in getting him to follow that path, even when he is convinced of its worthwhileness. But how do empiricists explain man's failure to follow his own obvious best interests? Empiricists lean too heavily on the effectiveness of argument based on experience, to guide men toward their own highest interests. They forget that after man discovers the good, he must discipline himself in the pursuit of it. The breakdown of the orthodoxies of the past resulted not only in the rejection of absolute moral standards, but in the abandonment of disciplines tested by ages of human experience which encouraged man to follow the good.

Dr. Frankel is on absolutely unshakable ground when he maintains that the empirical method cannot be avoided when "the universal moral rule is to be applied to the specific case." But how can the metaphysical or theological be avoided, when one seeks to establish any kind of "moral law," universal or limited? Experience always validates a true moral law. But the law and its discovery by human beings always precedes its validation by experience. How does that happen? The sanctity of the life of the individual was pronounced long before experience validated it. Or perhaps experience has not yet validated even this moral law? Experience has not unto now been able to convince even so-called civilized nations of the validity of this moral law. Thus also the Senate of the United States to this day cannot agree on the basis of human historic experience, to outlaw genocide. And, indeed, on what grounds, other than metaphysical, would it be wrong to eliminate some of the primitive tribes in the heart of Africa, to make room for white men? Above all, empiricists must explain how it happened that in the twentieth century the most brutal form of genocide was practiced by the philosophically and scientifically most advanced people of Europe.

What some of those who are not interested in defending old orthodoxies are asking of relativists and empiricists is a simple question in essence. It is this: Are there any principles which a man ought to feel obligated to obey, even at the cost of his life? If there are, what are they? And why should they be obeyed? Are there any principles which a nation should obey, even at the possible risk of its existence? If there are, what are they? And if there are no such laws, are we to assume that the physical existence of the nation is the highest moral value?

Comment by Barna Horvath:

The author holds that "an element of choice or preference is uneliminable from moral judgments," yet these are not capricious, because "choices are natural events which take place in accordance with (at least theoretically) ascertainable laws and have identifiable consequences which do not depend on the hopes or desires of the choosers." This shows that the author takes teleological rationality for *choice,* and the question is whether this accounts for freedom.

I am afraid it does not. Or does Professor Frankel hold that free choice is the same thing as the phenomenon that a stream of water chooses always the valley? It is true that in *social* freedom—as in all other cases of *external* freedom—we are concerned only with *removing* more and more of the external impediments of behavior. Whether behavior is determined internally, we do not have to inquire. But this does not cancel the problem whether individual behavior—quite apart from its social freedom or determination—is internally free. For this individual moral freedom gives meaning to social freedom. It is vain to deny that the human mind is confronted here by one of the greatest puzzles.

I think that freedom is an unresolved problem, and that empiricism no less than metaphysics is in an awkward situation in the face of it. They have no other way, if they want to treat the question on its merits, than to make concessions to each other. They have to incorporate a foreign element into their respective systems of thought. This is called sometimes "moderate" determinism and indeterminism. But neither of them can claim in good faith that all is in order, after the foreign element has been admitted.

When Diogenes was told he could not act freely, he stood up and went around his barrel. If this is taken for the empiricist's answer, it is hardly satisfying. For rational choice is not the same thing as free choice, and causally determined (necessary) choice is hardly a choice at all. Rationality is, of course, an important element or condition of freedom, and it may well be that most of our frustrations, in the present situation, are due to lack of insight into teleological relevancies. But this does not mean that a calculating machine or "electronic brain" is free, although it may be a powerful instrument of freedom.

A "free agent" is *per definitionem* undetermined in its choice to act. By "personifying" it, we simply take it from the causal context, and treat it as an independent "point of imputation" to which we may impute blame or merit, sin or virtue, obligation or claim, punishment or reward. This "normative" order of ideas seems to be radically different from their causal order. We may move on the lines of either order, but their underlying assumptions are utterly different. Hardly can we imagine one and the *same* behavior both as causally determined and as *deserving,* as a point of normative imputation, moral praise or blame, or legal reward or punishment (apart from future motivation, reformation, and prevention). You have to *forget* that the event is causally determined, before you can persuade yourself it deserves (*pro praeterito*) to be visited by normative consequences. If you doubt this, imagine yourself trying to justify in conscience capital punishment, inflicted upon a criminal by yourself!

I wanted to point this out, in order to prove that empiricism, no less than metaphysics, is at a loss in the face of the problem of freedom: the first because it has no place for "free agents"; the second because it cannot reconcile them with causality, pervading the empirical world. In admitting that choice supposes unalterable limits, recommended on moral, not physical grounds, Professor Frankel has already admitted that there are within nature somehow *empty spaces,* left for rational-moral "normative imputation." As he calls choices also "natural events," his meaning of freedom can be only that natural events somehow *"embrace"* those *empty spots* of freedom.

This would mean that causality has *holes.* Rickert thought that causality holds only in the realm of events, considered as mere examples of general laws, whereas anything considered as *historically unique* escapes them. Nobody would try to explain causally, by laws of natural science, historical personalities, such as Marcus Aurelius, Beethoven, or Franklin D. Roosevelt (although their diseases may be so explained).

Perhaps uniqueness, which is, after all, empirical and the mark of any *individual,* brings this transition from causality to moral imputation nearer to the empiricist. Where causality loses its power of explanation, we have to resort to other types of law. The whole theory of probability, out of which the *statistical* conception of causality has developed, started with the assumption that where, as in certain types of gambling, causal effects are practically undiscoverable, chances and hazards are, nevertheless, governed by laws.

What I wanted to emphasize here is that neither empiricist nor metaphysician has much reason for complacency in the face of the riddle of freedom. The first, because one and the same thing or event cannot be both free and causally necessary. The second, because freedom makes little sense without teleological rationality, and this supposes causality.

The paradox might be formulated thus: freedom is possible, only if causality has holes or gaps, but it makes sense, only in so far as causality has no holes or gaps (at least not many holes in addition to the agent's freedom).

I completely agree with the author that an appeal to human interests provides "a conception of 'ultimate' social authority which serves the same normative purpose for which absolutists provide their own alternative conception of authority." I approve also of his praise of "successful compromise" and "a pluralistic society, offering a variety of values" which may be a better safeguard of "social cohesion" than "a society initially committed to a unitary scheme of fixed and final ends."

Is this anything else but the very creed of the Free World, now facing the threat of totalitarian absolutism? Under the sway of the latter, empirical relativists and metaphysical absolutists are equally deprived of their freedom. Within the Free World, they have the same reason to reject totalitarianism unconditionally. What is, then, the difference between them arriving at the same "unalterable" conclusion from widely different starting points? I think, the explanation of this is that just as you cannot feel passive (causally determined) at the moment you *act*, in the same sense you testify to your belief in a principle as absolute (at least for that action) by *acting* on it.

Comment by Mortimer R. Kadish:

Dr. Frankel, it seems to me, has defended well and clearmindedly the rights of free, empirically directed inquiry to construct in morals and in politics humanly adequate norms for human behavior.

Yet, much as I agree with the substance of what Dr. Frankel has to say, one of his theses disturbs me, at least in the form in which he has put it here: Dr. Frankel suggests that to introduce "metaphysical" or "theological" considerations in deciding issues of morals and politics, is in principle mistaken. Now I, too, see, or think I see, a close affinity between contemporary metaphysical or theological treatments of politics and morals, on one hand, and conformist, sometimes authoritarian, points of view, on the other. Yet, despite the tactical opening left to the proponents of the method of authority, it seems to me important to emphasize the point—which Dr. Frankel's effort to exclude metaphysic and theology at least obscures—that fundamental views concerning the nature of man and society, knowledge and inquiry, the truth or falsity of which is empirically verifiable, are implicit in democratic practice.

Dr. Frankel, I know, insists wholeheartedly upon the procedural presumptions of democratic behavior; I am suggesting that the presumptions of such behavior are also substantive. "Men," he writes, "can differ widely over first principles, or even whether there are any, and there can still be broad agreements as to such 'tried and true' moral and political principles as good faith, equity, the rejection of hearsay evidence, or the rights of *habeas corpus*." "Can" is the key word. Of course there "can" be such agreements given differing first principles. But also for certain classes of "first principles" there may necessarily *not* be. And that is precisely where Dr. Frankel's essential quarrel with theoretical absolutism arises. Further, Dr. Frankel will want to say that when his "tried and true" principles become more than advertising slogans for the *status quo,* they depend in a very direct sense upon pervasive views (of a verifiable character) concerning social structure, intelligence, the nature of persons, etc. But then either metaphysic and theology will contain as at least latent content, considerations of this sort, or they will not. If metaphysics and theology do, then they are not *ipso facto* irrelevant. If they do not, freedom need not be defended against a species of nonsense.

More generally, however: procedural considerations, not only in political life, but in every domain, are separable in principle from substantive conceptions of fact only through rendering procedure arbitrary. If we cannot give evidence of the truth of the proposition that such and such is a better procedure than another, then all that remains is the dictum of whim or authority to support or deny the belief. But evidence depends in the last analysis upon knowledge of fact, however general that knowledge may be. Accordingly, it should occasion no surprise to discover that a practicing democracy depends as much upon certain of the more pervasive hypotheses of modern science for justification as upon the translation of the method of that science into the terms of practical behavior. That the value of freedom thereupon loses absolute certainty, will strike the empiricist, who prefers reasons to certainty, as a positive recommendation of the view advanced here.

There is a moral to be drawn from the above remarks—a moral I think quite consistent with Dr. Frankel's actual practice in his paper: absolutisms and orthodoxies are to be contested, not only by showing that more than one hypothesis may justify even a desirable phenomenon—so preserving the intellectual basis for cooperation among different groups; the attempts of various candidate conformities to preempt the idea of democracy may more effectively be discountenanced by accepting the gauntlet of relevance and denying the truth of the dogmas upon which those conformities rest.

Professor Frankel's reply:

There is a sense in which I am sympathetic with Professor Kadish's remarks, if I interpret them correctly, and a sense in which I think I am not. As I tried to make plain in my paper, I believe that neither metaphysics nor theology do, in fact, avoid empirical considerations. Consequently, I agree with Dr. Kadish that they contain, "as at least latent content," substantive considerations that are in principle empirically verifiable. Indeed, I think it wise "to accept the gauntlet of relevance," not only in order to deny the truth of metaphysical or theological dogmas, but also even to learn some truths from them occasionally. Certainly I deplore (as Dr. Kadish's remarks suggest he does as well) what is fortunately becoming the less popular tendency among certain empiricists to reject out of hand some of the most suggestive systems of thought in our tradition on the basis of a pat decision that they are "meaningless."

The difficulty, however, is that those who hold "metaphysical" or "theological" beliefs so frequently reject, on their side, the relevance of an empirical interpretation of these doctrines, and insist that it is some "transcendent" meaning that characterizes metaphysics and theology. This is unfortunately not a difficulty of my own making. Professor Kadish says, "Dr. Frankel suggests that to introduce 'metaphysical' or 'theological' considerations in deciding issues of morals and politics, is in principle mistaken." But what I am saying is that it is mistaken to introduce considerations which are *in principle metaphysical or theological,* in the sense suggested above. In a sense, my paper is a plea to metaphysicians and theologians "to accept the gauntlet of relevance."

Of course, if some one claims to hold a "metaphysics" (as, for example, certain empiricists do), but is prepared to subject it to the ordinary tests to which other beliefs are subjected, I certainly will not argue a question of terminology. Accordingly, the issue between Professor Kadish and myself seems to reduce to a question about those elements of beliefs which are held to have a more than empirical meaning. At this point, Dr. Kadish writes: "Freedom need not be defended against a species of nonsense." I wish he were right. But it seems to me that, on the record, nonsense, especially "hifalutin" nonsense, has more seriously harmed the cause of freedom than have falsehoods, clearly expressed. Indeed, it is in part because so much of what passes for ideas is, in fact, nonsense, that the old liberal dream that we shall grow in wisdom by the free interchange of ideas so frequently fails to work out. I am afraid that the struggle against nonsense is a recurrent responsibility of those who are interested in maintaining or creating an environment in which Dr. Kadish's kind of truth can be found.

The possible issues raised by Dr. Kadish's very suggestive criticism perhaps reduce to two. It may be that Dr. Kadish holds some view that there are "primary" or "basic" human interests, in the light of which all other activities may be evaluated. This is a modernized form of the old Natural Law argument which is becoming increasingly popular, and it raises a host of very complex issues into which I cannot go. Under the present circumstances, I can only record my present disinclination toward such a view.

Again, there may be only a terminological issue between us. In the first place, I think that such procedures as *habeas corpus* are quite sufficiently justified by certain common sense experiences in politics, which need not be dignified as "a fundamental view." In the second place, I should not want to say that a democracy, by definition, must employ scientific hypotheses. Certainly a democracy can make mistakes, can act in ignorance or blindness, and still be a democracy. (Indeed, it is for this reason, among others, that political decisions are observed to be so often mistaken—call this "a fundamental view" if you like—that democratic procedures like the civil liberties, which make it possible to retrieve one's errors to a certain extent, are set up.) For such reasons I should myself wish to use a term, such as "democracy," primarily to characterize the procedures by which social decisions are reached, rather than the content of those decisions—except in so far, obviously as the substance of a political decision is incompatible with the maintenance of those procedures. And it is also for this reason that I stress methodological considerations in the clarification of the presumptions of democratic behavior.

Comment by Chaim Perelman (translated from the French):

I would like to make one comment. Professor Frankel says: "Certainly the one thing on which all empiricists are agreed is that statements about the relations of means to ends are the only responsible type of moral discourse."

While I share almost completely in the views of Professor Frankel, and find his article most noteworthy, I should like to point out a defect which his argument shares with a goodly number of ethical theories based on an empiricist approach. This defect, due doubtless to utilitarian influence, consists in limiting "rational" analysis of value-judgments to those analyses which confine themselves solely to the "means-ends" relationship. This arbitrary restriction, the principal cause of the inadequacy of empiricist moral theories, seems to me more the result of prejudgment than of an examination of the modes of argumentation actually used in moral thought. Aristotle long ago indicated, in his *Topica*, several other "rational" means of establishing moral preferences. It seems to me that the processes which allow us to judge a person by his acts, and conversely to appreciate his acts in virtue of what we know of their author—different though they be from the "means-ends" relation—constitute nevertheless a "very responsible type of moral discourse."[1]

Comment by Quincy Wright:

I find Professor Frankel's philosophical discussion of absolutism and relativism very refreshing. It comports with my idea of "truth" to say that a system of thought integrating propositions which predict and control, is more "true" than such a system integrating any other kind of propositions. When the system applies to phenomena in the social or moral field there are complications. A system of thought may make itself "true" in the above sense merely by being generally accepted in a community. Anthropologists can, for instance, predict the behavior of the Hopi Indians through knowledge of their system of thought and values, although that system might be wholly "untrue" as a guide for predicting or controlling the behavior of the Arunta, the Andamans, the Afghans, or the Americans.

These considerations induce me to raise a question about Professor Frankel's answer to the objection, which he cites, to the empiricist view that "the worth of human decisions can be measured in terms of their consequences for human interests." The objectors ask: How do we know that such a human interest as "happiness" is "good"? Professor Frankel answers: "The question is not an empirical one but a matter of definition." Empiricists, he says, define values in terms of human interest, and consequently when disagreements arise over values, the answer is to be found in evidence and among the important sources

[1] Cf. Chaim Perelman and L. Olbrechts-Tyteca, "Act and Person in Argument," *Ethics*, July, 1951.

of evidence are human interests. It seems to me that this insufficiently emphasizes that human interests differ from culture to culture. Consequently one must seek evidence in the specific culture or value system which the parties to the disagreement accept as defining their "interest." If these parties belong to different cultures, then comparison of common elements of the two cultures or study of the developing universal culture, can be appealed to. Perhaps the concept of a "Universal Culture" is the modern terminology for "natural law." Evidence of the values of that culture may be sought, among other sources, in the Universal Declaration of Human Rights promulgated by the United Nations General Assembly in 1948.

Obviously, if there is a universal culture, it is in an embryonic stage. Consequently, disagreements about values or about what are "human interests" among people or groups of different culture cannot be settled without much toleration and compromise. As Professor Frankel points out, the evidence suggests that efforts to achieve universal acceptance of any value system have been more productive of war and disorder than have efforts to tolerate the coexistence of diverse value systems. It is refreshing to find that he finds logical support for the conclusion, to be drawn from this evidence, that belief in the relativity of values is more conducive to harmony than belief in absolute values. It is indeed surprising to find that persons can be found at the present time to argue for the opposite point of view. This can be explained perhaps by the human propensity to neglect the time element in society. While appreciation of the relativity of current values and toleration of diverse systems seems to be a condition for stability under present conditions, it may be admitted that the shrinking of the world and the increased abundance of contacts among all value systems require efforts at synthesis with the object of evolving some universal standards.

Professor Frankel's reply:

I am grateful to Professor Wright for giving me an opportunity to clear up a possible source of misinterpretation. When I used the expression, "human interests," I did not mean to suggest some set of universal biological traits, but rather existent human interests as socially conditioned, and as varying from culture to culture. Indeed, I am doubtful of the validity of any attempt to reestablish a version of "natural law" on the basis of certain universal biological drives.

CHAPTER XXXVIII

The Concept of Political Freedom

By FRANZ L. NEUMANN

Professor of Government, Columbia University

THERE IS ONE striking fact in our teaching of political science, namely, the growing interest in the study of political theory. It is my observation that some students prefer political theory to other branches of political science because they believe it to be simpler. No facts and figures, but ideas (or more fashionably ideologies) are the subject of political theory, which is thus more interesting than the allegedly pedestrian study of government and administration.

But there is a more charitable, and perhaps more justified, explanation for the upswing of the demand curve: the deep concern of the students with the validity of our value system, or perhaps even the inability to understand it rationally. It is to the honor of the students that they turn to political theory for an answer to the perplexing problem: are there objective values, not depending upon acceptance or rejection even by majorities, not simply being individual and arbitrary preferences; how can one perceive them, and how do they manifest themselves concretely in any given historical situation?

What can political theory do to help answer these questions? To many, politics (and history) is simply the struggle for political power. Ideas are mere ideologies, rationalizations of any given power position, valid if they help attain the desired objective, invalid if they fail to do so. The significance of political theory is thus exclusively its propagandistic and manipulative value.

Politics is, indeed, the struggle for power. But in that very struggle, some (or one group, or state) may indeed promote an historically progressive principle, the other may not. The one may represent merely egoistic and particular, the other national or even universal interests. The thought structure of the former would indeed be an ideology; that of the latter an idea.

It is, so I maintain, possible to determine objectively which groups (or states), in the political struggle, do more than just fight for egoistic, particular interests. We can determine where the interests of humanity are preserved.

To this end, we must analyze the crucial concept of political theory: that of political freedom.

I

Political theory is solely concerned with the freedom of man and with nothing else. From this follows one important insight: political theory must always be critical of existing political systems, for none can embody fully the idea of freedom. A conformist political theory is no theory, it is propaganda. The task of the political theorist is then to criticize, not to eulogize a system. And the standard of his criticism can only be: the concept of political freedom.

What, however, is freedom?

II

The Juristic Aspect of Freedom

Very often and particularly in the Anglo-American tradition, freedom is defined as absence of restraints. It was thus formulated by Hobbes, and has quite a long and honorable record. Thus conceived, freedom is legal or juristic freedom. This definition is correct, if it is designed to describe *one* aspect of freedom; it is wrong, if it is meant to describe the whole content of freedom.

This juristic definition of freedom is based upon the confrontation: citizen *versus* state. Man is free, to the degree that the state does not intervene within his sphere of freedom.

This formula involves a whole philosophy: the view, namely, that man exists outside of the state. To Plato and Aristotle, the conception of man (and mankind) as opposed to the political community, was unthinkable. Man's freedom, on the contrary, was tied to his status as citizen of the *polis*. The separation of man (and of mankind) from the political structure within which he lived, is the work of the *Stoa*, and found its first legal formulation in Cicero. But the spread of this basic conception is, without question, the work of Christianity. Freedom of man *per se,* and not simply the rights of citizens, involves the recognition of the fundamental equality of man: there can be neither slave nor free, there can be no distinctions as to race, nationality, status. Each man, because he is created in the image of God, is capable of salvation. This trend culminates in the formulation of Kant: man is always an end in itself; never can he be or be considered merely as a means to other ends.

The political consequences of this conception of freedom must be made clear. It follows first and foremost that the state (no state) can swallow up man's private sphere in its entirety. We cannot accept the view that the freedom of man is tied exclusively to the political system within which political freedom operates.

Consequently, the antithesis: man *versus* power (that is, the state) is correct.

Yet it is also true that the state does intervene in our private sphere and one can define the state as a coordinated system of intervention with the private competence of the citizen.

What, then, is the significance of the juristic concept of liberty? Two men, so widely apart as Cicero and Voltaire, have given almost identical answers—Cicero in his formula, "The laws are the foundation of liberty which we enjoy. We all are the laws' slaves that we may be free": and Voltaire, in a still more precise manner, "To be free, is to depend upon nothing but the law."

Clearly then, liberty and restraint by law go together. But in a very specific manner. There exists always a presumption in favor of the individual's freedom against the coercive power of the state. The state must prove that he has the right to intervene. He can prove it only by reference to the "law."

What then is the law? It is clear that the definition of law assumes major significance. These definitions of law do exist: the law as the command of the sovereign; the law as the sum total of natural rights; the law as the general statement of duties imposed upon us (the so-called generality of the law).

If law were nothing but the command of the sovereign, one could not possibly define freedom. Then the sovereign could, indeed, act arbitrarily. The law would then not protect, but rather oppress. This is precisely the function of law in totalitarian states.

It is precisely here that the United States has made the decisive contribution to the conception of freedom. There is probably no other country where the conception of the rights of the individual, as preceding the power of the government, is so widespread as here. The culmination of the development may perhaps be found in Justice Jackson's statement in 1943. "If," he says, "there is any fixed star in our constitutional constellation, it is that no official, high or petty, can prescribe what shall be orthodox in politics, nationalism, religion, or other matters of opinion, or force citizens to confess by word or act their faith therein."[1]

It would go too far to develop here the concrete principles following from the single and simple statement that there always is a presumption in favor of the individual's right, and against the power of the government which must prove its power by reference to general law. There follow the absolute impossibility of *ex post facto* (retroactive) laws; the prohibition of bills of attainder; the doctrine of judicial independence (because, as the state has to prove its right of intervention, the organ that intervenes cannot possibly be the same that decides upon the right of intervention).

The whole legal system of liberalism thus follows from the simple principle. Yet, there remains a doubt.

What is the doubt?

III

The Historical Aspect of Freedom

Is this juristic liberty really the total content of liberty? If it were so, why should we need democracy? The statement that juristic liberty can be protected in a constitutional monarchy cannot possibly be challenged either on theoretical or historical grounds. (See Section IV below.)

There is a second doubt, equally relevant: the juristic element of the concept of liberty is essentially static and negative, while society permanently changes. This difficulty has been excellently stated by Justice Jackson in the same decision. "The task of translating the majestic generalities of the Bill of Rights . . . into concrete restraints on officials dealing with the problems of the twentieth century, is one to disturb self-confidence. . . . We must transplant these rights to a soil in which the *laissez-faire* concept or principle of non-interference has withered at least as to economic affairs, and social advancements are increasingly sought through

---

[1] West Virginia State Board of Education v. Barnette, 319 U.S. 624 (1943), p. 642.

closer integration of society and strengthened governmental controls."

Justice Jackson's statement leads to the third doubt of the adequacy of the juristic concept of liberty. The formula liberty *versus* government seems to comprehend two statements: the one, that our liberty increases with the decrease of governmental power (and *vice versa*); the second, that liberty has but one enemy—the government.

None of these implications can possibly be accepted.

The first can be refuted in two ways: historically and theoretically. First, is it really true, one may ask, that liberties of the citizens decreased wherever the state expanded its activities, and were greater in periods of contraction of governmental action? If we look into the history of Europe or the United States, we could not possibly say so. Second, is it really inconceivable that the government intervenes to safeguard and even deepen the citizen's individual rights? Can we really think of individual rights in terms of a state of nature? I believe not.

This, of course, is tied up with the falsity of the second implication of the formula liberty *versus* government, namely, that only government threatens our liberty. Can we really assert this? Is the threat from private organizations and private power positions not sometimes more dangerous than governmental intervention? Is it not the very aim of the state to secure, to use Rousseau's term, that the general will prevail against any and all aggregations of private social power?

I have raised three doubts against the claim that the juristic concept of liberty exhausts liberty. The last two I shall take up now. The first (the relation of political structure to liberty) I shall take up last.

The mere legal definition of liberty forgets to take into account the process of social change, namely, history. The historical element is the second constitutive element in the concept of political liberty. What does this mean? I want to show the intellectual stages in the formulation of the historical element of liberty.

1. The first stage is Greek natural philosophy, particularly Epicurus and his Roman disciple, Lucretius. Epicurus set himself the problem of discovering laws governing external nature so as to liberate men from the terror inspired by nature. Once one has understood the necessity governing external nature, he can use it for his own happiness and freedom.

2. The second step is best embodied in the philosophy of Spinoza. He attempted the discovery of psychic laws, so that reason could prevail,

man could free himself from his passions and prejudices, could live according to reason, and thus become free. Freedom is thus defined as the ability to control one's passions.

There are thus two steps: the Epicurean, the understanding of the lawfulness of external nature; the Spinozist, the understanding of the lawfulness of internal nature.

3. There remains the third and final step to be taken, the understanding of the process of social change, that is, of history.

This is the contribution of the eighteenth century, and the unquestioned merit of the Italian Jean Baptiste Vico. Here is the first attempt to understand history not as metaphysical or theological, but as a social process. History, according to Vico, is the conflict between man, nature, and culture. While we cannot accept the cyclical theory which he expounded, he initiated the study of history as a science.

So did Montesquieu. It is he who insisted on the interdependence of society, and rejected the attempt to isolate specific elements and to attribute consequences to such isolated elements.

From Vico and Montesquieu, the road goes to Hegel and Marx. Both developed theories of historical development, the one seeing in history the progress of an idea, the other the struggle of social classes. Both consequently accepted Spinoza's formula: freedom is insight into necessity. A man who understands what is happening and why it is happening, is thereby free.

This formula is obviously wrong. If the historical element alone would constitute freedom, we could not change anything; and we would preach reaction, because it would be useless to interfere with the historical laws.

But without the historical element the concept of freedom would be empty or dangerous. History prevents us from repeating old formulas regardless of changes that have occurred. It shows the relativity of many time honored formulas. History also prevents utopian radicalism.

Instead of discussing this problem theoretically, I shall attempt to illustrate it at two concrete instances: the significance of the concepts of sovereignty and of property.

It is fashionable today to defame sovereignty. Such a view follows quite logically from the mere juristic view of liberty, but it is neither theoretically nor historically valid. For what is the historic role of sovereignty? In a period of feudal rule, there arose central power, establishing one central authority, one law, and one administration. How could our commercial and industrial society have emerged without this central authority which, at least, established a minimum of uniformity and order?

That leads to the second example: the role of property. By property, we understand man's control of a part of external nature. Property is safeguarded, because one felt it to be the necessary instrument to assert man's rights. It is rarely realized that the founder of our liberal theory of the state, John Locke, justified property as a natural right, solely because he conceived of man's property as the result of man's investment of his labor in external nature. Property, according to Locke, is legitimate, because it represents the transformation of the raw external nature by man's efforts.

This intrinsic connection between the personality rights and property has been lost in the course of the historical development and under the pressure of vested interests. Freedom may well be threatened by property concentration, by private social power. It is then the function of government to redress this balance, so that man can actually assert his rights which the constitutions protect. Liberty and property do not necessarily go together. The protection of property then should depend upon its role as an instrument in asserting one's liberty.

Thus, let me repeat: the juristic element of the conception of freedom is essential, but not adequate. Without taking into account the historical process which alone makes freedom concrete, we cannot arrive at an understanding of the meaning of freedom in a specific historical situation.

IV

The Volitional Aspect of Freedom

Yet our first doubt remains unsolved. I put it this way: if liberty is merely the absence of restraint, if the formula, liberty *versus* government exhausts the concept of freedom, how then can one justify democracy? Is it not true, I asked, that this liberty can be secured as well in a constitutional monarchy, a system where the executive power rests totally in the hands of a monarch who is merely restrained by laws in the arbitrary exercise of his power?

The answer lies in the recognition that the two elements in the concept of freedom are still not adequate. Law protects us; history shows us the possible road; but only man can, through his action, change reality; he alone can, through his own effort, realize his freedom and that of mankind.

While neither Plato nor Aristotle showed any preference for democracy, both insisted that only through active participation in political life can freedom be attained. The withdrawal from politics denies the third element of human freedom: the action of man. The culmination of this activist trend in the history of the concept of freedom is probably to be found in the work of Fichte. His aim was the development toward absolute perfection from a limited to a less limited condition, until the end appears as absolute freedom from all restraints, as absolute independence and self-activity. Here is clearly expressed the one, vital, element of human freedom: the need for human action.

But to stress only this actionist element is false and dangerous. It negates that we have obligations to our fellow men, that we cannot assert self-perfection at the expense of others. The juristic element of restraint is thus sacrificed.

Secondly, to stress action and action only, regardless of historical situation, makes for anarchism or Fascism. One then preaches (like Bakunin, who was deeply influenced by Fichte) revolutionary action for the sake of revolutionary action; or one preaches, as did Mussolini (equally influenced by this theory) the virtues of an heroic life against the so-called bourgeois liberty.

Yet the element of human action is indispensable, for neither God nor history is willing to grant man, without his efforts, the boon of freedom. Man can realize his potentialities, can approximate a state of freedom only through action—that is, through participation in political life. That is the theoretic base of democracy.

The democratic form of government is the only one which institutionalizes the activist element of man's freedom.

V

Summary

All three elements are vital, none can be dispensed with. All three are threatened.

All three are non-existent in totalitarian states. There is there no liberty against government. The presumption in favor of the individual's right against the coercive power of the state, is there reversed. The state has the right to intervene at discretion; law loses its protective function and becomes a mere instrument of coercion. Man is no longer considered an end in itself, but becomes a tool in the attainment of ends alien to his destiny.

But the totalitarian systems equally violate the second element of the concept of freedom: history. If history has a meaning, it can only be that the tremendous potentialities given to us by modern technology, are to be used for the improvement of man's lot. Yet, in the totalitarian systems, modern technology becomes an instrument of oppression, and of annihilation of mankind.

And I need hardly add that the third element of the concept of political freedom, participation in politics, is denied.

Yet this analysis must not lead us to be smug about our own freedom; it must be applied to our own system as well.

This is not my task today. I shall merely indicate the problems.

Liberty as a juristic concept is in danger. The critics of liberal democracy (the French traditionalists, Spengler, and many others) asserted that democracy is incompatible with juristic freedom, because democracy has the tendency of imposing conformity upon the members of the community. This danger exists: it will undoubtedly grow.

The second element—the historical element—is equally threatened. It is likely that the requirements of the cold war will make necessary a delay in the dedication of technological progress to the betterment of the conditions of man. If it is a mere delay, nothing can be said against it. If it is more, a dangerous situation may arise.

The third element, human activity, participation in politics, is equally difficult. The difficulties are inherent in the complexity of modern government, in the process of bureaucratization, in the remoteness of government from the people. Let us be reminded from time to time that participation in politics is not merely voting, but an active share in the performance of governmental functions.

Thus, tremendous problems do exist for us. I have tried to bring out that political freedom is not mere protection of one's right by law; that it is not static, but dynamic; that it is not granted, but must be fought for.

Comment by Barna Horvath:

There is a sense, I admit, in which political thought has a wider field of application than legal thought. This is so because we do not know all law, or how to apply it in all cases, while the twilight zone between uncertain principle and elusive fact is the field of operation of the political genius. I may mention the crucial problem, in international law, of the difference between legal and political disputes. But the political field is wider than the legal, only in the sense that the *search* for law is going on in a wider field than is its application, according to clear and fixed rules, standards, and principles. This does *not* mean that political freedom is somehow above or beyond the legal one. As certainly as moral freedom is autonomy and *not* arbitrariness, political freedom is the fruit of wisdom that *finds* the law, and not of political cunning that circumvents or shuns it.

Comment by Roy Wood Sellars:

An excellent analysis. But was not the city-state somewhat totalitarian? And did not Cicero and Seneca, together with the preceding Epicurean and Stoic philosophies, institute the difference between the state and society? A man is more than a citizen of a state. Christianity took up this theme but in too supernaturalistic a way.

If we regard the state as an historically developed, political organization of a society, we can note both its functions and its inadequacies. Assigned functions vary with the times and social pressures. Hence the need of cultural and political debates and decisions. Democracy seems to me to be an instrument of freedom, to the extent that it aids and abets the conditions of a good life for all. But political democracy is an abstraction, apart from the whole institutional setting of a given society.

CHAPTER XXXIX

The Universal Declaration of Human Rights: An International Effort at a Synthesis of Freedom and Authority

By JOHN H. E. FRIED[1]

I

EFFORTS TO RECONCILE the rights of the individual with the power of the authorities, did, of course, not begin with the writing of the first Bills of Rights toward the end of the eighteenth century. The history of politics, and also of morals and religion, could largely be told in terms of such endeavors; and who would count the victims and the heroes of this struggle?

The particular device of Bills of Rights coincides with the emergence of the modern constitutional state. Between the early 1800's and the 1930's, the number of constitutions containing or referring to, a bill of rights, increased steadily. There was also a tendency to proceed, from a catalogue of *procedural* or *"prohibitive,"* to a catalogue of *substantive* or *"positive"* rights. Never, however, did an *international* Bill of Rights exist.

It would be hypocritical to maintain that Bills of Rights have always been honored. But the rise and spread of Fascism challenged the very foundations of the Bills of Rights. Not only was the *in*equality of persons and peoples proclaimed as doctrine; the doctrine was translated into practice, and culminated in horrors of which Auschwitz and Majdanek were merely among the most conspicuous. Characteristically, the Second World War was incubated by this doctrine of *in*equality and, in turn, was a prerequisite for its "application." Technology was severed from the rationalistic soil from which it sprang, and harnessed to a newly released, atavistic tribalism: a new type of "authority" thus made its ap-

[1] The views expressed are those of the author as an individual.

pearance, glittering with loudspeakers and bombs. This authority utilized many of the old values which it borrowed and falsified. Freedom went into eclipse, but license was widely granted. The repercussions of the experience have not yet ended.

On the other hand, the cataclysm acted as catalyzer. Revulsion against the torture chambers blended with determination to strive for positive national, social, and economic aims. At a time when the individual appeared hopelessly and infinitesimally small, it was necessary to reassert that man is the unit that counts. If Roosevelt's Four Freedoms, despite their revolutionary implications, especially in the fields of international affairs and economics, are accepted as a truism, this only indicates their timeliness.

II

The Charter of the United Nations refers to "human rights" in no fewer than seven places, thus making the promotion and protection of human rights an *international* responsibility. One result of the "United Nations' Human Rights Program" has been the drafting by the Commission of Human Rights,[2] and the adoption and promulgation (December 10, 1948) by the General Assembly, of the first *"universal"* declaration of human rights.

The Universal Declaration was bound to be a composite instrument embodying ideas which are shared by, or acceptable to, different political, ideological, and economic systems.[3] This is its strength.

The spirit of the Declaration is well shown in the principles enunciated in the preamble. The keynote is struck in the statement that the "recognition" (not the bestowal) of the "inalienable" rights, is "the foundation" of the three major values: *"freedom; justice; and peace in the world."*

---

[2] The following seventeen countries were represented in the Commission: Australia, Belgium, Byelorussian S.S.R., Chile, China (vice president), Egypt, France (vice president), India, Iran, Lebanon (rapporteur), Panama, the Philippines, the Union of Soviet Socialist Republics, the United Kingdom, the United States of America (chairman), Uruguay, and Yugoslavia.

[3] The debates stretched over two years and covered a great deal of ground—from the question of the abolishing of the death penalty in peace time, to the question of whether "all human beings are endowed with reason and conscience" (on which point there was agreement) by God, or by nature. The thoroughness of these discussions shows that the governments attributed great significance to the Declaration, although it was understood from the beginning that the Declaration would not constitute a binding international treaty. In the following quotations, the italics are mine.

These three major values are *interdependent*. "Recognition of the inherent dignity and of the equal and inalienable rights of all members of the human family" is, as the preamble says, the "foundation" of "freedom, justice and peace in the world."

The opposite doctrine is rejected for moral and for empirical reasons: "disregard and contempt for human rights have resulted in barbarous acts which have outraged the conscience of mankind"; against these, are set the Four Freedoms, accepted as "the highest aspiration of the common people" ("freedom of speech and belief[4] and freedom from fear and want").

As the rights are "inalienable," they are preexistent. Hence, in an interesting echo to ideas of the enlightenment and the monarchomachs, and to the feudal concept of the *jus revolutionis,* the Preamble acknowledges the natural right, or the fact, that "man [may be] compelled to have recourse, as a last resort, to *rebellion* against tyranny and oppression."

Positively "friendly relations between nations" are declared to be "essential." This is one of the central themes of the Universal Declaration. Because, as we shall see, a fair international order is proclaimed as an *individual* human right, it is only logical that "the development of friendly relations between nations" is declared to be "essential."

The determination to achieve *higher economic standards* is recognized as legitimate, and a prerequisite for larger freedom: "the peoples of the United Nations have . . . determined to promote social progress and better standards of life in larger freedom."

Although the Declaration shows no doubt or relativistic attitude about the "highest aspirations of the common people," it is aware of the dangers of ignorance and of false education (Article 26, 2). The rights and freedoms cannot be fully realized without "a common understanding," that is, unless they are commonly understood ("a common understanding").

III

Within this framework, the Declaration formulates a wide range of separate, positive rights and freedoms—but always stressing their interdependence, and also specifically declaring that "everyone has *duties* to the community." As long as we keep these two points in mind—namely, that the various rights are conceived as *interdependent,* and as matched

[4]Here, Roosevelt's version ("freedom of worship") has been widened. (See Article 19.)

by *duties*—we can divide the rights enunciated in the Declaration into several categories:

"Human rights" (*droits de l'homme*)—rights which are proclaimed for "everyone," regardless of citizenship. These rights presuppose that the "authority" *abstain* from *arbitrary* interference—*e.g.*,

> No one shall be subjected to arbitrary interference with his privacy, family, home or correspondence (Article 12). (Cf. Article 15, 2, Article 17, 2);

or that the "authority" take *positive action* to guarantee the rights. *e.g.*,

> Everyone has the right to an effective remedy by competent national tribunals for acts violating the fundamental rights granted him by the constitution or by law (Article 8);

"Political rights" or citizenship rights (*droits de l'homme et du citoyen*) *e.g.*,

> Everyone has the right to take part in the government of his country, directly or through freely chosen representatives (Article 21, 1). (Cf. Article 2, 2);

"Economic, social, and cultural rights"—rights which are proclaimed for everybody, irrespective of citizenship, as a responsibility of *society e.g.*,

> Everyone, as a member of society, has the right to social security[5] and is entitled to realization, through *national* effort and *international* co-operation and in accordance with the organization and resources of each state, of the economic, social, and cultural rights indispensable for his dignity and the free development of his personality (Article 22).

Together, the catalogue of rights and freedoms shows a blending of equalitarian, libertarian, religious, *laissez-faire,* and socialist ideas.

IV

The present paper can only outline some of the basic doctrines which permeate the Universal Declaration and are of wide significance, because they have been accepted by the General Assembly of the United Nations without a dissenting vote.

[5] "Social security" is used here in its wider sense, not in the restricted meaning of "social insurance."

It is possible to outline a broad, universal doctrine of the "Fair State," the "Fair Social Order," and the "Fair International Order."

Evidently, the framers of the Declaration were able to achieve this broad doctrine, only by *not* committing the United Nations to any governmental or economic system. Nevertheless, the Declaration is remarkably specific and concrete on what makes the fair state, the fair social order, and the fair international order.

First, there are the postulates on what makes the "fair state." There are the "evident" demands—such as for fair trial (Article 10, 11), freedom of thought, conscience, and religion (Article 18), freedom to hold opinions without interference (Article 19), freedom from arbitrary arrest (Article 9), the right to leave any country including one's own (Article 13, 2), etc.

The Universal Declaration, in enumerating the attributes of the fair state, avoids the word, "democracy,"[6] for good reasons, because of its frequent abuse. However, it does proclaim:

> The will of the people shall be the basis of the authority of government; this will shall be expressed in periodic and genuine elections which shall be by universal and equal suffrage and shall be held by secret vote or by equivalent free voting procedures (Article 21, 3).[7] (Cf. Article 21, 1.)

There are proclamations concerning the fair social order—the rights to own property (Article 17, 1), the right to *work,* the right to free choice of employment, the right to just and favorable conditions of work, the right to protection against unemployment (Article 23, 1). Large as the implications of this last mentioned single paragraph are, the Declaration becomes much more specific. For example:

> Everyone has the right to a standard of living adequate for the health and well-being of himself and of his family, including food, clothing, housing, and medical care, and necessary social services, and the right to security in the event of unemployment, sickness, disability, widowhood, old age or other lack of livelihood in circumstances beyond his control (Article 25, 1). (Cf. Article 23.)

---

[6] The word, "democratic," appears once, in a self-explanatory sense, in the reference to "a democratic *society.*" (See below.)

[7] This Article is one of the twenty-three and one half which in the paragraph-by-paragraph vote of the General Assembly were adopted unanimously, *i.e.,* without dissenting votes and without abstentions. The Declaration has thirty Articles.

While this program implies a great deal of action on the part of the authorities, the Declaration limits the range of the norm-giving prerogative of the authority ("the law"). It proclaims that the "law" may restrict the exercise of rights and freedoms of individuals, "solely" for the following purposes: to secure "due recognition and respect for the rights and freedoms of others," and to meet "the just requirements of morality, public order and the general welfare in a democratic society" (Article 29, 2).

The fact that the phrase, "just requirements of morality, public order and the general welfare in a democratic society," is elastic, cannot be denied. On the other hand, the very catalogue of rights and freedoms contained in the Declaration as a whole, provides a great deal of substance, and many concrete yardsticks for these concepts. Also, aversion against the omnipotent state is unmistakably expressed in this rule.[8]

The framers of the Declaration were, of course, aware of the often made objection that "escape clauses," which permit the limitation of guaranteed rights, leave in Bill of Rights but an empty façade of pompous words. The Declaration intended to avoid the pitfall—and, as it seems to this observer, with remarkable success.

Even in the freest of societies, man is surrounded by laws infringing on his "freedom"—from the speed limits on the road, to the building code for his home.

The Declaration made the limitation of the norm-giving prerogative of the authority substantively meaningful, by stating that only the requirements "in a democratic society" justify regulations; furthermore, it must only be requirements of morality, public order, and the general welfare. Any other collective aims are precluded. To give a random example, citizens may not be drafted into the army, in view of territorial aspirations of their country.

On the other hand, the Declaration says, *"a* democratic society." It implies that there can be different types of "democratic societies"—as long as they adhere to the principles laid down in the rest of the Declaration.

---

[8] The provision proclaims that the individual may be limited in the exercise of his rights and freedoms *"only* by law"—and not, that is, by any wanton discretion of the authority; this has to be read in conjunction with the carefully worded guarantees against arbitrary police actions, arbitrary court actions, etc., etc. The spirit of the provision is clearly expressed by the restrictive words, *"solely* for the purpose . . ."; *"due* recognition . . ."; *"just* requirements . . ."

The Universal Declaration of Human Rights

Beyond that, partisanship in favor of any particular "democratic society" would have been sociologically chimerical and politically unrealistic.[9]

The provision which limits the lawgiving prerogative of the authority adds that "these rights and freedoms may in no way be exercised contrary to the purposes and principles of the United Nations" (Article 29, 3).

We see here again that the principles of the fair international order—as expressed in the Charter and spirit of the United Nations—are carried over from the international field into the national field, and, indeed, onto the level of the individual. This is important and new.

The Interdependence between, and Identity of, Individual Rights and Public Morality

The universal Declaration of Human Rights is constantly conscious of the interdependence between the different rights and freedoms of man; and of the interdependence between, and, indeed, identity of, individual rights, the public order, and the international order. The fair state, the fair social order, and the fair international order continuously condition and reflect each other. *The acceptance of this monistic view in the Declaration is another of its most noteworthy aspects.* Most strikingly, it is expressed in the following words: *"Everyone is entitled to a social and international order* in which the rights and freedoms set forth in this Declaration can be fully realized" (Article 28).

This states clearly that promises of separate "human rights" will not be of great help, unless there exists a social order propitious to their realization; and that even a social order of such kind will not fulfil the "highest aspirations of the common people," unless there is a propitious international order. Hence, the logical conclusion is drawn, namely, to declare that a social order and an international order of such kind is the right of every individual.

If this should sound self-evident—or, let us say it, trite—so much the better. General acceptance of this doctrine would testify to a profound change of attitude on a fundamental problem.

The cleavage between individual morality and group morality is one

[9] It is interesting to recall, however, the phrase, "*just* requirements of morality, public order and the general welfare . . ." The version upon which the Commission on Human Rights agreed did not contain the word, "just." The addition of the word, "just," unanimously adopted by the General Assembly, indicates the degree of revival of natural law concepts in the world.

of the age old problems of humanity. As long as the individual may not steal an apple, but a nation may steal a province, as long as hunger, discrimination, exploitation, preventable disease, and ignorance make largely illusory the enjoyment of freedoms theoretically granted—a reconciliation between freedom and authority is impossible. If the principles which govern organized authority—that is, which govern political action and the behavior of states—are conceived as being fundamentally different from those which govern the actions of individuals, the problem remains one of authority *versus* freedom and remains insoluble.

In an era when the cleavage between the rules for individual behavior and the practices of states is tragically wide, the Universal Declaration of Human Rights *wishes to abrogate the disparity between the explicitly requested morality of the individual, and the implicitly accepted morality of the "reason of state" (authority)*. The fair public order, the fair social order, and the fair international order, are postulated as the rights of the individual. The three major values—freedom, justice, and peace—are identical for individuals, for groups, for states, and for the international community as a whole. These three values are, in turn, interdependent.

This approach disposes of some questions which have baffled philosophers and political scientists: does the community exist for the individual? does the individual exist for the state? which has the "higher" value? which is a means, which is an end? It tends to solve these questions by dissolving, or by overcoming, them.

To be sure, in our time, when the sheer technological and physical power of organized authority becomes ever more overwhelming, Napoleon's word will remain true, that *la politique, c'est le destin*. The word could be varied, to say that *international* politics make our destiny. This fact makes the approach of the Universal Declaration of Human Rights all the more realistic.

V

In conclusion, it may be appropriate to emphasize specifically a few other basic attitudes which are implied in the Universal Declaration of Human Rights. They are:

a. A rejection of any "organic" theory of the state; and of any other theory of the state which would attribute to the state metaphysical quali-

The Universal Declaration of Human Rights

ties, and, thus, by implication, always make the individual the expendable tool of the state.

b. A rejection of any race theory which would imply qualitative differences between different races.

c. A rejection of historical determinism. This is particularly important in the field of international affairs, and first of all with respect to the occurrence of *war*. If international calamities, crises, and above all, wars are "inevitable," then it would be a mockery to write into the Declaration that "everyone is entitled" to an international order propitious to the full realization of human rights—which, in turn, are summarized as freedom, justice, and peace.

d. The implied rejection of the concept of the immunity of "acts of state." The vague and, so often, misused concept of the "act of state," as if it were not an act of men made of flesh and blood, but divested from general morality and beyond the scrutiny of the common multitudes, is incompatible with the principles of the Universal Declaration. (It should perhaps be noted that the pretension of a Hitler—that the "leader" makes the most crucial decisions pursuant to his peculiar "inspiration"—is only a particularly crude form of this doctrine; and that more subtle forms of it are not unknown in democratic states.)

The Universal Declaration of Human Rights is optimistic. In this time of widespread gloom, it not only flatly rejects any doctrine of the inevitability of apocalyptic conflagrations; it also rejects doctrines, not uninfluential now, which stress the nightside of human existence. It is dedicated to a rationalistic and dynamic progressivism.

Or, it may be more nearly correct to say that the Universal Declaration is *conditionally* optimistic. The two year deliberations which preceded its final adoption, showed that its drafters were acutely aware of the fact that, for the first time, the yearnings of the peoples are matched by commensurate technological potentialities; but that the crisis deepens. The Universal Declaration is a solemn warning that we are at the crossroads, with enormous possibilities to one side, and the danger of complete collapse to the other, and that half measures will not do.

CHAPTER XL

Authority as the Validation of Power

By MORDECAI M. KAPLAN
*Professor of Philosophies of Religion,
The Jewish Theological Seminary of America*

BOTH AUTHORITY and freedom are variables. Being functions of each other, variation in the one corresponds to variation in the other. Though society is possible only through the exercise of authority by some and the surrender of some degree of freedom by those who are subject to that authority, the extent to which one may assume authority or be compelled to yield one's freedom is one of the most complex problems of human relations. *The one aspect of the problem which will be singled out in this paper as in need of being dealt with is the concept of authority as distinguished from mere power to coerce.*

It is evident that the term, "authority," is intended to convey something more than the mere fact of exercising power to coerce. It implies a characterization of that power as exercised in accordance with some principle, norm, or standard, which is recognized as binding or permissive by those of social and political status equal to that of the one who wields it. If it is also recognized by the one who obeys, the latter no longer experiences the restraint of his movements as a loss of freedom. Such obedience is then demanded and submitted to as a kind of "higher freedom." It is apparent how easily the concepts of authority and freedom lend themselves to word jugglery by which tyranny may make itself out to be an angel of blessing. This gives us the merest glimpse into the complexity of what may seem the simplest case of conflict between authority and freedom.

I

Human society did not come into existence with a ready rationale and a program by which to order its various social, political, economic arrangements. By the time man attained self-awareness society had long been in existence. Those who were stronger or more cunning were able to hold under control or to deprive of freedom those who were less strong or cunning. With the advent of self-awareness, however, man sought to explain to himself the connection of events in the world about him and to validate the control which the few exercised over the many.

The person who reflected on the situation was generally the master or ruler. It was he who was more likely to have the mind for reflection and the leisure to engage in it. That is all the more amazing, because one might imagine that such a person might well be content with the power which was his. When occasionally a slave or a subject rebelled, it was merely as a reaction to pain or deprivation. He would strike back blindly in the same way as the hen strikes back at the hawk that has pounced on it. Perhaps some such display of resistance would stir the mind of the master to an awareness of the master-slave relationship, and with awareness would arise the need for validation. Man has always tended to interpret his own will to power as the drive of a will outside himself, sanctioning his own exercise of power. He projected his will onto some transcendent being or god. The topmost ruler, especially the founder of a dynasty, would generally excel both in physical and mental power. By the same token that as king, he was able to hold the rest under his control, as priest, he was able to validate for himself the exercise of such control. He might also have been able to validate for himself the exercise of such control. The chief warrior or king would then also be high priest.

In time there would arise a priest guild that had as one of its main tasks the validation of the power exercised by the ruling class. The priest not only allayed the fears of the ruler, by assuring him that he wielded a power bestowed by God. He also poured oil on the turbulent spirits among the subjects. None of this was deliberate craft or deceit. Far from it. What could be more natural than for man to assume that what existed in his physical environment or in the social order was the way the gods wanted it to be, and that what the gods wanted was for his best interest.

On that assumption it was not for man, whether ruler or subject, to determine the limit of authority. Only those who could decipher the will of God could be entrusted with the task of delimiting authority.

It never occurred to those who promulgated the theocratic validation of authority to probe behind the actual distribution of power, and to find out how those who enjoyed it happened to come into possession of it.

Their assumption that all authority derived from God, was at the basis of the equally prevalent belief that all laws and customs were obligatory by reason of their divine source. Every ancient civilization boasted of some divinely revealed code. It was only in Greece where human self-awareness came to be further advanced than anywhere else, that law deliberately recognized as manmade first emerged. It was there also that thinkers went in search of a human source for the validation of authority.

II

The theocratic conception of authority was accepted universally and was the basis of all authoritative social arrangements and institutions, including the state, until the period of the Renaissance. It lived on in the doctrine of the divine right of kings. The fact is that in its traditional sense that conception of authority still leads a very vigorous existence in the teaching of the Roman Catholic Church. From its point of view, the entire democratic development of Western civilization, which has sought a different validation for the exercise of power from the traditional one, is on the wrong track. It uses the present tension and fear of global devastation as evidence of what it considers man's tragic aberration. It overlooks, however, the fact that in olden days, when the traditional view of authority reigned supreme, mankind was subject to evils which, in comparison with the goods they then enjoyed, loomed no whit less frightening than the contemporary ones.

Those, however, who can no longer subscribe to the traditional conception of authority are far from having found a satisfactory substitute. The one substitute which, since the eighteenth century has explicitly or implicitly served as a basis of Western democracy, has been the theory of social contract. That theory may be said to assume the following hypothetical situation: If by some chance or mutual consent the members of a society were to be entirely emancipated from the power of the ruling class, they would then, of their own free will and consent, surrender to those now in power as much of their own freedom as they would receive for, in return, security, protection, guidance, peace. The power which would then be exercised by the rulers would be authorized power or authority, in that it would be derived from the free consent of the governed.

The revolutionary character of this contractual conception, although it is seldom realized, is to negate entirely the idea that reason affords any justification for one human being lording it over another. Every human being, in so far as he is human, is king in his own domain. As, however, every person's domain overlaps other persons', all persons living in contiguity are compelled to come to terms with one another. Those who are capable of exercising leadership, organization, administrative ability, should offer their services in exchange for deference, emoluments, revenue, and production of goods and services. The leadership of the one in power is as much a form of service as the work done or emolument offered by the one who obeys. The fundamental validation of dominion over others does not derive from some transcendent or divine source. That validation derives from the rational procedure of a *quid pro quo* transaction.

The problem of authority and freedom thus reduces itself to one of getting the quid and the quo to be as nearly equal as possible.

It is an indisputable fact that those who exercise power seldom recognize the limits to which it must be subjected. Power inherently tends to expand. The contract once consummated, so to speak, the ruler, the master, or the boss, tends to do as he pleases. Kohelet a long time ago observed that "one man rules over another to his hurt." That situation, it is assumed, can best be met by a process which is in a sense a reenactment of the original contract. Each election is a kind of renewal of the social contract, when only those who are likely to keep the limits of the power voted to them are, theoretically at least, to be vested with authority.

Where then is the catch? It is in the fact that *in the transition from the theocratic to the democratic conception of authority the significance of opening up of new sources of power was lost sight of*. Before the commercial revolution, possession of land constituted a source of power, and the possession of power was validated by the religious authorities as a matter of divine course. But with the commercial revolution and the enlargement of the scope of production, the problem of authority and freedom grew more complicated. Exchange and machinery became sources of power which competed for control over the masses with the original source of power that had inhered in land. The English revolution of 1688 and the French revolution of 1793 were successful bids for power on the part of the newly risen merchant and manufacturing classes. But something in the human being which prevents him from being satisfied with the possession of power as naked force, least of all when that power is utilized against one's fellowmen, reasserted itself. The revolt against feudalism, therefore, had to be justified in terms of principles that would be acceptable to the rising classes.

Those who promulgated the contract theory, in order to validate the power of the commercial and manufacturing classes, were no more inclined to look into the way those came into possession of power, than those who promulgated the theocratic theory had been inclined to look into the origin of the landed or feudal classes. But the contract theory recognized the legitimacy of the claim to some utilitarian advantages on the part of the masses for the freedom which they surrendered. When those expected advantages did not materialize, and wage slavery, poverty, ignorance, began to increase, some people woke up to the fact that the problem of validating authority was not to be solved simply by some theory providing some plausible reason why those who are in possession of power should continue to hold it.

The only way to deal with the problem of authority is to note realistically, what kind of people actually wield the power whereby the freedom of others is delimited. It is soon discovered that those in possession of the means of production and exchange wield the economic power, which is the form of power that affects human life more profoundly than any other. On the other hand, those who are invested with political authority can exercise that authority only as long as it conforms to the will of those who control the economic power of the country.

III

The separation of political from economic power was a marked advance on the feudal system. When one no longer had to be lord of a manor in order to be a member of a cabinet or parliament, and especially when later one did not have to possess a property qualification to vote, the only considerations that would be expected to move those in authority to exercise their power appeared unquestionably to be those of abstract justice and the well-being of the governed. Actually, however, that separation of political from economic power turned out to be a delusion. Big Business is in a position to dictate the choice of candidates, the formulation of the programs, and to influence the final elections and the measures to be passed or defeated by those who are elected. The very separation of political from economic power removes all responsibility from Big Business to render a full *quid pro quo* accounting. It provides the window dressing behind which dominion can be carried on without validation in reason or justice.

How then has it really been possible for people, by and large, to delude themselves into believing that the millennium would come with the separation of political from economic power? The answer lies in the failure of people to have sufficient imagination to realize that, in a machine or technological age, an individual laborer or artisan is entirely at the mercy of the owner of the machine, who can dictate the wages and conditions of employment. Yet somehow people who are supposed to be wise and just have displayed a hysterical fear of trade unionism, as though that meant the end of all just authority and self-controlled freedom. Collective bargaining is still suspect. Only since the "New Deal" have trade unions been granted legal status; their place in society as a counter to the tremendous monopoly of power in the hands of Big Business is only gradually being recognized.

The recognition of collective bargaining in economic relations, is nothing more than the day to day application of the contract principle, of the *quid pro quo* exchange, to the most immediate and vital concerns of life. This is by no means intended to imply that trade unionism is a final solution of the problem. Unions are themselves organizations of power, and create many opportunities for the abuse of power. In our country we are now in the stage of experimentation with various methods of bringing out the greatest good latent in unionism and averting the many evils to which it is liable. We are, however, still very far from having arrived at a stable equilibrium between the economic power of management and that of labor.

Even assuming, however, that labor has succeeded in acquiring sufficient power to bargain with management on a *quid pro quo* basis, there is the danger that this very equality between them might simply mean a race between them for power over a third party, the consumer. The consumer group—actually the same middle class and labor group as is involved in the conflict between management and labor, now in the role of consumers—is victim of that conflict. Not until a way be found to mobilize and organize the power that inheres in the consumer group, will the spiralling of prices due to the struggle between labor and management for a larger share of the profit ever come to a stop. At present, the *political* authorities can afford to disregard the consumer group, just as they disregarded all labor claims in preunionism days. *If Western democracy is to be successful in applying impartially the social contract validation of power to all people alike, and not merely to one or another class, it will have to build up the consumer group into a power that will hold the balance between labor and management.*

If the exercise of power is to be validated, not along theocratic lines, but on the basis of the *quid pro quo* principle implied in the social contract theory, the check and balance system will have to be far more thoroughgoing than the classic division of political power into legislative, judicial and executive. The check and balance system will have to be applied to the economic powers wielded respectively by management, labor, and consumer public.

IV

The social contract theory, we have seen, approaches the problem of authority on the basis of the following three assumptions: a) The tradition that God ordains who shall rule and who shall obey is an assumption which those in power adopted to justify their exercise of power. b) In reason, there is no possible basis for assuming that power of body or mind entitles one to coerce others. c) The only source of authority can be a contract in which there is *quid pro quo* exchange.

The time has come when theorizing about the validation of power is no longer merely an intellectual exercise. The issue has to be brought to the surface, in order that our struggle for democracy be not merely a blind, sentimental allegiance to a cause which we intuitively fail to grasp. Not only for the sake of democracy must we be aware of each of the three assumptions implied in the social contract theory on which it is based. We must also reckon with each of them, in order to be fully cognizant of what underlies the two contemporary rivals of democracy.

Both Fascism and Communism, subscribing to the first assumption, reject the *traditional* validation of authority. Such validation would of necessity reinstate the power of the Church which is the main vehicle of that tradition. But they take sharp issue with democracy on its two other assumptions. Both Fascism and Communism assume that human society is as natural a fact as life itself. As society is inconceivable without the stronger commanding the weaker, so dominion or the wielding of power over others is inherently legitimate and requires no further validation.

According to both Fascism and Communism, the question which should concern human beings most is what kind of capacity or power in general do they need most, and what social arrangements can best help them to achieve such capacity?

V

According to Fascism, the power or capacity man needs most is that which enables him to ward off enemies, to wage war against those who are liable to despoil him of his possessions or to enslave him. The nation then becomes the one organization of power to which every citizen must give undivided allegiance. No subordinate allegiance to family or friend, to religious, social, or intellectual group dare compete. The one great objective, to which all else must be secondary, must be to make the nation as strong as possible. It must always be prepared for war. War for conquest is justified, as merely an anticipation of attack on the part of other nations which are the natural enemies of one's own nation.

Underlying the philosophy of Fascism—and to an even greater degree of Nazism—are two propositions which are deprecated in democracy: a) The will to dominion is so much part of man's nature that to tamper with it, to treat it as evil or even as in need of being brought under control, is to run counter to human self-fulfilment. b) The human being can achieve his self-fulfilment or salvation only through the medium of the nation. Any tendency to look to transnational values or media for salvation is bound to detract from one's allegiance to the nation.

The first of those propositions, which calls for the "transvaluation" of the values which have figured in the Judeo-Christian tradition was promulgated by Nietszche. He it was who lent respectability to the idea that many people had come to believe but did not dare to express. Thrasymachus, in Plato's *Republic,* and Machiavelli, his apologists to the contrary notwithstanding, may be viewed as precursors of the same conception of power. In Fascism and Nazism, the "will to power" is formally accepted as the norm of all human conduct which is to lead man to his self-realization.

The second of the foregoing propositions, which would have horrified Nietzsche, declares the nation's being and greatness as the ultimate purpose of the individual's existence. The nation is nothing less than God incarnate. Nothing less than a religious mystique will do to set forth the intrinsic character of a nation and its claims upon the citizen. Such a mystique would be incompatible with having every Tom, Dick, and Harry decide who is to lead the nation. Only the one who possesses the charisma that fits him to be the vicar of God as incarnate in the nation, can be the *Duce* or *Fuehrer*. His dictatorship is original, lifelong, and absolute. The authority of his subordinates is derived, terminable at his will, and relative. In obedience to his and their dictates consists the "higher freedom" of the citizens.

VI

Communism has an entirely different answer to the twofold question: what kind of power or capacity do men need, and what social arrangements can best help them achieve it?

According to Communism, what men need most is to produce the maximum amount of goods. Not the capacity to overcome enemies but to produce so much wealth that none shall be in want: that is the function of society. That would remove the main cause of war. What is wrong with democracy now is that, on the one hand, it condemns the very exercise of dominion as wicked and puts in its place the fiction of social contract, while, on the other hand, it permits the few who have economic power in the form of capital to exploit *ad libitum* those who are devoid of such power.

Although Communism treats the exercise of power as inherent in the very nature of society, it does not altogether disregard the need of giving it the status of authority. Authority, Communism holds, is validated in so far as it furthers productivity. Hence the type of productivity which prevails in any era determines not only the kind of power which is to be authorized or recognized as legitimate, but the entire pattern of cultural and social values and ideals. Thus the very meaning of validation changes in the Communist universe of discourse. In tradition, validation assumes the existence of some absolute norm sanctioned by divine origin. In democracy, validation assumes such norms as are sanctioned by reason. In Communism, validation is merely recognizing natural necessity as normative and preventing man's will from interfering with it.

Karl Marx sensed that to stop at that point in the evaluation of economic power was merely to diagnose what was wrong with the existing social order, from the standpoint of authority and freedom. To move the masses to take action, to give his politico-economic theorizing elan and drive, Karl Marx set it within the context of a philosophy of history. He made out history to be a dialectic progression based on class struggle.

All this has helped to identify the proletariat as the class which is at present in the process of remaking civilization. This it is doing by setting up its own dictatorship or authority in place of the dictatorship or authority of the capitalist regime. The struggle for power on the part of the proletariat is thus part of the process of human history which cannot be held back any more than the ebb and flow of the oceans. *For Communism, the proletariat plays the same mystic role as nation does for Fascism.* The proletariat is God incarnate. A recent article in *Pravda*, in answer to the one by Herbert Morrison, quoted in support of its own contention, the saying, "The voice of the people is the voice of God." The dictator is the vicar of Communism's God, and the mouthpiece for his voice. The Party is Communism's priesthood. Once again implicit obedience is man's "higher freedom."

What has been said so far of Communism is both expressed and implied in the writings of Karl Marx. Stalinist Communism, however, is much more than that. It is a synthesis of class struggle and Fascist nationalism, with Russia as the nation of destiny. To the mystique of dialectic materialism Soviet Communism has added the mystique of Dostoievski's "Holy Russia" and Panslavism. It does not require much imagination to realize the fanatical zeal with which Soviet Communism inspires the Russian masses. They are given the illusion, not merely of being free from arbitrary exploitation, but of exercising the only kind of authority that is compatible with the highest freedom. The increase in productivity and the potential rise in living standards, which are prevented from becoming actual merely by the warmongering of the capitalist nations necessitating feverish war preparations, are offered as evidence in support of that illusion. The facts are so manipulated as to obscure the tyrannical slavery which has had to be instituted to achieve the notable advances in productivity.

VII

There never would have been any Fascism or Communism, if democracy had not stopped short in its analysis of authority and freedom, and had not been contented with divorcing the state or political power from church and nobility. There would have been no need for looking either to nationalism or to the class struggle for a way of solving the problem of authority and freedom. Let us hope it is not too late for democracy to wake up and to apply itself to the task of carrying out its social contract theory of the social order to its logical conclusion. The state would then hold the balance in the three cornered struggle for power: management, labor, and consumer public. The resulting formula for the amount of power each may wield would then give such power the character of authority. Such authority would define the amount of freedom to which individuals and groups are entitled.

In addition, it is necessary for those who wish to promulgate democracy to bear in mind the psychological role of mystique in both Fascism and Communism. The fact that mystique is resorted to in the propaganda of both *isms* should not prejudice us against the intrinsic significance and indispensability of mystique in any cause, it must appeal to the heart and the imagination as well as to the mind and the reason. The function of a mystique is to give cause in a cosmic setting, where it takes on the character of inevitability which is certain to overcome inner resistance and inertia. So far the wholesome fear of demagogy has inhibited the advocates of democracy from growing emotional about it, or referring to it in cosmic terms.

This inhibition must, for the sake of democracy itself, henceforth be overcome. There is no reason for hiding under a bushel the light of cosmic significance which inheres in democracy. In the first place, the very proposition, that no man has the right to wield power over another, and that all domination should be a form of service in a *quid pro quo* arrangement, signifies that man is the first creature that refuses to be intimidated by brute force. The very need of having his exercise of power over others validated and rendered authoritative, however gropingly and erringly man has tried to meet that need, points to a "Power that makes for righteousness" not alone within him but also beyond him, even as the will to live points to a Power beyond all living beings that makes for life. Democracy thus possesses a mystique which calls upon man, individually and collectively, to metamorphose himself into a being that will be rid of the tendency to tyrannize over the weak and to be intimidated by the strong, and that will look to cooperation and love, instead of to struggle and hate as instruments of happiness, self-fulfilment, or salvation.

CHAPTER XLI

Autonomy and Theonomy

By EDGAR S. BRIGHTMAN
Borden Parker Bowne Professor of Philosophy, Boston University

I. *Postulates of the Discussion*

THE PRESENT DISCUSSION will not be from the point of view of anthropology or sociology, psychology or economics (Marxist or capitalist), important as all those approaches are. It will be an inquiry in social philosophy; more specifically, in social metaphysics, assuming that metaphysics includes not merely the traditional ontology, cosmology, rational psychology, and theology (or modern variants of them), but also a metaphysical theory of value (axiology). The writer accepts a personalistic theism as a philosophical truth (not as a necessary truth, but as a probable hypothesis). As a democracy allows differences of opinion, it is taken for granted that such a discussion would be of some interest to anyone concerned about democracy, regardless of his own personal convictions.

The specific *postulates* of the present paper, are, therefore, two.

1. *The relations of freedom and authority are functions of beliefs about values.* This postulate does not mean that social relations are caused by beliefs. This would be one-sided and false intellectualism. On the other hand, it would be even more one-sided to overlook man's conative nature, or to ignore William James's definition of the self as a "fighter for ends." The ends for which a self strives are ends in which, in some sense, he believes. Many social processes, then, are guided by beliefs in ends to be attained, or ends that are worthy of respect and devotion. These ends are man's ideals or norms; they are prized. The fulfilment of such an ideal norm is what we call a value. It is, of course, true, as has been implied, that much of social process is determined by events which are not voluntarily chosen as ends, and may not be valued at all. Nonvoluntary or involuntary aspects are present in all social process. Man does not

control the climate or the weather (save perhaps for rare "rain makers"); man cannot choose his own heredity or create by his will the laws of nature or prevent by his will any influence of society from affecting him. Yet whatever be the effects of heredity and environment on man, whatever be one's theory of causation or determinism, or social process, everyone makes a distinction between those situations in which he is relatively free and those in which he is not free at all—or free only either to acquiesce or to perish. Freedom is always relative. Absolute freedom, unrestricted by facts or laws of any sort, is a fiction. Real freedom is freedom within limits. Freedom is essentially a power to choose and carry out what the individual prefers under the circumstances. To put it otherwise, freedom is a power to choose from among the attainable values.

Authority is defined as a power which prescribes either what values are to be attained, or how they are to be attained, or both. The physician is an authority because he shows how health may be attained; if his prescriptions are not followed, nature may cause increasing illness or death. A church is an authority because it defines certain spiritual values and prescribes the conditions of attaining them. A state is an authority because it prescribes the conditions of political cooperation and well-being. The nature of the enforcement of authority varies with individuals and institutions. But the point of the first postulate is that both freedom and authority derive from beliefs about values. Unless values are believed in, freedom and authority are both aimless and empty.

There is a second postulate.

2. *Theism is true*. Because this postulate has been and is shared by many millions of Jews, Mohammedans, Hindus, and Christians, as well as others, it is socially useful to assume it here, rather than to debate it. By theism is meant the belief that God is a conscious and perfectly good, spiritual being (that is, a person). Such a God is purposive and benevolent, wise and loving, immanent and transcendent. From this postulate we shall omit reference to the differences that arise from beliefs in special revelations, and different churches, hierarchies, rituals, and creeds. These differences exist and are potent cultural forces; but our inquiry centers about the significance for democracy of belief in God, whatever additional beliefs may or may not exist.

II. Definitions Presupposed

1. *Autonomy is the belief that a person should acknowledge as true and binding only those principles which he voluntarily imposes on himself.* This does not mean arbitrary anarchy and self-will. It means, rather, that, in dealing with persons, the Platonic preference for persuasion rather than violence is to prevail; that no belief or mode of conduct should be "forced down the throat" of a citizen of a democracy; that "the consent of the governed" is presupposed in all good government. In short, autonomy is at the heart of democracy. The right of revolution was accepted in 1776, because autonomy was taken for granted—an autonomy that means, on the one hand, that conscience is more fundamental than any civil authority, and, on the other, that social obligations autonomously accepted are imperatively binding. It is a dangerous principle; yet democracies which recognize it seem to have outlived heteronomous rivals that have denied the rights of the individual.

2. *Theonomy is the belief that the basic laws of the universe* (the laws of physical nature and of ideal values alike) *are laws of the will of God and constitute the conditions of all possible and valuable achievement.*

III. Inferences from the Postulates and Definitions

1. There is no more essential conflict (or difficulty for freedom) inherent in the claims of autonomy and theonomy than there is in the fact that all freedom exists within limits, and that all values rest on conditions which man did not originate.

2. Theism implies that man's freedom (his autonomy) is a gift (or creation) of God, allowing man spontaneous initiative and choice within a limited field. God has created creators, presumably because He values free persons more than He would value puppets or robots. It is obvious, also, that He has created an immense variety of persons, to whom He has given an indefinitely wide field of choice as an arena for struggle and development. The misuse of freedom by man is a price God is willing to pay for man's freedom. God's authority, therefore, is an authority that not only recognizes, but even creates, freedom. The ideal of democracy doubtless has developed as a result of many complex influences; but to deny that faith in a good God Who creates man as free and responsible has played a large part in the development of modern democra-

cies in Europe and America, is to deny historical, social, and psychological facts.

3. Value experience (apart from any theory of revelation) implies that one purpose of God—perhaps His basic intrinsic purpose—is the development of respect for persons. All value exists in, of, and for persons. No state of affairs of which no person is or could be conscious— no matter how breathtakingly beautiful or sublime it would be if experienced—could be called valuable or good in any intelligible sense. Unrealized value is valueless, as unheard avalanches are soundless. The actual world is a world of actual and potential value (and of disvalue also, to be sure) for persons, value that can be adequately realized only as persons respect each other. In a word, true love is a condition of true value. As related to belief in God, this means that theonomy prescribes autonomy. It is God's will that persons respect themselves and each other individually and cooperatively. That there could be a society of goodwill without belief in God, is conceivable; that believers in God may fail to carry out in practice the implications of their belief, is an all too evident fact. But that belief in God is a logical and psychological source of goodwill and of universal cooperation, cannot well be denied. In short, God is love.

4. God requires that men live socially. It could also be said that nature, or the biological ongoing of life, requires sociality. (Even hermits have parents, heredity, and memory of social relations; or, if nurtured by animals, develop social relations with them.) But to say that God requires social living is not a mere repetition or endorsement of the natural fact of sociality. It relates that fact to its source in a God of love, and to the ultimate purposes of such a God. Religious beliefs do not contradict scientific facts; religion puts science into a larger setting—the setting of ultimate good.

5. Social life is a moving imbalance, or dialectical process of freedom and authority; or, theistically speaking, of autonomy and theonomy, of man's self-assertion (be it search for truth or rebellion against its restraints) and God's purposive guidance. There is grave and tragic difference of belief among theists as to how this imbalance may best be expressed and preserved in actual individuals and institutions. But, whatever their institutional or doctrinal differences, all theists believe in man's moral responsibility and in God's purposive guidance, as well as in God's respect for man's free choice.

The imbalance or dialectic, to which attention has been called, presupposes extraordinary patience on God's part, and extraordinary confidence that man's freedom will respond eventually to divine love and purpose. Without such response—on some level—the principles of reason and love are either forgotten or subordinated or wrongly related. When that happens in a human society, either freedom or authority runs riot. When freedom runs riot, we have anarchy: lawless rebellions against just governments, wildcat strikes, unprincipled individual living. When authority runs riot, tyranny, autocracy, and relentless cruelty are in the saddle, as has so often occurred in human history. Anarchy does not prove that freedom is evil; autocracy does not prove that authority is evil; but their abuses serve as a constant reminder that the will of God is that men shall seek and maintain a living society in which freedom and authority, conscience and law, shall both be respected. Imperfect human wisdom and faltering human wills are a guarantee of an imbalance between the factors. The disastrous consequences of an excess of imbalance are a reminder that the dialectic of history (a history both this-worldly and other-worldly) should move on to a fuller actual reconciliation of autonomy and theonomy. That it will continue to approach such a reconciliation is the faith of theists, a faith that is not an assertion of necessary, linear, uninterrupted progress, nor of confidence that scientific knowledge alone guarantees devotion to and realization of all ideal ends. Nor is such faith necessarily a pure optimism; it has always been compatible with full recognition of human sin and rebellion, and has often acknowledged obstacles and sources of suffering and delay in the universe other than the will of God and the will of man—call them demons, or the Abyss, or the receptacle, or matter, or the Given, or what you will. But all theists, whatever their gloom and despair about the present may be, have looked forward to a future—either in this world or the world to come—in which a society shall exist wherein loving theonomy is the basis and guide of free autonomy. The imbalance of social forces does not mean the doom of free society for a theist. It means rather that the force of intelligent love is the most attractive, as well as the most powerful force in the universe.

6. It follows that theonomy is a primary social force toward tolerance, peace, and progress on the highest level. This is not to say that theistic belief is always such a force. It is all too evident that theists have hated and fought and deteriorated. The history of theistic cultures has been

in these respects hard to distinguish from the behavior of atheistic cultures. But theonomy is not to be identified with the behavior of theistic believers at any stage of history. Theonomy is the rule of God in the universe. Wherever there is tolerance, love of peace, and real progress, there are actual evidences of the rule of God. When theists become intolerant they are deviating from the rule of God; when they become warmongers, they are distrusting God; when they deny or impede progress, they are skeptical of the power of God in the world. Theism implies theonomy; and theonomy implies both respect for autonomy and confidence that autonomy, enlightened by reason and guided by love, will cooperate with theonomy on an increasing scale.

The view here presented presupposes that theists will respect atheists; that believers will cooperate with unbelievers for the common welfare; and that God's love for all men, regardless of their differences of opinion about each other and about Him, is far more comprehensive than is usually supposed by religious individuals of any creed. The existing intolerances of the left are scarcely more gentle than the worst intolerances of the right. The existing social conflicts can be solved only by social behavior *as if* there were a just God of love supreme. Actual theists assert that *there is* such a God. Is there any ground for devotion to tolerance, peace, and progress that is more cogent than God? One practical and immediate lesson may be drawn from these considerations, namely, that it is both socially and religiously more important for theists to become better theists, than it is for them to expend so large a proportion of their energies in denouncing Communists or other real or supposed atheists.

Comment by Swami Akhilananda:
We would like to suggest that the abuses of religion and theonomy are due to the lack of stabilization of the emotions and proper discipline. Theonomy can become operative in human society and inspire people to mutual love and respect, only when the belief in God is made dynamic in personal living. It should be emphasized here that higher values of life, namely, conquest or subordination of the disintegrating human urges or "inordinate affections," are essential for the establishment of a harmonious social order with individual autonomy. We want to make it clear that theonomy can be successful when autonomous individuals go through the required practices for successful living on the plane of theonomy, with consequent integration of the emotions and development of will power. Otherwise, there is every chance of keeping the ideal of theonomy on a mere intellectual level, rather than on a practical level, resulting in all sorts of social evils on which the critics of religion are already passing judgment.

The lives of the great mystics belonging to different religious groups prove to us that conviction of the presence of God becomes more and more dynamic, only when the individuals control their lower urges and express the highest qualities of love, patience, forgiveness, and endurance.

Comment by Rudolf Allers:

Although the general tenor of Professor Brightman's essay is such that I can wholeheartedly subscribe to it, and although I especially agree with the author in what concerns the compatibility of autonomy and theonomy, there are some points on which discussion appears not only possible but required.

One of these points—to raise them all would be too lengthy—may seem of minor importance for the general topic; I believe, however, that it is rather fundamental. I refer to the paragraph dealing with "value experience."

It seems to me that the view proposed in this passage is dangerously subjectivistic. It results from an identification of value and end, as goal of human aspiration. But is it true that all value exists in, or, and for persons? Value may be defined without reference to human ends. It may be defined as the state of perfection, that is, that state in which a maximum of potentialities of a being is actualized. Thus, a crystal is more perfect, and, hence, represents a higher value than the amorphous pebble. Not because it pleases our eye or guarantees purity to the chemist, or any such reason, but because in the crystal a "perfection," not actually existent in the pebble, has reached actuality.

"Unrealized value is valueless." Yes and no. First, it is potential good. Secondly, it is envisaged, in human action, as a good to be realized by the person's actions. Thus, it is effective, and it is because of its axiological character. Something unreal cannot be effective; something valueless cannot become an end.

Wherefrom might a good intention derive its goodness, if not from the fact that it aims at the realization of a value which is not realized? An intention does not become good *ex parte post.*

So far as I can see, there is some incompatibility in asserting the existence of a Divine Law, on one hand, and denying reality to values unless they be realized in human actions. "And God saw every thing that He had made, and, behold, it was very good."

Professor Brightman's reply:

There is, of course, a difference in fundamental philosophy between Professor Allers and myself. He is an Aristotelian realist; I am a Lotzean personalist. Yet on reconsideration, I think that he can see that the subjectivism he finds in my position is not so dangerous as he fears. Let me (following Scholastic practice) make a distinction. There is "dangerous" subjectivism and "nondangerous." The "dangerous" kind derives all values, all norms, all ideals, from man alone—individual man or social man. The "nondangerous" kind finds all reality—God, man, nature—to be nothing but personal consciousness of different levels and kinds. It finds human consciousness to be dependent for its powers and its very existence on the will of the divine consciousness. It locates all values in the persons who feel them, to be sure, but for personalism man is not the measure; for it, as for Plato, God is the measure. The norms (the ideas of Plato or Plotinus) by which all values are truly measured lie in God's knowledge, which we human seekers approximate as best we can. Is this "dangerous" subjectivism?

Comment by Hoxie N. Fairchild:

I warmly agree with Professor Brightman's general thesis, but believe that at certain points it could be presented more effectively.

"Autonomy," he says, "is the belief that a person should acknowledge as true and binding only those principles which he voluntarily imposes on himself." But does this person believe that the principles which he voluntarily imposes on himself are shaped by the independent, self-sufficient powers of the human mind? Does he say, with Emerson, "No law can be sacred to me but that of my own nature"? In that case we have an autonomy which either ignores God entirely, or romantically attempts to deify manmade value. We cannot say that this is not "real" autonomy so long as thousands of people, many of whom insist on calling themselves religious, interpret the term in this way. It seems to me that the religious person can be described as autonomous only when he voluntarily imposes on himself those principles which he believes to be reflections of the will of God.

Similarly, there is still a widely held theonomy which denies the voluntary element in man's response to the will of God. Hence it seems to me that there is real danger of conflict between autonomy and theonomy. The conflict disappears only when autonomy is defined theonomously as free acceptance of God's will, while theonomy is defined autonomously as God's desire that man should accept His will freely. I do not think we can be Hegelian about it, for the only autonomy and the only theonomy which can be harmonized do not stand in a thesis-antithesis relationship. They must be thought of synthetically from the beginning, each defined in terms of the other.

Earlier, Professor Brightman says of his second postulate, *Theism is true:* "Because this postulate has been and is shared by many millions of Jews, Mohammedans, Hindus, and Christians, as well as others, it is socially useful to assume it here, rather than to debate it." Although I seldom find myself talking in the accents of John Stuart Mill, I would suggest that it is never socially useful to assume the truth of a disputed proposition, merely because it has been held by millions of people. I personally believe that theism is socially useful, but I am forced to grant that the proposition is self-evident only to theists. And the social usefulness of assuming that theism is true, does not necessarily follow from the social usefulness of theism.

Professor Brightman's reply:

I appreciate the clarity of Professor Fairchild's comments, but it seems to me that he is reading in ideas which I did not state or intend.

When I speak of autonomy, he asks whether I mean that the autonomous principles are "shaped by the independent, self-sufficient powers of the human mind?" My reply is twofold: (1) it seems to me impossible to conceive that man's powers exist in a vacuum, independent of the use of reality; and (2) the vital question for democracy is not whether every autonomous person agrees with Professor Fairchild and me about man's dependence on God, but rather how a fair-minded democrat should treat the autonomous person, even when he deviates from a recognition of God. This, it seems to me, is overlooked by my critic.

Professor Fairchild's second point quite misconstrues my intent. Not for one moment do I believe or did I say that the belief of millions in God proves or tends to prove the truth of that belief, any more than the popularity of sin proves sin to be right. I remarked that the belief of millions makes it "socially useful" to assume belief in God for the purposes of this discussion. Surely my critic would not suppose that the socially useful and the true are the same!

Comment by Barna Horvath:

The contribution, by the author of this paper, to the investigation of *Postulates of Theories of Freedom and Authority* is, to begin with, the statement that the immediate form of our problem is *not philosophical* and becomes so only by considering the wider issues of values acknowledged and their sources, issues which enter into the individual's submission to, or revolt against, authority.

Professor Brightman, approaching the problem from the vantage ground of *social metaphysics,* proposes as postulates of the discussion, the *axiological* proposition that our problem is a *function of beliefs about values,* and a *theological one,* namely, that *"personalistic theism"* is a philosophical truth (probable hypothesis).

But, interestingly enough, there is no reference to values in the author's *definition* of autonomy. And in the definition of theonomy, it is declared merely that the will of God is the source of the basic laws of the universe (part of which concern "ideal values").

The definition of autonomy as the belief "that a person should acknowledge as true and binding only those principles which he voluntarily imposes on himself," seems to formulate the sufficient reason of freedom rather than its dependence on "beliefs about values" or theological hypotheses.

Indeed, it is no negligible problem whether freedom (in the sense of autonomy) is but the *consequence* of values realized or violated, or their condition and *source*. It may be argued that the laws we impose upon ourselves, laws necessarily pointing to values, make us free, and that, consequently, our freedom is dependent on values realized (or violated) by ourselves. This is the *objectivistic* interpretation. But it may be argued also that, in the field of autonomous morality, the laws are binding and engendering values, only because we impose them on ourselves freely, and that, therefore, the value of anything moral derives only from our freedom. This is the *subjectivistic* interpretation.

I believe the latter interpretation is somewhat nearer to the accepted meaning of autonomy. Whoever is autonomous, is *lawgiver* to himself, and every "value" of such laws, and of the obedience to them, derives from the *legislator*. In case of moral autonomy, this legislator is our own free will. On the other hand, autonomy is far from arbitrariness, and, therefore, it is the natural fountainhead of law and value.

Freedom is necessarily connected with values, either as their source or offspring; but *it* is not so sure whether we have to speak of values at all, in order to explain freedom and authority. Both seem to be the function of necessity or causality, law, source of law, and their negatives; whereas value seems to be a more remotely connected conception. As a matter of fact, the classical problem of free will has been discussed for centuries, without any reference to values, merely as the problem of a choice, free from necessity, and, as it were, arbitrary in its complete indifference to motivation (*liberum arbitrium indifferentiae*).

The author considers freedom as "relative" and "within limits." Such freedom, he holds, is "a power to choose from among attainable values." Authority, on the other hand, "is defined as a power which prescribes either what values are to be attained, or how they are to be attained, or both." Consequently, "both freedom and authority derive from beliefs about values."

"Belief" seems to be something *subjective,* while "value" is defined as "fulfilment of ... an ideal norm." It is obvious, then, that the author prefers a subjective interpretation, and conceives of value as something *subsequent* to norm or law. In this case, the first postulate is *not* necessary, because freedom and authority are functions of norm or belief, immediately, and of value (norm-fulfilment), only more remotely. Freedom, in the sense of autonomy, means obviously making or imposing laws on ourselves; values come into the picture, in the sense of the author, only later, with the fulfilment of such laws.

Quite apart from the formulations of the author, it is undeniable that free choice implies evaluation. The big problem is, however, whether freedom is the *creature or the creator* of values.

We may now consider usefully the author's second, theological, postulate. He defines theonomy as "the belief that the basic laws of the universe (the laws of physical nature and of ideal values alike) are laws of the will of God and constitute the conditions of all possible and valuable achievement."

From this definition it is possible to argue back to the problem of values. If values originate in the (free) will of God, freedom is certainly prior to values. The same will hold of the free will of man; this latter is no creature of creatures, but of the Creator, for —as the author so eloquently remarks—"God has created creators."

It is characteristic of *theonom positivism* (Occam) that it derives moral laws from the arbitrary will of God. St. Thomas Aquinas, on the other hand, has answered rather cautiously, the question, whether natural law derives from God's being or will. His answer is that its *content* derives from God's being, its *validity*, however, from His will. To Occam, it is conceivable that God reverses the moral order, so that murder becomes virtue and honesty sin. To St. Thomas, this is not conceivable because God's will cannot contradict His being (from which immutable principles of good follow).

Now we may answer the question of the *first* postulate. Freedom has a subjective, as well as an objective element. The first is the living source of its validity, the second that of its content. The subjective element is that a man can choose as he pleases; the objective element is that he has to choose in a certain way, in order to remain free, and that, in order to do so, he has to accept and obey certain laws (or principles or values).

In order to bring out this, it is not necessary to speak in terms of value. But it is no mistake either to use this rather modern terminology, provided this language does not reduce value to "belief," "evaluation," or "fulfilment." To signify something akin to the objective element of freedom, "value" must cover the whole field of freedom from a particular angle, namely, the angle of the *contents* of law a man has to respect, in order to become or remain free. Freedom itself becomes, then, a value, and, as the sum total of those contents, the supreme value. In this sense, a man may, indeed, "choose freedom," meaning by this phrase a continuous progress in freedom, beginning with a first, happy choice.

As to the *second* postulate, the author proposes it because it is "socially useful," because "the existing social conflicts can be solved only by social behavior *as if* there were a just God of love supreme," and because there is hardly "any ground for devotion to tolerance, peace, and progress that is more cogent than God."

This proposition seems to be vital in a conference which bears in its very name the idea of cooperation between science, philosophy, and religion. We should distinguish, however, between the fruitfulness of such cooperation in general, and the claim that religious truth is an indispensable postulate of the solution of a particular theoretical problem.

In this sense, I do not believe that a recourse to theism is necessary, in order to clear up the particular problem of freedom and authority, or, to put it more modestly, that this thorny problem would present less *theoretical* difficulties, if recourse is taken to theism.

From a *practical* point of view, however, I admit that religious belief may serve as the solid *backbone* of freedom. This is a reason why it is dreaded and persecuted by totalitarian countries. A man who has found his freedom in God, has found also an easy solution of authority. Protected by the Highest Authority, he will obey or resist the lesser ones, as they are confirmed or condemned by the former.

In general, the cooperation between science, philosophy, and religion is most fruitful, if each respects scrupulously the autonomy of the other, as provinces of one and the same culture. Science, in our time, has worked miracles, but failed, as yet, to make mankind as a whole much happier. Yet in science methods of verification are more developed than in philosophy and religion, and this is the reason why a mathematician or physician, for purposes of his own research, has little need of philosophy or religion.

Philosophy stands on a lower level of verification than science, but treats problems vital to presuppositions both of science and practice; its only weapon is reasoning pushed as far as reason still yields answers even to ultimate questions. That the miracles of science are not turned into general human happiness, is due chiefly to the weakness of philosophy or its lack of persuasion. Nevertheless, it is clear that in this field reasonable argument is the only admissible criterion to which even theological truth has to submit, if it wants to grow into a philosophical one. The times are gone when philosophy was *ancilla theologiae*.

But this does not mean that theology or religion has not its own legitimate, autonomous field of knowledge. Only in this field the air becomes still thinner than in philosophy, and methods of verification are—from a scientific point of view—still more doubtful. Yet the problems dealt with are momentous. Indeed, the most valid claim of religious truth to our attention is that scientists and philosophers alike who *deny* it, perhaps as unwarrantedly as it is *affirmed*, might be turned into fools, *should* it be verified one day.

In spite of their autonomy, there is some *atmospheric* influence of each field on the others. It would be a good thing for philosophy and religion to become scientific; the lower standard of verification in these fields is also a failure and frustration of science. This makes philosophy and religion *desirous* of science. Science, on the other hand, gains width and depth, if it is at least informed of the problems it is unable to solve. The scientist, as a man, surely gains by considering the fine idea of the author that "the force of intelligent love is the most attractive, as well as the most powerful force in the universe."

Professor Brightman's reply:

Professor Horvath's comment on my paper is of a rare and admirable sort. Instead of attacking, he seeks to understand. His paper is mostly a careful and enlightening analysis of what I have said; it is a model of internal criticism. If all international relations could be on this level, the world would be more cooperative and more peaceful.

A few points in reply may illumine the thoughts further. It is true that "there is no reference to values in the author's *definition* of autonomy," that is because the principle of autonomy, while essential to personality and to ethics, is not the whole of ethical theory. For a full theory "freedom," as Professor Horvath says, "is necessarily connected with values."

Belief, Professor Horvath thinks, is "something subjective." It is true that it occurs in a subject or person, but it is directed toward objective reality. All knowledge is but tested or "warranted" or "confirmed" belief, in my view.

In holding that ideal values are laws of the will of God, I do not mean to agree with Occam; I am closer to Thomas Aquinas. But I would prefer to say that both validity and content of norms derive from God's being; actualization of them, from His will. That autonomy is valid, is a truth not created by will, but discovered by it.

My paper did not aim to show that "a recourse to theism is necessary in order to clear up this problem of freedom and authority" (although I do actually believe that no alternative solution is satisfactory). My aim was only to show the democratic and social implications of belief in God. My view of reason as coherence, forbids me to accept entirely the suggestion that "theology or religion has . . . its own *autonomous* field of knowledge." No field can be entirely independent of all other fields, there is no absolute autonomy, save the autonomy of The Whole. Perhaps Professor Horvath's "atmospheric influence" hints at this. I thank him for his penetrating remarks.

CHAPTER XLII

Freedom and Authority

By BEN ZION BOKSER
Rabbi, Forest Hills Jewish Center

FREEDOM IS THE condition which underlies the possibility of any organism's growth toward self-realization. The need for freedom derives from the fact that growth is not automatic, but that it depends on certain indispensable resources, in the environment or in the organism itself. In its highest context freedom is a necessity throughout all existence, and it is not concerned solely with human life. A flower will not grow to the fulness of its hue and to the greatest riches of its fragrance unless it is given an ample measure of sun and rain and the stuff of nourishment which it sucks up from mother earth. And its growth will be dependent also on the absence of impediments, like rocks, which might fall upon the tender plant and crush it before it has had a chance to blossom, or like weeds, which might deny our precious flower the space it needs for its full unfolding.

The conditions of growth depend in part on whether or not the society in which we live makes available to us the resources adequate for our needs. It is in this sense that justice is a condition of freedom. Regardless of how goods and services are produced or distributed in a society, the criterion of freedom is always made manifest by the destiny of the individual. Does his world make available to him *de mahsoro,* in accordance with his needs? Unless this condition is satisfied, there is no freedom.

There is one major difference between freedom as required by an organism in nature and freedom as required in human life. Nonhuman organisms proceed in their growth without factors of voluntarism. The cycle of man's life is more complex, and it involves the exercise of voluntary choices. Man carries within himself instinctive vitalities that comprise the energizing ferment of his life. But by nature these vitalities are not organized into a pattern. They wait to be refined, to be directed, to be integrated into some comprehensive pattern in which each shall be given its proper scope for the service of life's larger goals. Thus man needs culture and discipline, the culture and discipline of the mind, as well as the culture and discipline of the will.

The training of the mind and the will, in turn, depend on the recognition of life's transcendent goals. In the absence of a clear vision of life's goals, one lacks the perspective from which to harmonize the conflicting pressures of his nature, or for that matter of the world beyond. We then become slaves of momentary whims or of some particular instinctive pressure which has then come to dominate us. The man who has become addicted to narcotics is free in the sense that he does what he pleases. He is not free in relation to the larger possibilities in his nature which he allows to remain frustrated. Indeed he has become a slave to his drug. But freedom is not the absence of passion. It is rather a passion for the highest, a passion for a great purpose and the capacity to proceed for its realization.

What is the great purpose which a person must thus seek to realize? It is the measure of his uniqueness as a person. Like that flower which has attained self-realization through the creation of its distinctive hue and fragrance, so does man attain the highest rung of his own growth when he brings to fruition the distinctive powers which inhere in him and which can be realized only through him. For that is the most significant fact about people—that for all the elements which they have in common, they remain essentially unique. Each person is an original creation, embodying distinctive excellences. There are no duplications in the hierarchy of life. There are phases of the question of life's teleology with which we cannot deal here. But this much is surely clear. It is obviously the purpose of man to grow toward the discovery of his distinctive self, and it is his function to express that distinctive self, as a means of serving the world into which he has come. Jewish tradition has expressed the conception of man's distinctiveness by the doctrine that each person is made in the divine image. In each person is embodied a unique aspect of that image.

The highest measure of freedom thus brings into convergence the human self with the will of God. Freedom is the capacity for self-realization. It is, from another perspective, the capacity to fulfil the will of God. A free man is not without a master. He is mastered by God and by the divine purpose for his life.

Freedom does not mean living without compulsions. Those compulsions emanate not only from nature but also from man. Those compulsions may be exercised from within the person himself, by his own mind and will, in order more effectively to realize consciously sought goals. Compulsions may also emanate from a source beyond man—from the social unit of which he is a part, such as the family or the state. When is the exercise of control by man over man consistent with freedom, and when is it not? Here we move into the considerations of authority.

The state no less than the family exists as an agency for the control or direction of life. Its goal must, however, be related to the general purpose of all life. It is the means by which individuals are enabled to grow toward their distinctiveness. The need of the physical resources on which life depends, the need for the education of the mind and the will, cannot be met by the individual through his own private effort. He must depend on a multitude of social processes, on the production and distribution of a variety of goods, on the creation of conditions of safety and health, to permit his unimpeded development. The implementation of these goals may curtail the actions of some people, but that curtailment is a means to a higher end. It is a means to the creation of justice, which is a condition of freedom.

The consent of the governed is an important prerequisite for the validation of the state and for investing its acts with authority. The noble goals it professes are not enough, for selfishness can readily mask itself by a pose of noble intention. Tyrants have invariably offered themselves as instruments of some great purpose, designed to benefit the people. But even if sincerely conceived, the purposes of government, as well as its establishment, must ultimately emanate from an act of free concurrence on the part of the people. Freedom is not the absence of determination; it is self-determination. According to the Talmud, even the Torah would have had no authority over the lives of the people, but for their freely given consent to live by it.[1]

This principle of consent makes government into self-government, and completes the prerequisites of its authority. Its compulsive acts are then consistent with freedom. Power used to curtail the actions of individuals or groups, is used authoritatively, if it is maintained with the consent of the governed, and if it is directed toward the goal of arranging for an order that will make available to each person the resources he needs for his self-fulfilment.

[1] *Abodah Zarah* 36a, *Shabbat* 88a.

The restraints imposed in the name of justice open new opportunities for life even to those who bear their burdens most heavily, but that is not their sole justification. The services of the welfare state illustrate some of the tangible benefits people may gain as a result of the regulatory powers of society. These gains, moreover, are not confined to any one social class. They who are taxed most heavily in order to create those services, gain through the greater stability which their society thus acquires. Where men are denied justice, the seeds of class war are planted, and its woes fall upon all alike.

The highest motivation of that restraint is in the dimension of altruism, which is one of the self's attributes. The pressure of an individual for his own assertion as a person is a necessity to gain the means of subsistence, to maintain an area of self-expression. It is a vital safeguard against his submergence and extinction. But the area of self-expression which every person requires for the fulness of his life, is, among other things, an area of service. Whether these restraints are assumed voluntarily or through the mandates of law, depends on a variety of circumstances. In the family they are usually assumed voluntarily. In the state voluntary restraints have generally proved insufficient. But their highest justification is the will to help others to the means of their self-fulfilment.

Every exercise of power, even if authoritative, has elements of ambiguity. The state—or the family—is always tempted to see itself as a final end. And those who wield power in its name often confuse their private interests with those of the larger group. Moreover, the decision to regulate or control in a given direction always includes contingent elements. It represents acts of discretion in which the general principle is only imperfectly embodied. Its control may be too rigid or not rigid enough; its laws may in fact favor certain people at the expense of others, making it possible for some to enjoy more than what they need of the resources that sustain life, and others not enough. Freedom, like justice, is therefore only a relative achievement. At the edge of freedom is power impinging upon it, authoritative power when legitimately used, or arbitrary power when illegitimately used.

Tyrants, to rationalize their use of arbitrary power, have occasionally pretended to be God. They have claimed infallibility which is an attribute of God and not of man. All human claims to absolutism, as all acts of arbitrary power, are idolatrous. All power exercised by men has only relative authority. An important safeguard of freedom is, therefore, a recognition of man's fallibility, including the fallibility of those who exercise the power of government.

One of the most common expressions of arbitrary power is the power employed against social deviants. The very business of society is to encourage originality in its citizens. It is to encourage their growth toward uniqueness. The suppression of deviants is the effort to create uniformity, but only where individuals are not fully grown can there be uniformity of life. Deviants may have to be curbed if they seek to impose their way of life by violence against the group. Then *they* make a bid for the mantle of tyranny. But an existent pattern of life in society must not be regarded as a final achievement that is beyond criticism. The deviants who project forms of life other than the one that dominates in their environment carry the seeds of new growth for society. They at least carry the challenge of criticism which all life needs for its periodic purification and renewal. Man fulfils his highest self not when he conforms to others but when he finds the distinctive note his own life can play, and when he does indeed play it.

We have treated here freedom as it bears on the life of the individual. It is similarly involved in the status of the group. Communities have a life of their own; they have distinctive characteristics, distinctive cultures, toward which they must grow, and which they must feel free to express in life. Their possibility of self-realization likewise depends on antecedent conditions, and the fulfilment of those conditions creates their freedom. And as they, too, have their being in a larger context—a world community—their freedom must remain consistent with incidents of curtailment. Nations have been reluctant to admit a sovereignty higher than their own, but the necessities of finally establishing a viable international order will eventually move them to concede it. The power that curtails an individual or a nation does so with authority if its motive is a larger justice. It is arbitrary power when it is pursued for ends other than justice.

Freedom is positive and it is negative. It means the presence of those conditions, economic, social, cultural, which govern the growth of man toward his uniqueness as a person. It means the absence of coercion in the choice of the directions of one's growth or in the expression of distinctive attributes toward which one's life has grown. Consistent with freedom is discipline, whether exercised by one's own mind or will, or by the judgments of the society of which one is a part and to which one has given his uncoerced allegiance. That discipline may curtail life, but it is vindicated by contributing toward the conditions which underlie freedom for ourselves or others in our society. A power that has been so vindicated has been invested with authority. And it is the fact of its authority which brings power into harmony with freedom.

Comment by Swami Akhilananda:
We are concerned by Rabbi Bokser's interpretation that a person is an unique being. Would it not be more effective, if we understand that diversity among individuals is based on unity of existence? It seems to us that if we overstress individual uniqueness, we are likely to lead the people to an egocentric and self-assertive attitude, even though Rabbi Bokser feels that "The highest measure of freedom thus brings into convergence the human self with the will of God." In the study of the history of mankind, we find that the more individual uniqueness is emphasized, the more is difference created without any basic unity. We beg to offer the suggestion that if we can find unity in diversity, we can eliminate many of the dangerous and anti-social elements from modern society, as we are all "made in the divine image."

Self-expression becomes dangerous when we forget our interrelationship with God. When we realize that there is basic unity in all human beings from the transcendental point of view, then we find the real basis for cooperation in our interpersonal relationships. Besides, this very understanding enables us to develop the motive of service by cultivating self-imposed self-discipline without repressing our inherent tendencies. In that case, there would be no danger of losing our uniqueness or individuality, if we remember that there is unity in variety, as we are made of one divine substance or the divine Reality.

Comment by Nels F. S. Ferré:
I have read Rabbi Bokser's paper with interest and appreciation. My only comment concerns a difference of emphasis. Service and community seem, to me, in the paper to be made too much a part of self-realization. As I understand man's relation to society, under God, he is as much a socius as an individual and as much an individual as a socius. In the same way, the stress on "deviants" frightens me. The more creative variety we have the better. My point of caution is not directed at this point. Nevertheless, the paper can abet an aristocratic individualism. Too many people are frustrated in our culture, because they do not succeed in being original. We must be thankful for creative deviants and encourage enriching variety, but I believe that these will come in a wholesome way the more we relax our striving for being different, original, creative. Obviously Rabbi Bokser enjoins freedom and authority for community; but, for me, the structural stress is too individualistic in its total emphasis. "The measure of his originality is the measure of his life's significance," is a rule which can become a crushing burden. Not even the excellent paragraph starting at the foot of page 486 can offset the total impact, for me, of this kind of thesis throughout the paper as a whole.

CHAPTER XLIII

Authority and Freedom

By NELS F. S. FERRÉ

*Professor of Philosophical Theology,
School of Religion, Vanderbilt University*

GENUINE AUTHORITY is for freedom. Such authority, concern for the common good, is of such a nature that the more it commands the more freedom is also made real. As a matter of fact, the more authoritative is the concern for the common good, the less it is experienced as authority while the more it is understood to be true freedom. The kind of love which is concern for the common good is most authoritative even while it is least authoritarian. Any age, perhaps particularly our own, needs authority to make general freedom real. The nature of such authority and of such freedom is our subject.

Our thesis is that absolute authority inheres only in the will of God which is the source and center of all concern for the common good. The will of God, being love, is always for the fullest possible measure of practicable freedom, and is finally for the perfect freedom of every creature.[1]

I. *Freedom and Community in Love*

The inmost nature of love is to bestow freedom on its objects. Love is not content with the respecting of each one as an individual. Love seeks fulness of community. Such fulness demands the finding of the highest development of every part of the community and the most satisfactory relations on the part of the community both within and without. Love therefore bestows freedom on all its objects because it is creatively concerned with them. Love wants each one to become genuinely

[1] For fuller elaboration of this thesis compare my series, *Reasons and the Christian Faith*. Volume I, *Faith and Reason*, Harper & Brothers, New York, 1945, deals with the problems of origins; Volume II, *Evil and the Christian Faith*, Harper & Brothers, New York, 1946, deals with ends; and Volume III, *Christianity and Society*, Harper & Brothers, New York, 1950, deals with our present practical difficulties.

himself, but knows that no one can become his fullest and truest self apart from cooperative enterprise. The authority of love is the organic constraint for a cooperative community of free and genuine individuals. The fuller and wiser the concern, the more freedom is fostered within the total conditions of man's organic need for community.

The Greek name for this kind of love is *Agape*. When Agape becomes the final authority we have an absolute which can never become fanatical. This we need. For mankind both longs for an absolute and dreads it. False absolutes, when seriously practiced, at best curtail freedom and at worst destroy. The history of religion records enormous cruelty and persecution. Religion, in general, is with real right considered to be a divisive factor. Narrow loyalties, served religiously, tear and destroy the social fabric. Many honest and competent thinkers have therefore dismissed religion as a unitive force of civilization.

Agape by its very nature, however, cannot be fanatical and divisive, for it is organically constituted by inclusive concern. This concern precedes religious and culture content. It is the ultimate unitive function which engenders and lives in the forms of freedom. As such it is definite without being specific. A child can depend upon a mother's love, if real, without knowing specifically from day to day what the mother is going to do or to give. There is thus an absolute unity presupposed in Agape which nevertheless acts as a lure to freedom. Agape includes by nature both the quality of belonging and the opportunity for creative self-expression.

Such concern, moreover, comprises a pedagogical principle whereby, as far as possible, each person or group is first of all accepted for himself where and as he is. The good is not forced on him, but offered to him at the point of concrete relevance. Persons are not subordinated to principles. Lives are not made means to moralisms. The good intention is not substituted for wisdom and concrete knowledge. The good will must rather be tested, as far as it can be, by the actual consequences which would ensue from its intentions. The more absolutely Agape is understood and accepted, therefore, the more inclusive and concretely wise it must seek to become. Concern for the common good, precisely as the nature of the ultimate, is consequently the greatest possible incentive to growth in freedom. Agape as the absolute insures as fully as possible man's intellectual, moral, and religious autonomy. That such freedom is, nevertheless, both social and responsible we shall see later.

Authority and Freedom

Nor can Agape as authority be artificial in nature. Freedom is in the nature of things. The child if held too tightly rebels. Man needs freedom. Personal needs are organic to the world out of whose womb the persons came. The authority for freedom is thus constitutive of the self and its world. A closed universe enacting exact equivalence of causal continuity we believe to be a methodological abstraction. We do not know, on the other hand, a world of merely random choices, of spontaneity in the sense of mere causelessness or of lack of prior motivation.

The freedom which we are discussing is, rather, conceived in terms of field theories where origination is both inside and outside the skin, where there is a give and take in the forces which impinge on the organism and a certain degree of plasticity in the selection of them and adjustment to them. The higher we rise into personal organisms, the more real this kind of freedom becomes.

Freedom may be looked at in some such terms as "the pattern of purpose" of a magnetic torpedo which changes its own course with every change in the course of the ship which it pursues. We believe personal purpose to pervade the Universe, in accordance with the total unity which constitutes our world a universe. Particularly such purpose pertains to the discrete personalities which respond selectively within this general unity of the universe. Agape is therefore never artificial but expressive of the nature of reality.

When concern for the common good constitutes the ultimate nature of authority, furthermore, freedom can never be arbitrary. There can then be no escapist otherworldliness. Neither can there be any "pious" individualism which evades social responsibility. Nor, again, can there be any externalism which relegates the bettering of the world to legislation. Agape is, through and through, personal and social in nature. Solitude is a precondition for society. Privacy is a necessary ingredient in full community.

God's love is thus a principle and power which intends and achieves satisfactory freedom. It is an absolute—the more it is accepted in actual practice the more true freedom is actualized. Sovereignty and liberty are thus symbiotic terms; they belong together within the nature of reality. We shall be free only as we know and accept the truth. This truth, furthermore, cannot be arbitrary because it involves inclusively the common good. Freedom is not for the strong alone. Freedom is not for the majority alone. Freedom is not for the mass alone. Freedom is for all. Except freedom be responsible to this end, therefore, we neither know nor do the truth.

Nor does freedom remain mostly a duty. When we become freed for the common good, we lose the fever of life, the illusions of a false individuality, and find the reality of our organic needs fulfilled. In the language of high religion, our duty becomes our song. The religion of law becomes experientially transcended and fulfilled by the gospel of love.

God bestows freedom responsibly. Only as we mature in insight and within the experience of concerned freedom, do we begin to glimpse the whole which was planned from the beginning. Penologists are now saying that the most important factor in raising socially oriented children is a father who is both strict and loving. God is such a Father. Agape is completely concerned but also completely unsentimental.

We must consequently learn freedom within the ambiguities of nature and history. If reality showed us a clear face, we should never know the freedom of real and riskful choice. The history of self and society God set within the uncertainties of nature, social processes, and finally of death. We are stubbornly self-centered from childhood, not puppets, mere qualifications of the absolute. At the same time we are restlessly driven toward others by our sense of duty and drawn toward them by our gregarious desires. Beyond human relations, too, we long to be right ultimately. We want to be more than socially adjusted. The unconditional demand of the right haunts us deep within, and the eternally good draws us toward the complete satisfaction of our being.

The finding of the will of God, Who achieves community, through the pedagogy of nature and history, is the goal and ground of creation. God's will, we believe, reaches beyond the confines of our death. The total meaning of this life is therefore organically understandable only within the larger meaning and logic of the eternal love of God. Nevertheless, because God has made and explains the nature of our lives and of our world, His will also provides the fullest meaning for life and explanation precisely for this world.

II. *Freedom and Authority in Institutions*

The authority for freedom which constitutes God's concern for the common good operates with and in the individual, but also through institutions, which are both expressive of the community and also instrumental in fulfilling the self. These institutions are primarily the family, the church, the school, and government.

The Family

The family is the group within which the child normally experiences its first understanding of authority and freedom. The parents should be authoritative but not authoritarian. The parents who continually decide for their children stunt their growth. The parents who allow the children too much their own way give them a false freedom and thus prevent their proper growth. Freedom should be responsibly and wisely bestowed, according to the development of the child and in relation to the other members of the family. The American home is threatened by sentimentalism more than by undue severity. The inviolability and sanctity of righteousness becomes real through parents who exercise authority for the sake of the children in a wise and understanding way.

Authority should know how to do away with itself as the children mature. There should be growth in freedom and the steady development of the assumption of responsibility. Authority should be *flexible, but full,* at every level of need. Freedom should be real, according to the measure of the child's ability and maturity, and increased at the rate of its maturing. When peace, order, and security are found at home, through strict and loving parents, the children are very likely to grow up well adjusted and creative members of the community. "Social engineering" can do no better than to secure the fullest possible conditions for a happy homelife, the continual living within the will of God for the common good.

To do so requires many conditions. In most cases and in the long run religious faith of a high and inclusive kind is the most important factor. Love in the individual and at home is found most fully when the parents genuinely believe in the love of God, and when they through authentic worship at home find the kind of community which bespeaks the reality of their faith. Romantic rationalism and naive idealism forget the stubbornness of sin. Through family worship the children are also allowed the knowledge of the prime source of authority for freedom. There they find the power to become delivered from the pressures of self and society. Love can be believed, for love seeks only the welfare of those who trust it. Love is therefore the essence of legitimate faith and faith in God's love expels fear.

In order that to faith may be added virtue, all the other conditions of a happy home are also to be sought. The family should belong to and actively cooperate with a high grade of religious community. The economic order ought to produce both real security and private initiative. Love lives not only by family worship and concern, but in relation to a society that abets and encourages, by its very social and physical makeup, the freedom in fellowship which is based on responsible concern.

The family combines the religious, the moral, the legal, and the physical aspects of authority. Family life to be effective, however, should be centered overwhelmingly in religious and moral suasion. Strictness should be clearly within the context of love. Shall we put the case this way? The exercise of physical sanctions should be at the minimum, though naturally there is an implicit physical force which backs up parental authority. Most important is the dependability of the moral order and of the love which backs it up. The parents should always be more interested in their children as persons than in principles, but they should also know that persons do not live well apart from principles.

The Church

The church, moreover, is the institution where religious motivation is the only legitimate force. The religious constraint should be solely the love of truth. With truth, again, we do not mean intellectual formulas, but the content of the living truth which is, first of all, God's will and, secondarily, the purpose for common good which underlies all creation and all social processes. The church is the place where authority ought to be present in its pristine purity. For this reason religious authority is the more legitimate, the more it respects and encourages freedom. By freedom we mean not individualism, but, rather, spontaneous or unforced concern for the common good.

Religious authority is characterized by inclusive freedom. The very nature of the family makes limited responsibility and concern a functional necessity. The main bulk of living centers in the concrete cares of a limited group. The self expands intensively in relation to a very few. The family thus at least tempts to exclusiveness, even in attitude.

The church should enact the unlimited family. It should stress by its very being, the extensive relation. The function of the true church is to uphold and to teach the authority which frees men from the fever of self and the divisiveness of limited loyalties and local groups. The authority of the church is the will of God, and the inclusiveness of this will ought to be reflected in its organization, worship attitudes, and actions.

With relation to the family, the church should have no authority except moral suasion and spiritual power. The family has a measure of real autonomy of thought and action which should be kept sacred, even by the religious group. No other institution can substitute for the family with full effectiveness. The basic function of the family is not mostly the control of sex, as some aver, but the creation of community. The intensive family and the extensive family, the church, thus complement one another.

The second basic aspect of the church's authority, though in a real way it belongs to the home, too, is making religion real. We know a great deal of how things ought to be, both personally and socially, but we do not do what we know ought to be done. The problem of authority is, therefore, crucially the problem of motivation. Apart from the solution of this problem we can have no more than some theoretical rat races. We have to overcome ignorance, indifference, and sin. If the church has mostly the authority of ritual, creed, or convention, it will fail mankind. What the church needs most of all is to be able to teach people how to worship at such a genuinely effective level that religion becomes a personal power and a social force for the good.

When worship helps set men free by the breaking of the power of sin and by the creation of free spirits, then alone will the church wield its true authority. When the church will help people to see beyond their limiting horizons toward the never closing reaches of the unlimited love of God, then the church will have the authority of the truth that sets men free. When the church achieves within itself freedom and faithfulness in fellowship under and within the love of God the church will illustrate its native authority.

The School

The intrinsic authority of the school is the authority of truth. All enforcement of rules for cooperation is instrumental. A serious responsibility is laid by truth on the teaching profession. In the name of truth much harm has been done. Some of it has been done by fanatics, loyal to a limiting insight; some of it has been done by indifferent teachers, without concerned commitment.

The truth of God's concern for the common good should be the ultimate unity behind all teaching. Care for the inclusive welfare ought to be the bedrock of teaching conviction. There can be no sectarianism in such an attitude and action. Here we have religion both beyond and behind democracy. Here we have the absolute beyond but also within the relative. Here we have the cohesiveness of ultimate truth with ample room for real pluralism of cultural and religious development. Here we have transcendence and creativity joined in a happy and productive marriage. The schools are set under authority because they cannot escape the ultimate obligation of truth to be concerned with the common good, but they are set under an increasingly liberating authority.

The schools need real freedom in order to achieve their own end. When the government is too near the school system with too heavy a hand on its controls, the schools are likely to reflect distortingly the interests of the party in power or the narrower interest of the country. The government itself needs to be scrutinized by the truth, as it is seen by those not directly involved in governmental decisions.

In a similar way the schools, in general, should be free from direct church control. The knowledge imparted in schools needs the context of religious faith and the power of religious motivation, but the church cannot take the place of the school nor lord it over the school. The church and school should both carry out their intrinsic assignments, but with the fullest possible cooperation. The Harvard report on *General Education in a Free Society* concludes that "to isolate the activity of thinking from the morals of thinking is to make sophists of the young."[2] Both in church and in school there ought to be cooperation on the part of people who see the total need of man for disinterested search for truth and its effective communication, on the one hand, and the obtaining, on the other, of the lively concern which gives spontaneous motivation to the general good.

The authority of the school is ideally truth. We can see that the church, as vested tradition, and the government, as vested interest, might plead their authority over against the school. A conflict is then bound to arise

[2] Report of the Harvard Committee, Harvard University Press, Cambridge, 1945, p. 72.

which, very likely, is better settled in favor of the school. The church and the government want to prevent the teaching of the truth which challenges their content of authority. The school, however, does not enforce its authority on either church or government, and should be free to find and to teach the truth that it finds. All the church and the government have to do, if the arena is free, is to point out the error of what is taught.

Naturally we are not dismissing the authority of the past. No teacher is free to disregard the horizontal transcendence of accumulated knowledge and insight. Education is basically a social act. *For this reason there should be thorough indoctrination of the good*. The matters of common concern and freedom ought to be instilled. To avoid commitment to truth or to the concerns of the content of truth, is to teach false attitudes and to encourage ineffective and bad action.

The new good must naturally always be tested by, and related to, the old good. Social stability depends upon the transgenerational accumulation of patterns of insight and behavior. Nevertheless, all human knowledge and wisdom is relative, in some measure, and the authority of past skill must also meet the test of the new vision. Today's needs demand revision of yesterday's good. The pragmatic test is always a valid aspect of any criterion of truth as a whole. With however much reverence for the past, the faithful teacher will never owe ultimate allegiance to any dimension of truth except the vertical: the eternally transcendent will of God from which new light is ever ready to break forth and to become created.

The Government

The authority of government is neither the natural order nor positive law. It is neither physical might nor political control. The final authority of government is, rather, the will of God for the general good. No government is, therefore, ever sovereign as such. The very concept of sovereignty on the part of a human institution is idolatrous deification. The government is under divine authority to legislate, judge, and enforce all matters with the view to the individual and the common welfare. Thus no one person or group, even a majority, has the right to exercise arbitrary authority over God's other creatures. Every political institution is under divine obligation to foster, maintain, and protect all possible freedom on the part of all people, both individuals and groups.

Practically this means democracy is divinely ordained. Democracy is not "majorcracy." Nor is democracy the running of a country or a community by a few on behalf of the many, without effective participation of the many. Representative government can in effect deny the true nature and authority of democracy and destroy the government of free people. Democracy is, first of all, the fostering and protecting of the common good under constitutional safeguards of individual and minority rights, both by preventing its being thwarted by some dissident minority and by frustrating any mob rule by the majority.

Courts also ought to judge according to the rules of the common and the individual good, being more conscious of God's will for the common good than of immediate pressures from partial interests, even on the part of the majority. Every intellectually and morally responsible person should have the right to vote. The machinery for elections ought to be safeguarded and so constituted as to encourage independent, informed participation. When church and school have true independence, they can assume particular responsibility for the finding and the dissemination of facts and evaluations beyond the immediate pressures of political interests.

Economic power, moreover, should not constitute *de facto* authority of government. We now have undue force both subtly and openly exercised by economic privilege. This is indirectly true, not only in terms of ease for voting, pressure on the employed, the power of money over the ministry and educators, but also through the control of means of communication and the backstage power over legislators. Kitchen cabinets usually have long ears for moneyed interests. Property exists under God, however, for the common good. Its function is to develop responsibility, initiative, concern, cooperation, and community. It is given for the development of both freedom and fellowship, both initiative and security. If social incentives are to rise in quality and intensity, we need to subjugate property to the common good with urgent but patient wisdom. Regulation, planning, or ownership by society, of the large framework of property would very likely remove the pressures of private groups which distort and destroy the common good.

On the other hand, there should be such genuineness of consumers' reward that real freedom would be encouraged, while individual initiative and responsibility would also be developed. The point is not, however, to destroy the openness of the capitalist system nor to do away with its real improvements, whether in production or in the living conditions as a whole, but rather to fulfil it by means of a creative capitalism which might also be called a democratic socialism. Such creative capitalism will require a new high level of social incentive which cannot be had apart from the proper exercise of the authority of home, church, and school. Totalitarianism of government and of property, on the other hand, destroys the genuine place which individualism and minority status should have. Marxism is a killing cure.

What we need, rather, is the progressive ridding of our system of its own contradictions and the development of its own strong points. This can be done only, we believe, as we continue in the general direction of the Social Security Act. The fire department, for instance, was once free enterprise with such slogans as "No money no squirty." We now know that fire is a social problem calling for social control. Such socialism is creative capitalism. The post office was once a private institution with conflicting and confusing rates. We now consider mail to be a problem for the country as a whole. Such socialism is creative capitalism. No formula can be drawn, but the rule can be laid down that property ought to be increasingly regulated or owned by society as a whole with a view to the common good, but that consumers' rewards and workers' movements should always be ample enough to encourage private responsibility and to support religious, educational, and social groups, endowing these with real freedom to criticize and to change the government. *In some such way* we shall arrive—granting the right social motivation and educational attainment—at a dynamic synthesis of freedom and security, of the recognition and reward of the strong, and of helpful concern for the weak. *In some such direction,* we believe, lies wise concern for the common good.

Obviously sovereignty has been exercised by nations in the sense of final, earthly authority. In one sense, of course, the nation has legitimately carried on final social and physical control: God's control is indirect and mostly through units of delegated power. Now the time has come, however, when the nation can no longer afford to remain sovereign, even in this secondary sense. Some form of effective supernational organization is necessary with the power of sanction, not so much over individuals and groups as over the states themselves.

The larger the unit of togetherness, however, the more the stress needs to be made that authority is for the sake of the fullest possible freedom in fellowship. Freedom is with and for others, not mostly as an abstract ideal but as a concrete experience. When the authority of God calls for worldwide government on one level, then, the authority for actual freedom calls at the same time for the utmost diligence in the maintaining of all possible local freedom for creative independence and initiative. Thus local government needs to be made even more real and vital. Every rung on the ladder of bigness needs also to be treated with care as to its distinctiveness, from the smallest to the largest. More care should also be exercised increasingly with respect to functional diversity.

Peace is not a matter of the external control of strife. A few hydrogen bombs centrally located might become the possible instrument for that! Peace is rather a matter of fulness of satisfactory relationships on every level of life and in every dimension of experience. The more authority is centralized, therefore, in terms of the needs of ever larger units of togetherness, the more liberty needs also to be developed from the smallest unit to the largest. Cultural pluralism and political diversity will find a real place for the nation. The state will not be abolished and absorbed, but fulfilled and protected, by doing away with nationalistic wars and the emergence of world government and world planning.

III. *The End of Authority*

Apart from the complete realization of the kingdom of ends, the end of authority is never completely reached. Our kind of history is not the place for this perfection, but even within our kind of history the nature of the end of authority can be observed and the more this end is concretely realized the better. We are not, then, talking of any proposed utopianism but rather of a possible measure of attainment toward which we must always aspire as individuals and as a society.

It is not enough to internalize authority. Ethics can be authoritarian in structure without external sanctions. A dictatorship or an autocratic theology can indoctrinate in such a way that individuals, even when away from the power of the authority, will *willingly* do what has been taught them. As a matter of fact, the psychological structuring of authoritarian ethics is usually such that motivation becomes a matter of habituated obedience. Freedom as riskful choice or as personal insight becomes a burden to those who have been kept immature. Voltaire sneered that a priest was worth ten policemen! Authoritarian ethics can thus be internalized and need not exist mostly as external authority. The difference between authoritative and authoritarian ethics is therefore not that of external and internal authority.

Authoritative as opposed to authoritarian ethics, however, can be discovered by the fact that it fosters genuine freedom. Freedom is authentic, not when people do what they want after they have once become indoctrinated by authoritarian standards, but rather when they do from personal insight and by personal choice the very things which accord with their fullest nature. *Authority can be judged as legitimate only by the genuineness with which it abrogates itself.* Love is interested in the doing away with itself as authority, in order to mature freedom and for freedom to mature. This abrogation takes place both externally and internally. Jesus said that he had called his disciples servants, but that now he would call them friends, for the servants do not know the what and the why of the master's doings. A friend does. The law exists to teach us the right relations which are for our own true good. When the lesson has been taught, the external compulsion is abolished. The authority has become our friend. We live no longer by law but by love.

The same thing is true internally. What was once done as a duty becomes done as a privilege. The duty becomes our song in the night of our pilgrimage. Where there is no law there can be no trespass. The community is no longer lived on the legal level. Morals are no longer the compulsions or even the constraint of the right. Ethical obligation gives way to the inclination of concern for community. Man's life becomes characterized less by obedience and more by spontaneity. Man becomes a free soul willingly and gladly accepting right relations. Authority is exchanged for freedom within the very citadel of life. The will of God for the common good becomes man's perfect freedom. Learning the better relations is no longer a mere duty or drudgery, but the desire of our life.

Instead of being over against God and others, we come to belong to the holy community within which true happiness arises. The shadows of the cave are exchanged for the light of the free day. Man is, to be sure, immeasurably far from understanding, let alone realizing, this freedom within the will of God, but the more His authority is understood and accepted, the more individual and social peace and constructive community is achieved. For the finding and the realizing of this end, there can be no patented formula. Man, however, has freedom to learn better social relations. His life is not as though it were in a chicken yard, where the chickens develop closed structures of pecking at each other! Man has freedom to learn better living relations. Though no formula can be concretely full, however, clear directives toward the personal and social finding of such conditions, are minds and lives open and ready for the concern which is as concrete as every individual, and as wide not only as the world but as the heart of God.

Comment by Swami Akhilananda:
In describing his conception of the function of the church, Dr. Ferré tells us that "The authority of the church is the will of God." We wonder how he can identify the authority of the church with the will of God, knowing the historical background of religious movements. It is disturbing to find that an institution is being equated with the will of God. There are many religions in the world which are still operating and inspiring millions of people who do not have an institution called the church. Moreover, aside from Hindus, Mohammedans, Buddhists, Taoists, and many Jews, there are innumerable Christians who would not be willing to equate the activities of the church with the will of God. May we suggest that the awareness of God, rather than the church, is fundamental in understanding the will of God. It seems to us that the attainment of the love of God and neighbor should be emphasized in the family and social ideal.

The authority of the government and other such institutions should also be regulated and controlled by the religious ideal—love of God and neighbor. Economic and political power is bound to be demoralized, which we see happening today, because individuals have abandoned the religious ideal. It seems to us that the emphasis ought to be given to religious practices, such as worship, prayer, and meditation, in order to keep the religious ideal bright in individual, family, and national life. Authority in any sphere of life is bound to be tyrannical and despotic, if the ideal of the culture is changed from awareness and love of God to the attainment of the greatest amount of pleasure.

Comment by Edgar S. Brightman:
Two questions arise. 1. Why is "authority" not explicitly defined? Are authority and freedom synonymous? 2. Does Professor Ferré take into account the social implications of all of his statements? For example, he says: "both in church and in school there ought to be a union of religious faith and knowledge"; and "there should be thorough indoctrination of the good." Then the social question arises, whose "religious faith"? Whose concept of "the good"? In a society in which there are Christians of diverse creeds, Jews who differ, secularists of many kinds, Hindus, Buddhists, Mohammedans, Bahaists, and others, what authority is to determine the content of indoctrination? Is it to be "God's love" (and then the secularists will go to the Supreme Court) or simply "love" (and then many will complain of lack of content). That the schools should impart information about religious faith and ideals of the good, is not unreasonable; but that indoctrination should occur in public schools, is a questionable democratic practice.

Professor Ferré's reply:
With authority I mean rightful power over others to direct and to control them. Such authority is for freedom, because the purpose of experience is to mature in creative and cooperative activities and satisfactions.

I believe that indoctrination of God's love is necessary, because democracy by its very nature enacts, when successful, this love. *God's love means educationally that concern for common good is in the nature of things.* The democracy which fails to teach cooperation as essential, denies its own nature. That the essential good is also ultimately real, is a proposition that must be settled on the basis of truth, by means of free investigation and open discussion. Naturally such truth cannot, in the nature of things, be forced on anyone, but the more this truth can be generally accepted, the stronger will be democracy.

Until we so believe, we are forced to teach, by action or inaction, that the very nature of democracy is founded either on falsehood or mere convention. Democracy will have strong social power, when it is generally realized that concern for the common good is not merely optional or desirable but actually in the nature of things.

Comment by Barna Horvath:

I am somewhat surprised to find that the author is more *interventionist* in his concrete proposals than one would expect, on account of his abstract definitions. For instance, he advises parents to be strict to their children, although "within the context of love," because "there are times when to 'spare the rod' is to sin against the children." I am afraid this is not the best pedagogy, nor easy to reconcile with the definition of genuine authority. Is not the *example* the best method of parental authority, and is not corporeal punishment poisoning the very well of such authority? Is it no exaggeration to speak of the "stubbornness of sin" in the case of small children, to whom corporeal sanctions might be applied with less tragic and detrimental effects than to older ones?

Nor can I suppress my doubts against the statement that *"there should be thorough indoctrination of the good"* in the school. Indoctrination is a term taken from the vocabulary of authoritarian or even totalitarian ideology, and means an educational method which is, in my opinion, hard to reconcile with either freedom or genuine authority. Even if, relying on another formulation, by the author, of his educational principle, namely, that "the matters of common concern and freedom ought to be instilled into the depths of young character," I am inclined to consider our difference of opinion terminological rather than substantial, I have to underscore the commonplace experience that the method of "indoctrination" sweeps away in an objectionable manner all the pedagogical advantages of methological doubt.

It is of course in the political and legal field that it becomes most difficult to draw the lines from the germinal principle of divine agape right to the problems with which government is faced. The appeal to divine authority means here the emancipation from earthly authorship, and, accordingly, we read that "sovereignty on the part of a human institution is idolatrous deification." But it seems to mean also, busy interventionism on the lines of "regulation, planning or ownership by society, of the large framework of property" and of "world government and world planning."

But I am sure the author is aware of the limiting principle: *corruptio optimi pessima.* In his opinion "Marxism is a killing cure." His own program, too, depends for its justification not only on the purity of philanthropy with which it is proposed, but upon considerations of feasibility and expediency. How much freedom is conditioned by this rational, in addition to the philanthropic, element is clear from the problem of judicial freedom, briefly treated by the author. Courts have to judge according to law, constitution, and statute. To ask them to be "more conscious of God's will for the common good than of immediate pressures from partial interests, even on the part of the majority," is a proposition to be rejected, in so far as it opens loopholes to judicial arbitrariness. It is a defensible view, only when it means that courts, in case of doubt, have to reconcile public opinion or the majority's interpretation with their own enlightened opinion. In this sense, every judgment is not only a legal, but also a moral action of the judge for which he bears full moral responsibility.

CHAPTER XLIV

Freedom and Authority as Functions of Civilization

By CHARLES W. HENDEL

Professor of Moral Philosophy and Metaphysics, Chairman of the Department, Yale University

I. *Our Need of a Theory of Authority*

"WE MUST THINK less about authority and more about liberty." This was Jean Jacques Rousseau's advice to his fellow citizens of Geneva in 1764, when they were involved in a bitter controversy with their government over certain constitutional powers and rights.[1] Today it behooves us to talk less about liberty and to think much more about authority than we do. Let freedom stand, superior in value and importance for man. But if we do not reckon with the function of authority and if we do not see how it is properly related to human freedom, we leave freedom in "splendid," utopian isolation, something in a far off shrine before which we bow as we go our ways in a present world in which some authority is always calling the tune.

Rousseau's advice was meant for the civilized world of the eighteenth century, and the world followed it, for those words were but expressing a tendency of history itself. During a century and a half after Rousseau's time liberty won first place in the hearts and minds of men. It is still gaining allegiance in the far corners of the seas of the East and in Africa. Yet among the modern peoples of older civilization today authority has taken a new lease of life, and it is having worldwide effects in contemporary civilization. Hence we must take it more seriously than we have done, and study what there is in it and what role or value it should have in the democratic way of life.

[1] Jean Jacques Rousseau, *"Lettres écrites de la Montagne, Lettre 7,"* The Political Writings of Rousseau, edited by C. E. Vaughn, University Press, Cambridge, 1915, II, p. 220, and Charles W. Hendel, *J. J. Rousseau: Moralist,* Oxford Press, Oxford, 1934, II, p. 301.

But Americans are apt to recoil at once from the very thought of such an inquiry. It goes against the grain to entertain the possibility that there might be any value whatsoever in authority. For we have been bred in a political tradition which is hostile to the idea. When our written Constitution was prepared, the greatest care was taken in defining how the newly established authority of the United States should be exercised, and more particularly what the lawful powers of the federal government should be in relation to those of the several united states. The people's liberties were taken for granted, vindicated in the successful Revolution, and now presupposed. Yet the people were not satisfied until their basic liberties were spelled out and made perfectly explicit in the first ten amendments. And precisely this has indeed been the portion of the Constitution about whose infringement we have become more and more sensitive. Other issues having to do with government are felt as a matter of serious public concern, chiefly when they have a plain bearing upon the freedom of the people. It has thus become habitual for us to be more concerned about personal rights and freedom than about the authority of government.

We are confirmed in such a habit of mind by our experience during the Second World War. And as we stand against aggression today from "authoritarian" states, we tend more and more to mark the differences between the two sorts of politics by claiming freedom as our cause and supreme concern, and by spurning the notion of authority so dominant in the policies we are opposing.

This attitude of rejection of the idea of authority is strengthened by a modern philosophical tradition. The progress of "free-thinking," as it came to be labelled, called forth repressive efforts of authority which have left in many a memory and a settled conviction that there is a radical and necessary opposition between the free spirit of research in science and philosophy or the freedom of expression in arts and letters, on the one hand, and an authoritarian spirit which is associated with both absolutist religion and government. This view has been only more firmly fixed in us during recent years, as we witnessed the authoritarian politics spreading over the whole of life, becoming totalitarian and invading the sacred precincts of the spirit.

In opinion we wholly reject authority as something opposed to our moral and political traditions; yet the circumstances of today require that we should accept it in some form. We are uncomfortably aware of a contradiction between our professed belief and actual practice. Even while we proclaim daily that we are fighting for freedom, we perceive that this very struggle will involve a greater and greater exercise of the collective power of the state. Nor can we dismiss this growing political power as merely a temporary affair. The trend toward government regulation and control was long a cause of concern even before the two world wars. This troubles us. We cannot envisage what kind of "free world" we are fighting for. No consistent image of it can be formed. We sometimes suspect that what we shall have in the end will be entirely different from the objective of all our efforts.

Such uncertainty confuses us and dulls the edge of our resolution. There is no simple issue that can be expressed in a pat phrase: freedom *versus* authority. The genuine problem is to find out how freedom and authority can coexist in the same universe, what respective functions and value each one has in life in a modern civilized community.

II. *A Fundamental Issue Concerning Authority Illustrated in a Contemporary Political Discussion*

An example is at hand in American political discussion which reveals a need of better understanding of the nature of authority. The public hearings of two joint committees of the Senate of the United States investigating foreign policy and the recall by the President of General MacArthur are an exhibit of a prevailing confusion about the nature of authority in a democratic order. At the session of June 5, 1951, the Secretary of State, Dean Acheson, was being interrogated. Senator Gillette asked about "the full power" which the United States had, "as a delegation of power from the Security Council to direct the war operation in Korea. Is it subject to a report to the Security Council and nothing more?"

Acheson: Yes, the command function was given to the United States. Yes, sir.

Question: And it is also your interpretation that the United States without an interposition of the Security Council or its agents can change the character of the war, can expand the war or contract the war in any way it sees fit, subject only to report of what it has done?

Acheson: I don't make that contention at all, sir. I have said that what the United States has been trying to do and what the resolution of

July 7 again referred to, was to give prompt and vigorous support to the resolutions of the 25th and 27th of June, 1950, to assist the Republic of Korea in defending itself against armed attack, and thus restore international peace and security in the area.

Now the military aspects of that campaign fall under the command direction, and if it becomes necessary in the military conduct of the war to move here or there or respond to this or that attack, then the command has that authority.

Question: Then why . . . did you, when you were contemplating the question of hot pursuit, when you were contemplating the question of blockade, take it up with the other nations? Was it a matter of courtesy or a matter of obligation?

Acheson: Well, it is very important that in carrying out this campaign we have the enthusiastic and warm support of all those who are taking part in it, and therefore we have endeavored to keep in closest touch, closest consultation with them and have a very continuous exchange of ideas and advice back and forth.

Question: Also, then, according to that interpretation of yours, we could take such action as we saw fit to close the war, to take the initial steps toward an armistice or any other treaty of closing hostilities without referring it to the Security Council of the United Nations.

Acheson: Well, the Security Council, or rather the General Assembly —the Security Council has not been able to act . . . The General Assembly thinks it wise, and the United States is endeavoring to follow the course which has tremendous international support and is not attempting taking unilateral steps of its own. . . .

Question: Well, the Assembly action of course is purely advisory, it is not binding.

Acheson: This is not binding but it is very important. It is a recommendation of the greatest importance. . . .

Question: Then may I go back to my question. . . . Do we have . . . the authority to take action to close the Korean war without submitting it to the United Nations . . . ?

Acheson: I should think the unified command would have the right, if it wishes to, to bring about an armistice. I think it has that right.

I doubt whether the military command would undertake to work out a solution of the political problems of Korea. I don't think that that is covered under the heading of command function in the military field.

I think the United States, as the military command, would consult in the closest possible way with its colleagues in this operation before making proposals about an armistice which have been put forward by the other side.

Question: I thank you, Mr. Secretary, I may say that I deplore your interpretation . . . repudiate it personally, . . .[2]

It was quite obvious that Senator Gillette and the Secretary of State differed on many points, but the crux of their difference was this—what is the character and the extent of the authority of the "military command" vested by the United Nations in the United States?

A. *A Citizen's Scrutiny of the "Debate"*

The differences between the two speakers were large and comprehensive ones concerning what we are to understand by delegation of power, authority, responsibility, obligation, rights, and freedom—all factors essential to a democratic civilization. That passage of words between Senator Gillette and the Secretary of State deserve to be examined in detail, noting the things on which they are agreed. First, the United States had been "clothed with authority" by a resolution of the Security Council of the United Nations, at the time of the invasion of Korea. This authority was thus a "delegation" of power which should thereafter be employed by the United States "to assist the Republic of Korea in defending itself against armed attack, and thus restore international peace and security in the area." To this end forces were made available from various countries, though the United States contributed by far the most. The authority vested in the United States was that of a "unified command" of all the United Nations forces. The United States was empowered with "the full function of command" for whatever military operations would be necessary to carry out the specific intent of that original resolution.

B. *Command Authority*

Now for the differing interpretations of this authority. In the interrogations of Senator Gillette there is an unmistakable trend, for they all harp on the theme of the "full power" of the military "authority." On this view, then, the authority possessed by the United States admits of no limitation. That previous resolution of the Security Council which had requested the United States to assume command of the forces of the United Nations had stipulated only that the United States should "re-

[2]The preceding quotations are from the record of testimony reported in the *New York Times,* June 6, 1951.

port" to the Council, and, the Senator asked, why do more than that? There is no other "obligation" attached to this authority.

The Secretary of State then conceded that the letter of the resolution had laid no further obligation upon the United States to do what he had nonetheless done, which the Senator deplored and repudiated, *viz.,* when the question of "hot pursuit" had come up, the Secretary "consulted" with some other members of the United Nations whose forces were part of the command. In the eyes of the Senator any such diplomatic consultation detracted from the "full power" and "authority" of the United States in this war operation. Here we see the Senator's conception of the authority enjoyed by the United States.

But who is it that possesses and exercises all this authority and freedom of action? The Senator refers to the United States only in his words, but seems all along to have an image of an authority in the person of General Douglas MacArthur. The Senator simply identified the whole authority of the United States with the military command of the General and then expressed his disapproval over any limitation upon the General's action which would hamper his power and freedom of action—as if that were a direct impairment of the very majesty of the United States.

It is apparent that the Senator is exalting authority and making a military sort of authority supreme. And the reason for so doing, it would seem, is that he wanted to justify General MacArthur, and condemn the Administration and the Secretary of State for hampering the efficiency of the military authority vested in the General.

C. *The Difference between Military and Political Authority*

The discussion moved to slightly different ground when the Secretary introduced his own interpretation of the authority possessed by the United States. He used a new term to define it, calling it "the command function," an expression which at once limits the authority. But the Senator was willing to accept the phrase, for evidently the word, "command," seemed good enough for his purposes. Then he went on to say that this power of command meant "that the United States *without an interposition of the Security Council or its agents can change the character of the war, can expand the war or contract the war in any way it sees fit,* subject only to report." (Italics mine). Here the Secretary spoke in emphatic disagreement. He reminded his interlocutor—and the public

—that the command was vested in the United States, only for a definite, specified purpose and with reference to a particular state of affairs. Consistently with this interpretation of the limits of the United States' authority, the Secretary, when he was faced with the practical question of action which might "expand" the war or "change its character," regarded it as a question to be dealt with on the political level and not to be left to military discretion. Hence he resorted to the diplomatic procedure of consulting with the other nations whose forces were under the unified command. Since it had become no longer possible for the United States to refer back to the Security Council for advice (that body having been put out of business by a Russian veto), one could best follow the course of action regarded as "wise" by the General Assembly, thereby assuring ourselves of continuing support.

D. *The Political Form of Authority*

But are we *bound,* the Senator asked, to follow the course indicated by the General Assembly or the other nations? The Secretary conceded that legally the resolutions of the Assembly had no binding force upon the United States. But leaving aside strict requirements of law, the advice given in a resolution of the Assembly is "a recommendation of the greatest importance, ... more than persuasive, ... a very important act indeed." And this is precisely the kind of consideration one must take into account in the political direction of the war.

But the Senator was interested always in the rights of military command. Surely the "command function" includes "the authority to take action to close the Korean war without submitting it to the United Nations." Certainly, the Secretary replied, the "unified command" does have the right, if it wishes to, to bring about an armistice. Yet "a solution of the political problem of Korea" was not the proper function of the "military command." The settlement is not our business alone, but that of all the nations concerned with international peace and security. So once again the Secretary insisted that consultation is requisite "before making any proposals about an armistice or before accepting proposals regarding an armistice which have been put forward by the other side." The Senator had had quite enough at this point and closed, deploring such an interpretation and repudiating it.

Now what the Senator there repudiated was nothing less than the traditional American ideas of responsible government, and, in particular, the idea of the necessary subordination of any military command to the political authorities of the state. The fact that there is such a contradiction between the Senator's own views and the tradition is partly obscured, because the argument is on unfamiliar ground, the international sphere. But we can see it clearly if we recapture in imagination the large, general way of thinking characteristic of the early founders of the American republic who reasoned about "all men" and about the interests, rights, and duties that held for all equally, for men of other nations as well as the American nation. The same principles had greater validity for them because they were universal.

E. *The American Way of Thinking about Authority*

According to this way of thinking it is an elemental lesson of life that when people are traveling on the same road and find any one of their number beset by enemies, they must look out for each other, as well as for themselves. With common resolution, then, they undertake their defensive war against their aggressor. They confer upon one or more the authority and power for the purpose of securing peace. That authority is rightly used as long as those in whom it is solemnly vested carry out the intentions of all those who are participating. In the case of any new ventures some further or new grant of authority would have to be procured. The declaring or proposing of terms of a peace to close a war is likewise the business of all those who first united to seek a peaceful and just order. It is not the decision alone of any general in the field, nor even of the leading state itself which has put most effort into the winning of the victory. The peace, the independent existence, and the welfare of every one of the parties, are all affected by the nature of the peace proposed. What right then has anyone to *object* to consultation at this juncture? Is it not requisite for him who has authority to seek the continued support of all, or as many as possible for any policy that is proposed? Is it wrong to acknowledge that there are other people besides oneself who have an equal stake in the things which are of concern to us, though they may be smaller, weaker, less vigorous and prominent at that moment in "world history"? Are we inconsistently to repudiate the democratic form of authority as inapplicable to the dealings of a democracy with other people?

F. *Authority and Responsibility*

The Secretary of State argued in that so-called "debate" in the large, generous spirit which has made the American republic the great power it is in the modern world. According to Mr. Acheson, authority in this situation is a right of action conferred by a deed of those who recognize a common danger, and desire appropriate unified action taken to meet it. The fact of one party being a large contributor, therefore, does not entitle it to assume an unquestioned preponderance, and consequently to act "as it sees fit," and without reference to others' judgment or advice. Any authority of this sort, authority received by delegation, is inherently a *limited* one. The party having it is not free to change the purpose for which it is granted, and is strictly obliged to conduct affairs in accordance with the understanding of all the parties to the united action. The person or state "having authority" is ever responsible to those who have created it.

G. *The Unprecedented Character of the Authority Derived from the United Nations*

There is, doubtless, a question in the minds of some as to whether an international "community" exists, and whether the United Nations organization represents a real community. Those who have such views are apt to think that nations in this international union or organization have actually very little authority to give. Now it may be conceded that the community of the nations is much less real and vigorous than any present national community. Yet we have learned from experience that we must unite early for common action to guard against threats to the very existence of any of the nations. We are trying now to demonstrate the validity and effectiveness of such common action—and we have an authority officially granted to the United States, one of the many parties involved, to execute this common will of the nations. The operation in Korea is the first demonstration of this democratic sort of authority in the contemporary world. No matter how we evaluate it in terms of the armed strength of those who have constituted this authority, its primary significance is *moral,* the fact that it springs from the will of the nations and represents an agreed-upon common undertaking. Whether or not this moral will is to live and grow stronger, whether we can together work increasingly for peace, freedom, and justice, now depends absolutely upon the way we employ authority in the present situation.

And if in the course of events the authority derived from the United Nations is not regarded as sufficient from our own point of view, we cannot merely assume more authority for ourselves than has been given. We would be imposing our own will and actually usurping the function of the United Nations, and practically destroying the hopes of mankind today for the development of a civilized technique of dealing with this increasing scourge of war. If we were to follow such a policy, our authority would vanish and only sheer power remain in its stead, the power of the United States, alone in a world disappointed, dispirited, perhaps even sullen, and certainly far less united than before against an aggressive power.

The idea of authority applied to this case by the Secretary of State is the very one which has made us what we are as a free nation. It is authority exercised with responsibility to those who give it. That means that it is not an arbitrary power which can disregard the community or set itself over against it. And there is no getting around this fact, too, that authority so conceived as rightful power does entail an obligation to consult and abide by the opinion and judgment of "the others."

In the inquiry we are studying, the Senator studiously sought at every turn to *exclude* binding obligations from the picture. The Secretary of State conceded to him that there was no obligation by law or the stipulation of a treaty. But there is the obligation which underlies all law and government in a democratic society, because it is the condition under which any party has the right to exercise authority. The Senator, however, tried to retain for the United States an authority *not* so bound by the judgment or advice of the community at large, but an authority free to act "as it sees fit." This would give authority with precisely that arbitrary character against which the first Americans themselves once revolted in 1776.

H. *The Essential Subordination of Military Command*

The American people at the beginning of their career as a nation plainly stipulated that the commander in chief of the military forces should always be their President, and the President precisely in his capacity as an elected official directly responsible to them. It is intolerable then, on American principles, to claim that a general in the field is ever invested with this authority. We expect our Presidents to exercise their own best judgment and not to surrender their authority or allow decisions to be made for them by commanders of the army. In any given case we may think a particular decision to be unwise, but it is far more important in every case that we should not have the determination of our policies in regard to peace and war made simply by any member of our military establishment. Otherwise we should no longer live under a constitution and the Republic would be in grave danger.

I. *The "Decent Respect to the Opinions of Mankind"*

"The last straw" for the Senator was the willingness of the Secretary of State to *consult* with the representatives of other nations in the United Nations, and to seek justification for any action contemplated by our military command which might have "changed the character of the war." Let us recall here that when first Americans launched their own Revolutionary War, they penned a Declaration of Independence to tell the world their reasons, and they took pains, in their opening sentence, to show a "decent respect to the opinions of mankind." And the present policy, which accords with this original American attitude, is precisely what a Senator of the United States can deplore and repudiate causing hardly a stir among his fellow citizens.

III. *The Persistent Problem of the Reconciliation of Freedom and Authority*

There are echoes of the past in this discussion within the halls of the American Congress. It repeats in a present context the long struggle in the modern world between those seeking to establish a social order of freedom and those holding back, with a different emphasis on authority. But the debate rehearses an even older argument that had been carried on time and time again throughout the whole span of what we recognize as Western Civilization. Robert K. Carr, writing on "Liberty Under Government" in *Freedom and the Expanding State* suggests: "In no small degree the history of human progress is told in the story of the varying success man has enjoyed in reconciling liberty with authority, authority with liberty."[3]

There is fairly current a delusive notion of a regular advance of modern thought from a primitive and absolutist view of authority in the sixteenth century toward the civilized view of liberty now attained. Yet peoples of other times achieved a civilization in their day, only by hard and careful thinking about both the actual conditions in which they lived and the better things they were striving for. Some of this practical wisdom we remember, but not all of it, and frequently we find ourselves, as at present, obliged to rediscover very illuminating ideas in the older traditions with which we have lost touch.

A. *The Early Modern Situation and the Theory of Authority*

Now it is quite true that thinking men of the sixteenth century were preoccupied with authority. It is remarkable that Richard Hooker, author of the *Laws of Ecclesiastical Polity* (1583), focussed attention on "the necessity of authority," this phrase being the title of a significant chapter in the book. We prefer to think of the Hooker who also defined true laws to be those made only with "the consent of the governed." This latter idea is the gold, the other the dross. Yet to Hooker there seemed good reason for both, and the fact that they appear together in the same well considered masterpiece of political thinking is instructive.

Europe was then the whole of the Western world and all Europe was in turmoil, on account of the religious and political dissensions after the Protestant Reformation. In the absence of any general authority—Papal or Imperial—capable of restoring "universal" peace and order, the practical maxim for these uncertain times seemed to be to seek peace, unity, law, and order, within the territory of each national state where allegiance was still possible to one ruler or prince. For there were princes who had the political competence and military leadership to unite the warring parties within their own respective domains and establish new vigorous states, independent and autonomous, and to represent in their own persons the new unity and all the glory of what James I of England later called, in his own fateful work on sovereignty, a "free monarchy."

---

[3]*Proceedings of the Academy of Political Science,* edited by John A. Krout, May, 1950, XXIV, 1, p. 4.

(1) Bodin: The Theory of Sovereignty under Natural Law

First among all the theorists of this new or modern order was Jean Bodin who launched the theory of sovereignty on its career in his *Six Books on the Republic* (1576). Now it might seem as if Machiavelli should be the man to notice in connection with the new power of the modern national state. For his *Prince* certainly taught the lessons of the way to gain and hold effective power. Yet it was Bodin himself who told men to disregard Machiavelli. The Machiavellian does not honor moral or religious law, but only uses it. And here was the crux of the matter for Bodin, who, consequently, took great care to warn his readers that his argument was anti-Machiavellian: the prince of Bodin's theory is a sovereign who always operates under the "law of nature."[4] Sovereignty is the power of the prince, but it must always be rightful or lawful power, exercised subject to natural law or God's law.

This was the form which the theory of authority took in the beginning when the modern state was in process of making. Sovereignty, though it meant supremacy of power, was not conceived as absolutely supreme. How could it be if there was, above all earthly powers and principalities, an Author of the universe? Supreme power in the absolute is in God alone, the Supreme Being, and consequently the handiwork of God contains an absolute order and law, the natural law, which no man, however puffed up with political authority, can ignore and violate with impunity.

Hence, according to Bodin, "all the princes on earth are subject to the laws of God and of nature, and to many human laws common to all peoples."[5] But what sort of supremacy is this sovereignty when thus limited to the human order? The definition is as follows: "The sovereignty is the absolute and perpetual power of a republic."[6]

The meaning of "absolute power" is "power to dispose of the goods, the person, and all the state according to one's will, and then to leave it to whom one wills, and all this just as a proprietor can give his own property purely and simply as he wills."[7] Sovereignty was thus conceived by analogy with ownership and the power with *right* that any owner has to dispose of what is his own. And Bodin intended plainly "right"

---

[4] Bodin on Machiavelli, see Jean Bodin, *Six Livres de la République,* Chez I. du Piys edition, Paris, 1583, *Preface.*
[5] *Ibid.,* "On Sovereignty," Book I, Chapter 8, p. 131.
[6] *Ibid.,* p. 122.
[7] *Ibid.,* p. 126.

and not only "power," for he later insisted that the sovereign is always obliged to respect the property of his subjects and must never impair or confiscate it, precisely because his own personal title to sovereignty is founded on the same universal right of property. And that universal *right* exists by virtue of the law of nature. Now all of this means that the sovereignty spoken of as absolute is nonetheless *limited* by the natural law. Hence Bodin even approved of the practices of the government of England, where the sovereign could not levy taxes upon those who had property without their own consent.

But sovereignty was subject to further limitation, in his own phrase, "to many human laws common to all peoples." This is a reference to the "laws of nations." Sometimes the term, "laws of nations," harked back to the old Roman *jus gentium,* an empirical body of laws found in fact among the various nations, which by their approximation to universality seemed to be witness to the ultimate law of nature and God. But there was a second usage, *viz.,* the laws obtaining in the *relations* of nations or states with each other. The statement that "all princes on earth are subject . . . to many human laws common to all peoples," means that sovereign princes are under obligation to respect the laws of nations in both the senses which we have noted. It is not only the case, Bodin appears to be saying, that certain laws are so universal that no prince dares to disregard them—such a law would be, at that time, the commercial law of Europe—but also that no prince is free to break treaties but is obliged always to honor them.[8]

Furthermore, so authoritative is the universal moral law of keeping faith or one's word, that Bodin thought of the sovereign as actually being bound by any agreements or contracts which he makes even with his own subjects who are nevertheless entirely within his power.[9]

So much stress on good faith seems positively utopian to our seemingly wiser, or perhaps more sadly experienced, age. But the thinking men of the sixteenth and seventeenth centuries perceived that the life of industry and commerce and the prosperity of all nations depended ultimately upon such "good faith." Here the prince, the exemplar of the nation, should set the example, and the old Greek adage was still pertinent: he who would command must first learn to obey.

---

[8] See Gerhard Niemeyer, *Law Without Force,* Princeton University Press, Princeton, 1941.

[9] Bodin, *op. cit.*, pp. 134 f.

a. "THE COMMAND FUNCTION" AND THE LAW

But still we wonder why Bodin ever spoke of the power of sovereignty so conceived as "absolute." With respect to what functions or actions is there any absoluteness? The essential and distinctive function of sovereignty is that "of giving the law to the subjects in general without their consent."[10] Consequently, "Law is the command of the sovereign."[11] The meaning is further elaborated through a comparison: "custom gets its force little by little and over a long period of years by the common consent of all, of the majority; but law issues in a moment and derives its vigor from him who has the power to command all; custom flows along gently and without force, but law is commanded and declared by power and very often against the wishes of the subjects."[12] A second feature of sovereignty is "the power to declare war or peace."[13] Laying down the law, and making war or peace—these constitute the marks of the "command" function which is characteristic of sovereignty in the sixteenth and seventeenth centuries.

This is, indeed, a great commanding power, and yet when Bodin discussed *Royal Monarchy* he recalled the limitation that a true monarch is one "who is obedient to the laws of nature," leaving to each subject his "natural liberty and property."[14] Consequently, any ruler who "tramples on the laws of nature abuses the liberty of free subjects . . . and abuses the property of others. . . ." is a tyrant.[15] The monarch has no right, as sovereign, save *under* those conditions of respect for law, liberty, and property.

b. "THE LIBERTY OF FREE SUBJECTS"

But how was the liberty of man to be conceived? "We call 'natural liberty' not being subjected, after God, to any living man and not suffering any commandment except that of oneself, that is, of the

---

[10] *Ibid.*, Book V, Chapter 8, p. 142.

[11] *Ibid.*, "The True Mark of Sovereignty," Book V, Chapter 10, p. 216, repeated on p. 430.

[12] *Ibid.*, p. 222. Cf. Aristotle on law as derived from custom and being its fulfilment, *Politics*, Book 2, Chapter 8, 1269a.

[13] Bodin, *op. cit.*, Book IV, Chapter 8, p. 224.

[14] *Ibid.*, Book II, Chapter 3, p. 279.

[15] *Ibid.*, Chapter 4, p. 287.

reason in oneself which is always conformable to the will of God."[16]

How, then, is it possible to reconcile liberty with sovereignty? The solution was given in terms of the whole system of ideas by which men like Bodin were thinking out the problems of their civilization.

C. THE SYSTEM OF NATURAL LAW OF PROPERTY

Bodin's argument was concerned with the idea of a republic conceived as an order of law in which peace and justice can prevail. Two factors of universal significance appear essential, one the sovereignty of the state, the other the property of the constituent members of the national state. But who were the particular constituent members? Not simply individual persons as such, but rather social units which comprised the society of the republic: "the family is the true source and origin of every republic and it is the principal member thereof";[17] and besides the many families were other established societies and fellowships: guilds, "corporations, colleges, estates, and communities."[18] So property was the property of the plurality of societies. And the sovereign authority of the state was limited by respect for all such property of the members of the state.

d. LIBERTY AND AUTHORITY WITHIN A SYSTEM OF LAW

Now the absoluteness of this limited authority appeared in the sovereign's role of commanding *men*. For there could be no commanding of things. In each guild or community some responsible person exercised a limited power of regulating the affairs of that group, and it was by commanding this representative that the sovereign exercised his preeminent role as an authority for the whole republic. The manner of the command was the important and distinguishing feature of this social order. In the first place, the sovereign should never act by decree, arbitrarily requiring one of the nobility or a representative of another group to do his own will. On the contrary, the function of sovereignty was *to make civil law* and to make it prevail throughout the land, but the most striking feature was that this civil law *was* commanded by the sovereign

---
[16] *Ibid.*, Book I, Chapter 3, p. 19.
[17] *Ibid.*, Book I, Chapter 2, p. 11.
[18] *Ibid.*, Book III, Chapter 7, pp. 474 ff.

"without the consent" of those subject to it. Yet all those who were thus commanded *by way of law* had a sphere of their own, in which they, in turn, commanded after the fashion of their own society. They were entitled to do some things on their own initiative. Thus the natural freedom of the members of Bodin's republic consisted precisely in their having that individual part to play in their respective domains. Their freedom was real but limited by the command function, which itself was, in turn, limited by the natural law of that whole hierarchical order of life. Thus freedom and authority were seen together in an order under Heaven and its overarching law.

The early discussions of authority in continental Europe are like a set of variations on a theme by Bodin. Each thinker had some immediate application in mind which modified and developed the essential idea. Bodin himself favored "pure, absolute monarchy," and the reason for this opinion can be inferred from his work and the history of the time. The circumstances demanded men of commanding political gifts who could, by their prestige, as well as by their power, force the warring parties within a nation to unite and form a more perfect state. Laws had to be enforced with "vigor," even "against the wishes of those who were subject to them." The emphasis was on unity of power, command, authority.

(2) ALTHUSIUS: SOVEREIGNTY, THE PEOPLE, AND NATURAL LAW

But the idea of sovereignty under natural law was not tied exclusively to monarchy. Johannes Althusius, who was experienced in the affairs of the free city of Emden, adopted the concept of sovereignty in almost a democratic form of the sovereignty of the people. There is the conception of a plurality of associations that take form naturally and by agreement —societies not forged by the sword or the military power—and the state is that comprehensive society in which there is a *jus majestas* or sovereignty. But the government that exercises the sovereignty is still "subject to the people and to the laws of the realm."[19] Furthermore, there are "obligations" to be observed. And even a popular sovereignty, though it has the function of making law, must work under law higher than that which it makes.

---

[19] Cited by O. von Gierke, from Althusius's *Politics,* translated by Bernard Freyd in a volume entitled, *The Development of Political Theory,* George Allen & Unwin, Ltd., London, p. 42.

(3) The Theory of Grotius's Law, Sovereignty, and Liberty

The development in the thought of Grotius deserves special attention, for he was advancing both a doctrine of sovereignty and a doctrine of liberty. *The Rights of War and Peace* (1625) was intended to show, by rational argument, that there are "laws of perpetual obligation," equally "suited to all times," which all governments and nations must observe, lest human society dissolve in warfare.[20]

Laws must *govern* war; what is a just war, however, should be well understood and defined; sovereignty must exist for the sake of peace with right; and what is right must be derived from the law of nature and God, "the Author of nature."[21]

On this view the sovereign has the right to govern by laying down positive law, as Bodin had described; but now it is man, more than the group or lesser associations, who enjoys the natural rights and liberties of action over his own property.

For Grotius was actually developing a theory of civil liberty applying to individual persons. Hence we can understand how John Milton, who was to write the *Areopagitica* and speak of "the philosophy of freedom,"[22] found it profitable to consult Grotius in Italy.

The teaching of Grotius was quite in accord with English traditions of liberties and rights dating from the Great Charter, and it subsequently inspired the conception of natural rights entertained in the eighteenth century and the principles of American liberty.

The political philosophy of Grotius introduced, however, an additional kind of freedom into a world at that time thinking much more about authority. The civil liberty of "natural right" is not valid without effective guarantees. Now seeing to it that no one, however strong or powerful, shall ever be excepted from the rule of law, is itself a function of government; it follows that the people should have a role in the government. In other words, to enjoy a genuine civil liberty, men must have political liberty as well.

---

[20]Hugo Grotius, "Preliminary Discourse," *Rights of War and Peace*, Barbyrac edition, English translation, London, 1783, p. xxvii.

[21]*Ibid.*, "What war is and what right is," Book I, Chapter 1, pp. 1–10.

[22]Cf. Charles W. Hendel, "Education and Politics: The Problem of Responsibility," *Goals for American Education*, Lyman Bryson, Louis Finkelstein, R. M. MacIver, Editors, Conference on Science, Philosophy and Religion in Their Relation to the Democratic Way of Life, Inc., New York, 1950, pp. 174 ff.

This practical demand was first met by a traditional theory of contract for government which Grotius refurbished for new service. The typical idea is that the original institution of government is a voluntary deed of all the persons concerned, by which they solemnly invest a representative person with authority.[23] Political government was thus born in freedom. For those who ruled, that original contract was to serve as a reminder of the source of their power, and of their own duty to employ their authority for the good of the state and the people. In those times, when authority apparently had to play a great role in restoring peace and unity, the right of the people to rescind their original deed was in theory never granted. Certainly resistance and rebellion were outlawed. Nor could individuals ever claim to judge of the working of their government.[24]

The government has a duty, it is true, but it would lack sovereignty if it ever had to defer to the will of the people manifested in any other quarter.

a. THE LAW OF NATIONS AND ITS DEFECT IN AUTHORITY *vis-à-vis* SOVEREIGNTY

But war was, for the most part, an international affair, and Grotius's supreme concern was with universal peace in all the civilized world. Here what had been the secondary theme of Hooker and Bodin became a main theme—the "law of nations." And the original anti-Machiavellian spirit, with which Bodin had opened this argument about sovereignty, again cropped out, in the conclusion of Grotius's book where he solemnly admonished all princes "to preserve good faith among men and to seek peace."[25]

But Grotius's final recourse to mere admonition betrays a weakness of the law of nations and its lack of authority. On the earlier view, the universality attributed to the law of nations made it seem a visible approximation to the eternal natural law of God, whence it had a borrowed authority. But Grotius, absorbed with the contract idea, had set out to recommend the "right" or "law of nations" to the individualistic temper of the time, by saying that it "derives its authority from the will of all,

[23] Grotius, *op. cit.*, Book I, Chapter 3, especially sections VI–XVI, pp. 62–77.
[24] *Ibid.*, pp. 69 ff.
[25] *Ibid.*, "Concerning Faith between Enemies"; "Concerning the Public Faith Whereby War is Finished: of Treaties"; "Of Faith During War, Of Truces and Conclusion," Book III, Chapters 19, 20, and 21, pp. 735 ff.

or at least, of many nations."[26] Can a free and absolutely independent sovereign state ever oblige itself to a law merely *authorized by a majority of states?* Can it even oblige *itself* when it has *once* given the sanction of its own will to the law? In the case of individual men, Grotius had said: "No man can lay himself under the obligation of a law, that is, a law to which he may be subject," for law must always come "from a superior."[27] How impossible, then, to expect a sovereign state to lay itself under an obligation to a law which comes from the will of a majority of the nations! In other words, what authority can such international law have for *sovereign* states?

Yet Grotius thought that there could be an obligatory law of nations. And the reasons for his view seem to have been twofold. The first sprang from his belief that the Christian religion was still a valuable force "in the universal society of mankind."[28] The second reason was that the strong interests of individual men in their own liberties and rights coincided with the cause of peace. The sovereign state was limited by having to pay regard to "the intentions of those who originally framed it,"[29] these intentions being obviously to promote a society in which they could peaceably enjoy their natural and civil rights.

The work of Grotius was the last great affirmation of sovereignty under religious authority, and it was at the same time the opening of a seam in the well knit system of thought fashioned by Bodin. The supreme law of nature was still "eternal" and "of perpetual obligation," because it was God's will and command. Sovereignties had supreme power over all who dwelt in the lands that God gave them, and *their* law was given without the consent of those subject to the law. Yet there was a sort of large general consent assumed when the people were conceived to have made over the right to govern them of their own free will. How far would this conception of individual freedom extend itself in the minds of men?

[26] *Ibid.*, Book I, Chapter 1, p. 15.
[27] *Ibid.*, Book II, Chapter 4, Section XII, p. 183.
[28] *Ibid.*, "Of Punishments," Chapter 20, Section XLIV, p. 442.
[29] *Ibid.*, Chapter 6, Section VI, p. 216.

B. *The Sharply Drawn Issue in the Eighteenth Century and the Story of Freedom*

The great argument of politics was resumed during what may be called the revolutionary period, beginning in the early seventeenth century. The answer to the royal claim to authority by "divine right" of kings was a counterclaim to their own personal liberty by divine right. When the army of Cromwell got the King of England actually into their power, a prisoner, they had to take counsel among themselves and with the Parliament, concerning the settlement of the war and the establishment of a new government. Among the many spontaneous, impromptu observations was this revealing description by one Mr. Wildman: "authority hath been broken into pieces."[30] Many present hoped to keep it so. (We can see here that it was not Montesquieu alone who taught the Americans later to distribute the powers of government.) But at that early time the English state or the Commonwealth, as they wanted to call it, remained in great danger and the situation cried aloud for authority.

(1) HOBBES AND ABSOLUTE AUTHORITY

At this juncture, exactly three hundred years ago, Thomas Hobbes emerged as a political philosopher. According to Hobbes, we must forget about divinity in politics, and think no more, too, about liberty. Men in a "state of nature," that is, a state where they had no government and law, enjoyed liberty, but it was now plain enough that with only liberty and without government they were heading simply for disastrous anarchy. Surely men have had enough of perfect liberty by this time to be ready for the important lesson about authority, before ruin finally overtakes them and they are thrown back into a complete anti-social savagery. Absolutely *sovereign* authority is necessary for the restoration of peace and a life in civilization.

Hobbes had here resorted to a scheme of thought destined to have a considerable vogue after him—the "state of nature" and the passage to the civilized state of affairs. The "state of nature" was that imaginary condition of man, when his life was not yet ordered by any law or

---

[30]"The Whitehall Debates," December 14, 1648, in *Puritanism and Liberty,* edited by A. S. P. Woodhouse, J. M. Dent & Sons, Ltd., London, 1938, p. 127.

political government. Think away all that these civilizing factors contribute to the existence of man, and you have the "natural" order of life. Now the particular account Hobbes gave of the natural order of things was designed for a purpose; it was *not* a description of anything that was actually the case. It was a conception intended to bring men to an appreciation of the great positive value of the civilizing function of government, so that they would *welcome* its authoritative rule over their lives. This was the great object of Hobbes's *Leviathan* (1651).

This was a new doctrine for England, and contrary to much in the tradition of government. Hobbes could not succeed with the minds of men if he simply flaunted the idea of freedom. He could with reason, of course, condemn the anarchic liberty of man, but he had to honor a certain modern claim to freedom that went with it in practice. For men as rational beings had discovered by their bold enterprise new places on earth for new empires, and they were becoming masters, too, of the universal forces ruling all nature. Why could they not judge and control, in turn, those political powers that exercised a control over their own existence? Hobbes had, therefore, to frame his argument so as to allow for some expression of the will of the individuals, while retaining for government its full unimpaired authority which made it a government. Consequently Hobbes employed the contract idea, and represented the original setting up of government as a voluntary deed or covenant by all of the individuals concerned. At this instant men were both free and rational—doing of their own free will what was perceived to be necessary for their own preservation. Thereafter they must let the government function and exercise its authority—make the laws of the state, enforce them upon all men alike, and rule out any disturbance of the peace.

Thus Hobbes threw a sop to freedom, and sought to persuade people to accept an authority that would be absolute. For after their first free deed of conferring authority upon their government, the people became bound "subjects." Consequently, it was not their business ever to set themselves up as judges of the good or ill performance of their government and to demand that it conform to their judgment and will. The government alone is the judge of what is right and for the public good, and its constant interest is always in the basic need of peace and security, and not any further ideas about welfare.

The people whom Hobbes was addressing were too intelligent to yield their freedom on such a plea. He had conceded too much when he invoked the convenant idea. These men could not forget that the authority in this political scheme came from themselves. With all his subtlety, therefore, Hobbes could not check the power of that idea in the minds of some Englishmen. And when they emigrated to America, and started new commonwealths there, and rebelled, in their turn, showing the same spirit their forebears had shown, and then set about making a constitution for their union, they constantly repeated and reminded each other of that fundamental principle that "all authority is derived from the people."[31]

That was the answer, of course, of men of action. Before there could be such firm and battling conviction, however, a whole century of philosophical thinking had taken place in Europe. Why should not men who are free enough to set up an authority which is to exercise *their* power in making the laws and ruling over them, why should they not have a *further* say in the whole affair? The political power is for a useful purpose, and it is their own purpose, and can they not decide whether that purpose is furthered and how far? Practically speaking, too, would not the modern type of men who were doing great new things in industry and commerce, as well as in things of the spirit, feel themselves quite competent to have an important part in the government and its law making? Princes depended on them. Why then should they not continue to play their initial role of free agents over and over again and never be merely commanded from above?

(2) Spinoza and Freedom

Here Spinoza made a telling point against the Hobbes who was so obsessed with peace and order: there always *will* be disorder where the laws are merely imposed, and not in accord with the "understanding" of the people. Hence Spinoza defiantly spoke a good word for democracy, as the most "natural," the truly stable, enduring form of government. And further the cultivation of the "human understanding" is of the greatest importance for life in society; and the true object of every government, as well as education, is "freedom of thought."[32]

[31] Alpheus Thomas Mason, "The Nature of Our Federal Union Reconsidered," in *Political Science Quarterly*, December, 1950, LXV, 4, p. 507, referring to James Wilson, cited in Jonathan Elliot, *The Debates in the Several State Conventions on the Adoption of the Federal Constitution*, J. P. Lippincott Company, Philadelphia, 2nd edition, 1896, II, p. 406.

[32] Spinoza, *Works*, "Theologio-Political Treatise," Bohn's Philosophical Library, G. Bell & Sons, Ltd., London, 1833–1834, I, Chapter XVI, and Chapter XX, p. 259.

(3) LOCKE ON FREEDOM AND AUTHORITY

John Locke was an exact contemporary of Spinoza, and likewise advanced in opposition to the authoritarian Hobbes a "philosophy of freedom." Whereas Spinoza had the classic ideas of democracy in view and abortive attempts at a free republic in the Netherlands, Locke had behind him the English tradition of liberty through parliamentary institutions, as well as Milton and the Puritans. Hence Locke's two *Treatises on Government* (1690) sought to convince people that the authoritarian form of government was contrary to nature and the liberal form alone right and true.

Locke pointed out the quite irrational inconsequence of the doctrine of unlimited authority: "by dressing up power with all the splendor and temptation absoluteness can add to it, without showing who has a right to have it, is only to give a greater edge to man's natural ambition—and so lay a sure and lasting foundation of endless contention and disorder, instead of that peace and tranquillity which is the business of government and the end of human society."[33]

But Locke recognized the necessity of authority. The "great question" was not "whether there be power in the world, nor whence it came, but who should have it . . ." and the terms on which it is had and exercised. "Political power, then, I take to be a right of making laws, with penalties of death, and consequently all less penalties for the regulating and preserving of property, and of employing the force of the community in the execution of such laws, and in the defense of the commonwealth from foreign injury, and all this only for the public good."[34] In so defining this power, Locke was plainly limiting it. He further asserts that the community never surrenders the control of the forces which it entrusts to any "representative" of itself, but always has the right to resume the political power of governance to itself and reinvest it in another "representative." Locke believed in the value of the practices of parliamentary government. The civil authority has power to act within limits set by the community, which is expected to voice its judgment from time to time, as long as the community endures.

[33] Locke, *Treatise I*, Chapter XI, Section 106.
[34] *Ibid.*, Book II, Chapter I, Section 3.

(4) ROUSSEAU'S HERESY

It was Rousseau's turn to be critic, hardly more than half a century after Locke—but critic is not a strong enough term, for he had the spirit of a heretic. He simply reversed the values in Hobbes's scheme of thought. What folly it would be, if men, initially free to act, proceeded to bind themselves into a voiceless subjection thereafter. And the much desired civilization brought by the modern state, where is its peace and its law, justice, good life for all? The actual record is one of worsening evils, war, injustice, and, worst of all, personal slavery. Such were the heretical views of the blast in the *Discourse on the Origin of Inequality* (1754).

But Rousseau asserted in later years that his own "principles" were identical with those of Locke. What were these common principles? One was a practical precaution, to make certain that no mere partial body of men shall ever be allowed to imagine that the power of the community is their property, made over to them by any solemn deed or contract. To avoid any misunderstanding here, Rousseau even refused to follow the pattern Locke had followed of describing the authorizing of government by contract. Government is established as a mere utility, as an appointment by the people to perform a function for the community which is always to remain the judge of the performance. Hence Rousseau would not allow the term, "contract," to be mentioned at all in connection with the instituting of a government.

a. FREEDOM AND THE REPUBLIC

There is then only one kind of contract which is admissible in the affair, because it alone is compatible with the freedom of man. Of that Rousseau discoursed in his *Social Contract* (1761). There it is granted, that men have usually found it necessary to supplement their native resources for their individual preservation with the superior power that comes from a union of all their forces, and thence arises the distinctively *political* power of which Locke had spoken. The crucial problem is how to reconstruct a form of society in which every individual person can remain free while living subject to the "political power" of the "community." For "man is too noble a being ever to be made to serve merely as an instrument to others' purposes."[35] So one must be careful to think of "the social contract" as a "compact," which rather conveys the sense that *many* men are here acting together, not a two party transaction between king and people. The original act that unites men into a society is a free act for the sake of every man alike, for his personal and individual freedom. The securing of liberty for each and all, that is the prime and irreplaceable object of the whole political organization. Peace, happiness, enjoyment of many new goods, *may* come to men through their civilization, but none of these is worth anything to man, if it is purchased at the price of man's personal liberty. Freedom is the condition of all other good and it is at last conceivable in this "republic."

The "sovereignty" of a society is nothing which any one person or any number of them constituted as a government *can* possess, for it is essentially the "general will" of the people as a community. Its object is always personal freedom.

Rousseau was not unaware how this sort of authority would be received. It seemed too much of an abstraction, a thing of spirit. What is truly concrete, that is, what is really identifiable in the life of civilized mankind as the evidence of a general will, is *law*.

b. FREEDOM, LAW, AND OBLIGATION

So Rousseau's thinking carried him to the theme of the meaning and value of law. And it is law as a norm, and not as an enactment, owing its existence to government. Genuine law is universal and equal in application. Under its regulation no person is favored, none prejudiced or placed in special jeopardy. Hence it is the rule of true law that can alone secure the desired general order of freedom.

But what "security" is that? There was a rankling taunt from Hobbes: "Laws cannot govern, only men can govern." Rousseau's retort was: laws can "oblige." Precisely because there is real obligation holding in the actual lives of men, it is not so necessary to have the state govern in the commanding manner of old. For the true laws of the community are expressions of the general will of those who have constituted it. After his book the *Social Contract* had been proscribed in France and even burned publicly in Geneva, Rousseau summed up the essence of his repudiated

---

[35] A citation from Rousseau's novel, *Julie ou la Nouvelle Héloise*, Garnier Frères, Paris, Lettre 2, *Oeuvres*, Hachette, Paris, IV, p. 373.

theory in these words: "What is it that makes the state one body? It is the union of its members. And whence arises the union of its members? From the obligation that binds them." And then Rousseau went on to ask, "What surer foundation can there be for an obligation among men than the free engagement of the one who obliges himself?"[36]

Here the modern argument revealed a new dimension of liberty. It had been foreshadowed in the *Social Contract* which had defined "moral liberty" as "obeying the law one prescribes to oneself." For Rousseau the case for freedom was now completed, within the limits of the system of ideas in which he was thinking. As civil liberty had pointed the way to the value of political liberty, which was necessary to it, so the latter yielded insight unto the necessity and basic value of "moral" freedom.

C. PEACE, FREEDOM, AND LAW

The difference between Rousseau's view of law and the view of those who had pleaded so hard for sovereign authority, consisted in this, that while they envisaged law as a command from without, Rousseau regarded it as an expression of the will of those who are governed by it. The basis of law consisted in the personal obligation which only free men can experience. What it comes to, then, is this, that obligation is more important than authority as the actual bond of civilized life and the means to peace among men.

Not that Rousseau ignored the possibility of political instrumentality for peace, any more than he had ignored the necessary function of government. The cause of peace had also been the cause of freedom in the modern world. With many writers in the eighteenth century, Rousseau proposes the organization of the nations into an effective body for common action to give international law its needed validity.[37] These ideas were the forebears of those that subsequently inspired the League of Nations and the United Nations. Nevertheless, Rousseau's own argument had already carried him beyond the mere reliance on "the force of government" in either international or internal affairs. Both situations posed one and the same problem for the lover of freedom. "To put the law really above man is a problem of politics which I compare to that

[36] Rousseau, *op. cit.*, "Lettre 8," p. 235. Cf. Hendel, *J. J. Rousseau: Moralist, op. cit.*, II, p. 301.
[37] Rousseau, *op. cit.*, "Projet pour la Paix Perpetuelle, 1755," I, pp. 370 ff.

of squaring the circle in geometry. . . . Until you solve that problem, rest assured that when you think you are making the law rule, it is in reality only men who will be ruling."[38] With that problem Rousseau brought a period to a close, with a part confession of failure, for he had to admit that Hobbes had accurately described what commonly happens, and the true form of the republic, the imagined society of men ever free, was nowhere in sight. Yet Rousseau believed in this form and way of life, that there was no other way to live as men ought to live. And seeing that was so, the problem ahead was how to make the law of freedom really transcendent.

(5) On Reading the Story of Freedom Aright

In reviewing the story of freedom, it is well not to exaggerate the differences between the earlier times and our own. We should not read contemporary authoritarian practices back into the sixteenth and seventeenth centuries, and then congratulate ourselves on how far we have come. In Bodin, Grotius, and even Hobbes, the sovereign's function was to deal with overt actions against peace and to enforce laws, so that the individuals would live together "sociably." Hobbes's sovereign had no direct concern with the opinions and beliefs of men, except as they showed in habits of behavior which were a present danger to the peaceful existence of men.

Here it has to be admitted that the Puritans, who fought in the name of liberty and righteousness, were the very ones who did invade the sanctity of individual and personal life. As revolutionists they were for liberty of conscience; as men with a zeal for righteousness they invoked authority over matters of the spirit. They knew well the importance of the spirit, but in their first commonwealth they were quite unable to work out a form of government in which freedom and authority were reconciled. In those Whitehall Debates one of the two major questions was, "Whether to have any reserve to except religious things or only to give power in natural and civil things, and to say nothing of religion."[39] In America later it was decided to take a position about religious things in the first article of amendment to the Constitution which forbade an identification of Church and State.

---

[38]Rousseau, *op. cit.*, "Considerations sur le Gouvernement de Pologne," translated by Charles W. Hendel, II, pp. 426 f., see Hendel, *J. J. Rousseau: Moralist, op. cit.*, II, p. 315.
[39]Woodhouse, *op. cit.*, p. 127.

IV. *The Supreme Importance of Law*

"Law forgotten, and remembered" could well be used to describe the course of modern thought from Hobbes to Rousseau's last thoughts on politics. But then Rousseau saw that "the Law must be really *above* men," and that obligation depends also upon the authority of law. In this conclusion, which was his final statement of "the problem of politics," Rousseau remembered Law.

What is law that men are mindful of it, men in all stations, those vested with authority, those who do the smaller business of life? It cannot be simply the law that men have "made."

Rousseau clearly saw this truth that both the freedom of the individual and the authority of government depend upon law for their validity. Yet he still treated law as an "institution" that men themselves set up or establish, so that law is by nature always "positive." But that was exactly what Hobbes had said, intentionally excluding social law in any sense, except that which a sovereign lays down and enforces. It is a paradox to say that law has authority for men, because they "make" it or "prescribe" it to themselves or "put" it above them. Law which is to perform the function Rousseau here discerned is not to be conceived in any terms that identify it with "positive" law.

(1) MONTESQUIEU AND HISTORICAL LAW

There were two significant lines along which further thought about law was to develop. Montesquieu in his *Spirit of the Laws* furnished abundant evidence of laws of every nation which were the historical product of a multitude of factors, some being human and moral in nature, others elements of circumstance. No man nor any body of men or government "makes" such law. The law is antecedent both in time and dignity to the activities of governments. Montesquieu himself called this "fundamental" law—for on it as a foundation the statesmen and governments should build. By reference to it they must do their legislating and arranging. Here law has a normative role, but it is not a norm which can be determined solely by reason but it must be empirically ascertained. Nations have a way of life which is the actual way they have become nations, and those who govern and direct the destinies of the nations should know and be guided by these fundamental principles of national life, which have authority in the sense that they are controlling practices of the nation.

Montesquieu's idea is basic to the conception of modern constitutional law. While written constitutions are in a sense made, quite as truly as positive law, nevertheless, the very idea of a constitution is that of a law under which the making of all particular laws and the exercise of the authority of government are subordinated. The law here is superior to the ruling of men. A constitution might thus serve to meet Rousseau's requirement. But here Hegel's objection must also be admitted: a constitution which is set up and amendable through conventions, is hardly likely to be the truly fundamental law which embodies the historical "spirit of the nation." A constitution may indeed have a certain cautionary value for a government, but it does not have the *profound* authority that will direct the spirit of man. The fact that people live under a written constitution is no guarantee whatsoever that they will conduct their affairs with a fine sense of personal obligation to each other and the community at large.

(2) KANT AND THE MEANING OF LAW

It was Kant who saw this argument about law to its ultimate conclusion. There is no disagreement between Kant and Rousseau on the point that man's freedom demonstrates itself in his self-legislation. But, according to Kant, it is truly *law* that must be prescribed. What Rousseau needed in his account of man was the motive of *respect* for law. The act of will here must be an act of reason; law, is at all times "the interest of reason." Thus, for example, the form of all knowledge is that of law. The idea of law determines us to seek our understanding of nature in terms of "lawful," that is, universal and necessary relations of what is given us in present fact and experience. The intelligibility of our natural world rests upon this affinity of the mind for law. And the moral life of man shows us the same authority of the idea of law in the reason of man. The most impressive aspect in man and all nature is law in its *objective character,* and it elicits the sense of awe or respect which men experience in contemplating the heavens or in moral duty.

There have been doubts as to whether this solution is sufficient for the problem of politics, but there is no question that it is to the point. The same is true of the older religious view of natural law and the law of

God. In both instances it is realized that for the general freedom of man there must be such a *supremacy of law* that it cannot be evaded either by adroit politicians in government or by subtle rationalizations of the individual "conscience." This is our own troubling problem today, in public and in private life.

V. *General Conclusions*

Freedom and authority can and must coexist in the same universe. The universe to which they are relevant is civilized human society. Men and women are the prime factors in the making of a civilized order of existence. They have made it by virtue of their own intelligence and moral powers, by their initiative, resourcefulness, industry, capacity for cooperative living, and by the objectives of life which have commended themselves as good. They realize the value of working in harmony, and become concerned about the unity of their society. They accept restraints, because they can see some good for themselves in their life in community. In short, morality is one of man's chief discoveries that make life in civilization possible. And the freedom of man has been essential to all discovery, initiative, self-restraint, and the interested efforts for both individual and general welfare.

But it is also a fact that man cannot have a civilized existence without the distinct agency of government. The state is a reality, and government is its function. And authority is an attribute of the state, acting through its government, which regulates, directs, makes decisions, and enforces its law upon men.

Both are necessary, then, freedom for *persons* and authority for *government*. They often appear to be in sheer opposition. In moments of conflict, as at present, freedom is "loved" and authority "hated." But the whole history of civilization has included within it a history of the effort to reconcile these two things in the actual politics of the period.

The contemporary approach to the problem is described by Robert K. Carr: "This pragmatic aim of Western man to get on with the business of reconciling liberty and authority . . . has been one of his outstanding characteristics since the revolutions of the seventeenth and eighteenth centuries."[40] However, the solution itself as Carr states it, is precisely that which the philosophers and jurists of those earlier and more ration-

[40]Carr, *op. cit.*, p. 6.

alistic days proposed. ". . . freedom in a civilized society is always founded on law enforced by government. . . . Freedom in the absence of law is anarchy.[41] . . . Liberty in the modern state is dependent upon authority for its existence."[42] But we should not forget the other practical truth, implied in this one, that for modern men who so value freedom that they seek to secure it by employing the forces of government, the government *has* authority for precisely that purpose, and so authority in turn depends for *its* existence on the freedom it serves. We must think of freedom and authority in their proper relationship which is that of interdependence.

Moreover they are both in a functional dependence upon a system in which there are other factors no less important than themselves. Law is one such additional factor. Authority and freedom are in right relationship when they are seen to entail definite rights of action according to law. In this sense, law is a norm or principle for government and not an enactment of government. Nor can it express merely the will of the generality of the people or of a governing body. There must be more "reason" to it, if it is to be the overruling principle under which the government and the people alike stand. It has to be conceived as "natural" or "divine" or "objective," in order to be the source of all limitation upon sovereigns and citizens alike and upon whole states and even all the nations of the world.

In this study we have only encountered further problems which are still to be solved, perhaps even stated. The immediate problem before us, however, is that of law which will be authoritative for men who value their freedom. What is wanted is a principle which will *define* the rights of man and the right of the state, and beyond that the rights of nations and the right of any organization which acts for the nations in order to secure all the rights and freedoms of man. So we must also think more about a system of rights as well as about law.

And further thought is needed about that which will command (in the moral sense) *obligation,* so that all parties, men, governments, nations, will discipline themselves, instead of needing to resort to force for the rule of law. A political decision must be capable of *justification* before the bar of the opinion of those whose lives it orders or affects. Hence, to take the example we have used, whenever the people of other

[41]*Ibid.*, p. 8.
[42]*Ibid.*, p. 12.

nations become alive to the bearing of an authoritative decision by the United States in the present war operation upon their own fate and fortunes, the situation of the authority is actually changed—we can no longer carry on as we would have done before the question arose, but must act by consulting the others. A "command authority" of the United States might take steps which so altered the conditions contemplated at the investiture of authority that we would actually lose title and all support for our actions, because it would have transgressed the freedom and independence of the other nations concerned.

How much authority should the state or its government have, on the one hand, and what are the rights and liberties of individuals and social groups? That is what has to be determined for each society according to the circumstances. For the reconciliation of freedom and authority has to be relevant to the particular conditions.

During the past war a philosophical writer, J. E. Turner, dealt with the question: "Is Liberty Compatible with Organization?" He rejected, as we have done here "the false antinomy between freedom and organization."

Naturally in a time when Europe and America were struggling for freedom that concept was uppermost in mind. But "the crucial task" is "to harmonize at one and the same moment individuality and cooperation." And cooperation comes about "only within a community of highly developed individuals, each of whom is guaranteed his due measure of freedom."[43] Thus freedom and organization are reconciled afresh for each novel situation.

But similarly the altered role of authority must be defined in any period. Authority, as we have chiefly known it, is closely associated with military business. The "necessity of authority" is clear in a war period. "Command authority" for the emergency becomes in the minds of those who exercise it a settled supremacy, so that the consulting of others becomes a sign of weakness and even an insult to the majesty of the state. But any people who are able by their moral and intellectual capacity to produce the power and wealth of a great nation can never be governed *domestically* along the lines of such authority, and in due time the government exercising it is compelled by their demands to resume its proper position. And what is that? To find and execute the law of the state and nation, and, in the case of a free people, to protect the liberty and rights

[43] *Philosophy*, London, July, 1942, XVII, 67, pp. 248, 249.

of every individual in the state. Authority comes down to earth in such a performance. But it is not to be buried under the earth any more than liberty (in the previous situation) is to be *submerged*. To seek to reduce authority to nothing, is to attempt an impossible elimination of the *political* function in a civilization.

The problem is one of finding the order or system of life in which the function of the free man and the function of the state are related in a fruitful way, with clear understanding on every hand of rights and obligations and the law of values of the whole order. But any such problem must be *worked out by all concerned,* working together. A government needs time to execute its policies; but it must also at reasonable intervals consult those who are being governed. Consultation is of the essence of good government. And freedom that is not *political* freedom, with power on the part of those governed to require attention to the judgment and decision of the people, is but an empty freedom.

Some may object that nowadays we should not resurrect authority as a "good" thing at all, but leave it to perish from the earth, when we shall have finished with our work and despatched the dragons of today who would consume our world with their authoritarian fire. Once upon a time, it may be conceded, authority did have the meaning here given it, of rightful power, power that honors law and seeks only the rule of law. But, it may be urged, authority today means to many people what they have witnessed in authoritarian governments—namely, ruthless exertion of their power, forcing their will upon other nations, and destroying any system of law and ideas which might encourage men to resist their aggressive will. Now it may well be that the searing experience of this age will be so deep in its effects that civilized men will never again want to use the word, "authority," except with detestation. But, if we were to surrender the term, we should have to provide something else to bear the meaning which it has consistently had in past Western history. Authority or sovereignty has meant power-with-right, whether right be conceived as natural or divine right, or as a title conferred by a solemn and free act of men.

There has been abundant criticism, of liberty, too, much of it with too great relish to be disinterested. The critics attack liberty as they look upon its meaning in the "liberalism" of the nineteenth century. It is condemned as a doctrine that necessarily leads to both unrestrained self-interest and personal irresponsibility. Today we have developed a profound consciousness of a general need among all people for social attitudes and the sense of membership in community.[44] This has favored a certain disparagement of liberty. But liberty has older and richer meanings than that.

There is a peculiar vogue in philosophy today which has been deliberately avoided here, and that is the abuse of the idea of freedom in existentialism. Freedom is talked about there as if it were an activity that refers to no agent, but is a substantial agency itself. Freedom has man by the hair and casts him about and man fears it, and we have a long story about something which we can recognize and can speak of in less lurid imagery as man's irresponsibility and lacking in courage to be himself.[45] But freedom in this school of thought somehow does not *belong* to anyone, not even to the spirit, as Hegel conceived it, to whom we ultimately seem to owe some of this strange abuse of the good word, "freedom." Such a usage of freedom works to the disadvantage of the individual, and by diminishing the importance of the person it may end by serving authoritarianism.

But what is authoritarianism? The mark of it is that whereas any civilized society depends upon liberty as well as authority, the government of such a society makes it authoritarian by turning its temporary power against liberty. It is not simply the possession of great power that constitutes the evil, as we see it, but the fact that the authority is corrupted by the nature of the policies it serves, and above all, by the disregard for the value of personal freedom. And the worst practices of authoritarian rule consist in perverting the very *means* by which people have in the past been able to achieve and maintain civil and political liberty, *viz.*, their resources of free expression in meetings and in print. The institutions that once prevented government from having its own way are turned against the possibility of men's ever developing free minds. The greatest danger from an authoritarian order is that it would not let a Spinoza or a Socrates live long enough to produce an idea that others could likewise find true or right, and by which they would judge of the works of their rulers and themselves, and unite then to take action about a state of affairs which they know to be evil.

[44] See Charles W. Hendel, *Civilization and Religion: An Argument About Human Values*, Yale University Press, New Haven, 1949. Cf. J. Middleton Murry, "Is the State an Abstraction?" in *Enquiry*, September, 1949, II, 3, London, pp. 29–31.

[45] See the forthcoming work by Paul J. Tillich, *The Courage to Be*, the Terry Lectures, Yale University, 1950, to be published by Yale University Press.

CHAPTER XLV

The Nature of Personal Freedom

By F. ERNEST JOHNSON

*Professor Emeritus of Education,
Teachers College, Columbia University*

IN APPROACHING A topic that owes its current interest to a contemporary problematic situation, it is important to notice first the nature of that situation. All significant philosophic inquiry has an existential aspect which conditions the manner in which perennial problems present themselves for solution in a given historical moment. The problem of human freedom, ineluctable so long as man is man, presents today a quite different aspect from that which it wore in the time, let us say, of the American Revolution. Against the background of an intolerable restraint, freedom appears as an undiluted good, unclouded by ambiguities. Man's freedom is then defined negatively, as a result of the removal of restraints.

But in a nation that has achieved a relatively high degree of independence and at the same time experienced stresses and strains because of inequalities of power and privilege, the kind of freedom that results merely from the absence of restraints is seen to be a poor affair. Then the problem of *order* looms large, and may become the prime consideration. In such a situation the threat to a free, democratic society is seen to be less from an arbitrary seizure of power than from popular clamor for a central power strong enough to maintain ordered human relationships in which security may be found. Plato's skepticism of democracy was at least in part well grounded: he discerned the threat to stable government that arises from popular failure to exercise restraint, or, as he put it, from an excess of freedom. The result is the destruction of order. A contemporary writer has said that we moderns should learn from Plato that the first business of government is to govern; it is a secondary responsibility to govern *well*.

What this adds up to is a restructuring of man's thought about freedom when his problem is no longer one of shaking off the shackles of alien oppression, but one of using his formal liberty to establish the basis of genuine freedom in a society of equals. In that statement I have intentionally distinguished liberty from freedom. Without overworking what may seem to be an arbitrary distinction, I wish from this point on to use the word, "freedom," to denote the achievement of a synthesis between liberty, conceived as absence of restraint, and social obligation, which imposes restraint.

When one attempts to say something meaningful about the nature of freedom as a personal possession, he can hardly avoid altogether the metaphysical problem which is involved. However, the line of thought that I am suggesting is, as I see it, not dependent upon the solution of the metaphysical problem. We may readily admit that a rigid determinism works havoc with any effort to defend convincingly the idea of moral accountability. One may even find something intriguing in the suggestion that there may be at the psychic level something corresponding to the Heisenberg principle in the physical world. That is to say, the concept of moral responsibility cannot make peace with philosophical necessitarianism. For this reason many of us find it necessary to posit contingency somewhere in the nature of things as a ground of moral accountability.

The fact is that the essence of freedom as a kind of moral experience has been recognized both by theologians and by positivists. "Of what importance is it," asked Calvin, "whether sin be committed with a judgment free or enslaved, so it be committed, with the voluntary bias of the passions. . . ?" The conscious exercise of choice is the essence of freedom. From a psychological viewpoint a man is free to the extent that he feels free. Freedom, one of the most eminent of positivist writers has said, "consists in the fact that I can act as I desire." This is, of course, but a modern rendering of Cicero's definition of freedom: *"potestas vivendi ut velis."* What I am contending here is that personal freedom, as experienced, has the same moral quality, no matter what may be the metaphysical assumptions underlying it. One is reminded of Bertrand Russell's remark that "there can be no argument *against* the physical world, since experience will be the same whether it exists or not." So it is, in the final analysis, with personal freedom.

This, it seems to me, adds immeasurably to the significance of personal freedom. It gives us a clue to an understanding of the conflict between those who insist that freedom should be defined in terms of absence of restraint—that is, the right to do as one chooses, and those who contend that freedom is to be found only in obedience to law. For the former are really seeking to preserve the right of persons as such to be exempt from compulsion to do the will of others, whether imposed by individuals, groups, or institutions; while the latter are seeking to define the conditions of inner spiritual freedom. To revert to our distinction between liberty and freedom, liberty is granted by the withholding of pressure, whether of restraint or constraint, but freedom is attained only as a realized capacity to choose what one holds to be preferable.

The classic example here is the agonized cry of Saint Paul: "So I find it to be a law that when I want to do right, evil lies close at hand. For I delight in the law of God, in my inmost self, but I see in my members another law at war with the law of my mind and making me captive to the law of sin which dwells in my members. Wretched man that I am! Who will deliver me from this body of death?" (Romans 7:22-24—Revised Standard Version). What Paul is struggling for is freedom in the only sense in which it is ultimately significant. Liberty, in the sense of power to choose, he takes for granted. But to be able to choose the good against an inner bent to evil—aye, there's the rub!

The Stoics' urge to live according to the law of nature reflects the same mood. "Who," says Epictetus, "chooses to live in error? No man. Who chooses to live deceived, liable to mistake, unjust, unrestrained, discontented, mean? No man." Bad men, he says, fall into evils they would avoid, and fail to obtain that which they wish. For, he declares, no bad man is free!

It would, of course, be a miscarriage of reason to infer that such considerations as these make liberty, whether political, social, or familial—liberty understood as resistance to coercion of mind and conscience—any less important than the literature of democracy represents it to be. But the duty to respect the liberties of others is an obligation arising out of the claim of persons as such, not out of any assumption that the bestowal of liberty of thought and action will make any one a free soul. The claim of persons to exemption from coercion—except as the well-being of the community requires it—is an ethical ultimate, because personality is an ultimate. The withholding of restraint out of respect for authentic liberties may actually increase the dimensions of the moral disaster awaiting the person who is hellbent; but this in no way lessens the obligation of others to allow him to make his own choices—again assuming that the social good does not require intervention.

I wish now very briefly to make application of this conception of freedom in three realms—politics, education, and religion. Let us begin with politics, because it is here that the challenge to the traditional claims of freedom is sharpest.

I said earlier that the increase in stresses and strains within our nation has shifted the historic focus of attention from protection against the infringement of liberty from without, to the maintenance of stability and order within. This shift became apparent as the Great Depression settled upon us, and made it glaringly evident that even the winning of a global war to make liberty "safe," gave no assurance that the fruits of liberty in terms of well-being would be duly garnered.

But with the mounting threat of Communist aggression since the end of the Second World War, this nation is challenged for the first time in its history by a power that has consistently and avowedly, since its inception, championed a wholly different theory of political and civil rights —a different conception of liberty. The characteristic American reaction is to revert to the old pattern of identifying our own cause with that of liberty—or "freedom," as we commonly say—and to assume that the survival of America will insure the perpetuation of the "freedoms" that we associate with democracy. I venture to suggest that we are neglecting an opportunity to make the present crisis an occasion for stocktaking with respect to Western democracy and for a reexamination of its major assumption, which I take to be that the maximization of individual political and social liberty is a primary good.

Let me illustrate. In an informing book, entitled *Public Opinion in Soviet Russia,* the author, Professor Alex Inkeles of Harvard, makes some observations that are as impressive as they are unusual, about freedom of the press. It would go without saying that the Soviet conception of freedom of the press is a travesty on liberty, as we in the West understand it. But this fact should not obscure what Professor Inkeles calls the "bipolar" character of the concept of press freedom: it involves both freedom and responsibility—or, as we should say in the context of the present discussion, both liberty and responsibility. He points out that "when press freedom is seen as a bipolar concept, it is the pole of responsibility that comes first in Soviet thought, and that exercising the right or the freedom is subordinate to the goals such exercise advances." Continuing, Professor Inkeles says:

> Hence, it is declared to be the responsibility of the press in the Soviet Union to see that elections are a success for the party, that the labor productivity of the people is high, and so on. If in serving these ends the press also provides an opportunity for people to enjoy freedom of the press, well and good; but this consideration of freedom is secondary in the Soviet Union to the responsibilities of the press, and may be and is sacrificed if need be. In the United States, the emphasis is placed on freedom rather than responsibility. Freedom of expression is the absolute value, at least for those who have the means to express themselves; if in so doing they advance the common weal or otherwise act to advance certain social goals and fulfil responsibilities to the society, that, too, is well and good. But this consideration of the common good is secondary to the freedom of expression and may, if need be, be sacrificed to that freedom.[1]

The point I want to make out of this is not only difficult to make; it is hazardous. To suggest that the kind of "responsibility" implicit in Soviet citizenship can be a discipline of inner freedom, is on its face preposterous enough. But the fact remains, I believe, that while the regimentation of Soviet life sadly needs the corrective our Western concept of individual liberty can furnish, the latter is itself in need of modification in the general direction of social responsibility that comes by way of acceptance of corporate discipline. Freedom in the moral and spiritual sense, or what I am calling personal freedom, can be as surely vitiated by the assertion of individual "rights" as it can be strangled by the hands of a police state.

The relevance to education of this concept of freedom is perhaps obvious already. It is in this area that stress on individual liberty has been most conspicuous for the past thirty years or more. What may be called the modern movement in education took its cue from the discovery of the wide range of individual differences among children within the limits of what is commonly called normality. The realization burst rather suddenly on educators that traditional school discipline and the curriculum

[1] Alex Inkeles, *Public Opinion in Soviet Russia*, Harvard University Press, Cambridge, 1950, p. 138.

itself put a premium on conformity, at the expense of naturalness and freedom of initiative and expression. It was a liberating discovery, and I believe the gains are vast and permanent.

But in order to prevent shipwreck, wiser minds in the movement had to stem the tide of the new educational "freedom" at the point where unimpeded spontaneity in overt behavior was mistaken for inner freedom. Social responsibility has come into the picture as a counterpoise to individual liberty; the individualistic elements have become subject to a corporate corrective; and responsible freedom is, I believe, coming into its own in general education.

Perhaps the best way to put this is to say that a well conceived revolt against arbitrarily imposed and repressive discipline tended to degenerate into an ill conceived nihilism with respect to discipline itself; but that the reaction has come, and discipline is coming to be regarded as an internalized autonomous experience in which growing persons adjust themselves to the social and moral realities of their environment. Education for citizenship is coming to be seen as a setting of the stage for furthering this process. What is authentic in the old individualism remains, but the "liberty" enshrined in it is being transmuted into inner personal freedom, autonomous and responsible.

Now a final word about the bearing of this discussion on religion. At the moment this is a rather explosive subject. I wish all of us who have any responsibility in the field of organized religion had the boldness to tackle it. Broadly speaking, the religious situation presents a close parallel to that which we have noted in the political sphere. The lines are drawn between what is called religious liberty and religious authoritarianism. Protestant and secular writers contend for the former with equal zeal and often in the same terms, though from different motives. The Roman Church is made the defendant, so to speak, and finds it difficult to state its case convincingly within the prevalent frame of reference. It happens that Protestant individualism and contemporary secular humanism, while wide apart in their deeper assumptions and intentions, are very closely matched with respect to their notions of liberty. They make a formidable combination.

In the context of this discussion both Protestants and secularists are preoccupied with "liberty." Roman Catholic apologists are ineffectually trying to convince non-Catholics that their rejection of religious individualism, with its emphasis on private right, is not inconsistent with freedom, which they believe must be conceived in relation to authority. As for the Jews, they are found on both sides of the line so drawn.

It should be said that this reference to Protestants, to be quite accurate, must be restricted to what may be called sectarian Protestantism—that portion of the Protestant community which adheres to a conception of the church as a "gathering" of persons who have, so to say, individually negotiated their salvation and become members of the voluntary "universal priesthood." Here the individual Christian is the primary consideration: the church is secondary. On the other hand, those communions—notably the Anglican and Lutheran—which accord primacy to the church, making the religious community the prior fact, cannot construct their idea of religious freedom on purely libertarian lines.

It is hardly to be expected that the wide chasm now existing will be speedily spanned. But both organized religion and the secular community have much at stake in the clarification of the "religious liberty" issue. I venture to say that on the non-Catholic side the main contribution to a better understanding will come from those who hold a sufficiently high conception of the church—or shall I say of the social basis of Christianity—to see that the secular notion of individual liberty is as inadequate in the religious as in the political sphere. For when religion is conceived as participation in the life of a corporate community, "liberty" passes over into the inner freedom that is fostered by a corporate discipline. Such an approach would still be attended by stubborn problems, but the two groups would at least have learned to speak the same language.

Comment by Swami Akhilananda:
May we take the liberty of stressing the dangers inherent in the modern movement against the old authoritarianism in education? It is evident in the life of modern youth that any disciplinary measures are resented. We admit that everyone should have proper opportunity and encouragement for individual growth, based on the recognition of individual differences. Individual initiative should not be crushed by authoritarianism, but a certain amount of discipline is absolutely necessary for cooperative living. A sense of responsibility and social consciousness must be cultivated, in order to foster proper self-expression without hindering the growth and development of others. Uncontrolled self-expression necessarily creates an egocentric attitude, along with all the evils that are observed in present day interpersonal relationships. The disturbances in the relationships of parents and children, husbands and wives, etc., can be traced considerably to the selfish, egocentric attitude of life. It seems to us that the destructive activities and many anti-social activities in school, college, and university life, which are disturbing the educators, can be traced to a great extent to the abuse of individual freedom without the sense of responsibility.

So we are compelled to think that broad basic religious ideals can eliminate the evils in the modern abuse of freedom. We do not hereby mean sectarian or authoritarian religious concepts. It is rightly said that we cannot serve God and Mammon simultaneously.

If we forget the basic goal of life and organize the educational system only for the purpose of obtaining information and increasing efficiency in technology and other applied sciences, then human beings are bound to degenerate. There are some philosophers and educators who seem to feel that scientific development will solve the problem of modern society. They advise us to give up the pursuit of the Eternal Reality. But when we study modern problems we realize that science is power without any guiding principle. Consequently, science and scientists can be used by anyone. In fact, this is occurring in different countries. We need a guiding and inspiring ideal, so that scientific knowledge and such other branches can be used for the betterment of humanity.

So we suggest that in order to understand the proper meaning and use of freedom, the educational system should be based on the fundamental religious ideal without any narrowness or sectarianism. Then alone can we expect to have real freedom, and at the same time control license, arrogance, and other anti-social activities. The goal of education ought to be the attainment of perfection that is already in man, as Swami Vivekananda says.

Comment by Rudolf Allers:

Most of Professor Johnson's essay appears to me as perfectly acceptable, even as very enlightening, and furnishing an appropriate basis for further discussion.

His comments on the problem of the freedom of the press deserve to be pondered. Perhaps, one might add that the press but too often confuses that in which the public is interested with that which is in the interest of the public.

There are only two points which I might question. One is the claim that man must be allowed under all circumstances to make his own choices, even if he is "hellbent." But we make use of force, if need be, to restrain a man from committing suicide. Should we not find ways and reasons to prevent him committing eternal suicide, too? Else, do we not become like Cain: "Am I my brother's keeper?" (Gen. 4:9.)

Secondly, I am more skeptical concerning the gains achieved by the recent changes in education. There is one test they do not stand. Were it true that naturalness and freedom of initiative and of expression, as modern educational theory conceives of them, are so helpful, then one would expect a definite decrease in the incidence of neurotic troubles. In fact, the opposite seems to be the case.

Comment by Edgar S. Brightman:

Professor Johnson's closely reasoned paper seems to me to be sound and much needed. There is nothing in it that I want to challenge.

There are, however, two points that, it seems to me, need supplementation. They are, first, the distinction between moral and political freedom, and, second, the function of corporate discipline.

As regards the first, the status of restraints is part of the ambiguity. Legislation imposes restraints on political freedom (or liberty); whereas the very nature of reality imposes restraints on moral freedom. Those restraints arise partly from the fact that freedom is a function of a thinking mind, and all free choices have to be made under the restraints imposed by the reasonings and principles of the mind. They arise also from the restrictions inherent in the field of choice, the free mind can choose only from what is given to it, and included in the given is the struggle against Paul's "body of death." The caused efficiency of each choice is another restraint; consequences will be what they will be. Moral freedom, then, is hardly the power to do what one desires, but requires also the wisdom to select the best possible from what is available. The idea of restraints is, therefore, inherent in moral freedom; and the duty of making the best of it is as essential to freedom as the right to choose. Such inner and essential restraints are quite different from political and legislative restraints. I would like to see fuller recognition of both types of restraint in the paper.

The second point, the function of corporate freedom, is even more important to explicate. The superiority of the Soviet citizens in regard to corporate discipline and responsibility, is an undoubted fact which should be frankly acknowledged and from which Americans have much to learn. However, there is a prior question which Professor Johnson does not raise explicitly and which should be raised, namely, the question, what is the function of corporate discipline? More simply: corporate discipline for what? Not every corporate end is a morally or economically or esthetically or religiously worthy end. What are the values which corporate discipline is intended to promote? The power of the state? The economic life alone? For myself, I strongly favor far more corporate discipline and legislation than we now have in America, but I want to have every such proposal for discipline tested by the norm of its effect on the individual persons in the body politic.

Comment by Stewart G. Cole:

Is not Dr. Johnson in his comments on the material of Professor Inkeles focusing one of the most neglected issues in American democracy and in the conflict between the democratic and the Communist ways of life? He is indicating that many advocates of the American way are still stressing the priority of the principles of individualism and moral freedom, and that the spokesmen of Communism are emphasizing excessively the authority of the principles of collectivism and moral discipline. Each represents a partisan position in a bipolar conception of the method of operation of a vigorous society. Cannot the advocate of each framework for human society benefit from the other's claim? A democracy, fit for the strains of human life of our times and in harmony with the trends in democratic morality and in the social sciences, will necessarily have to learn to strike a mediatorial balance between the claims of individualism *and* collectivism, freedom *and* responsibility, rights *and* obligations, in the multiple types of interrelationships of its people. We in this country need to grasp and embrace a substantial "ethics of responsibility," to bring our way of life into harmony with the implications of the American Creed.

Does Dr. Johnson not suggest an oversimplified analysis of the situation in drawing the lines between "what is called religious liberty and religious authoritarianism"? There is a conflict in religion, as between those who organize their faith socially by the principle of liberty, and those who depend considerably upon the principle of authoritarianism for ecclesiastical control. Aspects of this tension are observable within every religious faith and between sects within a particular faith. But what we need to look at here, in keeping with the foregoing interpretation of Dr. Johnson's thesis, is a more subtle weakness in religious strategy. It not only operates as a basis of tension between Protestants and Roman Catholics, but it involves each major religious faith and every denominational group in a moral problem within a particular faith. One phase of this problem is how to get devotees to assess reasonably the relative importance of the principles of individual freedom, social responsibility, *and* a fine moral balance between them, in the exercise of every activity in their faith. A collateral problem is how to motivate a religious group, whether a local parish, a denomination, a federation, or a major faith, so that it will practice the ethics of (a) liberty, (b) responsibility, *and* (c) a fitly conceived balance between liberty and responsibility in its full range of activities, including its relationships with corresponding groups of other religious faiths.

Comment by Karl W. Deutsch:

I am impressed by Dr. Johnson's paper and particularly by two of the points he raises:
1. There is, says Dr. Johnson, a neutral or collective element in freedom, including religious freedom, as well as philosophic or political freedom: "discipline," as Doctor Johnson sees it, "is coming to be regarded as an internalized autonomous experience in which growing persons adjust themselves to the social and moral realities of their environment." Could we be told more about the structure of this "internalized autonomous experience"? How does this "autonomy" work? Perhaps we might also add physical and technological realities to the "social and moral" ones to which adjustment must be made.
2. "When religion is conceived as participation in the life of a corporate community," Dr. Johnson concludes in his paper, " 'liberty' passes over into the inner freedom that is fostered by a corporate discipline." Which of the existing religions and "corporate disciplines" does Dr. Johnson have in mind? Perhaps not the "corporate" of the seventeenth century New England Puritans over Catholics, Quakers, and the reluctant Roger Williams? Nor perhaps does he mean the "corporate discipline" of the Roman Catholic Church in Spain over Protestants or agnostics—or that of any one of the religious factions in Israel over the rest of the community. But if so, where and how is common agreement to be found? Ought it not to have been found, at least in part, by methods resembling those of science, that is, by proposing patterns of behavior for individuals and groups, and judging these patterns of morality or religion by their observable verifiable consequences?

Comment by Nels F. S. Ferré:

I have read Professor Johnson's wise and weighty paper with real interest. Especially was I happy to note what he says about discipline as integral to education. Knowledge is a social act, and the best of it merits reverence as well as experimentation. Somehow the seriousness of life makes it inadvisable to make the authority which results in freedom simply subject to the learner's whims or to experiments in group dynamics. Though truth is open to constant individual and social testing, those who educate must, as far as possible, handle both the truth and the learners within the concerned discipline of those who are themselves under an Authority Which constitutes the ground and reality of their own freedom.

Comment by Roy Wood Sellars:

I agree heartily with the general purport of Professor Johnson's analysis of personal freedom. It does have two dimensions, or directions, usually spoken of as freedom from and freedom for. Demand for freedom from what are felt to be restraints and constraints is *justifiable,* when it can be shown that such curbing of personal desire and judgment is in the service of beliefs and institutions which are outworn and can be intelligently challenged. I suppose the democratic tradition is that the burden of proof is upon constraint.

But *freedom for* implies effective autonomy and the qualities which persons need to make the most of their lives within society. On the social side, it involves supporting institutions to give the proper conditions. On the personal side, it implies developed personal qualities of self-control and rationality. Ethics has concerned itself with the qualities and virtues essential to moral autonomy. Discipline is hardly separable from the eliciting of judgment and understanding.

I am not quite certain that Professor Johnson's stress upon order and discipline within a redefined freedom is not overweighted. There must be *criteria,* such as personal and social welfare and achievement. And institutions, likewise, have their responsibilities. For instance, churches desire freedom from control and autonomy. But they, also, must justify their methods and goals. I suppose my query is whether Professor Johnson did not neglect this aspect of the question too much.

CHAPTER XLVI

The Dialectics of Freedom

By RUDOLF ALLERS

*Professor of Philosophy, Graduate School,
Georgetown University*

THE FORMULA, "freedom and authority," suggests, as do many such formulas of similar structure, that there exists between the two terms a perfect opposition and that they are mutually exclusive. They may be, indeed, defined in such a manner as to make this opposition appear inevitable. But it is not certain that they must be thus defined.

Nor is it certain that to an opposition of terms must correspond in reality the same opposition of the referents. It is submitted in this essay that this mutual exclusiveness does not exist, and that, to the contrary, the two terms are correlated to each other so as to make each of them, or rather each of the referents, dependent on the other. A relation entailing interdependence and contradiction is called dialectical. Hence, the title.

The thesis, then, is that freedom, to be truly what the name means, requires the existence of authority and even brings it forth. Likewise, that authority is meaningless unless exercised over free persons.

The Philosophical Standpoint

How such a problem as that of "freedom and authority" appears to the individual student depends on his general philosophical standpoint. Terms are equivocal; ideas allow for very different interpretations. Each author takes for granted his own interpretation and his own terminology, and assumes tacitly that every other one uses terms in the same sense. I shall, therefore, define as far as possible the fundamental standpoint from which the problem will here be envisaged.

As it is impossible to give a detailed explanation, let alone a formal justification of these fundamental ideas, I shall simply list a number of propositions in dogmatic form. This procedure will, or so I hope, have at least the advantage of rendering impossible arguments arising because of equivocations.

The following propositions, then, are fundamental for the argument of this essay:

1. It pertains to man's nature that he have a free will. If this is not assumed, all discussions on freedom or similar problems become meaningless. If he is not free, man is caught in the inexorable cosmic process, and it may as well be his fate to be made the passive subject of totalitarian power as to indulge in the illusion of liberty.

2. Man's will exercises a "ruling power"—*dominium politicum,* says Aquinas—over all appetitions. If man is in full possession of his capacities, he need never become the passive playball of some forces, not even of his "instincts," the existence of which in the normal adult is anyhow questionable.

3. Like all appetition, will aims at the realization of the good. By virtue of the fact that it still is to be realized, the good which is the end pursued by will is not yet real. All will aims at a future state of affairs, which is judged "better" than that existing at present. But no judgment can have a compulsory power over will which, while still aiming at the realization of some good, is not forced to aim at that good which is judged as greater: *Video meliora proboque, deteriora sequor.*

4. Among the goods which are possible ends of will there are some whose goodness consists in nothing other than their ability to provide satisfaction. Their goodness depends largely, though, perhaps, not exclusively, on their relation to man's desires. There are others which "exist"—in the peculiar mode in which values and other non-material things may be said to exist[1]—independently of their ability to provide satisfaction. They are good because they embody "objective values."

5. The objective values form a definite order which originates from the intrinsic nature of the values. This order is, however imperfectly, discoverable. The theory of "relativism" in regard to values is unfounded, not countenanced by facts, and deleterious to any attempt at defending any view on human affairs as being better than another. Especially, if there is no objective order of values, does it become impossible to maintain that man is entitled to liberty or that a liberal political constitution

---

[1] Cf. Nicolai Hartmann, *Das Problem des geistigen Seins,* Walter de Gruyter, Berlin, 2nd edition, 1949.

offers any advantages over one which turns man into a mere atom of a greater whole. Without the acceptance of the idea of an objective axiological order, criticism of ideas not approved by ourselves becomes utterly meaningless. We then have no answer to the contention that others may prefer what appears as execrable to ourselves.

For the end of the present discussion it does not make any difference in what manner the objective order is conceived. I am convinced, personally, that axiological objectivism requires the idea of a *summum bonum*. But as long as it is admitted that some sort of objective order of values exists and may be, however faintly, envisaged, a discussion on what is better and what worse will make sense.

Three Aspects of Freedom

A well known distinction opposes "freedom from" to "freedom for." The former term refers to the absence of all obstacles rendering impossible or insufficient the satisfaction of the so-called "basic needs." If one is agreed on these needs, the types of freedom-for may be determined. The notion, however, entails at least two difficulties.

The first becomes visible when one considers that every freedom-for may encounter obstacles. Freedom-for presupposes, therefore, a peculiar kind of freedom-from. Obstacles which oppose the satisfaction of basic needs appear as simple denials of the corresponding freedom-from. This freedom is itself basic and not related secondarily to another freedom. But what is comprised under the heading of freedom-for, that is, for ends not related to basic needs, requires as a condition that there be a secondary freedom, secondary in the sense that it is subservient to the other. In other words, the distinction is not of that clarity which some seem to attribute to it.

The second difficulty is more serious. Satisfaction of basic needs is not definable because of the wide range from the lowest degree of satisfaction to any higher degree. One has only to consider the meaning of "freedom from want." It is impossible to indicate how far supply must be increased to fulfil the condition of freedom from want. There is the level of mere subsistence on which the basic needs for food, shelter, and so forth, are indubitably satisfied. But an existence on the mere subsistence level is not at all "satisfactory."

Any freedom may be viewed, first, as determined by the ends for the realization of which man is made free; and, secondly, in regard to the degree in which such realization is possible. The first consideration may be called "vectorial," the second "scalar." Most discussions on freedom take account only of the vectorial aspect; they seem to presuppose that freedom is essentially unlimited. From the remarks made by several writers on these problems, one gathers that they apparently view any restriction of freedom as unjustified, and fear that even a slight restriction threatens freedom. But limitation is not only not tantamount to derogating freedom, but is a condition without which freedom cannot exist.

Apart from the twofold aspect of being determined by its vectors and its scalars, there is a third aspect of freedom which often seems to be neglected. The possession of freedom on the part of the individual and its recognition on the part of the community or the legal constitution is one thing; the exercise of freedom another.

In ordinary life man recognizes that there may be conditions under which full use of his freedoms is either unadvisable or wrong. The general freedom or right to say what one thinks, may be, and often is, restricted by the demands of prudence and of charity, not to mention custom. Freedom is not threatened nor abrogated, if account is taken of such conditions. In fact, nobody but some extremist will claim that his freedom is curtailed by such considerations. Neither does man, generally, admit that he or any of his fellows is free to do evil. It is tacitly understood that freedom is only for good.

One has, therefore, to distinguish a subjective and formal side of freedom, on one hand, and a material and objective, on the other. Subjectively and formally, man may be free to utter any sentiment, opinion, judgment, on anything whatsoever. Materially and objectively he may be subject to restrictions, both in regard to vectors and scalars.

Relativism and Changing Human Nature

The recognition of limiting conditions does not contradict the principle stated above that values are objective and stand in a recognizable order. The changing conditions allowing or restricting freedom are sometimes used as an argument in favor of relativism when they appear successively in history or simultaneously in different civilizations. These facts are alleged as a proof of human nature being subject to change; man has no longer, according to this view, the same nature he had thousands of years ago, and it is hoped that his nature will change to the better the further civilization progresses.

That this change, should it take place at all, will be for the better is, of course, a mere postulate or even nothing other than a fond hope. It is part of the creed of progress as the eighteenth century imagined it. However, none of the enthusiastic advocates of progress, so numerous in the seventeenth and eighteenth centuries, believed in a changing human nature. *Les philosophes* thought rather of human nature as essentially good, of this goodness realized in a "state of nature" and deteriorated by social and cultural factors. How this good human nature could ever give birth to such deteriorating forces remains an unexplained mystery. The modern idea of progress, though a descendant of that alive around 1750, is no longer the same as it was at first; it is the product of an unholy alliance between the notion of moral and cultural perfection and that of biological evolution.

It is necessary that a few words be said on this particular interpretation of "progress." In this regard, the following quotation appears to the point:

> ... the problem of values must be faced. Man differs from any previous dominant type in that he can consciously formulate values. And the realization of these in relation to the priority determined by whatever scale of values is adopted, must be accordingly added to the criteria of biological progress, once advance has reached the human level. Furthermore, the introduction of such criteria based upon values ... alters the direction of progress. It might perhaps be preferable to say that it alters the level on which progress occurs.

These lines are taken from the concluding chapter in Professor Julian Huxley's work, *Evolution*.[2] Only one additional remark seems necessary. Professor Huxley justly says that the "level is altered on which progress occurs." One has, however, to consider that with a shift of level is associated also a shift of categories. That is, progress assumes a totally different character on the new level, even though it remains progress nonetheless. Aristotelian or Thomistic Scholasticism would insist, and I believe correctly, that progress is not an unequivocal but an "analogical" term.

Whatever formulation one may prefer, one thing stands out clearly:

[2] Julian Huxley, *Evolution*, Harper & Brothers, New York–London, 1942, p. 575.

that to equate progress in civilization with evolution amounts to the logical fallacy of a *metabasis eis allo genos*.

It is because of this fallacy that the advocates of a "changing human nature" become involved in self-contradiction. It is hardly an exaggeration if one attributes to these men the idea that the progress from older forms of political constitution to that of democracy entails not only a definite advance and improvement of human situations, but also a change of human nature: progress gives birth to the "democratic man."

But were human nature to change, it could not do so in a sudden cataclysm. Man would change gradually and some individuals would change more and others less. Some parts of mankind or even of a nation would advance more quickly than others. The effect must be a growing inequality. The final result might well be the emergence of a race of "supermen," rather as Nietzsche conceived of these fantastic creatures. Men would have to cease to believe that they are "born equal," or each of the new race will have to arrogate the name of *homo sapiens* to himself, while degrading his less fortunate brother to the status of *homo servus*.

Of course, nothing of this kind will happen. The talk about changing human nature is, after all, but an outcome of a certain benevolent but improvident enthusiasm which one need not take seriously, were it not that it apparently appeals to many uncritical minds.

The Complexity of Truth

It is the uncritical mind to which many things are "self-evident." It would be well if both the philosopher and the average person realized that their most cherished beliefs may not be as well founded as they love to think. What is evident to an orthodox follower of Lenin fails to convince a Western democrat. The latter's conviction that "men are born equal" was inconceivable for a member of the privileged estates of the *ancien régime*. And not because of presumptuousness, or lust for power, or any such reasons; these men simply "knew" for sure that inequality is the law of human nature. All problems present different aspects according to the frame of reference within which they are envisaged.

It is not otherwise with the conception of freedom. If one distinguishes with Mr. T. G. Weldon[3] three fundamentally different conceptions of

[3] T. G. Weldon, *States and Morals*, Whittlesey House, New York, 1947.

the State—the Democratic, the Organic, and the Power State—the consequences differ considerably in regard to the interpretation of freedom.

It is important that one see clearly in this respect. If a proposition is not of such a kind as to be truly evident—and of these there are very few; its evidence rests on that of another more general proposition which may be justly called a "prejudice"—not by way of disparagement, but in the literal sense—and it is precisely the examination of this implicit presupposition on which hinges the validity of the allegedly evident statement.

"Whatever," writes Mr. Weldon, "the authors of the Declaration of Independence asserted to the contrary, the inalienable rights of men as such to life, liberty, and the pursuit of happiness, are neither self-evident nor demonstrable."[4] Exception may be made to the last two words. It might be possible to arrive at a demonstration, if certain presuppositions are made and, perhaps, even made evident.

It may be that the authors of the Declaration of Independence were not as assertive as Mr. Weldon thinks. The American Declaration says: "We hold . . . ," but the French *Déclaration des droits de l'homme* makes a statement of unconditioned generality. One asks whether or not the authors of the Declaration were conscious of the fact that any such proposition can be held evident only within a definite frame of reference, whereas the doctrinaires of the Revolution did not hesitate to proclaim universal truth.

Theoretical discussions, as well as the handling of practical affairs, would profit were men more conscious of the primary assumptions they make, and which, once made, disappear from conscious thought because they are taken for granted.

One of the most disastrous of these implicit assumptions—though it is often not implicit at all, but openly professed, still without any further examination—is that that truth must be simple. One asks in vain, why? There is no reason whatsoever to assume that reality is essentially simple. This is so little the case that a philosopher once placed on the title page of a work the motto, *Simplex sigillum nec veri nec falsi*.[5] Simplicity has nothing to do with truth; it is not a criterion of truth, and simple statements are as much liable to be false as are complicated ones.

The problem of freedom is as complicated as any other of the funda-

[4]*Ibid.*, p. 128.
[5]J. Cohn, *Theorie der Dialektik*, F. Meiner, Leipzig, 1923.

mental questions. Its complication is of its essence, and not, as some seem to believe, the result only of recent practical situations. It is not because some people see fit to propagate Communistic ideas among the students of American schools that the problem of limitations of "freedom of speech" or "academic freedom" emerges. It has been there, in fact, all the time. The actual situation has only rendered more people aware of this problem.

Some Views of Freedom

It seems to be the opinion of many that freedom is essentially unlimited, and that all limitations are the result of unwelcome necessities. Man in his ideal state should, according to this conception, enjoy unrestricted freedom. He could not possess unlimited scalar freedom, because the finiteness of his capacities would force him to renounce the achievement of ends he might imagine. But he would be free to move along any vector he might choose.

Such was, apparently, the idea of John Stuart Mill. He recognized, of course, that unlimited freedom is a utopian dream and that the concrete human situations render certain limitations inevitable. The inevitability of limitations, however, can be seen as founded on different reasons. Mill reveals clearly his position when he writes: "If grown persons are to be punished for not taking proper care of themselves, I would rather it were for their own sake than under the pretence of preventing them from impairing their capacity of rendering to society benefits."[6] It is not a convincing argument for an author to say that "he rather would." Mill, too, starts with some "evident truth," the nature of which is stated in the motto on the front page of his essay. It is taken from W. von Humboldt: "The great leading principle . . . is the absolute and essential importance of human development in its richest diversity." Absolute and essential, indeed, only if certain presuppositions are admitted as "evident."

The intellectual climate in which Mill moved is that of an ontological nominalism, an ethical autonomism, and an anthropological subjectivism. Only within this frame of reference may Humboldt's principle be said to be absolute and essential, or may Mill feel as he does.

[6] John Stuart Mill, *On Liberty and Considerations on Representative Government*, edited by R. B. McCallum, Oxford University Press, Oxford, 1948.

Mill's utilitarianism is, of course, not a primary attitude; it flows from the general philosophy indicated above. Mill's avowed preference, by virtue of which he "rather would" this and not that, cannot be derived from his utilitarian conception. It is not the utilitarian principle that allows for an answer to the question: Useful for whom?

Suppose that a small fraction of a large population feels quite unhappy, unless its members are permitted to preach their ideas openly and unreservedly. But the majority feels differently; most people feel unhappy when they hear these ideas preached. The conflict cannot be solved on the basis of any "felicific calculus." Nor can one appeal to "expediency," because the question, "Expedient to whom?" is unanswerable.

All such questions must be placed in a much wider frame than that of utilitarianism or, for that matter, any kind of "anthropological subjectivism." These problems require that they be envisaged from the angle of a conception within which man's place in reality can be defined.

It must be noted that this conception need not yet be metaphysics in the proper sense. The problems remain the same also when they are viewed as pertaining to a merely "phenomenal world." Man's being (*esse*) is to be (*existere*) in a world, as Heidegger justly emphasized.[7]

And it is particularly to be in association with his fellows, what Heidegger calls *Mitsein*. This is pure description. But, "to be in a world" is not yet "to face a world." Man's position is customarily viewed as if he were facing a world which would be, so to speak, "outside of himself," and of which to become or not to become a part is left to his decision. But the fact is that he is part whether or not he be aware of it. He is so much part of the world that he cannot think either of himself or of the world without taking account of the other. Man without a world is as empty as any Kantian concept without intuition, and without society he becomes undistinguishably merged with the chaos of nature[8] and never attains the actualization of his strictly human capacities and so never the "development in its richest diversity."

Consequently, there cannot exist any independence of man in regard to the laws which govern both nature and society. Whatever his freedom, it is limited by his relations to his fellows, severally and totally as society. These relations, to say it once more, are not "outside" of or added to man's nature, but constitutive of it. So also are the limitations of freedom

[7] M. Heidegger, *Sein und Zeit,* Niemeyer, Halle a.S., 1927, pp. 114 ff.
[8] The expression is, so far as I know, Feuerbach's; the idea is, of course, much older.

not extraneous to freedom but essential aspects of it. Freedom exists only when and as limited.

Were freedom not limited and did its exercise not encounter resistance it would not be. The concept which considers freedom as essentially unlimited is, in truth, the result of a "secularization" of the notion of divine freedom. But this process yields meaningless results because man has no means to understand God's freedom and in arrogating for himself what he believes to be an attribute of divine nature, he forgets that all statements of this kind are "analogical," or, as St. Augustine said, that God *melius scitur nesciendo*. By rejecting the idea of God, man does not acquire the right to credit himself with the attributes the faithful predicate of divine nature.

It is not the fact that man's nature is limited nor that many ends are mutually exclusive of each other, which bothers those who conceive of freedom as essentially unlimited. They will admit that "one cannot have the cake and eat it." Although many feel like the little boy who was asked, on his birthday, whether he wanted to listen to the band or go donkey riding, and replied: "I want to ride the donkey to the concert."

Nor are these people disconcerted too much by the fact that one cannot pursue all imaginable ends, though they believe that all opportunities should be open to all men. Goethe's advice to seek infinity by moving in all directions within finitude—*Willst Du in's Unendliche schreiten, geh' im Endlichen nach allen Seiten*—is suitable, perhaps, only for few people. What man demands is not that he become actually an infinite being, but that he be free to choose among an infinite number of ends. And choose "freely," that is, uninhibited by any conditions extraneous to his being.

But there is no infinite number of ends. However numerous, their number is finite. To the finiteness of being corresponds the finiteness of freedom, both in its vectorial and its scalar aspects.

The exercise of freedom, like that of any power in man, is possible only if there is something on which, and, therefore, against which, this exercise is effected. As Spinoza put it: *Omne ens in suo esse perseverari conatur*. The concept of a basically unlimited freedom is self-contradictory. It is not the mere fact of consideration to be taken of others and their rights which limits human freedom, as some formulas seem to imply. Thus Lord Acton wrote that freedom consists in "the assurance that every man shall be protected in doing what he believes his duty, against the influence of authorities and majorities, custom and opinion."[9] This definition will appear acceptable to many. It is, however, far from being clear and requires comment.

"Every man" can mean, obviously, only every man sound of mind and fully responsible. Neither the child nor the fool can be allowed such freedom. A schizophrenic may see his duty in doing the most unreasonable and dangerous things. He is, of course, free inasmuch as he is human; he, too, possesses "inalienable rights." But he cannot act as a responsible member of society.

It is only a part of the truth, if it is said that the fool must be prevented from doing harm so that the normal people may be protected. Obvious though this be, it is secondary. The primary thing is that the fool's actions are wrong and his sense of duty perverted.

The definition of Lord Acton, therefore, presupposes that the "sense of duty" be of the right kind, within the framework of a theory of objective right and wrong. One is led, automatically, as it were, back to the notion of the "natural law."[10]

A further qualification seems necessary. The mere "sense of duty" is not enough; it ought to read "considered sense of duty." It is easy for man to believe that he is prompted by a sense of duty, whereas, in truth, he is obeying passion or some egoistic desires. Mr. James Branch Cabell, in his *Jurgen*—a book as clever as it is fantastic—has a young man remark, "I shall always do my duty as I see it—but, then, I was born with bad eyes." Some are, maybe, born that way; but more acquire this defect later. The sense of duty or conscience must be enlightened by reason. One may dislike custom and opinion, authority and the will of majorities; but they may still voice what is just.

Without making use of some criteria outside and above one, one cannot arrive at a final judgment. If to behave as the definition of Lord Acton suggests were the essence of freedom, society would have no right whatsoever to impose restrictions on any individual, not even on the fool.[11]

To discover all the implications of a "sense of duty" one would have to

---

[9] Lord Acton, "The Theory of Freedom in Antiquity," *The History of Freedom and Other Essays,* edited by Reginald V. Lawrence and John Neville Figgis, Macmillan & Company, Ltd., London, 1907, p. 3.

[10] Cf. M. J. Hillenbrand, *Power and Morals,* Columbia University Press, New York, 1949, especially pp. 69 ff.

[11] A consistently subjectivistic and relativistic conception would, in fact, have no plausible reason for putting restrictions on the fool. The only reasons are those that are practical, such as protection of the others.

unravel the many threads interwoven in this idea. The influence of Christian ethics and Kantian moral philosophy, of Shaftesbury's "moral sense," and of the interpretation given to it by Hutcheson and Adam Smith, of Reid's "commonsense," and of the French Enlightenment, and others, too, would have to be appraised. For these men, moral truth appeared as not less objective than any other truth; perhaps, even more objective than many other truths. They believed in the "natural law," even if they did not stress the point.

But the notion of the "natural law" had undergone a subtle modification since the time of Thomas Hobbes. With him the natural law became a law of nature, comparable to those physics discovers. No longer is the natural law a reflex of the *lex aeterna* and implanted somehow into the minds of men, but it becomes more and more like the laws of human nature. It then depends on the view one has of nature in general and of human nature in particular, what consequences he draws. Hobbes concluded that human nature is possessed only by lust of power and fear of death; thus he arrives at his well known political philosophy. Others thought better of man's nature, and believed that his inclinations are fundamentally good; in so far as they are, they follow the "natural law," and inclination then becomes a criterion of the right. It would seem that any doctrine denying to the good some kind of objectivity must arrive at either the one or the other conception. In both cases, man's freedom is jeopardized. He becomes the slave either of a self-created tyranny in the Leviathan, or of his inclinations and impulses which he has no means to evaluate.

If the notion of an impulsive, subjective "sense of duty" be taken without qualification, it endangers the very idea of freedom. But suppose that the notion of this sense of duty be sufficiently clarified and rendered unequivocal. This sense discovers what man ought to do, what ends he ought to pursue. Therewith, however, the "autonomy" of will comes to an end. Man appears as subject to laws which are extrinsic to his nature.

This is only apparently the case. If one realizes that the opposition of ego and non-ego, as it usually is made, is based on a misinterpretation of reality—of which man is part—and has to be replaced by the "dialectical" formula indicated above, the objection loses its validity. Man by obeying the law which he encounters as not his, in fact, obeys the law which is his, because he is, as a part of reality, subject to this law which governs also his own being. Not the idea of "heteronomy," to speak in

Kant's terms, but that of an exaggerated "autonomy" is contrary to human nature and man's dignity.

It would seem that the best definition of freedom is still that suggested by Anselm of Canterbury: freedom is *rectitudo voluntatis propter se servata,* righteousness of will preserved for its own sake.[12] Righteousness implies that there be precepts to be observed. Freedom is significant only, if and in so far, as it is limited by principles.

The limitation is both vectorial and scalar. Reference has been made above to the obvious fact that ends may be incompatible with each other and that this incompatibility limits the exercise of freedom. Envisaged from the angle of determinant principles, this limitation appears in a new light. It is not simply a material impossibility, a result of man's restricted power, of his incapacity to pursue manifold ends at the same time, but the necessary consequence of the order of vectors. It is superficial to claim that all vectors are of the same dignity. They form an order, and thus stand to each other in the relation of higher and lower.

Utilitarianism, relativism, and similar doctrines are open to the unanswerable objection that the principle on which they rest is arbitrary and undemonstrable. Why should the "greatest happiness of the greatest number" be sought? Why should the opinion of one group, be it however numerous, prevail over that of others? Why should a man be permitted to utter publicly whatever ideas he may cherish?

An Example: Freedom of Speech

To examine a special instance, some limitations of "freedom of speech" are, probably, recognized by most people. They agree, on the whole, that man is not free to slander his fellow, to use offensive language, to divulge secrets confided to him, openly to preach immorality. The idea of what constitutes improper or offensive language, or immorality, or slander, may vary. But some general agreement seems to exist.

"Freedom of speech" figures among the "inalienable rights." But what precisely this freedom implies is not defined. As the words stand, they seem to indicate that freedom of speech is an unequivocal term, hence that all speech under all conditions is covered by the formula. That this cannot be the case becomes clear, if one takes account of the recognized limitations mentioned above.

[12] Anselm of Canterbury, *De libero arbitrio,* c. 13.

Speech, as referred to in the formula, is not the more or less pleasurable exercise of the articulatory organs. It is, first, significant utterance, and, secondly, directed at an audience. As many things may be signified, the question arises whether or not one has to do with one vector only. Is speech on this or that, to this or that person or group, one and the same thing? Its oneness becomes questionable if account is taken of what is expressed or communicated.

If freedom of speech is curtailed in some respect, it does not follow that its existence is denied or its exercise threatened. Freedom of speech does not imply that a man is free to say whatever he wishes under whatever conditions. If, therefore, it were to be claimed that certain things cannot be taught to immature minds, that other things should not be publicized, that uninhibited discussion of still other things is contrary to the interest of the community, or any such restrictive measure were taken, freedom of speech would not necessarily be endangered or abolished.

Those who are afraid of losing this freedom or of the democratic principle being imperiled, base their indignant protests on the idea that freedom of speech is a right vested in the individual person and independent of all extraneous conditions. In other words, their argument is that of an unlimited subjectivism, implying the notion of unlimited freedom. So far as restrictions are recognized, they are envisaged as imposed by necessity, not as inherent in or correlated to freedom. Obligations are enforced; they do not pertain to the nature of freedom itself.

This view is basically not too different from that of Thomas Hobbes. This philosopher, too, recognized a fundamental equality of all men, which, with him, was founded not on rights that were inherent in human nature, but on the capacity of every man to damage and kill his fellow, either by brutal force or by stealth. Mutual obligations do not arise from either human nature or a "natural law," but from dire necessity; because they are in a certain sense "unnatural," they must be imposed and maintained by the power of the tyrant.

Thomas Hobbes was not a democratic thinker. Democracy seems to imply respect for every man's person and, therefore, derives the obligation, under which everyone stands, not from necessity but from the very essence of its fundamental conception. Obligation and freedom belong together. To be obliged by the positive law, the political constitution, the moral principles, even by custom, is not in contradiction to man's freedom, and does not diminish it in the least.

It will be objected that man finds the principle of obligation in his own conscience. This is what Lord Acton implied. But conscience—like memory—is easily deceived. Many a man has deluded himself in believing that he was obeying his conscience, when in truth he was prompted by totally different motivation. If a man were to make what conscience seems to suggest at a given moment his only guide, he would make himself into the supreme lawgiver.

It is inevitable that doing one's duty be, at times, unpleasant. The "good feeling" of having done one's duty is often but a poor compensation. Nothing could be more false than the idea that men act only for the sake of some pleasure they expect as a sort of reward for having done their duty. Christian morals do not tell man to do good because he then will be rewarded; he ought to do what is good—or, in the terms of Christian doctrine, what is the will of God—simply because it is good. He is told to love his neighbor as himself, not to earn thus some reward, but because his neighbor is invested with all the dignity which is man's.

Self-interest, however "enlightened," is not a foundation of morality nor of human society. The idea of an unlimited freedom is born out of self-interest, not a very enlightened one, it is true.

Freedom, Authority, and Democracy

It is claimed that all restriction of freedom endangers democracy. This seems to be fallacious. True, there are forms of undemocratic political life in which freedom is restricted. But one cannot conclude therefrom, that all limitation of freedom—beyond the barest necessity—is for that reason anti-democratic.

One might risk the statement that this overemphasis on freedom is the manifestation not so much of a democratic as of an adolescent mentality. No life requires more that those who lead it be mature than does democratic life. The immature mind is not fully responsible. The greater is the misfortune if the immature are entrusted with responsibility.

The essence of democracy is that—ideally speaking—every citizen be fully responsible. If democracy fails, it is because the citizens were not aware of their responsibilities. Of these responsibilities, one of the greatest is to see to it that the good be realized as far as this is within human power. As it is not an infringement of freedom to prevent a man from doing harm to himself or others, so also is it not a diminution of freedom if men are hindered from spreading evil.

Freedom is and cannot be but freedom for the good. If we are agreed that the democratic form of life is a good or that this form of life approximates the ideal form of a community more than any other, then it follows that what is contrary to this ideal is evil. And evil is to be prevented.

It is on this point that the question of authority finds its answer. Nobody doubts that some authority has to exist for the sake of maintaining civic order. The law must have its executive organs. But not all law is written. Some of the most fundamental laws are neither written nor stated explicitly. They must be observed, because they are the very laws of man himself. That he does not recognize them as such should make no difference. What is fundamental is often discovered last and through a long and laborious search.

All authority exists for the sake of an end. Authority is established that a good may be realized, or, if real, preserved. In the life of a community this good is ultimately that of all, or the common good.

Authority is the formal aspect of that power by which a person or an institution deserves to be called *auctor rei publicae*. The *res publica* is not simply the state or the territory or the might of a nation; it is primarily the common good. There is nothing more "public," or more in the interest of the public, than the common good.

The common good is not freedom. Freedom is, rather, that endowment of human nature which renders possible the pursuit of the good. This ought to be clear, for freedom may be as well—and has unfortunately been quite frequently—for the pursuit of evil.

Freedom is, to say it once more, not freedom for everything; it is only freedom for the good. Freedom of speech, too, falls under this definition. No college would permit any member of its faculty to give a course on "successful adultery." It does not matter whether or not this—fictitious—college professor be convinced that adultery is all to the good. That it is objectively not good, is all that counts.

It is, therefore, no deprivation of freedom if people are hindered in spreading ideas which are the opposite of what is—with cogent reasons—believed to be the good.

Who says freedom, says limitation. Who says democracy, says limitation. The limitation of which so much has been said on these pages, is something wholly other than forcefully imposed "domination"—in the sense Professor Santayana uses the term in his latest work[13] and not extrinsic to but inherent in freedom.

The very idea of democracy is perverted and deprived of its efficacy, if it is detached from its original and solid foundation on the belief in an objective order of goodness within which democracy has its definite place. If we abandon the concept of such an objective order, we lose every right to defend democracy for any reason other than that we just happen to like it.

But if such an objective order is recognized, it must be also recognized that man's freedom has its intrinsic limitations, and that freedom cannot exist unless these limitations be recognized.

One cannot have democracy and deliver it to an unbound subjectivism and relativism. Human nature is one, and so is the order of life. The "moral law within ourselves" which "aroused ever renewed admiration" in the mind of Kant, is the moral law outside of us. A man oblivious of himself and dedicated to the good, achieves by this his greatest perfection. He is free when he consents to the fact of his limited nature and realizes that obligation is not imposed from without, but is the "dialectic counterpart" of his very freedom.

Two words ought to be written so that everyone may have them before his eyes. They should adorn the walls of our schools, and they should resound in the minds of every citizen:

Democracy obliges.

Comment by Swami Akhilananda:

May we suggest that if democratic society does not have a clearcut understanding of the supreme value of life, then its members are bound to be confused, being impelled by the so-called national urge of self-expression. By the supreme value, we mean the understanding of the higher nature of man or the manifestation of the divinity of man or, again, the attainment of love of God. When a man realizes that the different members of society are veritable manifestations of God, or children of God, as St. Paul says, then alone can selfishness, greed, love of power (the anti-democratic tendencies) be overcome. History proves that the humanistic idea of the "sense of duty" or "moral sense" or "common sense" cannot withstand the temptations of selfishness or self-assertion based on the egocentric attitude of life. It has been found through experience that mere humanism or even a conceptual understanding of higher religious values do not stabilize a man and help him to overcome anti-democratic tendencies.

So we would like to suggest that in order to achieve what Professor Allers advocates,

[13] George Santayana, *Dominations and Powers*, Charles Scribner's Sons, New York, 1951.

strenuous self-imposed self-discipline, rather than repression, is absolutely necessary, in order to establish real freedom and real democracy. Otherwise, selfish, self-expressive freedom will impede the harmony of society. Moreover, this very attitude will gradually destroy the equilibrium of a personality. We feel that proper and required self-control cannot be attained unless the emotions are integrated on the basis of higher values. Furthermore, the emotions can be integrated, harmonized, and manifested, only when the will power is harmonized and strengthened through the practice of concentration and meditation and such other spiritual practices. So real philosophy and spiritual discipline must go hand in hand, in order that we may achieve the goal that we are all trying to achieve, namely, personal and social integration.

Professor Allers's reply:

The ideas expressed in the Swami's comment appear to me as being in perfect agreement with my own, which they, in some manner, complement.

I am, indeed, convinced that "self-discipline" is a primary requisite to achieve freedom and to establish social harmony, so far as such can exist. Likewise, I am certain that "selfish self-expressive freedom" will inevitably lead to its own abolishment and engulf legitimate freedom, too.

Henri Bergson believed once that after the First World War there would dawn on mankind what he called an "ascetic age." We know that he was sorrily mistaken. By now, it should be evident that unending self-indulgence, the craving for ever more comfort, more pleasure, more possessions, is neither consistent with the idea of liberty, nor with the actual state of human affairs.

I also side with Swami Akhilananda in regard to the fact that nothing is needed more than the recognition of higher values, which man does not make but discovers, and, which, once envisaged, reveal to man the existence of what I have called the objective order of goodness.

The appreciation of my ideas shown in this comment is highly welcome. Its author and myself may, probably do, think differently on many things. But there is, I like to think, necessarily, a definite and fundamental unanimity of all those who believe that spirit and not matter rules the world.

Comment by Edgar S. Brightman:

The principle of the dialectical relations of freedom and authority—of the individual and society—seems to me to be thoroughly sound. It has affinity with some of the great insights of Hegel regarding freedom, and is subject also to some of its dangers. Only one critical comment arises in my mind. Although Professor Allers is fully and correctly aware of the need of limiting freedom by authority, is he equally aware of the reverse need—that of limiting authority by freedom? May authority exceed bounds? When, if ever, is authority wrongly used? How is an evil state or church to be adjudged evil and be controlled or condemned? Is Professor Allers willing to apply to the evil authority the same norm that he applies to the evil freedom, "that it is objectively not good, is all that counts"? And who is to decide what is objectively good or not good, if the authority is evil?

Professor Allers's reply:

Dr. Brightman's thoughtful remarks call for some distinctions.

1. Authority can be misused or exceed bounds as much as every other human behavior. If authority is sought and exercised for its own sake, as a display of power, or gratification of personal desires, it is wrong. Its intrinsic badness results from the failure to recognize the true meaning of authority, which is that it exists for the sake of those over whom it

is placed. For the sake of, however, does not mean that all whims or claims be satisfied, but that the objective good, that is, the "perfection" of those under authority be achieved.

2. Thus the use or misuse of authority is measured by the objective order of values, as is freedom.

3. The question of control or condemnation or of practical behavior, in regard to the misuse of authority or of freedom, is of another nature. It is, probably, impossible to say who is to decide. In moral problems the vote of the majority carries as little weight as the decrees of the despot. One may, however, hope that a more satisfactory state of affairs can be approximated, once the idea is abandoned that there does not exist any objective criterion of right, and when people will come to realize that denial is not injustice, nor "frustration" equalling tyranny. If people were agreed on the existence of an objective order of values, even if it were difficult to discover, it would be conceivable that both authority and subjects would submit voluntarily to some sort of arbitration. The judgment of such a "supreme court" would not be infallible; but it would be the closest approach to truth, and preferable to an endless wrangling or the appeal to violence.

Dr. Brightman points at the Hegelian background of my remarks. Of course, one cannot discuss any dialectical situation without recalling Hegel's ideas. We might recall also that for Hegel history meant the advance toward freedom and authority, a means for ensuring this advance. But freedom was not for Hegel an ultimate goal; it appeared to him as the condition under which the spirit will realize itself perfectly, *an und fuer sich*. But the spirit is truth, and "truth is the whole." That is, the perfect state, if it is to be attained at all, must be conceived of as an equilibrium of the whole and the parts, of the common and the private good, of freedom and authority.

Comment by Barna Horvath:

Dialectics of freedom may mean (1) developing the problem of freedom, through contradictions involved in it, to an apparently insoluble one or (2) offering a solution to the problem. In the first sense, which may be called perhaps Platonic or Kantian, the task of the philosopher is to dissolve the "dialectical appearance"—an undertaking extremely useful, but apparently no concern of this paper. In the second sense, which may be called perhaps Hegelian or Marxian, dialectics can hardly be recognized as a scientific, logical, or philosophical method. From a logical contradiction, be it even called *coincidentia oppositorum,* strictly nothing can be logically concluded. Consequently, dialectics, in so far as it leads to any new result, is only a spuriously logical, and genuinely *empirical,* method. But we do not find in this paper the empirical conditions of freedom and authority specifically investigated. All the author claims is that freedom is not unlimited, and, therefore, some limitations do not threaten it. Yet what we should like to know is *how far* limitation of freedom is compatible with freedom and *just what* kinds of limitations are permissible.

The preceding remarks concern only the *method* of this paper. As to the *substance* of Professor Allers's view, I find it in his idea that freedom, as well as authority, are only *instrumental* to the common good. This common good "is not freedom," and yet it is the objective order of values justifying all freedom and all limitation of freedom, ultimately delegating all authority.

As usual, the commentary ends where the difficulty begins. Is it not difficult to think of authority as existing "for the sake of an end," for the sake of not even recognized "fundamental laws," and yet delegated, in a democracy, by the people? What happens in case the people and the authorities think differently of the common good? Who judges of the "cogent reasons" by which something is "believed to be the good" (believed by whom? the people? the authorities?) to the effect that it is "no deprivation of freedom, if people are hindered in spreading ideas which are the opposite of" that good? Is the merely definitional statement that "the meaning of authority is that the pursuit of the good be rendered more effective," enough assurance for the conclusion that "its being established does not either diminish or endanger freedom"?

The difficulties concern only the political casuistry of freedom, not its moral core. Yet in their own field, the difficulties are real, and perhaps the best statesmen suffered most from divergent visions of the common good, seen differently by themselves and by public opinion.

In so far as moral freedom is concerned, Professor Allers thinks of it as "that endowment of human nature which renders possible the pursuit of the good." I doubt whether his statements that "freedom may be as well . . . for the pursuit of evil" and "freedom is . . . not freedom for everything; it is only freedom for the good," can be reconciled, or whether moral responsibility for evil done might be justified, were the second statement true. Perhaps the term, "freedom," is applied in different senses.

But if the pursuit of the good, at least, is only made possible by the endowment of freedom, it is obvious that freedom must have a limitative *function* and a pervading *methodological significance* for the pursuit of the good. This means also that it cannot be contrasted with the "table of values" which may be realized *only* in the realm of freedom.

In a characteristically existentialist way, the author uses the formula, "Man in the World and the World comprising Man," to refute "any independence of man in regard to the laws which govern both nature and society." They are not "outside," but constitutive of, human nature, and, consequently, limitations of freedom are not extraneous to, but essential aspects of it. The author goes to the extent of declaring that "man by obeying the law which he encounters as not his, in fact, obeys the law which is his," and that "autonomy" is more dangerous than "heteronomy." Subjectivism, empiricism, and relativism are rejected, though the author himself stresses the point that "the question is not simply of freedom, but of freedom exercised here and now and under certain conditions." Sense of duty, moral sense, commonsense, utilitarianism, and autonomism are rejected as arbitrary and undemonstrable. It is natural to ask whether the author's existentialist interpretation of the limitations as constitutive of the very essence of freedom, is more demonstrable.

Indeed, we may ask whether, if this interpretation be correct, there are limitations at all, incompatible with freedom. Did the author *define* freedom at all?

It is true that "to the finiteness of being corresponds the finiteness of freedom," and that "freedom brings with it obligation, because . . . so many vectors are open to man that he is in need of a principle by which to decide which vectors to follow and how far to follow them." But we should not forget that moral obligation and principle are *freely* accepted and obeyed.

I would go even so far as to share the author's opinion, that emotional ethics of the "sense of duty" entails the danger that "not deliberate but impulsive action then appears as the right thing," and that "without making use of some criteria outside and above one, one cannot arrive at a final judgment."

I would go so far, however, only because I believe that the main trends of ethics which are, after all, the fruits of our classical and Christian civilization, should be reconciled rather than contrasted.

Naturalism, utilitarianism, and Kantian ethics of duty, are so many stages in the refinement of ethical principles. They are supplementary of, not contradictory to, one another. Pleasure, greatest happiness of the greatest number, and rigorous duty, mean, all of them, freedom in an ever deepening sense (egoism, altruism, respect for law) and may be taken for our maxim of action in a reversed order (1. duty, 2. altruism, 3. egoism). But this reconciliation is possible only when the genuine sense of freedom—to free ourselves

The Dialectics of Freedom

from the chains of pain, selfishness, and, at last, to emancipate ourselves from all external motives—is preserved, and an indefinite progress in this sense remains open.

Professor Allers emphasizes the point that "Who says freedom, says limitation. Who says democracy, says limitation." To him, "Democracy obliges." May I add that it also *liberates*? And if it obliges more than aristocracy or monarchy, is it not because it liberates more and appeals to a moral law not quite "outside of us," but also "inside of us"?

If I am wrong, however, and Professor Allers is right that the laws of reality, external to him, are man's own laws—that he needs no autonomy because, even obeying the laws governing the universe, he obeys only his own conscience—well, in this case I would ask what is the difference between this view and the rejected determinism, relativism, and empiricism? Is not man "caught in the inexorable cosmic process," is he saved from being "the passive subject of totalitarian power" and from indulging "in the illusion of liberty," when his free will amounts to nothing more than to the *inverted* freedom of making his own, whatever the limitations, authorities, and causal realities, happen to be imposed on him?

Professor Allers's reply:

The searching comments of Professor Horvath contain, among certain points on which I shall touch presently, two that I do not quite see in relation to my remarks.

The first is the interpretation of my position as "characteristically existentialist." The only reason I can discover for this is my referring to Heidegger's ideas. But one may well approve of an author's ideas without adopting his philosophy. I am not conscious of belonging to any of the existentialist sects. Nor do I conceive of the formula, "man in the world . . . ," as characteristic of existentialism.

I beg to add that I fail to understand how from the acceptance of the said formula it results that a man is delivered up to the play of the cosmic forces and committed to a deterministic view. As I see it, man is free to act according to the laws of his own nature, that is, of reality, or not to do so; in the latter case he will pay the penalty. Therein consists the "dialectics" of the human situation.

My distinguished critic seems to find a contradiction between the statement that "freedom is for the good," and the other that it "may be for the pursuit of evil." It may be used for the pursuit of evil, or rather, may be misused. One has to distinguish between freedom as a condition of human action—and as such it permits the pursuit of any goal, because it is freedom of choice—and, on the other hand, freedom as a constituent feature of human nature, as which it is destined—if such an expression be permissible—to increase the amount of goodness in the world, that is the maximization of actualized goodness.

It may be debatable whether or not freedom can be "defined" at all. It may be that it is one of those notions which are undefinable, as is, for instance, that of life or also of health; or, for that matter, any of the primary data which can be "pointed out" in some manner but not defined.

Moral obligation and principle are, indeed, "freely accepted and obeyed," in so far as man may reject even what is evident. Perhaps the fundamental difficulty is found with the notion of an "objective order of values." If such an order "exists"—whatever this term may mean when applied to values—then there exists also an antecedent obligation, not a moral one, in the usual sense, but one imposed by the nature of being, and so man's own, to accept that obligation and that principle which are in accord with this objective order. This leaves untouched the "psychological freedom" of choosing what is objectively wrong. This freedom, however, might prove, on closer examination, to be not truly freedom but slavery, unfree acceptance of prejudice or surrendering to passion.

I cannot concede that naturalism, or utilitarianism, or even Kant's moral philosophy are "so many stages in the refinement of ethical principles." The first two appear to me anything but refinements, and Kant's lofty ideas suffer, as Scheler seems to have demonstrated, by their abstract formalism.

Professor Horvath sees a dilemma in the notion that man forms part of his situation and is under the same laws as the world he faces, on one hand, and the idea of freedom, on the other. I do not think that this dilemma exists. Man, indeed, achieves his end, that is, the perfection of his being, by complying with the objective order; but he need not do so. It is the peculiarity of man's position that he is free to accept the laws under which he stands, or to ignore them. In the latter case he will pay the penalty; but his freedom is nonetheless intact. It is within the range of man's free nature, that is, his free will, to act in his true interest or against it. The laws with which he ought to comply are precisely laws of "oughtness," not comparable to those of which science speaks as determining the course of physical events.

One may consider this freedom of man as a paradox. But it appears as such, only as long as one believes that reality must be resolvable into simple principles. Reality, however, is not simple.

Comment by Ignatius Smith, O.P.:

Dr. Allers has done a service to many areas of thought by his expositions of fundamentals.

Expecially excellent in this presentation is the explanation of two pivotal propositions. The first is that liberty, to be kept free, must be kept under control. The second is that authority is necessary in every group and in its turn must be controlled.

CHAPTER XLVII

An Outline for a Comprehensive Inquiry into the Problem of Authority and Freedom

By SIMON GREENBERG
*Provost and Professor of Homiletics,
The Jewish Theological Seminary of America*

Definition of Authority and Freedom

MAN'S MOST universal characteristic is his need to act. Anything which in any degree determines his actions is to that extent exercising authority over him. We make no distinction between authority and power. Where there is no power to influence action, there is no authority. Nor do we distinguish between physical and spiritual power. An idea's impact upon a mind is as compelling as, often more compelling than, the impact of the policeman's club upon the head. Nor do we identify authority with that which is just or good or true. Power to influence human action does not limit its association to the just or to the true. Whatsoever or whosoever possesses power to influence human action, is to that extent, therefore, exercising authority in human affairs.

"To influence human action," does not necessarily imply the power to make a human being conform to any given law or ideal or pressure. The need to resist any of these also implies an exercise of authority by them over the human being. Hence whatsoever forces itself upon the attention of a human being and compels him to take it into consideration when determining upon any given action, is to that extent exercising authority over him. An inescapable polarity exists between authority and freedom. The realm of the one inexorably implies and limits the realm of the other.

No one ascribes to man an absolute freedom, for that would connote that man knows himself to be completely independent of all conditions. There are those, however, who deny that man possesses any freedom.

They maintain on theological, philosophic, or scientific grounds, that man is the inevitable product of forces determining his every thought and act. Indeed, from the standpoint of such an absolute determinism, one cannot rightly speak of forces exercising authority over man, for man is nothing more than the sum total of his acts and thoughts, and each of these is but the product of forces interacting among themselves.

If either of these doctrines were true, then this inquiry would *ipso facto* be futile. Where there is no possibility at all for the exercise of freedom, the concept of authority does not apply; and to a situation in which authority can never be exercised, the concept of freedom is irrelevant.

Elaborate refutations of the doctrine of absolute determinism have been formulated. But the rejection of the doctrine is not dependent upon the cogency of the logical arguments mustered against it. Logically, both sides of the discussion have able proponents. The average individual wavers in his estimate of his true position in the world. The prevalence of a sense of fatalism among men gives substance to the philosophic contention that man is in no way a free agent. At the same time, the sense of power to choose among various alternatives, a sense repeatedly experienced by the average human being almost every moment of his life, has nurtured the equally widespread conviction of human freedom.

Except for some closeted philosopher pronouncing all of creation to be the product of his "ego," or some bold romantic proclaiming that he is "the captain of his ship" and the "master of his soul," the average human being knows that his acts can never be completely independent of the conditions which precede them. Every act is performed within the framework of a given situation and the available alternative it presents. In well-nigh the same manner do the consequences of an act influence the act, once the actor develops even the rudimentary power to envision consequences.

However, the manner in which and the extent to which the preceding conditions or the following consequences are to enter into the act, *are not determined by the conditions and consequences themselves*. For these may at times cancel one another out, and, therefore, all of them cannot possibly enter into the act. For example, a parent aware that his child is in a burning building experiences simultaneously a sense of fear and love, and a vision of physical pain or sense of guilt. The outcome of the struggle between fear and love, pain and guilt, is determined by a factor other than any of them, namely, man's power consciously to formulate a judgment and make a decision.

Man, in so far as he is man, cannot refuse to exercise that power. He is as much under the compulsion to pass judgment as he is to act. He can never be completely deprived of his human freedom, as long as he continues to possess the mental capacity to judge rationally.

But the use of man's mental capacity to pass judgment and to act thereon may be gravely limited by two factors:

1. *Ignorance of the true nature of the conditions preceding or following the act.* A man seeking a path out of a dark forest, if he has no way to determine the direction in which he may find help, has as little power of choice as the driven leaf.

2. *An excessive limitation on the number of conditions which may precede, or follow upon, his act.* A man confined to a prison cell may exercise his power of judgment in deciding upon the act he chooses to perform. But the area within which he can maneuver intellectually or physically is highly limited.

Under the best of circumstances man exercises his freedom of choice under a cloud of ignorance of varying density. For in human relations neither all of the preceding conditions nor all of the subsequent results of a given act can possibly be known. Moreover, even such knowledge would not necessarily be enough to determine which of the possible acts under those conditions would be the best one. For that implies a knowledge of how the ultimate purpose of the universe can best be served within that situation.

Because at the present stage of man's development we do not possess infinite knowledge, nor a universally accepted and clearly defined *summum bonum,* no two men having the same knowledge at their disposal will necessarily arrive at the same conclusion. All we can, accordingly, say at the present juncture in human affairs, is that the greater man's knowledge and the more fertile his imagination, the greater is the choice of alternatives before him, and, accordingly, the greater the possibility and the necessity for man to exercise his freedom.

In so far as man must of necessity pass judgment upon alternative paths of action open before him, once he becomes aware of them, one can justifiably describe man as a creature who has been "condemned to freedom."

Man's attitude toward the possible consequences of his actions is in essence, however, different from his attitude toward the preceding conditions. The preceding conditions are given data, but the consequences of an act are not yet given. They first come into being after man acts. The anticipated consequences may not materialize. But in so far as a man's acts are guided by anticipated consequences, he acts as a goal making creature. His judgment becomes inescapably involved, not only in evaluating given data, but in evaluating desirable consequences. A man's estimate of the desirable consequences has been as decisive a factor in human action as the facts inherent in the preceding conditions. The Bilu who left Russia to settle in Palestine in the eighties, and the Jews who migrated to America, were both influenced by the same factual conditions. They differed radically, however, in their vision of the desired goal.

To summarize: the concepts of authority and freedom presuppose the following conditions: (1.) The existence of at least two subjects in contact with one another at least in one area of their being. (2.) The presence within each of the two subjects of a drive toward uninhibited action, in accordance with its own nature or desire. (3.) The exertion of unequal pressures upon one another. The more powerful of the two can, therefore, at the point of contact, influence the action of the other. Where no actual or theoretic resistance is possible, no authority exists. Where there is no actual power exercised, no authority exists.

Factors Exercising Authority in Human Affairs

The factors which exercise authority in human affairs may be grouped under four categories:

1. The forces of the external physical universe.
2. The forces inherent in the mental and physical endowment of the individual.
3. The forces of the individual's social heritage.
4. Supernatural forces, whose existence is violently challenged by some, but acknowledged by those to whom God is a living reality.

The Relationship Between the Authoritative Forces and the Individual

It is our assumption that at the core of the human personality is a reality whose existence is independent of all of the factors included in the preceding four categories. This reality which we shall designate as the "ego," functions within the framework of the factors included in the four categories. It reacts to them and is shaped and molded by them. It, in turn, may often shape and mold them.

The ego's reaction to any situation depends upon two things. 1. Its own inherent nature. 2. The manner in which its nature has been influenced by the external forces infringing upon it.

No two egos are ever exactly alike, any more than two human bodies are ever exactly alike. And the external forces act upon each ego in combinations and interactions that are unique. The ego in reacting to these external forces itself undergoes inescapable modifications. It accumulates its own store of memories and experiences, which it utilizes in reacting to the subsequent situation. Hence, no two results of the confrontation between individual egos and any given authoritative factor can be exactly alike.

The manner in which any of the factors within the four categories exercise their authority over the ego depends upon:

1. The extent of the actual power possessed by them.

2. The ego's knowledge or belief about the extent of that power and the manner of its exercise.

3. The ego's skill in inventing ways to emancipate itself from that power, to cooperate with it, or to utilize it.

A full discussion, therefore, of the problem of authority and freedom in the life of man, would involve the exposition of the manner in which the factors within the four categories of authoritative forces interact with the ego upon whom they are exerting their pressures. We shall illustrate briefly by an example of the type of inquiry we envisage.

I. *The Authority of the Laws of the Physical Universe*

One of the assumptions of preatomic science which remains relatively unchallenged is that the "laws" of the physical universe exert their pressures uniformly throughout the universe, and, therefore, also upon all human beings.

The most primitive human intellect could not help noticing certain regularities in nature. That these "regularities" exercised inescapable authority over human beings, was equally obvious. No human being could halt the setting of the sun or the coming of the rainy season. No one could escape death. These physical processes of nature determined when man was to sleep, when he was to plow and plant, and when he had cause for mourning or for celebration. But as man developed and became conscious of these laws, the manner in which they exercised authority over him underwent profound change. That change was due, in the first place, to man's growth of knowledge of the manner in which these laws function, and, secondly, to his interpretation of the nature of these laws.

Gravity does not exert its pull upon "A" in a manner different from that in which it exerts its pull upon "B." If, however, "A" should become aware of gravity and the manner in which it operates, he may learn how to react to it in a manner different from "B's." He may invent the airplane. That does not mean that he has denied the existence of the force of gravity. He has merely found a new way of acting within the law and under its full authority. Modern man, flying in heavier than air machines, has a far greater regard for the authority of the law of gravity than does primitive man, who is equally subject to it without being conscious of it. But he has also discovered that subservience to these laws has opened for him new vast realms for freedom of choice in action.

Not only man's knowledge of the manner in which the laws of nature function, but also his opinion of the true nature of these laws, determines a large area of his activities. Thus the notion that the regularities in nature were due to impersonal, unchangeable forces in no way related to or concerned with man and his doings, did not occur to man until he began to philosophize, to conceptualize his experiences, and to order them into some kind of rationally acceptable system.

Aristotle's doctrine of the eternity of matter was the philosophic formulation of the principle that the physical universe is essentially independent of all moral or spiritual forces, and governed by laws of its own. This was the one doctrine of "the philosopher" which medieval theologians, with very few exceptions, found absolutely unacceptable. They must have intuitively felt that to set the vast realm of physical nature beyond the reach of God, was to set up an intolerable duality in the world and to limit God's omnipotence well nigh to the point of impotence. Even though they noticed the regularities in nature, they did not attribute either independent existence or immutable regularity to them. There were, to be sure, "ordinances" that governed "heaven and earth," but they were "appointed" by God (Jeremiah 33.25). And He who "appointed" them could modify them at will and would in the future assuredly do so (Isaiah 51.6; 66.22).

Atomic physicists are no longer as sure as their predecessors were about the immutability of the laws of nature. By and large, however, they remain equally certain that these laws are completely indifferent either to moral consideration or to man's interests, and are independent of any forces, spiritual or physical, superior to themselves.

An individual's conviction on this basic issue is the most important single factor determining the essential character of his spiritual life. The laws *per se* are authoritative, in that they cannot be disregarded with impunity. Man's conviction about their essential nature becomes authoritative, in that it determines a whole series of actions related to the laws themselves and to many other aspects of human life.

II. *The Forces Inherent in the Mental and Physical Endowments of the Individual*

Many attempts have been made to eliminate the dualism between body and mind, by making the one a function of the other, but none has established an absolutely irrefutable case for itself. The problem of the relationship between body and mind remains one still requiring a solution. That they are intimately and indivisibly interrelated, no one denies. That there are areas within which they act independently of one another, is also widely conceded. In so far as each has its area of independent action, it is subject to its own distinctive group of authoritative factors which play their part in determining its action.

A. *The Factors which Exercise Authority Over Man's Mind*

Just as man cannot escape the authority of the physical laws of the universe, he cannot escape the authority of the laws which govern his subconscious and self-conscious mind. Locke, Hume, Berkeley, Kant, and a host of others have attempted to formulate the conditions which make human thought of any consequential nature possible. Their differences, though many and significant, do not add up to the significance of the one thing in which they all agree, namely, that human thought is not absolutely free. The mind, may, as modern psychology inclines to emphasize, be more dependent for its judgments upon the emotional and physical state of the body with which it is associated, than upon external stimuli and its own inherent dispositions. Be that as it may, it is certain that man's power of thought is not absolutely free to think or to conceive, without any relation to the outer world or to the inherent nature of the mind *per se*.

Thus there are many things of which the mind cannot form a picture, even though it may think of them as theoretically possible. The mind cannot conceive empty space, or infinity, or anything which exists and does not exist at one and the same time. Nor if it is healthy, can it maintain that four plus two are seven.

The mind's limitations are equally marked in the realm of moral values. Man cannot *mentally fully comprehend any moral value*. He cannot grasp it *in toto*. He cannot determine with certainty, either its origin, or its ultimate validity, or its absolute relevance to any given human situation. There are those who believe that the mind may yet be able to achieve the full comprehension of the mathematical infinite, as well as of moral and ethical values. When it does achieve that, it will be a mind in essence different from our own. But until that occurs, we are all equally subject to the laws and limitations of the mind, the only differences among men being whether they are aware of these limitations or not, and whether they take those limitations into consideration in arriving at conclusions which are intended to determine action.

B. *The Factors which Exercise Authority Over Man's Body—Our Biological Inheritance*

Man has a physical body with a vast number of impulses, instincts, cravings, and desires, which determine an infinite variety of human actions. Their authority, however, differs from that of the authority exercised by the laws of nature and of human thought. Each of our several biological needs and desires does not exercise a *uniform* pressure in the case of every individual. Nor do the biological endowments of any one individual exercise the same pressures uniformly upon him over an extended period of time. Nor are the impulses and instincts of the body as relentless and inflexible in the exercise of their authority. The pangs of hunger, the urgings of sex, have been defied by men at will for long periods of time.

Moreover, a law of the physical universe, or of the mind, cannot be obeyed to the point where it becomes destructive of itself. The laws of the physical universe and of the mind set exact limits for themselves, neither accepting less nor demanding more. The drives, impulses, and needs of the biological inheritance, however, urge us to "over-obey" them to their own destruction. Hence the boundaries of their sovereignty over our acts must be set for their own good, not by them, but by some other power at our disposal, such as our knowledge, reason, and will.

However, man cannot possibly free himself completely from the importunities of his biological heritage, nor can he disregard them. He must *do* something about them either by conforming to their insistent pressures or by exercising energy in curbing those pressures. In either case, a vast number of his visible and invisible acts and audible and inaudible thoughts are, in whole or in part, very definitely determined by them.

III. *The Authority of the Social Heritage*
A. *Definition of Social Heritage*

The term, "social heritage," includes all aspects of the environment into which a child is born, except the external physical universe. While an individual may become a Robinson Crusoe, he cannot be born or grow up as one. He is, of necessity, a member of a human society, which includes, among other important factors, the basic universal institutions of the family, the state, the church, and the climate of opinion regarding right and wrong, beauty and ugliness, the appropriate and the inappropriate, that prevail among those with whom the individual is in contact during his life time.

Within the framework of the primitive tribe the authority of the organically indivisible social heritage was well nigh as absolute as that of the laws of physical nature. Except under the rarest of circumstances, the individual could not separate himself from his tribe, and live. He could not revolt against the authority of his family or his priest, without having the authority of the whole tribe turned against him. He could find no ally in the state against the priest, or in the priest against the family. They all constituted an unbreachable front. The tyranny of primitive society must of necessity, have crushed an infinite number of creative, adventuresome spirits; yet there was no consciousness of suppression of the human personality.

As a society grew in number and extended over wider areas, as peoples with differing social heritages were incorporated into empires, the maintenance of such an organic unity became increasingly difficult. Empires, such as the Roman Empire, which abandoned the ideal of primitive organic social unity, opened the gates to greater exercise of personal freedoms. But in smaller homogeneous units, even when they were culturally as far advanced as the city-states of Greece, the social heritage exercised an authority sufficiently powerful to compel Socrates to drink the hemlock.

In every society there is a strong tendency toward a monolithic social structure, for a society could not function at all as a society, if each one of its more significant component parts were completely unrelated to the other. There is an inevitable overflow from one area to the other. The climate of public opinion may sustain the maxim that "to the victor belong the spoils," or, "you do not hit a man when he is down," and it will affect the action of the state, and a man's attitude toward his adversary. The state may be organized on the principle of elected representative government, and that principle may then affect the institutions of religion. The institution of religion may also, in turn, affect the state. Thus, in the United States, though we have a constitutional provision forbidding the use of the organs of the state for the advancement of any one religion or religious denomination, Sunday, Christmas, and Easter, are, nevertheless, legal holidays.

The complete autonomy of the state, the church, and the family would lead to a social chaos, just as their complete social integration must end in spiritual stagnation. No society has as yet found the point at which there is the most desirable relationship established between the drive toward social integration and the pull toward individual autonomy.

One thing is certain, however, and that is that personal human freedom is, to a large extent, dependent upon the degree of autonomy enjoyed by each one of the major components of a society, as well as by the degree of freedom granted to the individual within each of the component parts. The possibility of finding refuge in the state, as against the church, and in the family, as against the state, furnishes that minimum area of maneuverability for the individual which is indispensable to his exercise of any significant degree of freedom. Hence, from the sixteenth century until the Bolshevik revolution in the twentieth century, the course of social development in the West, at least, was toward an increasing autonomy for the main institutions of society, as the basis for the increasing freedom enjoyed by the individual. It was left to the modern totalitarian states to set as their conscious goal a return to the primitive ideal of an organically indivisible human society, whose social heritage should also be one and indivisible.

We shall discuss briefly only four areas of the social heritage: the state, the family, the climate of public opinion, religion. They are, of course, not the only areas within the social heritage. The economic system and the educational system are also of the utmost importance. But we shall not include them in this discussion.

A. *The State*

The state, in its authority over the individual's life, has the following characteristics:

1. The state has an identifiable group of individuals who are charged with the duty of enforcing its authority.

2. The state's authority can assert itself against recalcitrants in a twofold manner.

a. *It can withhold desired goods.* It can deny a citizen who violates its laws the benefits accruing from citizenship. These restrictions may limit the area within which he might fulfil himself as a human being. But they may still leave a fairly wide area open for him within which to pursue happiness and find satisfaction.

b. *It can inflict positive punishment.* It can restrict an individual's movements by prison walls. It can confiscate his belongings. It can even claim his life.

3. The authority of any given state is not as indestructible as that of the laws of the physical universe. States can be destroyed, and the authority of any given government can be overthrown.

4. Its authority is exercised over only a limited geographic area. One can, therefore, escape from its authority by removing himself beyond the area of its jurisdiction.

5. The areas of human behavior over which it exercises authority *are not inherent in its nature or structure*. Those areas may be increased or diminished, depending upon factors existing beyond the limits of the state *per se*.

6. Its effectiveness varies with the competence of the individuals who exercise its authority.

7. Most important of all, we judge the moral quality of a state's authority by examining the motives which lead individuals to subject themselves to it, or to revolt against it. The moral quality ascribed to authority embodied in a state, is in inverse proportion to the extent to which the state is called upon to exercise its police power. It is one of democracy's basic tenets that a state and its laws stand morally condemned, if the exercise of its authority necessitates a constant threat of force and a frequent use of it.

This proposition touches upon one of the basic dilemmas facing all law makers and state builders, namely, is law the crystallized moral conscience of the society it is intended to govern, or is it the forerunner of that moral conscience. If we assume that "The essential function of authority is to direct the multitude toward its common good," we still have to answer the question, "Who is to decide what the common good is?" Totalitarians, who are certain of what the common good is, have no such intellectual problems, and hence face no moral dilemmas. They judge the moral quality of a government by the quality of its purposes and by the extent to which it *succeeds,* whatever its methods, "to direct the multitude toward its common good," as they define that common good. It cannot be denied, however, that the virtue inherent in a society in which a virtuous authority is exercised with a minimum of recourse to the police power or the fear of it, is greater than the virtue inherent in a society in which a virtuous authority is exercised with much greater recourse to the police power or the fear of it.

B. *The Family: The Authority of the Parents*

Parental authority over the child originates in the concern which the parent feels for the child's welfare and in the complete dependence of the child during the years of infancy and early youth upon the love, protection, and largesse of the parents. The nature of the relationship between parent and child undergoes radical changes as the child matures. The character of the parental authority, therefore, of necessity also changes.

In many aspects parental authority, particularly during infancy and early childhood, is much broader than that of the state. There are no fixed limits to what a parent may demand of a child in matters of food, or of dress, or of behavior at the table, or of relations to other children, and in an infinite number of other spheres of action. In all civilized societies, however, limits on the direct punishment a parent may inflict upon the body of a child for disobedience, have been set.

While the principle which guided parent-child relationships until comparatively recent times, was that of "Spare the rod and spoil the child," it is now generally recognized that it is the part of wisdom, as well as that of kindness, to eliminate punishment, or the fear of it, from the relationship of parent and child as rapidly and completely as possible. Only slightly more efficacious than the fear of punishment as an inducement to obedience to the parent, is the motive of winning the parent's approval or favor. There is virtue in pleasing a parent *per se*. But the child should be conscious that when he is doing something because his parent desires it, it is being done not in order to gain a favor, but as an act of love and gratitude which carries its own reward.

Regardless of how determined a parent may be to permit his child to grow up free of parental indoctrination, he cannot possibly succeed, unless the child is geographically and spiritually completely removed from the parent. Nothing can destroy the inveterate human trait to imitate one's elders and superiors. The parent's standards are the first to impinge upon the consciousness of the child. Chronological primacy is of high importance in initiating basic tendencies in esthetic tastes, in moral values, and in intellectual judgments, and in setting the fundamental patterns for later habitual behavior.

In addition, the parent has the opportunity to press his point of view consistently and freely upon the child, before the child becomes old enough to spend most of his time beyond the reach of the direct supervision of the parent. Finally, the parent is the child's first natural "hero," and he has the opportunity of maintaining that position for a goodly number of years in the child's life.

Nevertheless, the ultimate goal of all parent-child relationships must be the development of the child, to the point where he will of his own free will and understanding either accept or reject the ideas, ideals, and standards urged upon him by his parent.

Parental authority declines as the child grows older and becomes increasingly free of fear of the parent's punishment, or of need of the parent's goodwill. Moreover, with advanced age comes wider experience, and this not only brings the child into contact with other individuals whose favor he may seek or whose disfavor he may fear, even more than that of his parents. It also acquaints him with ideas and practices which may appeal to his reason, or satisfy his temperament more than those presented to him by his parents.

The child in later life may in action reject the teachings of his parents, but the pressure of those teachings will to some degree always be present with him. Early teachings which are rejected in later life have to be constantly counteracted consciously or subconsciously. They are, moreover, associated with a natural biological bond which can never be completely severed. No child can completely reject his parent, without in part rejecting also himself. Those aspects of a parent's life which are conceived by the child as belonging to the parent's essential, conscious being cannot be rejected by him, without some feeling of pain and regret. In the same way a parent, regardless of how generous, broad-minded, and tolerant he may be, cannot see a child rejecting his fundamental convictions, without pain or regret, because in the rejection of his profoundest convictions the parent cannot but see himself partly rejected. Nor can any one feel himself rejected by those nearest to him, and remain completely indifferent.

C. *The Authority of Public Opinion*

In relation to any single individual, "the public," as here used, consists of all those under whose observation he actually comes or can imagine himself as coming at regular or irregular intervals. The authority of such "public" over any individual derives from the instinctive human desire to have every one in whom we recognize the capacity to formulate a judgment, pass a favorable judgment upon us, so that we may be loved, admired, approved, or, at the very least, not rejected by them. Though this desire for the approval of others might have originated in the biological instinct for self-preservation, it has differentiated itself from it. Man's need of the approval of his fellow man, is spiritually indispensable to him. The king hungers for the approval of the slave or beggar, even as they seek the approval of the king. No normal human being can be or is completely indifferent to the opinion of any other human being who is within the orbit of his experience.

Public opinion has no police force at its disposal. But it can under some circumstances inflict punishments which human beings fear more than bodily pain, and bestow rewards more highly treasured than those any prince can bestow.

Everyone is subject to the authority of the opinion of a variety of publics. There is the public opinion of the family, the neighborhood, the professional group, the trade union, the industrial association, the city, or county in which one resides. Each of these groups develops a climate of opinion of its own regarding few or many matters. The whole code of social etiquette, of professional courtesy, of good sportsmanship, of style in dress and address, all belong to this amorphous, constantly changing, area of public opinion.

The pressure of the authority exercised by the public opinion of any group upon any one of its members, depends upon a considerable variety of factors among which are the following:

1. The extent to which the individual believes his physical or economic security to be dependent upon the goodwill of the other members of the group. The politician in a democracy who stands for reelection at regular intervals is far more responsive to the opinions of his public, than is a member of that public whose economic security is assured by income from invested capital.

2. The intensity with which a man feels the need to have his vanity fed. We have all met the man who would "sell his soul" for the plaudits of the multitudes.

3. The frequency with which the individual finds himself in the presence of the same group. It is very difficult, almost impossible, for an individual to dissent seriously from the opinions of the group within which he spends all or most of his time.

4. The extent to which the group *consciously recognizes* the right of any of its members to dissent from its opinions. That is what America has done by writing into the Constitution provision for freedom of speech, worship, and public assembly.

5. The extent to which the individual can spiritually bear the intellectual or social disapproval of the members of his group.

6. The extent to which the individual recognizes the other members of his group as his spiritual, cultural, and intellectual equals or superiors.

7. The significance which the group or the individual attaches to any matter regarding which the individual dissents from the group.

8. The clarity and conviction with which the majority of the group embrace and espouse an opinion.

D. *The Authority of Religion and Religious Institutions*

Religion is that phase of men's thoughts and acts which is rooted in the conviction that there exist essences or an essence superior in power and wisdom to man, and concerned in one form or another with man. Institutions of religion may and do serve many useful purposes of a sociological and psychological nature. But their unique and distinctive purpose has always been to bring man into a relationship with that superior essence, in the conviction that when such a relationship is properly established, it redounds to man's highest welfare.

Among those who believed that there do exist essences wiser and more powerful than man and concerned in one way or another with man, there were those who believed that this concern was of a malevolent nature. Others believed it to be a beneficent concern. In either case institutions were projected whose purpose it was to bring man into the happiest possible relationship with those superior and wiser essences.

E. *Religion and the State*

These institutions exercised direct authority over all those who came to seek their benefits, for they could make demands upon their votaries in return for the services rendered. But the matter did not always rest there. In a monolithic, socially indivisible society the actions of any one individual were believed to have a direct effect upon the attitude of the superior powers to the whole group; hence the relations of any individual to the institutions of the religion of his group were the concern of the whole group. Hence the religious institutions, through their own agencies or through the agency of the state, felt fully justified in using all means at their disposal to compel the individual to follow their dictates.

This approach was possible, only as long as religion was regarded as a matter of doing the "right thing," regardless of motives. But once men became conscious of the place of motives in their relationship to the superior powers, and once they awakened to the element of injustice in the doctrine of total group guilt for every member's transgression, the place of force in the religious life had to be redefined.

An Outline for a Comprehensive Inquiry

Unfortunately, religious leaders were not at a loss to find new justifications for it. The place of force in religion was justified, either on the principle that it would help keep others from following a wrong course, or that it would drive the "evil" spirit out of the punished individual and restore a proper attitude within him. During the past three centuries, however, especially in the West, a growing segment of opinion within religious and political thought has sought to dissociate religious institutions from the control or the support of the state, and the state from control by religious institutions. While there is no unanimity of opinion on what the proper relationship between these two realms should be, there is, nevertheless, a strong sentiment that a state which identifies itself with specific religious institutions is exposing its population to the dangers of religious bigotry and persecution, and a religion which leans too heavily upon the strong arm of the state is not only admitting failure in effectiveness but exposing itself to inner corruption. For we would set it down as an axiom that the quality of an act may be described as religious, in so far as (a) its intent is that of establishing a relationship with an essence outside of man conceived to be wiser and greater than man, and (b) in so far as its performance is not due to the use, or threat of physical violence by another human being.

How then is religious authority exercised? We shall list the various channels through which religious authority is exercised in the chronological order in which they appear in the life of the average individual.

1. Religious authority is exercised through the medium of the religious institutions, rituals, and ceremonies that become part of the social heritage.

2. Through example religious leaders set standards of conduct and open channels for spiritual experiences whose authority over the lives of others is immediate.

3. The religious doctrine makes its own immediate impact upon the individual, and establishes its power over him by his recognition of its truth and relevance.

IV. *The Authority of the Supernatural*

In the preceding section we discussed the institutions of religion as part of the social heritage. We have said, however, that religious institutions have as their purpose the establishment of a relationship between man and essences superior to him, *that would redound to the highest welfare of the individual and the group.* Obviously, once that highest welfare is defined and its definition accepted, it, too, becomes an authoritative force, indeed potentially the most authoritative force in the life of a group or an individual. But how is that highest welfare defined? How do men arrive at the knowledge of the best means to attain that highest welfare and at the best method to establish the most desirable relationship between themselves and the essence or essences superior to themselves? We are now asking the most fundamental question in human life, namely: How does man function as a goal making creature? for once man formulates for himself his definition of his highest welfare he sets up within himself a drive toward the attainment of that welfare. It inevitably influences all his judgments of desirable consequences. Hence, what we are asking is: How does he arrive at his moral and ethical ideals? What is the origin of such "self-evident" truths as that all men are equal and are endowed with certain inalienable rights? That human life is and should be sacred and inviolable? That universal peace is desirable and attainable?

The answers to these questions group themselves under two basic categories: 1. Naturalism. 2. Supernaturalism. The naturalists contend that one need not go beyond the forces latent in man himself and in his physical and social environment, in order to discover the source of man's highest ideals and moral aspirations.

The supernaturalists maintain that the ideals of justice, peace, mercy, love were revealed to man by a Power superior to him. This Power impinges upon the consciousness of man, and sets before him or reveals to him the goals which are alone worthy of his greatest efforts. Once these goals are clearly envisioned by man and the supernatural source or their origin recognized, they exercise a powerful, often an irresistible, influence upon his actions.

We know as little about the manner in which the supernatural impinges upon us, as we know about the manner in which the mind forms an image of a tree, despite the numerous attempts made to explain this commonplace phenomenon. But no one, therefore, denies the reality of the phenomenon. This being but an "outline" for a more comprehensive inquiry into the problem of authority and freedom, we shall not now enter into a discussion of our conception of the supernatural and of its place in human affairs. We shall merely state that we believe it to be the source of our conceptions of the highest ideals that man as a goal seeking, rather than as a goal creating creature, has set before him. We further assume that the supernatural impinges with uniform pressure upon all human beings, and that no one can escape its influence completely. But each one reacts differently to it, just as no two human beings react alike to a sunset or a thunder storm. Those who deny the very existence of the supernatural are not thereby emancipated from its influence, any more than the generations who denied that the earth traveled around the sun, thereby placed themselves beyond the effects of the earth's annual journey. Their denial affects only the extent to which the influence of the supernatural may enter into their personal lives, just as man's ignorance of the earth's roundness limited the extent to which that fact could enter actively and positively into man's physical progress upon the earth.

These then are some of the chief areas within which human beings experience authority and exercise freedom. They are all interrelated and the freedom one enjoys within any one of them depends upon, and, in turn, influences the freedom he enjoys in any of the others.

CHAPTER XLVIII

Metaphysical Background of the Problem of Freedom

By STERLING P. LAMPRECHT
Professor of Philosophy, Amherst College

FREEDOM HAS BEEN the occasion of eulogy more often than of analysis. It is a term of many, though vaguely affiliated meanings, which need to be carefully distinguished. Freedom always has a dual aspect. It is always freedom from something (usually undesired and perhaps undesirable) and also freedom to something else (usually desired and supposedly desirable). The context is required to make clear what these somethings are. Economic freedom may be freedom from want, and consequent freedom to the possession of such material goods as bring personal satisfaction and increase the range of opportunities for various kinds of achievement. Political freedom may be freedom from fear of war, and consequent freedom to participate in a social order in which certain stabilities promote the means of wise planning for an at least partially foreseeable future. Religious freedom may be freedom from compulsory performance of enjoined rites and consequent freedom to alternate rites which seem appropriate to certain individuals or groups. Freedoms are always specific and are as diverse as human desires.

All such freedoms entail a certain view of man and his place in nature. They involve the supposition that man may significantly choose among different courses of action and thus contribute to the fashioning of his destiny. This supposition raises a number of fundamental problems, problems about the nature of time, about the processes of change in the world within which man must act, about the relation of human affairs to the rest of nature. Freedom is of course a concept of importance for ethical theory and moral practice. But like many other ethical and moral considerations, it raises issues in regard to the nature of the world within the texture of which man occurs, a world which not only existed before the advent of man within it, but also conditions every aspect of his living. Therefore, we need to consider the metaphysical issues in the background of the problem of freedom.

The position of this paper is that man has a measure of freedom because all events in nature are genuinely contingent. This position stands directly opposed to any view which regards the course of events as the working out in time of an inevitable trend. The opposite of freedom is, not authority, but inevitability. Many philosophies have held the course of change in nature generally and the course of human history, consequently, to be inevitable. The Augustinian position, at least in one common interpretation, finds in the almighty will of God, a timeless decree, of which the course of time is a necessary, if never completely realized, expression. The Hegelian position finds the Absolute Idea working through thesis and its logically necessary antithesis, to a momentary synthesis which is, in turn, but a new thesis for further dialectical development. Orthodox Marxism, a kind of Caliban to the Prospero of Hegel, finds in the play of economic forces the ruthless and irresistible manifestations of the drive of omnificient material substance.

These and other philosophies, differing profoundly in many other respects, agree in regarding the course of all change as an inevitable march through time from earlier event to later event. Sometimes, with defiant self-renunciation, the spirit of man is treated as, in an ineffective way, exempt from the necessity of nature, that is, to the extent that he is free in imagination and so may witness the change about him with amused irony, even perhaps with cognitive justice. But even then, he is regarded as bound in his body to the natural mechanisms he witnesses, and as powerless to interfere with the course of events or to alter the displacements of matter upon which even his spirit depends. More normally, however, the thinking of man, the feelings, and the volitions of man, are all viewed as part of the inevitable course of events.

This paper defends the position that inevitabilism is false, or, more positively, that, granting realistically all that the present of the world is, together with all that the past of this present world is, we may yet fashion, within the limits of our degree of skill in handling present potentialities, any one of a number of different futures. The future, when it becomes a present, will be exactly what it determinately is: its actuality

Metaphysical Background of the Problem of Freedom 599

will be its actuality, and its potentialities will be its potentialities. But the future, while still future, is indeterminate or is in the making. The future will be continuous with the present, limited to the range of potentialities of the present, but not inevitably any one of these plural potentialities, rather than any other of them. We may, therefore, properly say that what the future will be is a function of what the present is. But we may not properly suppose that this simple statement sums up clearly and exhaustively the complexity of the pattern of change in nature. Analysis of the present is requisite, in order to explain how certain potentialities of the present are selected and brought into actuality, and other potentialities of the present are thereby eliminated from being altogether. All the potentialities of the present could not become actual, because in their actuality these potentialities would be incompatible. Inevitabilistic theories of time and change flourish in the absence of such analysis, taking each present as a simple thing which generates the next present, and ignoring the diversities of potentiality contained within any present. Analysis of the present brings to light interrelated but distinguishable factors, some of which are coercive and others of which present options which indicate that to some extent we live in "an open universe."

All changes in the world around us are interactions. Iron ore does not inevitably evolve into steel girders, instead of railroad couplings. A military situation does not inevitably evolve into victory, instead of defeat. Iron ore and a military situation are, like all physical materials and like all social conditions, subject matters with diverse potentialities which change according to the manner in which some agents treat them. We here discover a distinction between two factors in all change: subject matter and agency. Both are actualities of the present, but their roles are different. The diverse roles are not obscured by recognition of the complexity of the interactions of nature. A physician who heals is agent and his patient is subject matter, even though, simultaneously with the healing activity of the physician, the patient also acts in various ways upon the physician. The wind is agent and the bending elm is subject matter, even though the elm diverts the wind somewhat from the course it would have taken. But the physician and the wind, in their roles as agents, are not subject matter; and the patient and the elm, in their roles as subject matter, are not agents. The distinction between subject matter and agent is absolute, even if the actualities to which the distinction can be applied are complexly interrelated and continually changing in those interrelations.

Philosophical errors arise whenever the distinction between subject matter and agent is overlooked. And the distinction is overlooked whenever the present, in all its complexity, is lumped together as the cause of the future. The present is not one thing. It is a vast number of things, each of which may at the same time be playing diverse roles in its relations to some of the others.

Any actuality, in its role as subject matter imposes two sorts of limitations upon an agent. In the first place, an agent is always limited by the chance as to what materials are available to it. And in the second place, the potentialities of these materials, if not single, are yet specific and hence confining. Either or both of these limitations may be partially surmounted when the agent happens to be a rational agent. The former can be surmounted to that degree to which the agent has sufficient information or ingenuity to secure materials appropriate for his ends; the latter, to that degree to which the agent discovers the fuller potentialities of the materials and elaborates techniques for exploiting them. The range of freedom to which a rational agent may rise has never yet been reached. But the eulogists of freedom ought not to become romantic and speak of it as without natural limits. The insistence of the world around every agent relentlessly restricts the range of activities to materials at hand and their specific potentialities.

The relentless insistence of the world in restricting the freedom of human action is by no means a tragic limitation. A freedom without limitations would be undesirable, and the idea of such total freedom is fanciful. Men need, in order to act with technical efficiency and moral power, to deal with the existing subject matters about them at the time and in the place where they are living. Men would be foolish to try to live in some age other than their own or in some place other than the environment of their bodies. So they would be foolish to crave some allegedly ideal subject matter which would, at their bare touch, become whatever their hearts' desire dreamed of. The good life for man involves the meeting of the existing situation, in its full concreteness, in the best possible way. The existing situation is always a human problem, often a trying problem, occasionally a crushing, and even a fatal problem. But to dodge the existing situation because it is a problem, is to imagine that freedom is greater when obstacles are absent. Just because agency is impossible without subject matter on which to operate, freedom is surely always within limitations relative to contingencies of nature, specific, finite.

The conflict between inevitabilism and the theory of this paper can be stated in terms of two conceptions of time. Inevitabilism views time as an advancing unilinear continuum. Moments, in this treatment of time, are like points on a line, each expressing in its turn the formula which establishes once and for all the character of the entire line. There is, among these points, an ordered succession, but there is not process. The temporal order, however, when realistically viewed is essentially process or act. Time is not itself an existent requirement which imposes its form upon events, any more than speed is an existing requirement which imposes its form upon motions. Speed is a measure applicable to motions, and time is a measure applicable to all processes or acts. Time is a measure of the relative durations of the productive processes of the many agents in the world. It is not a form into which processes must be fitted, though, when processes have already occurred and are viewed in their place in history, time appears as such a form. But past time is not actual time, any more than a past action is an actual action. Action or process is present actuality, and time is its measure. Viewed as having already occurred, process and time are concepts for the analysis of the subject matter upon which processes may now occur. But, thus viewed, they have lost their dynamic character. To treat the dynamic present as a mere continuation of the past, is to lose sight of the most insistent character of process. For process is continually producing the past by adding to that past. When any agent acts upon any subject matter, that agent brings into actuality some one of the potentialities latent in that subject matter, and at the same time pushes what that subject matter was into the past. Time in its occurrence is far different from time as an historical order. Time in its occurrence reaches out into the future (in its bringing into being what before was but latent) and relegates to the past (in its making what formerly was actual a no longer active element of the situation). Or, to put the point more nearly accurately, processes reach out into the future and relegate to the past, and time is the measure of the way one process overlaps or is overlapped by other processes. The earth spins some 365 times upon its axis, while the earth moves but once in its orbit about the sun. A presidential administration in the United

States overlaps many changes of sentiment among the people who constitute the electorate. So all processes have relations to one another which can be called their temporal order. But processes in their occurrence have a dynamic character which is lost from view when those processes have been completed and are considered in their dead finality. The historian, therefore, in so far as he chooses to devote himself to the completed events which lie behind him, is not analyzing the dynamic processes of nature in their occurrence. He is analyzing the subject matters which impose limitations on all present agents. But important as this analysis is, it ignores—and this is said, not in condemnation, but in recognition of the due function of history—all reference to the dynamic or creative role of action upon that subject matter.

A frequent objection to the view defended in this paper may properly be considered at this point. The objection is this. The agent may well be different from the subject matter upon which it acts. But it acts in the way it does, because it is just the kind of agent it is, and was so produced by forces which were its antecedents. Therefore, the argument runs, the agent, as well as the subject matter, is wholly a function of the past. And hence the entire process of change in nature proceeds by necessity from past to future.

This objection follows from taking the attitude of historian to the description of the present course of nature. That is, it follows from taking the agent as one of the given factors by operating upon which a calculated result can be foreseen. And so to take the agent, is to put it among the factors which are subject matter for action. For the calculation of outcome is as much an operation upon the subject matter as any other operation would be. Moreover, the presence of just that agent at just that moment is contingent. The agent, if it be a rational agent (like man), can choose between alternatives presented by different potentialities of the subject matter. And the agent, if it be a non-rational agent (such as a blast of wind), is, in its conjunction with its subject matter at just that time and place, a matter of chance. There is no warrant for supposing some other-than-natural agency through whose other-than-natural activity the chance contingencies are to be explained as over-all determination. Choice by rational agents we know to occur: we know that fact by empirical evidence. The course of nature before man or other rational agents appear—that course of nature now when man has appeared but apart from the relatively few processes in which man participates—that course of nature must be conceived in such fashion as to make logically and factually possible the kind of rational agency which man is observed empirically to perform. And, therefore, we must affirm contingency of nature generally, as well as rational choice by man. When we view the course of nature as solely subject matter without agency, we are guilty of a kind of mythology (however much that mythology may masquerade by talking the language of scientific discourse), according to which the course of events is driven along by antecedent compulsions, and natural change is a kind of unfolding of subject matters without the mediation of efficacious agents. This mythology, popular in the nineteenth century and surviving in certain quarters in our own day, is due to ignoring the distinction between subject matter and agency in any and all events.

Another objection to the view defended in this paper comes from a misconception of the nature of scientific laws. Laws of nature, viewed properly, are neither subject matter nor agency. They are the purely formal element in the course of events. They are generalized statements of certain uniformities which ensue when a given kind of determinate agent operates in a determinate fashion upon a determinate kind of subject matter. But they do not bring about the events which they enable us to formulate in general terms. They are not forces. They do not themselves operate at all. Agents who are rational and have knowledge of the laws may anticipate consequences of alternative choices, and may thus guide events, more or less successfully, to desired outcomes. Knowledge of the laws of nature is in this case a means of increased freedom, not a restriction of action to inevitable destinies. The laws of nature are not existent factors until and unless they are recognized and used by minds capable of formulating them. They, like other abstractions such as beauty or ugliness, are a way of knowing events. And knowledge is a technique of accomplishment, not an enslavement of the knower in a network of necessity. The laws exist, when known and used, as patterns of change which nature makes possible and among which rational agents may then choose with a degree of freedom. They define conditions which ensue necessarily upon the action of agents but do not cause the choices of those agents. Men cannot make bricks without straw, nor can they nourish their children on stones rather than on bread. The laws of nature describe the consequences of the various courses of action which lie in the various potentialities of the subject matters upon which various agents may act. Relatively to brute and unconscious agents, the laws of nature define the consequences of the contingent conjunctions of those agents with the subject matters those agents chance to encounter. Relatively to rational agents, however, they define the area of choice, so that knowledge of the laws emancipates choice from routine happenstance, and turns choice into enlightened decision.

The metaphysical considerations defended in this paper are the background for a discussion of the problem of freedom and authority. Freedom is the exploitation by rational agents of the contingencies in nature, in the pursuit of ends chosen among the potentialities of available subject matters for action. The alternate to freedom is, not authority, but necessity. The limits of human freedom are not now known and doubtless will never be known. But nature surely sets limits to freedom, even if men may properly continue indefinitely to push back the present limits of their choices and to dream, in Francis Bacon's words, of "the effecting of all things possible."

Authority, when used as a term in conjunction with freedom, needs careful definition. In a very broad sense, authority is a name for any pressure which given subject matters with their specific potentialities exercise upon agents. The concrete situation, physical or social, then exercises authority over any agent which confronts it. We are perhaps accustomed to use the term, "authority," more narrowly. But it is advisable to realize that the looming threat of brute unconscious physical forces and the attempted coercions of one's human fellows are in one respect akin. Both are factors in the situations a man faces: they are present in the subject matters which a man must take account of if he is to deal with them successfully, which, in their actuality, set limits to his freedom, and, in their potentialities, offer diverse courses of action to his free choice. The legislation of constitutional assemblies, the decisions of established courts of law, the pull and push of crowds of men, the occasional outbreak of rioting—these, like the specific nature of iron ore or of uranium, are subject matters to deal with, to act in the light of, to strengthen or to weaken, to promote or to divert, by the responses which a man makes to their actuality and their potentialities. Both physical and social situations exercise authority over a man's actions and his range of choice.

Then, in a third and more colloquial sense, authority is a name for the effective exercise of force by agents upon subject matters. This force may be blindly exercised, as by a descending avalanche, or stupidly exercised, as by an avaricious employer, or wisely exercised, as by a gifted leader of affairs. We speak of a drink as having authority: the drink does something to him who takes it. In similar fashion, we speak of the law courts as having authority: the courts, the decisions of judges, and of juries, do something to litigants and prisoners at the bar. Authority is in this sense a measure of the effectiveness of agencies.

In all of these three senses authority is a constant and inescapable aspect of the course of events in nature, whether these events be inanimate physical events, or events in which human beings participate, guide, and foresee. Therefore, authority is not an alternative to freedom, any more than size is an alternative to shape. We should not be free in a world devoid of authority, because without authority there would be neither subject matter nor agencies; there would be no world at all. The recognition of the unescapableness of authority in events is a correlate of the recognition of the unescapableness of limitations to effective freedom.

The word, "authority," is today often abused. It is treated as a term of reproach, as a dyslogistic term. It is loosely spoken of as something men should seek to escape entirely. But this linguistic confusion should be firmly met. Authority may of course be exercised in sinister fashion, to effect the debasement of human lives. It has been so exercised most tragically in our own times. But the remedy for the malicious employment of force is not to repress force. For one force can be repressed by no means other than by exercise of a greater force in opposition to the former. We cannot escape the exercise of force if we would live at all.

A corrective for the abuse of the term, "authority," is to be found in a careful choice of words to express contrasts among the authorities men exercise. Perhaps we may find such words in the use of power, as the desirable exercise of force, and violence, as the undesirable exercise of force. Authority would be wholesome when the exercise of force occurred in the fashioning of beneficial social institutions, in the creation of great art, in the conferring of opportunities for moral growth and achievement. Authority would be harmful when the exercise of force occurred in contrary ways. Authority may thus be either power or violence, according to the worth of the ends it promotes. There is bound to be as much authority in the noblest human enterprises as in the most debasing; for we live in a world whose actuality is process, whose subject matters are specific, and whose agencies are dynamic and hence forceful.

Comment by Edgar S. Brightman.

Professor Lamprecht is facing a problem that man must face if he thinks very far. His thesis that "man has a measure of freedom because nature is genuinely contingent," is one on which theist and naturalist may agree, provided "nature is genuinely contingent" means (as I assume it does to Professor Lamprecht) that "nature has a measure of genuine contingency." I doubt, however, whether Hegel and Marx deny contingency as Calvin does.

That "inevitabilism is false," that "all changes in the world . . . are interactions"; that "agents" are "limited in their action"; that "the temporal order is . . . process or act"; the application of these principles to freedom and authority—all this is both reasonable and relevant.

CHAPTER XLIX

The Problem of Authority and Freedom and the Two Fundamental Alternatives of Thought

By LOUIS J. A. MERCIER

Professor of Comparative Philosophy and Literature, Graduate School, Georgetown University

THERE ARE NECESSARILY two ultimate fundamental and contradictory alternatives of thought: dualism or a belief in God and a created universe, with man distinct in nature; and monism, materialistic or idealistic, which merges God and man in nature, and hence is best known as naturalism. With reference to man, they may be contrasted as Theistic Humanism and Atheistic Humanism.

Our outlook upon authority and freedom depends entirely on whether we believe in God antecedent to the universe and in God's order, physical, moral, and supernatural, a doctrine gradually developed from Aristotle to and including most of the eighteenth century; or whether we believe in a self-existing universe in constant evolution, a doctrine not unknown in pre-Socratic days or since, but raised to an all embracing system only from the late eighteenth century through our own.

This paper will, therefore, first discuss the problem of authority and freedom from the point of view of dualism, and then from the radically different outlook of monism.

I. *The Dualistic Theistic Doctrine*

1. FREEDOM

We must distinguish freedom of thought and freedom of the will. Then we shall have to consider authority and the coercion it may exercise on both.

a. FREEDOM OF THOUGHT

Freedom of thought is evidently based on avowed ignorance. If I think I know indubitably that two plus two equal four, I am not free about thinking that they equal five. What we are after when we talk about freedom of thought is really freedom of research when we do not know whether a statement is true; and the aim of freedom of research is to put an end to freedom of thought.

Can we have assured knowledge (like our knowledge in the physical sciences) as to what should be the behavior of man? The Theist would answer: at least the reason may gain considerable knowledge of the divine law which pertains to the conduct of man. Objective morality is based on the belief that God created natures which have consequent relations; at the very least, the essentially different natures of inanimate beings and animate beings; and, within animate beings, plants, animals, and man.

Because man has intelligence, he is able to distinguish natures and, at least, some of the relations between natures, and consequent duties and rights. Because he has a free will, he is able to live according to these relations, or to refuse to live according to them, and this constitutes subjective morality or immorality.

For instance, understanding the relations of God to man (Creator and creature), it may be seen that the Creator should be worshipped, thanked, loved, that these are duties and inalienable rights, and that no outside authority should interfere with them. Understanding his own nature as an intelligent autonomous being, both animal body and spiritual soul, man may see that he has a right to life, to liberty, and to the fulfilment of the ends of his capacities (happiness); that he also has a right to the means thereto; that he must develop and safeguard his physical and mental powers, and cultivate the self-mastery of his animal appetites. Understanding that his fellow men have the same nature he has, he should recognize that they have the same rights.

Natures, natural relations, duties, and rights flowing from them, constitute God's moral order, part of God's total order, physical, moral, and supernatural. They make up the natural moral law. Their violation is evil. Hence "do good and avoid evil," is the primary principle of the natural law. Its secondary principles are well represented in "the Ten

Commandments" and their implications. To live according to the natural law, is to be a just man, to practice justice.

b. FREEDOM OF THE WILL

As to the freedom of the will, there are various statements from those who believe in it, as the Theists do.

If you say that the will necessarily follows the intelligence, then there is really no freedom of the will. This has been called the Socratic paradox. Every man wishes necessarily his happiness: the possession of the good as known by intelligence. Hence things are good in proportion as they are useful to produce happiness. Therefore the happy man is the virtuous man, and the virtuous man is the wise man, the sage. No one does evil voluntarily. Sin is due to ignorance. So the will, determined by the intellect, is not free.

It is further held: in heaven, we shall know God's essence enough to love Him necessarily. We shall not be able to turn away from Him, to sin. "No one who sees the essence of God can willingly turn away from God, which means to sin."[1]

The consequence of making the action of the will finally depend on the intelligence, is that either knowledge determines the will, and the will is not free, or the will is free, in proportion to our ignorance, hence to our imperfection.

The opinion that the will does remain truly free, is called "voluntarism." It asserts the independence of the will in regard to the intellect.

Voluntarism does not mean that the will need not be enlightened by the intellect, but that even when it is so enlightened, it remains free, free even if the perfect good were known. It may always say, no, no matter how enlightened by the intellect. Even in the next life its abiding love of God will not be due to the vision of the essence of God but to a free act of love. The will may say to God and man: "I shall not serve. I know the right but I will not do it." The will would then be the possible affirmation of the self, through action, in accordance or against the dictates of the reason, or, as we shall see later, of the sense appetites.

[1] St. Thomas, "Summa Theologica, I," *Basic Writings of St. Thomas,* edited by Anton C. Pegis, Random House, New York, 1945, Qu. 94, a.i, p. 903.

St. Thomas is not considered a voluntarist. However, in his articles on the will,[2] he asks: "Does the will desire something of necessity?" He answers, yes, but only in the sense that the will necessarily seeks "its last end which is happiness." But when he asks: "Does the will desire of necessity whatever it desires?" he answers, no. St. Thomas also recognizes that "the will may move the intellect, as it moves all the powers of the soul (except the vegetative) to their respective acts."

Moreover, according to the Catholic doctrine of sin, "The true malice of mortal sin consists in a conscious and voluntary transgression of the eternal law." "A sin is from certain malice when the will sins of its own accord, and not under the influence of ignorance or passion."[3] This seems to be in conformity with voluntarism.

The will then being free, man is not naturally regulated. Man alone in nature is unregulated, autonomous. Animals are regulated by instincts. How can man regulate himself?

The situation is not simple. Because man is an animal (though a rational, volitional animal), he has animal appetites. Some are necessary for the maintenance of life: appetite for food, drink, rest, sex. Some tend to excess. They crave more intense and diversified stimulation. They have a *libido sentiendi*. Hence they tend to move the will as much as the reason does, and the will has to oppose their tendency to excess to regulate them. Moreover, these sense appetites may not only try to move the will, but they may even move the reason, or move the will to move the reason, to find means for their more intense satisfaction, *e.g.,* to develop intoxicants, to pervert sex. Only man can be a pervert, because only he can use reason to find means to become so.

The will, it is true, may find in the reason reasons to oppose the sensual appetites, but, on the other hand, the reason may side with the sensual appetites, erect them into legitimate ends (cf. aspects of hedonism and "romanticism,") and the will may also side with them deliberately, or be overwhelmed by them.

Furthermore, the will, as a power of the self to act, has an appetite of its own—happiness—but it may seek this happiness in sensual satisfactions. Then, too, this appetite for happiness, unregulated by the

---

[2]*Ibid.,* I, Qu. 82, pp. 777–792.
[3]A. C. O'Neil, "Sin," *Catholic Encyclopedia,* The Robert Appleton Company, New York, 1913.

acceptance of the knowledge that it is to be found only in God's will, means self-will, self-assertion. So the will may have an unregulated appetite of its own—the will to power, the *libido dominandi*.

This may suffice to indicate that the rational animal is not naturally a going ethical concern, and that there has to be in man something superior to reason and will, if he would lead an ordered life.

There is a good hint of this in St. Thomas's analysis of the state of Adam as created by God. Adam was in a state of rectitude. "This rectitude," says St. Thomas,[4] "consisted in his reason being subject to God, the lower powers to reason, and the body to the soul ... Now, it is clear that such a subjection of the body to the soul, and of the lower powers to reason was not from nature, or otherwise it would have remained after sin (natures do not change). Hence evidently the first subjection, by virtue of which reason was subject to God, was not a merely natural gift, but a supernatural endowment of grace ... If the loss of grace dissolved the obedience of the flesh to the soul, we may gather that the inferior powers were subjected to the soul through grace existing in the soul."

Therefore, according to this view, man needs an element of restraint above the reason and will. "The fall" would not consist in a change of nature, or in a complete corruption of nature, but in a fall from the supernatural state to the natural state in which man is a disordered being, with the reason and the will very imperfect instruments for its ordering. In any case that is the state in which experience reveals man to be.

Here is where the theology of "revealed religion" enters, first intruding into psychology. The question of supernatural grace becomes central. This question of grace is the dividing line between natural theology and natural ethics, which belong to philosophy developed by reason, on the one hand, and dogmatic theology, which interprets revealed religion, on the other. There is no doubt that the question of supernatural grace to secure the righteousness of a free will, presents difficulties. How all these questions have exercised theologians may be seen very objectively and candidly presented in the *Catholic Encyclopaedia*'s articles on Grace, Predestination, Tolerance, etc.

But returning to mere philosophy, the question remains: if experience reveals that reason and will are not sufficient to regulate the sensual appe-

---

[4] St. Thomas, *op. cit.*, I, Qu. 95, art. 1, p. 911.

tites and the libido of the will, and we do not accept the doctrine of grace, is there any possible way to propose a remedy? This has seldom been attempted. It was, however, recently done by the late Irving Babbitt of Harvard University, in a manner which reveals, on purely experiential grounds, the acuity of the problem.

Babbitt did not want to consider the problem in terms of "revealed religion," or even of an avowed Theism or Deism. He opposed the romanticists and hedonists, all those who consider the cultivation of the sensual appetites as good, the utilitarians who make material progress the final end of man, and the sentimentalists who credit man with more natural fraternal sympathy or benevolence than he has; and, on the other hand, those in the Socratic tradition, particularly the Stoics, who hold that the reason determines the will or that the will easily sides with right reason. Finally, he denounced our more recent naturalists who, while proposing to discover the true and the good by experience, disparage the findings of the experience of the past. To all these he opposed the fact, which he held to be experientially ascertainable, that man had libidos not only of the senses but of the will, and, he added, of the reason.

His solution was that we experience not only disordered appetites, a constant tendency to excesses, a centrifugal tendency including the libidos of the reason and will, but also a centripetal principle, a veto power, a higher will, which opposes the tendency to excess of the sensual appetites and the libidos of the reason and will.

He urged meditation on these facts, and called this meditation high religion, as opposed to the stoic pride, the mere rationalization of experience, or the divinization of the natural appetites. He then proposed to school the will with the help of what he called the higher imagination and the use of the now more enlightened reason.

From both the Christian and the Babbittean positions, we may at least gather that the possible need of an element besides reason and will is part of the problem of conduct, and that "revealed religion," "dogmatic theology," as distinguished from philosophy, is fundamentally concerned with that needed third element. Babbitt's assertion of the needed presence of a "higher will" in man, stressed this third element the more that he wanted to avoid discussing it in terms of Christian grace. But, evidently, it stands in the same relation to the possible inclining of the natural will to right conduct as does Christian grace: a power transcendent to the reason and the will, though Christian grace is much more than a power of restraint.[5]

2. CIVIL AUTHORITY AND THE FREEDOM OF THOUGHT AND OF WILL

Both the need of putting an end to our freedom of thought as to right conduct by rationally working our way to an understanding of objective morality, and the complexity of the problem of the freedom of the will are basic to the discussion of the problem of civil authority. For authority is a power, outside the individual, which may, and, in fact, must, interfere with his thought and decisions.

Now, the church depends for its knowledge on "revelation," while the state depends for its knowledge on reason. Therefore, the church may not coerce the individual to accept its dogmas, because they are not knowable through reason alone. They cannot be accepted without faith, and faith is not purely a rational matter. Moreover, even though God may reveal a law, He may not compel its acceptance, because He has created man free. So a church which claims to represent God should leave man free to accept its message. If God is the Author of the nature of man, endowed with reason and free will, God and those who claim to be His representatives are necessarily guarantors of the freedom of man.

But the same is not true for the state. The state cannot respect freedom of thought, because its end is to secure the common good in this world, and this cannot be done, except on the basis of a common rational acceptance of an objective morality. The state always forbids what it considers wrong, from murder to the passing of a traffic light.

We may see the same principle by following the natural development of society. Because man by nature must live with fellow men to survive and develop, he is naturally social. A social group is a natural institution.

In the family the basis for the legitimacy of authority is at once revealed. It may be the individual good of the father or of the sons to rest; but the common good demands food for wife and children, protection from animals, etc. So there must be organization of efforts and authority

---

[5]Cf. L. J. A. Mercier, *The Challenge of Humanism*, Oxford University Press, Oxford, 1933; *American Humanism and The New Age*, Bruce Publishing Company, Milwaukee, 1948.

for this organization. This authority belongs most obviously to the father, who is the natural head of the family.

Families multiply, presently we have family groups which must be united for survival and development. Here we may see the natural origin of sovereignty: the authority, being a natural community need, has naturally a community origin. If it cannot be exercised by all, it belongs to all to delegate it to one or many. Thus is popular sovereignty founded in nature, though as nature comes from God, so does ultimately all authority. This is the position of St. Thomas.[6]

The only question left is whether authority will be justly exercised. How can that be determined? What is justice? Evidently, it must be a code above both the ruler and the ruled, based on the objective reality of natures and of their relations; otherwise there may be the imposition of the whims, personal interests, or arbitrary will of the ruler.

We thus get the following propositions:

Authority remains legitimate, if it rules according to a rational, objective code of ethics which rational men can recognize as objectively true, and freely accept.

Authority ceases to be legitimate, if it rules arbitrarily, according to a subjective code which rational men cannot accept.

The state is an organization for the common good, and the state has the right to coerce the individual in the name of the objective common good. This is to take his freedom from the individual, but not to do him an injustice. This is because, as the code is objectively true, he should in justice accept it.

Does the state then take away freedom of thought? Necessarily, as it considers that it is not ignorant of the objectively moral. There is no legitimate freedom of thought against objective truth. There can be freedom of thought, only when there is no assurance of objective truth. Both the state and the individual are bound by the natural law. The only question is then what belongs to the natural law.

So we find the following theses in standard books of theistic ethics.[7]

1. The Eternal Law applies to man and is proposed to his reason. As it exists in the mind of man it is aptly called the Natural Law. Its injunctions constitute the specific law of human nature.

---

[6]Cf. St. Thomas, *op. cit.*, I–II, Qu. 90, article 3, p. 746. Also Bernard Roland-Gosselin, *La Doctrine Politique de St. Thomas D'Aquin*, Rivière, Paris, 1928.

[7]Cf. *e.g.*, T. J. Higgins, *Man as Man, The Science and Art of Ethics*, Bruce Publishing Company, Milwaukee, 1948.

2. The Natural Law consists in practical universal judgments which man himself elicits. These express necessary and obligatory rules of human conduct, established by the Author of human nature as essential to the divine purposes, and promulgated by God solely through human reason.
3. The Natural Law is one, universal, and immutable.
4. No man whose reason is developed can in any way be ignorant of the primary principle of the Natural Law: do good and avoid evil. Nor is invincible ignorance possible of the secondary principles, such as those of the *"Ten Commandments."* At times man may be inculpably ignorant of some tertiary principles, such as divorce and polygamy, because they depend on rather involved processes of reasoning.
5. Where inadequate, the Natural Law must be supplemented by positive law (law promulgated by the state), but positive law must be based on, or at least not contrary to, the Natural Law.
6. Independent of any positive law, there exist natural rights which follow from the Natural Law.
7. Man is by nature a social being.
8. Authority is an essential property of any society.
9. The Natural Law confers on parents social authority to guide their children to the proper ends of the family. The primacy of this authority resides in the father.
10. To parents alone belongs the inherent right to educate their children.
11. The State is a natural society.
12. The Natural Law commands men to establish States, forbids that the State should be an end completely unto itself. It is but a means to the good of men.
13. The function of the State should be more than the safeguarding of rights, but the Natural Law forbids the State to take direct, complete, and perpetual care of its citizens.

More particularly, on authority the Theist has the doctrine of Suarez, which might be said to develop the implications in that of St. Thomas: the recognition that authority was from God to the multitude and transferable to one or many.

First, sovereignty comes from God, for it is in accordance with human nature to live in society, which naturally requires authority. God as the immediate source of human nature, is the immediate source of authority.

Secondly, authority is never immediately from God to kings in a monarchy, or senators in an aristocracy, but to the people, who may formally or implicitly delegate this authority to either one or several for the common good.

Thirdly, if the chosen sovereign violates his trust of working for the common good, he becomes tyrannical, and the people may withdraw their allegiance, though not without good cause nor before the exercise of patience.

All this is fundamental American doctrine. In fact, the three Suarezian theses are to be found at the beginning of the Declaration of Independence, and the historical connection can be traced.

The upshot of this presentation of the relation of human freedom to authority is that there must be authority in social groups, that it must be exercised in the name of reason, that it is possible to get to an objective code of morality by reason, and that, when the state imposes its authority on the individual in the name of this objective code of the natural law, it does not violate his liberty, because this code is not against reason, and freedom should be used according to reason.

3. The "Social Contract"

Two doctrines developed before the nineteenth century need to be examined in connection with the question of authority and freedom: the doctrine of the social contract, and the question of the relations between church and state.

The great point about the doctrine of the social contract in relation to authority and freedom, is whether human rights continue to be considered to be based on man's original God-given nature, and thus antecedent to the contract, man being looked on as naturally social and political; or whether political rights are held to come from the contract.

In the latter case the political status of man, initiated by the contract, becomes the source of rights. The way is opened to the absolutism of the state in morals and religion, and, consequently, to totalitarianism. Thus Hobbes (1588–1679), speaks of a contract, in which the individual transfers all his rights to the supreme authority of the state, so that the ruler is not only the sole arbiter of right and wrong in the moral order, but of the true and false in religious belief. Spinoza (1632-1677) similarly considers the power of the sovereign limitless. In the social contract of Rousseau (1713-1778) the individual surrenders all his rights to the state. He presumably remains free, because he has willed this surrender and will have to conform only to the consequent general will. But Rousseau entrusts to the state the imposing of natural religion, as well as of whatever laws the majority may pass, possibly against natural rights and duties. Thus we have again a totalitarianism.

In the former case the state's chief function is the protection of inalienable rights. Thus Locke (1632-1704) accepts the idea of the social contract, but the people remain sovereign; if the civil government violates natural rights, the people may withdraw their allegiance even through a revolution. Montesquieu (1689-1755) is close to Locke. He, too, is a Theist, and believes in an objective moral law, and recognizes that the civil law must be based upon it. So freedom is the power to do what one should do under natural law, with no coercion to do what one should not under the same law.

It was then fortunate that neither Hobbes, Spinoza, nor Rousseau were influential in the development of American political thought; and that, on the contrary, Montesquieu and Locke were, with their doctrines which safeguarded natural rights anterior to the state, supposedly established by the social contract.

4. Church and State

The question of the union of church and state in relation to authority and freedom is a particularly difficult one.

To those who believe in a revelation of truths above the reason and in the keeping of a church, it may seem rational that church and state should unite to uphold both revealed truth and rationally ascertainable truth.

After the collapse of the Roman Empire and the "barbarian invasions," the bishops of the Catholic Church often were the only ones left to exercise civil authority, and later had inevitably much to say as to who should exercise it (cf. history of Clovis). Hence the union of church and state became a natural development, with the Church looked upon as a supreme authority in matters of morals, national and international. The dream of the Middle Ages then naturally became that of a Christendom, a United Nations, with a superauthority in the Catholic Church, represented by its head, in matters of faith and morals.

Here, we may note that today we are also aiming at an international society which would exercise authority in matters of morals over all nations. Instead of papal bulls we would use as sanctions the atomic bomb. But we evidently cannot exercise such an authority without a common code of morals. Hence, the further importance of a natural law rationally ascertainable.

But if the state takes on the imposition of one interpretation of revelation, besides that of a rationally ascertainable code of morals, the question arises whether it is not bound to violate the religious conscience of some. Cf., *e.g.,* the imposition of a state interpretation of Christianity in England; the Puritans, escaping from it, but setting up a state guardian of their own faith in the new world; Louis XIV persecuting the Huguenots for the sake of the unity of his realm, though, at the same time asserting a supremacy over the Catholic Church through "Gallicanism," etc.

Now, it is recognized that freedom from coercion as to revealed religion is a natural right. Hence, where there are many faiths based on varied interpretations of revelation, the state should exercise no authority in such matters.

This does not mean that the state should be atheistic, for the existence of God is ascertainable by reason, nor that it should be indifferent to revealed religion, as it is a safeguard to natural law. On the contrary, the state should recognize as a natural right the practice of religion, as long as it does not teach any doctrine contrary to the natural law.

This is eminently American doctrine: no establishment of religion, but recognition of the existence of God, of the natural law, and freedom of religious worship, which leaves open the possibility of the dispensing of "grace," considered as a needed element in the solution of the problem of conduct.

II. *The Monistic Atheistic Doctrine*

The trend, at least in our academic circles, has been away from this traditional American doctrine, toward a monism which is necessarily atheistic, and which, therefore, saps the foundation upon which morality was based on the whole from Aristotle to the end of the eighteenth century.

What happened at the end of that century was the great radical shift, from the conviction of a rationally grounded dualistic philosophy of God and the universe, and of the special rational nature of man, to a radically new conception of the nature of ultimate reality.

Belief in the antecedent reality of an abiding God was given up in favor of a philosophy of total change, of total becoming. This really constitutes the first complete successful philosophical revolution since Aristotle. Its evolutionistic outlook, strengthened by an atheistic interpretation of Darwinism, was imported to the United States, and became largely taken for granted in our academic circles. We have been "ringing out the old and ringing in the new" ever since. It was crystallized most candidly in the 1933 manifesto of the self-termed "religious humanists," who are really humanitarian naturalists.

There it bids us disown Theism, Deism, and even modernism, consider the universe as self-existing and not created. It denies the traditional dualism of mind and body, and defines man as a part of nature that has emerged as the result of a continuous process.

So there is no God, no spiritual soul, no immortality, no antecedent reality, and hence no antecedent morality, no possible inalienable rights dependent on man's God-given nature. There is no abiding moral law, only new ways of adaptation to the constant evolution to be discovered. The high purpose to do this for the good of all will be called religion; and traditional religions based on Theism will be considered deceptions which hinder the progress of humanity.

It should be evident that this doctrine brings in a totally different conception of authority and freedom, which is antithetical to the American conception of both based on Theism. If righteousness is to be evolved in the here and now, its formulation will necessarily belong to the state. There can no longer be appeals to inalienable rights, as they were based on Theism. Authority becomes absolute, and freedom is no longer to be found in the free, because rational acceptance of an abiding moral reality, but in the coerced acceptance of what is held by the state to be the righteousness of the present moment of evolution.

The consequences of the doctrine are written large in the history of the nineteenth and twentieth centuries.

Nazi philosophy, as may be easily shown by a study of Hegelian historians and theorists down to Rosenberg's Nazi bible, *The Myth of the Twentieth Century,* was based on the belief that the present moment of evolution was represented by the superior German race, and that its victory would represent the triumph of the highest evolution of the good. Had not Hegel written that the victorious state represents the highest approach to the ideal?

The same holds true for the atheistic Communism of the doctrinaires now ruling Russia, who are to be distinguished from the Russian people. The evolution of their doctrine is well known, from idealistic Hegelianism to its materialization in Marxism. So, even more formidably than with Nazism, there emerged a theory of authority which is a complete denial of freedom, a barring of all thought contrary to materialistic atheistic monism, and a coerced adoption of an economic doctrine which is held to be the key to a greater material happiness for all.

As the problem of social justice to all was far from solved by the Western world which, largely dechristianized, developed during the nineteenth century an unethical capitalism and an exploiting colonialism, it is only too true that atheistic Communism had a chance to appeal to many as an ideal worthy of religious fervor. But its process of progress is nonetheless the exercise of ruthless authority destructive of all legitimate freedoms.

In the face of all this, the pertinent question for us is what the adoption of monistic atheistic evolutionism may do to our own institutions, and our conceptions of authority and freedom.

Already we see a trend toward the denying that our government should continue to recognize Theism. We are asserting that the teaching of a religion in a private school, though a constitutional right, is a bar to state aid, even in services now claimed to be state functions. The denial of the legitimacy of private schools would be but the next logical step. For if evolutionary monism is the only true doctrine, it should be imposed on all citizens through a monopolistic state education. This state education should train men to discover what should be held to be true in the ever changing present.

All the past beliefs of the Western world and even our American institutions may thus be held to be outmoded developments, which should yield to the pressure of the wave of the future. Logically, too, our growing cultural propaganda to other nations should not be the propagation of our traditional Theistic American doctrines, but that of our new evolutionary naturalism, so that, while supposedly opposing Russian thought, we would spread the atheistic philosophy back of both.

All this is necessarily, according to evolutionary monism, the acme of freedom. All efforts to maintain belief in the dualistic Theistic philosophy on which this nation was founded, and which is still back of the creeds of Catholics and traditional Protestants, Jews, and Mohammedans, and still dominant in our own political, as opposed to our academic circles, can be but the imposition of a tyrannical authority.

The shift from the dualistic to the monistic conception of authority and freedom is only a little more than a century old, and it has already brought about the dislocation of the Western world.

On what basis not only the Western world but the whole world will be constructed in the coming years, is really a question of which of the two fundamental contradictory alternatives will prevail.

Appendix

The radical opposition between dualism and monism does not mean that the dualist may not profit by some of the points made by the monist.

Theistic philosophy is a philosophy of the abiding transcendent to and in the changing. Therefore, it should not stand for stagnation. Although it should be adamant on the abiding truths based on God-given natures, it should recognize that there are constant shifts of conditions going on, which necessitate new utilizations of abiding truths. This is the problem of standards. For instance, the three unities were standards for the classical theater. The necessity for clearness of the play remains as a standard, but it may be achieved other ways. So with many customs. Women should not be wantons, but what parts of the body they may expose from ankle to face is susceptible to variation. Economic solutions may also need to be greatly modified, as the possibility for the production of wealth increases.

The dualist may thus learn from his adversaries, always being ready also to recognize their sincerity of thought, even though always earnest in pointing out the defects of their premises. The materialist is radically wrong in making conduct depend so exclusively on material conditions, but the improvement of material conditions is certainly a factor in the development of the common good, and, in fact, is still lagging far behind for most of the human race. An educative process may well be condemned if too didactic. There may be nothing wrong in the still Theistic pedagogical progressivism of Francis W. Parker (the real founder of progressivism) with his insistence on motivation, on starting with experience to get at the general truth about God's order, and on the need of self-expression. There is something radically wrong only in the atheistic progressivism based on the denial of an antecedent abiding reality.

The dualist should be the first to believe in progress. In fact, he should constantly strive to bring out that belief in an antecedent reality is the only foundation for a true progressivism. Progress is vertical rather than horizontal. You have the horizontal freedom, freedom of research, when you are looking for a mine, but it is fruitless till you have discovered the antecedent existence of the mine. Then you dig in, and progress vertically with genuine results.

So with truth. You have but the freedom of ignorance when you are looking for it, but you have the freedom of exploitation when you have found it. Not only in proportion as you have tapped God's antecedent physical order, may you progress scientifically; but only in so far as you are tapping God's antecedent moral and supernatural order, may you hope to progress morally and spiritually.

Ultimately, genuine freedom is the freedom of the children of God, and authority should only be a help to secure that freedom.

Comment by Edgar S. Brightman:
On this learned paper, with the bulk of which I am in hearty agreement, I offer only two comments. (1) As an idealistic, personalistic theist, I wish that Professor Mercier had explicated further his understanding of his dualism ("God and a created universe") and shown the bearing, specifically, of the idea of matter on authority and freedom. (2) I read: "If God is the Author of the nature of man, endowed with reason and free will, God is, and those who claim to be His representatives are necessarily guarantors of the freedom of man." If this means only that belief in God entails belief in freedom, well and good. But I find some ambiguity in the words, "claim," "representatives," and "necessarily."

CHAPTER L

The Location and Dislocation of Freedom

By MORTIMER R. KADISH
Assistant Professor of Philosophy, Western Reserve University

THAT FREEDOM IS located in rational choice, that the problem of freedom is to create within a culture the conditions of rational choice; such is the primary burden of this paper from which certain inferences concerning the significant dislocations to which freedom is heir shall be drawn.

This thesis, of course, places no claim to novelty. But in times when freedom increasingly comes to be regarded as a possession vaguely equivalent to a legal code, a tradition, a national interest, to the dream of the *status quo* for an eternity of the *status quo*—when, in a word, to be free is to be respectable[1]—it may be opportune to show how freedom might have a rather different sense.

I

Perhaps the greatest theoretical obstacle to the understanding of freedom inheres in the traditional formulation of the question of freedom: "How is freedom possible?" The classic question implies freedom as such, out of the context of the particular situations within which men behave freely. Three kinds of responses, therefore, have been framed: that "freedom" is in any imaginable situation impossible; that it is possible only in some non-empirical sense; that for all situations the possibility of freedom is intrinsic. Each response leads to a similar denouement.

The determinists say that choice is impossible because there are never any real alternatives. If someone asks why a man chose as he did, we answer the question to the extent that we state why for this individual at this point all alternate courses were necessarily out of the question.

---

[1] There are, of course, a variety of respectabilities, some decidedly less beneficent than others—as, for example, those manifested in the societies we call "totalitarian."

Past possibilities, the argument runs, seem real only to the extent of human ignorance of past history; future possibilities seem genuine only because we fail adequately to grasp the present. Furthermore, these considerations hold not only for human choices but even for the proverbial fall of the sparrow. To assert that freedom is *not* possible, is to assert that the only behavior is *necessary* behavior.

Observe, however, that determinism precludes *on principle* the meaningfulness of freedom as choice among alternatives. It is not that free choices do not happen to occur in our world; the point is that they *could* not occur. In brief, the attempt to *deny* the possibility of freedom question implies a purely formal theory, and throws into considerable doubt the referential character of the question.

Nevertheless, the choice of determinism is an issue of the gravest practical importance. When the determinist has been led to use the language of freedom, which he can hardly avoid on all occasions, he can mean by "freedom" only *assent, acceptance,* of *the* one possible thing. Historically, this "one possible" has taken many forms. It has been recognized in the State, in the Order of Nature, in the Will of God, in the Inevitable Revolution; and located anywhere in time or in eternity. In all cases, however, the final method for the fixing of men's beliefs inevitably becomes the method of authority—the determination of opinion by what "the one possible" inexorably demands.

On the other hand, if no one is free, who can be blamed? Even those who refuse to accept a *status quo,* refuse necessarily. Now arises the doctrine of the freedom of the metaphysical will, which, to save the possibility of blame, asserts in effect that the freedom question must be answered *both* negatively *and* positively ("yes" for the transcendental will, and "no" for the knowable universe). Once again the effect of a question which refuses empirical meaning to its subject makes itself felt. For if all events are indeed caused, then any instance of human freedom, if we are to salvage that freedom, automatically becomes some sort of nonevent. Hence one approach may designate freedom as "noumenal" rather than "phenomenal," and mean by this, presumably, that only the non-experiencing mind as such can experience freedom. The doctrine of metaphysical freedom amounts, therefore, to the allegation that any choice freely made is necessarily groundless—and that I will be held strictly responsible for it!

Yet to identify freedom with causelessness deprives the chooser of any reason for choice within the domain of causality and experience. Freedom of the will reaches the same denouement as absolute determination: choice is nonsense. It is hardly surprising that theories of the metaphysical will have been associated with systems of revealed morality as absolute over human choice as any of the forms of the *status quo* to which determinism lends sanction.

The third possible answer, the unqualifiedly affirmative one asserts that not only man, but the universe, every particle of it, has free will. (The smaller the particle gets, the freer.) The question, "How is freedom possible (when all events are caused)?" is in effect countered by the equally dialectical question, "How is law possible (when the universe is composed of individuals)?" As there can be nothing which is non-free, man's free choice has been naturalized into the great community of Things As They Are.

But, alas, chance implies that for any particular choice situation choice is pointless; for whatever happens to happen—and all things now happen to happen—becomes the only possible justification for whatever it was we decided to do. In this net result, determinism goes no further. And it is at this point that one encounters the significant element of identity which unites the traditional responses to the freedom as possibility question: none of them allow choice to be mistaken, except in the sense that a choice might run counter to the main current of some moral or physical *status quo*. In Peirce's language, they do not and cannot distinguish between a right way and a wrong way; and, therefore, they operate effectively only as apologetic for the preestablished legitimacy of some given state of affairs. And since none of them allow a verifiable distinction between choice and non-choice, it would seem that philosophy might be altogether within its rights in dropping entirely what now appears as a totally misleading formulation.

May one not avoid the predicaments that formulation encountered by examining the possibility of freedom as qualified and in context? Might one not then salvage a vital question, and, in apparently empty responses to the wrong problem, find leads to answers for the correct one?

II

Let us, then, modify the question, "How is freedom possible?" into the question, "When and under what conditions is genuine choice possible?" Let us exhibit, if we can, how determinism, indeterminism, and the doctrine of the intrinsically free will, have fixed upon phases of decision genuinely and seriously relevant to this problem.

Any evaluation of "free choice" must accept the fundamental insight of the determinists: that human behavior has a causal dynamism which makes it part of the natural world, and, in principle, predictable. For far from eliminating the genuineness of choice a causal nexus, properly construed, makes choice possible.

If, however, the determinists have not seen that causality need not eliminate choice, it is perhaps because they held the processes of choosing identical in structure with processes like the transformation of water into ice. Then man has indeed no more choice than water when the thermometer drops. Given the origins of modern secular determinism in the generalizing of the mechanics of the seventeenth and eighteenth centuries, it is hardly surprising that the philosophy of that period should regard intelligent behavior on the model of a relatively simple mechanical system—or else expel it from the universe entirely into a special and groundless domain of freedom as such. But when an expanded physical science will even manufacture "feedback" mechanisms capable of discriminating among presented alternatives, switching action appropriately, and using "experience" to guide future discriminations, the old mechanical analogy has become completely gratuitous. "Choice among created alternatives," taken as a whole, may itself constitute a naturally determined fact.

Accordingly, biologists have sought the dynamism of choice in behavior seen now as the function of a nervous system, of effectors, affectors, energy systems requiring the restoration of equilibria, etc.; and psychologists have found choice determined by a motivation-perception adjustment complex. The laboratory rejects the dichotomy established within an older science between "will" and "law." No longer can the inquirer consider "natural," behavior dominated by purely "physical" drives, while "intelligence," disembodied, derives from itself its own impalpable laws. To dichotomize "reason" and "passion," makes each empirically unintelligible. And so we substitute for a chooser whose course of action is unilinearly determined by the impact of force upon force, a chooser whose "nature" consists in a complex motivation-intelligence dynamism operating within a milieu defined by genuine potentialities.

A dynamism such as this, far from making choice unreal, gives it material content. Only a determinate organism integrated within its environment has a reason to choose. Because that which happens within its environment makes a difference to the organism, and those transformations which the organism undergoes effect that environment; therefore, not only is choice grounded, it is also justifiable through the determinate and predictable significance of causally induced changes within organism and environment. Thus, needs are satisfiable precisely because the organism is constituted to explore its environment and to persevere in the exploration until those objects which satisfy those needs *causally* induce the stoppage of that exploration. Accordingly, predicting with a good probability what one would actually do under certain circumstances, becomes the prerequisite for intelligent choice. And the possibility of making a genuine *mistake* in the process of choice exists only because of a dynamism which will persevere with a causally altered behavior, once an adjustment fails to meet its requirements.

The analysis of choice can hardly stop with the location of the dynamism of such choice in biological configurations. Recent inquiry suggests that human choices are also societal in their constitution, as well as in their effects. Accordingly, any discussion of choice must locate its dynamism in the institutions and habits of societies—must, in effect, find rationality and motivation, social.

The Cartesian Compromise, because it surrendered to empirical inquiry the physical world, made impossible the understanding of rationality in its societal significance. But that compromise once rejected, then we are in a position to perceive how the dynamism of intelligent choice, when peculiarly human, arises through a complex of institution, community expectation and interest organized to overcome difficulties. Accordingly, even abstract science, contemplated not as truth but as human process, has a sociology; and what that sociology discovers constitutes the "dynamism" of that science.

In summary, then: it has been suggested that genuine alternatives are possible on both biological and sociological levels only because on both levels behavior may possess *the apparatus for self-correction*. Human organisms and societies record their failures as well as their successes, and "necessarily," under certain conditions, alter attitudes to deal with them. Hence freedom. It is to this insight that determinism leads, in the context of a properly formulated question about freedom.

Now let us turn our attention to the indeterminists who argue basically that individuals are unique, separate, and, therefore, unpredictable. Does indeterminism, then, have no import for an empirical theory of the conditions of freedom which recognizes a causal dynamism? Such a conclusion does not follow, once one recognizes that the entire issue of responsibility without which questions of choice lack all moral import, depends upon distinctiveness between the chooser and his encompassing environment. Some *one* must exist to be held responsible. Otherwise, the very process of holding accountable loses its point as a means of inducing desired change. Indeterminism has exploited this fact and so secured a spurious credibility as the last refuge of individual responsibility.

What does it mean to be a *this*-chooser, an individual? When does a specific organization of needs, history, and discriminating capacities become a person? This is by no means a simple question when one considers the problems of modern social psychology in studying the processes of identification. The indeterminist, or "pluralist," furnishes us with a first approximation in this direction when he discovers the universe of experience to be composed of "plurals," of relatively isolated systems.[2] For this discovery suggests that the entities we are dealing with in the study of choice and freedom are autonomous organizations, relatively isolated systems, for which "warranted" choice is somehow possible.

Common practice and assumption seem to accord with such a suggestion. So children and the insane are not regarded as full persons, because one would not think of asking them to be accountable for their choices. And if a Bureau of Supplies and Accounts commits some grievous error, it is not the stenographer who types the error who is held as a person by the organization within which the Bureau has its identity, but the director in his representation of the Bureau as a relatively autonomous organization.

Choices of the sort for which we hold people responsible do not occur, except the following conditions be fulfilled:

a. The chooser must have its "person" defined by participation in a variety of social roles. For an organization those roles may appear in the form of procedural habits, legislation, managerial regulations, etc.

---

[2] The pluralist, of course, is William James, and the essay in which he equates pluralism to the assertion of the existence of relatively isolated systems, "The Dilemma of Determinism," *Essays in Pragmatism,* Hafner Publishing Company, New York, 1948.

Similarly, for the individual: to the degree a man is lawyer, doctor, beggarman, thief, certain kinds of choices may be expected from him.

But consider what occurs when a human being "chooses" *outside* the context of any role. Then, as with the insane under comparatively enlightened conditions, only a *causal* study is relevant. He has acted but he has not chosen—he "doesn't know what he is doing." The true relation of his behavior to the role structure of the community is lost upon him.

b. The "person" who chooses must react in specified and predictable ways under certain stimuli and not under others. If the aforementioned Bureau of Supplies and Accounts should respond to pressure upon one and all of its members in performing its service—if, in effect, "channels" should be entirely interrupted—it would soon disintegrate as an organization. Similarly, the individual who could not *ignore* wide ranges of stimuli, reject them from all consideration in his conduct, would soon disintegrate as a determinate personality.

c. The autonomous organization which is a "person," must involve somehow the apparatus for meeting role-determined situations. This recognition of the requirements of the situation is not only the condition of sanity in the individual; it is also the condition of the operation of our Bureau. One must know what is relevant and be prepared to act in terms of what is relevant. In this sense the potentiality of warranted choice is a precondition of being held "responsible" and a "person."

In sum, then: the indeterminist-pluralist focus suggests that freedom consists of independence for the chooser; and we translate its results by saying that a precondition of freedom consists in the autonomous functioning "person" that a chooser must be. An implication or two, worth noting, follows for the consideration of freedom.

Our analysis asserts that "persons" are social constructs. But if persons are genuinely *made,* not preestablished substances as radical indeterminism proposes, then they may be destroyed, subverted by guile or superior force or the blunt facts of social change. Accordingly, the problem of creating the conditions of freedom will impose the consideration of ways and means by which to *preserve* persons—such as a reasonably efficient police force and a Bill of Rights expressive of the civil habits of the community.

Nonetheless, if freedom involves protecting persons, it by no means follows that the problem of freedom be *restricted* to the preservation of all *status quo* persons in all their rights and privileges. Such an easy solution for the problem of persons is simply a mask for interest. A positive, never silenced question undercuts the question of how to preserve persons: namely, which persons should be preserved and which should be modified or perhaps eliminated?

It is popular today to attempt a partial answer to the question by insistence upon the "inviolability" of the human personality. But the notion of inviolability is clearer perhaps in what it denies than in what it affirms. Presumably we would all want to say that a society which practices genocide or the "liquidation" of social classes has answered the question wrongly. But many have maintained the inviolability of the person only to defend prison sentences which deprive the individual of most of his rights as a person. Others have even argued that birth control constitutes an assault upon the personalities of the unborn. Such issues cannot be solved by appealing to even the most attractive *a priori* principles. Nor have legalistic approaches fared better. Willy-nilly, then, we are involved in making and breaking persons, sometimes consciously, more often unawares. The point is to do so with knowledge of what we are about and in the light of a careful assessment of the consequences.

Now let us see what may be gleaned from the doctrine that there exists some sort of intrinsic freedom prior to and presumably causal to behavior. It was fairly obvious in our discussion—and, indeed, has been obvious for some centuries[3]—that except as a response to a wrong problem intrinsic freedom made little sense. Nevertheless, this curious doctrine does exploit the sense and feel of living choice.

Modern writers, theologians, romantics of every sort have made the sense of guilt and the terrible giddiness of choice in a dislocated society the nerve of their inquiries. There is certainly some evidence to suspect that the kind of experience to which the neo-theologians of the new and utterly bereft will, refer, may actually interfere with the operation of that dynamism of rational choice underlying "mental health." Still, the question is: where does the climate of decision have its origins? I should like to suggest, following the major trends in psychiatry and analysis, that the answer lies in the relation of the chooser and of the choice situation as he reacts to it, to their histories. The relation of the chooser to his past—in the broadest sense of the word, to his "education"—consti-

---

[3]Consider, for example, David Hume's trenchant chapters "On Liberty and Necessity" in his *Treatise*.

tutes that condition of free choice which is symptomized by and operates through a conscious climate of decision. So it is that elements in a human history, elements perhaps derived from earlier and less mature periods in that history, obtrude into the treatment of real predicaments only to lead to the infinite variety of disasters covered by the expressions, "neurosis" and "madness." It is perhaps through this sort of intrusion that blame, hatred, guilt, terror, "nausea," become intelligible.

The point is that the chooser may have established himself with respect to some particular situation as an autonomous "person," he may possess to a maximum degree the selective dynamism which makes rational choice possible, yet his freedom to choose may be utterly made waste by the spontaneous rising up of elements of an irrelevant past—or, for that matter, in a happier person, may be advanced with a new exhilaration by a base in matured relationships.

We have encountered, then, a third condition for human freedom: developmental health. Perhaps, therefore, when people talk today of the "primacy of the individual," we may state the empirical import of what they have in mind as follows: that only that society is "free" whose members possess the resources to behave responsibly with respect to their social roles and intelligently with respect to the predicaments which exact their consideration, rather than compulsively and with fear. We might translate the burden of this section's analysis: freedom is a function of mind, political life, and harmony within the soul.

III

The analysis so far has consisted in the general method of fusing the processes and conditions of choice with those of rationality. To locate freedom with any degree of adequacy next requires the stipulation of criteria according to which one could state the kinds of circumstances under which the overall social dynamism involved in choice has maintained or failed to maintain that delicate equilibrium that makes rationality in action possible. The problem of the equilibrium of freedom is the problem of determining the limiting cases of freedom, those points in the careers of cultures and persons at which the balance fails. They occur when choice has reached an impasse.

Suppose that any choice the State Department might make would lead the nation to war. Such a situation would exemplify an "impasse" in diplomacy. Or, suppose an individual trying to decide a conflict among fundamental loyalties where no more inclusive loyalty supervened—and you have a second instance. A third class of impasse is less disastrous but no less difficult: consider cases in which the unformed character must decide among alternative careers, or instances in which a man attempts to make preferential choices in the arts, when for the life of him he can discover no basis for preference. Lastly, recall such trivial instances as when we find ourselves poised in a moment's agony before an overrich menu and beneath the eye of an expectant waiter.

All of these have certain elements in common. First and most obviously, all demand some sort of action. We are not choosing for the fun of it. Secondly, the alternatives available are equally acceptable or unacceptable. Thirdly, no external force compels us to accept one thing rather than another; the impasse lies solely in the nature of the choice to which we are committed. Fourthly, and more significantly, we shall assume that no increment of knowledge about the alternatives will change their complexion significantly. I know that this is, very often, not the case; but perhaps it is by no means as rare as more optimistic moralists assume. When these four conditions obtain, choice has reached "an impasse"—not because *any* choice then made will represent a *mistake,* but because it has become impossible to *distinguish* between a right and a wrong way.

Consider now the elements of difference among our examples: first, there is an obvious distinction involved between forced and avoidable choices. We *could* walk out of the restaurant; the United States cannot walk out of the world (as some propose), nor can we put aside loyalties to the degree that we are loyal. Secondly, it is also obvious that the two forced choices are momentous, not only for the life careers of the choosers but for the careers of the numerous persons with which they might intersect; the fourth is trivial on both counts; the third significant, in all probability, only for the chooser.

Impasses which are forced and momentous are "primary," those avoidable and (relatively) trivial, "secondary." Primary impasses tend to stultify future experience and to disrupt the personality; secondary impasses, may even provide beneficial opportunities for the growth of new interests, tastes, and activities. Clearly, the boundaries between the two sorts of impasse are not to be sharply fixed.

But it is the first kind of impasse which is peculiarly relevant. The assessment of an impasse for what it is involves no "value" judgment upon the part of the assessor, and a way lies open for determining the existence of the equilibria which sustain freedom, or, what is the same thing, the practical possibility of correct choice: *given a culture, or some subarea of a culture which holds a chooser responsible for selecting a course of action within it, then the equilibrium of freedom will properly have been adjusted within that culture or subarea which minimizes the occurrence of primary impasses, and improperly adjusted when those occurrences are maximized.* The culture which succeeded in minimizing primary impasses would, in the fullest sense, constitute the "Open Society" about which so much has been written of late: a creative society, expanding in sensitivity and depth, clearminded and, what amounts to the same thing, clearpassioned.

But the analysis of impasse has a more specific value for the diagnosis of culture patterns, and, accordingly, for the setting up of standards. For any instance of primary impasse, we may, by referring back to last section's discussion of the conditions of freedom, expect one of the following sorts of dislocation to have occurred:

a. A dislocation of the dynamism of reflective behavior within the cultural areas within which the impasse appears. So, for example, the recent Kefauver Committee, to the extent that it substitutes for an examination of the complex origins of organized crime, the damnation of its wickedness, and for a remedial program constructed upon the results of that examination exhortations to morality and religion, does rather little to control the legal, social, and economic processes responsible for the crime the Committee thinks to stem. This combination of moral exhortation and mythology, by making of inquiry primarily a means for titillating the sense of righteousness, represents a radical dislocation of the social dynamism of reflection.

b. A failure in the complex systems of social roles or identifications in virtue of which autonomy of function, and hence a clearcut allocation of responsibility, may be achieved. In an evolving society, split by clashing interests, we should be able to predict a Hiss, even if we had never seen one. But the essence of the true "subversive's" predicament consists characteristically not in an interest in thirty pieces of silver, but in a deeply felt perception of impossible-to-reconcile roles—the tragedy of moral impasse.

c. A carry over of either individual or cultural "neurosis" to a situation which might not otherwise result in impasse. Analysts have well documented this point.

d. A malfunctioning derivative of a combination of the preceding. (These are probably the more numerous cases.) Consider, for example, the intrusion of developed industrial technologies in communities the social structures and histories of which are oriented to very different technologies. Around every phase of life in which the new technology strikes the community, the community's past rebels and tends to block the successful solution of even technological problems. In such a community, primary impasse might be the rule. Nor need we look for illustration only to those cultures to which a Point Four program might apply or misapply; the history of the industrial revolution in the West illustrates the point quite fully.

Free choice, then, has dynamically related conditions knowable by their fruits. Within that area of experience within which we can distinguish a right way *and* a wrong way, and act upon the distinction, "freedom" exists; where the very foundations of corrigibility disappear in the predicament of impasse, so does freedom.

IV

We must, in conclusion, show how the general problem of creating the conditions of rational choice might be translated into a multitude of questions pointed more or less sharply at present predicaments. For does not our inquiry suggest that "freedom" as rational choice is a revolutionary idea, an idea denoting present process and a constant remaking, an idea which is genuinely the ideal only of the uncommitted? For the last. time we may take up the leads which early in this paper the metaphysicians provided:

Questions concerning the dynamism of intelligence. Such questions have received their classic formulation in terms of the concepts of freedom of speech, assembly, and thought. The foregoing analysis requires expansion of that formulation in terms of the concrete conditions of *present* choice. Today communication and opinion-formation no longer occur solely or perhaps primarily in terms of face to face interactions but are mediated by press combines, radio, television, advertising, large scale indoctrinating systems of public and private education. If, therefore, the dynamism of intelligence is to be maintained such questions as the control of radio, television, newspapers, by special interest groups must be raised and reraised—and raised in such a way that we do not substitute "freedom of speech" for an inquiry into the actual conditions of communication.

Moreover, that dynamism, under modern conditions, must be extended far beyond its traditional scope. The statistically illiterate will judge with accuracy the record of professional baseball players; but they fail with a vengeance in appraising intelligently the performances of governmental and industrial administrations. Yet active and informed audiences are preconditions of effective social behavior. How to create them? Consider the problem of rationalizing intergroup behavior. Is the only mechanism available to break the network of hatred, a Brotherhood Week? Surely, it is at least worthwhile to consider the careful scrutiny and utilization of *all* the complex interpersonal formations in business and play in terms of which "prejudice" occurs.

Questions concerning social autonomy. Individuals being conceived as tight little centers of self-interest, it was perhaps inevitable that freedom be defined primarily as the absence of impediment—with the consequent problem of explaining how one might convince one independent universe to be responsible for another. And so the central problem of creating significant persons, since it must be met somehow, is met *sub rosa,* and only haphazardly.

As a result, concrete problems such as the problem of creating universities capable of performing their announced functions, become unmanageable; and an autonomy of organization necessary to conduct genuine inquiry and the teaching of that inquiry is swamped in the pressures of trustees, church, government, and a public opinion by no means inevitably benign. The same problem occurs elsewhere, in labor, in business. And it is a real problem because freedom, in the phase of autonomy, or person creation, implies also the task of creating linkages. So that in essence, the problem of autonomy becomes the problem of converting business, labor, university, from social force to "responsible" organization —an organization, that is, given sufficient play and sufficient development to perform its functions where those functions integrate in the complex of the community. The alternative is bifurcation in the community, destruction of the focus of personality.

Questions, therefore, of "freedom of enterprise," of "academic freedom," of the "freedom" of labor, interpreted outside of the atomistic mythology of much current discussion, constitute the current exchange value of social autonomy as a condition of freedom. The question of determining which, if any, of such "freedoms" be entirely abrogated within the community in the effort to avoid impasse, is itself a major question which the above formulation is not intended to dismiss.

Questions concerning the formation of histories. Free choice has, of course, its historically created climate. The creation of an atmosphere which would sustain the individual in his role-guided efforts at social reconstruction, constitutes, therefore, a major function of educational institutions; and the reflex of orthodoxy which tightens nerves all about us today suggests a major failure in those institutions.

Yet surely the previous discussion suggests that the teaching of "democracy" and "freedom" as faiths, the vociferousness of which goes toward establishing a secure place in the community, must engender attitudes hostile to the rational reconstruction of social organizations and, hence, to democracy and freedom as rational process. What procedures are available for creating a saner atmosphere? Presumably, they will involve not only instruction for the young but reeducation of the comparatively mature; not only the reconstruction of formal organs of education but the informing of the numerous and complex institutions of American life with the liberal—free—spirit. Only some such fundamental remoulding of the social mechanisms of memory and indoctrination seems likely to eliminate the kind of response implicit, for example, in the electoral successes of McCarthyism.

Of such a nature are the questions which compose the general problem of choice and freedom. Obviously, they extend into the furthest reaches of politics, economics, morals, philosophy. The hope for their eventual solution, however, rests on the realization that those questions extend downward as well as to the most delicate and personal areas of contemporary experience. In consequence, we shall know that we have begun to answer the questions of freedom by our acute discomfort; and our ease and self-righteousness will signify that they have escaped us.

Comment by Edgar S. Brightman:

The very valuable contribution of Professor Kadish is excellent within its limits. Those limits are defined by the first sentence, "Freedom is located in rational choice." Here's a sound definition of *ethical* freedom; but in our search for a democratic way of life we must also consider political freedom. Political freedom must include (within limits, to be sure) the right to choose irrationally. How many voters in how many elections make rational choices in their capacity as free citizens casting the Australian ballot? This objection does not detract from the merits of the soundly argued paper. It is intended only to indicate a necessary supplement.

Comment by Nels F. S. Ferré:

Certainly we can accept neither a mechanical determinism nor a causally indifferent freedom. Both are untrue to experience and to fact. The real question is his own statement of it: "When and under what conditions is genuine choice possible?"

When, however, he argues that "human behavior has a causal dynamism which makes it a part of the natural world and, in principle, predictable," he has unfortunately prejudiced the issue. Freedom is within the natural world; it is in fact. Freedom has a causal context and a motivational bias. Freedom is as concrete and complex as the situation of choice and the intellectual-emotional history of the chooser. The final issue of freedom, I also believe to be predictable. Man chooses his real good when he is truly aware of and convinced of it.

But between this distant event and any present choice, freedom consists precisely in the fact that man's choice is not predictable, even in principle, even by God. Freedom can no more be reduced to cybernetic naturalism than to mechanical naturalism. A self-adjusting mechanism is not a human purpose, nor is a human purpose a human being. Even a self-correcting mechanism pursuing a shifting target, or any "feedback device" in sociological method, is a creation of human thought, a reflection of human operations in one particular way, not the full orbit of human reality.

Any discussion of freedom on a level lower than man's total nature and destiny, is necessarily partial. But on its level it can render great service analytically and concretely. Professor Kadish has contributed weightily to the clarification of the subject of this Conference.

I particularly like what he says of the bearing of social roles, cultures, and an "open society" on personal freedom. His discussion of mental health means to me maturation of freedom. The prophets and seers also have a supercultural condition for culture to which or whom they respond to remake culture, cause it to be healed, or advance beyond itself. There is thus always available to those who know an inclusive fundamental loyalty —God's concern for the common good.

There is no "primary impasse" for a religiously aware and committed person. But all false impasses should be eliminated by the creative society. Professor Kadish warns of the great danger "of a generation of committed men, of people who have no recourse." Unless we maximize democracy in the concrete, I can foresee anguished frustration, but I fear more a generation of uncommitted men, men who having lost faith, forfeit their freedom, who substitute academic lore for religious reality.

Comment by Barna Horvath:

The method of Professor Kadish is to show that a too abstract question about freedom leads determinism, indeterminism, and the doctrine of the intrinsically free will, equally to a meaningless freedom, accepting invariably the inexorable demands of some authority; whereas a qualified question, put in context, can be answered more fruitfully, while all three above doctrines contribute some grains to this meaningful idea of freedom as rational choice.

The basic objection to the three doctrines is that "none of them allow choice to be mistaken." The question is only whether these doctrines, if refuted in the abstract, can be used for showing the possibility of freedom as qualified and in context.

As in this section of the Conference the *Definition of Freedom and Authority* stands to question, let us remark, first of all, that in the criticism of the three doctrines leading to authoritarian beliefs, the concept of authority is used in different senses. In the case of determinism, "the method of authority" is said to mean "discovery of what 'the one possible' inexorably demands"—in other words, causal necessity. In the case of indeterminism, it is "revealed morality." In the case of intrinsic freedom, it is chance.

But causal necessity, revelation, and chance are surely not authority in the same sense. Freedom may be defined perhaps as the negation, or contradictory opposite, of necessity (or, more particularly, of compulsion). Professor Kadish emphasizes, correctly according to this use of the terms, that freedom is *definitionally* excluded by determinism. Authority, however, could not be defined as the negation of freedom, as it seems to mean something more or less *freely* accepted. But of course authority is still a far cry from freedom. The difference of meaning seems to point to some finer kind of influence in the case of authority than in that of power or coercion. Whenever we speak of the authority of experts, for example, there seems to be no trace of curtailment of freedom in the meaning of the term, any more than in the fact that we cannot know everything, and are, therefore, obliged to rely on others.

Authority, in the genuine sense of the term, seems to be a freely and rationally chosen guide on account of its superior ability to lead us on paths where we would stumble and fail without it. Even the finest kinds of authority mean, of course, dependence; whereas freedom means independence. Blind belief in authority may be more detrimental to freedom than physical coercion. But there is also, at the opposite end of the scale, almost completely free, rational use of authority, *e.g.*, when we consult the best available sources of information on any subject before we form our own independent opinion. Intelligent utilization of authority does not exclude free criticism and is as compatible with freedom as the use of instruments in general, although blind following of authority may lead into servitude. But the change of free into blind following, changes also authority into power and tyranny. We have to conclude, therefore, that authority is dependence on another man in the course of our own efforts, short of power, compulsion, or domination, but, also short of complete freedom.

Perhaps it is now clear that causal necessity and chance cannot be called authority, whereas revelation may be so called.

It is forcibly brought out by the author why determinism furnishes the conditions of rational choice. Because only an "organism integrated within its environment has a reason for choice." Possibility of prediction and of genuine mistake make choice rational. In short, causality is the precondition of teleology. Both are but the same series, looked at from opposite ends, while causes turn into reasons.

If "caused and justifiable" choice would explain freedom, determinism were enough. But determinism has been rejected in the abstract; can it then explain freedom in a context? The author claims only that it explains the *mental element* in freedom, or freedom as a function of mind: rational choice. If determinism has to be supplemented, in order to explain freedom, this implies the admission that freedom is not quite the same thing as rational choice or teleology.

On the other hand, does determinism suffer to be *supplemented* by indeterminist elements?

A determinist will answer that there is no need of supplementation. Freedom is the recognition of necessity. As "caused" choices are "justifiable," we may regard the subjective illusion of freedom simply as a useful device of nature, and need not trouble ourselves by the causal determination of our or other's acts. We punish, in order to prevent or reform; not in retribution or retaliation.

Let us see, next, why does Professor Kadish turn to indeterminism in order to "locate" freedom, after he has rejected it in the abstract. He does so in order to explain *responsibility*. The conditions of responsible choices are seen in "persons," defined by participation in social roles, who "react in specified and predictable ways under certain stimuli and not under others," meet "role-determined situations," or "act in terms of what is relevant." Such persons are "social constructs."

If this "autonomous functioning 'person' "—autonomous in spite of its social construction and possible elimination—is the *second* precondition of freedom, its *third* condition is seen—utilizing the doctrine of intrinsic freedom—on "developmental health," meaning by this term the climate of decision created by "histories" of the chooser and the choice situation.

The result of this combination of doctrines is that "freedom is a function of mind, political life, and harmony within the soul." What follows is the explanation of dislocations by a "theory of impasse," and some practical application to present day problems.

The concessions made to indeterminism follow the pluralist idea of "isolated systems" and the existentialist idea of the "sense and feel of living choice." The turn to indeterminism is marked by the appeal to *subjectivity* and *history*. But this means, to the author, only an appeal to *social constructs* and *psychoanalytical conditions* of mental health. We may doubt whether this interpretation does not reverse the indeterminist elements of subjectivity and history again into their determinist explanation on the line of causality.

Comment by Wayne A. R. Leys:

Professor Kadish has performed the philosopher's clarifying function in showing verbal difficulties in the question: "How is freedom possible?" "Under what conditions is rational choice possible?" is a more fruitful question.

If I understand the thesis, it is that freedom of choice is possible when a person after deliberation prefers one goal rather than another and when the preferred goal is attainable. If, on the other hand, a person finds no basis for preference of goals, or if his preferences and efforts cannot achieve the better goal, the person is at an impasse and is not free.

Such a definition of freedom is, no doubt, capable of clarifying discourse. I can see no objection to it, if it is allowed that "freedom" is sometimes used to express other meanings.

The only difficulty I felt in reading the paper was that of identifying the context in which the constructive suggestions would have an advisory effect. To whom is the advice addressed? And for what purpose? Although the problem is stated in very general terms, the opinions expressed toward the end of the article do not have a universal application. They would be easier to understand if Mr. Kadish would indicate the area of human enterprise which he intends to criticize.

Mr. Kadish's comments on the Kefauver investigation suggest that leaders and propagandists should not create the illusion of a choice between alternatives that are not known to be practicable. But I have been under the impression that some controversies deal with uncertain futurities and that leaders sometimes achieve the "impossible" by acts of faith. By the definition, stated above, such leaders and their followers do not have a genuine choice, but I see nothing objectionable in betting blind when the odds are incalculable.

The comment on the Hiss case seems to be addressed to people who are worried about subversive activity and wish that it could be stopped. There is no suggestion that a definite person, official, or group, can carry out a program of action that will substitute a "genuine, rational choice" for the moral impasse of the marginal man who is caught in the conflict of cultures. The advice seems, therefore, to enjoin Stoic resignation to the existence of moral impasses, or tragic, impossible choices for some individuals.

The later remarks about creating universities and other institutions, that are capable of performing their announced functions, are apparently addressed to policy-makers. My experience is limited; but, having participated in the founding of one college, I can say that the creation of the conditions of freedom is a complicated business. In making provision for "autonomy" one makes assumptions about the goals, the work, the functions, that the students and faculty will prefer. The resources that are collected and the machinery that is established will, however, permit autonomy for some and deny it to others, for the simple reason that preferences differ. This raises the question whether much rational freedom (in Mr. Kadish's sense of the term) is possible, except in a homogeneous society.

Although I am personally fond of freedom, I doubt that concentration on the problem of preventing impasses will do very much to increase the amount of freedom in the world. I doubt whether much freedom is achieved by gift. It is true that persons born into a civil rights democracy enjoy more freedom than persons born into a despotism, but the persistence of freedom seems to be due to the social inheritance of a certain assertiveness and certain restraints, rather than to the prior existence of Bills of Rights, etc.

Perhaps, the objection which I am expressing could be better stated in this way: some social machinery is more conducive to freedom of choice than other social machinery. To that extent I agree with Mr. Kadish. But one of the conditions for the survival and use of such social machinery is an aggressiveness which says, "Damn the impasses; full speed ahead." Such initiative (coupled with willingness to let others pursue their interests if they do not make too much trouble) depends upon childhood training, economic resources (above the starvation level), literacy, and other factors. These conditions can be changed, to some extent, by deliberate action.

Professor Kadish has formulated an excellent question. His answer needs empirical evidence. On impressionistic grounds I believe the evidence will complicate his answer.

CHAPTER LI

A Case Study in Freedom through Authority

By JOHN LaFARGE, S.J.
Associate Editor, "America"

OUT OF THE many fields explored by the Conference on Science, Philosophy and Religion, few would seem more fruitful than that chosen for the 1951 meeting: the relation of Freedom to Authority. A glance through the papers submitted shows the interest of their writers. A more careful study reveals the subject's complexity, once you embark upon a deeper philosophy of these two great poles of all human conduct and of the structure of all institutions. The Conference was born out of a concern for freedom, and the years of its development confronted it with the difficult task of choosing between the specious and the genuine in types of authority, a task related to the most vivid experiences of our lives. Yet when we try to fit these experiences into the framework of any exact definitions, we may feel like the physicist Walter Heisenberg, who observed that scientific research was like unravelling a tangled ball of yarn. You start in the middle with a couple of free ends, and trust that a final disentanglement will display a vast rational plan behind all the world's complexity.

One of the "free ends" in our present discussion is obviously that of an immediately observable human phenomenon that is both religious and social in character. Brief attention to such phenomenon may add a certain perspective to the more theoretic treatment, with which naturally most of the writers are concerned. My choice comes simply from the circumstance that in the spring of 1951, when on a short study trip through Germany, I happened to witness the public veneration of the bodily remains of a man who during his lifetime occupied an extremely clear, well defined position toward both those poles of conduct under examination, that of freedom—personal and social—and that of authority, civil and religious. My purpose in mentioning him is not to describe an irrelevant tangent to our discussion by publicizing an interesting religious celebrity, but simply to suggest what any individual case study might reveal. In this instance, various decisive points of reference are familiar to me from my own observation.[1]

Rupert Mayer, S.J., was an outstanding preacher of the word of God, and an extremely influential personal counsellor, particularly to men—singly and in groups. He was the leader in active welfare work among people of all beliefs and affiliations in Bavaria. During the late 'twenties and the 'thirties he made himself anathema to Hitler and the Nazi regime by his repeated public contradiction of their teachings, both in word and in practice. He was one man in the city of Munich who ceaselessly heckled Nazis and Communists alike in the cafés and beer halls. As a result, he suffered imprisonments over a space of seven years, although he had won decorations for bravery and had lost a leg as an Army chaplain during the First World War. Freed by the Americans on May 11, 1945, he collaborated generously with the liberators, and resumed his active career, but died shortly after, on November 1 of the same year. He was buried in the crypt of the St. Michael's Hofkirche in Munich. (The church was badly damaged by the war but is now in regular use.) There his tomb is visited year in and year out, by some three thousand persons daily, who kneel in silence and ask grace from God for the daily battle with poverty, social disorder, and sin.

I

The following are some points that may bear upon our discussion.

1. The people, of all walks of life, ages, and conditions, who pay this extraordinary respect to the memory of Rupert Mayer honor him for what he was: a resolute opponent of dictatorial authority. Yet they are not, I imagine, of the revolutionary type. They are the same by nationality, many possibly are alike by native temperament to the crowds that had flocked to hear Hitler at the Festsaal but a few blocks away. Yet the authority—in a wide sense—of Father Mayer's personality and ideas compelled them where Hitler's "authority" had failed.

2. The man who exercised this compulsion during his life and has continued to exercise it even six years after his death, was no "problem-

[1] Cf. Anton Koerbling, *Pater Rupert Mayer*, Schnell & Steiner, Muenchen, 1951.

atic" case. His was a completely uncomplicated personality, devoid of resentments and singularly trustful of his fellow human beings. It was better, he used to say, to be fooled ten times running than to miss helping one deserving person out of the ten. Those who differed from him, as to religion or other matters, he approached with the same directness that he showed to those who shared his beliefs. He sharply censured the government of the Third Reich for creating divisions, as he saw them, between the people of different beliefs in the community who could live together in happiness and peace, if they but respected one another and lived up integrally to their own beliefs. He had only one way of speaking and acting, and signed a declaration while in prison, typed on the Gestapo letterhead, that if he were ever to be released he would continue preaching and speaking in public as, where, and in the same manner as he had done before arrest. With equal directness, he asked the presiding Nazi official at one of his many hearings: "What kind of authority does your state exercise, when you see ordinary citizens' teeth chattering and faces blanched in your presence?"

II

Yet here is the paradox, about which so much discussion turns and will continue to turn in all our deliberations. This man—whom I present as a category, not as a unique personality—derived intellectual conviction and the inner strength of will to reject an anti-human authoritarianism, in virtue of his uncomplicated acceptance of an absolute spiritual authority: God's moral law, governing the relationships of man to man and of man to governments; and of a spiritual teacher whom he considered divinely authorized to expound it. Such a belief was not the result of any psychological yearning; nor was it a form of escape from the cold analysis of visible reality. It was a conclusion drawn simply from the nature of things as one man saw them, and from the experiences and data which appeared to him to fit into the general scheme of the world, the relations of that world to its Creator, and the relations of man both to the world and to God.

Moreover, this anti-authoritarian had dedicated himself, at an early age, to an obediential way of life—that of a religious order—for the express purpose of realizing in the most perfect fashion this essential relation of God-world-man in his own personal case. The severe yoke that he placed upon his own will and judgment by this extra dedication was completely voluntary: it was the pattern that he chose to follow, not one that he would prescribe for countless others who shared his own fundamental beliefs and life philosophy. Basic to this specialized and supererogatory way of life was a twofold concept as to liberty itself:

1. Man's liberty, man's immediately ascertainable power to determine his own life (one of the first ascertainable "free ends" in the tangled yarn of our existence) is a gift that comes to us from a Divine Creator and leads to Him. Fundamentally man is made that he may seek God and find Him. It is basically a positive gift, a *liberty for,* in advance of its being a liberty *from* or a liberty *against.*

2. The complete fulfilment of this liberty is achieved when it is fully dedicated to the Source from which it arose, and this fullness of dedication can be achieved under certain circumstance through the hands of a fellow human being, whose voluntarily accepted governing or paternal authority is nonetheless an instrument of that inner liberty to which governor and governed alike are dedicated.

In every individual way of life, every individual pilgrimage to God, the completely unifying force is that of love, with its correlative rejection of hate. "We must hate evil," said Mayer, by "we" meaning all of us without exception, "but we cannot tolerate hate and aversion to our fellow human being."

III

Certain conclusions may be suggested from the foregoing considerations.

1. There is obvious need for a study of the *positive* concept of man's basic, existential freedom: that concept which asserts that the highest form of liberty is a response to the ultimate love which is the source of the world's being and is the finality of the world's development.

2. Such a positive concept of inner liberty is compatible with the acceptance of a spiritual authority—in teaching and in governance; indeed, implies such an acceptance, once we accept the idea of a transcendent God Who at the same time is immanent to human conduct. Furthermore, a person can win a universal and reasoned respect from his fellow human beings by the very fact that he has synthesized these two poles of conduct in his own personality. The veneration paid to the individual

whom we have cited is not the veneration of devotees or enthusiasts or fanatics, but the humble tribute of men and women who have drunk the bitter deprivation of human liberty to the dregs.

3. The fact that religious men are ordinarily distressed by the lack of respect shown to spiritual authority, constitutes a periodical temptation to bolster such authority by an appeal to political power or even to physical force. The man who is "outside the State"—to use the expression of Professor Neumann[2]—necessarily suffers a certain isolation that is not the lot of one for whom the State is coterminous with all morals and religion. Hence the temptation to end that sense of isolation by a facile recourse to the temporal power. The fact, however, that some have sought the wrong solution—and that some today may advocate the same—is not a reason for diffidence in the authority of God, but rather for a diligent recourse to the deeper study of the nature of that authority, a more determined effort to prevent such betrayals by the shortsighted.

4. Dorothy Lee, in her lucid contribution from the field of anthropology,[3] shows how among certain peoples who possess a highly integrated type of culture, the political authority is, as it were, immanent in the very structure of their lives. They instinctively recognize an order to which all citizens belong, but which itself is superior to any one individual. Their "authority" is nonetheless genuine and compelling by the reason that it possesses a certain degree of immanence.

Yet the authority of God is, as it were, immanent in the very nature of things, even though, in the Judeo-Christian concept, it is the authority of one Who is uniquely transcendent, Who "Is" of Himself, where all others "are" by and through Him. The response to that authority is not a compliance to a mere external compulsion, but is the very breath of that inner life by which the creature ascends to fellowship and union with the Creator. Hence the instinctive feeling of those who accept this authority that its rejection is an essentially *inhuman* act, the introduction of an essential negativism and deathlike nihilism into the living texture of human life. Hence a very real concern over the policies of those elements in our nation who would try to erect this negativism into a form of political or educational monism, even though sold to the public as a democratic process.

[2] Cf. Franz L. Neumann, "The Concept of Political Freedom," pp. 442 f.
[3] Cf. Dorothy D. Lee, "Freedom and Authority as Integral to Culture and Structure," pp. 335–343.

From its very concept, authority, in the deepest sense of the word, as opposed to mere authoritarianism or compulsion, implies an acceptance by reason and an acceptance by love. This may explain why the most effective and the most compelling resistance possible to the forces which seek to impose tyranny upon mankind, is often found in the persons of those men and women who have no hesitation in responding with a free gift of their own liberty to an ultimate Authority Whom they conceive as God of love.

Comment by Swami Akhilananda:

Father LaFarge gives us a very clear conception of true liberty and true authority. He also illustrates his points with the inspiring life of Father Mayer of Germany. We are indeed grateful to Father LaFarge for the presentation of this beautiful character who represents the real meaning of liberty and authority.

We would like to emphasize this very conception of authority, because there are many critics who become extremely susceptible to the idea of authority in the field of religious life. It is true that there have been many abuses of religious authority; and many critics support their own views of these abuses with facts from history. However, they do not consider the true meaning of religious authority, which is based on divine love and the cultivation of the practice of the presence of God.

We fully support the viewpoint of Father LaFarge that authority from a religious person's life is accepted by a liberty seeking person, because the religious person is established in the transcendent reality, and because he realizes that liberty really comes from God and not from his own power and position. We want to emphasize that the authority of a religious man which is shown for the service of another man or society, is purely based on love, as he realizes the divine Presence in him and in others.

So, in order to synthesize liberty and authority, we must individually reach the transcendent Reality, God. The more we realize that Reality, the more we manifest love. Then the authority does not seem to be harsh or authoritarian; it rather becomes a loving expression in harmony with reason. Thus we can refute the arguments of the critics against religious authority. Moreover, this kind of life can alone counteract the totalitarian or military type of authority.

CHAPTER LII

The Freedom of Civilization

By PAUL SCHRECKER
Professor of Philosophy, University of Pennsylvania

HARDLY ANY PROBLEM arising within the condominium of politics, ethics, and the philosophy of history has been discussed so much in recent years as that of Freedom and the freedoms. As a matter of fact, it is no new problem; every step forward on mankind's tortuous path to Freedom has manifested itself by the recognition of some new freedom. From the challenge voiced in 399 B.C. by Socrates, who in the face of death proclaimed every man's right and duty to follow his moral conscience rather than the unjust orders of traditional authorities, to the latest discussions of a right to freedom from fear and want, immense progress has been achieved, even though reverses have occurred and will continue to occur. But now, for the first time the world at large begins to realize that freedoms ought to be safeguarded on a worldwide basis. The Charter of the United Nations declares indeed the "universal respect for, and observance of, human rights and fundamental freedoms for all" to be one of the main pursuits it proposes to promote.

As long as the discussion turns around general confessions of faith it seems easy to come to terms, at least verbally. To proclaim, for instance, the dignity and worth of the human person, is something scarcely any government would refuse openly to do. But when it comes to defining and specifying legislative or judicial or administrative norms which would violate this dignity and this worth, divergences which appear to be irreconcilable emerge. Even within one nation, such fundamental freedoms as that of enterprise or the right of equal access to educational facilities, are explosive issues. Moreover, it is highly controversial whether all the demanded or granted freedoms are consistent within one system of law. And, finally, it is obvious that every particular freedom must suffer limitation for the sake of the preservation of the others, as well as of Freedom. But how much?

If such difficulties arise within one nation, how can we hope to define the legitimate claims of human dignity and worth in a way agreeable to nations so widely separated by their national civilizations, traditions, aspirations, ways of life, and institutions, as are our Western world (itself far from being One World), the Arabic states, Russia, and China? Just as widely as the conceptions of human dignity and worth varied in the various epochs of history, so they vary also among contemporaneous nations. The fact that up to the eighteenth century women were not taught generally to read and to write, was not felt then, even by themselves, to be a denial of their freedom to learn. And, as everybody knows, Aristotle and after him most of the Schoolmen considered slavery as a natural, necessary, and morally unobjectionable institution. Even nowadays we must aver, however reluctantly, that some freedoms, such as that of research, of opinion, or of the press are being considerably curtailed, even in the freest nations, and that in so far as they are claimed to exist, they cover, in the various nations, diametrically opposed practices.

These considerations should, however, not discourage us. On the contrary, only by analyzing the nature of the resistance which historic reality opposes to the diffusion and stabilization of freedom may we hope to get a more adequate insight into its essential structure and phenomenology. What is, in fact, the lesson we may derive as to the seeming relativity and patent metamorphoses of the freedoms? We see them emerging and slowly developing. We see them vindicated first by some lonely crier in the desert, then gradually spreading until they become understood and protected by society. Sometimes, but more rarely, we also see some well established freedom eclipsed in a society or nation, because its actualization would impair powerful vested interests. We must not conclude from such experiences that justice is the interest of the powerful or nothing but a screen for class interests. The fact that a certain freedom emerged only at a definite point of the historic process, does not prove that it did not exist before, but only that it was unknown, unrecognized, and perhaps unnecessary before. Has it been just to grant liberty only to a few and to refuse it to the others—who may not even have missed it then—because human equality has been a relatively late discovery? We might, with exactly the same right, contend that the theorem of Pythagoras became true only when it was discovered. Or did the theory of relativity cease to be true in Germany and Russia when it was suppressed because of the alleged race or capitalistic odor of its inventor?

If the question is raised this way, it will be realized at once that a sharp distinction must be made between freedom *in abstracto* and the specific historical forms under which it is actualized or refused. But at this point the difficulty grows formidable. For how are we to define freedom in a way so general and so flexible that it will adapt itself readily to very disparate cultures and ways of life, without, in the very process, losing its meaning in an empty slogan? To accomplish such a definition, we must attempt to find a common expression for the various freedoms (and the corresponding human rights) which, in the course of time, have been claimed or granted by civilized mankind. Now, it is not likely that any serious objection will be raised when it is affirmed that each freedom aims at guaranteeing possible satisfaction, or the pursuit of satisfaction, to some fundamental and aboriginal aspiration of man. Material needs such as those of food, shelter, reproduction, sleep, are certainly not the only ones inherent in human nature; man shares them with the animals. Even the most primitive cultures have produced spontaneously some rudiments of language, art, knowledge—however implicit—religion, economic, social, and political institutions, be it but in the form of very undifferentiated and unspecialized patterns of conduct. This fact, substantiated by all ethnological and prehistorical discoveries, obliges us to concede that man does not live by bread alone. Each one of the collective achievements we meet in all human societies manifests an omnipresent though more or less developed aspiration of civilized man. The term, "civilized man," is almost redundant. In fact, man before or without civilization is a mere fiction. There is no evidence, for instance, for man's ever having been without the instrument of expression and communication called language. Similarly, we discover in every civilization, primitive or rational as it may be, a deeply rooted craving for a meaning of the individual's life which transcends his limitations in time and space, a desire which, with a very general word, may be called the pursuit of salvation. Again we find in every civilization a desire for knowledge—and not only the need for technical skills—which manifests itself in many various forms, from magic, myths, and legends, up to methodically organized rational research. Nor is there in any civilization a complete lack of artistic elements giving evidence for a primordial though frequently inarticulate desire for esthetic satisfaction. And again, we must assume, a native human aspiration for security and justice, a desire which may be highly developed, self-conscious, and rationalized, or merely instinctive and implicit, or even frustrated and atrophied, but which never is missing entirely. And finally, the essential limitation of human power, lifetime, and the resources needed for the preservation of the individual and of the species, provokes the ubiquitous attempt to produce an optimum ratio of expenditure and effect, in short, economic patterns.

Regarded from this viewpoint, civilization in its entirety appears as a gigantic and ever changing human undertaking to satisfy the primordial and irrepressible aspirations constituting human nature. The whole of human history may be considered as a very slow approach toward this asymptotic goal, often marking time, sometimes even retrogressing, but never resting. One of the conditions which aggravates this perpetual strife of mankind is the fact that the various human aspirations do not always cooperate but very frequently compete for supremacy, not only in the individual but in society as well. Not only is there a constant rivalry between the material and the spiritual needs; even the spiritual needs themselves are far from cooperating fraternally. How often has religion set out to supplant science and rational knowledge, or a specious scientism set out to ridicule the desire for salvation! How frequently has the craving for security assailed the desire for justice and even for the very fountainhead of civilization, liberty! There is no people exempt from the danger referred to by Alexander Hamilton when he spoke of nations which "to be more safe, at length become willing to run the risk of being less free."

It must be admitted that those primordial needs are not equally distributed. In some individuals the craving for salvation is more developed than the desire for knowledge or wealth, in others the esthetic aspiration prevails over that toward security, and in many the material instincts are hypertrophied to a degree which allows only the most scanty expenditure on behalf of justice, knowledge, or esthetic elation. This is also true as to entire epochs and nations. Ancient Athens, Rome, and the Middle Ages are remembered for widely differing achievements. In our own times, differences of national civilizations which hamper the quest for "mutual understanding" might be more easily overcome, if they were understood as manifestations of differing hierarchical orders of the basic aspirations. In French civilization, for instance, to a larger proportion than in other nations, the national effort is devoted to the satisfaction of the esthetic desires, with the result that other aspirations—economic, political, and so on—are partly frustrated.

The onesidedness or unbalance of every civilization may serve as a clue to understanding the diversity of the systems of freedoms which the various epochs and nations have carried out in practice. May we not presume, at least tentatively, that every civilization will grant predominant concern to those freedoms which implement the satisfaction of the prevailing aspirations? But the historical experience at first seems to contradict such a thesis. The European Middle Ages certainly witnessed a hegemony of the religious aspiration, and yet the idea of religious freedom was absolutely alien to this epoch. And in nineteenth century France, Flaubert, Baudelaire, and many others were persecuted because of their creations in belles-lettres.

Yet, it may be precisely by such example that an understanding of the freedoms and their relationship to Freedom can be attained. What is happening, actually, when a particular freedom is denied recognition? The satisfaction of one of the aspirations of civilized man is threatened by the punitive sanctions established in another field of civilization. If, *e.g.,* debarment from civil rights, professions, or certain educational opportunities are incident on a person's adherence to a certain religion, his freedom of religion is violated. If an individual's desire for knowledge incurs disadvantages in any other field or frustration of his other aspirations, the freedom of research, education, or information is suppressed. When a man's political convictions entail sanctions, an analogous lack of freedom prevails. In short, any menace brought to bear by one field of civilization on the pursuit of human aspirations articulated in another field is a deprivation of freedom. Every freedom thus manifests the autonomy of a particular human aspiration and its right to claim protection of this pursuit against encroachment by any other.

Thus there is a constant competition of the various human aspirations for the available means of satisfaction, and hence a perpetual seesawing of the patterns of behavior in which now one and now another human drive prevails for a time. The oscillation may be small, in which case civilization presents for a time the aspect of a balance—however precarious—or it may be so conspicuous that the historian cannot but recognize it and state that an epoch of human history has ended and a new one is beginning. From the Middle Ages to the Renaissance, from the latter to the Enlightenment, for example, a shift in the hierarchy of human aspirations evidently has occurred. Subepochs are marked by a shift which leaves the leading province in its hegemonic position but rearranges the order of precedence among the other human pursuits. We see similar shifts occurring in the lives of individuals, *e.g.,* Pascal abandoning his scientific work in favor of his pursuit of salvation, or Albert Schweitzer going from music to medicine.

Evidently, any such change entails alternations affecting, not only the kind of creativeness to which the epoch or the individual is devoted, but concomitantly the system of freedoms actually carried out by work. For every leading province tends toward assigning places to the other ones, using their achievements for its own purposes, limiting their autonomy, and thus encroaching upon the freedom of the aspirations articulated in the subdued fields. It would be difficult to overlook, for instance, the fact that in a civilization which not only proclaims but actually puts into practice the primacy of the economic, all the other fields, science as well as art, religion as well as politics, and even language, are deprived of their autonomy and freedom. And it is a trite historical experience that whenever the political province has predominated, the neighbor provinces have met this same fate. It is a nice, epigrammatic example of such a situation that, during the trial of Lavoisier, the accuser before the revolutionary tribunal pronounced the memorable words: *"La République n'a pas besoin de savants."*

While it is true that religious, political, and economic hegemonies involve the greatest jeopardy to the autonomy of the other provinces and freedoms, it should not be overlooked that primacies of the other aspirations also occur occasionally, even though on a minor scale. Monopolistic claims of science in the form of an excessive intellectualism or of pseudo-scientific panaceas, of art in the form of estheticism, and even of language in the form of purism, may sometimes be observed to obstruct the free satisfaction of aspirations in other fields. The justification of wars by a reference to the progress of human knowledge or to the eternal epics they have provoked, may stand as an instance of such hypertrophied claims of cultural provinces. And as to language, the discrimination against linguistic minorities may illustrate the historical experiences we have in mind.

Thus every field of civilization claims ascendancy over the others and sets out to curtail or even to abolish the free satisfaction of the aspirations articulated in them. Yet the monopolistic ascendancy of the political, religious, or economic fields over the others, not only represses the autonomy of the subdued provinces, but weakens and eventually eliminates the freedom articulated in the dominating province itself. A few examples may illustrate this essential *solidarity of the freedoms*. When the religious province predominates, as during the Middle Ages or the period of early Calvinism, the civilization thus constituted not only refuses to grant freedom in the political, esthetic, economic and scientific fields; it also abolishes religious freedom, and sets punitive sanctions on any deviation from the particular religion or sect which has achieved this ascendancy. When a civilization has raised economy to hegemony, there can be no freedom in other provinces, as has been pointed out before; but there will not be any free choice of the forms of production, distribution, and so on. In a politically dominated civilization, as when the desire for security outweighs all the other aspirations of civilized man, political freedom itself will be forced to yield to the particular form of government actually dominating the epoch. And the same would be the effect of the predominance of any other of the provinces. To refer to but one characteristic example: in *milieux* in which the intellectualistic drive prevails, say, the academic world, there is a strong tendency to curtail intellectual freedom and to enthrone one particular method, one particular system, one particular intellectual pursuit, and to discriminate against the others.

What is the reason for this solidarity of freedoms? It is simply the constant interaction and interdependence of all the provinces of civilization in the course of the historical processes. The patterns of each province have to adapt themselves continually to changes in all the others, so as to allow the conjoint satisfaction of all human aspirations. Freedom consists precisely in this reciprocity. When, on the contrary, one province achieves hegemony, it tends to obstruct this reciprocity; the other provinces have to adapt to it. The consequence must necessarily be that the frustrated desires in the subordinate fields will eventually burst forth in a revolution which dethrones the hegemonic province, puts another one in its place, and begins the process anew. Revolutions are effects of a lack of Freedom—in the leading province as well as in the subordinate. For, this dominant province, locked up against influences emanating from the subdued fields, eventually becomes petrified and unable to reflect in its own patterns variety and pliability. Take the example of Soviet

Russia. Its economic form is maintained in a state of dogmatic rigidity; and the ascendancy of this pattern does not tolerate in the other provinces (science and the arts, for instance) development of any patterns, methods, styles, which would antagonize the prevailing dogma. Hence no challenge to the primacy of the economic can issue from outside the economic province, which becomes petrified. This process will continue until enough frustration is accumulated in the other fields to overthrow the economic hegemony.

This solidarity of the freedoms raises, however, a crucial problem. For, no more than they can exist without each other, can they coexist without limiting each other. The very idea of Freedom demands categorically that the practice of any of the freedoms be prevented from encroaching upon the exercise of the others. Freedom of religion, for instance, does not authorize the erection of a temple to Moloch on Times Square, for the sacrifice of first born children. Or, to quote a more serious example, Supreme Court Justice Robert H. Jackson has maintained in a recent opinion that "Newspapers, in the enjoyment of their Constitutional rights," namely, the freedom of the press, "may not deprive accused persons of their right to fair trial," by an out of court campaign to convict.

A word concerning sanctions must here be inserted. All punitive sanctions established by a civilization are exclusions—partial or total—from participation in civilization. If a man is put into jail, exiled, debarred from certain pursuits, disfranchised, discriminated against, fined, or fired, he is thereby excluded from satisfying some of his civilized aspirations. Such sanctions may be just and equitable or unjust and iniquitous. We need not commit ourselves here to any theory and definition of right and wrong nor even presuppose the possibility of any absolute meaning of these terms. The only norm that must be admitted is that every man has a right to civilization, and should not be excluded from it more than necessary to maintain civilization itself, that is, through an act of self-defense of civilization. If we could refer to any absolutistic system of ethics, the problem we have to face now would be easy, namely, is there anything of the kind usually called "the hierarchy of values" which would be able to create an absolute order of precedence among the several aspirations of civilized man, a standard which would indicate which actually practiced hierarchy is right and which is wrong? Unfortunately there is no such standard, or rather each province of civilization has its own. Who or what instance is then to decide between these several and incompatible claims for sovereignty? If this power is delegated to the state, a supremacy of the political province is thereby established which will unavoidably lead to its own petrification, and consequently to a stagnation in the whole of civilization. Suppose religion is called upon to establish the standard looked for. It will first use this power to suppress religious freedom and then the other freedoms including the political, as evidenced by the medieval theory of the two swords. And if science is to be the arbiter, a decision would have to be taken first as to whether this role is to be assigned to Platonic or to Epicurean, to metaphysical or to positivist method. In consequence, freedom of science would certainly fall as the first victim.

What follows from these skeptical considerations? If not the impossibility, at least the undesirability, of any standardization of the hierarchy of the provinces of civilization or of the aboriginal human aspirations. They are not equally distributed among the various civilizations nor among the various individuals, and one can hardly present any evidence that they ought to be. Esthetes, intellectuals, politicians, religious people, businessmen, purists—types of human characters all of which are more or less lopsided—are those who drive the wheels of civilization. The perfectly balanced individuals may be good company even though somewhat boring, but they are certainly not the creative type.

Freedom of civilization, as distinct from the several freedoms, thus can have no meaning other than to be the guarantee that whatever a man's aspirations may be, his pursuit of them will not be subject to sanctions, by a particular civilization. The common denominator of all freedoms is, therefore, the freedom to be civilized; the fundamental right is the right to civilization. For civilization is indeed what distinguishes human society from mere animal associations.

Nobody can reasonably wish for a uniformalized and monotonous world civilization. Even if it could be imposed by force or propaganda —and I do not believe that such a tendency subsists on only one side of the Iron Curtain—it would not last. If we are to have an International Bill of Rights, let us not be too specific. Let us be democratic also in regard to the various fields of civilization, and consider a sort of federal union among them as the desirable goal.

Let us wish that Freedom of Civilization, that is, the right to participate in and not to be debarred from it without having sinned against it, be the Supreme Law of this Federation. Something of this kind seems to have inspired the framers of the Declaration of Independence. If happiness consists in the satisfaction of the aspirations inherent in human nature, and if civilization is the ever changing set of patterns devised for this satisfaction, then the right to civilization and the right to the pursuit of happiness prove to be but two expressions for the same Freedom.

This conclusion may receive also a different expression. Any particular civilization over which one province holds exclusive power is totalitarian. One has but to mention Calvin's regime in Geneva or the sway over an entire civilization held by the Kremlin, to realize that political totalitarianism is but one specific form of a more general type. Moreover, there is, of course, an indefinite number of degrees of freedom and servitude between the full recognition and practice of the right to civilization, that is, Freedom, which is an asymptotic ideal, and the almost complete denial of any such right to the individuals who in that case are but the fuel driving the Famous Ship of State or of Economy or of Religion or of any other hypostatized and deified particularism. All totalitarianism appears thus as a revolt against civilization. To outlaw such regimes is impossible, of course, without an international authority of sufficient power. But this is also true as to an International Bill of Rights. It can have no greater efficacy than ideas have, in general, in the historical process. This power, whatever skeptics may think of it, is certainly very far above zero. It must increase proportionately as the freedoms contained in such a Bill are not unsystematically compiled catalogues resulting from diplomatic compromises, but are derived from a central idea. To discover such an idea is a task incumbent upon philosophy, and particularly upon ethics and philosophy of history. To stand aside, as a philosopher, in this struggle and to be content with a semantic analysis of what, as an alleged value-judgment, is thought to be neither true nor false, is equivalent to an unconditional surrender of authority to brute power, and therefore to an abdication of philosophy.

If, however the right to civilization is, as I submit, the fountainhead of all specific human rights and freedoms, the nuclear idea of which the single freedoms are but integuments, a common basis may be given thereby from which any future discussion would be able to start. It may be objected that the proposition: every man has a right to civilization, is again nothing but a value-judgment, neither true nor false because unverifiable, and consequently nothing more than the statement: I like civilization, or I do not like to be deprived from participation in it. Such an interpretation might be countered by defining civilized people as those who like civilization and dislike to be deprived of it. And only civilized people I suggest, ought to be admitted to such a discussion.

Comment by Barna Horvath:

Is Professor Schrecker right in holding that *freedom of civilization* is the central idea for all freedoms and human rights? I would agree without reserve, did not his concept of civilization seem a bit too wide, threatening to become meaningless. To him, the term "civilized man, is almost redundant," and civilization comprises all "undertaking to satisfy the primordial and irrepressible aspirations constituting human nature." And freedom of civilization has "no meaning other than to be the guarantee that whatever a man's aspirations may be, his pursuit of them will not be subject to sanctions, by a particular civilization."

For my part, I prefer a somewhat narrower concept of civilization. Perhaps the point of divergence between our views is that I attach more weight, particularly in the present historical situation, to the preservation and restoration of the treasure of our traditional civilization than to that boundless experimentation with new programs of which even the great Justice Holmes was an ardent advocate. Where *this* may lead to, is obvious to all from conditions prevailing in a considerable part of the globe. I do considerably value openmindedness, but to throw away existing treasures for never realizable visions is not openmindedness to me.

To these treasures belong, among other things, the great achievements of constitutional legal development as embodied in the Constitution and legal institutions of the free countries. And *this* is the narrower sense of civilization to which I want to refer. Professor Schrecker is afraid that delegation to the Constitution of the power to decide over the "precedence among the several aspirations of civilized man," would establish a "supremacy of the political province," and this "will unavoidably lead to its own petrification, and consequently to a stagnation in the whole of civilization." Accordingly, he objects to "any standardization of the hierarchy of the provinces of civilization or . . . of the aboriginal human aspirations." This principle is carried so far as to qualify any civilization "over which one province holds exclusive power . . . totalitarian." At the background of all this, the idea seems to be that "more or less lopsided characters"—esthetes, intellectuals, politicians, religious people, businessmen, purists—"drive the wheels of civilization," whereas "the perfectly balanced individuals . . . are certainly not the creative type."

I am in agreement with the author that a wholesome pluralism of various aspirations is preferable to a standardized hierarchy. This means that it would be unwise to enact a rigid scheme of preferences. Nevertheless, eventual conflicts are and will be decided from time to time in the constitutional way, by legislatures, courts, or, in some cases, by the executive. I do not think that the problem has much theoretical or practical importance.

As to the part played in "driving the wheels of civilization" by "lopsided" and "perfectly balanced" individuals, I must confess that, in the present situation, I decidedly prefer the latter type.

CHAPTER LIII

Authority: Intellectual and Political

By GUSTAVE WEIGEL, S.J.
Professor of Ecclesiology, Woodstock College

THE LEGEND HAS it that in the days when Henry Ford made all his cars black, he was asked to give buyers a choice of colors. His answer is said to have been that the public could choose to have any color in their Ford cars, provided it were black. Ford hit here on a basic truth that is often overlooked in discussing the question of choice. It is a fact that many people wanted black Fords, and for such persons the absence of other colors was no felt infringement on their liberty. That liberty can exist under a condition of inflexible determination, is not even a paradox but a bald statement of truth. If the agent chooses *ab intrinseco* the path to which he is determined, he moves freely along it, even though he cannot move along any other. If you were to tell such an agent that he was not free, the proposition would be to him quite meaningless. As a concrete problem touching concrete reality, freedom demands only that the agent act because he wants to act in a determined fashion, rather than because someone else wants him to act in that way.

This introduction necessarily brings up the whole meaning of freedom. It is one of the slippery notions that tantalize all thinkers. The freedom we are discussing here is the liberty of the citizen. If asked, the average man would say that he understood by the term the power to do what he pleases. Such a description can be accepted as a working formula, though its precise meaning is none too accurate. It is, after all, a brute fact that no man can do all that he pleases. Where truth is recognized, he is not free to ignore it. Two and two are four, at least as a formal proposition, and a man is helpless to deny it. What he sees to be true, simply compels his assent, and there is no field for choice, even if the truth is disagreeable and it would please him if it were not true. An agent may act arbitrarily in a fashion contrary to the truth he holds, though not even this is possible, if he has perceived the truth itself rather than the mere arguments that point to a truth unseen. A man may lie about the truth that he has perceived, but the perception has determined him in such a way that choice and freedom are simply irrelevant to his inner assent. We are free to forestall perceptions, but once the perception has been realized, whether chosen or not, our freedom just disappears.

On the physical level the restrictions on freedom are painfully evident. No matter how much it please him, the free agent will not be able to jump over the Empire State Building. No matter how much a man submerged in water wishes to breathe air, he cannot do so, because, given his manner of taking air, the environment simply does not have enough in a form useful to man to permit breathing.

When man is in society, he is restricted by more than his physical environment. If every citizen were to do what he pleases, some would kill others, take by physical force the food that other citizens had acquired, interfere with their activity. The unrestricted liberty of one would be destructive of the liberty of the other. Society, in consequence, is a context that supposes that a citizen cannot do all that he pleases.

Yet in spite of these inevitable restrictions the maximum of possible liberty is the legitimate desideratum of all men in society. The good life supposes that the citizen has the power to do what he pleases, within reasonable limits, and the state is not justified in restricting liberty, except on grounds of rational necessity. Only the reluctant restriction of civic liberty with a view to safeguarding society itself, is proper to government.

Now the state through its instrument, the government, can restrict liberty in two ways; first, by physical coercion, and, secondly, by its authority. Even when the governors exercise physical coercion, their action is different from that of the bandit who also uses this kind of pressure. The physical coercion of the state exercises the state's authority, and therefore the ultimate restriction of the liberty of the citizen *qua* citizen is the authority of the state.

The word, "authority," is a veritable chameleon. Forcellini in his Latin Lexicon gives seventeen different meanings of the word, and the dependence of one meaning on a previous one is not always too clear. Let us indicate some of the more current meanings of the English word: right or moral capacity to do something; the power to govern; prestige because of superior knowledge; the testimony of a witness; arbitrary use of governmental power.

It is clear that not all the meanings of authority are really opposed to civic liberty. However, the arbitrary use of governmental power is certainly a violation of the citizen's right to freedom. It will, therefore, be the duty of the citizen to resist any attempt on the part of the governors to act as if the authority they hold were absolute, unconditioned, and unlimited.

That the governors must have some authority, that is, the right to command and rule according to reason, is evident. The community cannot exist by a spontaneous consent of the citizens in all matters that need regulation, for in many instances a spontaneous uniformity of minds will not arise. Nor is a meeting of the citizens possible for every instance where a consensus could be achieved by free discussion, because the citizen cannot spend all of his time in political reunions.

However, before we discuss the power to govern, we must discuss another form of authority. Is political authority the only form of authority relevant in discussing the liberty of the citizen? The answer will have to be negative after a study of the notion of intellectual authority.

It is clear in logic that the authorities cited by a man in debate are not proofs. They are only persuasive media. However, such "proof" is much used in civic life. Thus in the courts and in the halls of the legislators specialists are called to give testimony, not only with reference to the facts directly relevant to the question at issue, but also to the general truths indirectly connected with the case. Of course, no one for an instant considers such men as infallible, even in the field of their authority. But there is in the mechanism a hint at something more interesting. Truth is considered as obligatory. It is taken for granted by every one, that though juror, judge, and legislator be free men, yet they must bow before what is.

Here we have an instance of the general principle we discussed when speaking of the inevitable limits of civic liberty. Truth is considered as normative for citizens and they must abide by it, no matter what they will. If a citizen wishes to cancel three accounts of $200, $300, and $400 with a check of $500, he will be compelled by the community to pay $900, and he will have no basis for complaint on the observation that his liberty is being curtailed. Nor will anyone believe in the sincerity of his claims, for it is taken for granted that he must *see* that 2 plus 3 plus 4 are 9, and if he sees it, he simply cannot act otherwise.

It is here that we have the great difficulty in our time and in all times. Governors are rarely complete Machiavellians. They justify to themselves and to others their arbitrary legislation and coercion by an appeal to truth. Hitler and his companions supposed with much or little sincerity that Germany was a substantial earth-spirit, somehow animating all Germans. The urges of this spirit were despotic and its inexorable mission was to dominate the world of inferior races. All that Hitler did was justified ultimately by him and his apologetes by this vision of the world and the real. Non-Germans considered this as the most fantastic nonsense, and it can be readily believed that no intelligent German really believed in it. Yet, there it was, and it curtailed the liberty of the Germans on every side.

The governors of Russia move in the same way with an important difference. They see the world as constructed by the thought of Karl Marx, explained, expanded, and defined by those in power. An amoral dialectic is dynamic in history and at the moment it is an urge to a classless society with communal ownership of resources, production, and distribution. This is absolute and all other things are relative to it. Conventional morality, a projection of class privilege, is quite irrelevant. Now this vision is not mystical according to the Communists. It is labeled as "scientific." Most sociologists and economists who work by the scientific method do not see the vision that the Communist enjoys. But whatever science may say, the Russian has no freedom to contradict this doctrine in word or work.

In the light of these examples, the fundamental principle that truth cancels out freedom in the human being, is a vexing truth. Every tyrant has appealed to this principle as a justification of his tyranny. However, it is highly imprudent to deny a truth just because possible evils arise therefrom.

In society the principle is valid only in so far as the truth is spontaneously perceived by the citizen body. It is not the function of government to force a citizen to assent to a proposition whose truth he does not see. Theories, therefore, that are mental constructions of some men must not be the ultimate basis of the governor's action, no matter how much he personally believes in them. Such theories might be pragmatically useful or they may be the framework of communal convivence, if they are spontaneously accepted by the community at large, but they cannot be rammed down the throats of men.

Therefore we must subscribe to the validity of the principle that truth can rightly curtail the liberty of the citizen, but we must modify the proposition so that it will read: commonly perceived truth is a limit to the liberty of the citizenry. We must insist that theories, either because they deal with imperceptibles or because they are mere constructs to unify perceptible factors, do not enjoy the status of truth, in so far as it affects the citizen's liberty.

This brings up the delicate question of Catholicism as an authoritarian religion. As the propositions accepted by Catholics as true, are accepted on the authority of the Church, the Catholic Church can certainly be designated as authoritarian. Does this mean that Catholicism, in theory if not necessarily in fact, is inevitably incompatible with democratic freedom? There is a tendency on the part of most non-Catholics to believe that the affirmative answer is the only one possible.

However, this tendency has arisen only because the different meanings of the word, "authority," are confused. The Catholic Church has never asserted that a proposition is true simply because she wills it so. She does not even proclaim that the content of her assertions are perceptible to common sense or even to herself. She claims only to be a witness to a testimony received from a primary witness. She believes that her propositions are true, because their content was delivered to her by a spokesman for absolute Truth. It is on faith, *i.e.,* assent because of the testimony of an authoritative witness who experienced the truth, that her propositions are held. What is more, she even teaches that unless a supernatural activity has taken place in the human spirit, her propositions cannot even be accepted in faith. Given such a divine activity, a perception, not of the contents of a proposition, but of the intellectual necessity of faith in the doctrine is engendered. The Catholic Church claims for herself the intellectual authority of a witness, not the political authority of a ruler.[1]

In the whole question of Catholic authoritarianism we must recognize that authority is used in the sense of proof, the proof of a witness, which has the epistemological virtue of inducing assent, as it does in every law court where the testimony of witnesses is the only source of knowledge

---

[1] In the community of the Church herself, she also has directional authority over her members, but this directive authority has no direct bearing on civic society.

concerning the facts of the case. Only a philosophy which by postulate denies that truth can be acquired in this fashion or that religious truth has anything to do with events or theory, will reject the possibility of achieving truth according to the Catholic scheme. Such philosophies, however, are justified only by postulates posited arbitrarily. If they insist on their postulates as true, they are authoritarian in the worst possible sense of that word. From the point of view of natural reason the validity of the Catholic Church's teaching can remain only an open question, for the mere analysis of the propositions brings forth no evidence that they be either true or false. Any philosophy that dismisses the doctrine as false because it does not recognize the principles of naturalistic empiricism or of a naturalistic rationalism, is just begging the question.

Hence the whole question of Catholic authoritarianism lies outside of the political field. We have already indicated that not all truth is restrictive of the liberty of the citizen, but only the truth that is readily perceived by men at large. Catholic theory does not consider its propositions to be of this class, though unfortunately Catholic practice has not always rested content with its own theory. However, the practice has given rise to a problem which interests all students of political organization. After all, in a Catholic community there will be a spontaneous adjustment of common life to Catholic dogma. This does produce a compulsion on those who are not Catholics, but let it be remembered that it is only the social pressure which the majority always exerts on the minority; it is not *per se* a political imposition if the Catholic community lives up to its own theory. The pressure will not be from the government down, but from the people up.

This phenomenon brings us to the last question: what are the limits of the restriction of liberty which can be legitimately imposed by governmental authority? The only answer can be that the norm for governmental restriction is the common good of society. Can we define the common good in more concrete terms? Perhaps it can be rendered more precise by saying that it is the prosperity and peace of all the citizens. Prosperity means an equitable access of the available resources required for human activity and evolution. Peace, if it means anything, means an environment that permits the citizen to act freely, provided he does not so intrude on his neighbor that the latter lose his prosperity and liberty. Government, therefore, is obliged to guarantee prosperity and liberty to its citizens. This is its function.

It is not an organ for the teaching of truth. It is a practical institution to maintain the conditions for good human life. Its only validation will be the result of its activity, which must be increased prosperity and peace. Are prosperity and peace possible without a given restriction imposed on the people? If they are, then the restriction is an unwarranted intrusion of government into the lives of the citizens, and no theory can whitewash such action. A government which tries to impose Marxism, Catholicism, Fascism, or any other *ism,* on the people is tyrannical.

This does not mean that governors must be indifferent to truth. It governs them as it governs all citizens, but the truth that is normative for all is that common deposit which is spontaneously shared by all. As a leader the governor should stimulate the people to a growth in truth, for leadership always supposes that the leader is richer in vision than the multitude to be led. However, the vision that he wishes to enhance and clarify must be the vision substantially present. Vision is a matter of culture, and this is not produced by the state, but precedes the state, and the state lives off it. If the community has a Catholic vision of reality, the governor is not free to destroy this vision with the powers entrusted to him by that community. If a Catholic governor tried to impose Catholicism on a spontaneously believing Marxist community, he would be abusing his authority as governor.

This principle will help to clarify the problem of the lot of a dissenting minority. It is usual for some of the people to have a vision of life quite different from that of the whole. Is it the function of the government to suppress this minority? Should the minority be liquidated by force? Or perhaps could it be isolated in a ghetto and carefully quarantined so that the majority would be able to follow its vision without disturbance or distraction? There is no one answer to these questions, valid for all circumstances. Much depends on the compatibility of the vision of the minority with that of the majority. Because the notion of majority is nearer to that of the general, the majority vision will inevitably be the intellectual framework of the conduct of the group. The minority has no right to demand that it be otherwise, because then the minority would be dictating to the majority, an unjust thing. If, however, the minority can follow its own vision without endangering the general framework of the community at large, the majority has no right either to annoy or molest the dissidents. On the other hand, should the free activity of the minority prevent the free action of the majority or be a real disturbance, the minority must have its liberty restricted in favor of the common good. Yet even in this instance, although the government can prevent the minority *from* acting because such action is an obstacle to the freedom of the majority, it cannot impose an action on the minority which makes it contradict what it sees to be true. In this latter case the minority would rightfully resist the dictamen of government.

If the governor cannot appeal to his perception of the truth as a justification of coercive action, neither can a minority make the same gesture to rationalize its disturbing action. Although liberty is one of the goods of citizenship, it is a relative and subsidiary good, subject to the highest good of society, the common weal. On the other hand, the common good, though it demands some basic unity of vision on the part of all the citizens, does not demand an isomorphic uniformity of *Weltanschauung;* in fact, variety contributes to the common weal by evolving the truth which is its basis.

The dynamism of this study is the assumption that society is a bigger notion than political organization. In such an assumption society, which must exist, takes on those forms of state which in a given historical setting are most propitious to the protection of society. The big reality is society; the smaller reality is the state, which exists only for the good of society. Given human subjects, society is also given, but the form of state organization is a variable, determined by history. States come and go, and even the historically continuous state passes through a process of evolution and transformation. Society, however, remains, and it alone is primary, though not an absolute, for it, too, must be referred to the great absolute, truth.

Comment by Nels F. S. Ferré:

Professor Weigel has written a careful analysis of the relation between intellectual and political authority, with special reference to the nature of the Roman Catholic Church. Certainly I should agree that enjoinments to do what one wants are no curtailment of freedom, unless they be given in such a way as to curb spontaneity or received with such immaturity as to effect rebellious response. Freedom should, I think, rather be defined as the spontaneous choosing with appropriate effectiveness what is according to one's nature to need or to do.

I cannot fully see the need for the distinction between the state's authority and coercion. Political authority is vacuous in our kind of world, apart from the power of sanctions. Naturally, authority may not be reduced to the status of physical power, as too many positivistic theorists aver, without losing the meaning and majesty of the concept of true authority. In this sense, I can see the need for a distinction which, to me, is made too strong in the case of the political field.

My own response to the proposition, "Commonly perceived truth is a limit to the liberty of the citizenry," is that it is somewhat academic. Most people never rise to the vision of the truth behind the general activities of life. Would not some such statement as the following be better: Democratically derived codes of social and political behavior both facilitate and thwart personal freedom?

The question of truth, however, is serious. If the Roman Church claims no more than the political right to witness to its claim to be entrusted with absolute authority, and to have its people effect a culture consonant with its witness wherever they predominate, giving due democratic liberty to others, we can have no objection to its position. Professor Weigel also humbly indicates the failure of this theory in practice. I see no reason that such a theory could not also be practicable, if the Church resolutely declared itself the Community of Christ's concern for all, and decisively enacted this declaration in history. The failing of the Roman Church, along with the other churches, has been its concern with its own power, possessions, and prestige, rather than with the losing of itself for the world, finding thereby increasingly its divine nature.

What I question most about the paper is the assertion that, even as majorities must not coerce dissidents in matters of faith, so minorities must not disturb majorities. The feel of the paper sounds defensive, as though Romans should be free from the witness to truth by others wherever the Roman Church now holds power or has numerical superiority. But non-Roman majorities might be disturbed by the Roman witness, however "decent and in order." Should the Roman Church, accordingly, silence its own minority witness?

Finally, I believe, the case comes down to the fact that for religion legitimately to be heard, it must speak the common language of the court of reason and be tested by authentic democratic processes. The more common truth and concern religion embodies beyond the general *status quo,* the more it must witness in patience, accepting misunderstanding and rejection. But its truth must always be *potentially* open to common verification. Its exceptional vision must potentially exemplify what anyone who is morally and intellectually mature can eventually discover and accept. The absolute of God's love for all, the Ultimate Concern for the inclusive good, is an authority which the more absolute its acceptance the more it makes for the fullest possible freedom, the spontaneous realization of one's individual and social nature, under God. The more the Roman Church espouses such a Christian claim, the more it can exhibit a universal theory and practice which need not be defensive, but creative and winning. Certainly Professor Weigel's own cooperative attitude and position exhibits to a very large extent what is needed.

Comment by Barna Horvath:

I agree entirely with the view that the state "exists only for the good of society" and that society itself "must be referred to the great absolute, truth." I do not agree, however, with the formulation that liberty, therefore, "is a relative and subsidiary good, subject to the highest good of society, and common weal."

I cannot accept this formulation, because the "common good" itself is defined by the author, and, correctly, in terms of freedom. It is defined as "prosperity and peace"; prosperity, meaning "an equitable access of the available resources," and peace, meaning "an environment that permits the citizen to act freely, provided he does not so intrude on his neighbor that the latter lose his prosperity and liberty." This correct formulation makes it clear that there is no *common* good that could not be translated into terms of *individual* freedom. Whenever we forget this, we are apt to make concessions to collectivism. Whenever we forget that freedom is justifiably limited only by freedom—which, strictly speaking, is no limitation at all, for a freedom violating freedom is no freedom any more—we invite tyranny.

The author's formulations are more fortunate as to authority than freedom. It is highly debatable, for instance, whether "liberty can exist under a condition of inflexible determination," "if the agent chooses *ab intrinseco* the path to which he is determined." This formulation pays lip service to materialism which would gladly admit that "freedom does not demand that the agent, given an existent order of things, have at his disposition different roads of action," but only "that he act because he wants to act." I think this is a dangerous formulation, because it prevents us from distinguishing between animal behavior and free rational choice.

Nor do I agree with the view that truth restricts freedom. Truth liberates. Nor is the man who cannot breathe because he is submerged in water, deprived of free will, but only of free action. The author seems to understand freedom as "power to do what he pleases." Moral freedom and responsibility presuppose rather *free choice of the will*.

On the other hand, I highly appreciate the author's courage to draw the necessary consequences of his view as to *resistance*. The doctrine of resistance, developed by both Catholic and Protestant "monarchomachs" during the religious wars of the sixteenth and seventeenth centuries is indeed the most crucial part of the problem of freedom and authority. In our philosophical speculations we are inclined to shut our eyes before the fact that resistance, both as theory and practice, has developed again in our times into an almost standing institution. This is most clearly seen in the fact that "partisans" of a civil war are treated more and more in a way analogous to the combatants of belligerent states, instead of as criminals.

Comment by Mortimer R. Kadish:

Professor Weigel's most provocative essay attempts, one gathers, to use the concept of truth as a norm to define the rights of individual liberty, on one hand, and of intellectual and political authority, on the other. The following argument, if I understand aright, is implicit in his position: (a) "As a concrete reality, freedom does not demand that the agent, given an existent order of things, have at his disposition different roads of action. It demands only that he act because he wants to act in a determined fashion . . ." (b) "Where truth is recognized, he (anyone) is not free to ignore it." (c) The truth, therefore, in depriving us of alternatives, does not deprive us of our freedom. (d) Hence, if we ground the right of authority upon at least the perception of truth, authority need never conflict with freedom—to the extent, that is, that both are legitimate.

Now I think the above argument is important, because in terms of the *substantive* notion of "truth" it seeks to present an alternative to the *procedural* concept of freedom and authority, as founded upon a method which in any particular case need not necessarily lead to "truth." I do not think, however, that Professor Weigel's effort succeeds: Proposition (a) seems mistaken, because, given an agent who chose to behave in a given manner and yet had no choice about it, ordinary usage of "freedom" suggests that this agent was indeed *fortunate*—but that he was not "free." Curiously enough, Professor Weigel himself assents to this point when he writes, "We are free to forestall perceptions but once the perception (of truth) has been realized, whether chosen or not, our freedom just disappears." That is, it disappears, because we have no *alternative* but to assent. Which brings us to (b). The familiar observation that we have no choice but to assent to the truth if only we have seen it, secures what self-evidence it owns from the fact that, strictly speaking, it constitutes a tautology. If I say even to myself, "It is true that it's raining," the very *significance* of that introductory "it is true" consists in the assertion that, whether I like rain or not, it is indeed raining. Accordingly, for me simultaneously to "see" the truth of a proposition and to refuse "inner assent" to it, is an impossibility, not because of some mysterious property of the truth, but because I would then have contradicted myself. Failing in my "inner assent," *of necessity* I could not have "seen" the proposition as true.

Why use the concept of truth as a basis for the discussion of authority, intellectual and political? Professor Weigel himself admits, with considerable candor, what he calls the "vexing truth" that "every tyrant has appealed to this principle" (the principle that truth cancels our freedom) as a justification of his tyranny. He even asserts that that great authority, the state, properly concerns itself with "prosperity and peace," not at all with the truth of world views. The relevance of truth so qualified, what remains? This, perhaps: That while in secular affairs, construed as matters of "prosperity and peace," he has indeed allowed for the operation of democratic politics, in vital matters *other* than secular ones—in matters of morals and education, perhaps, and in whatever concerns them—he has succeeded in reasserting the ancient Platonic doctrine of the intrinsic authority of Truth and Knowledge. In terms of what Professor Weigel calls "concrete reality," this amounts to a justification of the method of *authority* over against the method of free inquiry in those pervasive questions of "faith and morals" many of which may well constitute focal points for social control.

CHAPTER LIV

Freedom and Authority in Education

By ROBERT ULICH

Professor of Education, Graduate School of Education, Harvard University

There is a universal and essential difference between the actions of the will and all the other actions.

The will is one of the chief organs in belief, not that it forms belief, but because things are true or false according to the aspect in which we look at them. The will which prefers one aspect to another, turns away the mind from considering the qualities from all that it does not like to see; and then the mind, moving in accord with the will, considers only the aspect which it likes, and so judges by what it sees.

Pascal, *Pensées*, 99.

Let it be a word, a proposition, a book, a man, a fellowship, or whatever you please: as soon as it is proposed to make it serve as limit, in such a way that the limit is not itself again dialectical, we have superstition and narrowness of spirit. There always lurks some such concern in a man, at the same time indolent and anxious, a wish to lay hold of something so really fixed that it can exclude all dialectics; but this desire is an expression of cowardice, and is deceitfulness toward the divine.

> Kierkegaard's *Concluding Unscientific Postscript*, translated by D. F. Swenson and W. Lowrie, American Scandinavian Association, New York, 1941, Book I, chapter 1, paragraph 2, page 35.

BEFORE ATTEMPTING to discover what "freedom" and "authority" mean in and for "education," let us first try to find what these three concepts mean in general. For this purpose we will consider them from a "personal," "institutional," and "transcendent" point of view. By "transcendent" we allude to those values which go beyond both the personal and institutional areas toward a sphere supposed to possess transphysical and universal character. We could also use the words, "spiritual" or "ideal." But let us keep in mind that in actuality there are no strict boundaries, but continual fusions among the three divisions.

We will prefer in the choice of illustrations such areas as are close to educational theory and practice, namely, philosophy and religion as the ways of thought which endeavor to interpret the meaning of human life and which, therefore, give goal and purpose also to education. Furthermore, we will often refer to politics as the activity which largely provides the social milieu for the educational process.

I. *Freedom*

1. *Freedom as Personal.* People often support their insistence on man's personal freedom with all kinds of arguments which a skillful skeptic may easily refute. Yet, faith in one's freedom, even defined badly or not at all, has been one of the main vehicles of self-confidence and moral progress. It expresses the desire to unfold one's energies unhampered by alien forces. The farmer who looks over his fertile fields rightly feels a sense of freedom, and so does the mountaineer who after a perilous ascent has his eyes gliding over widening horizons. Freedom here is the same as power and independence, or control and conquest. Where would man be without it?

But man is a conqueror and mountaineer not only in relation to physical nature, but also in relation to himself. During the whole Greco-Roman antiquity and later ages inspired by its example, a man was considered free who had understood how to harness the wild horse of passion to the noble horse of wisdom and have the first agree with the latter.[1] According to Aristotle, action which is enforced from outside or done unconsciously is unfree, whereas a free man is he who has the source of action within himself.[2]

But this sense of personal freedom has also dangers. There are psychological forms of "feeling free" grounded in nothing but a vulgar urge for self-assertion. "Nobody can tell me what to do; I am a free man." The sense of independence expressed here may create hatred, crime, and revolution. Even to the Greek philosophers a Christian may object:

---

[1] Plato, *Phaedrus,* 237, 238, and 246.
[2] Aristotle, *Nicomachean Ethics* III, 1, 1110a; III, 3, 1112b; "that man is his own source of doing."

"How great must be the sin of pride in a man to make him believe that he is the source of his own doing, perhaps that he even can redeem himself out of his own will. Who is he who could say that he is the source of his actions? There is only *one* kind of personal freedom: that of surrender to a will higher than man's own, the freedom that comes from grace." Even Aristotle could have pointed at many of his own writings, according to which the free development and the rights of claims of the individual are contingent upon, and consequently limited by, society.

2. *Freedom as Institutional.* In the famous "Funeral Address"[3] Thucydides has Pericles say: "Thus liberally are our public affairs administered; thus liberally, too, do we conduct ourselves as to mutual suspicions in our private and everyday intercourse; not bearing animosity towards our neighbor for following his own humor, nor darkening our countenance with the scowl of censure, which pains, though it cannot punish." Here we have a beautiful combination of personal with institutional or public freedom; the Athenian can be a liberal, or free man, because he lives under a liberal, or free "form of government."[4]

No wonder that the founders of this country's liberty were inspired by the Greek conception of a free republic. In recent times Chief Justice Charles Evans Hughes rephrased large parts of Thucydides's ideas about institutional freedom, when he said: "This sense of sympathetic relation should increase respect both for individual interests and for community (or 'institutional') interests and should give a better understanding of what is involved in each. They are not in opposition; properly speaking, they cannot be divorced."[5]

But history knows of many institutions which have become the tombs of the spirit that once created them. If man fails constantly to revive in himself the creative animus, the organization may go on, it may even grow bigger and decorate itself with the title of noble purpose, but inwardly it becomes hollow. A republic, then, may still call itself "free," or "democratic," but the charisma is lost; there is no courage, no attraction, no ever widening embrace.

Often observers from outside discover the decay earlier than the heirs

[3] *The History of Thucydides,* translated by S. T. Bloomfield, Longman, London, 1829, II, 37.
[4] See also Aristotle, *Politics,* 1280a, 1291b, 1294a, 1317ff.
[5] Charles Evans Hughes, *Conditions of Progress in Democratic Government,* Yale University Press, New Haven, 1910, p. 13.

at home. Such was the situation of inner and outer corrosion of the Roman empire, of France and Russia before their great revolutions, and of Germany before Hitler. Such is the question which many of us may ask with respect to our whole Western civilization. Does it still carry with it the stamina which once caused it to start the fight for man's liberation? For now liberty can no longer be used by all kinds of white men for extending the frontiers of power all over the earth. It is now the dream of many nations, and these many are willing to fight for it.

But why does the institutional, or public, or political life of man so often degenerate? Because there is not sufficiently alive in him the third, or transcendent, aspect of freedom.

3. *Freedom as Transcendent.* Freedom as a transcendent quality of human life is closely related to religion. Our own Judeo-Christian tradition shows amazing contrasts in the interpretation of the relationship between man and God. Among the early Christian authors and the Scholastics man's will is essentially free, but for its proper realization it needs the grace of God. St. Augustine, *e.g.,* says that man's "will is then truly free when it refuses to serve vice and sin." On the other hand, "free will must not be defended in the opinion that there be no need of God's assistance."[6]

But Luther, who together with Calvin and Zwingli fought the authoritarianism of the Catholic Church and wrote his treatise, *On a Christian Man's Liberty,* nevertheless defends in his treatise, *On the Servitude of Will,* written against Erasmus of Rotterdam, strict theological determinism. The true Christian, according to Luther, is free in his right to defend his religious conscience against false ecclesiastical interference, but he will always live in the consciousness of his complete dependence on God.

Yet, it was exactly this logically difficult mixture of personal freedom and utter metaphysical dependence which made Protestantism of various kinds the champion of the modern concept of democratic liberty.

Similar difficulties appear in secular metaphysics. Spinoza's metaphysical determinism does not, from his point of view, exclude a considerable degree of individual freedom. In *Ethics* II, proposition XXXV, he says: "Men deceive themselves when they suppose they are free." However, man can be "as little dependent as possible on fortune's aid,"

---

[6] *S. A. Augustini Opera Omnia, Editio Parisina Altera,* 1889, VII, 580c; III, 2204 D. See also Index, *"Arbitrium."*

if he "lives in conformity with reason," and "strives as much as possible to escape being influenced by . . . passions."[7]

Modern American Pragmatism and psychology avoid a systematic treatment of metaphysical problems. There are many books on psychology where "will" and "freedom" are hardly mentioned—if at all. But avoidance of a problem is no solution. We have, consequently, in modern Pragmatism and psychology a most embarrassing mixture of scientific mechanism and human teleology. Consequently, there is little progress with respect to the understanding of man as a whole. Here the modern philosophical movement of Existentialism sets in with its radical inquiry into the problems of human existence. It remains to be seen whether the groping leads to definite results. But at least there is groping, awareness, and depth.

II. *Authority*

What is true of the concept of freedom, namely, its undefinability as a consequence of the variety of meanings and configurations in history, is true also of the concept of authority.

1. *Authority as Personal.* The voluntary identification of people, young and old, with that which in consequence of its inherent excellence is considered authoritative, is the driving force in the formation of all social norms. Without it people are a congeries of men, but not a community. But has not many a sensitive character been cracked by the parents' love of authority, and are there not many teachers who, rather than feeling the attachment of their pupils as a heavy, though joyful, responsibility, delight in it as a means of self-aggrandizement? And have not many potentially free men never arrived at their true selves, because they were not able to free themselves from the weight of false authority? Thus Ralph Waldo Emerson, in the context of his thinking, was right, when in his essay on "The Oversoul" he said that "the faith that stands on authority is not faith." It is the same fear of the stifling influence of authority on human creativeness which has lead certain modern educators to ban the mere word, "authority." But in banning this word one may scare away the forces that establish humility, rightful respect, and vision of the better.

[7] IV, prop. SLVI; also V, prop. III: "A passion . . . is so much more under our control . . . the better it is understood by us."

2. *Authority as Institutional.* In Pericles's Funeral Address we find in close proximity to the sentences already quoted the following words: "we are, in our public and political capacity, cautiously studious not to offend; yielding a prompt obedience to the authorities for the time being, and to established laws; especially those which are enacted for the benefit of the injured."

Likewise, in close proximity to the sentences already quoted from Justice Hughes's *Conditions of Progress,* we find: "The liberty of the individual in communities must of course be restrained by the mutual requirements imposed upon each by the equal rights of others, and by the demands of the common welfare."

In both statements we have a clear description of institutional authority. Yet, perhaps more than falsely used personal authority can falsely used institutional authority become a deadly evil. Authority vested in an institution has on its side the machinery of organized power and extends over a higher number of men. Modern totalitarian dictatorships have not persuaded their followers by telling them that they were going to be enslaved. When Marx proclaimed the dogma of the "dictatorship of the proletariat" as a transitory political necessity, he earnestly believed that thus could be achieved not only better conditions for the worker, but for human society as a whole. Hitler promised the Germans to use his authority for the "abolition of democratic corruption," the restoration of German liberty, and even for the revival of religion.

> O, what authority and show of truth
> Can cunning sin cover itself withal![8]

3. *Authority as Transcendent.* The religious mind believes that authority—like freedom—abides not in man, but in transcendent power.

For the Jew and Christian, authority has its source in divine revelations; earthly institutions possess only derivative authority. The martyrdom of the early Christians was caused by their refusal to acknowledge the authority of the Augustus above the authority of the Divine; again, the medieval battle of papacy against empire was (in its ideological aspect) the battle of St. Peter against the emperors. Also today the insistence of religious orthodoxies on their final authority in education is a symbol of the belief that the Transcendent must not yield to any man-made social construction.

[8] Shakespeare, *Much Ado About Nothing,* IV, 1.

But also here, dangers lurk around the corner. Transcendence is "vision toward" the Perfect, challenging all that exists, yet never within human achievement. But often in human history spiritual authority became so narrowly conceived that it lost the force of infinite judgment and became a means for the defense of vested interests. Rather than feeling itself in the service of the Divine, an institution made itself divine, that means, it became an idol. It pronounced its infallibility; it reigned over the conscience of man and became involved in earthly strivings and jealousies. For while God is One, of idols there are many, and they must fight each other. Under such circumstances the idea of chosenness, which can have a profound spiritual meaning, glides over into terrible arrogance.

III. *Education*

Is there any hope that we might rescue ourselves from the grip of all these contradictions by relating the concepts of freedom and authority to the concept and practice of education? Unfortunately not. Rather than being a guide toward clarity, education has often been used for the evil as well as for the good.

1. *On the Personal Level* education may be motivated by the desire of improving oneself and his fellowmen, but it may also be motivated by merely competitive instincts. St. Basil told his followers in his *Address to Young Men on the Right Use of Greek Literature*:[9] "We Christians, young men, hold that this human life is not a supremely precious thing. . . . Neither pride of ancestry, nor bodily strength, nor beauty, nor greatness, nor the esteem of all men, nor kingly authority, nor, indeed, whatever of human affairs may be called great, do we consider worthy of desire, or the possessors of them as objects of envy; but we place our hopes upon the things which are beyond, and in preparation for the life eternal do we all things that we do."

Compare with this the education which the Renaissance Humanist Aenea Silvio, who became Pope Pius II, recommended for Prince Ladislaus of Hungary in his *De Liberorum Educatione*,[10] or the education

---

[9]See *Yale Studies in English*, edited by Albert S. Cook, XV, *Essays on the Study and Use of Poetry by Plutarch and Basil the Great*, translated from the Greek with an introduction by F. M. Padelford, Henry Holt & Company, New York, 1902. Also see *Three Thousand Years of Educational Wisdom*, edited by Robert Ulich, Harvard University Press, Cambridge, 1947, p. 135.

[10]Ulich, *loc. cit.*, pp. 205 ff; see also pp. 287 ff. (Montaigne).

which, despite all Christian flavoring, was going on in the knightly academies of Europe during the seventeenth and eighteenth centuries, and there appear two completely different aspects of personal education even within the same so-called Christian culture; one for humility, the other for "glory" and "advantage."

Our modern public education no longer uses the term, "glory." The democratic concept now prevailing, stands for such concepts as equality, mutual responsibility, tolerance, mobility, and the possibility of human progress. But since, often under the direct influence of professional educators, the metaphysical and largely Christian background of democracy has sunk more and more into oblivion, we often educate much less for real and vigorous democracy, than for a strange mixture of "growth," "citizenship," and "efficiency."

2. *On the Institutional Level of Education* modern states have contributed enormously to the welfare of their peoples. On the other hand, the more governments become dependent on the support of the masses —even if they tyrannize and despise them—the more they tend to use education as an instrument of institutional power politics. Education, then, is essentially another form of authoritarianism.

Napoleon already said in 1805:

> There cannot be a firmly established political state unless there is a teaching body with definitely recognized principles. If the child is not taught from infancy that he ought to be a republican or a monarchist, a Catholic or a freethinker, the State will not constitute a nation; it will rest on uncertain and shifting foundations. . . .[11]

Naturally, every culture that believes in itself tries to transmit its mores to future generations. This is not only a society's right, it also is its duty. Often, however, the preservation results from the desire of privileged groups to dominate the people. We have the vices of nationalist chauvinism and imperialistic designs. Thus tradition through education becomes shot through with threads of conscious and unconscious crime. Youth, not sufficiently mature for constructive criticism, are taught not

---

[11]See F. M. Kircheisen, "Thoughts and Plans," *Napoleon's Autobiography, Personal Memoirs of Bonaparte Compiled from his own Letters and Diaries,* translated by Frederick Collins, Duffield and Company, New York, 1931, p. 246. See also, I. L. Kandel, *Comparative Education,* Houghton Mifflin Company, New York, 1933, p. 49. Also E. H. Reisner, *Nationalism and Education,* The Macmillan Company, New York, 1922, p. 35.

only to love, but also to hate; not only to preserve, but also to kill; not only to stand for truth, but also for falsehood. Even if the older generation itself may be divided with respect to the value of a particular subject, those teaching it teach it nevertheless as if it were beyond doubts and criticism. Unfortunately there are hundreds of big and small totalitarianisms everywhere in the education of mankind.

3. *Education on the Level of Transcendence.* Only through his power of transcendence or spirituality can man escape the narrowness of his self and his institutions. The greater this power, the greater is also his chance to understand both the potential blessings and evils in freedom and authority.

As a matter of fact, any good education directs the pupil's mind to see isolated detail (even his own nation can be a frightfully isolated detail) in a larger context from which it receives meaning. Good education makes every subject matter "transparent," so that the pupil can "look through it," as it were, and see it embedded in ever widening areas of belonging. And where can these areas of belonging end but in a transcendent whole for which, according to our faith, culture, upbringing, and experience, we may have different names, all, however, being reverential symbols of the cosmic vision which is man's noblest privilege.

Yet in education, transcendence becomes blasphemy, if it changes from continual openness toward a closed system of dogmata.

Fortunately, we have in every nation people who, inspired by a wholesome education, are aware of the transcendent and uniting ideals of mankind. At the same time we have sects and sections torn asunder by supposedly "eternal" loyalties they are unable to reconcile with the existence of different ideas.

Several undesirable types of personality may emerge out of such a sectarian education. We all have occasion to observe the type which finally prefers the false peace of conventionalism to the risk of inner search. Often he will not hesitate to attack with the ardor of a self-concealing bad conscience those who still dare question. Another type whose "eyes have been opened" becomes disenchanted and relativist, denying that the tentative and somehow conflicting character of all human enterprise can be reconciled with the idea of an embracing meaning which gives us a feeling of direction and belonging. In spite of all necessary relativism we still are allowed to believe that man's sense of truth is not only a psychological deception, but the reflection, however dim, of an essential principle in the world order which points finally at an ultimate unity of truth. Only in the light of such a vision can man, in education as well as in his whole life, acquire the necessary sense of what is important and what is unimportant.

The education that goes the way toward uncritical conventionalism or absolutism gives life a false meaning; the education that goes the way toward radical relativism makes life meaningless. Either one is equally harmful.

IV. *The Deeper Level*

Let us ask the fundamental question: Why is it that everywhere in organized human life we observe at least a beginning of freedom, authority, and education?

The answer is that all three, freedom, authority, and education, represent *existential categories, i.e.,* elemental factors in human life. They are modi or structural tendencies through which the mysterious power of Life expresses its creativeness in the individual lives of men. They are parts of, and functions in, man's ever self-transcending existence, just as the existential categories of thinking, solitude, gregariousness, love, and fear. Whenever man grows out of the state of mere vegetating into the state of mind peculiar to him, namely, of reflection and directed action, these existential tendencies grow with him and penetrate all that he does. They are not arbitrary inventions; they are his inner companions, whether he welcomes them or not.

Life, if developing in man to its fullness, creates curiosity, inquiry, the adventure of acting and thinking; and for realizing these tendencies freedom is necessary. On the other hand, a full human life is impossible without some degree of order, discipline, emulation, security, and organization, and this means authority. Hence all the more coherent and persistent activities carry with them both the trend toward freedom and the trend toward authority. Is there not in any vivid individual, as well as in social life, something like a desire for continual expansion (= freedom) and a desire for contraction, or preservation of the self which wants to master the otherwise chaotic impressions by aimfulness and direction (= authority)? One might think in this context of Goethe's idea of "exhaling" and "inhaling," of Herbarts's ideas about *Vertiefung* (projecting oneself into a foreign object of interest) and *Besinnung* (recollecting oneself under the dominance of a leading idea), or of Spencer's ideas about differentiation and integration.

After all, if freedom and authority represent, as we called it, "existential categories," they must be found in the individual, as well as in the collective thinking and behavior of men.[12]

The test of creativeness is not absence of either freedom or authority, but their proper balance, which will never be static, but one of *dialectical complementation*.

We may refer once more to the history of Christianity, which has, after all, exercised the greatest educational influence on the Occident. If early Christianity had remained in its state of mystical enthusiasm, without the authority of a cult and a strong communal organization, if despite all inner scruples[13] it had not finally decided to adopt large parts of pagan worldly education, it would probably have lost itself in the welter of sects which swept from Asia and Africa all over the Roman Empire. The often disenchanting fights between the Arians and Athanasians, the bishops of Rome and the bishops of Byzantium, and the persecution of the pagans, are signs of the elemental struggle for security through the medium of authority, and for authority through the medium of security.

On the other hand, Christianity would have become a pond without wells had there not been the "heretics," suspected and prosecuted by the Church, and yet providing its living conscience. The great mystical individualists revived "the spark" in man's soul which helped him to pierce the crust of cult and dogma and to arrive at divine freedom.

The same rhythm between freedom and authority we can observe also in the history of Protestantism. The early German Protestants under Luther's guidance banned Aristotle from the universities. They wished to cut down the thicket of sophistication of the "pagan philosophy," and to open the glade through which man could look freely into the eyes of the Eternal. Yet, after the revolution Luther's friend Melanchthon had to remind his academic colleagues that without the authority of an

---

[12] The profoundest that has been said about this whole problem, is, from my point of view, to be found in the philosophies of Soren Kierkegaard, Karl Jaspers, and Martin Heidegger, generally connected with the often abused term, "Existentialism." See also, Andivon.

[13] Compare St. Augustine's *De Ordine* and its praise of Platonic and Pythagorean wisdom, with his *Retractationes, De Doctrina Christiana* and *De Catechisandis Rudibus*.

established system of logic, as provided by Aristotle, the new movement would be unable to escape the pitfalls of aimless religious revelry. Thus, if we might name it so, Protestant Aristotelianism replaced Catholic Scholasticism and created a new and not less formidable orthodoxy. It was then again mystics, or "pietists," such as Jacob Boehme and Count Zinzendorf, who freed Protestantism from spiritual suffocation.

So one could show the rhythm of freedom and authority in education in the history of our whole Western culture from Plato's *Republic* onward to the present American struggle between the "progressives," and the "essentialists."[14] The same struggle between freedom and authority could also be described in the history of the belles-lettres. And it would be easy to point at similar phenomena of expansion and contraction, or of liberation and conservatism also in our political history and present.

V. *Application to Educational Principle*

After all that has been said so far it would be vain to hope that we could arrive at general and accurate definitions of freedom and authority, and of their right proportions. The rightness or wrongness of these proportions will always be contingent on the specific civilization, and the *Weltanschauungen* and purposes of particular groups within a civilization.

However, we can expect some clarification, if we combine the insights gained so far about these existential phenomena in human history, with modern progress in educational research, psychology, anthropology, and other social sciences.

Then the following propositions urge themselves upon us:

1. The more advanced a culture, the more it desires to use education for the full self-realization of the individual, *i.e.*, it aims toward freedom.

2. People in an advanced culture will also be sufficiently realistic to acknowledge the importance of authority.

3. Rather than juxtaposing freedom and authority as hostile forces, a mature culture and its education will try to relate them to each other in *dialectical complementation*.

4. The principle of dialectical complementation is necessary also for

[14] See Theodore Brameld, *Patterns of Educational Philosophy,* World Book Company, Yonkers-on-Hudson, New York, 1950.

the understanding of other factors of life which constantly impinge on education, *e.g.,* liberty *versus* control in national life, change *versus* stability in history, equality *versus* differentiation in social structure and selection, tolerance *versus* discrimination in the field of conviction.[15]

5. While it is the sign of a mature person that he is able to accept authority of the productive kind without inner rebellion, in the practical operation of education the immature person will need a higher degree of authority than the mature, though often he will rebel against it. But good education will use authority in such a form that it does not block the way toward freedom of self—authority "from without" should always try to change into authority "from within."

6. When the dialectical-complementary relation is understood, there should be no need for the continuation of the age old conflict between so-called "liberals" and "disciplinarians" in education, between "child-centered progressives" and "authoritarians." All such distinctions are signs of lack of balance. Even Bertrand Russell, who for some time was considered one of the most radical progressives in education, writes in his *Freedom and Authority in Education* ". . . one who advocates freedom in education cannot mean that children should do exactly as they please all day long. An element of discipline and authority must exist; the question is as to the amount of it, and the way in which it is to be exercised."[16]

The question, however, has to be raised: Why is such balance so difficult of achievement? Or, when accomplished for some time, why does it so easily break into antithetical hostility?

The answer is: Dialectical complementation of seeming contrasts by means of synthesis becomes impossible the moment there is no higher level of criteria to which to relate the individual problem. There must be a transcending intuition from the single phenomenon in question toward an embracing context which provides meaning and aim to the on-going life process. All events in human existence run into the danger of isolation and self-idolization unless there is vision of what we may call "wholeness."

---

[15] In reading such standard works as Elton Mayo's *The Social Problems of an Industrial Civilization*, 1945, or Roscoe Pound's *Social Control Through Law*, one will discover, though under a different vocabulary, the same emphasis on the dialectical relationship of freedom and authority.

[16] In *The Century Illustrated Monthly*, CIX, December, 1924, p. 172.

7. Because of the existential and consequently permeating character of the categories of freedom and authority, the failure of dialectical complementation within greater contexts of meaning must show its effects everywhere. For example, political parties then no longer recognize each other as complementary factors within the social whole, but each fights the other with the desire for absolute power. Scholarship and the arts lose their inner continuity. There appears the trend toward *l'art pour l'art,* knowledge for knowledge, originality *à tout prix,* departmentalization and the strife of schools. So also in education without the dialectical sense of wholeness, freedom and authority must become hostile absolutes. Freedom becomes license, while authority becomes tyranny. The other component factors of education get out of proportion; information and instruction become more important than the inner formation of man; intellectual "training" strangles sound emotional development; general education stands against vocational and professional education and *vice versa;* prolonged school attendance as such becomes confused with higher cultural achievement.

8. As already indicated, in the light of the principle of dialectical complementation also the concepts of "personal," "institutional," and "transcendent," as they were used in this paper, lose their exclusive characters. With a wholesome balance of freedom and authority, personal freedom will never be merely personal, for the person will recognize his dependence upon, and his responsibility for, the institutions within the framework of which he lives. He will also recognize that his personality will dry out without the sense of transcendence. Nor will the institutions try to live on themselves alone, realizing that without transcendence toward the human individual, on the one, and the embracing purposes of humanity, on the other side, they will sooner or later decay, even if they grow bigger and bigger. Nor will the idea of transcendence hover above the universe of man like a distant cloud, but will be the force that reveals to man and his organizations ever widening horizons of being.

9. From strict adherents to positivistic philosophies one will probably hear the objection that such terms as existential categories, transcendence, and wholeness, are "meaningless," because they have no clear referents in concrete reality. If by referent is meant an isolated and tangible object then, of course, all the ideas here are meaningless. But then sympathy, love, aspiration, hope, are also meaningless. On the other hand,

if by "referent" is meant a force which we constantly meet in ourselves and our social and spiritual environment, then all the categories used here are full of meaning.

Whenever a culturally significant movement starts, be it a great religion, or a great battle for political liberation, it will always reveal a transcendent power which aims toward a goal understood to be of universal validity. This "ideal" character survives and spreads even when the initial movement is materially defeated as, *e.g.*, in early Christianity which waited in vain for the coming of Christ, and yet became one of the world religions. It happened with the English revolution which ended in the Restoration, and yet laid the groundwork for a new concept of society. And it was the case with the French revolution which turned into bloodshed and the Napoleonic dictatorship, and yet made it impossible for absolutism to dominate Europe.

If our present civilization will be unable to achieve the dialectic-transcendent synthesis between freedom and authority, it will not survive. If it proves itself capable of this synthesis, it will not only survive, but grow far beyond its present state of achievement.

Comment by Swami Akhilananda:
Professor Ulich presents a very constructive and inspiring paper. His analysis and evaluation of present day education and his interpretation of freedom and authority are extremely helpful to any thinking person in the field of education.

Dr. Ulich is correct in his reference to "authority as transcendent," when he says that religious groups should not demoralize themselves with all sorts of superstitious habits and attitudes, but should remain well established in the consciousness of the transcendent Reality. Religion loses its power when the leaders lose the sight of Reality. Consequently, religion cannot inspire the various functions of a culture. Education then fails to retain its real value, and becomes a tool in the hands of interested parties, whether they are feudal rulers, capitalists, dialectic materialists, or other such totalitarians. So it is the imperative duty of Platonic philosophers, and of Hindu, Jewish, Christian, and other mystics, to keep the ideal bright by remaining conscious of the ultimate Reality, and by transmitting the ideal in all the phases of life. All the activities of life should be subordinated to the supreme value, or what the Hindus call *Paramartha* (supreme goal), namely, the awareness of God or transcendent Reality. It is indeed high time that the teachers and religious leaders of various groups realize their responsibilities and devote themselves to the fulfilment of the goal of life. This is the only way that present day civilization can be saved.

Comment by Rudolf Allers:
Convinced of the "dialectical" nature of freedom, and, in fact, of every essential aspect of human existence, I cannot but feel deeply gratified by discovering basically the same ideas in Dr. Ulich's essay. I may, perhaps, be permitted to add that I also find myself in agreement with and moved to gratitude by the truly "humanistic" approach the educator of Harvard has chosen. Humanistic in the twofold sense of an

appreciation of the "humanities" and the emphasis on the human side of the problems, as set over against an all too inhuman scientific view.

Whether one shares Hegel's ideas or not, one cannot but realize that his fundamental position deserves consideration: that dialectics, the opposition of thesis and antithesis, demands a resolution in a synthesis which has to be more and something other than a mere compromise. Also, that the task of synthesis is unending, that every synthesis is bound to give birth to a new dialectical tension and that thus the need of synthesis arises anew. This, at least, we ought to learn from Hegel, that all onesided positions are intrinsically false and will lead to a stagnation, which, as contrary to the reality which is ours, cannot but end in a catastrophe.

It is, perhaps, a matter of predilection and choice to view freedom and authority as "existentials," in the sense of Heidegger, or as pertaining to human nature and thus terms of an "essentialist" interpretation. The main point, which Dr. Ulich has made so clear, is that the two belong together, that the one cannot be without the other, and that each of the two, when separated from its dialectic counterpart, loses its significance.

The question is, indeed, not that of freedom *vs.* authority, or of freedom or authority, but of freedom and authority. All "radicalism" sins because of its onesidedness; it is truly an "unrealistic" attitude. One ought to distinguish between radicalism, on one hand, and intransigency, on the other.

Comment by Edgar S. Brightman:
First of all, I would like to congratulate Professor Ulich on his excellent "Hegelian" quotation from Kierkegaard.

His analysis of freedom and authority as personal, institutional, and transcendent is clear and helpful, although the social function of the transcendent in a democracy could be examined fruitfully, and the presence and relevance of the person on all three levels needs recognition.

The concluding propositions commend themselves to my approval.

Comment by Barna Horvath:
It is a great merit of this paper to trace the interdependence of personal, institutional, and transcendent freedom, as well as authority. Moreover, education is a field in which we find perhaps the finest type of authority engaged in unfolding, in the pupil, the subtlest experience of freedom. To investigate the problem of freedom and authority in this context, seems to be most promising, chiefly because we might hit here upon the most intimate interaction of freedom and authority.

I think one of the finest ideas of the author is that "good education makes every subject matter 'transparent,' so that the pupil can 'look through it,' as it were, and see it embedded in ever widening areas of belonging"—areas ending in a transcendent whole. In this sense of widening horizons until the last questions are asked and pondered upon, in the sense of struggling with last questions, it may be that the author's opinion is correct that "only through his power of transcendence or spirituality can man escape the narrowness of his self and his institutions."

On the other hand, I do not see very well the advantage of treating freedom, authority, and education as "existential categories," or of advocating their "dialectical complementation." Every real gain in this field of inquiry seems to be the result of introspection, observation, and clear reasoning in theory, and of trial and error, inventiveness and perseverance in practice. "Dialectical complementation" that, if the author is to be believed, "becomes impossible the moment there is no higher level of criteria to which to relate the individual problem," seems to add little to the enumerated methods.

CHAPTER LV

Liberty and Authority: Constitutional Aspects of the Problem

By ROBERT C. HARTNETT, S.J.
Editor-in-Chief, "America"

MY PURPOSE IN this brief exposition of the problem of liberty and authority is to outline certain constitutional aspects of the problem of balancing these two essential elements in our political system. I am not trying to present a rounded study, but merely to set the stage for a fruitful discussion.

Let me make clear now exactly what I am going to try to do. First, I shall point out how this problem of balancing liberty and authority was faced and met by the men who founded this nation. Two traditions were set up from the beginning. They were in conflict, and the conflict is still with us. Then, rather abruptly, I wish to focus attention on the special problem of balancing liberty and authority where the functions of the state have been broadened to include what we now call the "welfare state."

The Two Traditions

The American Revolution was fought in the name of liberty and against the tyrannical use of authority. Naturally, our political forefathers were not anxious to set up another tyranny to replace the British. So they set up *State governments* in which the legislatures, regarded as the guardians of the "liberties of the people," were strong and the State executives, or governors, comparatively weak. In setting up the Continental Congress they likewise favored liberty at the expense of authority.

Their own experience during the so-called "critical period" of 1783–1787 taught them the necessity both of a real Federal Union *and* of a stronger political authority. I suppose the question of liberty *versus* authority, in the concrete terms of the powers of government, was never so thoroughly thrashed out as it was in Philadelphia from May to September, 1787, and in the State ratifying conventions during the months following.

The *decision* was in favor of a *strong* central government. The same generation of statesmen that wrote the Declaration of Independence, with its ringing phrases extolling freedom, also wrote the Federal Constitution, with its sweeping delegation of powers to the Federal Government. They gave Congress unlimited powers of taxation, for example, for the twin purposes of providing for the "common defense" and the "general welfare." They empowered Congress "to make all laws which shall be necessary and proper for carrying into execution" the powers *explicitly* granted in the seventeen clauses of Art. 1, sect. 8.

In a word, they reversed the Articles of Confederation by writing the doctrine of "implied" powers into the Federal Constitution. In this way they made sure that Congress would never lack a constitutional warrant for any power it needed to do what it was supposed to do. These sweeping powers were stubbornly opposed. Alexander Hamilton was equally adamant in demanding them. "A constitution cannot set bounds to a nation's wants," declared Hamilton at Poughkeepsie; "it ought not, therefore, set bounds to its resources."

The Constitution likewise, after exhaustive debates, set up *a very strong executive*. The wording of the Constitution is as pregnant with executive power as any free people would ever tolerate: "The executive power shall be vested in a President of the United States of America." Some of his powers are later specified—as commander-in-chief, as head of the executive department, with power to make appointments, etc.—but the main grant, I think, consisted simply in making him *the executive*.

It is very much the same with the Federal judiciary. "The judicial power of the United States shall be vested in one Supreme Court and in such inferior courts as the Congress may from time to time ordain and establish." This power, too, is further specified, but the whole thing occupies but a page in somewhat small print. They knew what they meant by "judicial power," and they endowed the Supreme Court with it, without many if's, and's, or but's.

In a word, the Founding Fathers knew that government had great public business to do and that it needed great authority to transact it.

Of course, the Federal Government is a government of *limited* powers.

Especially in the Bill of Rights these limitations to protect the freedoms of the people are made very secure. The Federalists were committed to "IMMUNITY FROM THE ARBITRARY" acts of government. Still, the impressive thing about the Constitution, looking back at it from the vantage point of today, is that the American revolutionaries packed so much governmental *authority* into it. When the French framed their constitution in 1946, they refused to give their executive the power our President has.

By and large, our Federal Constitution embodies the kind of balance between liberty and authority which the Federalists regarded as essential. In the *Federalist Papers* one single theme underlies Hamilton's contributions: that *means* must be proportioned to *ends* and the end is a *strong* government, so set up as to provide natural *checks and balances* against abuse of authority, with the entire system made *responsible to the people*.

Washington, Madison (at this time), John Adams, Gouverneur Morris, James Wilson, John Jay, Rufus King, young John Marshall, and scores of others all concurred in this theory of the ideal pattern of republican government on a national scale: energetic, but safe as far as freedom was concerned. The principle of judicial review, clearly implied, was to be perhaps the strongest safeguard against governmental tyranny.

This was the theory incorporated in our fundamental law. It was further incorporated in legislation in the first Congress setting up the executive departments and the rest of the apparatus of government. The Federalists, in this way, made the Union a going concern. Its success amazed even themselves.

In Washington's first administration and immediately thereafter, however, opposition to this system and this theory developed. Madison mysteriously moved over to Jefferson's side. The old revolutionary ferment began anew, this time against the Federal Government. This demands a bit of explanation.

Jefferson himself had nothing to do with framing the new system. As Secretary of State he claimed that he went along with policies in which he did not agree. The fact is his theory of government was quite different from that of the Federalists.

Jefferson had what I might call an American Civil Liberties Union mentality. His only concern seemed to be with *liberty*. Though he took just about every possible position on every fundamental question at one time or other in his long lifetime, he said, in a letter from France in 1787,

"I own, I am not a friend to a very energetic government. It is always oppressive."[1] He also wrote, just after the proposed Constitution was published: "Their President seems a bad edition of a Polish king."[2] Washington grew extremely impatient with the onesided politics of the Jeffersonian party. "Let that party," he wrote in 1799, shortly before his death, "set up a broomstick and call it a true son of liberty—a democrat— or give it any other epithet that will suit their purpose, and it will command their votes *in toto.*"[3]

I have no space to develop this division of American public opinion. But I would like to make two remarks about it.

First, I think it has resulted in an inner conflict in the United States between our *political institutions* (which are essentially Federalist) and *the way we think about them* (which is, especially in the case of "liberals," most literary people and even the "common man," Jeffersonian).

Secondly, and I mean this to be a challenging statement, it has encouraged people like Paul Blanshard and Bishop Oxnam to excogitate an alarming conflict between the constitution of the Catholic Church and the American constitutional system. They picture American democracy in completely and extravagantly Jeffersonian terms: all it consists of is *liberty, liberty, liberty.* Never a word about authority. They then proceed to picture Catholicism as a sort of caricature of Hamiltonianism: *authority, authority, authority.* The two are in irreconcilable conflict. The reason is that both have been grossly misrepresented, both in theory and in operation.

The Problem in the Welfare State

The problem of balancing liberty and authority was comparatively simple so long as our political society remained comparatively simple. The chief areas of conflict in the early days were the Alien and Sedition Act, the tariff and the banking system.

In the 1840's, however, we embarked upon an "experiment," the full implications of which then passed unnoticed. This was the transfer to the

---

[1] *The Life and Selected Writings of Jefferson,* edited by Koch and Peden, Modern Library, Random House, New York, 1944, p. 440.
[2] *Ibid.,* p. 435.
[3] *The Writings of George Washington,* edited by John C. Fitzpatrick, United States Government Printing Office, Washington, 1931–1944, XXXVII, 313, from a letter to Governor John Trumbull.

state (in this case the several States) of the function of *popular education*. We more or less stumbled into the problem of the "welfare state," about a century before the term was invented and almost that long before the problems it involves were appreciated.

The "welfare state" consists in a fundamental change in the *functions* of government. These functions are expanded, not necessarily in conflict with the traditional theory of governmental functions, in order to meet altogether new needs. Let us suppose, what I believe true, that the theory of the functions of the state incorporated into the American constitutional system, State and Federal, attributes to the state the authority to promote the general welfare by positive means. Hamilton, and the Federalists generally, certainly entertained this concept of the end of the state. In some respects the Jeffersonians did, too, though they seem to have restricted such positive functions very much, mostly denying them to the Federal Government but admitting them, at least in the field of education, in the case of State governments.

Still, by and large, the conditions of life in a predominantly agricultural society allowed people to meet their social and economic needs, as they understood them, without state intervention. In general, such modern social problems as unemployment, lack of adequate housing, and inaccessibility of expensive medical care did not exist. Other problems, such as the care of orphaned children and the care of the destitute aged, could be managed through private means, either in families or charitable institutions privately supported. The "broken home" problem hardly existed, so that the problem of foster care of children was small scale and manageable through the large family system. I suppose there were mental defectives—the "village idiot" became a meaningful phrase in our language—but nobody knew anything about psychiatry or the insulin shock treatment and people lived in large houses, often on farms. "Queer" persons were taken care of the way the chronically sick were taken care of—privately or in voluntary charitable institutions.

Notice that several factors combined to prevent the problem of social welfare from outrunning private means of handling it. The *scope* of the problem was not very great, because living and working arrangements were more ample, casual, and flexible, and social misfits could be readily absorbed into the pattern of rural and uncongested, unhurried city life. It was not very great because cities, which breed so many social problems, were small and living quarters in them still large. Moreover, neither education nor medicine had advanced to a point where expensive facilities were required to provide their services. The *level of needs* was therefore low. Such needs as people had and recognized could be met rather simply, without state intervention.

Education was the first social need to be shifted from private and voluntary to governmental responsibility. This was an epoch making shift. It meant that the functions of the state, from being mainly *protective* in the old sense of maintaining law and order became also *curative* and *promotive* of social well-being.

Now the distinctive power of the state is its *coercive* power. The most obvious need of such power is for *national defense* and the defense of *social order* against violence, such as robbery and murder. Once we put education into the state system, however, we empowered the state to use its coercive power—primarily the power to tax—to support a *cultural* agency.

I feel sure that the state has the right to tax, indeed, the duty to tax, in order to *make available the means of supporting schools for all*, regardless of their economic status. Popular education is essential to the functioning of popular government. The Founding Fathers clearly recognized this truth. I have no quarrel whatsoever with the state's moving into this area *as far as concerns taxation and the regulation of education to insure that its civic purposes are met*.

The problem of the "welfare state" arises from this circumstance: *the civic purpose of education is not its only purpose*. Education has manifold purposes: *self-development*, for *individual* as well as *social* and *civic* ends and *religious instruction* bulk large in the complex of purposes education has. Even in achieving social and civic purposes, the state should not *dictate* civic ideals and principles. These should be generated freely, through all the cultural resources a community has as its command— through religious agencies, through private and free investigation and research, through the family, etc.

In a word, the state has certain rights in education; it can, I feel, demand that the political philosophy on which our democratic system is based be taught to all its citizens. It can require courses in civics and American history. But the state has no right to dictate the *content* of such courses, to tell us what books we must use in civics and American history, to impose, if you wish, an official ideology on us. It certainly has no right to filter out the religious content of education, if there are ways—as I think there are—of avoiding such an "educational crime." It has no right to impose a system of ethics as applied to literature, or to make one version of a theory—say in teaching biological evolution or in teaching psychology—the official theory.

Yet we have got ourselves involved in this sort of thing by making popular education a department of state. The limitations on freedom are, to my mind, alarming. The state has put its power and resources behind a universal, almost monopolistic and, for all practical purposes, secularistic brand of education. It amazes me that people who think TVA is "socialistic" do not think the public school is "socialistic." TVA, after all, deals with flood control and that sort of thing, which undoubtedly fall within the competence of the state. Education deals with *ultimate values*. To do what we have done, namely, to coerce people into paying taxes to support what is for all practical purposes a state monopoly of popular education *of a kind that does not even satisfy tens of millions of American citizens* is, to my mind, a form of tyranny.

Now, having made this mistake, we have got used to it and accepted it as "normal" and "American." The problem of the "welfare state," as I see it, is that this tyranny will spread into *health* services, *relief, family,* and *child care* and all the rest.

In my opinion, this barging of the state into social life is clumsy and unnecessary.

CHAPTER LVI

Altruism and Masochism

By WILLIAM PEPPERELL MONTAGUE
Johnsonian Professor Emeritus of Philosophy
Columbia University

A RECENT READING of the book, *I Leaped over the Wall,* has once more brought home to me the strangeness of the persistent supposition of an affinity between helping others and hurting oneself, which has resulted in a fusion of an ethics of altruism with what may be called an ethics of masochism.

The ideal of furthering the needs and desires of one's associates and, through sympathy, feeling grief in what grieves them and joy in what gladdens them, is the heart of Christ's teaching of the abundant life. And it is a teaching in which the claims of ego and alter are harmonized, for it means that man can deepen and broaden his own life by sympathy for the lives of others. It is thus a completely life affirming ethics, and the most true and most beautiful of moral ideals.

What has come to be associated with it is a life denying conception of the good life, involving an ascetic frustrating of the material interests of the self—an ethical outlook described by Nietzsche as the inversion of all values. It allies the Devil with the World and the Flesh, and envisages one's desires as tainted with evil and therefore to be thwarted. This masochistic ideal has found expression not only in Protestant Puritanism and Catholic monasticism but in Buddhism and other forms of religious ethics in India and elsewhere, though not in the ethics of Hebraism. Particularly in its Christian version, the good life is then interpreted as dual, calling for a fight on behalf of one's fellows and a fight against oneself. This combination of an affirmative and a negative principle mystifies me. I have never been able to understand why the conjunction of the two ideals is so widespread and regarded by so many as a proper conjunction.

I was first made vividly aware of the problem one Christmas of my childhood, when I received a football. I still remember the angry bewilderment with which my pleasure was neutralized, when I found that none of my comrades was allowed to join me in play with the new toy, because the day was Sunday and on that day pleasures were wrong. A few years later I was reading the novels of Walter Scott and feeling revolted by the gloomy manners and customs of the Roundheads. And it was the same kind of experience that I had recently while reading of convent life and the hardships assumed by the zealous inmates as obvious instruments of the holy life. Of a piece with the football incident of my young days are all the evidences I have encountered of what seems to me a most strange sanctifying of uncalled for self-denial and thwarting—hair shirts and fasting, celibacy practiced as a virtue, forswearing of card playing and playgoing and dancing. And of course these are but a random fraction of the ways in which one's own well-being has been regarded as of an importance at least equal to the importance of promoting the well-being of others.

What reasons then have been alleged for this widespread dual code of ethics?

In the first place, we may note that those who take quite literally or as a fundamental allegory the Biblical account of the temptation and fall of man in the Garden of Eden, have insisted that sin has so poisoned the world and normal human interests that those interests and what pertains to them are too base to be improved or harmonized. As the argument runs, all man's "natural" tendencies and desires are vile; and because his desire for sensory enjoyment and everyday worldly pleasures are the most universal and natural, it is these that must above all others be condemned. In the history of Christianity there have been two contrasted ways of apportioning duties of ascetic practice. In the monastic regime of Catholicism, hatred of sensory gratification was carried to an extreme, but exaggerated asceticism was limited to the chosen few, leaving for the majority a right to live a life of normal happiness. In the case of Puritanism, the austerest form in general of Protestantism, there was an ascetic code though of a definitely less exaggerated degree than that of Catholic monasticism. But its diminished intensity was accompanied by a greatly increased extensity. While there were no monastic orders, everyone was exhorted to adopt a semi-monastic austerity that involved drabness of costume, a general repudiation of worldly pleasures, and a universal sourness of the whole community.

Something further and at first sight more apparently reasonable in the way of defense of repudiating sensory pleasures comes from those who argue that continual practice of self-denial constitutes an all important discipline by which character is strengthened. But what those who make this point too often forget, is that there is plenty of opportunity to develop one's character in a positive way, instead of in the negative Puritanical way. Surely expending one's powers in trying to bring joy to others, should be rated as infinitely more commendable than expending them in a struggle to renounce personal pleasures when these do not involve injuring any one else. But actually many who, in theory, subscribe to the dual principle of altruistic and masochistic ethics, seem in practice to rank masochistic virtue above altruistic. All too often they are so preoccupied with thwarting themselves that they are oblivious of the call for sympathy and help of others.

It is of course true that the pursuit of personal pleasure does often not only involve sacrificing the well-being of one's fellow men but also interferes with one's own more enduring and higher good. In these cases one should certainly condemn the pursuit of fleeting, present satisfaction. But this does not mean that immediate pleasure is evil, just because it is immediate, nor that it is intrinsically opposed to more remote and higher kinds of satisfactions, though these are of course less easily attained and often call for strenuous efforts that bring present discomfort or pain. My own conviction is, nevertheless, that no satisfactions, however trivial and shortlived, are in themselves bad, except in so far as they interfere with those that are larger and more enduring.

So I am left with my original puzzle. Is there perhaps some consideration that I have omitted which would explain and justify the supposed connection between the altruistic ideal of making life more abundant by promoting the well-being of others and the masochistic ideal of making life more meager by hurting oneself? I can myself discover no reasonable solution of the problem, so I am appealing to you for help in clearing up my very fundamental bewilderment.

Comment by Rudolf Allers:

I do not presume that I shall be able to solve to his satisfaction the puzzle which worries Professor Montague. But his remarks touch upon a question of fundamental importance both for moral philosophy and the practical conduct of life. It seems to me, therefore, that everyone who holds a considered opinion on such matters is under the obligation to profess what he believes. Be it only that he may say to himself: *Dixi et salvavi animam meam.*

Perhaps, it was particularly unfortunate that Professor Montague encountered the idea which, for brevity's sake, I shall call ascetic, in the shape of the incident at Christmas. Childhood impressions, though they do not make up all of our later attitudes, are apt to remain effective. Christian asceticism and the doctrine of self-denial exist also in other forms.

One understands, of course, that the ideal of monastic mortification is rather alien to many, especially modern minds. It is the more so, because it is hardly ever understood correctly.

Let me quote: "Man is created that he honor, love and serve his God and thus achieve the salvation of his soul. All things that are created, however, he may use, in so far as they prove not a hindrance for the attainment of his goal." These are the first words on the so-called *fundamentum* in the *Spiritual Exercises* by Ignatius of Loyola.

It is not forbidden to man that he find pleasure in many things. Even St. Augustine, a strict moralist if there ever was one, acknowledged that there are many things man may enjoy, provided he does not forget his main goal. In an interesting passage in *De Trinitate,* St. Augustine lists these goods: beauty and the richness of the harvest on the fields, art and music, and other things, even wealth. Nor has it been the doctrine of the Church that people be glum and despondent. The words of St. Paul, *"Gaudete; et iterum dico gaudete,"* were never forgotten.

The Church distinguishes between precepts everyone has to fulfil for the attainment of man's ultimate end, and others which are called "counsels of perfection." The monastic life is among the latter. It is consequent to the ideas of Calvin that the "counsels" became, so to speak, the daily rule.

Nor is it correct to envisage the precepts of the ascetic life as merely of a negative character. When the blessed Henricus Suso had stayed eleven years in the convent, had mortified himself in all manners, had been so afraid of the sinful world that he even disliked serving at the door, one night, so he tells in his charming autobiography, an angel appeared to him and said: "My dear, long enough have you been here taking care of your soul; now go out and care for others." And he left the next day.

The ascetic ideal truly does not deserve to be qualified as masochistic. Masochism is a perverted form of an exaggerated self-love, of seeking one's pleasure in a definitely abnormal way. But that love which Christian doctrine calls charity, *agape,* is not self-seeking. It is precisely *caritas quae non quaerit quae sua sunt.*

It may be impossible for someone of an essentially non-Christian approach to understand that people retire to convents to live a life of contemplation and mortification. But, even the "outsider" might realize that they lead this life not primarily for themselves. It does not mean much to the "outsider," but it is nevertheless true that these ascetes live a life of sacrifice "for others." Their prayers, their meditations, their sacrifices are "offered up" for others.

Does the life of the scholar become meager because he repudiates immediate pleasures? No. Neither does the life of the Christian.

I cannot help feeling that the problem with which Professor Montague is so much concerned, is, in truth a pseudo problem. In the form in which he states it, it simply does not exist. Of course, it is quite true—and very regrettable—that there are many of the Faith who do not understand the true significance of an ascetic life. But the failure to understand on the part of some, or even of many, has no bearing on the true nature of the idea.

Comment of Stewart G. Cole:

The writer has stated, somewhat trenchantly, the ethical position of Puritan Christianity as it operated widely a generation ago. This dual and self-contradictory conception of the good life, although still controlling as a practical code in some conservative Protestant groups, has pretty well run its course in most of the American churches. Few representatives of the major denominations would share any longer Dr. Montague's particular "bewilderment." They and their brethren have surrendered most of the principles of masochism in their characterization of Christian ethics.

The weakness of their position ethically lies, as some of us see it, in the vague implications of the principles of altruism, which they affirm with respect to some of the most baffling problems of human life in our times: for instance, what Christianity's moral decisions are going to be with respect to the subject of the holocaust of world wars, to the human use of atomic energy, to the conflict between the cosmologies of science and historic religion, to the confusions between the economic viewpoints of the "free enterprise" system and the well-being of the masses of mankind, to the tensions between spokesmen of Roman Catholicism and Protestantism in this country, to the unchartered relationship of the ethics of democracy and the position of the Christian faith, and to the conflicting frameworks of the philosophy of the Christian religion as expressed by the so-called "crisis" theologians and those who adopt a straightforward, this-worldly approach to the meaning of life and the nature of God and His providential interest in man.

In recent decades the spokesmen for Christian ethics in Protestant circles have become somewhat experimental in their procedure. Judging by the muffled voice of the church on such subjects as have just been mentioned, they still seem to be at the stage of "trial and error" in their deliberations.

Here centers the real bewilderment within the Christian fellowship that threatens the soundness of the church's position. In one basic respect it poses a conflict between those who rest their ethical position upon some type of theological or ecclesiastical authority and those who would interpret the Christian position by free inquiry and realistic problem-solving.

CHAPTER LVII

Government in Islam

By GUSTAVE E. VON GRUNEBAUM

Professor of Arabic, The University of Chicago

Preliminary Statement

THE FOLLOWING IS an attempt to describe in a small number of propositions the essential structure of Muslim government. Attention is focussed on the classical period of Islamic political science from Mâwardî (d. 1058) to Ibn Taimiyya (d. 1328).
To facilitate discussion occasional references have been added.

Bibliographical Note

Abû Ya'là	Abû Ya'là al-Farrâ' al-Ḥanbalî (d. 1065), *al-Aḥkâm as-sulṭâniyya*, Cairo, 1356/1938.
Ghazzâlî	Abû Ḥâmid al-Ghazzâlî (d. 1111), *Iḥyâ' 'ulûm ad-dîn*, Bûlâq, 1289/1872. Especially Bk XIX: *Kitâb al-amr bi'l-ma'rûf wa'n-nahy 'an al-munkar*, in vol. II, pp. 283-334.
Ḥillî	Ibn Muṭahhar al-Ḥillî (d. 1325), *al-Bâbu 'l-Ḥâdî 'Ashar*, trans. W. McE. Miller, London, 1928.
Ḥisba	Ibn Taimiyya (d. 1328), *al-Ḥisba fî 'l-islâm*, Cairo, 1318/1900.
Ibn Ḥaldûn	Ibn Ḥaldûn (d. 1406), *Prolegomena*, ed. Quatremère, Paris, 1858; trans. de Slane, Paris, 1862-1868.
Ibn Jamâ'a	Ibn Jamâ'a (d. 1333), *Taḥrîr al-aḥkâm*, ed. trans. H. Kofler. In: *Islamica*, VI (1934), pp. 349-414; VII (1935), pp. 1-64; *Abhandlungen fuer die Kunde des Morgenlandes*, XXIII, 6 (1938), pp. 18-129.
Laoust	H. Laoust, *Essai sur les doctrines sociales et politiques de Taḳî-d-Dîn Aḥmed b. Taimîya*, Cairo, 1939.

Mâwardî	Mâwardî (d. 1058), *al-Ahkâm as-sultâniyya.* Ed. M. Enger, as: *Mawerdii constitutiones politicae,* Bonn, 1853; trans. E. Fagnan, *Mawerdi: Les statuts gouvernementaux,* Alger, 1915.
Nizâm al-Mulk	Nizâm al-Mulk (d. 1092), *Siyâsat-Nâmah,* ed. trans. C. Schefer, Paris, 1891–1897.
Sabine	G. H. Sabine, *A History of Political Theory,* 2nd ed., New York, Henry Holt & Company, 1950.
Siyâsa	Ibn Taimiyya, *Siyâsa šar'iyya,* trans. H. Laoust, *Le traité de droit public d'Ibn Taimîya,* Beirut, 1948.

I

The purpose of man is the service of God, *'ibâda.*

II

Complete *'ibâda* requires the existence of an organized community of believers.

III

The existence of such a community requires government.

IV

The primary purpose of government is the rendering possible of *'ibâda.*[1]

V

The primarily moral purpose of the state is manifest in
A. *a.* The ranking of the *hisba, i.e.,* the obligation to command the good and prohibit the bad, *al-amr bi'l-ma'rûf wa'n-nahy 'an al-munkar,* as the foremost civic-religious duty;[2]

[1]Cf. Siyâsa, p. 20: *Les fonctions publiques doivent avoir pour fin dernière de tendre à améliorer la condition religieuse des hommes.* E. Pritsch, Die islamische Staatsidee, *Zeitschrift fuer vergleichende Rechtswissenschaft,* LIII (1939), poignantly terms religion the *'staatsbildende Prinzip'* in Islam which makes for the *'grundsaetzliche Einheit der politischen und religioesen Gemeinschaft'* (pp. 36 and 71).

[2]Cf. Ghazzâlî, II 283; *hisba* as *al-qutb al-a'zam fi 'd-dîn.* This is a development from Koran 3:100; it is generally held to be a personal obligation, *fard 'ain* (thus Mâwardî,

Government in Islam

b. The derivation by political theory of the purpose of government from the *ḥisba* obligation.[3]

c. The conception of the office of the *muḥtasib*, or (market) inspector (and censor) as a specialization of the general duty of the *ḥisba*.[4]

B. The acceptance of Canon Law, *šarī'a*, as a limitation of the government's judiciary and executive powers. The limitation applies to both commission and omission of action. As, for instance, the execution of canonical punishment is a religious act, the government is not free to increase or to cancel the prescribed penalty. (Cf. *Siyâsa*, p. 100 (Laoust, p. 605). Already Ibn al-Muqaffă (d. 757) clearly defines the caliph's power in this vein

---

p. 404/513; Ghazzâlî, II, 288ff.). *Ḥisba*, p. 53, looks upon it as a collective duty, *farḍ kifâya*—an attenuation dictated by considerations of public order. The history of the *al-amr bi'l-ma'rûf* formula needs to be traced. (Some Islamic material is collected in A. J. Wensinck, *The Muslim Creed*, Cambridge University Press, Cambridge, 1932, pp. 106 f.) St. Augustine, *De doctrina christiana* IV, iv, 6, considers *et bona docere et mala dedocere* as the first duty of the *divinarum scripturarum tractator et doctor*, the *defensor rectae fidei ac debellator erroris*—a suggestive parallel the common basis of which may be looked for in Stoic natural law whose objective and universal validity is here restated in terms of a universal personal obligation.

[3]Cf. *Ḥisba*, p. 6. The obligation of the *ḥisba* (but not the term) is included in the five fundamental theses of the Mu'tazila. Cf. Aš'arî (d. 935), *Maqâlât al-islâmiyyîn*, ed. H. Ritter (Istanbul, 1929–30), p. 278: "The Mu'tazila are agreed (al-Aṣamm dissenting) on the obligatoriness of *al-amr bi'l-ma' rûf wa'n-nahy 'an al-munkar* if its execution is possible; it may be done by tongue, hand or sword—whichever way one is able." It deserves notice that al-Aṣamm, the lone dissenter (d. 850), held an official position as judge under the caliph al-Mu'taṣim (833–842). The same al-Aṣamm is referred to by Ghazzâlî as the sole representative of the view that the *umma* can dispense with an *imâm*; cf. I. Goldziher, *Der Islam*, VI (1916), 173–77.

[4]This is well brought out by Mâwardî, pp. 404–432/513–553. Functionally and probably historically, the *muḥtasib* is the successor of the *agoranomos* of the Greek and Hellenistic cities. For a convenient summary of the *agoranomos'* duties cf. J. Oehler, "*Agoranomoi*" in Pauly-Wissowa, *Realenzyklopaedie* . . . , I, 883–85 (1893). Outside of Egypt where they were chiefly notaries, ". . . *erstreckt sich ihre Competenz auf den Marktplatz selbst, . . . Ferner haben sie die Aufsicht ueber den Verkehr am Markte, besonders den Kleinhandel; . . . Ihre Aufsicht aeusserte sich in der Sorge fuer die eukosmia und das me apseudein durch Aufrechterhaltung der Ordnung. Schlichtung von Streitigkeiten zwischen Verkaeufern und Kaeufern, Untersuchung der Waren nach Qualitaet und Quantitaet, Ueberwachung des Gebrauchs richtiger Masse und Gewichte, ueberhaupt durch Erlassung einer bestimmten Marktordnung ueber Zeit und Ort des Verkaufes. . . . In Processen, die sich auf ihren Wirkungskreis bezogen, hatten sie den Vorsitz; . . .*" G. Vajda, *Journal Asiatique*, 1948, 325, saw the connection between *agoranomos* and *muḥtasib*, but failed to note the different basis of the two offices and the different manner in which they are integrated in their respective social systems.

(*Risâla fî'ṣ-ṣaḥâba,* in: Muḥammad Kurd'Alî, *Rasâ'il al-bulaghâ'*, 3rd ed., (Cairo, 1946/1365), pp. 121–122; similar though less specific, the Syrian jurisconsult, Auzâ'î (d. 774); cf. J. Schacht, *The Origins of Muhammadan Jurisprudence* (Oxford, 1950), p. 119). It should be noted in this connection that the division of governmental powers in legislative, judiciary, and executive is not to be found in Islamic public law and is used here only for the sake of convenience. Muḥammad 'Abduh, *Tafsir,* IV, 185–192; V, 443, 465–466, tried not very convincingly to trace the division to the Koran.)

VI

In a community constituted for the purpose of *'ibâda* no grounds for inequality among the legally responsible, *mukallaf,* Muslims may exist —except that the Prophet ranked the believers in order of their piety.

VII

Hence
(A) All Muslims are equal before the law except in so far as their *isonomia* is modified by
   a. the social heritage of earlier ages or cultures such as slavery and the depressed status of women; and
   b. the national or political stratification of the moment (rule of the Arab aristocracy, of the Turkish and Circassian *mamlûks* over Egyptians and Syrians, and the like).
(B) The impossibility for any non-Muslim to be a full member of the community of true believers. So the non-Muslims are neutralized in largely self-governing religious communities of their own whose relation to the ruling *umma Muḥammadiyya* are settled by treaties that tend to degenerate into unilateral contracts.

VIII

Plato and Aristotle, trusting man's natural light, considered the good life inseparable from participation in the state which, to them, is a value in itself.

The Middle Ages, Christian and Muslim alike, taking a dim view of man, look upon the state as the indispensable stage for the good life which leads through obedience to salvation. The value of the state is derived from its moral purpose.

IX

The legal basis of an assignment of duties to the government and at the same time the basis of governmental independence *vis-à-vis* both individual and community, is the distinction in Canon Law between *farḍ 'ain,* personal, and *farḍ kifâya,* collective obligation.

X

In its task of guaranteeing *'ibâda* the government is actually faced with three sets of tasks:

(1) Safeguarding the Muslim community *vis-à-vis* the non-Muslim world with "safeguarding" usually interpreted to mean "expanding"— the resulting duty is *jihâd,* Holy War. The conquest of unbelievers as such is pleasing to Allâh. Missionary activities often follow but rarely accompany *jihâd*. The near identity, at certain periods, of nation and religious community caused any foreign war to be thought of as *jihâd*. The inclusion in the concept of *jihâd* of war against heretics, parallels Augustine's *bellum Deo auctore* against the heretics who are to be compelled to rejoin the Church (the much quoted *coge intrare* which Brun of Querfurt (d. 1009) was the first to direct against the heathen). War on non-Christians with a view to their subsequent conversion was advocated by Pope Gregory I, but never accepted as Church doctrine. (For the Christian *bellum iustum* and related ideas cf. C. Erdmann, *Die Entstehung des Kreuzzugsgedankens* (W. Wohlhammer, Stuttgart, 1935), especially pp. 1–29 (and p. 97 for Brun of Querfurt).)

(2) Safeguarding the Muslim community against
    a. schism; and
    b. heresy.

(3) The enforcement of the stipulations of the good life as set forth in Canon Law on the basis of revealed text and tradition and in application of generally agreed to principles of elaboration or interpretation; or else, the establishment and maintaining of the conditions with which those stipulations can be carried out and enforced.

XI

The interest of the community in the continuity of the individual political unit within the area under Muslim rule, or *dâr al-islâm,* is slight as compared to the interest in the integrity of the whole. *Eleutheria, i.e.,* autonomy rather than freedom, is insisted upon only for the *dâr al-islâm,* not for the "accidentally" existing states among which the *dâr al-islâm* is distributed at any given moment.[5]

XII

The intellectual justification of the Roman Empire was the consummation of cultural unity through political unification (or again the realization of the Stoic *cosmopolis*); that of the Spanish, economic self-sufficiency and the prevention of scarcity; that of the British and the American (in its early phase), the moral obligation to extend the area of good government.

By contrast, the extension of Muslim rule is *objectively* justified as the duty to spread the superior truth which, as a way of life, can be fully realized only under a Muslim administration; *subjectively,* by the feeling that leadership and its honor belong to the "best community," which is Islam.[6]

[5] Cf. the characteristic passage, *Siyâsa,* p. 88 (= Laoust, p. 601).

[6] For the Spanish ideal of *los abastos* cf. M. J. Bonn, *Encyclopaedia of the Social Sciences,* VII, p. 607. The consciousness of economic aims, characteristic of the Mercantilistic period, coexisted in Spain with other motivations of imperialism, *viz.* "the conviction that the duty of civilized nations is to undertake the political, economic and religious tutelage of more primitive peoples; the eager willingness of government and people to perform this duty and to accept the material rewards involved" (J. H. Parry, *The Spanish Theory of Empire in the Sixteenth Century,* Cambridge, Cambridge University Press, 1940, p. 1).

In his study "The Sociology of Imperialisms" in, *Imperialism and Social Classes* (Augustus M. Kelly, Inc., New York, 1951, pp. 3–130; appeared first in *Archiv fuer Sozialwissenschaft und Sozialpolitik,* 1918/19, XLVI, pp. 1–39. 275–310, as "Zur Soziologie der Imperialismus,") J. Schumpeter defines imperialism as "the objectless disposition on the part of a state to unlimited forcible expansion" (p. 7). In discussing the motivations of Muslim expansion (pp. 45–56) Schumpeter emphasizes the secondary character of the warlike teachings of Islam, relative to the warlike traditions of the Arabs that formed the first Muslim community (and whose background he analyzes with considerable sagacity). The will to conquer of a specifically religious community remains fundamentally mere will to convert the non-believers. "In the course of this mission of conversion and in the political interests of the Church, the military subjugation of one country by another might on occasion be desirable, but it was never an end in itself. . . .

XIII

To appreciate Muslim sentiment it must be realized that to Medieval (and much of ancient) thought, Western as well as Eastern, *being* was susceptible of gradation; that the higher an entity's place in the creaturely hierarchy the more did it participate in *being* and the closer it was to *pure being*, or God; and finally, that as in God *perfect being* and *summum bonum* coincided, a hierarchy of moral values paralleled that of ontic values. So the higher *virtus* of the Muslim as the sole possessor of ultimate truth called forth his higher honor, or *šaraf*, in the societal order.[7]

XIV

Anticipating the Muslim attitude, the Christian Fathers and with especial forcefulness Augustine, insisted that a just state is one in which the true religion is taught, *i.e.*, since the advent of Christianity only a Christian state can be just. The chief purpose of the government of this state must be "contributing to human salvation by preserving the purity of the faith."[8]

XV

The duty of the government to suppress schism and heresy is to be carried out in obedience to the views of the *'ulamā'*.

In contrast to both the Sassanian and the Christian Roman (and Byzantine) governments the Muslim state did not employ organized religion as part of its administrative machinery, which is one reason why

---

What needed to be spread was the rule of dogma and the corresponding organization of religious, not political, life. In this process natural instincts of pugnacity could be vented only incidentally and rarely. This is clearly seen from the characteristic fact that the devoutly Catholic Spaniards never dreamed of giving a religious motivation to their overseas conquests, though these conquests did indeed serve the interests of the Church" (pp. 53-54). Schumpeter recognizes the fact that Islam did actually expand its area through conversion, especially in India and under the Mongols. "But this does not change our diagnosis of Arab imperialism" (p. 55, note).

[7] Cf. Max Scheler's remarks on medieval thinking, *Die Wissensformen und die Gesellschaft,* Der Neuer Geist Verlag, Leipzig, 1926, p. 133.

[8] The quotation is from Sabine, p. 192.

it was not, as a rule, concerned with enforcing complete agreement on theological and legal doctrine.[9]

XVI

The community through its *'ulamā'* revises periodically its concept of itself determining who is and who is not to be considered a member of the traditional community, *ahl as-sunna wa'l-jamā'a,* or in theological terms, what is to be considered orthodox, what heresy. In Sunnite Islam such self-definition is usually done with a view to preserving the unity of the *umma Muḥammadiyya;* in the sects a tendency to further fragmentation prevails.

XVII

Schism arose from dispute over the person of the legitimate ruler of the Muslim community. It developed into *heresy* due to
  A. The infiltration into political argumentation of traditional, that is, pre-Islamic thought-motifs (such as the epiphany of god in the ruler; dynastic legitimism—in the case of the *Šī'a*);
  B. Moral absolutism (the extreme egalitarianism of the *Ḫārijites* and their exclusion of the sinner from the community, which will be better understood when viewed in the light of Section XIII above);
  C. Historical accidents such as the multinational character of the community.

XVIII

Muslim public law does not start from a definition of the state, but from that of the *imāma,* the leadership of the community. The concept

---

[9] Ibn al-Muqaffa', a secretary of state, failed in his attempt to persuade the caliph Manṣūr (754–775) to eliminate, for reasons of administrative convenience, disagreement in matters of religion and law. In this proposal, Ibn al-Muqaffa', a Persian but recently converted to Islam, took up a tradition of Sassanian statecraft; cf. his *Risāla fī 'ṣ-ṣaḥāba,* pp. 126–127, and Schacht, *op. cit.,* p. 95.

To Constantine the Great (d. 337) religious uniformity was possible of attainment because of his (fundamentally Stoic) belief in the oneness of human reason, and it was politically necessary because of its concomitant, the absolute validity of the right world order, the *koinos nomos* of any human society; cf. Eusebios of Caesarea, *Vita Constantini* II, 65, and F. Kampers, "Rex et sacerdos," *Historisches Jahrbuch,* 1925, XLV, pp. 502–503.

of the state is alien to Muslim political theory in its classical phase and down to Ibn Ḥaldûn (d. 1406).

Here lies the essential difference between the political thought of Islam and that of the Christian successors of the Imperium Romanum. Christian thought never divorced itself from the Roman concept of the territorially circumscribed organization of power, and the limits of the Roman Empire lingered on as the natural borders of the ideal state. More precisely put—the Catholic Occident was, on the whole, satisfied to formulate its political aspirations in terms of the so-called Western Empire, but anxiously strove to maintain the religious unity of the entire *orbis Romanus*. The Byzantine Orient, on the other hand, never abandoned the claim to supremacy over the totality of the *orbis Romanus*, but did not make any effort to unite the Christian *oikoumene* under orthodox leadership. (For the Byzantine view of their empire cf. the excellent statement of G. Ostrogorsky, *Geschichte des byzantinischen Staates,* Munich, C. H. Beck (O. Beck), 1940, pp. 16 f.)

In this connection it is relevant to note that the idea of a succession of a limited number of empires which, on the basis of the Book of Daniel, effectively influenced the philosophy of history in the West, did not leave any mark on the political science of Islam.

Consequently, it is never the nature or concept of an *umma* as such that is discussed but only the conditions of membership in the *umma Muḥammadiyya*.[10]

[10]Cf. the works of the Šâfi'ites, Mâwardî and Ibn Jamâ'a, the Ḥanbalites, Abû Ya'lâ and Ibn Taimiyya, and the Šî'î, Ḥillî.

In Ibn Ḥaldûn's work social grouping as such is discussed before the different types of community leadership such as *mulk* and *ḥilâfa* are investigated.

Mâwardî's and Ḥillî's definitions of the *imâma* may follow as illustrations and as indications of the sharply contrasting approach of Sunna and Šî'a to the problem of rulership.

Mâwardî, p. 5. "*L'institution de l'imâmat a pour raison d'être qu'il supplie le prophétisme pour la sauvegarde de la religion et l'administration des intérêts terrestres."* It is then described as a necessary institution. The character of the necessity of the *imâma* as rational or canonical is under dispute.

Ḥillî, Section 174 on p. 62. "The Imâmate is a universal authority in the things of religion and of the world belonging to some person and derived from the prophet. And it is necessary according to reason. For the *imâmate* is a kindness (from Allâh; *luṭf*), and we know absolutely that when men have a chief and a guide whom they obey, who avenges the oppressed of his oppressor and restrains the oppressor from his oppression, then they draw near to soundness and depart from corruption."

XIX

The community as such is interested principally in being able to lead the good life; it is less interested in who administers it. 1. This attitude, 2. the conviction that government and transgression of the Law are inseparable, and 3. as time wears on, the political situation and especially the subjection of the community to foreign rulers lead to

A. Widespread disinclination to collaborate in government; it is particularly those classes that control the Canon Law by the systematic development of the principles of lawfinding and by the practice of delivering legal opinions, or *fatwà*'s, when consulted on doubtful points, that stay aloof from politics and administration; the result is an increasingly deep cleavage between legal theory and executive practice;

B. Growing indifference to the legality and the moral level of the particular government or the particular governmental act, provided it remains possible for the individual believer to carry on his life under the law, and provided the government protects the main concerns of the legal schools and of popular piety;

C. Recognition of the *de facto* ruler as *de jure;*

D. The feeling that a bad ruler is better than civil disturbance, let alone no ruler at all.[11]

XX

It should be remembered that the Christian Fathers, too, hold the bad ruler entitled to obedience, even as regards uncanonical acts. And before them the Epicureans and Stoics like Seneca had declared that a tyrant's rule was acceptable, seeing that he removed the outer obstacles to the philosophical life by taking charge of governmental functions.

---

[11]Cf. *Ḥisba*, p. 55; G. E. von Grunebaum, *Medieval Islam,* Chicago University Press, Chicago, 1946, pp. 168 f., for quotations from Ghazzâlî and Ibn Jamâ'a. For the concurring Iranian tradition cf. Abû Manṣûr at-Ta'âlibî (the famous philologist; d. 1038), *Histoire des rois des Perses,* ed. trans. H. Zotenberg (Paris, 1900), p. 483. (This history was written before 1021; for the authorship of the work cf. F. Rosenthal, *Journal of the American Oriental Society,* 1950, LXX, pp. 181 f.)

Everywhere cultivation of the inner man as the goal of life has tended to estrange man from political activity.[12]

XXI

The government is compelled to develop a system of executive law, sometimes called *qânûn,* and executive jurisdiction, the *maẓâlim* courts, side by side with the *Šarîʿa.* In the very nature of things this system is more flexible, more realistic, more effective. The *ʿulamâʾ* are able to justify it on the ground of its serving the *maṣlaḥa,* the public interest.

XXII

Limitations by the government of the freedom of the individual (to use a concept foreign to classical Islam) are justifiable 1. in view of its duty to prevent damage being done to any Muslim and 2. by the public interest, *maṣlaḥa.*

XXIII

The power of the government is not limited by any political rights of the individual Muslim but by the *Šarîʿa* in so far as it
- A. Denies to the government certain functions (such as legislation, properly so called), and
- B. Prescribes its course of action in some areas (such as its dealings with non-Muslims within the *dâr al-islâm* and to some extent also outside it; the kind of penalties to be imposed wherever Canon Law has arrived at a ruling; the admissibility of various economic, social, and cultural practices).

XXIV

The *ḥisba* implies the right to criticize the government. But it bestows freedom of speech without protecting against governmental reprisal.

XXV

The *ḥisba* may be carried to what amounts to armed intervention not against the government but against the trespassing fellow Muslims.

---

[12] For the characteristic attitude toward the unjust ruler of Pope Gregory the Great (590–604) cf. Sabine, p. 194. For Seneca's view cf. *Ad Lucilium* LXXIII.

XXVI

The right to resist the government is admitted on moral grounds: A command entailing disobedience to God must not be obeyed.[13]

XXVII

Since, however, the community is primarily interested in the preservation of its own stability, theory in effect seriously limits the *ḥisba vis-à-vis* the government.[14]

XXVIII

Apart from actual rebellion extra-legal recourse against (individual acts of) the government is had through the protests and admonitions of the religious élite.

A. The *'alîm* whose *fatwà* may demonstrate the incompatibility of the governmental action with Canon Law or Tradition. The government parries by introducing innovations under the protection of *fatwà*'s which it solicits from a *muftî* whose authority is largely derived from government appointment. The negative *fatwà* of an *'alîm* discredits but does not annul the executive act against which it is directed.

B. The zealot, ascetic or *ṣûfî* "saint" (who may be one and the same person).[15]

XXIX

In actual administration the government uses side by side, *šarî'a*, *qânûn*, *Reichsrecht* and *Volksrecht* (*i.e.*, local customary law, or *'urf*) and builds up its official apparatus without much regard to the stipulations of Canon Law.[16]

---

[13] *Siyâsa*, p. 2 (= Laoust, p. 598). Cf. *Hisba*, p. 55, the reference to the Mu'tazilite view that extends *hisba* to the duty of *qitâl al-a'imma;* and p. 87, Ibn Taimiyya's own view that one should not obey anyone *fî ma'ṣiyat Allâh*. This doctrine goes back to the seventh century A.D.

[14] Cf. Ghazzâlî, II, 306–310—of the eight degrees, *darajât*, of the *ḥisba* only the first two are applicable against the ruler.

[15] His intervention is well illustrated by the stories told by Ghazzâlî, II, pp. 320–334.

[16] Cf. Mâwardî, pp. 272–307, 333–377, on the different legal situation prevailing in different parts of the Empire.

XXX

The definitions of the function of the *imâm* that range from realistic description to utopian portrayal of the ideal country as represented in the ideal ruler, and to *Geschichtsmetaphysik* in the Šīʿite *imâm* and the Mahdî, constitute an attempt to legalize or protect actual government or the actual condition of the state.[17]

XXXI

The Šīʿite concept of the *imâma* combines
A. Ancient God-king memories;
B. The Platonic idea of the best man as the ruler; during the transmission from Plato through Fârâbî (d. 950) to Tûsî (d. 1274) and Ḥillî perfection becomes infallibility; and
C. The idea of permanent divine guidance of the community through the ruler's union with the Active Intellect (Fârâbî) or in more conventional language, through the perpetuation of the Prophetic office by the divinely inspired *imâm*.

By contrast the Sunnite (and the Christian) rulership merely signify the office of presiding over the coercive organization that is indispensable for the attainment by individual and community of the *summum bonum*.[18]

XXXII

Although under the impact of Iranian traditions the Sunnite caliphs were ceremonially exalted beyond the requirements of their office, their function continued to be that of guarantors of the legality of the body politic. If the theologian approved of their ceremonial remoteness, he did so solely in the belief that awe of the ruler would stabilize the state.[19]

---

[17] To reconcile theory and practice, Ibn Taimiyya gives the sovereign the qualification of a *mujtahid* (Laoust, p. 228). After the fall of Baghdâd in 1258, the caliph in Cairo represents the desire of public law to secure the continued validity of community life; cf. Laoust, pp. 45-48.

[18] This concept of rulership did not, of course, preclude, either in Islam or in Christendom, popular belief in the charismatic character of the prince.

[19] In early Arabic *ḥalîfa,* caliph, means "protector" which is also the meaning of the word *Koran* 38:25, the very passage from which the later theologians deduced the concept of the caliph as the successor or vice-gerent of the Prophet and, in later usage, of God; cf. I. Goldziher, *Revue de l'histoire des religions*, 1897, XXXV, pp. 336 f.

The contradiction inherent in the political attitude of Islam is due to the fact that *a*. on the one hand, the true purpose of man's life is otherworldly, but that *b*. on the other hand, its fulfilment depends on the functioning of a body politic of which each Muslim is a member by birth and from which he cannot withdraw.

The Christian never did need a state to fulfil the other-worldly purpose of his existence. The Roman Empire was rather an obstacle to the good life, unless the Christian's relation to it be viewed as a test. Withdrawal from it was both permissible and possible. In fact, such withdrawal remained possible even from the Christian state because the essential concerns of the soul continued to be administered by the clerical polity.[20]

The early history of Christianity and this dichotomy of Christian government preserved the West from the organizational breakdown that was the consequence of the unrealizable expectation which Islam had to place in the state.

To sum up:

XXXIII

Islamic thought is authoritarian. Political absolutism parallels the theological absolutism of God's relation to His creatures.[21]

XXXIV

Within Sunnite Islam, *lawful* government is confined to assisting in the realization of the good life as recognized at any given moment by the *ijmâ'*, the consensus of the learned, whose authority is verifying (*konstatierend*) rather than normative (as is the authority of the Russian Orthodox Synod in contrast to that of Pope and Council in the Roman Church). The extreme wing of the pious denied the existence of lawful government in Islam after the period of the "orthodox'" caliphs, *al-ḥulafâ' ar-râšidûn, i.e.,* after 661 A.D.

---

[20] Even the best *civitas terrena* cannot, in Augustine's view, ever form part of the *civitas Dei*. The very existence of a state is to be accounted for only as a need created by the essential sinfulness of the human condition. Cf. G. Tellenbach, *Libertas. Kirche und Weltordnung im Zeitalter des Investiturstreites* (Stuttgart, W. Kohlhammer, 1935), pp. 35 ff. (with discussion of scholarly views).

[21] Ideally, God is the head of the state. His visible representative is the Prophet whose political and administrative functions have devolved on his legitimate successors. Oligarchic government occurred on rare occasions only to be transformed into the customary monarchy after a short time. Theory never took notice of such developments.

Actual government resembles rather closely medieval government elsewhere.

This is to say that the spasmodic assertion of governmental authority did, in practice, favor particularistic tendencies. Political (as distinct from religious and intellectual) interests would operate on the parochial rather than the imperial level. The ruler's influence was apt to decline with distance from his residence; in the later period, many a sultan led the migratory life typical of the German emperors. Administrative techniques were poor, rights and duties easily forgotten for want of archives and loss of documents (the papal curia, the *dîwân's* of the caliphs in the good period and those of Egypt appear to have been the only effective chancelleries of the early and "high" Middle Ages). The conviction of the unalterability of the Law is accompanied by much uncertainty with regard to its content.

It should perhaps be noted that despite theoretical differences and actual hostilities between Sunnite and Šī'ite governments their administrative practices would seem to have been more or less the same.

XXXV

Within Šī'ite Islam, the cleavage between aspiration and accomplishment, or rather between actuality and its theoretical justification, is less pronounced and less painful, because the hidden *imâm* as the direct representative of God's will is legislator, as well as executor. Legal change is thus more readily accounted for than in Sunnite Islam.

XXXVI

While Islam is in one sense the political community *par excellence* it has tended to make the pious Muslim more and more non-political.

Comment by John LaFarge, S.J.

Members of the Conference, I am sure, will feel greatly indebted to Professor von Grunebaum for the skill and clarity with which he has opened our eyes to a topic unknown to all but a few specialists in this country. With the United States now deeply involved in the Near and Middle East, an understanding of Islam's concept of freedom and authority is of the highest practical as well as theoretical importance.

In Section XXXII, I wonder if it was his intention to convey the idea that the Augustinian view of the state—as "only a need created by the essential sinfulness of the human condition"—should be regarded as *per se* and *simpliciter* the Christian view. In the concept of Thomas Aquinas, widely accepted by Catholics at the present time, the state corresponds to man's need for an organized system looking toward his temporal welfare, an essential need which would exist, even if, by hypothesis, man were not sinful. While an individual might find it more perfect to "withdraw" from the state, in order to devote himself to some special vocation, such as solitary contemplation, it would be a disaster, in this Thomistic concept, if the generality of mankind followed such a procedure. We have a moral and *religious* duty to care for the good of the temporal order, which has a validity of its own, even though the ultimate and supreme goods are those which are eternal. Even the individual person who has "withdrawn," the hermit or contemplative, still has the duty to assist the temporal state by his fervent and constant prayers for its welfare.

APPENDIX

Freedom and Authority in the Realization of Values

By DAVID N. IINO

Lecturer and Assistant to the President, International Christian University, Tokyo

SOCIALLY AND POLITICALLY the Japanese people are beginning to have more freedom than before. The right use of this freedom will be the hope of Japan in the future. Yet instances of its misuse are many. Further, many of the people have not been able to avail themselves of the newly given freedom, and the reasons for this are worth studying.

At the same time some of the authorities of the old Japan have lost their prestige. New authorities are beginning to emerge but the people react to them in various ways. Which of them are the most valid? The relation between freedom and authority is a very important problem in contemporary Japan. Practical considerations about it claim our supreme attention. Yet we must begin with brief theoretical studies of these two concepts.

1. *What Freedom Means*

The amount of freedom we have is much more limited than most people assume. Everything which exists is related to all the rest of the universe more or less. Nothing is free in the sense of being independent of this relationship. The conscious person is dependent upon its environments which are physical, social, subconscious, logical and ideal, and metaphysical. Whatever freedom we have is relative in complex ways.

Within certain limits we have the power to desire, choose, and direct. This power is our freedom. It presupposes the absence of those obstacles which hinder our ability to think and to act. It includes capacity to carry out plans. It also includes the power to change these plans and have new experiences. Further, it includes efficiency in action. It is "spiritual determination," as distinct from "mechanical or organic determination." As Walter Moberly says, God has forfeited a part of His own power and has given a relative independence of its own; this is human freedom.[1]

As Ralph Barton Perry holds, every freedom has its negative and positive sides. There is "a freedom from" and "a freedom to and for." The former is not true freedom, unless there is at the same time capacity, as well as an absence of external restraints. It means little that we are prevented by no barrier or forbidden by no authority. We must be free, in the sense of being able to take the initiative, so that something worthy may be achieved.[2] Creative thought or action is different from day dreaming. The new Constitution may provide many forms of freedom, but what is more important is that the people use them in significant ways.

A better social order will be realized first through freeing the *status quo* from cramping and thwarting obstacles of external restraints, disorder, inequality, injustice, conflict, and war. These obstacles and disvalues hinder our freedom to and for the valuable things of life. Under ideal conditions the value experiences which we would like to enjoy freely come under the following ten categories: natural, economic, bodily, recreational, work, social, character, esthetic, intellectual, and religious values. But this freedom is marred by the above mentioned obstacles and disvalues. To remove these hindrances we must have such character and social values as justice, order, and freedom. These values conflict with one another or degenerate into something else unless they are placed under the pull of religious values such as our faith in God's love and judgment. Further, we need the Christian understanding of the limitations to what the secular man can do. This is Reinhold Niebuhr's insight, and seems to me valid.

This attempt to realize a freer society, is illustrative of liberty under law, which is a more effective freedom than the allegedly unlimited freedom. The latter is a narrowly restricted freedom of lawlessness. Free competition makes men and institutions plunder one another. It will prevent them from doing what they please. The above social policy is chiefly philosophical and religious. But it is also political, in the sense that government control has to support it. But control through govern-

---

[1] Walter Moberly, *The Crisis in the University,* Student Christian Movement Press, London, 1949, p. 152.
[2] Ralph Barton Perry, *Puritanism and Democracy,* The Vanguard Press, New York, 1944, pp. 512 ff.

mental laws alone cannot distinguish between art and lewdness, science and dogma, education and indoctrination. This depends upon private organizations such as school, family, church, where the control of taste and conscience can be performed.

2. Kinds of Freedom

We have thought of freedom in terms of the realization of the ten different values and also of its positive and negative sides. The meaning of freedom will become clearer if we study it from slightly different angles. First we discover freedom of thought. This, as well as other kinds of freedom which we shall consider, has its negative and positive sides. Clear thinking is impossible unless we are free from indigestion or fatigue. The positive use of this freedom is either meaningful or not, depending upon whether the object of thought is true, beautiful, good, or not. Often we waste our time by dwelling on malice or revenge. Dr. Niebuhr refers to the sensitive individual, whose freedom over history creates indeterminate new possibilities in it, has "a final pinnacle of freedom" where he is able to ask questions about the meaning of life and the historical process itself.[3] Unless the full moral and religious height of the individual's freedom over the community is explored and defended, a high ideal like that of the world community would not be created. From this height he surveys the ages and aspires to "a purity of life" which makes the actual community "a constant source of frustration as well as fulfilment."[4] Here the most important thing is the discernment of the noblest ideal to whose authority the individual should respond through freedom of thought.

When many such ideals are thought about the individual has to choose the best one out of all these. This is freedom of choice. This freedom is best utilized through coherent thought about all the facts and values of human experience.

Third, we have freedom of action. The thinker may have beautiful aspirations. Yet he may be either inactive or hesitant. On the contrary, action which is hasty or devoid of cooperation will result in a failure. Here prudence and cooperation must guide the freedom of action.

[3] Reinhold Niebuhr, *The Children of Light and the Children of Darkness*, Charles Scribner's Sons, New York, 1944, pp. 82 ff.
[4] *Ibid.*, pp. 82 f.

Fourth, there is civil liberty. Ralph Barton Perry says that it has at least five distinct meanings: (1) legal liberty; (2) political liberty; (3) liberties of speech, press, assembly, religion, those rights embraced under the formula of common law rights; (4) those liberties which have to do with allowing individuals and groups to give effective public utterance to their own opinions; (5) the constitutional liberties which limit the powers of the executive and legislative branches of the government. There are several ways in which government may become the enemy of freedom. When it deviates from its public function due to the private self-interest of the ruler; when it is paternalistic toward the people; when it is inefficient; when it is totalitarian; it is the enemy of individual freedom. Moreover, when the altruistic sentiment of the citizen is misused for the sake of the aggressive purposes of the government, his freedom is violated.[5]

Fifth, there is cultural freedom. This is the unhampered activities of science and art, morals and religion. Culture is the medium through which all values are experienced. There should be freedom and harmony in our expression of all the values if we want to be truly cultured.

3. *Freedom, Responsibility, Foresight*

Where there is no freedom there is no responsibility. An automaton is not responsible for what it does. Freedom gives birth to responsibility. The free person has the responsibilities of realizing as many values in his own conscious experience as possible, of improving society with the cooperation of his fellows, and of making as valuable a contribution to the world as he can. As to his responsibility of discerning and obeying the highest and best authority, we shall write later.

All these responsibilities are to be fulfilled in the future. So John Dewey is right when he says that study and foresight are the only roads to free, unimpeded action. Knowledge of present realities and future possibilities is needed for those who want to be efficient in execution through freedom. We do not control the future by using the present. We use the foresight of the future to improve and enlarge present activity. Freedom is actualized by thus using desire, deliberation, and choice. As to the validity of foresight, Dr. Brightman has a fine passage. He says that relatively few correct predictions about the future course of history can be

---

[5] *Ibid.*, pp. 527, 529 ff.

traced to scientists or philosophers; many such are ascribed to saints and prophets, poets and seers, who see things from the perspective of religious values. It is highly probable that the philosophy of history contemplated by religious thinkers, like Reinhold Niebuhr or Herbert Butterfield, is more nearly right than that by secular historians or philosophers. As A. N. Whitehead points out, there can be no preparation for the unknown. Foresight depends upon understanding of as much reality as possible. In practical affairs it is a habit and the product of insight based on coherent thought.[6]

4. *Authority*

Authority is the right to command and enforce obedience. The individual is free to obey some law. Empirically we recognize many authorities. We recognize the authorities of parent, state, church, teacher, Bible, voice of conscience. The authorities of men and institutions are valid only when they represent the ideal values which we have considered. The ten unique values stand for some unique value experiences which are authoritative. Natural values stand for the laws of nature; economic values the laws of economics; bodily values the laws of hygiene; recreational values the laws of fair play; work values the laws of doing our work effectively and with joy; social values the laws of friendship, cooperation and peace; character values the moral laws; esthetic values the laws which govern the experience of enjoying and creating such values; religious values the laws of worship of and cooperation with God. As Dr. Brightman holds, these values coalesce with one another and each of them is unique. So any institution which stands for each one of these values is uniquely authoritative, while we need all the other institutions which represent all the other values. The authority of each institution is in the uniqueness of its value but the coalescence of all these values makes this authority interdependent with all the other institutions embodying other values. For instance, the school stands chiefly for intellectual values, though it stands also for social, religious, bodily, recreational values to a certain extent. The church represents religious values but it should stand for other values which make the church life more meaningful than otherwise.

[6]Edgar S. Brightman, *The Future of Christianity,* The Abingdon Press, New York. Cincinnati, 1937, pp. 27, 118, 113.

Freedom under law is a fuller freedom than the nominally unlimited freedom of lawlessness. Hence the necessity of obeying the authorities of these values. But as Nicolai Hartmann points out, each value tends to dominate all the others. This is its *Wiederhaken*. So there must be law among values as well as disvalues. As religious values are the most coherent of all the values, the latter should eventually be ordered under the supremacy of the former through such character and social values as justice, order, equality, and freedom. This is our social policy and we have already touched on it. But religious values are not entirely free from the danger referred to by Hartmann. Rather the danger is here greater than with any other values, because they are higher and greater authorities. The greater the power, the greater the danger of the misuse of that power. All authority, whatever its function or ulterior purpose, tends to become a vested interest; lust for the power and the emoluments of office tends to grow in proportion to their range and duration.

Another danger we have here is that religious values are, after all, our experiences of laws of God. These experiences may be errors or inadequacies characteristic of all human experiences of values. The church is a human institution, and the Bible includes some human elements which need to be interpreted by its adequate coherence with the rest of human experience. Further, human nature is sinful, in the sense that will-to-power, misuse of power, pride, greed, desire to monopolize the values available to us so as to make our positions secure, will to dominate others, and other sins based on fear, lack of religious faith, and insecurity—all these tend to cause us to use our freedom for wrong purposes. Thus consciously or unconsciously we obey the authorities of disvalues and of the wrong interpretations of the ideal values. Here repentance, prayer, and worship will help. Training in synoptic and coherent thought which will enable us to discern the highest authorities is a help. Training the will power, so that we may be ever definite in devoting ourselves to these authorities can also help us. As Temple writes, "the authority of divine revelation is its capacity to satisfy those aspirations which God has implanted in us." "The authority of God over the soul does not arise from anything external but from the intrinsic nature of God and of the soul —of God as creative, holy love, and of the soul as creative, yet free to respond to love and holiness with willing obedience and with worship." It takes the best insight, the most coherent thought, and the most consecrated will, to be able to see the right relationship between freedom and authority. Some people are good in obeying authority but not so good in discerning the right authority whose command they should obey. Others are good in using their freedom for some good purposes for a short period of time but lack in endurance and consistency. Still others are lacking the will power, so that they change the object of devotion from time to time, as they are tempted to do so by either outward circumstances or by the persuasion of their associates. To use Whitehead's language, sporadic spontaneity is composed of insights thwarting each other. Deeds of freedom must be coherent with one another, with all ideal values and with God. These ideals of God are the right authorities, the commands of which we should obey through free creativity.

5. Practical Considerations

Is Japan freer today than before the past war? Such comparison is not easy. The answer to this question will vary, depending on the particular sense in which present Japan is compared with prewar Japan. The student of philosophy, who does not have enough relevant statistical data on this matter, has to be content with intuitive comparison between the two situations, in terms of the achievement of values on the part of the Japanese people.

From the standpoint of the enjoyment of natural values, Japan is not so free as she used to be, because today she has to get along without Korea, Formosa, the northern and southern islands which used to belong to her. She is more overpopulated today than ever before. The shortage of residences is so acute that some people live in houses where the enjoyment of sunshine, fresh air, and spaciousness is impossible. Japan has no freedom to acquire more natural resources.

About economic values, too, Japan has less freedom today. The amount of these values enjoyed by Japan is about ten times as little as those which America has. Here reasonable guidance on birth control will be a help. The authority of such guidance must be respected by the people through free will; otherwise it will not bring about the desired result.

At present food like rice and sugar is still rationed by the government. Some building material like glass is 1,000 times as expensive as it was in 1945 when the war came to an end. During the past six years, however, the Japanese economy has picked itself up remarkably from the depth of almost total ruin. Last year [1950] agricultural, forestry, and marine production reached the level of the 1934–1936 base years; industrial and mining output went up to ninety-four per cent of that of those years. Some of the credit for this recovery must go to the hard work on the part of the Japanese people. But it must never be forgotten that America has spent 2,000 million dollars for the rehabilitation of Japan during the past six years. Moreover, the American economic aid has also taken the form of goods and materials, in addition to cash.

After all has been said the fact still remains that more than one-fourth of Japan's national wealth was destroyed during the war, and further rehabilitation of this country will not be easy. We have an extremely small middle class and the misuse of economic power on the part of the privileged minority is great. If we are to be freer in realizing economic values, at least three authorities are needed: socialism, democracy, and Christianity. All of these are particularly difficult ideals to realize here, because in the recent past the first two were regarded by the Japanese authorities as dangerous concepts, and today the people know little about them. The third is comparatively powerless in Japan. Each of these concepts has many meanings and the important thing is to grasp the right interpretation of it so that the combination of them may give us the best authority of economic guidance in the months and years to come.

Our enjoyment of bodily values is limited not only by economic conditions but also by unhealthy habits we have. The belief that night air is so bad for health that the bedroom should have all the windows closed is one example of them. We are not so free to enjoy animal proteins and fats, especially dairy products. So the Japanese diet is not well balanced. All this creates a problem.

Poverty restricts the freedom to realize recreational values. Yet within certain limits the situation can be improved through the following considerations. The taste of the people must be so changed that they may come to prefer inexpensive, wholesome recreations enjoyed by all the members of the family to the costly forms of recreation, which are intended exclusively for the father. Government officials and managers of business firms give parties for the alleged purposes of having official consultations or entertaining guests. Such parties serve recreational purposes for these officials and businessmen. They are unnecessarily expensive and should be done away with as much as possible.

For many Japanese people work values are missing. They are unemployed or have to be satisfied with the kind of work they are not interested in. This is true in any country today. Sometimes the situation is so tragic that a radical transformation of the *status quo* is needed. But often that is an impossibility. A safe rule is somehow to get hold of a foothold in society and do one's work there as well as possible. If one happens to be a Christian, he may discern in that work a sense of divine calling.

In the realm of social values Japan has sinned greatly since the Meiji Restoration in 1868. The peace of the Orient and the Pacific area has been disturbed by the policies of militaristic Japan, especially in 1941. The culture of the Japanese people has been notoriously unsociable. The domination of the warrior class, feudalism, excessive devotion to the emperor at the expense of social ties among the citizens themselves, and emphasis placed on reticence and reserve—all this is indicative of the fact that the Japanese people were not free to realize social values.

It is in this realm that Japan is undergoing a revolutionary change in the postwar era. The beginning of this era is characterized by at least three ideals; the renunciation of war; a democratic revolution; and the destruction of the anti-social elements in tradition. Japan's new Constitution declares that sovereignty lies in the people and that the Diet, consisting of representatives elected by the people, is the supreme organ of this sovereignty and the only legislative organ of the state. This is a radical improvement over the old Constitution based on the sovereignty of the emperor. The new Civil Law places more emphasis on the importance of social values than the old one did. The three principles of the latter used to be:

1. Principle of respecting private property (the system of private ownership).
2. Principle of the freedom of the contract (everything can be decided by the contract of only those who are concerned with the contract).
3. Principle of fulfilling one's own responsibility (only those who committed an error are responsible for it and no one else will be held responsible for this error).

This old Constitution has one essential characteristic which is individualism. The new Constitution is characterized by the following three principles:

1. Principle of the welfare of society.

2. Principles of fidelity and sincerity (prohibition of the misuse of privileges is a necessary corollary of these principles).

3. Principle of the sacredness of the individual (the equality of the privileges of the sexes is a corollary of this respect).

The first two principles are society centered, though the third is individualistic. Here there is no contradiction because society consists of individuals whose welfare would be impossible unless they live in good society. The new Constitution aims at the unification of the welfare of society and the individual, of law and morality.

Under the new law we have much more freedom socially. For instance, we are free to abrogate the old system; men and women who have come of age are free to marry without their parents' consent, while the old law required that men under thirty and women under twenty-five should have their parents' approval before they could marry. This newly acquired freedom means that free marriage imposes more responsibility on the individuals concerned.

Through the centuries the Japanese people have been trained to be obedient to the commands of parents, government authorities, emperor. Now that much social freedom has been given them they need to receive special training and discipline. When the old authorities are questioned they are not sure how they could discern the authorities which are valid. They do not know how to avail themselves of new authority. They either are lacking in initiative to use it progressively or misuse it. What is needed here is cultural, moral, philosophical, and religious enlightenment, on which we touched in the first part of this paper. Social values are particularly needed by the Japanese people. Yet as Dr. Brightman writes, social contacts must have values like loveliness, truth, goodness, or God. Kiyoshi Ikeda of Keio University has written a book entitled, *Freedom and Discipline,* in which he describes the life of an English student at the public school, which stands for the happy combination of freedom and discipline. Ikeda says that sportsmanship is almost equivalent to religious faith for the English student. In the spirit of fair play lies the source of the right authority, the command of which the English gentleman obeys through his free will. It is an attitude against taking advantage of unfair handicaps the competitor has. It is the spirit of competing with each other on equal footing. Such a combination of freedom and discipline we Japanese people must emulate if we are to become respectable social beings. The right self-expression rather than reticence, undiscourageable goodwill rather than formality full of anti-social red tape, must characterize the Japanese people of the coming age.

The Japanese have more freedom of speech and of press now than before. A result of this is the appearance of many cheap publications in bookstores and the deliverance of speeches which are lacking in the values of truth, beauty, morality, and religion. What is needed in Japan today is the right guidance of the taste of the people so that they may come to appreciate good books rather than sensational magazines, inspiring speeches rather than utterances appealing merely to the worst in human nature. Freedom in this realm, given suddenly to the people, is dangerous unless there is at the same time such guidance as this.

For one who loves both America and Japan there is an important problem; that is, the realization of a better understanding between the two countries. The kind of social relations which he would like to have realized between them will be those of mutual appreciation and cooperation which can transcend the fluctuating conditions, political, economic, and military. The obstacles to the realization of such ideals are many:

(1) Any human relations are likely to be vitiated by pride, injustice, will-to-dominate, misunderstanding. But between two different countries these sins of human nature are made more unmanageable due to differences in racial, cultural peculiarities.

(2) Superiority or inferiority complexes which are consciously or unconsciously cherished by either the American or the Japanese people aggravate the situation.

(3) Difference in the standards of living makes the problem more complex than otherwise.

(4) The presence in Japan of the authorities of the Occupation Forces and missionaries have made this problem more complicated than otherwise. It is not the American official at GHQ who is proud or paternalistic but the Japanese who is assigned to his office or a Japanese who works closely with the American missionaries that is arrogant toward other Japanese people. This shows that moral education is needed for the Japanese people.

Despite all these obstacles the highminded people in the two countries would like to bring about the above ideals. Japan will remain a poor nation for a long time to come. She should regard it as her special mission to realize these ideals rather than military, imperialistic ambitions. She can understand America better than the Russians can: she can understand Russia better than America can, because economically and culturally Japan finds it easier to appreciate the hard conditions under which Russians live.

Japan stands at a crossroads. Whether she should take the road of the easy going, desperate way of living or the road of such consecration as has just been stated so that she may be something of a mediator between the greatest nations of the world, much depends on the way the Japanese people use their freedom in keeping with the most authoritative ideals of philosophy and religion.

International conferences like the Peace Treaty Conference will take place in the near future. It is the keen aspiration of this writer that those who will represent Japan at these meetings will be men of high character and noble outlook on life. At any rate is it too presumptuous for Japan to aspire to make up for the past sins by becoming the second Israel of God? Should she not try to become a champion of the cause which has been missing in the old Japan more poignantly than anything else?

The cooperation between the nations should not be confined to cultural, social, spiritual relations. There can be free cooperation in the realms of science, philosophy, ideologies in general, and religion. Exchange of ideas and ideals in all these realms is most desirable and worthy of sincere consideration.

At any rate America and Japan may set a new example of breaking the vicious circle of fear, hatred, and misunderstanding, and show it to the world. Today Japan is freer to move in this direction than ever before.

One of the most significant ways in which we can use our freedom is that of "actual organization of the whole experience of value by the will," that is, the achievement of moral values. The Japanese people have been moral chiefly in negative ways. They are good in realizing virtues like submissiveness, reticence, obedience, self-sacrifice, endurance, self-control, generosity. The realization of these negative virtues requires the exercise of the free will. But there are positive and dynamic virtues like adventure, aggressive goodwill, initiative, criticism according to ideals, the power to see it through, devotion to truth, loveliness, goodness, and religion, at the cost of death itself. The Japanese people should train themselves so that they may come to take the initiative to realize these positive ideals. Loyalty to the parents and the emperor was characteristic of them in the past. It is wise to retain this loyalty and yet dedicate this same moral attitude to the object worthy of our supreme loyalty, namely, the Spirit of infinite love and complete justice.

Nicolai Hartmann mentions the value of *Fernstenliebe,* love of the remotest. This is needed by the Japanese people as they set out for the task of the regeneration of Japan. This task will be hard to realize and it will take them a long time to achieve it. Hartmann stresses also the value of the *Schenkende Tugend,* radiant virtue, which is seen in one who is so full of excellent moral values that all those who come near him and have any contact with him will be the recipients of some rare values. Such a virtue also is needed by those who want morally to orient themselves anew.

One of the weaknesses of the Japanese people is that they are apt to say, "It cannot be helped," too soon. This is defeatism which must be gotten rid of through their free will.

Another weakness is that they have had some mean forms of race prejudice against the Chinese, Korean, and Russian peoples. The Sino-Japanese and Russo-Japanese wars, and Japanese imperialism have created these attitudes in the past. This is high time for them to free themselves from such prejudices. Some Japanese people today have lost their former pride and are suffering from the sense of inferiority complex or self-pity or despair. Here the Christian understanding of the divine possibilities of man can help. The Christian view of human nature is paradoxical, in the sense that it is more optimistic about the higher destiny of man and at the same time it takes a more serious view of his sin and evil than any other anthropology.

How about the freedom of realizing esthetic values in Japan today? If one characteristic of the people is to be mentioned that must be one of pure sentiment and genuine appreciation. They are not intellectual, nor religious, but emotional. The scope of Japanese art is small. But there is pathos and luster in it, sweetness and sentimentality about it. These war years and their aftermath have marred and cheapened it. Yet potentially there is a promise in this realm.

About the rehabilitation of Japanese art a few suggestions may be made. First, it should gain the right authority of the beautiful and sublime. In other words, moral and religious values which have been missing in Japanese art, should be introduced into it. Art should not only be attractive and refreshing but also ennobling, so that it might inspire people into resuming their daily tasks with renewed enthusiasm and a nobler outlook on life.

Second, the Japanese are now free to study the academic foundation of Western art, for instance, the musicology which is back of Western music, so that their own art may be less whimsical and more in keeping with the Western standard of artistic scholarship. Japanese art should gain the authority of academic recognition. This does not mean, however, that the simple loveliness of Japanese painting, as well as the pathetic turns and cadences of Japanese music, should be discarded.

Third, this postwar era can provide a rare opportunity of making Japanese art a new creation, in the sense that all the poignant frustrations and humiliating lessons which the Japanese people have learned in this period will color their art, so that it may be a perpetual reminder of this epoch and of the fresh national and ethnic departure which they are determined to take among the ruins of the sinful war.

In the old Japan the people were not able to enjoy intellectual values freely. Provincialism which prevented the free interchange of ideas and ideals, prohibition of critical inquiry, stress placed on blind obedience, the enforcement of too many taboos and secrets concerning the Imperial household and the military tradition—all this tended to inhibit the intellectual faculties of the people. No wonder Japan has produced no great logician or philosopher. Logical clearness, cogency, or coherence should be upheld from this time on rather than emotionalism, Shamanism, or uncritical, unconditional devotion which the Japanese citizens were supposed to have toward the emperor. When Buddhism was introduced to this country, not the more philosophical sects but the comparatively simple and emotionally appealing sects of it were adopted. Once these sects were here the people tended to change them into something still simpler. Nowhere else in the world has Barthianism been appreciated so much as in the Japanese Church. One of the reasons for this seems to be that this theology does not appeal to reason but to love of the unconditionally authoritative. Until quite recently the Japanese teachers of theology and philosophy were not interested in American philosophy, chiefly because they were emotionally against it.

What is needed in Japan is, first of all, intellectual stimulation from the rest of the world so that she may come to remove the shell of academic isolationism. In the second place, she should respond to such stimulus by taking the initiative to carry on scholarly research. In the realm of intellectual values the right authority should be that of clear thinking and logical coherence. Within Japan herself there are some walls of isolationism which prevent the free interchange of ideas and ideals. There is not enough opportunity of having scholars of different universities and institutions come together, so that they may exchange their views. What is taking place in the Conference on Science, Philosophy and Religion sets a good example for the Japanese scholars and government officials.

As the Buddhist philosopher, Hajime Nakamura of Tokyo University, points out, the Japanese people have respected family, nation, patriots who died for the nation, the emperor himself, so that these finite objects have been regarded as if they were supremely valuable. They have not had enough respect for the universal laws of God which transcend these. The Japanese word for God is *"kami."* But it means also many other things such as hair on the head, what is above or superior, the authorities of the government. The authority of the state religion Shinto used to prevent the people from discovering the God of science, philosophy, and universal religion. Today for the first time in the history of Japan the people are truly free to study and discuss the supreme authority of God. Now that Shinto as the state religion is down, the people are free to see that no human grouping has absolute authority. The stability of family, economic order, nation, is rooted in the loyalty of each member to something more sublime than any of these human institutions—the spirit of mercy and judgment, that is, God.

Until the end of the war they did not have the true freedom of belief. They were supposed to believe in Shinto and after that they were free to choose their own religion. But today they have a truer freedom of belief. However, there is one thing which bothers a conscientious believer in Christianity. The government authorities protect it, in the sense that business projects which are in the name of the Christian church are free from tax while Buddhist temples and Shinto shrines are financially handicapped greatly, not having any such privilege. As a result we find some deeply consecrated Buddhist priests and Shinto workers, but some of the Christian ministers do not have such grace. Such regulations will not serve eventually to protect Christianity because this partiality will engender in the Christians the spirit of self-righteousness or of reliance on others. They will become either lazy or degenerate, unless they are humble enough to rededicate themselves to the cause of the Kingdom.

The authority of Christianity lies in the fact that it is more coherent with the facts of experience than any of the Oriental religions which live in Japan. Such authority also depends a good deal upon the way the Japanese Christian lives his religion. Genuine repentance must be his starting point. He is free to become a Christian gentleman who is really helpful and efficient. The first duty of the Christian carpenter is to make good tables. He is free to become a Paul who has moved the course of history. He can be so cooperative with his fellowmen who may be either Buddhists, Shintoists, or Communists, that by inviting them into the fellowship circle of the Christian world he may make them enjoy a unique experience of mercy and usefulness. He may try to take part in politics actively so that eventually this may become a Christian nation. The Church in Japan may be full of weaknesses, but individually the Christians may exert a good influence upon the rest of society. Saving individuals alone will not realize a better society. But the consecrated, radiant, effective Christian can become a beacon to faith in this troubled world.

CONTRIBUTORS TO "FREEDOM AND AUTHORITY IN OUR TIME" *

SWAMI AKHILANANDA, *Ramakrishna Vedanta Society*, Boston

RUDOLF ALLERS, *Graduate School, Georgetown University*, professor of philosophy; author, *Psychology of Character, Self-Improvement, The Successful Error*, and others

GEORGE E. AXTELLE, *School of Education, New York University*, professor of education

DAVID BIDNEY, *Indiana University*, associate professor of anthropology and philosophy; Guggenheim Fellow in anthropology, 1950; author, *The Psychology and Ethics of Spinoza*

BEN ZION BOKSER, *Forest Hills Jewish Center*, rabbi

ADDA BRUEMMER BOZEMAN, *Department of International Relations, Sarah Lawrence College*

EDGAR S. BRIGHTMAN, *Boston University*, Borden Parker Bowne professor of philosophy; Conference on Science, Philosophy and Religion, fellow; author, *A Philosophy of Religion, Nature and Values*, and others

LYMAN BRYSON, *Teachers College, Columbia University*, professor of education; Conference on Science, Philosophy and Religion, first vice president; author, *Science and Freedom*, and others; editor, *The Communication of Ideas*; co-editor, 2nd, 3rd, 4th, 5th, 6th, 7th, 8th, 9th, 10th, 11th, and 12th Conference symposia

KENNETH BURKE, *Bennington College*, course in theory and practice, literary criticism; author, *Counter-Statement, Permanence and Change, Attitudes Toward History, Philosophy of Literary Form, Grammar of Motives, Rhetoric of Motives*, and others; translator of numerous books; contributor to leading magazines

EDMOND N. CAHN, *New York University*, professor of law; *Association of American Law Schools for the Twentieth Century Legal Philosophy Series*, member, editorial committee; *Conference on the Social Meaning of Legal Concepts, New York University*, chairman and editor of its *Proceedings*; contributor to *Annual Survey of American Law*; author, *The Sense of Injustice*

JULIUS COHEN, *College of Law, The University of Nebraska*, professor of law; author, *Materials and Problems on Legislation*

STEWART G. COLE, educational consultant; Conference on Science, Philosophy and Religion, director

W. G. CONSTABLE, *Department of Paintings, Museum of Fine Arts, Boston*, curator; Conference on Science, Philosophy and Religion, director; author, *John Flaxman, English Painting 1500–1700*, and others

THOMAS A. COWAN, *Law School, Wayne University*, professor of law; author, *Readings in Ethics, Administrative Law in Action, Readings in Jurisprudence*

KARL W. DEUTSCH, *Massachusetts Institute of Technology*, associate professor of history; Conference on Science, Philosophy and Religion, fellow

GRAY LANKFORD DORSEY, *School of Law, Washington University*, assistant professor of law; author, "Two Objective Bases for Worldwide Legal Order," in *Ideological Differences and World Order*, edited by F. S. C. Northrop

KERMIT EBY, *The University of Chicago*, associate professor of social sciences; author of pamphlets, *Letters to Dad, Political Primer*, and others; contributor to national, religious, and labor publications

HOXIE N. FAIRCHILD, *Hunter College of the City of New York*, professor of English; Conference on Science, Philosophy and Religion, fellow; author, *The Noble Savage, Toward Belief, Religious Trends in English Poetry*, and others

JAMES K. FEIBLEMAN, *Tulane University*, graduate professor and head of department of philosophy; author, *The Theory of Human Culture, Aesthetics, In Praise of Comedy*, and others

NELS F. S. FERRÉ, *Vanderbilt University*, professor of philosophical theology; author, *The Christian Understanding of God, Christianity and Society,* and others

LOUIS FINKELSTEIN, *The Jewish Theological Seminary of America,* president and Solomon Schechter professor of theology; Conference on Science, Philosophy and Religion, president; co-editor, 2nd, 3rd, 4th, 5th, 6th, 7th, 8th, 9th, 10th, 11th, and 12th Conference symposia

PHILIPP FRANK, *Harvard University,* lecturer on physics and mathematics; *Institute for the Unity of Science,* co-founder and president; Conference on Science, Philosophy and Religion, director; author, *Foundations of Physics, Modern Science and Its Philosophy, Einstein: His Life and Times,* and others

CHARLES FRANKEL, *Columbia University,* associate professor of philosophy; author, *The Faith of Reason;* editor, *Rousseau's Social Contract, Introduction to Contemporary Civilization* (1st edition); contributor to various journals and magazines

JOHN H. E. FRIED, formerly, Special Legal Consultant to the War Crimes Tribunals, Nuremberg

ROYAL M. FRYE, *Simmons College,* professor of physics

ELI GINZBERG, *Columbia University,* associate professor of economics and director, "Conservation of Human Resources" project; author, *The House of Adam Smith, A Pattern for Hospital Care, Occupational Choice—An Approach to a General Theory, Agenda for American Jews,* and others

MARK GRAUBARD, *Graduate School, College of Science, Literature and the Arts, The University of Minnesota,* teacher of the history of science; author, *Man, the Slave and Master, Man's Food, its Rhyme and Reason,* and others, and of many papers on biochemistry

SIMON GREENBERG, *The Jewish Theological Seminary of America,* provost and professor of homiletics; Conference on Science, Philosophy and Religion, director; author, *Ideas and Ideals in the Jewish Prayer Book, The First Year in the Hebrew School: A Teacher's Guide,* and others

LOUIS HARRIS, *Elmo Roper Organization,* research executive

ROBERT C. HARTNETT, S.J. *"America,"* editor-in-chief; author, *Equal Rights for Children, Federal Aid to Education;* editor, America Press pamphlets: "The Right to Educate," "Education for International Understanding"

Charles W. Hendel, *Yale University,* professor of moral philosophy and metaphysics, and chairman of the department; Conference on Science, Philosophy and Religion, director; author, *Jean Jacques Rousseau: Moralist, Citizen of Geneva, Civilization and Religion,* and others

BARNA HORVATH, *The Graduate Faculty of Political and Social Science, The New School for Social Research,* visiting professor; formerly, *Hungarian Academy of Sciences,* member; *The University of Szeged,* professor of law; *The University of Budapest,* lecturer on ethics and on international law

R. GORDON HOXIE, *University of Denver,* assistant professor of history; *Social Science Foundation,* general editor; chairman, University Committee on International Relations Programs; author, *John W. Burgess, American Scholar,* and others

DAVID N. IINO, *International Christian University,* Tokyo, lecturer and assistant to the president; author, several essays; translator of Conference on Science, Philosophy and Religion papers into three Japanese books

F. ERNEST JOHNSON, *Teachers College, Columbia University,* professor emeritus of education; *National Council of Churches of Christ in the United States of America,* executive director, Central Department of Research and Survey, and editor of *"Information Service";* Conference on Science, Philosophy and Religion, director; author, *The Social Gospel Re-Examined;* editor, *World Order: Its Intellectual and Cultural Foundations, Foundations of Democracy, Wellsprings of the American Spirit,* and others

Contributors to "Freedom and Authority in Our Time"

MORTIMER R. KADISH, *Western Reserve University*, assistant professor of philosophy; Rockefeller Foundation, Special Fellowship (to August, 1951); contributor to journals in the field; author, *Point of Honor*

MORDECAI M. KAPLAN, *The Jewish Theological Seminary of America*, professor of philosophies of religion; author, *Judaism in Transition, The Meaning of God in Modern Jewish Religion, The Future of the American Jew*, and others

WILLIAM H. KILPATRICK, *Teachers College, Columbia University*, professor emeritus of education; author, *Foundations of Method, Education for a Changing Civilization, Philosophy of Education*, and others

HANS KOHN, *The College of the City of New York*, professor of history; author, *The Idea of Nationalism, Prophets and Peoples, The Twentieth Century*, and others

LAWRENCE S. KUBIE, M.D., *School of Medicine, Yale University*, clinical professor of psychiatry; *New York Psychoanalytic Institute*, faculty; Committee on Psychiatry, National Research Council, member; author, *Practical and Theoretical Aspects of Psychoanalysis*

DANIEL L. KURSHAN, *Citizens Budget Commission, Inc.*, executive director

JOHN LAFARGE, S.J., *"America,"* associate editor; Conference on Science, Philosophy and Religion, vice president; author, *Interracial Justice, The Race Question and the Negro, No Postponement*, and others

STERLING P. LAMPRECHT, *Amherst College*, professor of philosophy; author, *Our Religious Traditions, Nature and History*

SUSANNE K. LANGER, author, *Philosophy in a New Key*, and others

GEORGE S. LANGROD, *French National Center for Scientific Research*, research director; *University of Sarrebruck*, professor of international law and comparative public administration; *International Academy for Political Science and Constitutional History*, secretary general

DOROTHY D. LEE, *Vassar College*, professor of anthropology

WAYNE A. R. LEYS, *Roosevelt College*, vice president and dean of faculties, professor of philosophy

ROBERT H. LOWIE, *University of California*, professor of anthropology; Conference on Science, Philosophy and Religion, director; author, *The History of Ethnological Theory, The Crow Indians*, and others

R. M. MACIVER, *Columbia University*, Lieber professor emeritus of political philosophy and sociology; Conference on Science, Philosophy and Religion, director; author, *Toward an Abiding Peace, The Web of Government, The More Perfect Union, The Ramparts We Guard*, and others; editor, *Unity and Difference in American Life, Discrimination and National Welfare, Great Expressions of Human Rights, Morals and Loyalties*, and others; co-editor, 4th, 5th, 6th, 7th, 8th, 9th, 10th, 11th, and 12th Conference symposia

JAMES MARSHALL, *Board of Education, City of New York*, member and past president; *New York Bar*, member; United States National Commission for UNESCO, member, 1946–1951; author, *Swords and Symbols: The Technique of Sovereignty, The Freedom to be Free*, and articles on education

RICHARD MCKEON, *The University of Chicago*, distinguished service professor of philosophy and Greek; Conference on Science, Philosophy and Religion, director; author, *The Philosophy of Spinoza*; co-author, editor, and translator of several books, contributor to scientific publications; co-editor, 12th Conference symposium

LOUIS J. A. MERCIER, *Harvard University*, professor emeritus; *Graduate School, Georgetown University*, professor of comparative philosophy and literature, and acting chairman of the department; author, *Mouvement Humaniste aux États Unis, The Challenge of Humanism, American Humanism and the New Age*, and others

WILLIAM PEPPERELL MONTAGUE, *Columbia University*, Johnsonian professor emeritus of philosophy; author, *Religion for the Modern World, The Chances of Surviving Death, The Ways of Things—A Philosophy of Knowledge, Nature and Value*, and others

GLENN NEGLEY, *Duke University*, chairman, department of philosophy; author, *The Organization of Knowledge*, and others

LEO NEJELSKI, *Nejelski and Company, Inc.*, Management Counsels, president

FRANZ L. NEUMANN, *Columbia University*, professor of government

HARRY A. OVERSTREET, *The College of the City of New York*, professor emeritus of philosophy; Conference on Science, Philosophy and Religion, fellow; author, *The Mature Mind, Let Me Think, Our Free Minds*, and others

EDWIN W. PATTERSON, *Columbia University*, Cardozo professor of jurisprudence; author of books on administrative law and insurance law, and of numerous articles on jurisprudence, contracts, and other legal topics

CHAIM PERELMAN, *University of Brussels*, department of logic and metaphysics

LUIS RECASENS-SICHES, *Graduate Faculty, The New School for Social Research*, visiting professor

GEORGE F. ROHRLICH, *United States Social Security Administration*, Division of Program Analysis, Bureau of Old Age and Survivors Insurance

PAUL SCHRECKER, *University of Pennsylvania*, professor of philosophy; author, *Work and History*, and others

ROY WOOD SELLARS, *University of Michigan*, professor emeritus of philosophy; Conference on Science, Philosophy and Religion, director; author, *Religion Coming of Age, The Philosophy of Physical Realism*, and others

HELEN SILVING, *New York Bar*, member; *Office of Alien Property, United States Department of Justice*, attorney; author, articles on law and jurisprudence

ERNEST J. SIMMONS, *Russian Institute* and *Department of Slavic Languages, Columbia University*, professor of Russian literature; *American Slavic and East European Review*, editorial board; author, *English Literature and Culture in Russia*, and others

IGNATIUS SMITH, O.P., *School of Philosophy, Catholic University of America*, dean

T. V. SMITH, *Maxwell School, Syracuse University*, professor of citizenship and philosophy; editor, *International Journal of Ethics*; author, *Atomic Power and Moral Faith*, and others

MARK STARR, *International Ladies' Garment Workers' Union*, educational director; author, various books dealing with labor

ADOLF F. STURMTHAL, *Bard College*, professor of economics; author, *The Tragedy of European Labor, 1918–1939*, and others

KENNETH W. THOMPSON, *College of Liberal Arts, Northwestern University*, department of political science

ROBERT ULICH, *Graduate School of Education, Harvard University*, professor of education; author, *Conditions of Civilized Living, Three Thousand Years of Educational Wisdom, Man and Reality, Crisis and Hope in American Education*, and others

RUPERT B. VANCE, *Institute for Research in Social Science, University of North Carolina*, Kenan professor of sociology; author, *All These People*, and others

GUSTAVE E. VON GRUNEBAUM, *The University of Chicago*, professor of Arabic

GUSTAVE WEIGEL, S.J., *Woodstock College*, professor of ecclesiology

JULIAN L. WOODWARD, *Elmo Roper Organization*, research executive; American Association for Public Opinion Research, president, 1950

QUINCY WRIGHT, *The University of Chicago*, professor of international law; author, *The Control of American Foreign Relations, A Study of War*, and others

*Positions as of September, 1951

Program

"FREEDOM AND AUTHORITY"

TWELFTH CONFERENCE ON SCIENCE, PHILOSOPHY AND RELIGION IN THEIR RELATION TO THE DEMOCRATIC WAY OF LIFE

TUESDAY, WEDNESDAY, THURSDAY, AND FRIDAY
SEPTEMBER 4, 5, 6, and 7, 1951
NEW YORK CITY

All sessions will be held at The Men's Faculty Club of Columbia University, 400 West 117th Street

TUESDAY, SEPTEMBER 4th

6:00 p.m.
Dinner meeting of Conference Fellows, the Chairmen and Co-chairmen
Main Room, 3rd floor

To help integrate the Conference discussion, Professor Lyman Bryson and Professor R. M. MacIver will serve as chairmen at each session, with a co-chairman.

8:30 p.m.

SECTIONAL MEETINGS[1]

DEFINITION OF FREEDOM AND OF AUTHORITY

Contributors

THURSTON N. DAVIS, S.J., *Co-chairman*
ARTHUR E. MURPHY, *Discussant*
RUDOLF ALLERS
SIMON GREENBERG
F. ERNEST JOHNSON
MORTIMER R. KADISH
JOHN LaFARGE, S.J.
STERLING P. LAMPRECHT
LOUIS J. A. MERCIER
WILLIAM P. MONTAGUE
PAUL SCHRECKER
ROBERT ULICH

Gustave E. von Grunebaum
Gustave Weigel, S.J.

Lounge, 2nd floor

POSTULATES OF THEORIES OF FREEDOM AND AUTHORITY

Contributors

William F. Albright, *Co-chairman*
Theodore Brameld, *Discussant*
Justin Wroe Nixon, *Discussant*
Anton C. Pegis, *Discussant*
Ben Zion Bokser
Edgar S. Brightman
Nels F. S. Ferré
Charles Frankel
John H. E. Fried
Charles W. Hendel
Mordecai M. Kaplan
Moorhouse I. X. Millar, S.J.
John Courtney Murray, S.J.
Franz L. Neumann
Gerald B. Phelan

Long Room, 3rd floor

FREEDOM AND AUTHORITY AS CULTURAL AND SOCIAL PHENOMENA

Contributors

Harlow Shapley, *Co-chairman*
Sigmund Timberg, *Discussant*
David Bidney
Kenneth Burke
W. G. Constable
Karl W. Deutsch
Gray L. Dorsey
James K. Feibleman
Philipp Frank
Eli Ginzberg
Mark Graubard
Charles S. Johnson
William H. Kilpatrick

Lawrence S. Kubie
Dorothy D. Lee
Rupert B. Vance

                        Entertainment Room, 2nd floor

FREEDOM AND LEGAL AUTHORITY

Contributors

Alan M. Stroock, *Co-chairman*
Ordway Tead, *Discussant*
Edmond N. Cahn
Julius Cohen
Harold D. Lasswell
Karl N. Llewellyn
Glenn R. Negley
Edwin W. Patterson
Helen Silving

                        West Room, 3rd floor

FREEDOM AND GOVERNMENTAL AUTHORITY, NATIONAL AND INTERNATIONAL

Contributors

Norman Cousins, *Co-chairman*
Harry L. Case, *Discussant*
Richard H. Heindel, *Discussant*
Ben M. Cherrington
R. Gordon Hoxie
Hans Kohn
Susanne K. Langer
George S. Langrod
Luis Recasens-Siches
Roy W. Sellars
Ernest J. Simmons
T. V. Smith
Quincy Wright

                      North end, Main Room, 3rd floor

FREEDOM AND AUTHORITY IN PRACTICAL LIFE

Contributors

Harry J. Carman, *Co-chairman*
Michael A. Heilperin, *Discussant*

Lewis L. Lorwin, *Discussant*
Lyman Bryson
Kermit Eby
Louis Harris
James Marshall
Leo Nejelski
Harry A. Overstreet
George F. Rohrlich
Francis H. Russell
Mark Starr
Adolf F. Sturmthal
Julian L. Woodward

South end, Main Room, 3rd floor

WEDNESDAY, SEPTEMBER 5th

10:00 a.m.

SECTIONAL MEETINGS (Continued)

2:30 p.m.

GENERAL SESSION

Thurston N. Davis, S.J., *Co-chairman*

Discussion of[1]

DEFINITION OF FREEDOM AND OF AUTHORITY

based on papers by

Rudolf Allers
Simon Greenberg
F. Ernest Johnson
Mortimer R. Kadish
John LaFarge, S.J.
Sterling P. Lamprecht
Louis J. A. Mercier
William P. Montague
Paul Schrecker
Robert Ulich
Gustave E. von Grunebaum
Gustave Weigel, S.J.

Prepared discussant

Arthur E. Murphy

Main Room, 3rd floor

Program

4:00 p.m.

GENERAL SESSION

William F. Albright, *Co-chairman*

Discussion of[1]

POSTULATES OF THEORIES OF FREEDOM AND AUTHORITY

based on papers by

Ben Zion Bokser
Edgar S. Brightman
Nels F. S. Ferré
Charles Frankel
John H. E. Fried[3]
Charles W. Hendel
Mordecai M. Kaplan
Franz L. Neumann
Gerald B. Phelan[3]

Prepared discussants

Theodore Brameld
Justin Wroe Nixon
Anton C. Pegis

Main Room, 3rd floor

8:30 p.m.

GENERAL SESSION

Harlow Shapley, *Co-chairman*

Discussion of[1]

FREEDOM AND AUTHORITY AS CULTURAL AND SOCIAL PHENOMENA

based on papers by

David Bidney
Kenneth Burke
W. G. Constable
Karl W. Deutsch
Gray L. Dorsey
James K. Feibleman
Philipp Frank

Eli Ginzberg
Mark Graubard
Charles S. Johnson[3]
William H. Kilpatrick
Lawrence S. Kubie
Dorothy D. Lee
Rupert B. Vance

Prepared discussant

Sigmund Timberg

Main Room, 3rd floor

THURSDAY, SEPTEMBER 6th

8:30 a.m.

Breakfast business meeting of the members of the Conference on Science, Philosophy and Religion, to transact necessary business of the corporation, including election of officers and new members.

Dining Room, 4th floor

10:00 a.m.

GENERAL SESSION

Discussion of[1]

FREEDOM AND AUTHORITY AS CULTURAL AND SOCIAL PHENOMENA

(Continued)

Main Room, 3rd floor

11:00 a.m.

GENERAL SESSION

Alan M. Stroock, *Co-chairman*

Discussion of[1]

FREEDOM AND LEGAL AUTHORITY

based on papers by

Edmond N. Cahn
Julius Cohen
Harold D. Lasswell[3]
Karl N. Llewellyn[3]
Glenn R. Negley

Edwin W. Patterson
Helen Silving

Prepared discussant

Ordway Tead

Main Room, 3rd floor

2:30 p.m.

GENERAL SESSION

Norman Cousins, *Co-chairman*

Discussion of[1]

**FREEDOM AND GOVERNMENTAL AUTHORITY
NATIONAL AND INTERNATIONAL**

based on papers by

Ben M. Cherrington[2,3]
R. Gordon Hoxie[2,3]
Hans Kohn
Susanne K. Langer
George S. Langrod
Luis Recasens-Siches
Roy W. Sellars
Ernest J. Simmons
T. V. Smith
Quincy Wright

Prepared discussants

Harry L. Case
Richard H. Heindel

Main Room, 3rd floor

8:30 p.m.

GENERAL SESSION

Harry J. Carman, *Co-chairman*

Discussion of[1]

FREEDOM AND AUTHORITY IN PRACTICAL LIFE

based on papers by

Lyman Bryson
Kermit Eby

Louis Harris[2]
James Marshall
Leo Nejelski[3]
Harry A. Overstreet
George F. Rohrlich
Francis H. Russell[3]
Mark Starr
Adolf F. Sturmthal
Julian L. Woodward[2]

Prepared discussants

Michael A. Heilperin
Lewis L. Lorwin

Main Room, 3rd floor

FRIDAY, SEPTEMBER 7th

10:00 a.m.

Critique of the Conference on Science, Philosophy and Religion, with special reference to the twelfth annual meeting and plans for the future.

Main Room, 3rd floor

[1]Papers available in mimeographed form. All oral discussion off the record.
[2]In collaboration.
[3]Text not received before program in press.

PARTICIPANTS IN PROGRAM*

Swami Akhilananda, *Ramakrishna Vedanta Society, Boston*
William F. Albright, *The Johns Hopkins University*
Rudolf Allers, *Graduate School, Georgetown University*
Hannah Arendt, *Jewish Cultural Reconstruction, Inc.*
George E. Axtelle, *School of Education, New York University*
David Bidney, *Indiana University*
Ben Zion Bokser, *Forest Hills Jewish Center*
Stephen Borsody, *Pennsylvania College for Women*
Adda B. Bozeman, *Sarah Lawrence College*
Theodore Brameld, *New York University*
Edgar S. Brightman, *Boston University*
Lyman Bryson, *Teachers College, Columbia University*
Ludlow Bull, *Metropolitan Museum of Art*
Kenneth Burke, *Bennington College*
Edmond N. Cahn, *New York University*
Harry J. Carman, *Columbia College, Columbia University*

Program

Harry L. Case, *Tennessee Valley Authority*
Edward A. Cerny, S.S., *St. Mary's Seminary*
Ben M. Cherrington, *Social Science Foundation, University of Denver*
Julius Cohen, *College of Law, The University of Nebraska*
Stewart G. Cole
W. G. Constable, *Museum of Fine Arts, Boston*
Norman Cousins, *"The Saturday Review of Literature"*
Thomas A. Cowan, *Law School, Wayne University*
Thurston N. Davis, S.J., *Fordham College, Fordham University*
Henry S. Dennison, *Dennison Manufacturing Company*
Karl W. Deutsch, *Massachusetts Institute of Technology*
Gray L. Dorsey, *Washington University*
Kermit Eby, *The University of Chicago*
Hoxie N. Fairchild, *Hunter College of the City of New York*
Allan P. Farrell, S.J., *University of Detroit*
James K. Feibleman, *Tulane University*
Nels F. S. Ferré, *Vanderbilt University*
Louis Finkelstein, *The Jewish Theological Seminary of America*
Philipp Frank, *Harvard University*
Charles Frankel, *Columbia University*
John H. E. Fried, *United Nations*
Royal M. Frye, *Simmons College*
Eli Ginzberg, *Columbia University*
Mark Graubard, *College of Science, Literature and the Arts, The University of Minnesota*
Simon Greenberg, *The Jewish Theological Seminary of America*
Feliks Gross, *Institute of International Affairs, University of Wyoming*
Louis Harris, *Elmo Roper Organization*
C. P. Haskins, *Union College*
Michael A. Heilperin
Richard H. Heindel, *United States Department of State*
Charles W. Hendel, *Yale University*
Hudson Hoagland, *Worcester Foundation for Experimental Biology*
John S. Hollister, *Institute of International Education*
Barna Horvath, *The New School for Social Research*
R. Gordon Hoxie, *Social Science Foundation, University of Denver*
Arno G. Huth, *The New School for Social Research*
Oscar I. Janowsky, *The College of the City of New York*
Charles S. Johnson, *Fisk University*
F. Ernest Johnson, *Teachers College, Columbia University*
Mortimer R. Kadish, *Western Reserve University*
Horace M. Kallen, *The New School for Social Research*
Mordecai M. Kaplan, *The Jewish Theological Seminary of America*
William H. Kilpatrick, *Teachers College, Columbia University*
Hans Kohn, *The College of the City of New York*
Lawrence S. Kubie, *School of Medicine, Yale University*
Daniel L. Kurshan, *Citizens Budget Commission, Inc.*
John LaFarge, S.J., *"America"*
Sterling P. Lamprecht, *Amherst College*
Susanne K. Langer, *Northwestern University*
George S. Langrod, *French National Center for Scientific Research*

Harold D. Lasswell, *School of Law, Yale University*
Dorothy D. Lee, *Vassar College*
Wayne A. R. Leys, *Roosevelt College*
Clem C. Linnenberg, Jr., *United States Department of Commerce*
Karl N. Llewellyn, *The Law School, The University of Chicago*
Alain L. Locke, *Howard University*
Lewis L. Lorwin, *United States Department of Commerce*
Robert H. Lowie, *University of California*
R. M. MacIver, *Columbia University*
Simon Marcson, *United Nations*
Jacques Maritain, *Princeton University*
James Marshall, *Board of Education, City of New York*
Eric Mendelsohn, *American Institute of Architecture*
Louis J. A. Mercier, *Graduate School, Georgetown University*
Moorhouse I. X. Millar, S.J., *Fordham University*
William P. Montague, *Columbia University*
Glenn R. Morrow, *University of Pennsylvania*
Arthur E. Murphy, *Sage School of Philosophy, Cornell University*
John Courtney Murray, S.J., *Woodstock College*
Glenn Negley, *Duke University*
Leo Nejelski, *Nejelski and Company, Inc.*
Franz L. Neumann, *Columbia University*
Justin Wroe Nixon, *Colgate-Rochester Divinity School*
J. Robert Oppenheimer, *Institute for Advanced Study*
Harry A. Overstreet, *The College of the City of New York*
Edwin W. Patterson, *Columbia University*
Anton C. Pegis, *Pontifical Institute of Mediaeval Studies*
Gerald B. Phelan, *The Mediaeval Institute, University of Notre Dame*
Arthur Upham Pope, *The Asia Institute*
I. I. Rabi, *Columbia University*
Luis Recasens-Siches, *The New School for Social Research*
Lincoln Reis
George F. Rohrlich, *United States Social Security Administration*
Elmo Roper
Joseph S. Roucek, *University of Bridgeport*
Beardsley Ruml
Francis H. Russell, *United States State Department*
Harold K. Schilling, *Pennsylvania State College*
Paul Schrecker, *University of Pennsylvania*
Herbert L. Seamans, *National Conference of Christians and Jews*
Roy W. Sellars, *University of Michigan*
Harlow Shapley, *Harvard University*
Helen Silving
Ernest J. Simmons, *Columbia University*
Robert J. Slavin, O.P., *Providence College*
Harry Slochower, *Brooklyn College*
Ignatius Smith, O.P., *School of Philosophy, Catholic University of America*
T. V. Smith, *Maxwell School, Syracuse University*
Ralph B. Spence, *Teachers College, Columbia University*
Mark Starr, *International Ladies' Garment Workers' Union*

Donald C. Stone, *Economic Cooperation Administration*
Alan M. Stroock, *The Jewish Theological Seminary of America*
Adolf F. Sturmthal, *Bard College*
Harry Tarter, *The College of the City of New York*
Ordway Tead, *Board of Higher Education, City of New York*
Kenneth W. Thompson, *College of Liberal Arts, Northwestern University*
Sigmund Timberg, *United States Department of Justice*
Robert Ulich, *Graduate School of Education, Harvard University*
Rupert B. Vance, *University of North Carolina*
Gustave E. von Grunebaum, *The University of Chicago*
Helen Hiett Waller, *"New York Herald Tribune"*
Theodore Waller, *United World Federalists, Inc.*
Gerald G. Walsh, S.J., *Fordham University*
Gustave Weigel, S.J., *Woodstock College*
M. L. Wilson, *United States Department of Agriculture*
Louis Wirth, *The University of Chicago*
Julian L. Woodward, *Elmo Roper Organization*
Quincy Wright, *The University of Chicago*

*Writers of papers and comments, and those expected to attend, as of August 24th.

Index

Abraham, 265
Absolutism, in philosophy, 420-430
Academies of art, 378
Acceptance, 8, 387
Acheson, Dean, 175, quoted, 509-510, 511-515, 517
Action:
 human, 448
 man's need of, 577-580
Acton, Lord, 564-565, 569
Actuality, 598-600
Address to Young Men on the Right Use of Greek Literature (Saint Basil), 677
Administration:
 and authority, 13, 16
 and policy choice, 36-37
 and policy-making, 18
 and responsibility, 15
 and trust, 15
 by experts, 22
 checking by, 20
 direction of morale, 37
 function of, 27, 38
 training for, 13
Advice:
 function of, 28-29
 theory of, 27
Advisory committees:
 of UNESCO, 20
 on vocational education in the United States, 20
Agape, 492-494
Agency, 599 ff.
Aggression, and the United Nations, 177
Akhilananda, Swami, comments by, 478-479, 490, 504, 549-550, 571-572, 646, 685
Alien and Sedition Acts, 690
Allegiance, and citizenship, 267
Allers, Rudolf, 555
 comments by, 10, 145, 213, 391, 430-431, 479, 550, 685-686, 697-698
Althusius, Johannes, 523
Altruism, 488
 and masochism, 695
America, South, 357
American Association of University Professors, 408
American character, 2-3, 7, 87

American Civil Liberties Union, 88
American Economic Association, 68
American Federation of Labor, 54, 58, 65, 68, 71, 75
 Labor's League for Political Education, 79
American Revolution, 127, 543, 687
Anaxagoras, 395
Ancien régime, 560
Angell, James, 133
Anselm, Saint, 567
Anytus, 396
Appraisal, of performance, 21-22
Aquinas, Saint Thomas, 482-483, 556, 610-611, 614-615, 715-716
Aristotle, 17, 123, 182-183, 228, 292, 301, 442, 448, 479, 582, 618-619, 648, 672-673, 681-682, 704
Armies, internationalization of, 143
Art:
 and democracy, 381-383
 decadent, 380-381
 elements of a work of, 377
 in modern times, 379-380
 in Russia, 156-157
 totalitarian, 380-381, 383
Articles of Confederation, 688
Arts, The:
 censorship, 380-383
 problems of freedom and authority in, 377-383
Asceticism, 695
Aseity, 197
Aspasia, 395
Atheism, monistic doctrine, 618-621
Athens, 650
Augustine, Saint, 564, 598, 674, 698, 705, 707
Augustus, Emperor, 676
Austin, John, 230, 231, 241
Attorney General, (U.S.), 4
Authoritarian personality, 1
Authoritarianism, in America, 3-4
Authority, 1, 16 ff.
 absolute, 527
 absolute, versus absolute freedom, 301-306
 and administration, 13
 and choice, 171

749

Authority (Cont.)
  and empirical philosophy, 420-421
  and force, 229
  and freedom, 159-167, 485-490, 491-504, 577-594, 607-622
  and freedom and orthodoxy, 419-439
  and freedom as functions of beliefs about values, 473-474
  and freedom as functions of civilization, 507-541
  and freedom in institutions, 494
  and freedom in structure of cultures, 309-316
  and good life, 95, 101
  and leadership, 13
  and personal freedom, 109-118, 137-146
  and power, 144, 297-301
  and responsibility, 201-215
  and state, 191
  as ambivalent ideal, 183
  as existential category, 680
  as institutional, 676
  as integral to culture, 335-344
  as legitimate power, 346
  as personal, 675
  as strategy of deference, 282
  as system of norms, 318-326
  as transcendent, 676, 685
  as validation of power, 461
  based on property rights, 53
  civil, and freedom of thought and will, 613-616
  command, 511-512, 516
  concept in Russia, 147-157
  concept of, 294, 304-305
  conflict with freedom, 322-323
  confusion with orthodoxy, 431-432
  defined, 297, 377-380, 474, 604-605, 638
  delegation of, 16
  derived from United Nations, 515-516
  difference between military and political, 512
  distributive scheme, 218
  educational, 497-498, 671
  end of, 602-604
  familial, 495-496, 588-590
  forces of, 580 ff.
  formulation of, 318-321
  four kinds, 231, 235
  freedom through, 641

Authority (Cont.)
  functioning of, 322-324
  governmental, 499-502
  harmony with freedom, 191, 197-198
  identity with freedom, 367
  in Greek culture, 340-341
  in growth of social groups, 271-288
  in industry, 45-51, 53
  in international relations, 103-108, 169-182
  in labor unions, 63-77
  in pre-British Burma, 338-340
  in prospect, 129-135
  in realization of values, 717-732
  in realm of poetic imagination, 365-375
  in relation to psychiatry, 385-391
  in retrospect, 121-128
  in social structure, 345-352
  in Tiv culture, 341-343
  in United States, 508 ff.
  intellectual and political, 659-669
  justification, 296
  legal, 222, 225-235
  legitimate, 614
  liberty and, constitutional aspects, 687-693
  lines of, 16-17
  meaning, 660
  moral, and legal imperative, 237-251
  necessity to freedom, 317-333
  need for a theory of, 507 ff.
  of physical law, 581-583
  of public opinion, 590
  of social heritage, 585-586
  of state, 587-588
  over man's body, 584-585
  over man's mind, 583-584
  persecution as pathology of, 393
  personal, 232
  political, 232, 513
  problem of, in cultural perspective, 289-307
  problems in the arts, 377-383
  relation of law to, 217-223
  religious, 496-497, 592
  role of, in interpretation of science, 361-363
  supernatural, 593-594
  supranational, 324-333
  traditional, 233

Index

Autonomy:
  and feedback of data from observation, 274-275
  and inner communication, 273-274
  and power, 284
  and theonomy, 473-483
  defined, 475
  in growth of social groups, 271-288
  social, 635-636
  structure, 272
Auzâ'i, 704
Axiology, 473
Axtelle, George E., comment by, 417-418

Babbitt, Irving, 612
Bacon, Francis, 604
Bakunin, Mikhail, 448
Barère, Bertrand, 256
Barthianism, 730
Baudelaire, Charles, 651
Beccaria, Cesare, 125
Becker, Carl, 134
Bellarmine, Cardinal, 398
Bergson, Henri, 164, 195, 572
Berkeley, George, 583
Bentham, Jeremy, 127, 207, 218, 227, 229, 241
Bevin, Ernest, 57, 356
Bidney, David, 289
"Big Business," 62, 64
"Big Labor," 64
Bill of rights, 170, 191, 451
Bill of rights, international, 655
Bill of Rights (U.S.), 444
Black Death, 140-141
Black, Hugo, 207, 214
Blackstone, Sir William, 241
Blanshard, Paul, 690
Boas, Franz, quoted, 289, 290, 306
Bodin, Jean, 519-524, 534
Boehme, Jacob, 682
Bokser, Ben Zion, 485
Bolshevism, labor program of, 55
Bonn government, 355
Borodino, battle of, 14
Bowdler, Thomas, 382
Bozeman, Adda Bruenner, comment by, 145-146
Brightman, Edgar S., 473, 720-721, 726
  comments by, 25, 85, 118, 333, 360, 432-

Brightman, Edgar S. (*Cont.*)
  433, 504, 550-551, 572, 606, 622, 636-637, 686
British Empire, 706
Brooke, Sir Alan, 16
Brotherhood of Railway and Steamship Clerks, 72
Brun of Querfurt, 705
Bruno, Giordano, 314, 399-401
Bryson, Lyman, 27, 315
Buchenwald, 6
Buddhism, 695, 730
Burgess, John, 128, quoted, 131
Burke, Edmund, 282
Burke, Kenneth, 365
Burma, 337-340
Butler, Nicholas Murray, 128-129
Butterfield, Herbert, 721
Byzantium, 681

Cahn, Edmond N., 201
Cain, 550
Caliphs, orthodox, 714
Calvin, John, 544, 606, 674, 698
Calvinism, 653, 656
  as ideology, 196, 198
Calvin's Case, 253
Campanella, Tommaso, 398
Caravaggio, Michelangelo, 379
Cardozo, Benjamin, 238
Carr, E. H., 150
Carracci, Annibale, 379
Cartesian compromise, 627
Castelli, Father, 397
Catholic Encyclopedia, 611
Catholicism, 344, 548-549, 552, 610, 617-618, 663-665, 667, 690, 695-696, 699, 714
Causation, law of, and moral freedom, 413
Censorship, in the arts, 380-383
Chamberlain, Houston, 406
Chaucer, Geoffrey, 125
Checking, by administration, 20
Child labor, 140
China, 337
Choice, 402-412, 579
  and authority, 171
  and free will, 109-110
  and freedom, 169
  and man's destiny, 597
  and scientific determinism, 413-415

Index

Choice (Cont.)
  freedom located in, 623 ff.
  in moral judgments, 425, 429-430, 434-435
  possibility of, 625-631, 633-634
Christ, 124, 165
Christianity, 442, 681, 685, 695-696, 698-699, 709, 714, 718, 724, 729-732
Christman, 397
Church, 124, 496-497, 504
  and state, 617-618
  good will and, 10
  power and authority of, 349
Cicero, 442-443, 450, 544
Citizenship:
  and allegiance, 267
  and freedom, 253
  as institution of public law, 263
  consensual, 260
  meaning, 254
  methods of acquiring, 266-267
Civilization:
  freedom and authority as functions of, 507-541
  freedom of, 647-657
Civil War (U.S.), 142
Clavio of Rome, 397
Cleisthenes, 123
Clement VII, 403
Clovis, 617
Codetermination (see Workers' Control)
Cohen, Julius, 217
Cohen, Morris, 246
Cole, G. D. H., 76
Cole, Stewart G., comments by, 551-552, 698-699
Command, lines of, 16
Commission on Human Rights, 452
Communication:
  and authority, 282
  in industry, 50
  in self-governing organizations, 271-288
  inner, and autonomy, 273-274
Communism, 6, 104, 107, 127, 163, 165-167, 186, 193, 356, 405-406, 408, 413, 467-471, 546, 551, 620, 662
  as religion, 357
  culture of, 299-301, 303
  distinguished from Marxism, 195
  in United States, 3-4, 88, 90-91
  Russian, 147-157

Communist Manifesto (Marx and Engels), 319, 328, 354-355
Communist Party, 198-199
  in Russia, 151-157
Communists:
  and human rights, 88
  indiscriminate labeling, 9
Competition:
  in industry, 46-47
  in world of affairs, 33 ff.
  new forms in business, 63
Compulsion, 389-390, 486-487
Conatus, 193
Concluding Unscientific Postscript (Kierkegaard), 671
Conditions of Progress (Hughes), 676
Conformity:
  and freedom, 2-4
  and security, 2
Congress of Industrial Organizations, 65, 68, 71, 75
  Political Action Committee, 79, 81, 91
Congress (U.S.), 688
  administration by, 18
  and security, 2
  immunity of, 6
  investigating committees, 2
Consciousness, and initiative, 276-277
Conseil Économique, 60
Consent, principle of, 487
Constable, William G., 377
Constituencies:
  and form of government, 41
  in policy-making, 39-40
Constitution (Japan), 725-726
Constitution (U.S.), 170, 301, 508, 591, 657, 688
Constitutional Convention (1787), 121
Constitutionalism, 191
  and liberty and authority, 687-693
Contingency, of natural events and freedom, 598
Contract, theory of, 531 ff.
Cooperation, 8
Copernican system, 361-363, 397-398
Copernicus, 402-404
Courts, and freedom, 171-172
Cowan, Thomas A., comment by, 221-222
Cremonius, Cesare, 397
Crime, involving moral turpitude, 204-213
Cromwell, Oliver, 527

Index

Cultural perspective, problem of freedom and authority in, 289-307
Culture:
  and education, 313-314
  and individual value, 113
  and inquiry, 314-315
  and tolerance, 314
  defined, 310
  fate of, 8
  freedom and authority integral to, 335-344
  hostility and, 8
  life relationships and, 8
  meaning for man, 114-115
  structure of, 309-316
  totalitarian, 298-301
  Western, 6, 103-108, 295, 416, 463
Czechoslovakia, 413

D'Alembert, Jean, 431
Dante, 125
Darwinism, 619
Da Vinci, Leonardo, 187
Decision-action process, 29-30
Decision-making process, 27 ff.
  alternative choices, 33
  and constituencies, 39-40
  competition in, 32
  morals and, 32
Declaration of Independence, 133, 561, 616, 656, 688
Declaration of Rights of Man, 253, 561
De Gré, Gerard, 348, quoted, 349
Deism, 612, 619
De liberorum educatione (Silvio), 677
Democracy, 9, 30, 304, 348, 350, 455-456, 463, 471-472, 500-501, 505, 543, 551, 568-569
  and communism, 331-332
  and free constituency, 41
  and living conditions, 170
  and metaphysical absolutism, 420
  and neo-liberalism, 196
  goals of work in, 358-360
  in the United States, 92-93
  international, 326-333
  Russian concept, 149-151, 153 ff.
Democratic innocence, 1
Democratic Party (U.S.), 80
  and labor, 82-84

Demokratia, 123
Denaturalization, 264-265
Department of Labor (U.S.), 76
Department of State (U.S.), 174
Depression:
  and *laissez-faire*, 353-354
  Great, 129, 355, 546
Determinism, 578, 623-627, 638
  and free will, 110-111
  historical, 459
Deutsch, Karl W., 271
  comment by, 552
Dewey, John, 129, quoted, 131, 218, 230, 720
Dialectical complementation, 681-686
Dialectics, 573
Dickinson, John, 238
Dignity:
  human, an end, 192, 196-197
  of man, 111-112
Directory of Labor Unions, 64
Discourse on Political Economy (Rousseau), 293-294
Discourse on the Origin of Inequality (Rousseau), 292
Discrimination, in higher education, 89
Distribution, in national economy, 97-98
Distributive scheme, of freedom and authority, 218
Dominance, 8
Dorsey, Gray Lankford, 317
Dostoyevsky, Feodor, 105, quoted, 148, 470
Douglas, William, 227
Dualism, 607-618, 621-622
Duccio, 379
Dynamism, 626-627

Eby, Kermit, 79
Ecclesiastes, 213
Economic Cooperation Administration, 175
Education:
  and culture, 313-314
  as existential category, 690
  freedom and authority in, 677
  in United States, 692-693
  institutional, 678-679
  personal, 677-678
  transcendent, 679
Egypt, 715
Einstein, Albert, 314, 361-362
Eisenhower, Dwight, 15

Eleutheria, 706
Eliezer, Rabbi, 201
Elijah, 202
Emerson, Ralph Waldo, 314, 675
Empiricism, 420-430
  utilitarian and pragmatic emphasis, 422
Encyclopedists, 125
Engels, Friedrich, 151, 299, 302, quoted, 319
England, 261-262, 264, 268, 706
Enlightenment, 193-194, 651
Ent, Doctor, quoted, 404
Epictetus, 545
Epicurus, 445
Equality, 1
  and leadership, 188
  as mean, 183-184, 189
  methodological, and functional idealism, 183-189
  myth of, 188
  under socialism, 165
Erasmus, 674
Escape from Freedom (Fromm), 2
Essai (Gobineau), 406
Ethelbert, 233
Ethics, and politics, 191
Evolution (J. Huxley), quoted, 559
Ewige-Student, 387
Execution, function of, 28
Existentialism, 573-575, 675, 686
  Christian, 197-198
Experience, and moral values, 220
Experts:
  and policy-makers, 27-28
  as advisors, 28 ff.
  functions in administration, 22
  related to problems, 30-31, 38
  services to public relations of firms, 39

Fabians, 56-57
Fair international order, 455-458
Fair social order, 455-458
Fair state, 455-456
Fair trade price, 63
Fairchild, Hoxie N., comments by, 10-11, 189-190, 479-480
Faith, and authority, 388
Family, 495-496
  and authority, 588-590
  power and authority of, 349
Fârâbî, Al, 713

Fascism, 1, 6, 104, 448, 467-468, 470-471
  as ideology, 194-195
Fear, and social security, 100-101
Federal Council of Churches (1947), 241
Federalism (U.S.), 687 ff.
Federalist Papers, 689
Feibleman, James K., 309
Ferré, Nels F. S., 491
  comments by, 85, 250, 344, 490, 552, 637, 666-667
Feudalism, 465
Fichte, Johann, 448
Firth, Raymond, 336
Flaubert, Gustave, 651
Force, and authority, 230, 580 ff.
Forcellini, 660
Ford, Henry, 659
Formosa, 723
Fortune survey, 92
Founding Fathers, 301
Four Freedoms, 130, 169
Fraenkel, Ernest, 242
Fra Lippo Lippi, 156
France, 262, 264, 267, 674
Franco, Francisco, 107
Frank, Philipp, 361
Frankel, Charles, 419
Frankfurter, Felix, 207, 214
Franklin, Benjamin, 125
Freedom:
  absolute, versus absolute authority, 301-306
  ancient, 123-124
  and authority, 485-490, 491-504, 577-594, 607-622
  and authority and orthodoxy, 419-439
  and authority as functions of beliefs about values, 473-474
  and authority as functions of civilization, 509-541
  and authority in institutions, 494
  and authority in structure of cultures, 309-316
  and citizenship, 253
  and conformity, 2
  and contingency of natural events, 598, 603-604
  and ecology, 161
  and equality, 183-184
  and fraternity, 183-184
  and idealism, 188-189

Freedom (*Cont.*)
  and law, 171-172
  and legal authority, 225-235
  and liberalism, 197-198
  and responsibility, 720
  and security, 104
  and value, 170
  and work, 353-360
  as ambivalent ideal, 183
  as existential category, 680
  as gift of God, 475
  as institutional, 673-674
  as integral to culture, 335-344
  as moral experience, 544, 550
  as personal, 672-673
  as range of choices, 281
  as relational concept, 217
  as social justice, 127-128
  as state of mind, 159-160
  as transcendent, 674-675
  changing concepts, 125
  Communistic, 165-167
  concept in Russia, 147-157
  concept of, 289-290
  conflict with authority, 322-323
  contrasted in community and business, 45
  contrasted in Russia and West, 147; 154
  corporate, 550-552
  defined, 577-580
  dialectics of, 555-576
  distributive scheme, 218
  economic, 126-127
  equilibrium of, 631-634
  exercise of, 87
  from want, 95-102
  genuine, 503
  group, 176 ff.
  guaranteed by law, 116 ff.
  harmony with authority, 191, 197-198
  historical aspect, 444-447, 449
  identity with authority, 367
  implementation, 195-196
  in abstracto and historic forms, 649 ff.
  in American culture, 45
  in education, 671
  in Greek culture, 340-341
  in growth of social groups, 271-288
  in industry, 45-51, 53-62
  in international organization, 169-182
  in international relations, 103-108
  in labor unions, 63-77

Freedom (*Cont.*)
  in organization, 24-25
  in pre-British Burma, 338-340
  in prospect, 129-135
  in realization of values, 717-732
  in realm of poetic imagination, 365-375
  in relation to psychiatry, 385-391
  in retrospect, 121-128
  in 17th-century England, 103-104
  in social structure, 345-352
  in Tiv culture, 341-343
  in United States, 87, 121-123, 128
  individual, 109-118, 121-135, 159
  individual and group, 170-171
  individual, limitations to, 169-171
  intellectual, 125
  juristic aspect, 442-444, 449
  kinds of, 719-720
  legal sense, 222
  limited, 600
  limited, and essential, 117-118
  limiting conditions, 557-558
  location and dislocation of, 623-639
  meaning, 225, 659-660, 718-719
  medieval, 124-125
  metaphysical background of problem of, 597 ff.
  modern, 125-135
  moral and political, 292-294
  moral, and scientific determinism, 409-418
  national, 126-127
  national and supranational, 324-333
  necessity to authority, 317-333
  of association, 91
  of civilization, 647-657
  of constituency, 41
  of elections, 90
  of enterprise, 92
  of inquiry, 91-92
  of press, 92
  of speech, 90, 227, 567-569
  of thought, 608-609, 613-616
  original, 222
  persecution as pathology of, 393
  personal, nature of, 543 ff.
  perspective, 289-307
  political and civil, 126-127
  political, concept of, 441 ff.
  political theory of, explained, 442 ff.
  possibility of, 624-625

Freedom (*Cont.*)
  problems in the arts, 377
  protected by civil liberties, 169-170
  protected by social and economic rights, 169-170
  real meaning still determinable, 221
  relation of law to, 217-223
  religious, 126
  solidarity of freedoms, 653-654
  subjective character, 159-160
  three aspects, 557-558
  three basic types, 291-292, 306-307
  through authority, 641
  to bargain colectively, 92
  to worship, 92
  unlimited, 562-564
  volitional aspect, 447-449
  want of, 95-102
Freedom and Authority in Education (Russell), 683
Freedom and Discipline (Ikeda), 726
Freedom and the Expanding State (Carr), 517, 537-538
French Nationality Code, 261-263
French Revolution, 125-127, 199, 256, 259, 464, 685
French traditionalists, 449
Freud, Sigmund, 396
Fried, John H. E., 451
Frye, Royal M., comment by, 11
Functionalism, 218
Future, as function of present, 598-600

Galileo, 397-399
Gallicanism, 618
Gandhi, Mohandas, 105
Gardner, Dr. John, 38
General Assembly, 143-144
General Education in a Free Society (Harvard), 498
General Motors Corporation, 58
Germany, 107, 255-256, 260, 262, 264, 355, 356, 380, 648, 662, 674
  and authoritarianism, 2, 8
Gillette, Senator, 511-514, 517
Ginzberg, Eli, 353
Giotto, 379
Glorious Revolution, 103, 108, 464
Glueck, Sheldon, 249
Goal, changing and memory, 275

God, 462-463, 468-470, 474-483, 486, 488, 490, 491-504, 571, 582, 598, 607, 610-611, 613-616, 618-619, 622, 644-646, 718, 722-723, 731
  and culture, 115
  as authority, 295
Goethe, Johann von, 188, 564, 650
Gogol, Nikolai, 153
Gompers, Samuel, 58, 80-81
Good, indoctrination of, 499
Good life, guaranteed by freedom and authority, 95-97, 101-102
Goodwill, 7
  in life relationships, 9
Gosnell, H. F., quoted, 350
Government, in Islam, 701
Goya, Francisco, 379
Grace, 612-613
Graubard, Mark, 393
Great Britain, 356
Great Depression, 129, 355, 546
Greece, 340-341
  ancient, 123-124, 416, 463, 586
Green, Leon, 238
Green, William, 58, 79-81
Greenberg, Simon, 577
  comment by, 433-434
Gregory I, 705
Grotius, Hugo, 244, 328, 524-526, 534
Group:
  dynamics, and leadership, 14
  identification, in industry, 47-48
Growth:
  dimensions of, 286
  of organization and individual, 286
  strategy of, and self-determination, 285-286
Grunebaum, Gustave E. von, 701

Hadrian, 36
Hamilton, Alexander, 650, quoted, 688, 689
Hand, Augustus, 206
Hand, Learned, 204-212
Happiness, as appetite of will, 610
Harris, Louis, 87
Hartmann, Nicolai, 722, 729
Hartnett, Robert C., S.J., 687
Harvey, William, 404-405
Hebraism, 695

Hegel, Georg, 103, 226, 230, 293, 446, 480, 536, 541, 572-573, 598, 606, 620, 686
Hegelianism, 196, 198
Heidegger, Martin, 563, 686
Heisenberg, Walter, 641
Hendel, Charles W., 507
Herbart, Johann, 680-681
Ḥillî, 713
Hillman, Sidney, 81-82
Ḥisba, 702 ff.
Hiss, Alger, 633, 639
Historical materialism, 301-302
Historical Materialism (Bakunin), 152
History:
 and freedom, 445
 as process of social change, 445-446
 formation of histories, 636
 theories of historical development, 446
Hitler, Adolf, 103, 340, 356, 406, 426, 642, 662, 674, 676
Hobbes, Thomas, 103-104, 193, 221, 296, 349, quoted, 404, 421, 430, 442, 527-529, 531, 534, 566, 568, 616-617
Holmes, Oliver Wendel, 233, 238, quoted, 249
Hoover, Herbert, 129
Horvath, Barna, comments by, 118-119, 198, 214-215, 222-223, 234-235, 250-251, 434-436, 449-450, 480-481, 505, 573-575, 637-639, 657, 667-668, 686
Hostility, 7
 in life relationships, 9
Hoxie, R. Gordon, 121
Hughes, Charles Evans, 673
Huguenots, 618
Human consequences, of freedom and authority, 218
Human nature:
 and free will, 111-112
 personalistic view, 114-118
 psychoanalytic theory of, 385 ff.
 subject to change, 558-560
 valuation by the law, 112
Human needs, in industry, 50-51
Humanism, 112, 118, 686
 as absolute, 196-197
 as authority, 296
 naturalistic, 11
 of empiricism, 425-426
 theistic and atheistic, 607

Humboldt, Karl Wilhelm von, 117, 562
Hume, David, 296, 583
Hutcheson, Francis, 566

'Ibâda, 702
Ibn al-Muqaffâ, 704
Ibn Taimiyya, 701
Idealism:
 ambivalence of, 183
 and monistic fanaticism, 189
 functional, and methodological equality, 183-189
Ideologies:
 and social philosophy, 193-194
 modern, 194
Idolatry, 488
Ignatius of Loyola, Saint, 698
Iino, David N., 717
Immunity, congressional, 4
Impasses, primary and secondary, 632-634
Imâm, 713
Indeterminism, 628-629, 639
Individual:
 and authoritative forces, 580
 biological forces of, 584-585
 dignity and worth of, 50-51
 mental and physical forces of, 583-584
Individualism, 191
Industry:
 competition in, 46-47
 concept of ownership, 46
 group identification in, 47-48
 impersonality of profits in, 46
 management problems, 49-51
 primitive state of management skills, 48
 specialization in, 47
Inevitabilism, 601, 606
Inferiority, individual, 186-188
Initiative, and consciousness, 276-277
Inquiry:
 and culture, 314-315
 freedom of, 4
Insecurity, and authority, 1
Institutions:
 as power structures, 345-346, 348-350
 freedom and authority in, 494 ff.
 government by, 347, 350
 interrelation of, 345-352
 obsolescence, 139
 political party, 350
 reform of, 140-142

Index

Intelligence, dynamism of, 634-635
International Alliance of Theatrical Stage Employees and Moving Picture Machine Operators, 72
International Conference of Free Trade Unions (Milan Conference), 58
International Congress of Catholic Artists, 382
International court system, 142
International law:
  and freedom, 172-173
  and United Nations, 173
International organization:
  dangers, 177-178
  freedom and authority in, 169-182
  long-, and short-run policies, 174-180
International relations, freedom and authority in, 103-108
Internationalism, 256-259
  democratic, 326 ff.
Interpretation, function of, 29
Iorio v. Day, 205-206
Ireland, 357
Islam:
  equality in, 704
  government in, 701
  political theory of, 708-709

Jackson, Andrew, 15, 129
Jackson, Robert, 207, 214, 444-445, 654
James I (England), 518
James, William, 473
Japan, 717, 723 ff.
Jaspers, Karl, 371
Jefferson, Thomas, 3, 129-130, 192, 396, 689-691
Jellinek, 223, 241
Jews, 6
  ancient, and freedom, 123
  and Germany, 8
Jihâd, 705
Johnson, F. Ernest, 543
Johnson v. United States, 210
Joint factory committees, 60-61
Jones and Laughlin Steel Corporation, 79
Jordan v. De George, 207
Joshua, Rabbi, 201
Jouhaux, Léon, 60
Joyce, William, 261
Jurgen (Cabell), 565
Jus civile, 253

Jus gentium, 253
Jus soli, 265-266
Jus sanguinis, 265
Justice, 488
Justinian, 233

Kadish, Mortimer R., 623
  comments by, 436-437, 668-669
Kan, 338
Kant, Immanuel, 106-107, 117, 185, 226-228, 230, 248, 292, 296, 297, 416, 443, 536, 567, 571, 575-576, 583
Kapital, Das (Marx), 354
Kaplan, Mordecai M., 461
Katayev, Valentin, 153
Keenan, Joseph, 79, 81
Kefauver Committee, 633, 639
Kelsen, Hans, 222, 231-232
Keynes, Lord, 357
Khomyakov, Alexander, quoted, 149
Kierkegaard, Sören, 196, 371, 686
Killers of the Dream (Smith), 185
Kilpatrick, William H., 409
King Lear, 374
Kistyakowski, V. N., 150
Knowledge, relation to power, 43
Koheleth, 464
Kohn, Hans, 103
Koran, 704
Korea, 723
Korean War, 59, 106, 179, 229, 509-510
Kothyarevski, S. A., 150
Kroll, Jack, 79, 81
Kubie, Lawrence S., 385
Kurshan, Daniel L., comment by, 25
Kutuzov, Prince, 14

Labor:
  and religion, 85
  child, 140
  emerging role in political economy, 79-85
  goals of, 51
  participation in management, 55-62
Labor Department (U.S.), 76
Labor movement, 466
  and Democratic Party, 82-84
  and New Deal, 81-82
  and Taft-Hartley Act, 66-67
  attack upon property rights, 53-54, 62
  check-off system, 66

Index

Labor movement (*Cont.*)
  closed shop, 65
  control of locals, 70-71
  control of members, 71-72
  court control, 68-70, 72
  delegation of power, 69-73
  discrimination in, 67-68
  future, 76-77
  in Europe and America contrasted, 53-62
  in France, 55
  in Germany, 56
  in politics, 79-85
  in United States, 58-60, 64
  leadership in, 74-75
  legality, 66
  philosophy of leaders, 80
  prohibition of strikes, 65
  union management, 69-75
  union officers and industrial management, 74-75
  union shop, 65
  yellow dog contracts, 66
Labor's League for Political Education (A.F.L), 79
Labour Government (England), 57, 60
"Ladder Plan," 61
Ladislaus, Prince, 677
LaFarge, John, S. J., 641
  comment by, 715-716
Laissez-faire, 353
  in United States, 122
Lamprecht, Sterling P., 597
Langer, Susanne K., 137
Langrod, George S., 159
Laski, Harold, quoted, 348-349
Lasswell, Harold, quoted, 51
Last Judgment (Michelangelo), 379
Lateran Council, 402
Lattimore, Owen, 4
Lavoisier, Antoine, 652
Law:
  and command function, 521
  and freedom, 171-172
  and man, 112-114
  and moral destiny, 116
  and morality, 247-251
  and responsibility, 201-215
  as general will, 532-533
  bad, and hard cases, 208 ff.
  defined, 443

Law (*Cont.*)
  historical, 535-536
  individual freedom under, 109-118
  international, 172-173, 243-245, 524
  "is" and "ought" in, 218-219, 221
  kinds of authority of, 225-235
  legal imperative and moral authority, 237-251
  legal validity, 231
  liberty and authority under, 522-523
  meaning of, 536
  of nations, 525
  relation to freedom and authority, 217-218, 221
  supreme importance of, 535
  three meanings, 238-239
  world, and world reform, 137-146
Laws of Ecclesiastical Polity (Hooker), 518
Laws (Plato), 362
Leadership:
  and authority, 13
  and equality, 188
  and responsibility, 15
  of labor union officers, 74-75
  training for, 13
League of Nations, 533
Learning, capacity, 278-280
Lee, Dorothy D., 335, 645
Legis Barbarorum, 253
Lenin, Vladimir, 152, 155
Leys, Wayne A. R., comment by, 639
Liberalism, 131, 191, 196-198, 422
Liberty (*see also* Freedom)
  and authority, 159-167, 507
  authority and, constitutional aspects, 687-693
  Jefferson on, 689-690
  of free subjects, 521-522
  twofold aspect, 644
Libri, Julius, 397
Life relationships, American, 9
Lincoln, Abraham, 129
Lindblom, Charles E., 64
Lippmann, Walter, 130
Locke, John, 127, 193, 296, 301, 447, 530-531, 583, 617
Lotze, Rudolf, 479
Louis XIV, 618
Love:
  freedom and community in, 491-494
  God's, 491-494, 504

Lowie, Robert H., comments by, 108, 306
Loyalty oaths, 4
Lucretius, 445
Lunacharsky, A. V., 155
Luther, Martin, 674, 681

MacArthur, Douglas, 41, 509, 512
Mach, Ernest, 361
Machiavelli, 103, 468, 519
MacIver, R. M., quoted, 346
Madison, James, 130
Maestlin, 397
Mahdî, 713
Maine, Sir Henry, quoted, 122, 244
Malinowski, Bronislaw, 296
Man:
  as end in himself, 111-112
  as fighter for ends, 473
  valuation by law, 112 ff.
Management:
  codetermination with labor, 55-62
  primitive state in industry, 48
  problems in industry, 49-51
Mandelbaum, Professor, 306
Mansfield, Lord, 233
Maritain, Jacques, 427
Marshall, George C., 15-16
Marshall, James, 13
Marshall, John, 19, 233
Marx, Karl, 127, 150, 293, 298-299, 301, 302, 307, 354-355, 406, 446, 470, 606, 662, 676
Marxism, 150 ff., 175, 193-194, 195, 198-199, 501, 598, 620
Maṣlaḥa, 711
Masochism, and altruism, 695
Mâwardî, 701
Mayer, Rupert, S. J., 642 ff.
McCarthy, Joseph, 4, 408
McCarthyism, 636
Meany, George, 81
Meiji Restoration (1868), 725
Mein Kampf (Hitler), 103
Melanchthon, Philip, 681
Meletus, 396
Memory, and goal changing, 275
Mercier, Louis J. A., 607
Merriam, Charles E., quoted, 347, 350-351
Messiah, 123

Metaphysics:
  absolutism of, 420
  and political philosophy, 419-420
  as background of problem of freedom, 597
Methodology:
  of equality, 186-189
  of ideals, 186-189
Michels, Robert, 69, 351
Middle Ages, 650-651
  art in, 378
Mill, John Stuart, 117, 127, 218, 286, 480, 562-563
Milton, John, 524
Miracle, The, 383
Moberly, Walter, 718
Mohl, Robert von, 128
Molière, 407
Moltke, Helmuth von, 249
Monasticism, 695
Monism, 607, 618-622
Monopoly:
  by business, 63
  by labor, 64
Montague, William P., 695
Montaigne, 314
Montesquieu, Charles, 125, 446, 527, 535-536, 617
Morale:
  and leadership, 14
  and policy-making, 19-20
  set by administration, 37
Morality:
  and empirical philosophy, 420-430
  and law, 247-251
  difficulty of absolute rules, 219
  moral authority and legal imperative, 237-251
  moral choice, freedom of, 414-415
  moral freedom and scientific determinism, 409-418
  public and individual rights, 457
  variability of judgments, 220
More, Sir Thomas, 125
Morrison, Herbert, 57, 470
Muhammad Kurd'Alî, 704
Muhammad 'Abduh, 704
Murdock, George P., 315
Murphy, Frank, 266
Murray, Philip, 79-81
Muslims (*see* Islam)
Mussolini, Benito, 448

Index

Mutual dependence, of world and ego, 118
Myrdal, Gunnar, 87
Mysticism, of Fascism, 194-195
Myth of the Twentieth Century, The (Rosenberg), 618

Nakamura, Hajime, 731
Napoleon, 14, 103, 199, 226, 233, quoted, 678
Napoleonic Wars, 194
National Association of Manufacturers, 91
National Industrial Recovery Act (1933), 66, 81, 232
National Prohibition Act, 232
National Service Bill, 356
National Socialism (Germany), 107, 242-243
Nationalism:
 and geography, 331-333
 criteria for, 331-333
Nationality, and citizenship, 255 ff.
Nationality Act of 1938 (U.S.S.R.), 260
Nationalization of industry, 61-62
 in England, 57
 in France, 57
Natural events, contingency of, and freedom, 598
Natural law, 191, 198, 243, 246, 250, 307, 417, 421-422, 430-431, 439, 519-524, 565-566, 615
Naturalism, and supernaturalism, 196-197
Nature and Sources of the Law, The (Gray), 204-205
Nature, as social, 417-418
Navaho Indians, 337
Nazism, 380-381, 405-406, 468
Negley, Glenn, 237
Negroes, and civil rights, 89
Nejelski, Leo, 45
Neumann, Franz L., 441, 645
New Deal, 81, 122, 129-130, 351, 466
New Freedom of Wilson, 122
New Nationalism of T. Roosevelt, 122
New Testament, 295
New York Times survey of freedom of speech, 90
New York Times tribute to Judge Hand, 207
Niebuhr, Reinhold, 718-719, 721
Nietzsche, Friedrich, 195, 298, 307, 316, 371, 468-469, 560, 695

Norris-LaGuardia Act (1933), 66

Occam, William of, 482-483
Office of Defense Mobilization, 356
Old Stone Age, 416
Old Testament, 253, 269, 295
Oliver Twist, 383
Ontology, and culture, 309-315
Opinion, public, and authority, 590
Organization, 271-281
 freedom and authority as aspects, 281-282
 freedom in, 24-25
 international, 169-182
 power in, 284
 spiritual function of, 13-25
Origins of Muhammadan Jurisprudence (Schacht), 704
Orthodox Synod, Russian, 714
Orthodoxy:
 and freedom and authority, 419-439
 confusion with authority, 431-432
 renewed quest for, 419
Orwell, George, 333
Osiander, Andreas, quoted, 403
Overstreet, Harry A., 1
Ownership, in industry, 46
Oxnam, Bishop, 690

Panslavism, 470
Paracelsus, 401-402
Paramartha, 685
Parker, Francis W., 621-622
Participation, in industry, 49-50
Pascal, Blaise, 182
Patriotism, 7
Patterson, Edwin W., 225
Patterson, Robert P., 206
Paul, Saint, 265, 545, 550, 571, 652, 698, 732
Paul V, Pope, 397
Peace, 502
 as balance of freedoms and authority, 179-180
 long-, and short-run policies, 174-180
 universal, 144-145
Pensées (Pascal), quoted, 671
Pentateuch, 265
Perelman, Chaim, comment by, 438
Perfection, 367
Pericles, 123, 395, quoted, 673, 676

Perón, Juan, 107
Perry, Ralph Barton, 718, 720
Persecution:
  and personality, 394
  as pathology of freedom and authority, 393
  by ambivalence, 409
  by creed, 405-406
  by impasse, 394-399
  by invitation, 399-405
  defined, 394
Personalism, 112-116, 118
Personality:
  goodwill pattern, 6-7
  hostility pattern, 6-7
Peter, Saint, 676
Petrillo, James, 73
Peucer, 403
Philosophes, 559
Philosophy (*see also* various fields)
  absolutism in, 420-430
  empirical and relativistic, 420
  idealism, 114
  present state of, 419 ff.
Philotimo, 340
Physical law, authority of, 581
Pinckney, Charles, 121
Pitt, William, 199
Plato, 123, 183, 292, 300, 362-363, 442, 448, 479, 543, 704, 713
Plotinus, 479
Pluralism, cultural, 502
Poetic imagination, freedom and authority and, 365-375
Point Four Program, 133, 634
Poland, 264
Policy-making, 18 ff.
  and constituencies, 39-40
  and experts, 27
  by administration, 27-28, 36
  by executives, 28
Polish Nationality Act (1951), 258, 261
Political Action Committee (C.I.O.), 79, 81, 91
Political freedom, concept of, 441
Political party, as power structure, 350-352
Politics, and ethics, 191 ff.
Pope, The, 382
Potentiality, of the present, 598-600
Pound, Roscoe, 227, 238

Power:
  and autonomy, 284
  and growth, 285-286
  and leadership, 13
  and power relations in the social system, 345-346, 348
  arbitrary, 488-489
  authority as validation of, 461
  ideology of, 298
  motives in practical affairs, 34-35
  of authority, 297
  of political party, 350
  perpetuation in business and politics, 37
  politics as struggle for, 441-442
  relation to knowledge, 43
  separation of political and economic, 465
  versus man, 443
Power politics, 179
  dangers, 176-177
Pragmatic dynamism, 80, 85
Pragmatism, 218, 675
Pravda, 470
Present, potentiality of, 598-600
Profits:
  human, 48
  impersonality of, in industry, 46
Progress, 559-560
Progressivism, 131, 134, 621-622
Property, 447
Protagoras, 395
Protestantism, 344, 548-549, 552, 681, 699
Psychiatry, in relation to freedom and authority, 385-391
Psychoanalysis, theory of human nature, 385 ff.
Ptolemaic Hypothesis, 398
Public Opinion in Soviet Russia (Inkeles), 546-547
Puritan Revolution, 103, 127, 685
Puritanism, 534, 552, 695-698
Pythagoras, 648

Qânûn, 711
Quakers, 552

Rabbi Eliezer, 201
Rabbi Joshua, 201
Race, 459
Railroad Brotherhoods, 65
Realism, 218
Reason, 191

Recasens-Siches, Luis, 109
Red-baiting, 9
Reform:
  democratic, 127
  of institutions, 139-140
  world, and world law, 137-146
Reformation, 126, 518
Reich, Third, 643
Reid, Thomas, 566
Rejection, 8, 387
Relativism, 558-560
Relativity, theory of, 361-362
Religion:
  and authority, 592
  and labor, 85
  and state, 592-593, 701
  goodwill and, 10
  revealed, 611-612
  supernaturalistic, 11
Renaissance, 463, 651
  and art, 378
Renault factory, 57
Repouille v. United States, 210-211
Republic (Plato), 228, 300, 682
Republican Party (U.S.), 351
Response, 6
  goodwill, 7
  hostility, 7
Responsibility, 16 ff.
  and authority, 201-215
  and clarity, 202
  and leadership, 15
  delegation of, 16
  evasion, 202-204
  policy-making and, 18
Rights:
  civil, 87-88
  exercise of, 89-93
  human, and United Nations Charter, 452-459
  human, economic, social, and cultural aspect, 454
  human, political aspect, 454
  individual, 3-4, 87, 324-326, 447-449
  individual, and public morality, 457
  of property and labor, 53-54, 62
Rohrlich, George F., 95
Roman Catholic Church, 463 (*see also* Catholicism)
Romanticism, 348, 377

Rome (ancient), 123-124, 586, 617, 650, 681, 706, 709, 714
Roosevelt and Hopkins (Sherwood), 147
Roosevelt, Franklin Delano, 81, 122, 147
Roosevelt, Theodore, 122, 129
Roper Surveys, 91-92
Rosenberg, Alfred, 406
Roundheads, 696
Rousseau, Jean Jacques, 125, 150, 185, 194, 283, 292-294, 296, 297, 300, 307, 416, 445, 507, 531-536, 617
Rumanian National Regulation of 1948, 258
Russell, Bertrand, 313, 544
Russia, 6, 14, 254-258, 260-266, 311, 319-320, 329, 356, 380, 547, 620, 648, 654-656, 662, 674, (*see also* Soviet . . .)
  art in, 156-157
  authoritarianism, 2
  censorship, 178
  civil rights in, 92-93
  Communism, 320, 325-333
  concept of freedom and authority in, 147-157
  irreligion, 11
  lack of free constituency, 41

Saftey-valve theory of the West, 122
San Francisco Conference (1945), 179
Sanctions, 654-655
Santayana, George, 571
Šarī'a, 703
Schmidt v. United States, 209
Scholasticism, 559, 648, 674
School, 497-499, (*see also* Education)
Schrecker, Paul, 647
Schweitzer, Albert, 652
Science:
  effect on moral behavior, 363
  role of authority in interpretation of, 361-363
  technical results as criterion of, 361-362
Scientific determinism, and moral freedom, 409-418
Scott, Walter, 696
Sears, Laurence, 3-4
Security:
  and conformity, 2
  and freedom, 95-102, 104
  dangers of, 101-102

Security (Cont.)
  international, 104-105
  long-, and short-run policies, 174-180
  national, and social security, 97-100
  search for, 2
Security Council, 509-510
Self-consciousness, 410-411
  and determinism, 414
Self-determination, and strategy of growth, 285-286
Sellars, Roy Wood, 191
  comments by, 306, 450, 552-553
Senate Armed Services Committee, 175
Senate Foreign Relations Committee, 175
Seneca, 450
Shaftesbury, Lord, 566
Shakespearean drama, esthetic of the, 365, 372
Shamanism, 730
Shapiro v. Gehlman, 72
Sheer exercising, 365-366
Shiites, 713, 715
Shostakovich, Dimitri, 156
Siderial Messenger (Galileo), 397
Silving, Helen, 253
Simmons, Ernest J., 147
Sizzi, Francesco, 397
Smith, Adam, 125, 127, 227, 301, 353, 355, 566
Smith, Ignatius, comment by, 576
Smith, T. V., 184
Snay v. Lovely, 70
Social Contract (Rousseau), 292
Social contract theory, 463-467, 616-617
Social Darwinism, 303
Social forces, unbalance of, 476-477
Social heritage, defined, 585-586
Social legislation, 98-100
Social philosophy, criteria for, 193-194
Social science, complexity and small stature, 218
Social security, 95-102
  aims, 97
  dangers, 101-102
  extension, 98-102
Social Security Act, 501
Social structure:
  freedom and authority in, 345-352
  democratic, 350
Socialism:
  Austrian, 55

Socialism (Cont.)
  British Guild, 55
  Fabian, 56-57
  Guild, 56
  Marxian, 54
Society, required by God, 476
Sociology, 556-557
Socrates, 395-396, 541, 586
Socratic paradox, 609
Soldier's Story, A (Bradley), 358-359
Solon, 123, 233
Sophists, 295-296
South America, 357
Sovereignty, 446-447
  theory of, 519 ff.
Soviet Central Committee, 155
Soviet Constitution (1936), 154-155
Soviet Political Dictionary, 153
Soviet Union of Workers' Deputies, 153
Spain, 357
Spanish Empire, 706
Specialization, in industry, 47
Spencer, Herbert, 190, 301
Spengler, Oswald, 449
Spinoza, Baruch, 193, 292, 296, 445-446, 529, 541, 564, 617, 674-675
Spirit, and strategy in organization, 287-288
Spirituality, 11
  and democracy, 9
Stalin, Josef, 103, 147, 151, 426
Standard of living, and freedom, 96-97
Starr, Mark, 63
State:
  and authority, 191-192, 587-588
  and church, 617-618
  and freedom, 126, 226-228
  and freedom of thought and will, 613-616
  and individual, 137-138
  and individual in Russia, 147-157
  and legal authority, 241-242, 245, 249
  and man, 112-114, 115-116, 443, 448-449
  and religion, 592-593
  authoritarian, 1
  fair, 455-456
  immunity of acts of, 459
  organic theory, 458-459
  power and authority of, 349
  Soviet, 149
  three types of, 561
  under Islam, 701

State *(Cont.)*
  welfare, 690-693
  world, 142
State Department (U.S.), 631
State of nature, 527
Statelessness, 259
Stockholm Peace Appeal, 178
Stoicism, 124, 442, 450, 612
Sturmthal, Adolf F., 53
Suarez, Francisco, 615-616
Subjectivism, 479
Sûfî, 712
Summum bonum, 557, 579, 707
Sumner, William G., 301
Sunnites, 708, 713-715
Superiority, individual, 186-188
Supernaturalism:
  and authority, 593-594
  Christian, 196-197
Supreme Court (U.S.), 63, 207, 227, 688
  crisis of 1937, 203
Suso, Heinrich, 698
Swift, Jonathan, 27
Switzerland, 261, 263
Symbolism, 366-375
Syndicalism, 54-55, 61

Tacitus, 14
Taft, Dr. Philip, quoted, 68
Taft-Hartley Act, 64, 65, 66-67, 82, 84, 233
Talmud, 201, 487
Taylor system of efficiency, 21
Temple, William, 722
Tennessee Valley Authority, 693
Testament, New, 295
Testament, Old, 253, 269, 295
Theism, 619-621
  dualistic doctrine, 607-618
  ethics of, 614-616
  personalistic, 473, 481
  truth of, 474, 480
Theocracy, 462-464
Theology, and political philosophy, 419 ff.
Theonomy:
  and autonomy, 473-483
  as primary social force, 477-478
  defined, 475
Thomism *(see also* Aquinas)
  as ideology, 197
Thompson, Kenneth W., comment by, 180-181

Thought:
  freedom of, 608-609, 613-616
  two fundamental alternatives of, 607-622
Thrasymachus, 468
Thucydides, 673
Tikopia clan (Solomon Islands), 336
Time, nature of, 601-602
Tiv (Nigeria), 341-343
Tocqueville, Alexis de, 20
Tolerance, and culture, 314
Tolman, Doctor Edward C., 408
Tolstoy, Leo, quoted, 14
Torah, 487
Totalitarianism, 348, 352, 357-359, 448-449, 501, 588
  and control of the individual, 164
  and lack of free constituency, 41
  and liberty, 132
  culture of, 298 ff.
Toynbee, Arnold, 280, 283
Transpersonalism, 112, 118
Trent, Council of, 379
Tripartitum of Werboeczy (1514), 222
Truman, Harry S., 41, 82, 106, 396
Truth:
  and intellectual authority, 661-669
  complexity of, 560
Turner, Frederick Jackson, 122
Turner, J. E., 539
Tûsî, 713
Twentieth Century Fund, 50
Tyranny, 488

Ulamâ, 707
Ulich, Robert, 671
Ulysses (Joyce), 382
Union, Labor *(see* Labor movement)
Union of Soviet Socialist Republics *(see* Russia)
United Labor Policy Committee, 65
United Mine Workers, 69
United Nations, 105-106, 533
  and citizenship, 259
  and freedom, 170-180
  and human rights, 128, 451-459
  and international law, 173-180
  authority, 174
  charter, 647
  Commission on Human Rights, 452
  effective power, 174-175, 177-178
  General Assembly, 143-144

United Nations (*Cont.*)
  membership, 143
  Security Council, 509-510
  steps to united world organization, 143
  World Court, 143
United States, 262, 264, 267, 586, 601-602, 687, (*see also* various departments)
  and authority, 508 ff.
  and Communists, 330
  and free constituency, 41-42
  contrasts of freedom in, 45
  contribution to concept of freedom, 443-444
  faults of industry in, 45-48
  occupation of Japan, 727-728
  policy toward Communism, 332
United States v. Francisco, 209
Uniting for Peace Resolution, 179
Universal Declaration of Human Rights, 118, 128, 170, 259, 261, 439, 451-459
Urban VIII, 398
Utilitarianism, 218, 307
Utopian radicalism, 446
Utopianism, 181-182

Value, 481
  and freedom, 170
  and political theory, 441 ff.
  as end of will, 556
  empirical, 424
  freedom and authority in realization of, 717-732
  in industry, 46
  metaphysical theory of, 473
  of human consequences, 218
  of human individual, 111-116
  of persons, 476
Vance, Rupert B., 345
Velázquez, Diego, 379
Vergniaud, Pierre, 256-257
Veronese, Paolo, 379
Vico, Jean Baptiste, 446
Vishinsky, Andrei, 147
Vivekananda, Swami, 550
"Void for vagueness" legislation, 203 ff.
Voltaire, 125, 443, 502
Voluntarism, 609
Von Grunebaum, Gustave E., 701

Wage, below-subsistence, 354
Wagner Act, 81, 233
Wallas, Graham, quoted, 350
War:
  and freedom and authority, 349
  as social institution, 140-144
Washington, George, quoted, 690
Watch and Ward societies, 382
Watt, Robert J., 73
Weigel, Gustave, S. J., 659
Weldon, T. G., 560, quoted, 561
Welfare, individual:
  and legal authority, 248
  and political philosophy, 228, 234
Welser of Augsburg, 397
Weltanschauung, 107, 666, 682
West, The, 6, 103-108, 295, 416, 463, 586-587, 593, 620-621
  and Japan, 730
Wheelwright, John B., 368
Whitehall Debates, 534
Whitehead, Alfred North, 417, 721, 723
Whyte, William F., 74
Widmanstadt, 403
Will:
  and problem of commitment, 277-278
  free, determinism and, 110
  free, man as, 109-118
  freedom of, 556, 609-610, 613-616, 623-639
  general, 194
  general and common, 293-294, 307
Will to Believe, The (James), 195
Williams, Roger, 552
Wilson, Woodrow, 13, 15, 122, 128-129
Wintu Indians, 337
Wishing, 412
Woodward, Julian L., 85
Woolsey, Judge John M., 382
Work:
  and freedom, 353-360
  ends of, 357-358
  external and internal problems, 354-355
  means of, 358
Workers' Control, 55-62
World Court, 143
World government, Eastern and Western concepts, 175
World War I, 572
World War II, 1, 451, 508, 546
  and labor, 59
World War III, 176

Wright, Quincy, 169
   comments by, 43, 438-439

Yeats, William Butler, 284

Zweck im Recht, Der (von Jehring), 218
Zimmerwald Manifesto (1915), 257
Zinzendorf, Nikolaus, 682
Zum Ewigen Frieden (Kant), 106
Zwingli, Huldreich, 674